a
comprehensive manual of
FOUNDATIONS AND PHYSICAL
EDUCATION ACTIVITIES
for men and women

a
comprehensive
manual of
FOUNDATIONS
AND PHYSICAL
EDUCATION
ACTIVITIES
for men
and women

GEORGE B. DINTIMAN
Virginia Commonwealth University

LOYD M. BARROW
Southern Connecticut State College

STACY A. FREY
Herbert H. Lehman College

VIOLET J. WADE
Herbert H. Lehman College

Burgess Publishing Company
Minneapolis, Minnesota

Copyright © 1979 by Burgess Publishing Company
Printed in the United States of America
Library of Congress Catalog Number 79-89671
ISBN 0-8087-0486-9

Burgess Publishing Company
7108 Ohms Lane
Minneapolis, Minnesota 55435

0 9 8 7 6 5 4 3 2 1

PREFACE

This book is designed for male and female students participating in a service or professional program of physical education at the junior college and college or university level. It includes two separate sections:

1. *Foundations* (Chapters 1, 2, 3)
2. *Activities* (Chapters 4-17)

The *Foundations* Section provides comprehensive material for an introductory course in physical education. It presents recent scientific data on Physical Education Programs, Fitness and Health, Weight Control and Preventive Heart Disease. An overview of physical education objectives and information on the place and importance of college physical education is provided in Chapter 1. In Chapter 2, there is a comprehensive analysis of the beneficial effects of exercise; of the components of physical fitness; of a critical overview of fifteen existing, worthwhile exercise programs with their contribution to fitness and their practicality for continued use throughout life. In addition, a thorough plan for the prevention of early heart disease is presented. This section enables the student to choose a program adaptable to his or her needs and interests. Chapter 3 examines the entire area of weight control through diet and exercise separating fact from myth and presenting sound principles for personal management of body weight throughout life.

The Activities Section includes a comprehensive analysis of each activity and a thorough explanation and discussion of every phase of the sport. Each chapter, devoted to one sport, consists of a description of the activity, equipment, skills and techniques, basic strategy, safety practices, weight training applied to that activity, definitions and list of terms, questions and answers on the rules, and a bibliography.

The inclusion of a weight training section for each activity is a unique feature of this handbook, providing the more advanced competitor with suggested exercises designed specifically to strengthen and improve explosive power and efficiency in the muscles involved in performing the particular skill. The weight training exercises suggested are explained and illustrated in Chapter 17. The definitions and list of terms section is included in order to facilitate learning by providing an opportunity to record answers on a completion-type test without reference to correct answers unless desired.

The Personal Record Sheet, located on a separate page at the end of the book, should be completed and submitted to the instructor on the first class meeting. This form provides a permanent record throughout the student's participation in the required program of his physical fitness, his skill, and his performance on written tests as well as his final grades.

The authors of this book are indebted to several groups of individuals who have assisted in the review and preparation of the manuscript. The following individuals have carefully reviewed and corrected the chapter on their respective activity: *Badminton*—Howard Hopkinson, former ranked badminton player in Connecticut, and Al Furbish, Physical Director, New Haven YMCA; *Fencing*—Albert J. Grasson, Fencing Coach, Yale University; *Golf*—Al Wilson; *Soccer*—Armand R. Dikranian, Soccer Coach, Southern Connecticut State College; *Volleyball*—Charles Pead, Director of Health, Physical Education at Waterbury YMCA, Regional Office of the U.S. Volleyball Association, former collegiate All-American at Springfield College (set-up man—1950); *Weight Lifting And Weight Training*—Barney Groves, Associate Professor of Physical Education, Virginia Commonwealth University; *Wrestling*—Tom Legg, Wrestling Coach, Virginia Commonwealth University.

G.B.D.
L.M.B.
S.A.F.
V.J.W.

v

CONTENTS

1

THE REQUIRED PROGRAM

Physical education at the college level is designed to provide some form of active participation for all students regardless of age, ability, level of physical capacity, or physical and psychological status. Education prepares an individual for effective living, and physical education as an integral part of the educational program prepares one to meet the physical demands of effective living. In order for physical education to contribute significantly to the challenges of education, programs must be scientifically developed and expertly administered, taking into consideration the unique needs and interests of the students in each institution of higher learning. Its place in the college curriculum is extremely important, and it should be held in high esteem, although at times it will be severely attacked by administrators and academicians who place the profession of physical education in a position where it must justify its role in the education of our youth. Perhaps such periodic, forced revision and examination of the unique contributions of physical education and of the degree to which objectives are being realized is healthy. Scientific evidence continues to mount supporting the value of physical education and its related programs in contributing to the total development of individuals.

In college physical education, student needs and interests are determined and well-defined objectives established in light of the information uncovered. Activities are then directed toward meeting these objectives. The entire program is constructed and executed in line with the objectives identified, and periodic evaluations are used to determine the degree to which objectives are being met. Sound testing pro-

grams are incorporated to identify skill and physical weaknesses and to assign students properly to correct activities and programs, as well as to equalize competition and provide homogeneous groupings for more effective learning. Students who demonstrate skill in and knowledge of various activities may meet their requirements by demonstrating passing grades on skill/knowledge tests, permitting additional flexibility in the election of activities.

College physical education requires the adequate use and coordination of seven areas:

A. *The Service Program.* This is designed for all students who are capable of active, vigorous participation in a wide variety of activities, including team sports, dual sports, individual sports, combatives, formal gymnastic activities, and recreational activities. Opportunity is provided for the election of specific activities, with emphasis placed on leisure-time or recreational sports. Group and individual instruction is provided in a teaching situation designed for the development of skills in "carryover" activities and games that are likely to be continued throughout life.

1. *The Adapted Program.* A wide variety of activities, games, sports, and exercises are provided (in close harmony with the medical office) and adapted to the needs, interests, capacities, and limitations of students who are unable to safely or successfully engage in the required program. Each student receives individual attention and evaluation prior to the initiation of the program. Supervision is provided throughout the four college years for individuals with permanent disabling conditions.

2. *The Body Mechanics Program* is a unique phase

1

of adapted physical education designed to identify and improve posture and body mechanics problems through games and exercises jointly prescribed by the health and physical education offices. This instructional and activity program is scheduled concurrently with the required program (they are separate areas) to allow rapid and easy transfer when disabling conditions are alleviated or eliminated.

3. *The Sports Appreciation Program.* This is designed to develop an appreciation for a wide variety of sports and games through a study of their rules, techniques, origin and development, cultural backgrounds, and strategies that will be conducive to intelligent and enjoyable attendance at athletic contests and informal play. Individuals who cannot be assisted by the adapted program because of serious and permanent physical or psychological conditions are assigned to this phase of physical education.

4. *The Developmental Program.* Students who do not meet minimum standards of physical capacity are assigned to this phase of physical education, which utilizes a wide variety of exercise programs, activities, games, and discussions to change dietary and health habits and to elevate general levels of physical conditioning as well as specific areas of weakness. The program also attempts to establish the need for continuous, progressive exercise throughout life and to expose students to the numerous existing exercise programs. The beneficial effects of exercise are thoroughly explained, and pre- and post-testing procedures are used for individual and group evaluation. Students classified as overweight or obese are also assigned to the developmental program for thorough study of the principles of weight loss through exercise and dietary control as well as through the implementation of a sound program of weight reduction under the close supervision of the medical office (see Chapter 2).

B. *The Recreational Program.* The maximum use of all institutional facilities provides for supervised free play for the entire student body, administration, and faculty on a periodic, scheduled basis. This voluntary program allows complete freedom of choice in all forms of acceptable leisure-time pursuits.

C. *The Intramural Program.* A diversified program of activities and games, paralleling the instructional class program, is provided and mass participation encouraged. Such groups as fraternities, dormitory floors, special organizations and classes are encouraged to compete, and team and individual point-and-award systems are emphasized in college- or

university-wide promotions on a year-round basis. An attempt is made to have as many students as possible participate (single elimination tournaments should be kept to a minimum and used only when absolutely necessary). Every student should be required to participate in one intramural sport annually. This program supplements the required program as a noninstructional laboratory experience and enables individuals to engage in formal competition to further develop and apply the skills acquired in the required program.

D. *The Intercollegiate Program.* Individuals of superior ability are provided with an opportunity to develop and display their talents to the fullest in highly competitive athletic events between institutions. This program involves only a small part of the total college population; however, it is an important and integral part of education when properly conceived and conducted, as in the majority of our nation's colleges and universities.

In summary, the Required Program consists of *active instruction,* the Adapted Program of *correction,* the Sports Appreciation Program of *inactive instruction,* the Developmental Program of *active exercise,* the Intramural Program of *practice,* the Recreational Program of *leisure-time pursuit,* and the Intercollegiate Program of *perfection and display of talent.* Activities and programs must be developed and conducted in close harmony in order to provide the best possible conditions for the student. Each program must be adequately staffed, promoted, and developed to meet the changing needs and interests of the student body.

COLLEGE PHYSICAL EDUCATION OBJECTIVES

"Objectives" refers to the desirable results for which the field of physical education strives. Such objectives serve as guidelines in class planning and conducting. They reflect the nature of society and the general aims of American education in terms of how this academic discipline contributes to efficient, effective, and happy lives. Such objectives at the college level vary, just as the emphasis placed on any discipline tends to fluctuate throughout the country depending upon individual and institutional philosophy and conditions. Objectives, emphasis, and the importance of physical education in the college curriculum tend to be altered by such conditions as the threat of war or a national crisis, by reports of high percentages of military rejects because of mental, moral, or physical deficiencies, by the physical-psychological strength of the nation's active military personnel, by automation and technological advances, by pleas from such high officials as the President of the United States and national committees, by the status of space-age competition between the major powers, by educational emphasis and the revamping of college curriculums, by findings that show American youth comparing unfavorably to the youth of other countries, by declines in physical capacity found in comparing college students of one generation to another, by government legislation of funds and leadership for physical education activities, and by educational leadership at all levels.

Although the terminology varies, there is general agreement among leaders in physical education concerning the general objectives of formal programs. Table 1–1 summarizes the frequency of objectives as listed by outstanding leaders in the field.

Organic Development

The development of organic power, or physical capacity, as discussed thoroughly in Chapter 2, as well as a complete reeducation of each student with respect to the effects of, need for, and importance and place of vigorous big-muscle activity in daily routines remain among the unique contributions of physical education. Strength, local and cardiovascular-respiratory endurance, flexibility, explosive power, agility, and speed are developed through carefully selected programs of conditioning and through activities that can be engaged in continuously and progressively throughout the normal life of an individual.

TABLE 1-1. Frequency of physical education objectives as listed by leaders in the field.

Authority	Organic Development	Interpretive Development	Neuromuscular Development	Personal-Social Adjustment
AAHPER	X		X	X
Bookwalters	X	X		X
Brace	X	X	X	X
Brownell-Hagman	X	X	X	X
Bucher	X	X	X	X
Clarke	X			X
Cowell-Hazelton	X	X	X	X
Daniels	X		X	X
Davis-Lawther		X	X	
Duncan-Johnson	X	X	X	X
Evans-Gans	X	X	X	X
Hughes-French	X	X	X	X
Irwin	X	X	X	X
Knapp-Hagman	X	X	X	X
Kozman et al.	X	X	X	X
LaPorte		X	X	X
Larson-Hill	X	X	X	X
LaSalle	X	X	X	X
Mathews	X			X
McCloy	X	X	X	X
Miller-Whitcomb	X	X		X
Nash-Hetherington	X	X	X	X
Neilson-Van Hagen	X	X	X	X
Nixon-Cozens	X		X	X
Obertcuffer	X	X	X	X
O'Keefe-Aldrich	X	X	X	X
Salt et al.	X	X	X	X
Seaton et al.	X	X	X	X
Sharman	X	X	X	
Staley	X			X
Vannier-Fait	X	X	X	X
Voltmer-Esslinger	X	X	X	X
Williams	X		X	X

SOURCE: Miller K. Adams, "Principles for Determining High School Grading Procedures in Physical Education for Boys." Unpublished doctoral thesis, New York University, 1959.

Interpretive Development

Actual participation in activities encourages creative and analytical thinking with minimum professional assistance from the coach or physical educator. Opportunities to make sound judgments and decisions based on the evidence and variables involved, as well as on past experiences, require unassisted, intelligent, and logical thinking by the student.

Neuromuscular Development

Neuromuscular development refers to the improvement of sports and game skills, body movement, and rhythm through continuous practice and instruction from the elementary school to the college years. Gracefulness, a minimum of energy expenditure, and improved skill in general are key areas of emphasis of physical education at the college level.

Learning of skills instills a desire for continued participation in carryover activities in post-college years. It increases the probability of continuous exercise throughout life. Individuals tend to engage in those activities in which success has been experienced and to avoid unsuccessful experiences in the future. Thus, the elevation of the level of skill in a variety of carryover activities is a primary concern of college physical education programs. The physical education profession has tremendous control over the development of skills over the years, with the elementary-school level (formative period) offering the greatest opportunity. The values of the development of skills are obvious: (1) less expenditure of energy, (2) increased enjoyment and satisfaction, (3) recognition, (4) safety, (5) development and maintenance of physical capacity, (6) wise use of leisure time, (7) vocational opportunities for a select few, (8) relief from tension, (9) development of confidence, (10) self-expression, (11) general improvement of coordination with carryover to everyday living, (12) aid to mental health, and (13) appreciation of excellent movement, form, and execution.

Personal-Social Adjustment

Although there are early claims indicating the contribution of physical education to social-psychological development, self-confidence, initiative, leadership, self-direction, feelings of belonging, character, and other difficult-to-measure qualities, until recently little scientific evidence was available to support such statements. An influx of experimental research has uncovered valuable information supporting the role of properly conceived physical education programs in improving personal-social adjustment at the various educational levels.

THE NEED FOR COLLEGE OR UNIVERSITY PHYSICAL EDUCATION

Most authorities agree that physical education is an integral part of the education of American youth and that it has a definite place at all educational levels. Its contributions are well substantiated, meeting needs that would not be met by other phases of education. The late President Kennedy,[1] in a message addressed to the nation's schools in 1961, pointed out:

The strength of our democracy is no greater than the collective well-being of our people. The vigor of our country is no stronger than the vitality and will of our countrymen. The level of physical, mental, moral and spiritual fitness of every American citizen must be our constant concern. The need for increased attention to the physical fitness of our youth is clearly established. Although today's young people are fundamentally healthier than the youth of any previous generation, the majority have not developed strong, agile bodies. The softening process of our civilization continues to carry on its persistent erosion. It is of great importance, then, that we take immediate steps to ensure that every American child be given the opportunity to make and keep himself physically fit—fit to learn, fit to understand, to grow in grace and stature, to fully live. In answering this challenge, we look to our schools and colleges as the decisive force in a renewed national effort to strengthen the physical fitness of youth. Many of our schools have long been making strenuous efforts to assist our young people to attain and maintain health and physical fitness. But we must do more. We must expand and improve our health services, health education and physical education. We must increase our facilities and the time devoted to physical activity. We must invigorate our curricula and give high priority to a crusade for excellence in health and fitness.

A statement by Dr. Wilson W. Elkins,[2] President of the University of Maryland, concerning the place of

[1] President's Council on Youth Fitness, "A Presidential Message to the Schools on the Physical Fitness of Youth," in *Youth Physical Fitness: Suggested Elements of a School-Centered Program*, Parts One and Two. Washington, D. C.: Superintendent of Documents, U. S. Government Printing Office, 1961.

[2] W. W. Elkins, "Physical Education—Part of the General Education Program," *Journal of Health, Physical Education, and Recreation*, 32:25 (1961). Reprinted by permission of the American Association for Health, Education, and Recreation.

physical education in general education at the university level is worthy of mention:

The purpose of education is to develop the potentialities of the individual. A complex variety of factors and agencies are involved in this development, and the schools and colleges have the primary responsibility of promoting intellectual growth. While carrying out this responsibility, proper consideration must be given to the interdependent parts which, taken together in sum total, constitute the personality. These parts cannot be separated, nor do they grow independently of each other. The intellect develops within the structure of the human body, and it depends upon a proper climate. In large measure, that climate is good health. The extent to which the individual, and ultimately society, will profit by the development of potentialities depends upon the fitness of the individual to fulfill his objectives. It is exceedingly important, therefore, that physical education be included in any general program designed to improve our human resources.

Health is more important than anything else. It is not the sole or the primary responsibility of the school or college, but the general welfare of society demands that it be given a place which will attract attention, assure interest, and command respect. However strongly one may feel about the responsibility of the home for physical fitness, the educational institutions must support and strengthen what is done on the outside. It is a well-known fact that if the general curriculum does not include a program of physical development and the essentials of good health, these will be neglected by the student and will not be adequately supplied by the home or other agencies.

The famous historian Thomas Woody [3] states:

Despite the fact that lipservice has been paid increasingly to the dictum "a sound mind in a sound body" ever since Western Europe began to revive the educational concepts of the Graeco-Roman world, there is still a lack of balance among those who write of education. . . . Physical exercise is necessary to the growth, the health, and the happiness of men, mental as well as physical. For man is a unity. His mind may be isolated for the purpose of study and discussion, but in actual life . . . when all labor is done by machines, it may someday be, man will still need healthy muscles and vital organs as a condition of healthy life. Such sturdy systems, if not developed by the normal labor of the day must be gained through substituted forms of exercise.

An interesting statement is made by Dr. George Gallup in his book, *Secrets of a Long Life*. After studying the exercise habits of a large number of individuals,

Dr. Gallup concluded that Americans are involved in a massive and continuous conspiracy to brainwash youth of all ages against physical activity.

Figure 1–1, comparing the potential and normal physical and psychic growths of man, supports the preceding statements and dramatically emphasizes the need for additional physical involvement by the masses from the elementary-school years to late adulthood.

In the area of activity and exercise, it is obvious that the American public would favor some type of "instant" exercise involving an armchair fitness program or "bottled" exercise that would permit an individual to reap the benefits of exercise while watch-

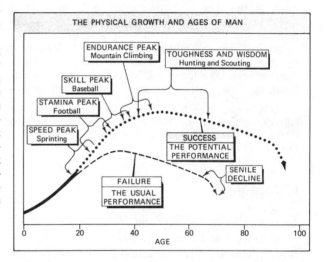

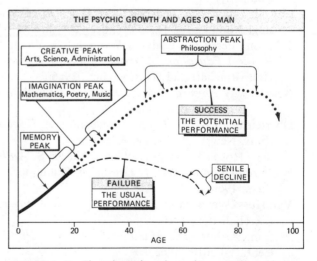

FIGURE 1–1. The physical and psychic growths and ages of man—possibility and performance.
SOURCE: From Joseph W. Still, *The New York Times Magazine*, November 24, 1957, © 1957 by The New York Times Company. Reprinted by permission.

[3] *Report of the Governor's Conference on Youth Fitness* (Springfield, Ill.: Superintendent of Public Instruction, State of Illinois, 1957).

ing TV. One pill would provide the cardiovascular and organic changes equal to 3 sets of tennis, running one mile, or swimming vigorously for 30 minutes. Another pill would account for 30 push-ups, 100 sit-ups, or a 2-mile walk. Pills, progressive in their effects, to turn the fat American slowly into an efficient, healthy organism again. While the public awaits such an unrealistic, impractical, and inefficient approach, years of unhealthiness pass, with the value of being a truly efficient individual never experienced.

Concerning leisure and predicted problems in the future, the late distinguished physical educator and philosopher J. B. Nash [4] states:

No great civilization has yet developed leisure and lived. In the time of Nero the active Gauls came to Rome and there were none to defend the walls. The Romans had become soft in body and spirit through luxurious living and misspent leisure. Education can set a pattern for leisure. Dr. Mortimer Adler, no educational liberal, Director of the Institute for Philosophical Research, charges that, "educators have failed to pro-

[4] J. B. Nash, "Who Is Educated." Talk given at the Buffalo Conference of the New York State Association for Health, Physical Education and Recreation, January 24, 1960.

vide men with the proper liberal arts training for his leisure hours. . . . The schools must assume some of the responsibility for laying the basis for leisure time skills; but here again, leisure is misunderstood, ridiculed and detested by the advocates of narrow disciplinary curriculum."

Also, the objectives of college physical education outlined previously are realized by a unique form of education through the physical that will not be fully met without the aid of physical education.

The place, importance, and role of college or university physical education is perfectly clear. The need is present, the value of programs is scientifically supported, and the beneficial effects of exercise are indisputable (Chapter 3). The value and importance of adapted physical education (Chapter 2) at the college level are obvious and provide the final chance for improvement in posture and body mechanics as well as for understanding the limitations and capacities associated with specific defects. The call for accelerated programs at the college level is heard from the President of the U. S., college presidents, philosophers, and numerous national committees. Both the challenge and the need will be magnified in the future.

BIBLIOGRAPHY

Barrow, Harold M. *Man and His Movement: Principles of His Physical Education.* Philadelphia: Lea & Febiger, 1971.

Bucher, Charles A. *Foundations of Physical Education,* 4th ed. St. Louis: The C. V. Mosby Company, 1976.

Cowell, Charles C., and Hazelton, Helen W. *Curriculum Designs in Physical Education.* Englewood Cliffs, N.J.: Prentice-Hall, Inc., 1955.

Johnson, Perry B., Updyke, Wynn F., Stolberg, Donald C., and Schaefer, Maryellen, *Physical Education: A Problem-Solving Approach to Health and Fitness.* New York: Holt, Rinehart and Winston, Inc., 1966.

Nash, Jay B. *Physical Education: Its Interpretations and Objectives.* Dubuque, Ia.: William C. Brown Company, Publishers, 1963.

Oberteuffer, Delbert. *Physical Education: A Textbook of Principles for Professional Students.* New York: Harper & Brothers, 1956.

Slusher, Howard S., and Lockhart, Aileene S. *Anthology of Contemporary Readings: An Introduction to Physical Education.* Dubuque, Ia.: William C. Brown Company, Publishers, 1966.

Van Huss, Wayne et al. *Physical Activity in Modern Living.* Englewood Cliffs, N.J.: Prentice-Hall, Inc., 1960.

Weston, Arthur. *The Making of American Physical Education.* New York: Appleton-Century Crofts, 1962.

Williams, J. F. *Principles of Physical Education,* Rev. ed. Philadelphia: W. B. Saunders Company, 1964.

Webster, Randolph W. *Philosophy of Physical Education.* Dubuque, Ia.: William C. Brown Company, Publishers, 1965.

2

FITNESS AND HEALTH

Scientific and medical advances have resulted in the elimination of numerous serious diseases. Successful treatment and control also exists for diseases previously labeled incurable or hopeless. Our advanced technology has given us the potential for long, healthy lives. Unfortunately, physical passivity or sedentary living in the United States counteracts this potential. Although more and more Americans are playing tennis, racquetball, age groups sports and engaging in aerobics, the "Fat, Sedentary American" is all too common. It is doubtful whether the American child and adult even approach the fitness levels of their European counterparts. Our average life expectancy is below that of several other less affluent countries. Diseases of the heart and blood vessels account for more than 50% of all deaths in the United States. Low levels of physical fitness must share a large portion of the blame.

No individual has "told it like it is" any better than Phillip H. Abelson, writing in the May, 1976, issue of *Science:*

"The public assumes that large expenditures for health care will bring better health. This assumption is questionable. During the early part of this century, life expectancy in the U.S. steadily increased, but it reached a plateau in 1954. In 1967, W. H. Forbes explored the relation between national expenditures in behalf of health and actual results. He concluded that we could halve or double the total expenditure without changing longevity. This was in the year when only $42 billion was spent.

Since 1967, others have pointed out that most of the deaths in the age range, 10-70, either are due to degenerative diseases or are fatalities arising from accidents, suicide, or homicide. The big killers are coronary heart disease, cancer, and stroke. Treatment for these diseases is

often costly. Their incidence is related in part to lifestyle, for example, sedentary living, poor diet, obesity, and smoking.

Because treatment of degenerative diseases is not uniformly successful and since the course of some of them can be altered by changes in the patient's behavior, there is increasing interest in preventive medicine. Frederick C. Swartz, M.D., has stated that our greatest health problem is in the physical fitness of the nation. Here the answer is the simplest and the cheapest, has the greatest application, and its reflection on the reduction of morbidity and mortality rates would be immediate and tremendous. It is entirely possible that a well-practiced physical fitness program begun early in life would increase life expectancy ten years . . ."[1]

Abelson continues, "substantially better health cannot be bought with 118.5 billion. Isn't it time the nation began to pay more attention to approaches that promise great improvement at little cost?"

This chapter contains an overview of all aspects of exercise and health to allow you to evaluate your current fitness level and make wise exercise choices meeting your interest and health needs. It provides you with an inexpensive approach to health through the nation's best health insurance—regular exercise.

BENEFICIAL EFFECTS OF EXERCISE

The Right Kind of Regular Exercise Produces a More Efficient, Healthy Body

One of the most apparent effects of increased leisure time on individuals of all ages involves the

[1]Abelson, Philip H., *Science.* May 14, 1976. Vol. 192, No. 4240, P. 619.

problem of lack of exercise and its consequences for health. The accompanying results have been obesity or overweight, sickness, increased susceptibility to diseases of all types, and a general feeling of fatigue. This problem, coupled with the common abuses of overeating, smoking, drinking, drug use, and lack of sleep have placed the average individual in a less than healthy state.

The beneficial effects of exercise have considerable support from research and expert medical opinion.

The statements below represent a summary of findings to date concerning the physiological and psychological effects of regular exercise. Exercise of a vigorous nature has been shown to:

1. produce organic changes in the lungs and circulatory system that improve normal living function and protect against stress and strain;

2. increase body weight and vital capacity of growing youths;

3. be a significant factor in the aging process: the aging, or degenerative, process may be delayed by exercise, and physical and mental health are preserved longer through exercise;

4. increase production of red blood cells in the bone marrow as shown in the hemoglobin count;

5. assist in maintaining normal blood pressure;

6. result in a more rapid return to normal heart rate and blood pressure as well as other body functions following exertion;

7. strengthen the heart muscle—no evidence has been uncovered indicating that a healthy heart is damaged through exercise;

8. assist in the maintenance of a healthy heart and prevention of cardiovascular disease and lessen the severity of an attack as well as enhance recovery;

9. increase the stroke volume of the heart (amount of blood ejected per contraction);

10. improve circulation throughout the body through changes in heart rate, stroke volume, and additional factors interacting to provide increased circulatory efficiency;

11. produce a lower resting pulse;

12. reduce obesity and overweight problems, which generally are a result of underactivity rather than overeating alone, and reduce body fat and weight through calorie expenditure and the call upon the fat tissue for energy supply;

13. improve respiratory efficiency and bring about a slower, deeper respiration than that of the sedentary individual;

14. improve the efficiency of the digestive system by increasing appetite and food intake and by accelerating the peristaltic action with subsequent speeding and increasing of the efficiency at which food is absorbed;

15. increase the strength, endurance, and size of active muscles;

16. strengthen weak muscle groups and improve posture and muscle tones;

17. assist in reducing, withstanding, and adapting to stress;

18. decrease triglyceride and cholesterol levels during and after exercise;

19. assist in reducing mental tension and anxiety through possible release of congested emotions in a socially accepted manner;

20. improve personal appearance and feeling of vitality.

COMPONENTS OF FITNESS AND HEALTH

Most individuals possess sufficiently high levels of physical capacity to perform daily routines effectively with some reserve energy. An individual may also be free from disease. However, such a minimum level has been acquired through daily routines and remains distant from the *potential* level. Such a level also fails to provide the individual with the many values of regular, vigorous exercise. It is therefore desirable to achieve a level considerably higher than the state acquired through normal daily routine through the initiation of an acceptable, vigorous exercise program of a progressive nature. The use of such a program will significantly improve the components of physical capacity discussed below.

The Most Important Objective of a Fitness Program is Improvement of Cardiovascular and Respiratory Endurance

The exchange of gases (oxygen absorption and elimination of carbon dioxide) and heart efficiency (increased cardiac output) are significantly improved through aerobic training such as running, bicycle riding, swimming, rope jumping, and other endurance programs. Both processes affect the ability to exert prolonged effort. This remains as the single most valuable fitness component for young adults and older individuals. Increased muscular bulk and superior strength are unimportant compared to heart and lung efficiency and the implications for preventive heart disease in the adult years.

"Girth Control" Requires a Combination of Sound Judgement, and Proper Eating and Exercise Habits.

The big belly with accumulation of fat in the abdomen is common among college age men and women, and is unhealthy for a number of reasons: (1) digestive problems are frequent, (2) the diaphram can be pushed up, separating the chest from the abdominal cavities, compressing the space for normal lung expansion and making breathing more difficult, (3) pressure in the abdomen is increased which can lead to varicose veins, hemorrhoids and other problems (4) loss of abdominal strength limits the ability of the stomach muscles to splint the back, leaving one more susceptible to lower back strains, and (5) accumulation of abdominal fat is a sign you are also acquiring fat in the walls of the arteries and heading for early heart problems.

Quick or gimic approaches to girth control are ineffective. Surgical removal of fat layers and stomach by-pass operations are dangerous choices and fail to eliminate the problems—overeating and sedentary living. The commonly used girdle, corset or tight belt also makes matters worse by pushing the fat inside the abdomen up against the diaphragm, increasing pressure on a hernia through the diaphragm or groin, and imparing both breathing and circulation.

The solution to girth control is the prevention or correction of obesity and the improvement of normal muscle tone in the abdominal area. While you are managing your caloric intake, certain exercises will assist in returning muscle tone and firmness. An acceptable mode of progression for the exercises listed below is to complete 10-15 repetitions of each exercise the first workout, adding 2-5 repetitions each subsequent workout until you are capable of performing 25 of each exercise. At that point, begin to repeat the 25 repetitions of each exercise 2-3 times each workout using a 1-3 minute rest period between each exercise. This high repetition approach is favored over fewer repetitions and use of weight behind the neck (overload principle) if your goal is to reduce abdominal fat and create definition of the stomach muscles (outlines of the muscles and a flat stomach).

Abdominal tensing—Contract all stomach muscles for 5 seconds while sitting in your office; relax and repeat, continuing 4-6 different times.

Bent-leg-sit-ups—Sit on the floor with knees drawn up toward the chest, feet hooked under a bed or dresser, hands behind the neck. Touch the left elbow to the right knee, alternating right elbow to left knee.

Curls—Lying on the back with knees bent slightly, curl the head and shoulder upward until shoulder blades come off the floor, hold one second and return to the floor.

Rowing—Lying on the back with knees bent slightly, bring the knees up toward the chest as you sit up.

Sit-up exercises with straight legs work the thighs and lower back muscles and are rather ineffective for the upper abdomen.

Body Flexibility Can Be Maintained Throughout Life

The extent to which the active muscles can be shortened and the antagonistic muscles elongated is determined by bone structure, the state of the connective tissue maintaining a particular joint, the soft tissues, and the state of the muscle itself. The last two qualities can be altered significantly by stretching procedures that produce increases in the total range of movement in a specific joint. Flexibility in the major joints can be improved in a relatively short period of time (2-3 weeks) through both *static* (steady pressure applied at the extreme range of motion in a particular joint) or *ballistic* exercises (bouncing to attempt to force the body beyond the normal range of motion). Static procedures appear to be much more practical and efficient (producing equal changes in flexibility) and have been found to relax the muscles being stretched, reduce the probability of injury, and eliminate much of the soreness accompanying ballistic procedures. Flexibility increases will be maintained following periods of inactivity for a period of 8-16 weeks and indefinitely when exercise is continuous. Flexibility is extremely high in the early years of life and tends to diminish with increased age and lack of exercise. This quality can be retained in the later years through stretching exercises.

PRINCIPLES OF CONDITIONING

Improvement in the Capacity of the Human Body to Perform Work is Based on the Concept of Work Hypertrophy

Although improving aerobic endurance, strength/power, muscular endurance, agility, reaction time, speed and flexibility require special routines, any improvement in the capacity of the human body to perform work is based on the concept of work hypertrophy. As show in in Figure 2-1, an individual functioning at level A who engages in some form of exercise will show a temporary decline (to point C) in working capacity immediately following the exercise bout. During the recovery phase, however, tissue will regenerate beyond the original level of conditioning (D) to point E. This is referred to as the exaltation phase (A-1) and it is at this point that an individual can perform more work than on the previous occasion with no more strain or effort. Use of this process can lead to continued improvement of conditioning levels as indicated by A-2, A-3, and A-4, providing certain basic principles are followed: (1) exercise must be sufficiently strenuous to cause a marked exaltation effect—the depth of the valley is in proportion to the intensity and duration of the exercise effort, (2) the next workout must occur within 36-48 hours; greater time lapse has a diminishing effect until one declines to the original level or lower, (3) sufficient recovery time must be allowed for the exaltation phase to develop; improvement will not occur and performance will suffer if exercise is initiated before the recovery phase is complete, and (4) each workout must be progressively more strenuous than the previous to ensure a deep valley, continued progression and increased capacity to perform exercise. The components of this concept can be applied to any exercise program.

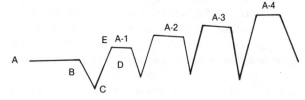

FIGURE 2-1. Concept of work hypertrophy A—Pre-exercise functioning level, C—functioning level following exercise, E—elevated functioning level following recovery, A-1—elevated functioning level at the proper point to reconvene exercise.

Law of Overcompensation. Vigorous exercise results in a destruction of muscle constituents. As the lost materials are replaced, nature overcompensates in order to prepare the body for still more strenuous efforts. The degree of overcompensation is in direct proportion to the severity of the exercise. This principle also explains the development of a callus on the feet or hands following activity that removes the superficial skin layers, and it explains the production of antitoxins (immunity) when the body is exposed to the disease-producing toxins.

Law of Progressive Resistance Exercise. For strength gains, muscles must be exercised against gradually increasing resistance. Increased loads (overload principle) beyond the demands regularly made on the organism determine the ultimate effectiveness of a program such as weight training. This principle is applied in exercise programs by increasing the resistance (amount of weight to be lifted or moved), increasing the number of repetitions (number of times you lift the weight), increasing the speed of contraction (speed at which you perform one repetition), decreasing the rest interval (amount of rest between exercises), and by a combination of each. The nearer a muscle is worked to maximum capacity, the greater the strength gain.

Training For Endurance (Heart Lung). Heart/Lung (aerobic) endurance can be developed through a number of different exercise approaches such as strenuous walking (4 m.p.h. and faster), bicycle riding, jogging, bench stepping, rope skipping, running in place, lap swimming, and various sports. Heart/lung efficiency has been found to improve by attaining a "critical threshold" in terms of elevating the heart rate through exercise. A critical threshold is a heart rate approximately 60 percent of the distance between the resting and maximum heart rates. For an individual with a resting heart rate of 70 and a maximum of 190, this critical threshold is 142 beats per minute (190 minus 70 = 120, 120 × .60 = 72, 72 + 70 = 142). You can identify your own critical threshold by determining your estimated maximum heart rate from Figure 2-2 and merely counting your radial or carotid pulse immediately after you stop exercising. If your heart rate is not at the critical threshold level, more strenuous activity is indicated.

FIGURE 2-2.   Estimated maximum heart rates by age.

Age Range	Estimated Maximum Heart Rate
20-29	200
30-39	190
40-49	180
50-59	170
60-69	160
70+	150

Training for Maintenance. Strength gained over a period of three months or more through weight training will decrease slowly with inactivity. The speed at which it subsides is somewhat proportional to the time spent acquiring the strength gains. There is evidence, however, that strength can be retained with one weight training workout weekly, through the establishment of a "maintenance load," or the amount of resistance and intensity required to hold the present conditioning level without regression.

Concerning endurance (aerobic), there is strong indications that maintenance requires nearly a daily or 5 times per week effort to avoid a drop in conditioning level.

Principle of Warm-Up, or Preparation for Vigorous Activity. Formal warm-up (preparatory activity simulating the efforts to follow, such as the use of jogging prior to a half-mile run) and infomal warm-up (preparatory activity different from the effort to follow, such as the use of calistenics prior to a half-mile run) have been used for years because of the possible assistance in both the prevention of injuries and improved performance. Research provides conflicting evidence, with some experimenters supporting the value of warm-up and others indicating no relationship between warm-up and injury or performance in various tests. Its importance may be an individual matter, with psychological value for some performers. Until the time when more conclusive evidence is available, experiment to determine its value in your exercise routine.

Principle of Slowly Diminishing Exercise Effort. Strenuous circulatory and respiratory endurance activity, such as distance running, requires a tapering off at the completion of the effort in the form of jogging for a substantial distance. If such a procedure is not followed, the venous return to the heart (assisted by the milking action of the muscles during the competitive effort) drops quickly and may cause blood pooling in the extremities, leading to shock or hyperventilation, which may produce lower CO_2

levels and muscle cramps. Walking, slow jogging or leisurely movement at the end of a workout would prevent this occurrence.

SELECTING AN EXERCISE PROGRAM

The One Best Method For Improving Physical Fitness Has Not Been Developed.

For the college student and adults of all ages the foundation or basic exercise program should place primary emphasis on the development of the heart and lungs through "Aerobic Training." The primary objective of an aerobic exercise program is to increase the amount of oxygen that can be processed by the body within a given period of time (Maximum Oxygen Uptake). An exercise program is judged by its demand upon the heart and lungs and caloric expenditure.

The type of program selected depends upon desired physical outcomes, time, and individual interest and preference.

Aerobics. The term "aerobics" was introduced by Dr. Kenneth Cooper to describe exercise that stimulates heart and lung activity enough to produce a training effect. The primary objective of such a program is to increase the amount of oxygen processed by the body within a given time period (Maximum Oxygen Uptake). Workouts and activities are classified according to demands placed upon the

FIGURE 2-3. 1.5 mile test for men and women. From: *The New Aerobics* by Kenneth Cooper, 1977. Used by permission of publisher, Bantom Books, Inc., New York.

1.5 MILE TEST: MEN

Fitness Category	Under 30	30-39	40-49	50+
I. Very Poor	16:30	17:30	18:30	19:00
II. Poor	16:30 - 14:31	17:30 - 15:31	18:30 - 16:31	19:00 - 17:01
III. Fair	14:30 - 12:01	15:30 - 13:01	16:30 - 14:01	17:00 - 14:31
IV. Good	12:00 - 10:16	13:00 - 11:01	14:00 - 11:31	14:30 - 12:01
V. Excellent	10:15	11:00	11:30	12:00

1.5 MILE TEST: WOMEN

Fitness Category	Under 30	30-39	40-49	50+
I. Very Poor	17:30	18:30	19:30	20:00
II. Poor	17:30 - 15:30	18:30 - 16:31	19:30 - 17:31	20:30 - 18:31
III. Fair	15:30 - 13:01	16:30 - 14:01	17:30 - 15:01	18:30 - 16:31
IV. Good	13:00 - 11:16	14:00 - 12:01	15:00 - 12:31	16:30 - 13:31
V. Excellent	11:15	12:00	12:30	13:30

FIGURE 2-4.   Aerobic training by fitness categories on the 1.5 mile test.

Rating	Weeks	Program	Comment
I. Very Poor	Initial Workout	On a track, begin running at a comfortable pace until you sense the onset of fatigue (mild). STOP IMMEDIATELY and note distance covered. Walk at an average pace until fatigue symptoms subside. Note the distance walked. Return to running until fatigue symptoms reappear. STOP. Record the total running distance covered during the two runing phases and one walking phase. This is your first "target." Until you can run this entire distance non-stop, do not add any mileage to your workout.	This is a run/walk workout. Do not overdo it on the first day. After several weeks you should be able to run the target distance non-stop.
	3rd Week	Begin LSD (long-slow-distance) Training— Use a pace that permits a pleasant conversation and causes only mild distress. Continue running non-stop for as long as possible. Rather than walk, slow the pace and attempt to finish the workout pleasantly tired but not exhausted. Do not be concerned about time.	Continue LSD training, add 30 seconds to 1 minute to each workout until you can run non-stop for at least 20 minutes
	6th Week	Test yourself in the 1.5 mile run again. If your category has changed, move on to the program for Rating II. If there was no change, continue LSD training until you can run 30 minutes non-stop.	
II. Poor	First	Use LSD training described above, covering a minimum of 1 mile each workout (non-stop) for several weeks before walk/ running 1-2 additional miles at the end of each workout.	Increase the number of weekly workouts to four
	3rd Week	Begin to time each mile, running at an 8:00 pace for as long a distance as possible. Attempt to achieve two miles in 16:00 or less.	Run a minimum of 6 miles weekly
	6th Week	Test yourself in the 1.5 mile run, moving to Category III if you qualify. If there was no change, continue LSD training until you can run one mile in 7:45 and two miles in 15:30.	
III. Fair	First Week	Continue LSD training at 8:00 pace.	Increase weekly mileage volume to 10-12
	3rd Week	Increase non-stop run to three miles	
	6th Week	Retake the 1.5 mile test, moving to Category IV if you qualify. If you do not qualify, continue to increase weekly mileage volume by 2-3 miles.	
IV. Good	First	Adapt the Fartlek Program to your conditioning level	An alternate method for time in this category is to add a minimum of 35 aerobic points weekly.
	3rd Week	Adjust Fartlek Program, attempting to complete the sample workout described in this chapter	
	6th Week	Retake the 1.5 mile test, moving to category V if you qualify. If you do not, continue Fartlek training for two additional weeks.	

FIGURE 2-4. (continued)   Aerobic training by fitness categories on the 1.5 mile test.

Rating	Weeks	Program	Comment
V. Excellent		Continue with whatever program you have been using if this was your original test category. Take the 1.5 mile test once monthly to judge the success of your maintenance program.	Increase the number of aerobic points weekly if you want to improve rather then maintain present level.

Each workout at all levels begins with a slow one-mile warm-up run/walk and ends with a ¾ to one mile slow warm-down

heart and lungs and caloric expenditure. An aerobic point value based on the caloric expenditure and oxygen demands of the exercise is assigned to each workout.

Stop reading for a half hour or so. If you are at home, measure off approximately 1.5 miles with your automobile. If you are near a one-quarter mile track, change into running attire and use that facility. Your first task is to self-administer the 1.5 mile run/walk test and determine your fitness category from Figure 2-3. If you have been inactive or are over 30 years of age, avoid the 1.5 mile test for 6-7 weeks and begin a walking program at Level I, Figure 2-4 The test can be dangerous for older individuals, those who have been inactive, are overweight or obese, or have high blood pressure. If in doubt, avoid taking the test and begin at Level I.

If you score in the "Poor" or "Very Poor" category, begin the walking program at Level I, Figure 2-4. If you score in the "Fair," "Good," or "Excellent" category, continue with your current exercise program. It would also be helpful to secure Cooper's book: *The New Aerobics* and follow the progression for your fitness category. The aerobic program allows you to choose from a number of exercise progams such as running, cycling, rope jumping, walking, swimming, tennis, handball, racquetball, basketball and other sports.

Other Aerobic Running Programs.   Aerobic running programs represent one of the most complete modes of conditioning.

Fartlek training is designed for the elimination of boredom as well as diversion from routine training, and has been used successfully by cross-country and distance runners in track and field. It is a personalized program whereby both pace and terrain are constantly altered in one continuous workout ranging from 20 minutes to three to six hours. Use of short sprints, walking, incline running up stairs or hills, track running at meet pact, backward running, and jogging provides a program geared to individual tolerance levels that can also provide training of a progressive nature on flat or hilly terrain of practically any surface.

Calisthenics.   Specific movements that utilize the body as resistance remain as one of the oldest forms of conditioning in existence. Exercises such as sit-ups, toe-touchers, trunk rotation, jumping jacks, push-ups, and a wide variety of others must be performed in a high number of repetitions, since the resistance is relatively low. Since resistance (body weight) also remains constant, the number of repetitions must be gradually increased, the rest interval between exercises decreased, the speed or rate or execution increased, and the duration of the workout increased. Use of weighted vests (ankle, back) or an exercise partner can alter the resistance variable, and thus further develop strength. Exercises must be carefully chosen to activate the major muscle groups and must involve endurance-type work to stimulate and develop the heart and lungs. A properly conceived program can yield significant changes in strength endurance, flexibility, and agility. The obvious disadvantages are boredom and lack of diversity.

Rope Jumping.   By counting the number of jumps per minute, regulating the rest period between different jumps and using some difficult high energy jumps, a program can be designed that will improve both agility and aerobic endurance. During the first week or two it may be helpful to warm up by jogging in place 50 to 100 easy steps. The program below includes three warm-up jumps (to be completed slowly) and five basic jumps (to be completed at the rate of 70-75 jumps per minute). Locate your level on the sample Ten-week program shown in Figure 2-5 and begin at that point, progressing each week as indicated. The Boxer's shuffle and single foot jumps are performed at the 70-75 per minute rate while the double jump is restarted when missed and continued for the specified number of repetitions.

FIGURE 2-5.   Sample Ten-Week Rope Jumping Program.

Week	Exercises	Sets[1]	No. Jumps	Rest Between Jumps
First Week	Warm-up jumps	1	15	Continuous
	Basic five jumps	1	15	2 minutes
	Practice session	1		15 minutes to learn jumps
Second Week	Warm-up jumps	1	20	Continuous
	Basic five jumps	1	20	2 minutes
	Practice session	1		15 minutes to learn jumps
Third Week	Warm-up jumps	1	25	Continuous
	Basic five jumps	1	25	90 seconds
Fourth Week	Warm-up jumps	1	25	Continuous
	Basic five jumps	2	15	90 seconds
Fifth Week	Warm-up jumps	1	25	Continuous
	Basic five jumps	2	20	90 seconds
Sixth Week	Warm-up jumps	1	25	Continuous
	Basic five jumps	2	25	60 seconds
Seventh Week	Warm-up jumps	1	25	Continuous
	Basic five jumps	2	35	60 seconds
Eighth Week	Warm-up jumps	1	25	Continuous
	Basic five jumps	3	40	60 seconds
Ninth Week	Warm-up jumps	1	25	Continuous
	Basic five jumps	3	45	30 seconds
Tenth Week	Warm-up jumps	1	25	Continuous
	Basic five jumps	3	50	15 seconds

[1]Number of times the specified jumps are completed—a one-minute rest period is permitted between sets when multiple sets begin in the Fifth Week.

Warm-up Jumps:

Two foot jump with an intermediate jump (double beat)—after the rope passes under the feet, a small hop is taken before jumping again to clear the rope.

Two foot jump (single beat)—no intermediate jump is taken.

Single foot hop (single beat)—the left foot is used for a specified number of jumps, followed by the right foot.

Basic Program

Boxer's Shuffle (single beat)—use alternate right and left foot jumping as the rope passes under.

Running Forward (Single beat)—jump while running forward; repeat running backward to starting position.

Cross-Overs (double beat)—jump with the rope turning forward, cross the rope by fully crossing the arms as the rope clears your head. Repeat with rope turning backwards.

Single Foot Hops (single beat)—same as warm-up jump; progress from slow to fast or pepper jumping.

Double Jumps (double beat)—the rope must pass under the feet twice while in the air. Perform one double jump, one single jump, one double jump, alternating until completing the specified number.

On the first workout day, locate your level on the sample Ten-week program and begin at that point, progressing each week as indicated. The boxer's shuffle and single foot jumps are performed as fast as possible; the double jump is restarted when missed and continued for the specified number of repetitions.

In summary, it is evident that choice of an exercise program depends upon the outcomes desired as well as on pressures of times, available equipment, and personal qualities. The degree to which a program contributes to the development of physical fitness depends both upon the activity selected and the extent to which the principles of conditioning have been applied. From an overall view, aerobic programs represents the most desirable choices; advantages of high caloric expenditure for weight control, heart/lung development and possible protection from early heart disease; and limited time demands make aerobic exercise superior to all others for the adult population of men and women.

Stop for a moment to evaluate your choice of exercise and its effectiveness. How frequent do you exercise? Does your program improve cardio-respiratory endurance? Does your choice allow for the systematic increases in intensity? From the information provided in this chapter, alter your program as it applys the basic principles of conditioning. Describe, in paragraph form, how your program should be changed to maximize benefits.

HOW TO EVALUATE YOUR FITNESS LEVEL

An integral part of any conditioning program is periodic appraisal of progress with reliable, valid, and objective tests used prior to the initiation and upon completion of a program. Numerous so-called fitness tests batteries exist that measure a wide variety of fitness components. None of these batteries successfully measure cardiovascular efficiency. Several principles should assist the college student in making wise test choices for personal fitness assessment:

1. Maximum oxygen uptake (VO₂Max) through direct calorimetry is the best single index of cardio-respiratory efficiency. This laboratory, one-on-one test, is becoming the international standard of heart-lung capacity. While this method requires a well-equipped laboratory and is impractical for testing large numbers of students, all other Field Tests must be evaluated in light of their relationship with this test.

2. Upper body (arm/shoulder) and abdominal strength/endurance are important test areas for college students.

3. The percent of body fat is a valuable index of fitness and can be determined using the skinfold procedure discussed in Chapter 3.

FIGURE 2-6.   Field Tests for College Students

Test	Purpose	Level	Comments
Pull-ups (Boys) Flexed arm hang (Girls)	Arm/shoulder strength and muscular endurance	Elementary Secondary College	High reliability, valid measures of upper body strength, critical to school age children
Modified sit-ups (Girls and Boys)	Abdominal strength and muscular endurance	Elementary Secondary College	30-second test is both reliable and valid; eliminates majority of problems associated with maximum number of sit-ups testing
12-minute test or 1.5 mile run	Cardiovascular efficiency	Secondary College	High correlation (.92) with Maximum Oxygen Uptake. Best performance measures of cardiovascular/respiratory efficiency in existence for this age group. See Figure 2-3 for fitness categories by time and age
Body fat	Percent of body fat	Elementary Secondary College	Important at all age levels. Accurate measurement possible with home-made cardboard or plywood calipers and nonogram
600-yard run/walk	Cardiovascular efficiency	None	Low correlation with Maximum Oxygen Uptake. Motivation and other problems make this unsuitable for elementary school age children and highly questionable for any age level
AAHPER and other fitness batteries	"Fitness"	None	Batteries measure items related to athletic performance; unsuitable for analysis of physiological functions. Fitness components such as agility, flexibility, balance, speed, etc., unimportant and yields no physiological data. Batteries are time-consuming, and in general, yield limited information.

FIGURE 2-7.   Test of Abdominal strength for Men and Women.

	Modified Sit-Ups
Equipment:	None
Validity:	Not reported
Reliability	0.91 and up
Procedure:	The number of sit-ups completed in 30 seconds is recommended in preference to counting the maximum number of repetitions with no time limit for several reasons: (1) the timed and untimed measures are highly correlated, (2) test administration time is saved, (3) the effects of motivation are minimized, and (4) extreme muscular soreness often accompaning maximum effort testing is avoided.
Test Administration:	Subjects lie on their backs, hands clasped behind the neck and the knees bent enough to allow a partner to place one fist underneath. A helper holds the feet down as the subject curls up off the floor and touches high right elbow to the left knee, alternating each sit-up. One sit-up includes the cycle from the prone position with elbows behind the neck to the specified upright position.
	Avoid use of straight leg sit-up or leg lift test. The iliopsoas muscle is the primary mover in the initial lifting of the trunk in these exercises, particularily when the back is arched during execution. Subjects should curl upward in the initial movement.

4. Typical fitness batteries include a number of items (softball throw, 50-yard dash, shuttle run, agility measures, flexibility items, balance items) that have no relationship to cardio-respiratory fitness, and must be termed unimportant items belonging in motor ability rather than fitness tests. Little useful data are revealed from batteries of this nature.

Figure 2-6 evaluates a number of specific tests and complete batteries. For the college student only 4 tests taking less than 30 minutes can provide an adequate fitness evaluation.

CARDIOVASCULAR HEALTH

Diseases of the heart account for 38.6 per cent of all deaths in the United States, and more than 4 million Americans now have cardiac disabilities. More than half of these 4 million are less than 65 years of age. In fact, heart disease is becoming increasingly common among people 40 years of age and younger. It is our fore-most health problem hitting more than a million times a year, and taking more than 600,000 lives while leaving many survivors with mental and physical handicaps.

The major diseases of the cardiovascular system include diseases of the heart valves, diseases of the electrical system (heart rhythm and heart block), rheumatic heart disease, congestive heart failure, congenital defects, and coronary artery disease. The latter, coronary heart disease, has reached almost epidemic proportions in some Western countries and is responsible for over one-half of all cardiovascular deaths with strokes accounting for approximately one-fifth. Evidence is increasing to support the hypothesis that coronary heart disease can be delayed or prevented with early lifestyle changes.

This section focuses on specific behavioral changes that potentially can influence the pattern of coronary heart disease. Major emphasis is placed upon providing information to increase your understanding of heart disease, to clarify the various theories including the role of risk factors, and to aid in making wise decisions for the prevention of heart disease.

HEART DISEASE

The normal heart muscle is extremely durable and continues to function as long as it receives sufficient blood supply from the coronary arteries.

A simple explanation of the function of the heart is provided in Figure 2-9. It is rarely the heart muscle that is at fault in causing a heart attack; rather, inadequate supply of blood to the heart, usually a result of clogged coronary arteries and their branches, brings about tissue death to certain areas of the heart muscle. The heart receives nourishment from two main coronary arteries which branch off the aorta. The right coronary artery covers the back side of the heart by branching into smaller and smaller arteries which penetrate the wall of the heart, eventually branching into tiny capillaries to supply oxygen and nutriments to the heart muscle and its electrical conduction system. The left coronary artery is divided into two parts which nourish the front and

left side of the heart. Through these coronary arteries, the heart maintains its own nourishment. Unfortunately, these coronary arteries are most susceptible to fatty deposit build-up and clogging.

"Coronary Thrombosis" may occur due to a clot in a coronary artery. Artery closure may be due to an accumulation of atheromas. In most cases, only a branch of an artery supplying a portion of the heart muscle is affected (see Figure 2-10). This may explain why many attacks are not fatal. Blockage in the

FIGURE 2-8. Tests of Upper Body Strength for Men and Women.

	Pull-Ups (Men)	*Flexed Arm Hang (Women)*
Equipment:	Horizontal metal or wooden bar approximately 1½ inches in diameter placed high enough for a student to hang off the floor with both arms and legs fully extended. Rings attached to a bar can also be used and permit a natural twisting of the wrists to occur.	
Validity:	See validity of back and grip strength.	
Reliability	0.981	
Procedure:	From a hanging position, subjects raise the body until the chin clearly surpasses the bar before lowering and completely extending the arms. The maximum number of legal pull-ups in 30 seconds constitute the official score.	
Test Administration:	Use near arm to prevent swinging action and encourage only vertical movement. Enforce exact form, eliminating all incorrect repetitions.	
Special Rules:	To initiate the pull-up tests, a forward grip (pronated) and a hanging position in which both the arms and legs are fully extended must be used. Swinging, jerking, kicking, partial extension of the chin over the bar, and flexed elbows prior to starting another repetition are violations in continuous action and avoid attempted rest periods while hanging motionless because this tends to induce rapid fatigue. To initiate the *flexed arm hang,* adjust the bar at the subject's height. The bar is grasped with palms facing away from the body. Subject is then lifted to a position with chin just above the bar, (chin may not contact bar), where she hangs for as long as possible. The score is the elapsed time subjects remain in the proper hanging position.	
Scoring Table:	Used in the combined scores of Roger's Physical Fitness Index. See also AAHPER Physical Fitness Test for Men (Chapter 3—"The Development Program" of the *Activities Manual*), Edwin A. Fleishman, *Examiners Manual for the Basic Fitness Tests,* NJ: Prentice-Hall, Inc., 1964. p. 45.	
Modifications of the Test:	If the subject fails to fully extend the arms or raise the chin completely above the bar, half credit is awarded for that attempt.	

Standards for Pull-ups (College Men)				*Standards for Flexed Arm Hang (College Women)*			
Percentile	Pull-ups	Percentile	Pull-ups	Percentile	Seconds	Percentile	Seconds
100	20	45	5	100	75	45	7
95	12	40	5	95	40	40	6
90	10	35	4	90	30	35	5
85	10	30	4	85	21	30	5
80	9	25	3	80	18	25	4
75	8	20	3	75	16	20	4
70	8	15	2	70	14	15	3
65	7	10	1	65	10	10	2
60	7	5	0	60	9	5	0
55	6	0	0	55	9	0	0
50	6	0	0	50	8	0	0

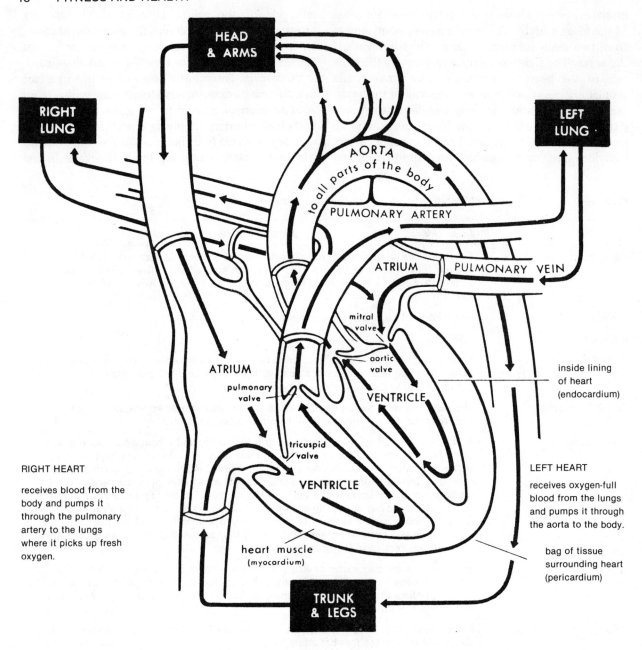

Figure 2-9.   Your Heart and How it Works.
©Reprinted with permission, American Heart Association.

Your heart weighs well under a pound and is long a little larger than your fist, but it is a powerful, long working, hard working organ. Its job is to pump blood to the lungs and to all the body tissues.

The heart is a hollow organ. Its tough, muscular wall (myocardium) is surrounded by a fiberlike bag (pericardium) and is lined by a thin, strong membrane (endocardium). A wall (septum) divides the heart cavity down the middle into a "right heart" and a "left heart". Each side of the heart is divided again into an upper chamber (called an atrium or auricle) and a lower chamber (ventricle). Valves regulate the flow of blood through the heart and to the pumonary artery and the aorta.

The heart is really a double pump. One pump (the right heart) receives blood which has just come from the body after delivering nutrients and oxygen to the body tissues. It pumps this dark, bluish red blood to the lungs where the blood gets rid of a waste gas (carbon dioxide) and picks up a fresh supply of oxygen which turns it a bright red again. The second pump (the left heart) receives this "reconditioned" blood from the lungs and pumps it out through the great trunk-artery (aorta) to be distributed by smaller arteries to all parts of the body.

larger sections of a coronary artery would diminish blood supply to a large area and generally result in death. Figure 2-11 shows the progression of plaque build-up in a coronary artery over a 30 year period.

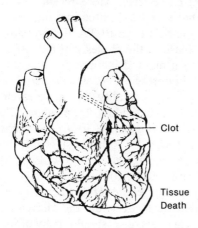

FIGURE 2-10.   Clot or blockage to a branch of the coronary artery (National Heart, Lung and Blood Institute, National Institute of Health).

"Angina Pectoris" refers to a symptom of heart disease caused by diminished blood supply to a portion of the heart muscle. When any muscle fails to receive an adequate blood supply (oxygen and nutriments), pain results. This condition is referred to as ischemia. When the heart muscle is involved, the victim experiences a tightness or pressure in the chest and pain that may radiate to the shoulders or arms. If angina is confirmed, a physician's care and lifestyle changes are indicated.

"Hardening of the arteries" (arteriosclerosis) and "atherosclerosis" are terms used to identify a disease process occuring in the *arteries* of systemic circulation; rarely does the disease involve the veins or blood vessels to the lungs. If the arteries supplying the brain are involved, a stroke occurs; involvement in the legs produce leg pain (claudication) and coronary artery involvement results in chest pain (angina pectoris) and heart attack. "Atherosclerosis" is a condition involving a progressive build-up of fatty material (triglycerides and cholesterol) inside arterial blood vessels to produce narrowing or blockage.

Chest pain may or may not be a symptom of a heart attack.

For the male over 30 years of age and the female over 40, any chest pain is often interpreted as a sign of a heart attack. In actuality, pain in the chest may be do to the chest wall (muscle, ligament, rib, or rib

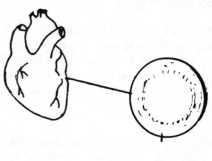

Clear opening (lumen) some plaque, no symptoms.   25-30 years of age

Early atherosclerosis, increased plaque, no symptoms; blood pressure may be elevated   10 years later

Rather advanced atherosclerosis, angina pain possible   20 years later

Coronary thrombosis. The small opening that remains may close depriving a portion of the heart without blood supply   30 years later

FIGURE 2-11.   Common progress of plaque build-up and a heart attack.

cartilage), the lungs or outside covering, the gullet, diaphragm, skin, or other organs in the upper part of the diaphragm. It is no easy task to distinguish between chest pain associated with heart attack and other pains. In general, these clues provide some assistance:

Possibly associated with heart attack: see physician	Probably not associated with heart attack
Mild, intense pain with a feeling of pressure or squeezing on the chest	A shooting pain lasting a few seconds (common in young people)
Pain beneath (inside) the breastbone	A pain at the end of a deep breath or pain that gets worse with a deep breath
Accompanying pain in the jaw or down the inner side of either arm	
Pain in chest, accompanied by nausea, sweating, dizziness or shortness of breath	Pain upon pressing a finger at the spot of discomfort
	Pain burning when stomach is empty
Shortness of breath and/or pulse irregularity	

For the symptoms unassociated with a heart attack, aspirin, Ben-Gay, heat and rest should help. If symptoms persist, a physician should be consulted. For heart attack symptoms, transport immediately to the hospital, monitoring blood pressure, breathing, and heart rate.

A number of different theories exist explaining the cause of coronary heart disease.

The Lipid Theory is based on the premise that a high number of fatty particles (lipoproteins) in the blood stream cause atherosclerosis or the accumulation of these particles on the walls of the arteries. The more fatty particles in the blood, the greater the propensity for accumulation within the arterial walls. Eventually, circulation through an artery is blocked or partially blocked. Depending upon the body part supplied by this artery, a heart attack, stroke, muscular weakness, senility, or a host of other ailments result. The process becomes more common with age and undoubtedly involves a long silent period of fatty deposit build-up beginning in the first decade of life.

Fatty particles that increase the tendency for atherosclerosis are called lipoproteins which consist of fat (triglyeride), a blood protein (to make the fat soluble or allow it to mix with the water portion of the blood), and cholesterol. Blood measurements of triglycerides and cholesterol provide an index of the fatty particles in the blood stream. Early investigators have found that exercise markedly reduced serum triglycerides but produced little or no change in serum cholesterol. More recent research has revealed that exercise resulted in a marked decrease in triglyceride-rich PRE-BETA lipoproteins, a significant decrease in the cholesterol-rich BETA lipoproteins, and a marked increase in the cholesterol-rich ALPHA lipoproteins. While early studies examined cholesterol in its totality, recent research looked at the affects on individual lipoproteins. *The lipoprotein fractions implicated in atherosclerosis are the "B" and PRE-B"* (both are significantly decreased through aerobic exercise). The ALPHA lipoproteins are not implicated. Although there may be no change in total serum cholesterol (increases in ALPHA lipoproteins can override the decrease in BETA lipoproteins), exercise should help prevent atherosclerosis by lowering the BETA and PRE-BETA fractions. Total cholesterol is a combination of what is formed by the liver and what is ingested in food. Triglyceride levels increase after eating a meal high in animal fat with elevation also related to excessive carbohydrate or protein in the diet. Of recent concern is the role of carbohydrates in the form of sugar.

Considerable evidence has been uncovered to support the Lipid Theory: (1) coronary heart disease is uncommon in countries with low cholesterol and fat levels in the blood, (2) the disease is highest in countries with diets rich in dairy and meat products (saturated fats), (3) individuals who have moved from the Orient and adopted the Western diet and lifestyle greatly increase the risk of coronary heart disease, (4) genetic errors in fat metabolism causing elevated lipid levels may result in death from coronary heart disease in the ealy 20's, (5) women develop coronary heart disease 10-15 years later in life than men, possibly due to the tendency of the female sex hormone to lower lipid levels, (6) diet induced elevated lipid levels in animals causes atherosclerosis, and (7) in males 30-49, a blood cholesterol level of 260 milligrams per 100 milliliters of blood increases the incidence of coronary heart disease to approximately three times that of those with levels below 180.

Since not all individuals with high blood lipids develop serious atherosclerosis, additional evidence is needed to isolate the exact cause or causes (genetic errors of handling fatty substances, diet, hereditary factors, stress, exercise habits, or a combination of several of these).

The Fibrin Deposit Theory is somewhat compatible with the Blood Lipid Theory.

It is suggested that sticky fibrin deposits on the inside of the arteries are the cause of atherosclerosis. Eventually, reduced flow or a complete block occurs. It is theorized that fibrin and fat are the culprit.

The Personality Behavior Theory as a cause of early heart disease was advanced by Dr. Meyer Friedman and Ray H. Rosenman (heart specialists) in the late 1950's. Individuals were classified as a Type A or Type B Behavior Pattern:

Type A Behavior—individual in a hurry, pressed for time, clock watcher, competitive, agressive, hates to lose, lack of patience and an underlying hostility.

Type B Behavior—unagressive person, not overly concerned with advancement in his job, not concerned with time pressures, more interested in his family than his career, a contented "cow" enjoying life just as it is.

In their early book, Friedman and Rosenman point out that in the absence of Type A Behavior Pattern, coronary heart disease almost never occurs before seventy years of age regardless of the fatty foods eaten, the cigarettes smoked, or the lack of exercise. In other words, Type B Behavior people can abuse their bodies by almost any known means because emotional stress is the cause of early heart disease.

Unfortunately, heart disease prevention is not so simple and little evidence supports this theory. It has not been proven that Type A or B behavior patterns are the key to the prevention of heart attacks. While some studies show a higher rate of heart disease among Type A Behavior persons, others do not. In fact, some research suggests that Type A behavior persons are less apt to suffer from early heart disease and that these individuals learn to cope with stressful situations.

In the revised edition of their book, the originators of the Personality Behavior Theory have changed the definition of a Type A Behavior Pattern. The modern Type A behavior now includes those personality traits described before plus someone who is overweight, eats a high fat diet including a high-cholesterol breakfast, has abnormally high blood cholesterol of over 300, high blood pressure, does not exercise, and smokes over two packs of cigarettes a day. The modern Type B also has the same personality traits plus low cholesterol, normal weight and blood pressure, a non-smoker, consumer of low cholesterol, low fat diet and exercises regularly.

The "modern" Type A Behavior Pattern covers a lot of ground. Stress is a factor in maintaining normal blood pressure for some people but, in general, stress affects people differently and may be more harmful to one than another. The original theory that emotional stress alone is the major cause of heart attacks has little or no support. The modern day version suggests that Type A Behavior in combination with other risk factors increases the chances of early heart disease.

The Risk Factor Theory suggests that heart disease is caused by a number of factors which appear to be additive. Presence of one factor in combination with several others greatly increase the chances of heart disease. Individuals, for example, who have high blood pressure, smoke and also have high cholesterol have eight times the likelihood of having a heart attack and six times the death rate of individuals with none of these factors. To further complicate the picture, the presence of stress or Type A Behavior in combination with other risk factors appears to make one even more likely to be a victim of early heart disease.

Risk factors include: (1) heredity, (2) hypertension, (3) hyperlipidemia, (4) obesity, (5) excessive cigarette smoking, (6) diabetes, (7) inactivity or sedentary living, and (8) age. With normal blood pressure and lipid levels and absence of smoking and diabetes, the chances of a male having a heart attack prior to age 65 are less than one in twenty. With one risk factor of these four, the risk doubles; with two, chances are one in two or fifty per cent.

Hereditary traits or the genetic tendency to develop atherosclerosis early in life greatly increases the risk of early heart disease. While a small percentage of individuals also apparently develop little plaque build-up regardless of living habits, others develop large amounts very early in life. In the past five years, three professional athletes of 23-39 years of age suffered serious heart attacks. Diagnosis by autopsy or by arterialography revealed rather advanced atherosclerosis. Apparently these young adults possessed the hereditary tendancy to aquire placque and hardening of the arteries. There is also some evidence to suggest that high blood pressure or the tendency to pass on hypertension from one generation to another is inherited. A history of early heart disease in your family is a caution sign for you to develop the right kind of habits very early in life. Although this is an absolute necessity for an individual from a family where one or more parents or grandparents suffered a heart attack or stroke prior to age 60, it may be sound advice for everyone.

Hypertension or high blood pressure accelerates arteriosclerosis and atherosclerosis. It also forces the heart to work harder and can lead to kidney damage. Coronary heart disease and high blood pressure are directly related. In adults, a reading of more than 140 during the contraction phase (systolic) or 90 during the resting phase (diastolic) of the heart cycle is above normal; a pressure of only 100/60 will maintain normal circulation. With readings of 160/95 the risk of a heart attack is 2.5 times greater than for those with pressures of 140/90. High blood pressure readings identified in youth of 130 or more resulted in a 50% increase in a heart attack death 20, 30, and 40 years later. Temporarily high readings in youth may be due to emotion or tension and are no cause for alarm. For longevity, health and slower deterioration of vessel walls, a lower reading is important. Approximately one person in ten has high blood pressure.

Numerous cases of high blood pressure among school children have been identified. The exact causes of hypertension are unknown and it can neither be prevented or completely cured. Control and prevention center around regular checkups, medication, regular exercise, weight control and stress control. Increases in blood pressure over long periods of time are generally due to high resistance to blood flow in the very small arteries of systemic circulation. In the U.S., no specific cause can be identified for approximately 80% of those with high blood pressure.

Obesity or overweight conditions are often accompanied by high fat levels in the blood, a higher incidence of arteriosclerotic disease, and high blood pressure. As a result, obesity is associated with a higher incidence of coronary artery disease.

Inactivity appears to contribute to early heart disease in a number of way. Lack of exercise is often associated with obesity, high lipid levels, and plaque accumulation (see the section: prevention of heart disease and stroke in this chapter for further discussion).

Hyperlipidemia or high lipid levels have been discussed previously under the blood lipid theory.

Excessive cigarette smoking, in combination with some of the other risk factors, appears to be a strong contributor to heart disease. The smoker who also has high blood pressure runs a greater risk of a heart attack than a non-smoker. Statistically, the incidence of heart disease is 70-200% higher among smoking males. The risk of heart diseases increases with the number of cigarettes smoked and inhalation habits (light, moderate or heavy inhaler). The risk is reduced when smoking is stopped. In a study supported by the U.S. Department of Health, Education and Welfare, 2,000 male smokers and 2,000 male non-smokers were examined on a regular basis for 6-8 years. Signs of atherosclerosis were absent when the study began. After 6-8 years, three times as many smokers died from all causes, most from arteriosclerosis. Unfortunately, arteriography was not used to determine the extent of atherosclerosis at any point in this study. Such a procedure would have been helpful for proper anatomical verification. Cigarette smoking appears to produce a number of changes, each with implications for coronary heart disease: increase the amount of cholesterol deposits in the arteries, increase heart pain in heart patients and decrease exercise tolerance to pain, increase the clumping of platelets which may be associated with the tendency to clot formation, and elevate heart rate (15-25 per minute), systolic blood pressure (10-20 milimeters of mercury) and diastolic pressure (10-20 milimeters of mercury).

In summary, it must be stated that no single risk factor has been identified without which coronary heart disease does not occur. Hypertension, hyperlipidemia, and diabetes may be the key factor with age, smoking, obesity and activity patterns playing important roles.

PREVENTION OF HEART DISEASE AND STROKE

Prevention or early coronary heart disease is pediatric problem and should begin in infancy.

Prevention is not entirely hopeless even for those with a family history of heart disease. Although "HEREDITY deals the cards," "ENVIRONMENT plays the hand" and much of what you do, experience, eat, will be the co-factor in determining your future health.

Atherosclerosis is a normally silent process, until middle age, affecting 80-90% of the adult population. For some individuals, it is evidenced by heart attack or stroke in the late 20's and early 30's. Autopsy reports of young American and Korean soldiers clearly suggests that the process can be quite advance by age 20-25. There is evidence of vascular fatty deposits in young children of school age. A preventive approach which includes moderate fat intake and sufficient activity would have to begin almost at birth and continue throughout the adult years. Diets very low in fats and sugars during the adolescent years are not advisable. Mass screening of elementary school children in the areas of blood pressure and blood lipid levels would greatly assist the problem and permit adequate management throughout the young and adult years.

Prevention should focus on the control of risk factors.

The regulation of those risk factors that can be managed would provide considerable protection.

As discussed in Chapter 3, body weight can be a misleading means of determining whether you are overweight or obese. In general, an individual who is more than 10% above recommended body weight on charts is classified as overweight, 20% above classifies one as obese. More accurately, a male who possesses more than 25% body fat and a woman with more than 30% body fat (see skinfold procedures described in Chapter 3) can be classified as obese. Control of body weight also aids control of blood pressure, blood sugar levels, and blood lipid levels.

Low salt diets are also recommended for patients with high blood pressure. In congestive heart failure patients, the kidneys retain salt and fluid resulting in fluid accumulation in the lungs, liver and legs. Restricting sodium intake (table salt, milk, bread) is probably a sound suggestion for everyone since evidence suggests our intake has been increased over the past ten years.

Cessation of smoking, management of diabetes, control of emotional stress, lowered blood lipid levels and increased physical activity round out a total approach to the prevention of heart disease.

The right kind of regular exercise plays an important part in preventing premature heart disease.

Exercise aids in the prevention of early heart disease by causing numerous physiological changes within the body. It is important to remember, however, that changes in *all* major risk areas cited previously are desirable: normal blood pressure, lowered blood lipid levels, elimination of smoking, and a return to normal weight. A change in only one or two areas cannot be expected to offer great protection.

The active person is 3-4 times less likely to ever have a heart attack and 3-4 times more likely to survive should one occur. The exercising cardiac patient who has suffered an attack is also less likely to have another. In addition, autopsy reports showed less cardiovascular disease in those who were active prior to death. Numerous other studies relate inactivity to early heart disease. Unfortunately, even in these studies, the so-called active person is classified by occupation. A carpenter, bricklayer, construction worker, for example, is considered highly active when in reality, such occupations do little to elevate heart rate and produce a training effect similar to that resulting from jogging, cycling, lap swimming, soccer, rugby, cross country, basketball, and other aerobic activities.

There is evidence that regular exercise relates in some way to each of the theories of heart disease discussed previously.

1. Exercise may aid in reducing the coronary risk factors associated with heart disease. Several of the risk factors are affected by regular exercise as shown below. Reducing the risk in four or five areas identified as contributing to early heart disease can be extremely important. Evidence recently presented by Cooper suggests considerable regulation or control of the risk factors and lowered incidence of heart disease for individuals of all ages (men and women) who can stay within the Good-to-Excellent Category on the 1.5 mile test for their age group.

Risk Factor	Effect of Regular Physical Exercise
Obesity and overweightness	Reduction of body fat, return to ideal weight
High lipid levels	Reduction of atherogenic fatty particles in the blood
Hypertension	Aid in the control of blood pressure
Tension and Stress	Increased tolerance for stress, release of tension and nervous or emotional energy
Lack of Physical Activity	No longer a risk factor for the exercising person
Genetic History	No change
Smoking	Changes in smoking habits are likely to take place
Age	Slows aging process

2. Exercise can help reduce lipid deposit atherosclerosis. A reduction in triglyceride levels can be expected with regular exercise such as jogging, distance swimming, cycling, sccocer, basketball, rugby, and other vigorus activites. This is not to suggest that an active person can continuously consume high calorie, high fat foods with the expectation that exercise will automatically regulate fatty particles in the blood. There is evidence, however, supporting exercise as an important factor in maintaining lower blood lipid levels which have been linked to heart disease. Both Pre-B and B Lipopotein fractions (both

implicated in atherosclerosis) are lowered during exercise and lowered even further one week after exercise. In addition, recent studies have shown that individuals with large amounts of high density lipoproteins (HDL) in the blood tend to be protected from early atherosclerosis and heart disease. Runners (joggers, distance runners, competitive runners) possess 50% more HDL than the non-exercising population. Aerobic exercise greatly increases the amount of HDL in the blood stream.

3. Exercise helps reduce fibrin levels in the blood. Regular exercise has been shown to cause the breakdown of fibrin in the blood and reduce fibrin blood levels which, in turn, may decrease the chance of a blood clot and the development of fibrin atherosclerosis.

4. Exercise induced coronary collateralization has been demonstrated in animals and not humans. In older men with chronic profuse organic heart disease, collateralization has been found regardless of exercise habits. Rarely does coronary collateralization occur in younger men even with exercise.

5. Exercise may increase the diameter of the arteries. Some protection may occur from possessing larger arteries since more fatty deposits would be required to cause occlusion.

There is considerable empirical evidence suggesting the importance of regular exercise in preventing heart disease

A number of claims (some supported by research and others only theoretical in nature) for exercise can be found in the literature. A summary of benefits expounded by advocates of running programs (aerobic) follow:

Running improves the lungs efficiency, expands the supply of blood for conveying oxygen to the body, extends the vascular system and lowers blood pressure. In addition, it improves muscle tone, relaxes the digestive system, lowers tension, and strengthens the heart by making it more efficient at slower rates and by extending the vascular system that supplied the heart with blood. Improved fitness through jogging has been shown to reduce coronary risk factors such as level of cholesterol, triglycerides as well as body fat, weight, blood pressure.

The circumstantial evidence in favor of exercise continues to mount. Opponents of exercise are decreasing and can only refer to its misuse in the form of sudden, unaccustomed activity that very definitely can prove harmful and even fatal to some individuals.

1. The Tarahumara Indians of Mexico begin distance running in childhood. Young men and some older adults may run 150 miles non-stop at altitudes of 7-8,000 feet. Heart and vascular disease are unknown to Tarahumar Indians.

2. The Masai race in Africa consumes a high fat and cholesterol diet (blood and milk). They may trot up to 50 miles daily (average 25 miles) as they hunt animals for food. Heart and vascular disease are unknown to the Masai race.

3. Atherosclerosis and heart disease was once unknown to the Japanese. Now it affects those who either moved to the U.S. or adopted the American lifestyle (inactivity and high intake of calories and animal fats).

4. Five hundred men who moved to Boston to live, who also had brothers in Ireland, developed much more heart disease, atherosclerosis, and died sooner than their brothers in Ireland who ate more calories and fat but led active lives.

5. Larry Lewis ran 6 miles every morning before work as a San Francisco waiter at age 104. He died at 106 of cancer. Numerous other cases can be cited of distance runners entering marathons at 60-100 years of age. In addition, coronary heart disease from atherosclerosis is much less evident in older distance runners than the sedentary population.

6. Cardiac Rehabilitation centers where victims of heart attacks are exercised, tested, and monitored are becoming more common throughout the U.S. Participants have been shown to reduce the risk of a second attack and increase their chances of survival should another attack occur.

STROKE OR APOPLEXY

The cause and prevention of strokes is identical to that of heart attacks.

The brain must also be continuously nourished. When blood supply to any portion of the brain is greatly reduced or cut off completely, nerve tissue in the brain is unable to function and body tissue controlled by this nerve tissue also ceases to operate. Depending upon the portion of the brain affected, a victim may experience loss of speech, loss of memory, partial paralysis, etc. Less than 10% of strokes are caused by embole or small clots from other body parts. The real cause or enemy is atherosclerosis. Those same fatty deposits that cause heart attacks also block arteries supplying the brain.

Mild strokes occur when the brain is deprived of inadequate blood supply for short periods of time (ischemia). These transitory ischemic attacks (T.I.A.) often result in momentary periods of paralysis, vision problems, or inability to speak. Generally, deeper brain cells are not permanently damaged although repeated episodes can bring about a number of personality changes. T.I.A.'s are warning signs of insufficient blood supply to the brain. Careful diagnosis and action can result in the correction of arterial disease outside the skull. Eighty per cent survive the first stroke with the likelihood of death increasing with age. Over twenty per cent of those who do recover have a second stroke within two years with over half of the survivors eventually dying from a heart attack.

Preventive techniques focus upon the prevention of atherosclerosis and high blood pressure. Specific preventive measures include:

1. Elimination of tobacco smoking.
2. Elimination of alcohol consumption, coffee and tea.
3. Elimination of obesity by controlling caloric intake, total fat, saturated fat and cholesterol consumption.
4. Initiation of a sensible exercise program to control weight and maintain good circulation.
5. Scheduling regular medical checkups for contributing factors such as anemia, diabetes, high blood pressure, diseases that may compress arteries in the neck.

EXERCISE   Definitions and List of Terms (Aerobic Exercise)

1. Flexibility exercises involving bouncing movements characterized by quick jerks and pulls upon the body segments at the extreme range of motion are termed _____ .
2. Energy expenditure, in calories, while the body is in a resting state is referred to as _____ .
3. The unit of measurement indicating the heat produced from food is a _____ .
4. The quality of a muscle that allows it to extend over a range of motion and still retain its normal contractility is _____ .
5. A warm-up procedure involving exercises that simulate that of the activity for which preparation is being made is termed _____ .
6. The increase in size of a muscle brought about through progressively increased loads performed in decreasing periods of time is called _____ .
7. A warm-up procedure involving exercises entirely different from those for which preparation is being made is termed _____ .
8. The conditioning principle involving work per unit of time, whereby maximum effort is made with gradually reduced time periods, is referred to as the principle of _____ .
9. Exercise programs that utilize muscle tension without movement of bony attachments are referred to as _____ .
10. A training program that permits both isometric and isotonic contraction is termed _____ .
11. The sense of perception of movement, weight resistance, and body position, as well as joint, muscle, and tendon sensitivity is termed _____ .
12. The amount of exercise dosage that enables an individual to retain or hold his present level of physical capcity is called the _____ .
13. The state in a muscle that provides a quality of firmness thought to be the result of the property of muscle elasticity is termed _____ .
14. The number of times one exercise or movement is performed is classified as a _____ .
15. The time span between each exercise, repetition, and set is an imporant training variable called _____ .
16. The technical ability of a muscle to complete movement with a minimum of effort and a maximum of precision is termed _____ .
17. Flexibilty exercises involving a held position of steady pressure, with no movement, in which body segments to be stretched are locked into a position of greatest possible length are termed a _____ .

18. The designated area where each circuit training exercise is performed is termed a _____ .

19. The capacity of a muscle to exert maximum force either statically or isotonically is termed _____ .

1. Ballistic stretching procedures	8. Intensity	15. Rest interval
2. Basal metabolism	9. Isometric training programs	16. Skill
3. Calorie	10. Isometronics	17. Static stretching procedures
4. Flexibility	11. Kinesthesis	
5. Formal warm-up	12. Maintenance load	
6. Hypertrophy	13. Muscle tonus	18. Station
7. Informal warm-up	14. Repetition	19. Strength

EXERCISE   Definitions and List of Terms (Heart Disease)

1. Lack of blood supply and oxygen to a portion of the heart muscle resulting in chest pain is a condition termed _____ .
2. The largest artery in the body carrying oxygen rich blood from the left ventrical throughout the body is the _____ .
3. The general term refering to arteries that have hardened, become thick and lost elasticity is _____ .
4. A condition in which arterial walls contain deposits of either soft, spongy or hard, calcified substances is termed _____ .
5. The amount of force exerted by the blood against the wall of the arteries is referred to as _____ .
6. The smallest blood vessels in the body that link the arterial and venous blood systems and provide oxygen and nutrients to tissues are termed _____ .
7. A chemical compound found in food of animal products only is _____ .
8. Newly developed branches of the coronary arteries that may provide alternate means of supplying sections of the heart muscle when a coronary blockage occurs are referred to as _____ .
9. The force of the blood against the arteries when the heart is resting is termed _____ blood pressure.
10. The blocking of a coronary blood vessel due to a clot is termed a _____ .
11. A clot that breaks free from a vessel wall and travels in the blood stream until it reaches an area it is unable to pass is referred to as an _____ .
12. Sticky susbstances that combine with blood cells to form a blood clot as the necessary part of healing a cut are termed _____ .
13. Tissue death to a body part due to lack of blood supply and oxygen is referred to as an _____ .
14. Inadequate blood and oxygen supply to a body part is termed _____ .
15. All fats and fatty substances are termed _____ .
16. Strands of fiberous tissue that attach to the inside of arteries form soft and mushy (if mostly fat particles) or hard (if scar tissue) _____ .
17. Fats derived from vegetables, lean poultry, fish, and cereal are labeled _____ fats.
18. Lack of oxygen and blood supply to the brain due to vessel blockage results in a _____ .
19. The force of the blood against the arteries while the heart is contracting is called _____ blood pressure.
20. Fatty chemicals of glycerol and fatty acids linked to atherosclerosis are termed _____ .

1. Angine Pectoris
2. Aorta
3. Arteriosclerosis
4. Atherosclerosis
5. Blood pressure
6. Capillaries
7. Cholesterol
8. Collaterals
9. Diastolic
10. Coronary Thrombosis
11. Embolus
12. Fibrin
13. Infart
14. Ischemia
15. Lipid
16. Plaque
17. Polyunsaturated
18. Stroke
19. Systolic
20. Triglycerides

BIBLIOGRAPHY

Annarino, Anthony A. *Developmental Conditioning for Women and Men.* St. Louis: The C. V. Mosby Co., 1976.

Chevrette, John M. and George R. Colfer. *Running to Fitness.* Kendall/Hunt Publishing Co., 1976.

Cooper, Kenneth H. *The New Aerobics.* New York: Bantam Books, 1970.

Dintiman, George B. *How To Run Faster: (A Do-It-Yourself) Book For Athletes On All Sports.* Champion Athlete Publishing Co., Box 2936, Richmond, Virginia 23235, 1979.

Dintiman, George B. and John Unitas. *Improving Health and Performance in the Young Athlete.* Englewood Cliffs, NJ: Prentice-Hall, Inc., 1979.

Edington, D. W. and V. R. Edgerton. *The Biology of Physical Activity.* Boston: Houghton Mifflin Co., 1976.

Getchell, Budd. *Physical Fitness: A Way of Life.* New York: John Wiley and Sons, Inc., 1976.

Hockey, Robert V. *Physical Fitness.* Dubuque, Iowa: Kendall/Hunt Publishing Co., 1970.

Johnson, Perry B. *et al. Physical Education—A Problem Solving Approach to Health and Fitness.* Holt, Rinehart, and Winston, NY, 1966.

Kennedy, John F. "The Soft American," *Sports Illustrated,* December 26, 1960.

Ricci, Benjamin. *Physical and Physiological Conditioning for Men.* Dubuque, Iowa: William C. Brown Company, Publishers, 1966.

Royal Canadian Air Force Exercise Plans for Physical Fitness. New York: Pocket Books, Inc., 1962.

Shepro, David and Howard G. Knottgen. *Complete Conditioning.* Addison-Wesley Publishing Co., 1976.

Sorani, Robert. *Circuit Training.* Dubuque, Iowa: William C. Brown Company, Publishers, 1966.

Spackman, Robert R. *Two-Man Isometric Exercise Programs for the Whole Body.* Dubuque, Iowa: William C. Brown Company, Publishers, 1964.

Steinhaus, Arthur H. *How to Keep Fit and Like It.* Chicago: The Dartnell Corporation, 1957.

3

WEIGHT CONTROL THROUGH DIET AND EXERCISE

DESCRIPTION OF THE ACTIVITY

Inactivity and overeating are the two most common causes of obesity. Activity can do much to offset weight gain and regulate overweight tendencies. Numerous studies of children reveal little differences in food intake of the obese and those of normal weight. Obese youngsters merely spend considerably less time in physical activity. Another study identified the winter (season of least activity) as the period of greatest weight gain for youngsters. Inactivity is the main cause of obesity followed by overeating. Social, genetic, and psychological factors may also result in overeating and obesity. In only a small percentage of cases is glandular and other physiological disorders related to weight problems although many obese people blame these areas. Studies investigating heredity and environment show that children of normal weight parents are obese as youngsters in about seven to eight percent of cases studied; with one parent obese, this rises to 40 percent and with both parents obese, it rises to over 80 percent. Identical twin studies with one of each pair of twins being reared in a different environment also indicate that herdity more so than environment determines obesity.

The widespread prevalence of overfatness and obesity in the United States is shocking:

1. Fifty percent of the male population between 30-39 years of age are at least ten percent overweight.

2. Sixty percent of the male population between 50-59 years of age are at least ten percent overweight, and 33 percent are at least 20 percent overweight.

3. The percent of overweight women under age 40 is lower than that of men, from ages 40-49 the percentage is identical, and in the over 49 category, more women are obese than men.

4. Approximately ten percent of the school population is obese with the percent rising to approximately twenty in some schools.

Obesity tends to shorten life due to atherosclerosis, high blood pressure, diabetes, heart-lung difficulties, early heart attacks, and other ailments. One long term follow-up study of 5,000,000 insured persons revealed that the death rate of obese men age 15-69 was 50 percent greater than the population of normal weight persons and 30 percent greater for persons who were classified as overweight. In addition, obese girls and boys are subjected to discrimination, prejudice, and social interactions are less.

Principles of Weight Control

The literature is saturated with weight control advice from numerous professionals and laymen. Unfortunately, much information is inaccurate and unsupported by scientific study. The following data represents a thorough review of research and expert opinion to provide the reader with recent, critical information that can be utilized in his personal control of body fat in the following areas: general, nutritional, and special diets, diet and exercise, and how exercise helps.

The amount of body fat is a much more accurate indicator of obesity than the amount of body weight.

Weight charts (see Figure 3-1) are inaccurate and should only be used as a guide in determining desirable weight. The major pitfalls are:

1. It is possible to be within the range of suggested weight and still possess excessive fat.

2. It is possible to be classified as overweight or obese (10 percent or 20 percent above suggested ranges) when you are at a desirable weight and possess little fatty tissue. Among thick muscled athletes with low body fat, this is common.

3. Some charts allow you to gain weight with age suggesting that it is fine to be fat at age 30, 40, or 50, but not at age 20. Actually, weight should decrease with age. If you weigh the same now as you did 20 years ago, you are probably overweight. Loss of muscle mass from earlier active years is now made up by an increased proportion of fatty tissue. Ideally, you should be five to ten pounds lighter at age 50 than your ideal weight of age 25.

4. The three categories of small, medium, and large frame (on some charts) encourages cheating. I have yet to meet anyone who took their recommended weight from the small or medium frame range; yet, everyone in this world cannot possibly have a large frame. A woman's frame is generally small until checking a weight chart. Males rarely consider themselves anything but large.

5. The key to obesity is not total body weight, but total body fat. Weight charts do not reveal the presence of fat.

There are several more accurate methods of determining body composition. Most of these fall under the areas of skinfold fat measures, underwater weighing, and anthropometric measures. Skinfold measures are the most practical for home and school use.

Scales and weight charts only reveal your weight and suggested ranges. Calipers and pinching show you just how much useless fat your body contains.

The per cent of total body fat can be accurately estimated by skinfold measures.

Since the majority of body fat lies just under the skin, it is possible to pinch certain body parts, measure the thickness of two layers of skin and the connected fat, and refer to two charts to estimate the per cent of body fat.

All measurements are taken on the right side of the body. The skin is pinched firmly between the thumb and index finger and lifted upward. The calipers are then placed about 1/16" under the pinch.

The proper location of each measure is shown in Figure 3-2. For women and girls, only two locations are needed:

A. **Tricep measure**—The skin is pinched on the back of the arm exactly halfway between the tip of the shoulder and elbow. The pinched skin will run vertical toward the shoulder and elbow. Two separate measures are taken with the average score recorded in millimeters.

B. **Illiac crest**—Find the pelvis bone on the right side and take a deep pinch. Place the calipers 1/16" behind the fingers toward the back. The pinched skin will run horizontal toward the stomach and back. Record the average of two measures.

For men and boys, three separate measures are used:

A. **Abdominal measure**—Take a deep pinch approximately one inch to the right of the naval; place the calipers 1/16" behind the pinch and record the average of two measures. The pinched fat will run horizontal.

FIGURE 3-1. Desirable weights for height. From: Food and Nutrition Board, National Research Council

Height[1]		Men Weight[2]		Women	
(cm)	(in)	(kg)	(lb)	(kg)	(lb)
152	60			49 ± 4	(109 ± 9)
157	62			52 ± 4	(115 ± 9)
163	64	60 ± 5	(133 ± 11)	55 ± 5	(122 ± 10)
168	66	64 ± 5	(142 ± 12)	59 ± 5	(129 ± 10)
173	68	69 ± 6	(151 ± 14)	62 ± 5	(136 ± 10)
178	70	72 ± 6	(159 ± 14)	65 ± 5	(144 ± 11)
183	72	76 ± 7	(167 ± 15)	69 ± 6	(152 ± 12)
188	74	79 ± 7	(175 ± 15)		

[1]Height and weights are without shoes and other clothing.
[2]Desirable weight include a range to cover small framed and large framed persons (±). Subtract the ± figure for small frame, add it for a large frame.

B. **Chest Measure**—Pinch the skin approximately one inch to the right of the right nipple. Place the calipers $\frac{1}{16}''$ behind the pinch and record the average of two measures. The pinched skin will run horizontal.

C. **Tricep measure**—same for men and women.

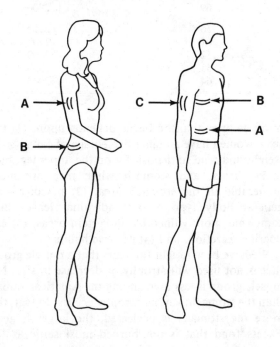

FIGURE 3.2   Location of Skinfold Measures for Men and Women.

What is desirable weight for you? It is almost any weight providing you possess limited body fat and fall within the acceptable ranges shown below:

Average Skinfold Thickness by Age and Sex*

	MEN 23-29	MEN 53-57	WOMEN 18-30	WOMEN 46-67
Chest	16.3	27.9		
Abdomen	19.1	26.0		
Illiac Crest			22.2	27.1
Tricep	13.7	15.4	21.9	26.9

*readings are in millimeters

Overeating begins early in life and develops weight problems that continue throughout the adult years.

In general, babies and young children overeat. This causes numerous difficulties in later life. Lets examine each in more detail.

Eating habits formed in infancy carry over to later life. A fat infant becomes a fat adult with a stopover as a fat teenager. In one experiment with rats, the milk of one mother was shared with four babies (plenty of milk for each) while the milk of other mothers was shared with as many as 22 babies (enough for small quantities for each). Rats from the smaller litters were fatter and healthier in appearance at weaning. After weaning, all rats had unlimited food available. The rats who were accustomed to eating less continued to eat less while the rats of small litters continued to eat more. After a short period of time, the thin rats overtook the fat rats in growth, showed much less heart and vessel disease and out-lived the fat rats.

Fat cells are formed early in life and may increase in both size and number until puberty. Although research is inconclusive, it appears that diet only decreases the size of fat cells; not the number. With a large number of fat cells formed, return to an overweight condition is much easier. This explains why adults who were heavy babies have difficulty keeping their weight down. These extra cells also may affect metabolism and result in the need for fewer calories to maintain normal weight than someone who has always maintained normal weight.

Atherosclerosis and cholesterol build-up may start in early life. There is increasing evidence that vessel damage begins in infancy and is directly related to the amount and type of food eaten.

There is little danger that a child will be malnourished; particularly if the child himself decides when to stop eating each meal. Forcing a youngster to "clean" a plate is a mistake. Forcing a child to overeat, making sweets plentiful and using them as a reward, and placing emphasis on the "fat" baby will only shorten lifespan, encourage premature heart disease, form undesirable eating habits that will be continued throughout life, and destine a child to a life of restricted eating due to a high number of fat cells formed in early life. A lean child with a great deal of energy and vitality is far more healthy and far more likely to be healthy in later life. There is no state of life when excess fat is desirable. A child should start off right and avoid over "stuffing." If his mechanism to "push-up" from the table when he feels full is destroyed, he is certain to need plenty of real push-ups in the adult years to control weight.

The exact number of calories needed daily depends upon the individual.

An individual's weight, age, sex, and activity patterns determine how much food is needed daily.

FIGURE 3-3.   Recommended daily deitary allowances by age, weight and height.

AGE (years)		WEIGHT (lbs.)	HEIGHT (in.)	CALORIES
10-12		77	55	2500
12-14		95	59	2700
14-18	BOYS	130	67	3000
17-22		147	69	2800
10-12		77	56	2250
12-14		97	61	2300
14-16	GIRLS	114	62	2400
16-18		119	63	2300
18-22		128	64	2000

Certainly, if no weight gain or loss occurs, you are consuming enough calories.

The Recommended Daily Dietary Allowances shown in Figure 3-3 below, for the moderately active person, were established by the National Academy of Sciences and provide a close estimation of needs for most individuals.

Use the chart as guides *only*. You may fall outside desirable weight or need to consume more or less calories depending upon your musculature and exercise habits.

You can determine whether you are in a state of caloric balance (food intake not excessive) by weighing yourself each morning.

Weigh yourself at exactly the same time of day and under the same conditions (preferably in the morning upon rising). When the total daily caloric intake is equal to energy costs or expenditure and calories lost in excreta, a caloric balance has been attained and no weight loss or gain will occur When you eat more calories than you use, these excess calories are stored as fat. With the accumulation of approximately 3500 excess calories, one pound of fat is stored. Remember, the body is extremely thrifty. Every unused calorie is stored as fat. Often, a change to an alternate food or drink will cause weight loss. An individual who drinks three glasses of milk daily (165 calories per 8 oz. glass), for example, takes in nearly one pound of fat per week (3485 calories). A change to skim milk (85 calories per glass) results in a weight reduction of one-half pound weekly or two pounds monthly.

Several factors determine where body fat forms when overeating and under-exercising occurs.

Where fat finally settles in the individual who eats more calories than he burns depends upon: (1) the sex—women have a higher percentage of fat to body weight and tend to deposit fat on the upper leg, buttocks, arms, and stomach while men are most vulnerable in the stomach area, (2) heredity—the general body type of an individual leaves him somewhat more vulnerable in certain areas, (3) endocrine secretion, and (4) exercise habits.

We have been taught for years that a muscle group that is not used will atrophy or decrease in size. No muscle group is less used among the American public than the stomach; yet, no atrophy occurs. In fact, the more the stomach is neglected, the larger it gets. Excess food that is not burned must settle as fat somewhere and it generally forms in an area where musculature is rarely stimulated. Fat will not accumulate around heavily used muscle groups. The upper leg and buttocks of men is generally firm and free from fatty tissue. Women, on the other hand, do not engage in vigorous muscle work involving these areas and, consequently, tend to build up fat.

The best protection from fat build-up is sensible eating habits and regular exercise. Keep in mind that fat deposits are a lot easier and a lot more fun to put on than to remove. The excess weight and the miles of new network of capilliaries to feed this new tissue also places excess strain on the circulatory system. Since the main pump or heart and the arteries supplying it seem to be the first to go as age increases, it seems a shame to hurry their destruction.

Weight control becomes more difficult with age.

This is mainly a result of inactivity, more time and money for fancy dining, and the fact that metabolic rates slow as one ages. By the time you are 70 years old, you need about 15% less calories than you needed at age twenty. As the years go by, eat less, exercise more, and dine at home. Parents should try to weigh less as the years pass since more of the body weight in later years is fat than during the younger active years.

Some body fat is desirable.

Athletes in contact sports should try to keep their weight slightly higher than normal as opposed to attempts to become one piece of lean meat. Fat deposits around the kidneys and other major organs offer needed protection from hard blows that could prove serious. Fat is not all bad and has a vital role, when the ratio of fat and muscle mass is normal, in providing both insulation and protection.

Weight gaining may be difficult and requires very careful planning.

To gain weight, you must take in more calories each day than your body needs for energy. Remember the body is thrifty and will store all calories that are not needed. On the other hand, if food energy is not available the body will resort to fat supply for energy and you will lose weight.

Although most underweight individuals have normal metabolism, they are generally jumpy and tense, causing energy to dissipate rapidly. On the favorable side, a thin person uses fewer calories to exercise than a heavy person. The only real solution then is to greatly increase your daily food intake. If this occurs with no increase in activity patterns and no existing medical condition affecting metabolism, you will gain weight.

Have patience. It is often very difficult to gain weight. Do not expect instant results. The following suggestions will assist in making your weight "gaining" program a success.

1. Undergo a thorough physical examination in an attempt to uncover medical reasons for your underweight status.
2. Maintain accurate records on the calories consumed over a period of 6-10 days. Compare daily intake to needs for someone of your weight and activity patterns. You are probably not eating enough.
3. Increase your food consumption by eating more high calorie foods, larger portions, seconds, and snacks. Become familiar with the high calorie foods to your liking and eat them daily.
4. Plan your diet around familiar foods and avoid foods (even high calorie) that you detest.
5. Avoid too many between meal snacks. Remember, carbohydrates will elevate the blood

sugar level and give the sensation of not being hungry. Thus, snacks can destroy appetite for meals when consumption should be high.
6. Avoid drinking with meals. This will allow you to consume more food before feeling full.
7. Cut down on bulky foods such as lettuce, carrots, apples, celery, and fresh fruits.
8. Always eat dessert, a second helping whenever possible.
9. Add a fourth meal just before bedtime; however, do not overeat and cause discomfort and difficulty in sleeping.
10. Secure proper rest, increasing sleeping time to ten hours and using early afternoon naps to conserve energy.
11. Continue exercising to maintain proper muscle tone. Reduce exercise volume if possible particularly in the off-season period. Since an athlete's desire to gain weight is coupled with need for increased bulk or muscle mass, exercise such as weight training or other strength training program is absolutely necessary.

NUTRITION AND SPECIAL DIETS

Fat should not be completely eliminated from the diet.

Fat plays a vital part in digestion, transportation of vitamins, and is the main fuel of some muscle fibers in most muscle groups. Also, it would be near impossible to eliminate fats from the diet. Meat is far from pure protein and is often tenderized with fat to improve taste. Unless one resorts to artificial foods, fats cannot be avoided.

Fat is the highest concentration of energy or calories and should be avoided *in excess*. Life magazine once carried a pictorial on the amount of fat in the American diet. Photos removed everything from common dishes except the fat to demonstrate its prevalence. The photos are short of shocking with fat content approaching an average of 35-40%—far too high.

Up to 65% of caloric intake should come from carbohydrates, 10-15% from protein, with the remaining from fats.

In terms of performance, energy derived from fats is less economical than energy drawn from carbohydrates and proteins. About 10-12% more oxygen is needed to utilize energy supplied from fats. Both your, long-term health and physical performance will improve if fat intake is reduced—only a magician could completely eliminate it.

Carbohydrates should not be completely eliminated from a diet.

Carbohydrates should be restricted, not eliminated. Exercise, for example, will draw from available carbohydrate supply for energy. If the supply is limited, the body must resort to fat for fuel resulting in loss of fatty tissue. Also, the brain needs a constant supply of glucose. This need is so essential that the body has a built-in mechanism to convert protein to carbohydrates when the supply is absent.

It is wise to cut down on cabohydrate intake (bread, sugar, cereal products, potatoes, etc.) but not to completely avoid these foods. A trained athlete will use almost all his carbohydrate reserves during exercise, whereas an untrained athlete will not. Once all reserves are used, fatty tissue must burn as fuel.

On the other hand, there is also evidence suggesting the need for high carbohydrate diet, particularly 24-48 hours before competition. Subjects were shown to have a slight increase in muscular efficiency after consuming a high carbohydrate diet. Some experts suggest that about 50 percent of food calories should be carbohydrates for athletes in vigorous training (40% is normal). This would not apply to the overweight athelete.

A diet is indicated as soon as you notice a weight gain of five percent, fall 10-15 percent outside your recommended weight, or posses an excess percent of body fat.

Controlled eating after splurges occur (eating out, parties) can prevent the need for a diet. The longer you allow excess weight to accumulate, the more difficult it is to remove.

There are other factors to weigh also before deciding to initiate a diet. Consider starting a diet:

1. At the onset of your vacation. You will save money and avoid additional weight gain during a relaxation time when everyone has a tendency to overeat.

2. After the November-December holiday season when temptation is reduced. Or, if you really are well disciplined, begin during the holiday season—you are certain to avoid 3-5 excess pounds.

3. After "cold and virus" season. The winter months are particularly troublesome due to flue epidemics and colds; avoid adding fuel to the fire with lowered resistance.

4. When finances are particularly low in your household. Chances of eating out and stocking "foodless" high calorie foods are minimized.

5. After finishing an organized sport such as softball, basketball, rugby, etc. Since the decrease in activity will not be followed by a decrease in appetite, this is a dangerous period requiring a change in eating habits.

If in doubt, start this minute. If obese and not just overweight, start a diet immediately in consultation with a physician.

Weight loss that occurs slowly through reduced calories and increased activity is more likely to be permanent.

As a general rule, weight loss should not exceed 3-4 pounds weekly. Also, a physician should be consulted when the desired weight loss exceeds 5% of body weight. A return to an obese or overweight state tends to occur within a time period proportional to that spent losing a specific amount of weight. Reducing over an extended period of time (minimum of three months) is preferred and generally results in the acquisition of sensible and different eating habits which are more likely to be continued in the future. *Rapid* weight loss, through "fasting" and other "crash" programs, can be dangerous and often results in a rapid return to old eating habits and an overweight condition. The extended period of time also involves the pleasant personal adjustment to clothes and new positive self-image so vital to weight control. Slow, controlled weight loss then, has the advantages of safety, permanency, and little or no loss of power for the athlete. It is unwise to try to take it off any faster than you put it on.

Improper dieting without exercise can result in skin wrinkling.

Since young people have an elastic skin, this is rarely a problem for the under thirty age group. For older individuals, wrinkles and folds do occur and will, depending upon age and the amount of weight loss, disappear over a substantial period of time. Slow weight loss over a long period of time is less apt to result in this type of condition.

Several factors then, determine the extent of wrinkles and folds that will appear:

1. **Speed of weight loss**—a minimum of 3-6 months is recommended when attempting to remove more than 5% of body weight.

2. **Age**—the older the individual, the less resillient the skin and the more prone one is to wrinkles.

3. **Amount of weight to be lost**—50, 75, 100, 150, 200 pound reductions can result in such ugly appearance in the stomach area that surgery may be needed to remove excess skin.

4. **Exercise**—daily activity is needed to maintain muscle tone, increase fatty tissue loss, and decrease lean muscle loss.

The basic problem is that skin is stretched, remains stretched after weight loss, and just does not fit the body—much the same as the problem of a new born baby.

Dieting causes the body to temporarily retain fluids much more than it did before the diet was started.

In the early stages of dieting, one often experiences a temporary retention of water (1-4 weeks) which obscures the actual measurable weight loss that occurs (vacated fat cells fill with water). This *temporary* water retention can be discouraging and cause the scales to record only moderate weight loss even when strict dieting has been employed. However, actual weight loss has occurred and will be more vividly noticed in terms of reduced pounds following this period. Many unhappy dieters discontinue the diet before this phenomenon passes.

Some sound diets requiring the consumption of large quantities of water avoid this reaction (increasing water consumption actually counteracts this tendency and results in the elimination of water). A more accuate measure of weight loss during the initial states of diet is the reduction of adipose tissue in fatty body areas. Mere observation and "pinching" fatty tissue or the skinfold measures described previously will reveal benefits even in the early stages.

Hunger can be controlled by consuming non-caloric and low caloric food and drink at the proper time.

There are two basic approaches to the control of hunger: (1) keeping the stomach relatively full, or (2) raising the body's blood sugar level. Both are effective. Several of the following suggestions help most dieters:

1. Keep busy at work.
2. Increase fluid intake both between meals and at mealtime.

3. Eat small amounts of candy such as one chocolate square about 20-30 minutes before meals (this raises the blood sugar level and gives the sensation of not being hungry).

4. Eat slowly to allow the blood sugar level to elevate before completing the meal (20-30 minutes). This will reduce the temptation to overeat or have dessert.

5. Eat bulky foods between and at mealtime: lettuce, carrots, apples, celery, fresh fruits.

6. Take numerous coffee breaks during the day. Do not use cream or sugar. Drink diet soda and other sugar free beverages.

7. Space allotted calories over five snacks instead of three meals to prevent hunger.

8. Season food with lemon, limes, onion, garlic, celery, saccharin, and grapefruit.

9. Go to bed early to avoid "midnight snacks" due to lowered blood sugar as the evening meal empties from the stomach.

Whole milk is a high calorie food containing saturated fats and is not essential to the diet.

The American male, the overweight female, and anyone who is vulnerable to atherosclerosis (includes practically all of us) would be wise to drink SKIM MILK. Resorting to skim milk eliminates damaging saturated fats and calories. In fact, if you drink four 8 oz. glasses of milk daily, a switch to skim milk will save you up to 320 calories daily, 9600 calories monthly, which represents more than 2½ pounds of fat per month—a substantial saving.

There is some justification for placing children on skim milk since cholesterol build-up begins early in life, as do weight problems, and the start of atherosclerosis. After an initial acclimation period of 1-2 months, whole milk will taste like cream and be unpleasant to you. Keep in mind also that although fortified skim milk has more calories than plain skim milk, it is probably the wiser choice for children. The fat in whole milk is not needed; we consume enough in meat and other dairy products.

Sweets can be completely eliminated from the diet without any consequences.

Most individuals get enough sugar in natural foods and do not need "empty calories" that only serve to destroy appetite and intake of important foods. A common mistake of mothers is to reward children with candy which immediately establishes the fallacy that sweets are better than other food. This reward procedure associates warmth and love with an undesirable food—a link that remains throughout life. Since food and emotion are associated in the child's mind, it would be far better to establish an association between good foods and reward.

Candy does elevate blood sugar level and curb appetite. It therefore can be used to the benefit of dieters who want to control hunger sensations. As an important source of energy, fuel, cell building, or aid to the function of systems, candy rates low. It also can form an eating habit that will help keep you fat in the future.

Weight reducing pills are dangerous and should be used only under the supervision of a physician.

Without careful supervision by a physician, the use of numerous drugs and drug combinations has been shown to be extremely harmful and sometimes fatal. The various drugs (prescription and patent medicine) employed to lose weight generally attempt to cause loss through (1) increasing metabolic rate or the rate at which the body burns up calories while at rest, (2) curbing the appetite by providing a feeling of "fullness" or (3) causing fluid loss. Amphetamines (Speed) and diuretics are the two most commonly used diet pills. Amphetamines toy with the thyroid gland, cause nervousness, speed up metabolism and require increasingly strong doses as the body builds up a tolerance, while diuretics result in rapid fluid loss. Both are a dangerous attempt at weight control. A physician should be consulted before starting any type of diet and certainly before ever using any drug or drug combinations for weight loss. Crash dieting with pills can destroy health and cause permanent damage to vital organs.

Six to eight glasses of water daily are critical to weight control and proper body functioning.

Water intake should not be restricted in anyway except under a physician's orders. Water is essential to the proper function of every body system. Drinking water immediately after an exercise session, immediately before, or during, will have no effect upon weight loss.

Water is also a diuretic and will help you to lose your fluids rather than retain them. Retention of fluids is common while dieting since water remains in the spaces freed by the disappearance of fat. This fluid generally remains for 2-3 weeks and often obscures actual weight loss.

The marjority (about 80%) of excessive weight is FAT, not water. If fat individuals would replace between meal eating with water, there would never be any misunderstanding again.

During the past 10 years we have moved toward a "waterless" society as we fill ouselves with juices, cool aid, sodas, beer, and other high calorie drinks. Consuming eight glasses of orange juice daily provides approximately the same number of calories as eight glasses of beer (120-150 per 12-oz. glass). Such high consumption can add approximately 8400 calories to the diet weekly or two pounds of fat. Water, on the other hand, eliminates hunger without adding even one calorie.

Special diets that force the body into a state of "ketosis" may be hazardous to Health.

When an individual decreases carbohydrate intake (most diets are high in protein and zero or low in carbohydrates), blood glucose is elevated. When the renal threshold of approximately 170 mg./100 ml. of blood is attained, glycosiuria appears (condition in which sugar or glucose is excreted in the urine), polyuria (excessive urine secretion) and thirst develop. Stored fat is now made available for energy causing a greatly increased production of ketone bodies by the liver. This process is called "ketosis" and is very conducive to easy fat loss. A 24-48 hour fast will cause the urine to show ketones.

Proponents of this approach indicate that is is desirable to keep an obese individual in a state of ketosis through a high protein, low carbohydrate diet to expedite loss of body fat. Carbohydrates cause the obese individual to release excess amounts of insulin which drive the carbohydrates into the fatty tissue cells and also inhibit the release of fat from the cells. While in a state of ketosis, insulin production is decreased and fat vacates fat cells more freely. It is also argued that short periods of ketosis are not harmful in any way.

Opponents point out that a prolonged state of ketosis may damage the kidneys. In addition, low blood sugar levels produce a number of additional undesirable symptoms such as discomfort, headache, and low energy levels. According to the American Medical Association it is a dangerous way to lose body weight and fat.

A diet results in loss of both body fat and muscle.

In most cases maintaining or attaining normal weight for individuals with the tendency to gain generally necessitates both diet control and exercise. To remain mildly or acutely hungry over the years may be the only solution to the impractical choice of avoiding exercise since its value far exceeds mere contribution to weight loss and regulation. A much greater number of calories can be eaten by the active individual without subsequent weight gain. Mere diet alone represents a truly difficult undertaking; however, the task is far from impossible with hundreds of *Weight Watchers Clubs* providing benefits to thousands of members without the benefit of exercise.

Obese people have also been shown to expend less energy during exercise than people of normal weight. Some overweight individuals do *not* have a high food intake; they are merely inactive. There is no doubt that exercise is a much needed addition to a diet for reasons of weight loss, improved muscle tone and conditioning level. Finally, it must be said that there is a difference between weight loss in terms of pounds and fatty tissue loss in terms of inches. A diet without exercise can result in about 30% fatty tissue loss and 70% lean muscle loss. With exercise and diet combined, this ratio can be reversed. It is undesirable to lose lean muscle mass when inches of fat remain. Muscle mass is useful tissue that is vital to movement and body function—fat is not. If you want to lose weight, make it fat.

SPECIAL DIETS

"Fasting" can be dangerous and should only be done under care of a physician.

There is some evidence that a 24-48 hour fast at the beginning of a diet breaks down an undesirable chemical balance and paves the way for more rapid weight loss. Long term fasting should only be attempted in a hospital under close supervision. This approach is used in various clinics for the extremely obese individual. It is good advice to avoid reducing caloric intake below the metabolic rate (amount of calories required in a 24 hour period while at rest, but not sleeping) This figure varies from approximately 1200-2000 depending upon the individual.

"Fast" only under the supervision of a physician. It is also wise to use a food supplement in the form of a multiple vitamin. Even wiser is an attempt to eat sensibly, avoid an obese condition and the need for fasting.

The disadvantages of fasting are that eating habits may not change, causing a return to the same foods that made you overweight when the diet ends. Also, inadequate fluid consumption can be dangerous even for a healthy individual. On the other hand, fasting builds will power and provides clear evidence that you can lose weight and that the cause of your overweight condition was not a glandular problem or metabolic imbalance, but being a gluttonous eater.

The Quick Weight Loss Diet can be an effective means of rapid weight loss.

The Quick Weight Loss Diet, often referred to as the "Water Diet" because of the strict requirement to drink eight 10 ounce glasses of water daily, has become one of American's favorite choices. Again, one should be cautioned to consult a physician before attempting such a diet. The diet is extremely simple to remember and follow:

1. A multiple vitamin is consumed daily.
2. Eight 10 oz. glasses of water must be consumed daily in addition to other calorie free fluids.
3. Carbohydrates are prohibited.
4. Foods that can be eaten include chicken (no skin), lean meat, fish (broiled), hard boiled eggs, cottage cheese, coffee and tea without milk or sugar. No vegetables are permitted.

Eating only one or two meals daily rarely results in weight or fat loss

It is nearly impossible for most people to skip a meal and lose weight. Their hunger becomes so intense at the scheduled meal that more calories are consumed than would have been eaten in two meals. It is also difficult to get the necessary daily vitamin requirements with one or two meals daily. Breakfast is the most commonly missed meal. After approximately 12 hours without food, it is the one meal that is absolutely necessary in your diet. Research indicates that late morning fatigue is likely if breakfast is missed. Obviously, if you exercise in the morning before breakfast and have not eaten since the previous evening, the only available fuel will be fatty tissue. On the other hand, when the body can utilize energy producing foods for energy, no loss of fatty tissue occurs. If carbohydrate diet is high, you will burn a greater proportion of carbohydrates with exercise. If intake is low, you will metabolize a greater amount of fat through exercise.

Missing the noon meal is the next most common and also represents a poor attempt at weigh reduction. A ten hour period of activity without food is too long and will result in tremendous overeating at the evening meal.

Do not skip a meal. Begin with a good breakfast and eat less quantity at each meal or eat six meals per day instead of three, consuming small portions at each. This approach has been shown to result in more weight loss than the three-meals-per day approach.

One food diets are hazardous to health and are not a sound choice of diets.

Nowadays more and more dieters turn to the "one food diets" (grapefruit, buttermilk, egg, poultry, fish, vegetable, steak, fruit, juice, melon, banana-milk, beer, yogurt, rice) to take off weight. Usually, dieters do this without asking their doctor for his okay. Actually, such diets can be pretty risky. The pitfalls are (1) that you may not get the necessary daily nutriments when you eat only one kind of food, (2) you may not drink enough water, thus depriving your body of fluid for proper functioning of the systems. (3) your resistance may be lowered, leaving you susceptible to disease or infection, (4) diets of this nature are usually short term, and don't help you change your eating habits. You just gain weight again after you stop dieting.

DIET AND EXERCISE QUACKERY

Special "Fad" approaches to weight and fat loss promising almost immediate slimness do not work.

The large majority of "gimmick" approaches involving a special apparatus or program are of questionable value. "Vibrators" result in little caloric expenditure and do not cause weight loss. "Spot reducing" has little scientific basis since research indicates that the greatest weight loss occurs in the area of highest fat deposits regardless of the body area or part exercised. "Steam baths" merely remove body fluids and do not cause weight loss. A steam bath simply does not burn up many calories; lying in the snow would be more beneficial since calories would be used to maintain body temperature.

"Wearing a heavy weight" around the waist throughout the day only burns up a few extra calories; however, the effect is negligible. The size of the waistline and muscle tone remain about the same after prolonged use. Do not become a victim of wild advertising claims. In May, 1971, the Federal Trade Commission prohibited the company marketing the Tone-o-matic weighted belt from misrepresenting that it is an effective substitute for exercise in reducing weight and waist size. This censor came after many months of radio, television and printed advertisements. To top it off, the Federal Trade Commission also indicated that the belt could physically injure some users. A fast, easy method of losing weight and stomach fat does not exist. The only belt that may be valuable is one that you place around your head and over your mouth—immediately after eating your first helping.

"Inflatable clothing" or "figure wraps" make the waistline appear as though it is smaller due to a shifting in fluids from one place to another but only for a short time. By the time you get home and drink a glass or two of water, you'll be back to normal—except for your pocketbook, where the loss is much more than water.

"Massage" burns very few calories and does not cause fluid loss. It is relaxing and can slightly aid muscle tone and improve circulation. Meanwhile, the masseur himself may lose a few pounds while you rest. And, to top it off, he gets paid for it.

FIGURE 3-4.   Energy cost of common activities.

Activity	Approx. calories per hour	Activity	Approx. calories per hour
Rest (Basal metabolism)	70	Dancing (fox trot)	266
Sitting at rest	100	Golf	290
Hand sewing	105	Walking (3.75 mph)	300
Bricklaying (6 per min.)	105	Horseback riding (gallop)	441
Dressing and Undressing	118	Tennis	450
Singing	122	Sawing wood	480
Typewriting rapidly	140	Swimming	500
Ironing (5 lb. iron)	144	Fencing	539
Dishwashing	144	Running (11 min. mile pace)	570
Sweeping	169	Skiing	600
Driving car	170	Wrestling	791
Shoemaking	180	Football (strenuous)	900
Walking slowly (2.6 mph)	200	Running (6 min. mile pace)	1000
Carpentry, metal working	240	Walking up stairs	1100

Laxatives are never used for the purpose of losing weight.

Laxatives are no more effective than the Roman practice of forced vomiting after a gluttonous meal to allow continous eating and socializing. Laxatives have a similar effect; however, they are a more dangerous practice and can cause gastrointestinal trouble. You need adequate fluid intake and nutrients while dieting. A laxative, taken on a regular basis, can prevent you from obtaining either, and cause dehydration and undernourishment. Be sensible. It is better to be fat than to be lighter and sick. It is impossible to defecate away unwanted pounds.

HOW EXERCISE HELPS

Even moderate exercise burns many calories and aids weight loss.

Energy expenditure tables such as that shown in Figure 3-4 have several limitations and must be interpreted accordingly: (1) tables are computed for an individual of average height and weight (male: 5'8", 150 lbs.; female: 5'4", 125 lbs.) and must be proportionally increased or decreased with deviations from this weight norm, (2) tables fail to include duration peaks where the expenditure may reach 1600-2000 calories per hour, and (3) tables fail to consider the fact that metabolic rate (amount of calories expended at rest) is increased through exercise and remains elevated 40-50 calories per hour for as long as 6-8 hours after cessation of activity.

If these shortcomings are applied to a male individual weighing 200 pounds who has run at a 6 minute mile pace for thirty minutes, according to the chart, he has expended only 500 calories or about ⅛ of a pound of fat (3500 calories = 1 lb. of fat). Adjusting this for metabolic rate changes and his extra weight we find:

Chart—150 lb. man		Actual—200 lb. man
6 min. mile pace for 30 minutes	500 calories	625 calories
Metabolic rate changes (40-50 per hour for 6-8 hours)	—	400
TOTAL	500 calories	1,025 calories (almost ⅓ pounds of fat)

The actual energy expenditure then, in this example, is more than two times that shown in the chart.

Adjust estimations accordingly when counting caloric expenditure. Weight loss without exercise is an unwise choice. Exercise is *the* most valuable means of controlling weight. The secret is to exercise daily as opposed to one all-out effort each month. A daily exercise expenditure of 1,025 calories can result in loss of two pounds weekly, eight pounds monthly, and ninety-six pounds in a year.

It is possible to initiate a sound, safe diet just right for your physical being and weight loss goals. Such a program should be jointly worked out with your physician. Some of the contents of such a diet will include:

1. Foods from the basic four food groups.
2. Three meals per day.
3. Sufficient liquids.
4. A vitamin supplement.
5. Absence of a diuretic or amphemetine-type aid.
6. Sufficient carbohydrates to avoid ketosis.
7. Reduced intake of saturated fats and foodless foods (sweets).
8. Elimination of between meal snacks.
9. Substitution of water for other high calorie fluids (sodas, milk, beer, etc.)
10. Caloric reduction to permit no more than 3-5 lbs. of weight loss per week; caloric intake of at least that required for basal metabolism.

Moderate exercise will not significantly increase appetite.

Exercise alone is recommended when desired poundage to be reduced is only minimum and, although a slower approach, this represents a much more sound, less risky method of weight reduction. Research shows that a newly started exercise program does not cause a great increase in appetite. Fat and excess poundage will be reduced by endurance programs such as distance running (1 mile or more), cycling, swimming, running in place and endurance activities (basketball, handball, tennis, rugby, soccer, lacrosse, wrestling, etc.) much more rapidly than any other means. A combination of both endurance running and *mild* diet (calories should be reduced no more than 15-20% when combined with exercise) will produce faster weight loss. An increase in appetite is thus controlled through diet and the caloric expenditure due to exercise is *not* offset by increased eating.

Exercising when very few carbohydrates are available in the body for energy may aid fat loss.

If the body has no energy producing foods (carbohydrates) to draw upon for fuel during exercise, it must resort to fat supply. The result is a reduction in adipose or fatty tissue in the areas of greatest concentration.

EXERCISE   Definitions and List of Terms

1. Activity rated by the amount of oxygen necessary for completion and performed through intake of atmospheric oxygen for fuel is termed _____.
2. A tissue in the human body containing fat cells is termed _____.
3. The unit used to measure the amount of heat released from food. One calorie supplies the quantity of heat required to raise the temperature of one kilogram of water one degree centigrade. This is a _____.
4. Calories taken in from food exactly equal caloric expenditures (calories of basal metabolism, calories of work metabolism, and calories lost in excreta) result in a _____.
5. Medicine that increases the secretion and discharge of urine and body fluids is referred to as a _____.
6. A condition resulting in excessive acetones or other ketones in the body that can be brought about by restricted carbohydrate and high protein intake. Such a condition tends to produce more rapid loss of body fat and is considered desirable when dieting under the care of a physician is termed _____.
7. The amount of calories expended while in a resting (not sleeping) state is your _____.
8. An extreme "overfat" condition estimated at 20 percent above normal weight indicated in weight tables or normal fat indicated in percent of body fat tables places an individual in the category of _____.
9. Possessing weight in excess of normal norms. If excessive weight is lean body tissue (muscle) and not fat, such a condition is not harmful. If excess weight is fat, it is classified as _____.
10. A procedure to estimate total body fat by measuring the thickness of two layers of skin and the body fatty tissue attached is _____.
11. The amount of calories expended while in an active state of exercise or work is referred to as _____.

1. Aerobics
2. Adipose Tissue
3. Calorie
4. Caloric Balance
5. Diuretic
6. Ketosis
7. Metabolic Rate
8. Obesity
9. Overweight
10. Skinfold Measures
11. Work Metabolism

BIBLIOGRAPHY

American Association for Health, Physical Education, and Recreation. *Nutrition for Athletes.* Washington, D.C.

Bogert, L. Jean and George M. Briggs, *Nutrition and Physical Fitness.* 9th Edition, Philadelphia: Saunders, 1973.

Buskirk, Elsworth and Emily Haymes. "Nutritional Requirement for Women in Sport." *Women and Sport: A National Research Conference.* Dorothy V. Harris, ed. Pennsylvania State University, 1972, pp. 339-374.

Mayer, Jean, "Exercise," *Family Health.* 7:43, February, 1975.

Mayer, Jean, "Nutrition's Future: Food for Thought." *Family Health.* 7:42, January, 1975.

Mayer, Jean, *Overweight: Causes, Cost and Control.* Englewood Cliffs, NJ: Prentice-Hall, 1968.

Mayer, Jean, "Water: You Can't Live Without It." *Family Health,* 7:27, September, 1974.

Mayer, Jean, "When You Think Food, Think the Basic Seven." *Family Health.* 5:40-41, December, 1973.

Oscai, Larry, "The Role of Exercise in Weight Control," *Exercise and Sports Sciences Reviews,* Jack H. Wilmore, ed. New York: Academic Press, 1973.

Passmore, R. and J. Durnin, "Human Energy Expenditure." *Physiological Review,* 35:801, 1975.

Stillman, Irwin M. and Sam S. Baker. *The Doctor's Quick Weight Loss Diet.* New York: Dell, 1967.

"The Perils of Eating, American Style," *Time.* 100:68-76, December 18, 1972.

Van Itallie, Theodore, "Trouble Losing Weight?" *U.S. News & World Report.* 77:56-58, July 22, 1974.

4

ARCHERY

DESCRIPTION OF THE ACTIVITY

Archery has evolved into two general types of competition plus several variations of these, all of which are basically similar. Target archery and field archery are the two fundamental modes of shooting. Several of the fundamental skill techniques of each are performed in different ways, and the targets and areas in which competition takes place are different for each type. Educational institutions are primarily interested in target archery; therefore, most of the space here will be devoted to it.

Archery, as a sport, is peculiarly adapted to individual rather than to team participation. It is simply the act of shooting an arrow from a bow at a target, which is marked off in graduated scales for purposes of scoring. No part of this action must involve any direct or indirect contact with another person or with any variable element over which an individual other than the archer has some control.

In formal competition, each archer stands on a clearly marked shooting line and shoots a given number of arrows at a target set up a designated number of yards away from that line. Archery contests are called *rounds,* and there are several of these, some of which are divided into different classifications for men, women, and juniors. The most common of these are shown below in Table 4-1.

Regardless of which round is used, the archer shoots arrows in groups of six, which are called *ends.* After each end the archers walk to the target, where one of them pulls the arrows from the target, beginning with those in or nearest to the gold, and two contestants record the scores for all arrows shot by each contestant. After all arrows have been recovered and scored, the contestants walk back to the shooting line and shoot another end. This is repeated until the total number of arrows for that distance has been shot. For example, in the American round, five ends would be required to complete each distance.

Archery competition takes place on an archery range, which should be designed for shooting in a northerly direction and clearly marked by parallel lines that are equally distant from all targets. The

TABLE 4-1. Competitive archery rounds.

Championship Rounds
1. FITA Men's Round:	36 arrows at each distance of 90, 70, 50 and 30 meters.	
2. FITA Ladies Round:	35 arrows at each distance of 70, 60, 50, and 30 meters.	
3. American Round:	30 arrows at each distance of 60, 50, and 40 yards.	
(For women, men and intermediate boys and girls and intercollegiate round)		
4. The 900 Round:	30 arrows at each distance of 60, 50 and 40 yards.	
	(Scoring is 10, 9, 8, 7, 6, 5, 4, 3, 2, 1.)	
(N.A.A. Championship Round) (Men, women and intermediate boys and girls)		
5. Columbia Round:	24 arrows at each distance of 50, 40, and 30 yards.	

Non-Championship Rounds
1. York Round: (men)	72 arrows at 100 yards, 48 arrows at 80 yards, and 24 arrows at 60 yards.
2. National Round: (women)	48 arrows at 60 yards, 24 arrows at 50 yards.
3. Junior American Round:	30 arrows at each distance of 50, 40, and 30 yards.
4. Junior Columbia Round:	24 arrows at each distance of 40, 30, and 20 yards.

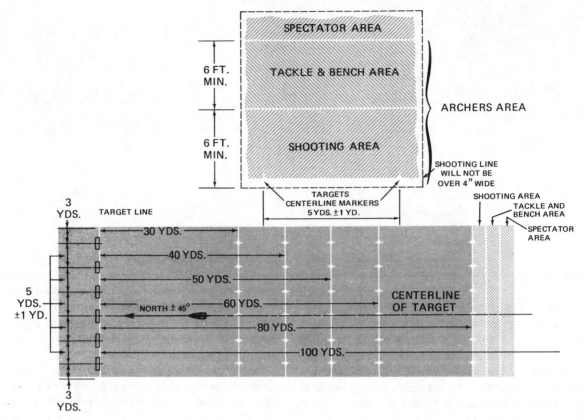

SOURCE: From the *Archer's Handbook,* National Archery Association, p. 15. Adapted by permission.

FIGURE 4-1.   The archery range.

TABLE 4-2.   Competitive archery rounds.

1. Men	17 years and up
2. Women	18 years and up
3. Intermediate Boys	15-18 years
4. Intermediate Girls	15-18 years
5. Junior Boys	12-15 years
6. Junior Girls	12-15 years
7. Beginners—Boys	less than 12

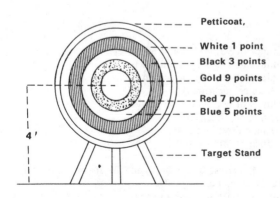

FIGURE 4-2.   The 48-inch target.

number of lines and the distance away from the targets will be determined by the round that is to be used; however, for beginners, there should be lines marked at 15 and 20 yards. These should be used during the learning stages. Archery ranges can also be set up indoors. In this case the distance and target size can be adapted to the available space. Some kind of backdrop is necessary to catch stray arrows that do not hit the target.

The official N.A.A. 48-inch target face is marked with different colors laid out in concentric rings. The scores for an arrow hitting in the various colors are: gold, 9; red, 7; blue, 5; black, 3; white, 1. When the arrow shaft is touching two colors, it is given the higher value. An arrow which hits the target face and falls off, and one which passes completely through it, when witnessed, are given a 7 point score at 60 yards or less, and 5 points if the distances are greater than 60 yards. A perfect score for an end is 54 points. According to the FITA rules, each of the five colors are divided and scored as follows: gold, 10 and 9; red, 8 and 7; blue, 6 and 5; black, 4 and 3; and white, 2 and 1. The target face for the two longest distances for men and women is 122 cm in diameter and 80 cm for the two shortest distances.

In team competition, four shooters make up a team, and the team with the highest total score wins. In college competition, the practice is used of permitting an unlimited number of players to shoot the required round and then selecting the four contestants with the highest total to make up the team score. Many school and college contests are telegraphic meets in which the shooting is done on a set date and at a set time, and the results of the team scores are sent in to a central location by telegraph or telephone.

Other forms of archery are clout shooting, flight shooting, wand shooting, and archery golf. The target for clout shooting is 48 feet in diameter, and is marked off on ground surface by concentric rings in a 12 to 1 ratio to the standard 48-inch target. The shooting line is located 180 yards away from the target. Scoring is the same as for target archery. In flight shooting the purpose is to obtain maximum distance, and therefore requires a specially designed bow and arrow. The record distance is somewhat more than a half mile. The objective in wand shooting is to score hits on a $2'' \times 6'$ wand, at a distance of 100 yards. One point is scored for each hit. Archery golf is played over a golf course with specially designed targets on each green.

EQUIPMENT

Each individual must be fitted with a bow and bow string, arrows, arm guard, finger protector, and quiver. Range equipment inclues targets, target faces, target stands, and backdrops if needed.

The Bow

Modern technology has provided many new bow designs and materials. One can now purchase bows made from wood, steel, fiber glass, or a combination of wood and fiber glass in laminated form. Yew, because of its peculiar makeup, is the best kind of wood for bow construction; however, Osage orange, lemonwood, and hickory may be used. The best and most expensive bows are recurved and laminated with wood and fiber glass. Most of these are too expensive for the group instruction archery found in school situations. The solid fiber glass bow, since it is relatively inexpensive and is very durable and effective, is the most functional bow for class instruction.

Bows may be constructed straight, reflexed, recurved, or deflexed. The straight bow has little or no angulation from nock to nock. The reflexed bow has a definite bend forward of both limbs. The recurved bow has a forward curve near the end of both the lower and upper limb. These are generally working curves which add to the cast of the bow. In the deflexed bow the upper and lower limbs are angulated backward. The working recurve is the best type of bow for school use.

Bows vary in length from 4½ to 6 feet. However, the length of the solid fiber glass bow for men should be at least 5½ feet. Expert archers will want bow lengths to fit their individual needs, but for learning purposes the 5½ foot glass bow is satisfactory.

The weight of a bow is measured in pounds of pull. The rated weight is generally measured from a 28-inch pull; therefore, when an arrow shorter than 28 inches is used, less pounds of pull will result.

Conversely when an arrow is used longer than 28 inches, increase in pounds of pull will result. In order to determine the exact weight of a bow, the following procedure can be used.

1. Divide the manufacturer's weight stamped on the bow by 20 and carry out the answer to two decimal places.

2. Determine the length of the particular draw in question.

3. If the actual draw is less than 28 inches, subtract this number from 28 and multiply the results by the number obtained in Step 1.

4. Subtract the answer found in Step 3 from the manufacturer's weight stamped on the bow. This will be the actual pull weight for that length draw.

5. If a particular draw is more than 28 inches, 28 inches is subtracted from the length of the draw in inches, and the result is multiplied by the figure obtained in Step 1. The quotient is then added to the manufacturer's weight stamped on the bow.

Bows with a weight from 18 to 80 pounds or more of pull can be purchased; however, for purposes of instruction it is best to use light bows so that students can concentrate on form rather than be forced to exert maximum effort to bend the bow. The weight selected for college men should be between 25 and 35 pounds. For high school boys and upper limit should not be more than 30 pounds For high school girls the maximum should be 25 pounds.

The more expensive laminated bows are constructed with a center shot design. This is a bow with a cutout in the handle, which allows the arrow to come out of the center of the bow rather than at the

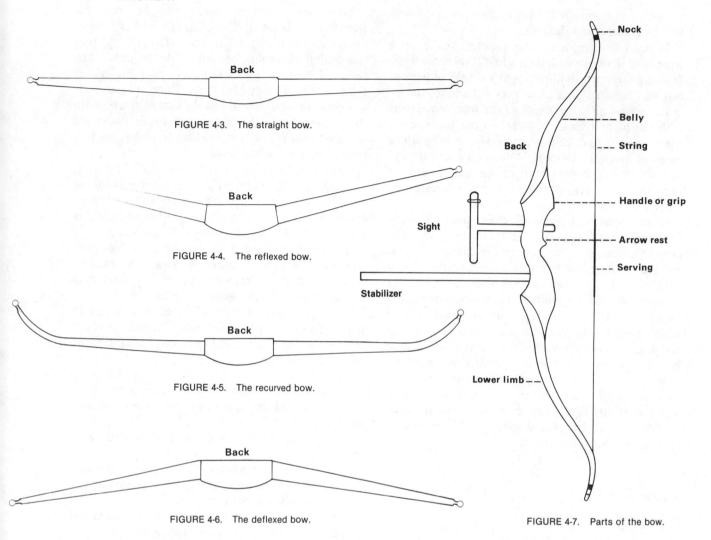

FIGURE 4-3.   The straight bow.

FIGURE 4-4.   The reflexed bow.

FIGURE 4-5.   The recurved bow.

FIGURE 4-6.   The deflexed bow.

FIGURE 4-7.   Parts of the bow.

side of it. This type of bow and those of other designs are made for both right- and left-handed archers.

Wooden bows require more care and maintenance than either glass or metal bows. They should be kept dry and waxed frequently. However, all bows should be stored in a cool, dry place; they should either be suspended from the upper nock or placed across two supports parallel with the floor; they should be strung only during the time they are being used for shooting and unstrung at all other times; and they should never be dented or bruised, drawn and released without an arrow, overstrung, or overdrawn, because any of these actions may weaken the bow or cause it to break.

Most bow strings are made from nylon, and dacron. The section of the bow string against which the arrow is nocked is wrapped with a fine thread to prevent wearing caused by the friction of the arrow nocks and the fingers. All are satisfactory; however, most manufacturers are now using nylon or dacron. They may be purchased with a loop on each end or with a single loop. In the former case, the string must be ordered to the exact length, of the bow or the bow cannot be correctly strung. In addition if the string stretches, the bow will be understrung. The single-loop string provides for adjustment to fit bows of different lengths and for stretch. The nonloop end is attached to the lower bow nock by a timber hitch. The double loop string is essential for a working recurve bow. It is made to fit the various bow lengths and can be shortened by adding to the number of twists and lengthened by decreasing the number of twists. However, it is recommended that not more than 10 or 12 twists be added to the manufacturer's finished product String length is important because it determines the brace height of the string. This is important not only because it is essential to accuracy in shooting but also because an overstrung or understrung bow can be a safety hazard and decrease its life.

The diameter, strength and weight of the string is determined by the number of strands it contains. The number of strands will vary from eight for a 25 pound bow to sixteen for a 60 pound one. The string with the fewest strands is lighter and faster than one with more. Most good archers want the lighest string possible if it provides sufficient strength.

Most good archers use stabilizers on their bows. These are metal rods that are attached to the back of the bow and extend varying distances (5 to 25 inches) out from it. Generally weights of varying sizes are attached to the end of these rods. The purpose of a stabilizer is to reduce or prevent the torque that is inherent in the release and initial flight of the arrow. Some archers will use two.

Bow Sights

Because practically all good target archers now use some kind of mechanical sighting device, this means of aiming should be taught early in the instructional program. Mechanical sights vary from a simple, big-headed pin stuck in a tongue depressor and attached to the back of the bow with tape, to the rather complicated commercial sight with both vertical and horizontal adjustments as well as interchangeable prisms. Simple but economical and effective mechanical sights are available. They can be classified according to the type of device found in the aperature; pin, post, peep and cross hair. These are sometimes interchangeable. They have both horizontal and vertical adjustments, and can be attached to either the back or belly of the bow above the arrow rest. Double sights, set from one to two feet apart, are also used by some archers. These provide a sighting design much like a rifle.

The Arrow

Arrows are made from wood, aluminum and fiber glass. Wood has been the most satisfactory in the past, but the fiber glass type has great promise because it can be uniformly constructed and possesses excellent shooting characteristics. Wooden arrows are either self or footed. A footed arrow has a short length of hardwood inlaid at the pile end of the shaft. The entire length of the self arrow is constructed from one piece of wood. The footed arrow is not used as much now as it was in the past because of the introduction of the aluminum and fiber glass arrows and because of the improvement in the production of the self arrow.

Practically all of the good archers use aluminum arrows because these arrows are the most accurate and consistent of any now available. They can be manufactured so as to control most of the variables such as weight and spine, therefore, each one reacts in exactly the same manner as it leaves the bow. Fiberglass arrows have similar characteristics as the aluminum but are not used as consistently by the better shooters, however, they are very durable and do not warp, bend or break easily. Both the aluminum and fiberglass arrows are more costly than the wood but because they last much longer they can be cheaper in the long run.

The pile is the forward end of the arrow. For target shooting, it is made from metal and is designed either with a gradual taper like that of a rifle bullet or with parallel sides that angle to a fast taper. The shaft is the part of the arrow from the crest to the pile. The section of the arrow from the bottom of the crest to the nock is the shaftment. When a wooden arrow is footed, the foot will be attached to the lower end of the shaft. The crest is the colored part of the arrow, which serves as a means of identification and is a part of the tradition of archery. The vanes, or fletchings, are the feathers or other material below the nock that guide the flight of the arrow. They are generally three in number—although hunting arrows often have four vanes—and are constructed from turkey wing feathers or from plastic. If three vanes are present, one is the index feather and the other two are hen feathers. The former is generally of a different color and is located perpendicular to the notch in the nock. The arrow is always nocked with the index feather away from the bow. The nock is the device at the back end of the arrow into which the string is inserted before the bow is pulled. It may be just a shallow slit cut into the shaftment itself, or it may be constructed from plastic, horn, or other material and glued to the back end of the shaftment. Plastic nocks are excellent for target arrows, since they are easily replaced if broken or lost.

Arrows are manuactured in various lengths and diameters. Standard lengths run from 24 to 28 inches; however, they can be purchased shorter or longer than those lengths. Most individuals will require arrows within this 4-inch range. The diameter of wooden arrows is generally 5/16 inch; however, 9/32 and 11/32 inches are also found. The diameter of fiber glass and aluminum arrows is less than that of wooden arrows.

The weight and spine are important characteristics to consider when purchasing arrows. The best arrows are matched in weight and spine and are called

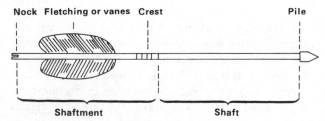

Nock Fletching or vanes Crest   Pile

Shaftment   Shaft

FIGURE 4-8.   Parts of the arrow.

matched arrows. The spine of an arrow is its rigidity-flexibility factor, which must be matched to bows within a certain weight range. It is the deflection or bend in an arrow when a two pound weight is rested at its middle with the two ends resting on a fulcrum. The manufacturers have machines which can measure this characteric accurately. The spine of an arrow is related to its movement as it is released from the bow. An arrow released by a right hand shooter will first deviate to the left just as it leaves the string and then back to the right before it corrects or stabilizes itself and travels directy toward the target. This is called Archer's Paradox. If the spine is too great, this deviation will be so wide that stabilization may not take place, or if it is not enough, it will never occur. In either case, accuracy will suffer. An arrow with a relatively flexible spine would shoot accurately in a 25-pound pull bow, but in a 50-pound bow it would not have sufficient rigidity and therefore would not fly true.

The care of arrows is extremely important. The arrows should be stored in a dry, cool place on a rack that will support them, and placed vertically with the pile end down and the vanes separated. Broken or splintered wooden arrows should be discarded, and warped or bent aluminum arrows should be returned to the manufacturer for repair. Broken vanes and nocks can be easily replaced, while life can be restored to the fletchings, or vanes, by steaming them lightly. Arrows which "snake" under the grass or bury themselves into the target beyond the vanes should be pulled out pile end first. The vanes should never be handled except for preening. Arrows should be examined after each *end*.

Each student should be fitted with arrows that are the correct length. This measurement can be taken in three ways. One method is to place the nock of the arrow against the sternum and extend the hands directly out in front of the body along the sides of the arrow. If the arrow is the correct length, the tips of the middle fingers willl just reach the pile end of the arrow. A yardstick can be substituted for the arrow

and the correct number of inches can be read from it. The second method is to place the nock end of the arrow against the chin and take the correct stance for shooting. The arrow is extended out along the left arm. If, with the hand closed in the bow-grip position, the arrow reaches the end of the third knuckle joint of the index finger, but does not extend more than the pile length beyond it, it is the correct length. A third way is to mark an arrow in one inch sections at the pile end, then have the archer take a full draw. The length of the draw will be seen on the end of the arrow.

Arm Guard

The arm guard is worn on the forearm of the bow arm for protection against the lash of the string after the release. It should extend approximately 6 inches from the wrist toward the elbow and be 2½ to 3 inches wide. Either leather or plastic is satisfactory as long as the material is rigid and thick enough to protect the arm.

Finger Protectors

The pressure and friction generated by repeated pulling and releasing of the bow string will cause the skin of the three functional fingers to blister or chafe. To protect against these possibilities, several types of finger guards are in use. The tab is a small piece of leather which fits on two fingers and covers the front portion of all three string fingers where they grip the serving. The glove is a more elaborate guard. It has covering for the three drawing fingers, is secured by a wrist band, and has no palm, or covering, for the thumb and little finger. A third type of finger protector used by some archers is the individual finger stalls, which are not joined, but patterned to slip on each of the three fingers separately. Regardless of which of these protectors is chosen, it must be made of soft, pliable material so that the student can grip the string properly and get the feel of it.

Quivers

Both for the convenience of the archer and the protection of the arrows, some kind of arrow container, or quiver, is necessary. There are several types of quivers: ground, shoulder, hip and bow. Ground quivers are used almost exclusively for target shooting and come in several varieties. The best type is made of heavy rust-proof metal with a rest for the bow as well as a circular loop for arrows. The body quiver is made from leather or synthetic material and can be worn over the shoulder or at the waist. The bow quiver is used mostly by hunters and attaches directly to the bow. It holds only a few arrows.

Target

Targets are made from rye straw or some kind of tough swamp grass. The best type of target is one in which the straw is made into long rolls that are wound into coils; these coils are then bound together with heavy cord. The standard size for an outdoor target is 50 inches. It is actually somewhat larger than this but made to accommodate a 48-inch target face. The face is not a part of the target, but is generally made so that it can be replaced easily. Constructed from either oil cloth or heavy paper, the better types of faces can be securely fitted to the target by the use of a drawstring sewn into the outer skirt. Straw bales may also be stacked to make archery targets. Targets also come in 25 and 36 inch sizes.

Target Stand

The traditional target stand is a tripod with legs approximately 6 feet long made from soft wood. The two front legs should have an 8-inch brace extending out at a 90-degree angle and placed 24 inches from the ground to form a rest for the target. There is now available a mobile-type target stand made from metal with rubber-tired wheels that enable it to be rolled to the range without a great deal of effort. A steel projection pierces the target at the top to hold is in place.

SKILLS AND TECHNIQUES

Stringing the Bow

Three methods of stringing the bow may be used. The first is the push-pull motion of the arms. One places the lower end of the bow against the instep of the right foot, with the back of the bow facing the archer. The right hand grips the handle and the heel of the left hand is against the back of the upper limb near the end. The thumb and index finger of the left hand grasp the loop of the string on each side of the bow. The right hand pulls and the left hand pushes. As the bow is bent, the left hand slides toward the nock. When the bend is sufficient, the forefinger and thumb place the string loop into the nock and the arms gradually relax their pressure until all tension is on the string. One must take care to see that the loop fits snugly into the nock.

The second way to string a bow is sometimes called the step-through method. It is particularly suitable for bracing recurved and heavy bows. In performing this skill, the student holds the upper limb with his right hand and places the lower end of the bow over the top of the arch of the left foot. The belly of the bow is facing forward and the entire bow is canted backwards about ten degrees. From this position the student places his right leg through the space between the belly of the bow and the string. The right hand brings the bow up with the belly against the back of the right thigh. The right elbow is pointed back, the right hand is placed on the back end of the upper limb and exerts pressure forward. As the bow bends the left hand pulls the loop of the string into the bow nock. When the loop is in the nock, the right arm gradually decreases the pressure.

The use of a stringer is a third method of bracing the bow. Several devices are available, but the most common one is a nylon cord with two leather loops or pockets attached to each end. It is used in the following manner. The bow is held by the left hand at the handle. The leather pockets are fastened to the tips of the bow; the longer one is at the lower end. The loop formed by the middle of the stringer is touching the surface, and the left foot is placed on it at the center. The bow is the pulled upward with the left arm until it is bent far enough for the bow string loop to be slid into the bow nock by the right hand. Both loops are then checked to determine if they are properly seated. This process is reversed to unstring the bow.

After the bow is strung it should be checked to ascertain if it has the correct tension. This can be determined by comparing the manufacturer's recommended brace height with the actual height. If this distance is greater than the manufacturer's rating, the bow should be unstrung and the bow string untwisted several turns to lengthen it. If this actual distance is less than that recommended, the string should be twisted to shorten it. If the bow is to perform efficiently this recommended distance must be secured.

Shooting Stance

When taking the shooting stance the archer straddles the shooting line with his left side pointed directly at the center of the target, his feet approximately a shoulder-width apart, and his weight evenly distributed. After this stance is taken the feet can be positioned in several different ways. If the *square stance* is taken, the toes are placed approximately parallel with the shooting line, or at their normal

FIGURE 4-9. The step-through method of stringing the bow.

standing angle so that if a line were drawn from the middle of the arch of the right (back) foot to the cener of the target it would bisect the middle of the arch of the forward (left) foot. The *open stance* is taken from the square stance by moving the left foot back 4 to 6 inches from this imaginary line. Some archers will take the square stance and pronate the left foot to about 45 degrees. This helps the bow string clear the arm after the release, and is recommended for those archers who are having trouble with this phase of shooting.

When the archer is ready to draw, his head is turned to the left, and his chin is held at the normal angle so that both eyes are looking squarely at the target. His head must be held in this position throughout the shooting process because it establishes the anchor point for the draw and release.

Bow Grip

The bow is gripped lightly during the time that the stance and nocking are being executed. However, after the draw is begun, the pressure of the pull will push the bow handle firmly against the suface of the hand between the thumb and index finger, therefore, any gripping is unnecessary and should not be done because it will cause increased torque and other prob-

lems related to relaxation affecting arrow flight. After the arrow has hit the target, the bow handle can be gripped lightly again.

There should be no palm pressure on the bow handle at any time during the drawing, aiming and releasing. The three remaining fingers are relaxed and slightly flexed, and do not touch the bow handle. A finger sling that is fastened to the thumb and index finger is worn by most good archers. It prevents the bow from falling after the arrow is released.

String Grip

The string is gripped by the first three fingers of the right hand. The index finger is above the arrow nock and the other two are below it. The string should be placed squarely across the fleshy part of these fingers at the first joint. When the bow is drawn, the fleshy part of the fingers will catch and hold the bow string. Both the first and second joints of these three fingers are flexed, but the third joints (big knuckles) are held extended and the wrist is held straight. The pressure of the index and middle finger on the nock should be minimal. The pressure of the serving on these fingers when the arrow is drawn will tend to flatten them and, therefore, increase their width. This will augment the pressure on the arrow nock which may require some adjustment in the grip to prevent undue pressure there. If this pressure is too great, the hold and release will be adversely affected. The problem is eliminated when a release aid is used. The three fingers used for the draw should be protected by tobs or gloves. The thumb and little finger are relaxed; the thumb drops down toward the palm, and the little finger is curled inward.

Nocking the Arrow

When nocking the arrow, the bow is held in the left hand and vertical, underneath the left hand and forearm. With the bow in this position, the simplest way to nock the arrow is to grasp it between the vanes and the nock with the right thumb and index finger and to place the nock at the proper spot on the string with the cock feather away from the bow. After the string is in the nock, the arrow is pushed snugly against it and the left index finger is placed over the arrow shaft to hold it against the bow in readiness for the draw.

Drawing

The grip on the string is taken while the bow is in the nocking position. As the bow is raised and turned upright to a vertical angle the draw is begun. The left arm pushes and the right arm pulls and the shoulder blades are squeezed together as the draw is complete. During this process, the right elbow remains level with the desired line of flight of the arrow. The left arm is pushed out to a fully extended, although not locked or hyperextended, position with the elbow

pointing away from the bow. At full draw the pile of the arrow, the left elbow and left shoulder, and right elbow form a straight line. The string is drawn back until the anchor point is established. This point may be high or low. The *high anchor* results when the index finger at full draw comes to rest just under the cheek bone with the end of it touching the corner of

FIGURE 4-10.   The bow grip—high wrist.

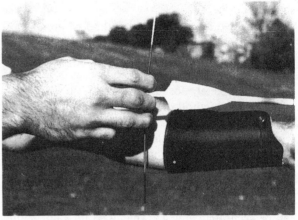

FIGURE 4-11.   The string grip.

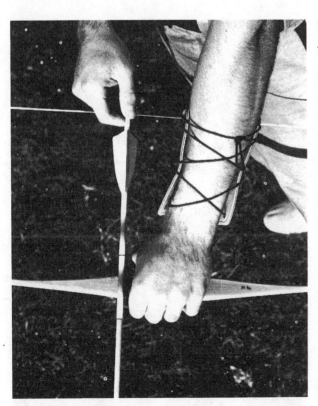

FIGURE 4-12.   Nocking the arrow. Bow is held vertical in tournament competition for safety reasons.

the mouth. If the index finger at full draw is rested just under the lower jaw bone, the *low anchor* has been taken. Some authorities feel that beginners should start with the high anchor. This is a kind of natural reaction exhibited by beginners because they will attempt to draw the arrow as close to their eye as possible.

It is essential that every draw is identical so that each arrow will be released with the same velocity and in the same manner. In order to accomplish this objective the anchor point must be the same for each release When the low anchor point is used, the string is drawn back until it touches the lips, chin or tip of the nose or all three simultaneously. The pressure of the string on these areas will inform the archer when the draw is complete. A kisser button that is attached to the string is used by some archers. It is drawn back until it comes to rest between the lips. When the high anchor point is used, the draw is continued until the index finger comes to rest against the right corner of the mouth or cheek bone.

All these actions bring the arrow back to its full length and place the string directly in front of the right eye so that when the archer aims, the string visually splits the arrow lengthwise. Women should draw only to the outside of the breast.

Aiming

There are three methods of aiming—point-of-aim, using a mechanical sighting device, and instinctive. The use of a mechanical sighting device has proven to be much more accurate than the other two methods. However, there is actually little or no difference between the fundmental skill techniques used in bare bow (point-of-aim) shooting and shooting with a sighting device.

Although the point-of-aim method of aiming has become obsolete for competitive archers, it is included here because it is sometimes used for beginners in schools and colleges, and because it should not be completely lost as a part of the past. The point-of-aim method is accomplished by aligning the eye, the arrow pile, and a given point somewhere in front of the shooting line with the center of the target. The point may be on the ground or on or above the target, but should be directly in line with the center of the bull's-eye. By sighting with the eye, with the pile and the target center aligned, the arrow can be accurately aimed at the target on a horizontal plane, but because the arrow at full draw is several

inches below eye level, the vertical line of sight from the eye to the pile is always angular rather than linear, therefore, precise vertical alignment is unattainable. In order to attain vertical accuracy, the archer must establish a point somewhere on the surface between himself and the target, on the target itself, or above and beyond the target. This is his point of aim for any given distance. As he moves in closer to the target, the point is moved back toward the shooting line. There is a point at which the range will be point blank. When the archer increases the shooting distance, the point is moved toward or beyond the target. This point must be both horizontally and vertically in line with the center of the target. Some kind of easily visible marker should be used to mark the point. The horizontal alignment can be checked by using the bow string to align the center of the bull's-eye with the point of aim.

The point-of-aim method cannot be used well until some degree of skill has been attained. In the early stages of learning, the instinctive method is best. Even after some skill has been developed, the point of aim must be established by trial and error. However, once it is found and marked, the archer

FIGURE 4-13.   The completed draw and anchor.

FIGURE 4-14.   The dead release and follow-through.

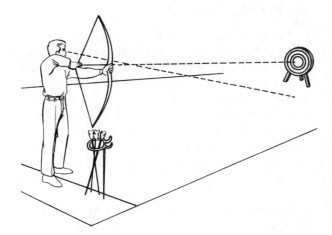

FIGURE 4-15. Point-of-aim sighting.

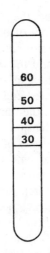

FIGURE 4-16. The range finder.

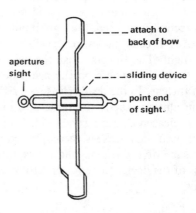

FIGURE 4-17. The bow sight.

aims at it and not at the target. In fact, he does not have to see the target at all because the point of aim is the spot on which his eyes are focused and at which he takes aim.

When the point of aim has been found for each of the distances that will be shot, it can be recorded on a range finder, which is a device used to establish a trial point of aim on a new range where the point markers are removed. A tongue depressor can be used to construct a range finder. When the point is established and marked, the archer holds the depressor in his left hand in full draw position and aligns the top of it with the center of the gold on the target. He then looks at the point-of-aim marker. Where the line of sight cuts the depressor, a mark is made and labeled for that particular distance. This procedure is used for each distance. If the point of aim is above the target, the depressor is inverted. Once the range finder is calibrated, it can be used on any range to establish the tentative aiming point for each distance.

When a mechanical sighting device is used it is mounted on the back or belly of the bow in such a way that the arm on which the actual device is located is above the arrow shaft. The archer looks through the aperture, which is one end of the sighting arm. The gold or bull's-eye should be put directly in the center of the aperture. The bow sight is adjusted by sliding the arm up or down and to the left or to the right until the proper setting for a specific distance is found. It is most easily adjusted by moving the aperature in the direction of the error; that is, if the arrows were hitting the target low and to the left of the gold, the aperture should be moved in that direction. The sighting arm is moved until the archer obtains a grouping of his arrows in the area of the gold. When this accomplished, a mark should be made on

both the horizontal and vertical section of the bow sight, so this same setting can be used, with minor adjustments, each time that particular distance is shot. When using the sighting device, both eyes may be kept open, or the left eye may be closed; however, it is better to keep both eyes open during the shooting process.

Holding, Release, and Follow-Through

After the draw is completed and the anchor is made, it is necessary to hold this position long enough to aim and release properly. The release is executed by relaxing the muscles of the forearm, wrist, hand and fingers to the extent that the pressure of the drawn bow string releases itself by uncoiling the relaxing fingers which hold it. Great care must be taken by the archer not to jerk the fingers loose from the string, pull to the right, or permit the string to creep forward before the final release. The string must be released at the anchor point and not somewhere out in front of or to the side of it.

There are two types of release and follow-through: the relaxed release and the dead release. In each of these types, the release and follow-through should be seen as one coordinated and related action in which the follow-through is the final phase of the shooting process. When the tension of the pull and hold is released from the muscles of the upper trunk, arms, and hands, certain movements are more conducive to accuracy in releasing the arrow than are others. Regardless of which release is used, the bow arm maintains its full draw position until the arrow strikes the target and the hand and wrist are relaxed. Also, the head remains steady with the eyes focused on the point of aim until the arrow arrives at its destination. The real difference between the relaxed and dead release is to be found in the movement and action of the right hand, wrist, and arm. When the relaxed technique is used, the right hand releases and then moves directly backward, level with the arrow's line of flight. The fingers brush the neck lightly and come to rest somewhere on the neck, below and in back of the ear. In the dead release the right hand remains in almost exactly the same position after the arrow is released as during the hold. When a release device is used the release is accomplished by relaxing the pressure of the thumb and index finger on the controls of the device thereby permitting the string to slide out.

Retrieving Arrows from the Target

After all arrows are shot, each archer places his bow on the bow rest and moves to the target. One of the archers removes the arrows from the target in descending order of their score, starting with the gold, and passes them to the proper person. The other archers record the scores. Care should be taken in removing arrows from the target. The proper procedure is to place the back of the left hand against the target face in a position so that the arrow is then grasped within a few inches of the target by the right hand. The left hand pushes against the target and the right extracts the arrow with an even, gentle pull. Arrows should never be jerked quickly from the target. If arrows have missed the target, they must be found before any archer shooting at that target returns to the shooting line.

SAFETY PRACTICES

The bow was employed for many thousands of years to kill both man and animal; it is presently still used for hunting. Archery can be a hazardous activity if certain safety precautions are not learned and followed. However, when used for target shooting, the bow should not be regarded as a weapon but as an instrument with great possibilities for recreation and pleasure. The following safety rules, if adhered to, will eliminate most of the hazards found in archery.

1. The archery range should be located in a cleared area, free from blind spots and with visibility on all sides, including behind the target.
2. The shooting line must be clearly marked and each archer required to use it properly.
3. The following negative rules must be enforced: never use a broken or splintered arrow; never loose an arrow straight up or into space—shoot only at a target; never overdraw an arrow; never draw and release the string without an arrow; never jerk arrows from the target.
4. Examine arrows after each flight to check for splinters and breaks.
5. Check the bow string for frayed or weak parts.
6. Always use protective equipment for the arm and fingers.
7. Obey the rules of shooting.
8. Do not remain in the vicinity of the target when others are shooting.

WEIGHT TRAINING

For many obvious reasons, participation in target archery does not make heavy demands on the individual's cardiovascular system. However, it does require reasonable strength and endurance of the muscles of the hands, arms, and upper trunk. These muscles can be strengthened and conditioned by weight training exercises that are properly selected and performed. Some suggested exercises are: wrist and arm curls (both regular and reverse), upright rowing, pull-overs, bench press, dumbbell curls from the side position, and wall pulleys. Descriptions of the correct execution of these and other exercise can be found in Chapter 17.

EXERCISE   Definitions and List of Terms

1. The _____ is the spot on the chin, lips, or nose to which the string is drawn and held before the release.

2. Some bows have an insert of hardwood or other tough material in that part of the bow handle where the arrow slides out. This is to protect the bow against wear and is called the _____ .

3. The narrow projection at the top of the handle upon which the arrow rests during the draw and release is the _____ .

4. That part of the bow opposite the belly is the _____ .

5. The part of the bow opposite the back is the _____ .

6. The distance between the inside of the bow handle and the bow string when the bow is braced is the _____ .

7. The process of putting the loop of the string into the nock of the upper bow limb is _____ or _____ the bow.

8. The inherent power of a bow to start the arrow and propel it is its _____ .

9. The _____ has a cut-out section in the upper handle that permits the arrow to be centered in the bow.

10. _____ is a type of archery competition in which the archers shoot at a target face 48 feet in diameter, marked out in concentric circles on the ground surface.

11. A serious fault in fundamental skill is to permit the string to slide forward from the anchor just before releasing. This is called _____ .

12. The colored portion of the arrow is the _____ .

13. In competition, arrows are shot in _____ of six.

14. The chief male official for an archery tournament is the _____ . The head woman official is the _____ .

15. The measurement taken by the fist and extended thumb at the bow handle to determine if the bow is strung correctly is called the _____ .

16. The feathers or other materials attached to the shaftment of the arrow to guide it are the _____ or _____ .

17. Archery competition for distance is called _____ .

18. The _____ is a type of vane which is fluffy and large and causes the arrow to lose speed rapidly.

19. An arrow which has a hardwood section fitted to the lower end of the shaft is said to be a _____ .

20. The _____ is the center section of the bow used for gripping.

21. The phase of the shooting procedure in which the string is fully drawn, and there is a pause for aiming is called _____ .

22. The odd colored feather on an arrow with three fletchings that is used as a guide to knocking is the _____ .

23. If the left shoulder is elevated and forced in toward the neck during the draw, the shooter is _____ .

24. The method of aiming in which the archer estimates the arrow flight without a mechanical device or previously marked spot is called _____ .

25. That part of the shooting procedure in which the fingers are disengaged from the string is called the _____ or _____ .

26. That part of the bow below the handle is called _____ .

27. The notch at the back end of the arrow is called the _____ .

28. When the pile of the arrow is drawn back behind the plane of the handle, the bow is _____ .

29. When the string on a braced bow is too high above the handle, the bow is _____ ; if the string is to near the handle, it is _____ .
30. When the shooter looks up too quickly to see where his arrow hits the target he is _____ .
31. That part of the target face outside the white area is the _____ .
32. The forward end of an arrow is the _____ .
33. During the release, when the shooter jerks the string fingers out and away from the face, he is _____ .
34. A method of sighting in which the objective focus is on a given spot which may be on the ground in front of the target, on the target itself, or above and beyond the target, is known as the _____ .
35. For any bow, there is a certain distance away from the target at which the point of aim will be directly in the center of the gold. This is called _____ range.
36. The container used by an archer to hold the arrows which are not being shot is a _____ .
37. The area in which target archery takes place is the _____ .
38. An instrument used to compute the approximate spot of the point of aim is a _____ .
39. A bow that has several inches of each end curved is known as a _____ bow.
40. A bow that has the limbs curved away from the belly when unstrung is a _____ bow.
41. The several classes of competition in archery are called _____ .
42. An arrow made from a single piece of wood is called a _____ arrow.
43. The section of the bow string that is wrapped with fine thread to protect it against wear from the arrow nock is the _____ .
44. That portion of the arrow from the nock to the lower end of the fletching is the _____ . The section from that point to the pile is the _____ .
45. The rigidity-flexibility factor of an arrow is its _____ .
46. The archer has taken his _____ when he assumes he correct position on the shooting line.
47. A device to protect the string fingers is the _____ .
48. The arc-like flight of the arrow from the bow to the target is called its _____ .
49. The section of the bow above the handle is the _____ .
50. A _____ is a two-inch by six-foot archery target.
51. The _____ of a bow is determined by its pounds of pull.

1. Anchor point
2. Arrow plate
3. Arrow rest
4. Back
5. Belly
6. Brace height
7. Bracing
8. Cast
9. Center shot bow
10. Clout
11. Creeping
12. Crest
13. End
14. Field Captain
15. Fistmele
16. Fletchings
17. Flight shooting
18. Flu flu
19. Footed arrow
20. Handle
21. Hen feathers
22. Index feather
23. Holding
24. Hunching
25. Instinctive aiming
26. Lady Paramount
27. Loose
28. Overdrawn
29. Overstrung, understrung
30. Peeking
31. Petticoat
32. Pile
33. Plucking
34. Point of aim
35. Point blank
36. Quiver
37. Range
38. Range finder
39. Recurved
40. Reflexed
41. Rounds
42. Self
43. Serving
44. Shaft
45. Spine
46. Stance
47. Tab
48. Trajectory
49. Upper limb
50. Vanes
51. Weight

QUESTIONS AND ANSWERS ON THE RULES (N.A.A. Rules)

1. *Q.* What position must the archer take on the shooting line?
   A. The archer must stand so that he has one foot on each side of the shooting line. He must not be closer than 18 inches to the center of the target lane or to the side boundaries.
2. *Q.* What is an end?
   A. An end is a flight of six arrows. This is the unit from which a round is made.
3. *Q.* May an arrow which falls from the bow inadvertently or because of faulty equipment be shot over?
   A. No, unless it can be reached by the bow from the archer's shooting position.
4. *Q.* What method of scoring is used in archery?
   A. A target face is divided into five areas by concentric circles, which are colored as given below. An arrow is scored according to the following values: gold, 9; red, 7; blue, 5; black, 3; and white, 1. An arrow which hits between the colors and breaks the inside edge of the scoring line is given the higher score.
5. *Q.* What score is given an arrow that hits the target and then bounces off?
   A. It will score 7 if the shot was taken from 60 yards or less, and 5 at distances greater than 60 yards.
6. *Q.* How is an arrow scored that passes completely through the target?
   A. It is scored exactly like an arrow which rebounds from the target.
7. *Q.* What system is employed to score arrows in tournament play?
   A. One member of the group shooting at a target is designated the target captain. He pulls each arrow out and calls the score to two other contestants on the target who act as scorers.
8. *Q.* How is a tie score resolved?
   A. When a round ends in a tie, it is resolved in the following manner and in the listed order: (1) the highest score at the longest distance; (2) then the next longest distance and in descending order until the shortest distance; (3) if a tie results after 2 and 3 above, it shall be resolved in favor of the archer with the most hits in the gold, then red, and so on; (4) if there is a tie after applying 1, 2, and 3, it shall be resolved in favor of the archer with the greatest number of perfect ends. If there is a tie after this, the round stands as a tie.
9. *Q.* What kind of bow may be used?
   A. Almost any kind of bow may be used as long as the bow is held in one hand, the string in the other, and no mechnical device is used to draw it.
10. *Q.* What kind of mechanical devices may be employed in shooting?
    A. Any type of sighting or aiming device, releasing devices such as tabs and gloves, foot markers, spotting aids, and ground quivers may be used except mechanical releasing devices which have two or more working parts.
11. *Q.* What kind of arrow may be used?
    A. Any kind, made of any material so long as, in the opinion of the officials, it does not damage the target unduly.
12. *Q.* How is an official archery range laid out?
    A. Shooting direction should be from south to north, targets placed 4-16 yards apart measured from the center of the gold, and the target and shooting lines plainly and accurately marked. Distances must be established in accord with the particular round being contested.
13. *Q.* How should the target be positioned?
    A. The target face must be angled 12-18 degrees away from the vertical and the shooting line, and the center of the gold must be 51 inches above the ground level.
14. *Q.* What field officials are required for tournament competition?

A. The following field officials are generally employed: Field Captain, Lady Paramount, and assistants to each of these.

15. *Q.* Is team competition held in archery?

A. Yes, a team is made up of four archers. In this type of competition, the team with the highest aggregate score is the winner.

16. *Q.* What rules apply to special types of archery competition, such as the wand, clout, and flight shoots?

A. Each has its own rules which apply to the specific conditions of the competition.

17. *Q.* What distance should be kept clear behind the targets and down the side lines?

A. A minimum of 20 yards should be kept clear.

18. *Q.* How are targets identified?

A. Numerals at least 8 inches high placed near the base must be used to mark each target.

19. *Q.* What are the penalties for violation of the rules?

A. The penalties for ordinary infringement of the rules are:

1. First violation . . . . Warning only
2. First repetition after the warning . Loss of the score for the high arrow in that end
3. Second repetition after warning . . . . Loss of the score for the entire end
4. Third repetition after warning . . . . Expulsion

If the first violation is flagrant or a serious breach of sportsmanship, the archer is expelled immediately.

20. *Q.* How are targets assigned?

A. The officials can assign targets in any manner they choose. However, every archer is reassigned to a different target after the completion of each round.

21. *Q.* How many archers are permitted to shoot at one target?

A. Not less than three nor more than five archers may be assigned to one target.

22. *Q.* Are practice rounds permitted previous to competition?

A. Yes. At least three uninterrupted practice ends must be shot at the longest distance. This must be followed immediately by the scoring round. No practice is permitted after postponement unless the delay is longer than 30 minutes.

23. *Q.* What are the starting and stopping signals?

A. Shooting is started by one blast of the whistle. Two or more blasts are blown to stop competition.

BIBLIOGRAPHY

Barrett, Jean A. *Archery* 2nd ed. Pacific Palisades, Calif.; Goodyear Publishing Company, Inc., 1973.

Burke, E. *Archery Handbook.* New York: Arco Publishing Company, Inc. 1960.

Elmer, R. P. *Target Archery.* New York: Arco Publishing Company, Inc. 1960.

Forbes, T. A. *Guide to Better Archery.* Harrisburg, Pa.: The Stackpole Company, 1955.

Gillelan, G. H. *The Young Sportsman's Guide to Archery.* New York: Thomas Nelson & Sons, 1962.

Klann, M. L. *Target Archery.* Reading, Mass.: Addison-Wesley Publishing Company, 1970.

McKinney, W. C. *Archery.* 2nd ed. Dubuque, Iowa. Wm. C. Brown Company Publishers, 1971.

N.A.G.W.S. *Archery-Riding Guide.* Washington, D.C.: AAHPER, 1974-76.

N.A.A. *Official Tournament Rules.* Clayton Shenk, Executive Sec., 2833 Lincoln Highway East, Ronks, Pa. 1973.

National Field Archery Association. *Official Handbook of Field Archery*. Palm Springs, Calif.: NFAA., 1976.

Reichart, Natalie & Keasey, Gilman. *Archery*. 3rd ed. New York: The Ronald Press Company, 1961.

5

BADMINTON

DESCRIPTION OF THE ACTIVITY

Badminton can be played either indoors or outdoors and can be enjoyed by the novice as well as by the highly skilled, and by the recreational-type player as well as by the tournament champion. In order to learn to play well, one must master many delicate and complicated skills and sound strategy. Speed, judgment, quick thinking, and stamina are essential factors in good play. The essential feature of the game is the process of hitting a shuttlecock, or bird, with a racket, back and forth over a net without letting it touch the floor. The bird can be hit only once to get it over the net. The object of the game is to play the bird in such a manner as to make it impossible for the opponent to return it. This is accomplished by placement, speed, deception, and change of pace.

Badminton is played either as a singles, a doubles, or a mixed doubles game. The singles game is played on a court 44 feet long and 17 feet wide. The doubles court is 20 feet wide and equal in length to the singles court. The court markings are the long service line, the short service line, the center service line, and the sidelines. The long service line marks the back boundary line for the service courts in doubles and is not used in any other way except for this purpose. The short service line establishes the forward limits of the service courts in both singles and doubles. The court is divided into two equal halves by a net stretched across its width at a height of 5'1" at the posts and 5' in the center.

Singles Game

The player who starts the game with the service is called the server. In this discussion, he will be called Player A. The player to whom the serve is delivered is the receiver, who will be called Player B. Action is initiated by the service. The player who has the first service must take a position within his right service court, and from this position, using an underhand arm motion, must strike the bird with the racket face, with sufficient force to propel it over the net and into the receiver's right service court. If the bird touches a boundary line it is considered to be in bounds. The serve is delivered by dropping the bird from the hand not holding the racket as the racket is brought forward in the serving motion.

After a good serve has been delivered by Player A, Player B must return the bird over the net and into the court of Player A. After the serve, the bird may be returned anywhere within the boundaries of the singles sidelines, baseline, and net. Play is continued in this manner until one of the contestants fails to make a good return or commits a fault. If it is Player B who makes the fault or does not return the bird, Player A scores one point and then proceeds to deliver his second service from a position within the left service court. If Player B fails to make a good return after this serve, Player A scores a second point and then delivers his third serve from the right service court. However, if Player A fails to return the bird, the service goes to Player B. In this case Player B becomes the server, Player A becomes the receiver, and no point is scored by either player because no points are scored on the change of serves. Points can only be scored by the server. Player B then proceeds to deliver his first serve from the right service court. The court from which the serve must be made is determined in the following manner. If a player's score is an even number or zero, he will serve from the right court; if it is an odd number, he will serve form the left court. Action continues in this manner until one player wins the game. The first player to

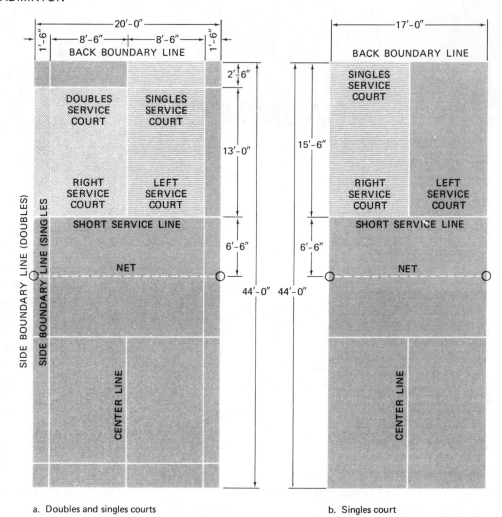

a. Doubles and singles courts

b. Singles court

FIGURE 5-1.   Badminton doubles and singles courts.

score 11 points in women's singles and 15 points in men's singles is the winner, except that a game may be set when the score is tied at 9-all and 10-all in women's singles, and 13-all and 14-all in men's singles. Setting is done in the following manner: when the score is 13-all, the player who first scored 13 points has the option of setting the game to 5 more points or letting it end at 15. If the score is 14-all, the player who first scored 14 points may extend the game to 3 more points or have it end at 15. In women's singles, if the score is 9-all, the game may be extended to 3 more points, and if 10-all, it may be extended to 2 more points under conditions identical to the men's singles.

Doubles Game

In doubles, two players on one team play against two players on another team. When one team has

completed its serve an inning has been played. The first serve in each inning is always taken from the right service court. In the first inning only one member of the team gets to serve. When he loses it, the serve goes over to his opponents. The first serve in each inning is called "first hand" and the second serve "second hand." When the serve is lost the hand is out and "side out" is called.

The doubles games is begun by a player of Team A delivering the serve to a player of Team B, both of whom must be within their own right service courts. After the serve is returned by the player on Team B who is in the right service court, either member of Teams A and B may play the bird until a fault occurs. However each player on the receiving team must receive all serves in an inning from the service court in which he started the inning. If Team B commits a fault or fails to make a good return, Team A scores one point, and the second serve is made by the first player to serve, from his left service court. After this, as long as Team A continues to make good returns and Team B faults or does not return the bird into Team A's court, the service is taken alternately from the right to the left and the left to the right service court by the first server of Team A until one member of Team A faults or does no make a good return. At this point, one inning, the first, has been completed and the serve goes to Team B, and the second inning starts. Team A becomes the receiving team, and each player receives the service from Team B in the service court he was in during the last rally in which the serve was lost. The procedure used by Team B for serving is identical with that of the first inning except that each member of Team B must serve before the serve goes back to Team A. Therefore, after the first inning each team has two hands in each inning. Play continues in this manner until one team wins. The system of scoring is the same as for singles. Only the serving team can score points, and no point is scored on the change of serves. The men's doubles game is won by the team that first scores either 15 or 21 points. Most play 15 points. The practice of setting in doubles is identical to that in singles.

EQUIPMENT

Items of equipment needed to play badminton, besides proper dress, are the racket, the net and posts, and the bird.

Racket and Press

Badminton racket frames are constructed from various kinds of wood and from metal. The grip should be covered with leather or other good gripping material. Some rackets are made from a mixture of materials, having a shaft made of metal or fiber glass with a head and grip made of wood. This type has become very popular. Nylon strings seem to be the most durable of all string materials; however, gut has great resiliency and is desired by many of the best players. Although no official specifications for racket weight, length, and size have been established, practically all rackets on the market today conform to a fairly standard length, size, and weight. When purchasing rackets, it is advisable to stay in the medium price range. Cheap rackets are generally not durable or functional, and expensive rackets lose their excellence on beginning and intermediate players.

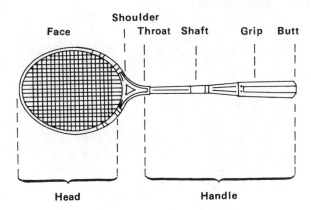

FIGURE 5-2. The racket.

Rackets must be handled carefully because they are light and fragile. They should never be struck against the hand, knee, or other hard object. When not in use, they should be placed in a press which is evenly and firmly tightened and they should then be stored in a warm, dry room. They should not be stacked or thrown into a box, but should be placed on a flat surface or hung from a peg. The press. should be light but rigid enough to provide sufficient support.

Parts of the racket are the head, face, shoulder, throat, shaft, handle, grip, and butt.

Net and Posts

The net should be made from quality cord string, woven into a ¾-inch mesh, 2 feet wide with a 3-inch white tape bordering the entire net. It should be of sufficient length to stretch across the width of the doubles court, and it should have a strong nylon cord or wire cable at the top and a strong rope at the bottom of each end for attachment to the posts. It should be attached to the post at a height of 5 feet 1 inch, with sufficient tension to raise the center of the net to 5 feet above the floor.

The top of the post must be at least 5 feet 1 inch from the floor or have an attachment for the net at that height. The posts must be placed on the side boundary line of the doubles court and be of sufficient strength and firmness to sustain a tightly stretched net.

The Bird

The bird is made either from a synthetic material or from feathers set in a leather-coverd cork head. The rules state that the official bird may have from 14 to 16 feathers and weigh from 73 to 85 grains. The cork head must be from 1 to 1⅛ inches in diameter and the feathers from 2½ to 2¾ inches long with a

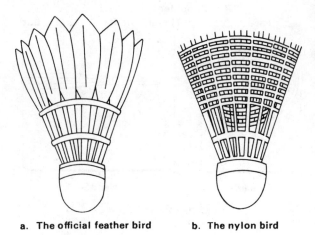

a. The official feather bird   b. The nylon bird

FIGURE 5-3.   The badminton birds.

spread at the top of from 2⅛ to 2½ inches. They are bound together firmly by thread or other material. The bird used in outdoor play shoud be heavier than that used in indoor play.

For class use in school and college, the synthetically made bird is recommended. While it does not have the same flight characterics as the feathered bird, the better ones are satisfactory and will last many times longer, are less costly, and take much more abuse than the feathered one.

SKILLS AND TECHNIQUES

To perform well in badminton fundamental skill techniques of correct footwork and body position, racket grip, and strokes must be learned. The correct movements in performing these skills will not feel natural in the beginning; therefore, practice and patience are essential. All explanation and description will be for a right-handed player of average ability. the degree of excellence that any player attains will depend upon his mental, physical, and emotional makeup.

Footwork and Body Position

Correct footwork and body position places the player in the most advantageous position for effective and controlled strokes.

The ready positions for singles and doubles are not identical. However, both are assumed in an alert but relaxed manner, with the body weight evenly distributed on the balls of the feet. The knees are slightly flexed, the body is bent slightly at the hip joint, and one foot is slightly ahead of the other. This staggered stance facilitates quick movement forward or backward. The head is up, facing the opponent's court, and the eyes are focused on the bird. However, the manner in which the racket and arms are held is different in singles and doubles play. In doubles, both arms are held out sideward and forward toward the net. The racket is held in the right hand wth the forehand grip and its head is pointed up and to the left. From this position, the player can move quickly either to the right or left. The position of the racket for singles can be a fit more relaxed; however, the ready position will vary according to the skill and dexterity of the opponent.

Movement to either the right or left side is best accomplished with either the pivot or the push-away step. The push-away step can be used effectively by most players. When the player is forced to move directly backward or forward, the push-away step with a hop is effective. The purpose of footwork is to move the body so that all strokes can be made to the best advantage.

Forehand Grip

The forehand grip is used for executing all strokes made on the right side of the body, including the serve, and overhead and around the head strokes. It is almost identical to the tennis Eastern forehand grip. It is taken by holding the shaft of the racket in the left hand with the broad surface of the face perpendicular to a line parallel to the floor and then gripping the handle with the right hand in a kind of hand-shaking clasp. This should result in a grip controlled mostly by the fingers in which the forefinger and middle finger are definitely separated from each other. Neither of the two remaining fingers are pressed closely together. The "V" formed by the thumb and forefinger should be placed directly at the top of the flat surface that extends from the edge of the racket face to the end of the handle. The thumb and fingers grip around the handle in a relaxed manner, with the end of the racket handle even with the heel of the hand.

Backhand Grip

The backhand grip is used for holding the racket when executing shots on the left side of the body. In this case, the bird is struck on the opposite side of the racket face from the one used in the forehand stroke.

A good method of taking the correct backhand grip is first to make the forehand grip, then to rotate the right hand approximately an eighth of a turn toward the left. This move will place the palm partially over the top of the racket handle. With the right hand in this position, the ball of the thumb is pressed lightly against the back of the racket handle instead of around it as in the forehand.

Strokes

Certain principles and techniques apply to almost all badminton strokes. One essential technique in executing all strokes is the use of wrist action. The only way that the fast movement necessary to drive the bird at great speed can be obtained in the racket head is through the use of the wrist snap. The wrist snap is a movement within the larger motion of the arm and body, and it must take place at the proper time during the execution of the arm stroke. The wrist snap should occur during the very end of the foward motion of the stroke just before the start of the follow-through. This means that the arm and body motion have brought the wrist almost even with the point of hitting the bird before the wrist snap is delivered. The longer the snap can be delayed, the greater the speed that can be developed in the racket hand. The degree to which the wrist is cocked and the rapidity with which it is uncocked will be determined by the objective of each stroke; however, even the most delicate shot requires some wrist action except in rare situations.

The grip on the racket is maintained mostly by the fingers, with some palm support; therefore, strokes are controlled to a large extent by the fingers and wrist. The body and feet, however, must be properly positioned before the arm and wrist action can be coordinated in producing the most effective strokes of all types. In general this means that in making all forehand strokes the left side will be turned toward the net, and in the execution of all backhand strokes the right side will be pointed to the net. In the backhand stroke, the right leg is sometimes extended so far to the left that the back is partially turned to the net.

The correct performance of several basic skill fundamentals is essential for effective play by both beginners and experts. These are listed here but will be referred to again under the skills to which they have special meaning. The following movements should be performed as described below during the execution of practically all strokes. 1. The body should be positioned behind the bird; 2. Weight transfer should take place from the back leg to the forward leg; 3. The bird should be hit with the flat face of the racket except when making special shots like some drop shots and half court and off-speed shots; 4. The bird should be contacted as high above the floor as possible; 5. Each shot should be placed as accurately as possible into the desired area; 6. The

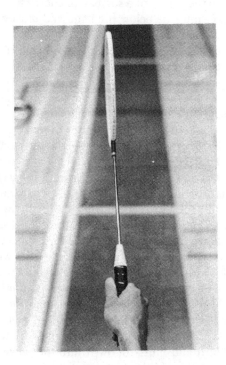

FIGURE 5-4.   The forehand grip.

FIGURE 5-5.   The backhand grip.

type of shot executed should be hidden as long as possible from the opponents; 7. Quickness and speed should be employed to get good court position; 8. The strengths and weaknesses of each type of stroke should be known and exploited.

The player should remember that most strokes are made with the feeling of hitting through the bird rather than hitting at it. This establishes the basis for wrist action and the follow-through.

Forehand Stroke. The forehand stroke is used to play all birds on the right side of the body and over the head. The full and complete action is similar to that of throwing a baseball with a sidearm or overhand motion. The left side of the body should be turned toward the net or toward the intended line of flight of the bird; however, the stroke may have to be executed with the body facing the net if there is no time to make the run to the right.

The backswing is coordinated with the turn of the body to the right and, if time permits, is even and deliberate. The elbow is flexed; the forearm is brought back as far as an imaginary line running from the net through the body. These movements place the racket head behind the upper, middle back. By the time the racket has reached its maximum backswing, most of the body weight has shifted to the right leg and the wrist is fully cocked.

The forward swing is initiated by starting the transfer of weight from the right to the left leg. As this motion gains momentum, the arm is coordinated with it in a whipping forward motion with full extension of the elbow. The wrist remains flexed until the hand is near the hitting point, at which time it snaps forward propelling the racket face quickly into and through the bird. Thus the wrist extension is the culmination of the entire stroke. The bird should be contacted away from the body and in front of the left leg so that the arm will have freedom to swing through its natural arc.

The follow-through is a natural continuation of the momentum generated by the forward motion of the body, arm, and wrist. It should continue in a smooth movement until it flows into full body recovery and balance and a resumption of the ready position on the floor.

Backhand Stroke. The backhand stroke is begun by turning the body toward the left to a position in which the right side is toward the net and the chest is facing the left sideline. However, in many cases there will not be sufficient time to make this body turn to the left, and the stroke will be made with an open stance. Some leaning of the body from the hip joint and knee flexion are essential. As the body moves in-

to this position, the backhand grip is taken and the right arm is drawn back toward the left shoulder, with the elbow bent at an angle of approximately 90 degrees. At full backswing, the right upper arm and forearm are extended across the chest and the right hand is in front of the left shoulder. The wrist is cocked from the little finger toward the thumb and most of the body weight has shifted to the left leg.

Execution of the forward motion starts with the initiation of the weight shift from the left to the right leg. The point of the elbow is driven directly at the bird, and, as the arm moves into the contact area, the elbow is extended to carry the hand to the point of contact, where the wrist snap explodes the racket face into the bird with speed and force. The little-finger edge of the hand, not the back of it, leads the hand movement. The bird should be far enough away from the body to provide ample space for freedom of arm movement and extension without drawing the right leg back away from the line of flight of the bird. The contact point should be in front of the right leg.

The follow-through is performed by permitting the racket momentum to continue and merge into the recovery and resumption of the ready position.

Service Stroke. In executing the service stroke, the left side of the body is turned toward the service court into which the bird is to be served, the left leg is ahead of the right, and the forehand grip is taken. The racket must be swung in an underhand motion similar to the action of a softball pitcher. The head of the racket must be below the hand and must contact the bird below the waist.

In executing the backswing the weight shifts slightly to the right leg, the arm is brought back, underhand, with the elbow only slightly flexed, and the wrist is cocked as the motion nears the end. The distance of the backswing depends upon the player and on the kind of shot he desires to make.

On the forward swing, the weight starts shifting forward to the left leg and the right arm is swung through in an underhand manner until it carries the hand into the hitting area, where the wrist snaps the racket into the bird. The hitting area will vary with individual peculiarities, however, in order to reduce the angle from contact point to the top of the net, the bird should be contacted as high as the rules will permit. This means that it may be struck from the ankles up as high as the middle thigh level as long as the racket head at contact is not higher than the top of the hips. The racket face meets the bird in front of and away from the body. The eyes must be focused on the bird and must follow it into the racket face. The follow-through in a continuation of the foward

FIGURE 5-6.   The backhand stroke.

swing and should help to move the body into the ready position for the next stroke.

The bird is held in the left hand at approximately waist level. It may be dropped into the hitting area or tossed onto the moving racket. Advanced players will generally use the toss technique and keep the body in a relatively upright position with only a slight lean from the hips. Beginners can start with a slight leaning of the body and the drop technique.

Three types of bird flights can be executed. The low, or drop, serve has a low trajectory over the net with just enough speed to carry it to or very near the short service line. Its highest point should be reached on the servers side of the net. In making the high, clear serve, the bird is hit high so that it falls vertically on or just inside the back boundary line, in singles or the long service line in doubles. It should rarely be used in doubles play. The drive service is one delivered with great speed, traveling low over the net, and reaching the center or rear portion of the opponent's court.

Overhead Smash stroke.   The motion in making the overhead smash stroke is similar to the service stroke in tennis. It is a powerful overhand motion that propels the bird downward with great speed into the opponent's court. The forehand grip and the body position of the forehand stroke are employed. The bird is contacted at the highest possible point approximately a foot in front of the head. Speed and power are developed by proper timing and coordination of the wrist snap with the body and arm motion.

The backswing requires that the arm be brought upward and backward over the right shoulder until the hand is behind and just above the inner deltoid area and at about ear level. The elbow is flexed more than 90 degrees, and the upper arm is approximately parallel to the floor. The wrist is fully flexed, causing the racket head to drop down behind the middle back. The body is twisted slightly to the right and bent backward, bringing the weight back on the right leg. The hips are pushed slightly forward.

The forward motion is similar to the overhand baseball throw. The weight starts shifting toward the

FIGURE 5-7.   The service stroke.

FIGURE 5-8.   The overhead smash stroke.

FIGURE 5-9.   The around-the-head stroke.

left leg as the body begins to untwist and move forward. This movement is led by the hips. The arm and hand movement is coordinated with the body motion. The wrist remains cocked until the hand nears the point of impact with the bird. At this time, the wrist is snapped and the forearm is rotated to the right, causing the racket face to contact the bird at great speed above and in front of the head. At the point of contact, the arm is fully extended and the racket face is at an angle that will propel the bird downward into the opponent's court. If a clear flight is desired, the bird will be contacted farther back and above the head with an upward angle of the racket face so that the bird is propelled upward rather than downward. The racket moves on through the hitting plane in a downward direction and is coordinated with the body weight as it shifts in the follow-through. The follow-through should help the player move into the ready position, but it often leaves him in a position that makes the next play difficult because of the force and power used in making the stroke.

Around-the-Head Stroke.   This around-the-head stroke is peculiar to badminton, and is used as a strong substitute for a high backhand. It is delivered much like the overhead smash stroke, except that the bird is on the left side of the body and high and near enough to the head to be played in a forehand, overhand manner, The body is bent to the left and the left leg is moved more toward the left than in the smash stroke, which places the body in a position

nearly facing the net. The arm motion carries the forearm above the head and as far to the left as is necessary to bring the racket face into the bird. The wrist is cocked on the backswing and uncocked at the point of contact as in all forehand strokes.

Lift Stroke.   Many situations occur in badminton play in which the bird is hit by the opponent so that it loses momentum and drops down almost vertically just as it crosses the net. A safe and good return in this situation will generally require a flicking or lifting motion of the racket with just enough force to return the bird over and low to the net, either in a hairpin arc or at an oblique angle from one side of the court to the other, but very close to the net.

This stroking movement is done with either the backhand or the forehand, depending upon the position of the bird. Execution generally requires the player either to lunge or to stretch in order to reach the bird. But in either case, the face of the racket is turned up and must be brought into the bird from below. This requires a flicking, lifting motion originating in a coordinated arm-wrist action.

Types of Bird Flights

Regardless of the type of racket stroke employed by the player, the characteristics of the flight of the bird can be varied extensively. The bird can be driven hard and low to the net, hit high and far into the backcourt, stroked lightly so that it barely makes it over the net, and hit at varying degrees of speed. Strokes describing the flight of the bird are: (1) drive, (2) high clear, (3) attacking clear, (4) smash, (5) drop, and (6) net.

The Drive.   The flight of the bird in the drive is characterized by a flat trajectory in which it travels low and fast over the net. It may be executed with either a forehand or backhand stroke and can be used as a passing shot down the sidelines, a quick cross-court shot, a fast defensive return of a smash, a quick shot into any open area, a shot directed at a player's body, or a serve. It is most effective when the bird is contacted at near net height or above, but contact can be made at a lower level. If it is played at a height below net level and stroked with full power, the flight will be upward. This can result in a set-up for a smash return by the opponent; however, if hit at partial speed the upward flight will be much less and it will drop much more quickly. Maximum speed of the bird necessitates vigorous body, arm, and wrist action. However, change of the speed of the bird is important for deception and for change of pace.

The High Clear.   The purpose of the high clear is to drive the bird high and far into the backcourt so that it will fall on or within a few inches of the baseline. The bird is driven with enough power and upward angle to propel it to a sufficiently high altitude so that when it loses speed its descent will be as vertical as possible. It is employed mainly as a defensive shot to provide a player time to gain good court position, to slow down the tempo, or to set up a situation favorable for using the drop or the attacking clear, but it can also aid in securing the offensive by driving the opponent back and forcing him to make a high, short defensive return. The flight must carry high enough and at a sufficient distance back so that the opponent cannot make an effective smash return. A few inches in length can make the difference between a good or bad shot. A bird falling vertically is more difficult to return than one falling at a slant, and it also forces the receiver to move behind the baseline in order to get behind the bird.

Great power is needed to obtain sufficient speed of the racket head to propel the bird in a high arc from a position near a player's own baseline to his opponent's baseline. It is relatively easy to produce such

power with the forehand and overhand strokes; however, it is more difficult when a player is forced to use the backhand clear from deep in his backcourt position. When using the backhand clear return, the player's body should be turned to the left so as to have the back rather than the right side to the net. This body position provides greater freedom from arm and wrist action and allows for maximum power and speed. Expert players use it mostly when forced to hit a low bird.

The Attacking Clear.   The attacking clear is generally executed from a position in the forecourt after a drop or short shot by an opponent who has moved up for the kill. The bird should be contacted as quickly and as high as possible so that quickness becomes an element of surprise. The arc is lower than for the high clear. The objective is to barely lift the bird above the opponent's reach so it will fall to the floor before he can retreat to play it. If the arc is too high, the opponent may have enough time to move into position to make a good return. It is extremely important for the player to make this kind of return with dispatch by intercepting the bird early in its flight and not waiting for it to come to him. When near the net, it can be executed with a quick, flick shot.

The Drop Shot.   The drop shot may be made from any position on the court and with any of the racket strokes. The purpose is to play the bird so that it loses speed just as it crosses the net and drops downward vertically into the opponent's court as close to the net as possible. The drop shot is used to

FIGURE 5-10.   The backhand and forehand lift stroke.

FIGURE 5-11.   The forehand lift stroke.

deceive one's opponent, to vary the pace, to put one's opponent on the defensive, to score a point, or as a defensive move if a player gets caught in the backcourt and cannot clear, drive, or smash.

A player must learn to execute the drop any distance from the net and with all types of strokes. In all cases, the bird should be hit at the earliest possible moment in its flight. Waiting provides time for the opponent to get set or to close the opening. The particular stroke used should appear, as nearly as possible, like a drive, smash, or clear; however, the key is in easing up on the wrist snap just before the racket face makes contact with the bird and slicing or cutting the bird. It is not a pushing motion, but a slowing of the racket head, resulting from releasing the wrist motion slowly rather than all out. This produces a slower flying bird tht will lose momentum quickly, and drop just as it moves across the net. The overhead drop is the most difficult to control but is highly effective when used as a change of pace with the smash and the high clear.

Placement of the drop may be at any point along the net, depending upon the location, speed, and direction of movement of the opponent. Good placment, however, can usually be found at or near either sideline. The cross-court flight can be extremely effective, but it must be completely accurate as it may be intercepted at net height and directed down the sideline away from the player.

The drop shot is often a point winner, but even though no point is scored, it can be depended on to force the opponent to hit the bird in an upward direc-

tion, thereby providing the player with the opening to move from defense to offense.

The Net Flights.   Two types of bird flight just over the net are the hairpin and the cross net shots. These have been referred to in relation to the lift stroke. The *hairpin flight* is one which carries the bird up and just over the net, where it drops nearly vertically into the opponent's court. Some of the better players will use a cutting motion by drawing the racket face across the bird as it is being stroked. It is used in situations where an opponent has dropped the bird very near the net and a clearing shot is difficult if not impossible, or it can be employed to catch an opponent, who has started backward in anticipation of a high clear return, out of position.

The *cross net flight* has a similar purpose and is used to produce like results. However, it is sometimes more effective than the hairpin because, if executed well, it carries the bird to the opposite side of the court. This compels the player to cover a long distance quickly and to change his plane of movement as well. If well conceived, the flight may start at or near one sideline and finish on the other side of the net near the opposite sideline. It can be a dangerous shot for the player using it if his opponent anticipates and intercepts it with a push or flick shot down the opposite sideline.

Much of the action and some of the most crafty strategy takes place near the net. Unless the bird is above the net level, the strokes in the net area must be made with an underhand motion and the bird must be propelled upward. Techniques for strokes made from near the net are somewhat different from those made elsewhere in the court because they are executed so deep in the forecourt that great power is not needed, but, instead, the bird must be stroked lightly and with finesse even though it is cleared to the baseline. The legs, body, and arms are used principally as extensions to help the racket reach the bird. The force necessary to make the stroke comes mostly from the forearm and wrist. The follow-through and backswing are reduced drastically.

When the opponent makes a poor return in which the bird is propelled well above and close to the net, it should be hit at a downward angle either with a push or a flicking motion. In either case care must be exerted to avoid committing a net violation and, therefore, the follow-through must be restricted.

BASIC STRATEGY

Individual fundamental skills are necessary in developing playing facility in badminton. Strategy in-

1. OVERHAND HIGH CLEAR
2. FOREHAND HIGH CLEAR
3. OVERHAND ATTACKING CLEAR
4. FOREHAND ATTACKING CLEAR
5. OVERHAND DROP SHOT
6. HIGH CLEAR SERVICE
7. SMASH SHOT
8. FOREHAND DROP
9. FOREHAND DRIVE
10. SERVICE DRIVE
11. DROP SERVE
12. HAIRPIN NET SHOT

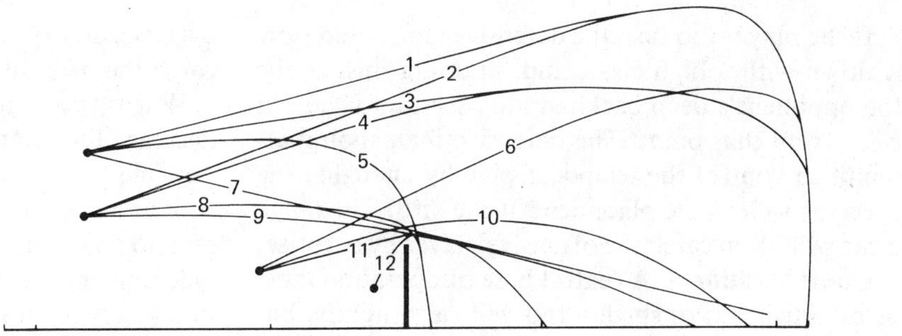

FIGURE 5-12.   Types of bird flights.

volves when, where, and to what extent each skill will be used. Decisions relating to these matters must be made instantaneously and during the full action of play. The drive, drop, smash, clear, and half-speed shots are used in combinations to produce favorable conditions for winning points. All of the various elements that go to make up the game must be fused into some kind of scheme or pattern of play. Although specifics in strategy are best related to either the singles or doubles game, there are some aspects of it which can be applied to play in general regardless of which game is involved.

General Offensive Strategy

The offensive and defensive status of opponents may change several times during one rally. Generally speaking, a player is considered to have offensive status when the bird has been returned to him so that it can be hit into his opponents court in a downward direction. In order to gain this favorable position, it is sound strategy for a player to force his opponent off balance so that he will make a weak return. When the situation presents itself for a player to move from the defensive to the offensive, he should play the bird as quickly as possible by moving to it rather than waiting for it to come to him. This hurries the opponent, makes use of the openings before they are closed, and will eventually force the opponent into mistakes which will result in a high, short return that may be smashed for a point.

Although the actual use of the smash is the best stroke for winning points, even the threat of it often opens the way for the effective use of other strokes, such as the drop, drive, attacking clear, and cross court. The drop can be used if the opponent starts back in anticipation of the smash; the drive can be hit at half speed down a sideline; and the cross-court shot can be played behind an opponent who is slow to move cross court to take a central position. When strokes are mixed in this manner, the opponent is

kept guessing as to what will come next. He is also forced to run, and to move up and back, as well as from side to side. If a point cannot be won from these tactics, the smash should clinch it. Therefore, when a good opening arises and the position is favorable, the smash stroke should be used. However, the smash should be utilized selectively. Continual execution of smash returns will cause undue fatigue, which may decide the course of the later stages of the game. It is also wise to pass it up and to wait for a more opportune moment if it must be executed from an unfavorable position.

General Defensive Strategy

Theoretically, a player is on the defensive as long as he is forced to hit the bird in an upward direction. When this situation exists, any slight mistake on the part of the defensive player could provide an opportunity for his opponent to deliver a smash or drive return. However, good defensive strategy will eventually provide the opening that will enable the defensive player to take the offensive. In order to bring this about, and to prevent the offensive man from overpowering him, the defensive player should keep the offensive player back from the net with the use of high clear, attacking clear, and passing drive shots. The offensive player should be moved away from his base of operation by a combination of drop shots and high clears. The high clear shot should be hit boldly and quickly. It is better to drive the bird beyond the baseline than to hit it short, because the opponent must make a decision whether or not to play it. Indecision in this situation will sometimes cause a poor return. If the opponent lets it go and it falls in bounds, the defensive man has a definite psychological advantage on other similar shots. The worst possible procedure for the defensive man is to hit short with the high clear, because then the offensive player can use a smash return for a possible point.

If the play is too fast, the defensive man could slow if down with a high clear, and, in doing this, probe the opponent's deep backhand to ascertain if he can clear from that point. The defensive man should attempt to control the tempo of play by changing the speed as well as the placement of the bird. The quick clear will often catch the offensive player by surprise.

Court Position. A central base of operation must be established. For singles, this will vary slightly, but should be on the center service line approximately four feet in back of the short service line. In doubles play, this position will be determined by the system of team play employed and will be discussed under doubles strategy. However, some kind of court position must be established as an operational base for play both in singles and doubles. After making a return stroke, the player should make every effort to return to this position before the opponent has had time to hit the bird for the return shot. If the base position cannot be regained in time, the opponent will have the opportunity to hit behind the player on the move, to make a shot which cannot be played or to force a weak return.

Returning the Body Shot. When the opponent smashes or drives the bird directly at the player's body, there is little time to maneuver into a side-to-the-net position and to free the arm for a normal backhand or forehand stroke. Therefore, it must be clocked or punched back over the net. In this situation, a backhanded, wrist and forearm motion is used in a flick shot. It is good strategy for a player to make the kinds of returns and placements that will forestall his opponent from counterstroking at the body. Drop shots, deep high clears, and passing shots are difficult to return at the body with a speed fast enough to cause trouble.

Returning the Smash. The smash is a difficult shot to return in any manner and extremely difficult to return effectively. But knowledge of certain factors may help to make an effective return more likely. First, a smashed bird slows down after a brief interval of rapid acceleration; therefore, if it can be played near the end of its normal flight, its speed will be much less than in the middle portion. A bird hit with a smash stroke from the baseline will reach the midcourt of the opponent, and by that time it has decelerated to the point where speed should not be the most important factor. However, waiting to stroke the bird near the end of the flight tends to slow the game down and give more recovery time to the offensive player; therefore, if the defensive man desires to speed the game up, he should intercept the bird as early in its flight as possible and block it back

over the net quickly. In this way, it is possible to catch the offensive man out of position.

When the defensive player definitely wants to decrease the tempo of play, he will wait as long as possible to make the return, then use either a drop shot or a high clear. The drop will force the offensive man to go on the defense, and the high clear will provide time for the defensive player to gain a good position and will put the offensive player so far back that a smash return will not be so devastating. Under no condition should the bird be returned directly to the opponent to give him an easy, forcing shot, neither should it be driven hard unless the opponent is completely out of position. In general, it is better to attempt to decrease the tempo of the game when on the defensive and when the bird is being returned after the smash stroke.

Placement. No stroke should be executed without an attempt at placement since random returns will never result in the development of a sound game. Each return should be made with a definite intent to place it at a spot or in a manner that will put the opponent at a disadvantage. Clear shots should be aimed to fall on the baseline, and so as to force a backhand or running return. Drives and smashes should be directed down the sidelines, cross court, into unprotected areas, and at the opponent's body. Drop shots should be used when the opponent is in the backcourt or when he is moving away from the net. The bird can be hit behind a moving player, which forces a difficult change of direction and quick movement on the player's part. Each return should be designed individually to meet the needs of the situation. The decision of which placement is best must be made on the spur of the moment and in relation to the demands of the specific situation; it cannot be predetermined.

Doubles Game

The doubles game is more offensively oriented than is the singles. This is true primarily because partners can cover for each other and in this way compensate for personal weaknesses. Furthermore, a doubles game gives better court coverage because, even thought the court is larger than for singles, only 22 square feet are added to each half of the court, and the length of the serving courts is decreased by 2½ feet from the singles service court length. These factors provide a more favorable situation for using the smash stroke because one of the partners is more likely to be in a better position to make it; and he can do so without undue fear of being out of position afterwards because it is possible for his partner to cover the opening which he may have left.

Teamwork and possible variations in floor positions add to the interest and complexity of the doubles game. There are three systems of doubles play that may be employed: (1) side-by-side, (2) up-and-back, and (3) rotation.

Side-by-Side. The side-by-side pattern of team play is based upon the division of the court into halves by the center service line. The area to be covered by each partner is clearly defined, and each is responsible for returning all birds hit into his area by the opponents. However, there are certain zones of confusion that must be resolved before effective teamwork can be developed. One of these possible zones of confusion is the area between the right and left courts. Partners must determine which of them will return the bird when it is hit into the middle of the court directly between them. This center-directed bird is generally played by the partner who can use the forehand stroke. For right-handed players, it would be the one in the left court; but this rule will not apply if one of the players is left-handed. The partners must also determine who will be responsible for playing the net returns of their serve. In this situation, good floor position can be best maintained if the server takes the short net returns of his service. He is already up toward the front of the court and there is some forward momentum with the delivery of the serve, both of which can place him in a more favorable position to play the short return than his partner. These are not hard and fast rules, and the assignments can be reversed or modified to meet a particular situation and individual strengths and weaknesses.

The side-by-side pattern is a strong defensive formation and is used for that purpose in the rotation and up-and-back systems. It provides excellent left-to-right and midcourt coverage, but is weak against the drop-clear combination because each player must cover the entire length of the half court, which is 22 feet. Therefore, if a player is forced back behind the baseline to play a bird and receives a drop return, he must recover quickly and travel several steps to make the play. Continued exposure to this kind of play will cause fatigue, which will be felt during the latter stages of a match. This pattern of play also makes it possible for the opponents practically to isolate one of the partners by directing all shots into his court thus forcing him to make all the returns. Once the player is isolated, the opponents can tire him out, play on his weakness, and harass him until he makes a poor return.

Up-and-Back. The up-and-back floor formation, in which the court is divided into halves with one player playing the front and the other the back half, provides a very favorable situation for offensive play because it places the partners in positions where there is excellent opportunity to employ the smash stroke. The better players generally use this system. The back player can take greater chances with the smash shot because he does not have to worry unduly about having to move up fast to cover a net shot or a short drive return; therefore, he can concentrate more on making the stroke. The front player can also smash

FIGURE 5-13.   Return of a body shot.

high weak returns, intercept cross-court and drive shots early, and have time to place all net shots, without having to anticipate the high clear shot, forcing him to move back fast to cover. He can play these strokes quickly, which diminishes the recovery time for his opponent and provides the split second necessary to take advantage of an opening.

The net player should position himself as far back away from the net as possible and still be able to play all drop and half speed shots that fall near the net. However, he must not hinder the play of his back partner in any way. If the opponent must return the bird from the right of his court, the net player will play somewhat to the left of his center service line; if the opponent is forced to return the bird from his left court, the net player will play on or very close to his center service line. His responsibility is to return all drop, cross court and weak shots, and, if possible, intercept straight ahead shots.

Because he has very little time to react to an opponent's return, the net player should take the ready position on the balls of his feet with the right foot slightly forward and the knees flexed. The racket should be held high up at shoulder level, and pointed to the left. The forearm and wrist should be cocked. There is generally no time to make a full backswing from this position. Concentration should be on the bird but the position of the opponents should also be known. His return shots should be deceptive and include drop, cross court, clear and cut shots.

However, the up-and-back system has a definite defensive weakness down the sidelines. The sideline drive, half-speed, and drop shots always pose a problem for adequate sideline-to-sideline coverage. Each player must cover the entire 20-foot width of the court. Even when the front player has a good position at the junction of the center service line and short line, it is difficult for him to play a bird hit directly down either sideline, and much more difficult to do so after he has been pulled over to one side. This makes for a situation in which the bird can be hit down the sideline away from the opponent, or, as he hurries to regain the good center position, it can be hit behind him.

Rotation. The rotation system is a combination of the side-by-side and the up-and-back patterns. It is employed to take advantage of their strengths and, at the same time eliminate their weaknesses. The rotation movement is usually made in a counter-clockwise direction and is initiated either when a specific and predetermined situation arises during play or on a signal by one of the partners. Generally, when on the defensive, the side-by-side position is assumed. But as soon as the partners move to the offensive, they rotate into the up-and-back pattern. When the bird can no longer be returned into the opponent's court at a downward angle, the partners rotate back into the defensive, side-by-side arrangement.

This system of play does not eliminate all weaknesses in doubles teamwork. Both players must make the shift from one pattern to the next, and if this change is not accomplished perfectly, the area which the slow partner is to cover will be open for a quick drive or smash and a possible point. Futhermore, because there must be movement during the

rotation, the opponents can, if they time it correctly, hit behind one or the other of the moving partners.

The Service. When serving from the right court, the server should take a position about 1½ feet away from the center service line, with the front foot approximately 2 feet in back of the short service line. When serving from the left court the same distance behind the short service line is maintained, but the distance from the center service line should be increased to approximately 3 feet.

Because of the short length of the service court in doubles, the basic serve should be the drop. The flight of the bird should be low, its trajectory should reach its maximum height just before it crosses the net, and it should then drop rapidly on or just beyond the short service line. These can be accomplished by contacting the bird as high as the rules permit. The bird should barely clear the net. This will force the receiver to hit up and prevent him from rushing the bird effectively. However, both the clear and drive serves should be employed occasionally to keep the receiver honest and to catch him when he attempts to rush. The clear can be used advantageously against a player who rushes the serve. In this situation, it should be hit just high enough to carry over his highest reach. If the arc is too high, the receiver will have enough time to recover and play the bird before it falls to the court surface. The drive service must be utilized judiciously for obvious reasons. If timed correctly, it can be troublesome to the receiver; however, because of its speed, it will be returned very quickly and can catch the server off balance. The server who uses it must always anticipate this quick reply and be ready for it. It is important that the preliminary movements be identical for all three of these serves. If this is not accomplished, there will be little or no surprise or deception involved.

Placement of the bird is very important. The drop serve may be effective if placed at any spot on or near the short service line; however, when serving from the right, the placement that should be used most consistently, if the receiver is in the normal receiving position, is at or near the junction of the center service line and the short service line. When the bird is hit to this spot, it narrows the possible angle of return, prevents the rush, and may force the receiver to respond with a weak backhand. Under certain conditions the bird can be served to the sideline area near the junction of the short service line. There is an element of danger in this shot, however, because it is a cross-court flight and can be quickly intercepted with a flick or push stroke and returned directly down the sideline beyond the reach of the server.

The drive serve can be valuable if it is used occasionally when serving from the right to place the bird near the junction of the long service line and the center service line. This will usually force the receiver to reply with a quickly executed backhand or with an around-the-head stroke.

The high clear serve should rarely be employed in doubles play because of the shortness of the service court. Anytime it is used, it provides the opposition with the opportunity to respond with a hard smash and thereby to gain the offensive, or even to win the rally.

The serving team must determine who will be responsible for handling the short returns of the serve. The most effective solution to this is for the server to make the play on any bird in front of him and for his partner to cover all other shots. However, some players prefer to divide the court lengthwise and let the player in whose side the short return is placed make the return.

Receiving the Service.   According to the rules, the receiver must be within his service court when the serve is delivered; however, certain areas in the court are more advantageous as a base of operation than are others. Generally speaking, the receiver should assume a position where all kinds of serves can be returned most easily. This location, for the right court, is some 2 to 3 feet away from the center service line and 1 to 4 feet in back of the short service line. The receiver's base in the left court would be the same distance away from the short line as in the right court but more to the center of the court. Naturally the locations of these stations are not fixed and should be adjusted somewhat according to the ability of a player to move up quickly to play the short serve and to go back to return the long serve. Under certain conditions, because of the shortness of the doubles service court, the receiver may stand very close to the short line itself. The racket should be held up and pointed to the left.

The receiving players must decide how they will return the various types of serves. The manner in which the drop serve should be returned will be resolved by the pattern of play utilized by the opposition, by their location, and by their strengths and weaknesses. In the first place, the short serve, if well executed, must be returned at an upward angle, thereby putting the receiving team on the defensive. Secondly, it should be intercepted quickly and at the highest possible point in its trajectory. If the opponents are in the side-by-side position, the bird can

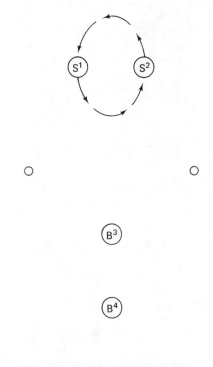

S¹ and S² are in the side-by-side position. When they move as the arrows indicate, they are playing the rotation system. B³ and B⁴ are in the up-and-back positions.

FIGURE 5-14.   Doubles patterns of team play.

be effectively returned by dropping it between their respective stations or by clearing it to the baseline. If the opponents are in the up-and-back formation, the bird can be dropped or driven to either sideline, which would start the front man moving, or cleared to the deep left baseline, which would force a backhand return from the back man.

In doubles play, the high clear serve should usually be smashed. If the bird is placed out toward the sideline, the smash down that line offers the quickest and often the most productive return. However, if the front man has moved too far to his left, the cross-court smash can be the best course of action. It must be remembered that the cross-court return always involves the danger that it will be intercepted and dropped, or pushed back just over the net away from the smasher.

Doubles Defensive Strategy.   In spite of the fact that the doubles game is more offensive oriented than the singles game, it is important to develop defensive procedures that will not only be a holding action but

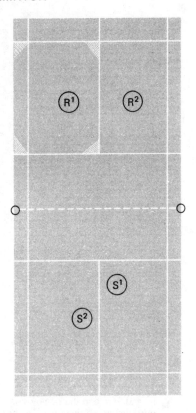 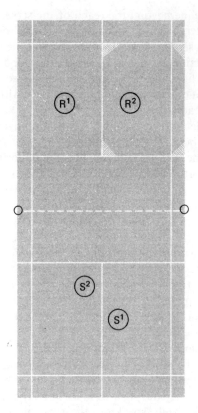

a. Player position when S¹ is
   serving to R¹ in the right
   service court. Shaded areas
   shows best serve placement.

b. Player position when S² is
   serving to R² in the left
   service court. Shaded areas
   show best serve placement.

FIGURE 5-15. Doubles court positions for serving and receiving.

also a means to move to offense. Certain tactics will aid in achieving these purposes. Because defense and offense are closely related to the characteristics of bird flight, it is important for the defense to return the bird in a way to force their opponents to hit it in an upward direction. Drop shots, net flights, and half-speed drives will aid in realizing this end.

A team must go on defense any time the opponents return the bird so that it must be hit below the level of the top of the net. The best defensive formation is the side-by-side position taken close enough to the net to enable either partner to return drive, drop and net shots yet far enough back to play the clear return. Each partner must assume a ready position with the racket up high and pointed to the left with the arm and wrist cocked. The full backswing is rarely ever possible from this position.

Careful selection and placement of each return stroke will help sustain continued defensive play and provide openings to move to the offense. The bird should be played away from the front man unless it

can be driven directly at his body about shoulder high. This is always a difficult shot for him to return because the bird must be stroked from an awkward arm and body position. However, if there is doubt about what counterstroke should be made, the high clear, driven to the baseline, will always provide respite for the defense and will slow down the action.

Doubles Offensive Strategy.   Because of the support given by a partner, the doubles game is very adaptable to offensive action. Each partner can make greater use of the hard smash and drive shots or take a chance on the cross-court flight because he knows that his partner can cover for him if he is off balance after the stroke or if he fails to execute it effectively. Futhermore, when playing the up-and-back or rotation pattern, the front man does not have to worry about going back for the high clear, and the back man can concentrate on the smash or hard drive without being too greatly concerned about rushing up to play the drop or half-speed drives. Once on the offensive, the partners should make returns as quickly as possible, without sacrificing placement and position, in order to keep the pressure on the defensive players and reduce their recovery time as much as possible. Pressure should be applied in this manner until a point is scored or the serve won.

Offensive strategy should also be concerned with opening up court areas by placing the bird so that the defense must move far to one side in order to make the return. Once opposing players are forced into this situation, the bird can be directed into the open space, or if the opponent is moving to cover that area, it can be hit behind him. This latter shot is extremely difficult to return. The smash and drop shots are the most effective in doubles attack. The best placement of the smash is in the mid-court area.

Weaknesses of the system of team play should be exploited. These have been discussed previously under the systems of doubles play.

Mixed Doubles.   Top players who compete in mixed doubles will use the up-and-back system of play because, at this level, the man has the more powerful strokes; therefore, he takes the back position and his female partner covers the front area. However, in ordinary competition, if the woman and man are near equal in playing ability, the reason for employing the up-and-back pattern is lost, and the rotation or any other system can be put into action. In any case, the basic strategy in mixed doubles will be similar to that practiced in men's doubles.

If the woman is a weaker player than the man, she will play the up position throughout, unless forced to cover the backcourt for a partner who may have been drawn out of position. It would be good defensive tactics to force her back into this position. When she plays this permanent up position, her base of operation is located at the junction of the short service line and the center service line. From this base, she should always keep her attention to the front and take full advantage of the openings made by her partner or of weak shots returned by the opposition.

Defensive and offensive strategy initiated against the mixed doubles formation should be like that of any up-and-back formation. The drop return of a clear serve or high clear should never be made against this formation because the lady will be waiting for it and may return it for a sure point. Drives hit directly at her shoulders, passing drives, and half-speed drives down the sidelines are effective.

The Singles Game

The singles player must cover much more territory than each of the partners in doubles because he is responsible for playing all birds that are hit into his 17-foot by 22-foot court area. For this reason, if for no other, singles is more of a running game than doubles and requires rapid movement, sudden changes of direction, and split-second decisions more often than does doubles. Also, the great relative length of the service court forces singles players to employ different serving tactics than doubles players. These factors, plus the fact that in singles a player acts alone without anyone to cover space or weaknesses for him, combine to make singles much more of a defensive game than doubles. Furthermore, there is no place to hide a weakness; the player truly stands alone, and a skillful opponent will surely probe every angle and shot until all short-comings are laid bare.

The Service.   The server in singles will take a position farther back in his service court than for doubles because he has no one to cover a high clear return for him, but the distance from the center service line is approximately the same as in doubles. The server starts out on the defensive because he must hit the bird at an upward angle. The basic serve should be the high clear to the baseline. This drives the receiver back and starts him moving from the opening play. The drop and drive serves should be used from time to time to keep the receiver off balance and to prevent him from playing deep in his court, a position that makes it easier for him to return the high clear serves. The same preliminary movements should be employed for each type of service. The direction and placement of the bird should be varied by a hit to the deep left, a drop to the front, a drive to the sideline, and others. After each serve is delivered, the server should move quickly to his base of operation.

Receiving the Service.   The receiver will take a position 4 to 5 feet in back of the short service line for both service courts; however, the distance from the center service line for the right court should be approximately 1 to 2 feet, and for the left court 3 to 4 feet. From these positions the receiver should assume the ready stance already described.

The receiver has an advantage over the server because he knows that the server must not only hit the bird in an upward direction but must also place it within the boundaries of the service court. The receiver is aware too that the great majority of the serves will be the high clear; however, he must be prepared to meet the challenge when the drop or drive serve is employed. The drop serve should be intercepted above waist level if possible. The receiver should not wait until the bird falls below that level because the lower the contact is made, the more difficult it will be to make an effective counterstroke because of the increased upward angle and the increased time it provides for the opponent to get set.

If the high clear serve is well placed, it should be returned most frequently with an overhead drop shot or a high clear flight. At times such a serve should be returned with a smash so the server will not get set for the other two. The high clear serve should never be returned high to the server's mid-court area.

A good sequence of strokes that can be put into use by the receiver is the drop shot to draw the server up to the net. This can be followed with the quick clear, and if the server anticipates another drop shot and starts to move up to the net quickly, the quick fast drive shot placed down the sideline could be very difficult to return. However, this arrangement of strokes or any other combination must necessarily depend upon the immediate situation and involves such factors as court position, type of counterstrokes, and speed and agility of the opponent.

Court Position. The base of operation after the serve may change to some extent with the course of action, but in general it should be located 8 to 10 feet back from the net on the center service line. The player may move from this location to take advantage of a particularly effective stroke of his opponent, to compensate for a possible troublesome angle of return, or in anticipation of a particular type of countershot. Also, when a player has executed a good smash, which has put his opponent in a disadvantageous position, he should move up a step or so toward the net to place himself in a favorable position for a point-winning return.

When compensating for the angle of return, if the bird has been directed to the opponent's right sideline, the base of operation should be moved a half step to the left of the center position. This move places the player closer to the left sideline, down which his opponent could place the bird with a smash or hard drive counterstroke. If the opponent chooses to return with a cross-court shot toward the right sideline, the bird must travel farther than if it were hit down the left line. This would give more time for intercepting it. Therefore, moving the base to the left balances the court for this particular situation. This principle would apply to a bird hit to the left sideline as well. When the bird is hit directly into the middle of the opponent's court, the base would remain on the center service line.

Singles Defensive Strategy. The singles game is more favorable to defense than to offense. This is true because of the size of the area to be covered, the nature of the bird itself, and the great variety of defensive tactics available to both players. Because of the large court space that must be defended, the player must establish a central base of operation from which all action will originate, and from which he will have the best chance of returning a bird hit in any manner. It is important for the player not only to move from his central position to intercept and return the bird to his opponent's court but also to move back to his central position quickly after the return stroke has been completed and remain on the balls of his feet ready to move in any direction. He should strive to regain good balance and body control and reach the base of operation before his opponent can make a return shot. If he is successful, he will leave fewer openings into which his opponent can hit the bird.

Many different kinds of bird flights are effective for defense, and, along with a continual change in speed and tempo, they form the fabric of defensive play. The drop and high clear combination, interspaced with the drive and part-speed shots, will not only serve the defense well but will also tend to induce a situation that will enable the defensive player to take the offensive. As the bird is moved around the court with the drop just over the net, the clear to the forehand and backhand, and the drive down the sideline, the opponent must move to return them. Eventually he will make a mistake that will give the player the offensive advantage or that will give him a point.

To play a sound defensive game, a player must have sufficient power to hit the high clear from baseline to baseline with either the forehand or backhand stroke. This skill must be mastered before a player can expect to play well. Also, any defensive strategy will include the use of the around-the-head stroke for returning high clears in situations where the backhand cannot be used effectively. Defensive players must also master the return of the smash and the use of the high clear when they are in trouble and want to slow down the tempo of the game.

Another important factor to consider in defensive strategy is the possession of the serve. When the opponent is serving, the player's game plan should be cautious and somewhat conservative because a mistake in judgement or a rash move may result in a score for the opponent. However, when the player is serving, playing tactics can be more bold and more chances can be taken because an error or fault will result in the change of serves rather than in a point.

Singles Offensive Strategy. The server should think offensively with the start of the serve in spite of the fact that the singles game does not lend itself to offense as well as does doubles. The serve should be placed so that the receiver must move to return it, and once this running motion is initiated, the bird should be hit thereafter so that there is no respite for the receiver. The opponent should undergo trial by a variety of strokes, flights, and speed. He should be felt out and tested until his strengths and weaknesses are made known. If a weakness is discovered, it can be better strategy to exploit it later on in the contest.

Midcourt placements should not be employed in singles unless the opponent is out of position and off balance. It is possible, however, to use the full-speed drive flight aimed directly at the body about shoulder height as a midcourt return when the opponent is playing a somewhat close base of operation. Otherwise, most placements should go to the right and left front courts, sidelines, and baseline, and into obvious open and unprotected areas. A player should never fall into a set pattern of returns, but should

vary a series according to the emerging situation. In the case of the clear and drop combination, if the opponent is coming up fast to cover the drop because he was caught by that combination previously, the quick flick clear can be used to propel the bird just over his reach. If the opponent hangs back in the center, the drop to the right or left can be employed. When the opponent has been driven back with a high clear and he makes a good return of it, the best counterstroke is the drop shot placed the farthest distance away from where he played the high clear. The extra step that is necessary to make the play could be the difference between losing and winning a point.

The offensive player should quicken the tempo of play by using drives, smashes, and quick interceptions. It is to his advantage to speed up play to the point where his opponent is unable to make a good defensive return and is forced to hit the bird high and short enough so it can be hit downward. When this situation occurs, the smash should be employed to win the rally.

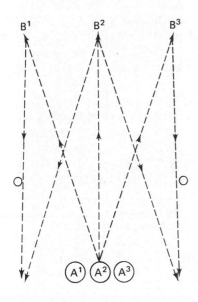

FIGURE 5-16.   Angles of return. When A returns the bird as in B¹, he adjusts the ready position to A¹. Position A² and A³ are taken when the bird is returned at angles B² and B³, respectively.

SAFETY PRACTICES

Besides the usual safety precautions common to participation in athletic events in general, there are a few specific safety procedures that relate directly to badminton. Adequate warm-up loose-fitting clothing, good sneakers, and sufficient light are safety essentials. In addition, badminton players should heed the following regulations:

1. When playing the close forecourt position in doubles, the racket should be held so it protects the facial area if a hard smash or drive shot is made directly at a player.

2. Doubles players should use a system of play and communication that will prevent collisions and situations in which one is struck by the racket of the other.

3. Stay off adjoining courts during a rally.

4. The racket hand should be kept dry. A towel should be provided for that purpose.

5. Boundary lines should be a sufficient distance from any obstruction and from another court to prevent collision with a wall, projection, or another player.

EXERCISE   Definitions and List of Terms

1. The initials of the governing body for badminton in the United States are _____ .
2. A unit of scoring in badminton is called an _____ .
3. The 1½-foot space between the singles and doubles sidelines is called the _____ .
4. _____ is a return stroke made by a right-handed player when the birdie is coming to him on his left side.
5. _____ is that portion of the court from the baseline up to 10-12 feet from the net.
6. The end line of a badminton court is often called the _____ .
7. The _____ is also called the shuttle or shuttlecock.
8. The line which divides the right service court from the left service court is the _____ .
9. The _____ propels the bird high and far into the back court so that it falls nearly vertically on or close to the baseline.
10. The stroke that sends the bird diagonally from one sideline toward the other is called a _____ .
11. When two players, called partners, compete against two other players the game is _____ .
12. _____ is the loss of a serve.
13. _____ is a stroke which propels the bird in a nearly horizontal flight just above the net.
14. The stroke which propels the bird just over the net, where it drops at a sharp angle toward the floor is a _____ shot.
15. The strung portion of the racket is the _____ .
16. _____ is a term used to indicate a rule violation, or a serve which is not good.
17. A stroke made mostly from near the net in which the wrist action is the principal source of power is called a _____ .
18. _____ is a violation in which the feet of the server or receiver are not within their proper court.
19. That half portion of the court next to the net is the _____ .
20. The stroke made by a right-handed player in which the bird is played on the right side of the body, and which is not the serve is called the _____ .
21. The _____ is completed when a player scores 15 points.
22. The manner in which the racket is held in the hand is called the _____ .
23. When the trajectory of the bird starts near and below the net and extends up and just over the net, where it falls toward the floor vertically, it is a _____ .
24. _____ is a term used to indicate that a player or a team has the serve.
25. _____ is a word used to denote that a doubles player has lost his serve. It is sometimes called a down.
26. _____ are the initials for the world organization which governs badminton on an international level.
27. When a side has had its turn serving, it is called a _____ .
28. The side that is serving is called the _____ . The receiving team is the _____ .
29. The name of the stroke in which the bird is driven hard and at a downward angle into the opposing player's court is the _____ or _____ stroke.
30. When a game is stopped for any legitimate reason during a rally or play a _____ is called and the point is replayed.
31. _____ is another name for the high clear.
32. The line which delineates the rear boundary line for the serve in doubles is called the _____ .
33. _____ is a term used to indicate the score at the start of a game and after a game has been set.
34. A _____ is three games. The winner is declared after one team has won two games.
35. _____ is a doubles game in which a man and a woman are partners.

36. When the bird is played close to the net and its trajectory is up and over the net, where it falls toward the floor, it is a _____ shot.
37. When the bird is directed to a specific spot or area, it is called _____ .
38. _____ is used to describe the course of play between the return of the serve and the scoring of a point or exchange of serves in which the bird is hit back and forth across the net by opposing players.
39. When the bird is returned by one player to an opponent it is sometimes called a _____ . However, the term _____ is most generally used.
40. The system used in doubles in which the partners move from the side-by-side position to the up-and-back position and vice-versa is called _____ .
41. The player who starts the game and puts the bird in play on each point is the _____ . The act of putting the bird into play is the _____ .
42. When a player makes a high, weak return that sends the bird into the opponent's mid-court it is said to be a _____ .
43. _____ is the name given to the procedure used to score when the game is tied at 13-13 or 14-14 in men's singles and doubles and 9-9 or 10-10 in ladies' singles.
44. _____ refers to a serve in which the bird clears the net but falls between the net and the short service line.
45. The line which marks the forward boundary of the service courts is the _____ .
46. _____ is used to denote the team that is serving.
47. _____ is the term used to indicate the player or team receiving the service.
48. _____ is used to specify the game in which there is only one player on a side.
49. The position that player takes with his feet and body while awaiting a return is his _____ .
50. _____ is a word used to describe the action of hitting the bird.
51. When the bird is struck so that it does not leave the racket in a clear and distinct manner it is a _____ . This is a fault.

1. ABA
2. Ace
3. Alley
4. Backhand
5. Backcourt
6. Baseline
7. Bird
8. Center service line
9. Clear shot
10. Cross-court shot
11. Doubles
12. Down
13. Drive
14. Drop shot
15. Racket face
16. Fault
17. Flick
18. Foot fault
19. Forecourt
20. Forehand stroke
21. Game
22. Grip
23. Hairpin flight
24. Hand in
25. Hand out
26. I.B.F.
27. Inning
28. In-side, out-side
29. Kill
30. Let
31. Lob
32. Long service line
33. Love-all
34. Match
35. Mixed doubles
36. Net shot
37. Out-side
38. Placement
39. Rally
40. Rotation
41. Server
42. Set up
43. Setting
44. Short
45. Short service line
46. Side-in
47. Side-out
48. Singles
49. Stance
50. Stroke
51. Throw

QUESTIONS AND ANSWERS ON THE RULES

1. *Q.* How is the game begun?
   A. The game is begun by a serve.

2. *Q.* Who serves first?

   A. The choice of serving or of end of court is generally determined by a toss of a coin immediately before play starts.

3. *Q.* How is the serve delivered?

   A. The serve is made by striking the bird with the racket in an underhand motion so that the bird is propelled over the net and into the correct service court. The bird must be struck by the racket below the level of the player's hips, and the racket head may not be higher than the hand when it makes contact with the bird.

4. *Q.* What is a good serve?

   A. A good serve is delivered as described above under the following conditions:

     1. The server must be standing in his correct court with his feet stationary. No stepping motion can be made.

     2. The bird must pass over the net and fall within the opponent's service court, which is diagonally across the net from the server's court—that is, right to right and left to left.

     3. The receiver must be ready.

5. *Q.* When is the service considered to have been delivered?

   A. A serve has been delivered as soon as the racket makes contact with the bird.

6. *Q.* What is the order of service in singles?

   A. The first serve is taken from the right service court; however, after that, when a player's score is zero or even, he will serve from the right court; when his score is odd, he will serve from the left service court.

7. *Q.* What position must the receiver assume when receiving the serve?

   A. The receiver must be within his own service court.

8. *Q.* How is a point made in badminton?

   A. Only the server can score. Each time the receiver fails to return the bird or commits a fault, the server scores a point. No point is scored by either side on the exchange of serves.

9. *Q.* When is a game complete?

   A. A game is finished when one side has scored 15 points in men's singles, men's doubles, and mixed doubles. However, a system of setting may be employed when the score is 13-13 and 14-14. When the score is tied 13-13, the side that first reached 13 has an option of setting the game to 5 more points or of continuing to play to 15. If the score is tied at 14-14, the side to first score 14 may set the game to 3 more points or play to 15. In either case of setting, the score starts at love-all. A game of 21 points is sometimes played. In this case the score may be set at 19-19 and 20-20. The game score for women's singles is 11 points. This game may be set, at 9-9, to 3 more and, at 10-10, to 2 more under the conditions given above.

10. *Q.* What is the order or service in doubles play?

   A. In the first hand of each inning the serve is delivered from the right service court. The next serve is taken from the left court, the next goes back to the right court, and so on in this manner until the serve is lost. In the first inning of each game the team that serves has only one hand. When that player or his partner fails to make a good return or otherwise faults, the serve goes to the opposing team. Both members of the other team get a hand at serving before it returns to the team which started the game. Therefore, after the first inning, a team has two hands.

11. *Q.* What is an inning?

   A. When one team has had its turn at serving, an inning has been completed.

12. *Q.* Who may receive the serve in doubles?

   A. Only the player to whom the service is being delivered may receive the service. If the bird is played by his partner, it is a fault and the server scores a point.

13. *Q.* How many serves does a player get?

A. A player continues to serve until he or his partner fails to make a good return or to deliver a good service or faults in some way. However, each player has only one chance to serve on each point. There is no second serve as in tennis.

14. *Q.* How may the bird be played after the service has been delivered?
    A. It may be played in any legal manner; that is, it may be struck with the racket by an underhand, sidearm, or overhand motion and must be propelled back over the net. It may not be "carried" or "thrown" from the racket face. In doubles, after the serve has been delivered and returned, either player of both teams may play the bird.
15. *Q.* What are the boundaries of the doubles service court?
    A. The court is bounded by the short service line, the doubles sidelines the center service line, and the long service line.
16. *Q.* What are the boundaries of the singles service court?
    A. The court is bounded by the shot service line, center service line, singles sideline, and the baseline.
17. *Q.* What is a net bird?
    A. During a rally, the bird may touch the top of the net as it passes over. A net bird is in play if it is otherwise good.
18. *Q.* What is the ruling if the server hits at the bird and misses it completely when he is delivering the service?
    A. It is not a fault and he must complete the serve.
19. *Q.* What are the common faults?
    A. The common faults are: (1) striking the bird before it crosses the net into the home court—a follow-through over the net is legal; (2) touching the net or its supports with the racket or the body while the bird is in play; (3) the server, while serving, contacting the bird above the level of his hips or with the racket face higher than the serving hand; (4) serving to the wrong service court, unless played by the correct receiver; (5) the bird falling short of the short service line or beyond the long service line on the serve; (6) the feet of the server or the receiver being out of the boundaries of the service courts when the service is being delivered; (7) either player making preliminary feints or moves to confuse the other before or during the serve; (8) the same player hitting the bird twice in succession or twice on one side of the net; (9) the bird touching the ceiling, falling out of bounds, failing to go over the net, or touching a player or wall; (10) an opponent obstructing, carrying the bird on the racket; and (12) stepping into the opponent's court when play is in progress.
20. *Q.* What is the penalty for fault?
    A. In singles if it is committed by the in-side, the serve is lost, and if made by the out-side, the server scores a point. In doubles, except for the first inning, a fault is committed by the in-side on the first hand, the serve goes to the partner. If it is made during the second hand, the serve goes over to the out-side. if made by the out-side, a point is scored by the in-side.
21. *Q.* What is a match?
    A. A match is two out of three games.
22. *Q.* Which side serves first after the game of a match has been completed?
    A. In doubles the side that won the game serves first; in singles the loser will serve first.
23. *Q.* What is the penalty for serving out of order, for serving from the wrong service court, or for receiving in the wrong service court?
    A. If the guilty side wins the rally, it is declared a let and must be replayed provided it is discovered before the next serve is delivered. If the guilty side loses the rally, the error shall stand and the positions shall not be changed. But, if the above errors are made and not discovered before the next succeeding serve has been delivered, the mistake will not be corrected.
24. *Q.* What is the meaning of obstruction?

     A. Obstruction is committed by a player who invades his opponent's court with his racket or his person or by a player's holding his racket up above and close to the net to block a smash return.
25. *Q*. What is the official bird?
     A. The official bird must weigh from 73 to 85 grains, have from 14 to 16 feathers 2½-to 2¾-inches long placed in a cork tip 1- to 1⅛-inches in diameter. The spread of the feathers at the top must be from 2⅛ to 2½ inches.
26. *Q*. What are the specifications for the net?
     A. The net is made of ¾-inch mesh, 2½-feet deep, at least 20-feet wide, and bordered with a 3-inch white tape. It is attached at each end to posts that are set on the side boundary lines an equal distance from each baseline and 5 feet 1 inch in height. The top of the middle of the net must be 5 feet above the playing surface.
27. *Q*. What is a carry?
     A. When, during a stroke, the bird comes to rest on the racket a carry has been committed. This is a fault.
28. *Q*. Are the boundary lines a part of the court area that they enclose?
     A. Yes.
29. *Q*. Is a wood shot good?
     A. Yes.
30. *Q*. Is the double hit legal?
     A. If the bird is hit twice in succession by the same player with two strokes, or by him and his partner, it is an illegal stroke and a fault. However, if a double hit occurs on one stroke made by the same player, and it is otherwise good, it is legal.

BIBLIOGRAPHY

American Badminton Association. *Rules Book*. San Diego, Cal.: (Mrs. Virginia S. Lyon, 1330 Alexandria Drive) The American Badminton Association, 1979.

Bloss, Margaret V. *Badminton*. 2nd. ed. Dubuque, Iowa: Wm. C. Brown Company, Publishers, 1971.

Davidison, Kenneth R., and Gustavson, Leland R. *Winning Badminton*. New York: The Ronald Press Company, 1953.

Davidson, Kenneth R., and Smith, Lenore. *How to Improve Your Badminton*. Chicago: The Athelete Institute.

Davis, Pat. *Badminton Coach*. New Rochelle, N.Y.: Soccer Associates, 1972.

NAGWS. *Tennis-Badminton Guide*. Washington, D.C.: National Association for Girls and Womens Sports of the AAHPER, 1974-76.

Pelton, Barry C. *Badminton*. Englewood Cliffs, N.J.: Prentice-Hall, Inc., 1971.

Rogers, Wynn. *Advanced Badminton*. Dubuque, Iowa: Wm. C. Brown Company, Publishers, 1970.

Varner, Margaret. *Badminton*. Dubuque, Iowa: Wm. C. Brown Company, Publishers, 1970.

Wright, Len. *Your Book of Badminton*. Levittown, N.Y.: Transatlantic Arts, 1972.

6

BASKETBALL
(MEN AND WOMEN)

DESCRIPTION OF THE ACTIVITY

Basketball is recognized as one of the most popular winter sports and is one of the common activities in physical education, intramurals, recreation programs, and informal competition. Recent rule changes have resulted in similar styles of play by both men and women.

A team is composed of five players, with two governing officials—an umpire and a referee. Each team chooses his offensive basket with preference given to the visiting squad. The game is begun with a *jump ball* at the center of the court by opposing players (centers). Teams then assume the tasks of attempting to enter the ball into their offensive basket and of preventing opponents from scoring at their end of the court. The ball is moved from one player to another by any means involving the hands. Two points are awarded for each score from play (field) and one point for each successful free throw. The team with the most points at the end of regulation time (two 20-minute halves in college basketball, four 8-minute quarters in high school basketball) is declared the winner. Should the score be tied at the close of the second half, as many 5-minute (college) or 3-minute (high school) overtime periods as necessary to break the tie shall follow.

The game is played on a hardwood court approximately 94 feet by 50 feet, with the official court markings as shown in Figure 6-1.

EQUIPMENT

The Ball

The regulation ball measures 29½-30 inches in cir-

cumference for college play (a minimum of 29 inches for high school) and weighs 20-22 ounces. The ball must be of an approved orange shade or a natural tan and must be of leather for all college games unless both teams agree to use a composition cover. Proper inflation is determined by dropping the ball from a height of 6 feet and measuring the bounce, which must be from 49-54 inches (to the top of the ball).

Clothing

Excellent quality shoes that easily provide a season of comfort are manufactured by several reputable companies. Socks of varying degrees of thickness that offer maximum protection against blisters and foot irritation are available. Knee socks offer additional protection against abrasions. Ideal pants for maximum efficiency should provide complete freedom of movement and contain small hip pads for protection.

SKILLS AND TECHNIQUES

Offensive Fundamentals

Passing. Regardless of the type of pass employed, there are certain common factors of execution. Proper form dictates the use of the thumb and fingers and not the palms, spread comfortably in a firm grip, with the passer stepping forward in the direction of the receiver. A quick arm extension and a wrist snap involving the thumb and fingers provide the momentum for an accurate pass. In the follow-through the palms are facing the floor. Only a slight backspin should be applied or the ball becomes difficult to handle for the receiver. The pass should

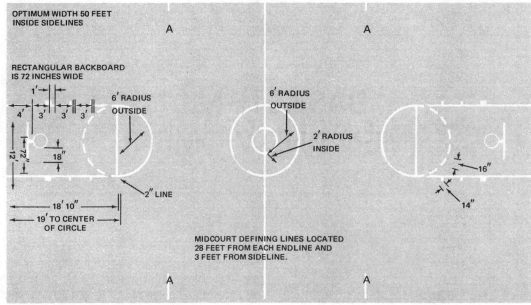

OPTIMUM WIDTH 50 FEET
INSIDE SIDELINES

RECTANGULAR BACKBOARD
IS 72 INCHES WIDE

6' RADIUS
OUTSIDE

6' RADIUS
OUTSIDE

2' RADIUS
INSIDE

2" LINE

16"

14"

18' 10"

19' TO CENTER
OF CIRCLE

MIDCOURT DEFINING LINES LOCATED
28 FEET FROM EACH ENDLINE AND
3 FEET FROM SIDELINE.

OPTIMUM LENGTH 84 FEET OR 94 FEET INSIDE
ALL LINES SHALL BE 2 INCHES WIDE (NEUTRAL ZONES EXCLUDED)

THE COLOR OF THE LANE SPACE MARKS AND NEUTRAL ZONES
SHALL CONTRAST WITH THE COLOR OF THE BOUNDING LINES

FIGURE 6-1.   Basketball court diagram.

be aimed at the area between the waist and shoulders of the receiver, and it should possess enough speed to avoid being intercepted and without increasing the difficulty of handling. Players must avoid "telegraphing" the direction of the pass and they must sharpen their peripheral vision by developing an awareness of the positions and movements of their teammates.

The *two-handed chest pass* is the most common method of advancing the ball upcourt or of "feeding" the ball to teammates from a short to a medium range. In this pass, elbows remain close to the body and parallel to the floor, the head and eyes are raised, and the knees remain slightly flexed as one foot moves forward in the direction of the receiver. Proper wrist snap is imperative if sufficient speed is to be attained.

The *two-handed bounce pass* is executed in a fashion similar to the chest pass. The bounce pass is effective in getting the ball to the pivot player and from a guard to a forward. Its use in high-speed, fast-break situations is questionable.

The *one-handed pass,* in the form of a bounce or chest pass, is effective in the short and medium range. In this pass the passer holds the ball with both hands, although supporting it with his left hand, and then steps forward to execute a one-handed push involving a quick wrist and finger snap.

The *one-handed, jump shot pass* is performed in a manner similar to the jump shot and offers an excellent chance of deception when properly used. Players should avoid leaping into the air, when not in shooting range, without an open receiver. This maneuver is only effective in situations where the

FIGURE 6-2.   Two-handed chest pass.

jump shot is a scoring threat.

The *two-handed overhead pass* is extremely effective for the tall player or against the defensive player yielding a height advantage. Using the foot action described for the two-handed chest pass, the passer employs a forceful wrist and finger snap, with the ball held high overhead. The ball follows a slightly downward flight with good speed, making an interception difficult.

The *hook pass* remains one of the most effective methods to initiate the fast break following a rebound—known as the outlet pass—or to feed the ball to a teammate when the passer is closely guarded by an opponent. Proper take-off is similar to that of the lay-up with the passer planting his jumping foot and making a half turn toward the receiver before leaping high into the air. A slight turn of the body, with shoulders pointing toward the receiver, follows as the passing arm moves sideward and upward reaching a fully extended position overhead. The ball is released with a snap of the wrist and follows a slightly downward path to the receiver.

The *baseball pass* is also effective in executing the outlet pass to initiate the fast break. It may occasionally be used when a long, full-court pass is necessary. The passer should simulate the elbow and wrist action of a catcher in baseball making a play at second base, with the ball brought back behind the ear. Special care should be taken to avoid a sidearm motion and spin that may cause the ball to curve. Body weight should shift from the back to the front foot as the ball is released. Due to the difficulty in controlling this pass, the hook pass and the underhand (one-handed) pass are frequently used instead of the baseball pass to move the ball to a distant receiver.

Receiving. Catching the ball when one is in a stationary position or when one is running at a low, medium, or high speed is one of the most basic and important fundamentals of basketball. As the receiver moves to meet the pass, his arms and his slightly flexed elbows are extended toward the ball. The fingers and thumbs are comfortably spread and cupped, and, along with relaxed wrists, help to cushion the pass by causing the hands to "give" as the ball contacts the fingertips. The receiver should "look" the ball into his hands with his thumbs placed outward on passes below the waist and inward on those received above this target area. It is important to squeeze the ball with the fingertips to gain control before an attempted fake, dribble, pass, or shot. The receiver should also protect the ball from the de-

FIGURE 6-3. Hook pass.

fender by assuming a slightly crouched position, with his elbows outward and the ball pulled away from the defensive player.

Dribbling. When dribbling, a player should avoid slapping at the ball. Instead he should maintain a cupped, relaxed hand, a relaxed wrist, elbows close to his body, and the fingers comfortably spread to push the ball forward and downward with the fingertips. Momentum for the little-needed push is provided by the wrist. The player's knees and trunk should be slightly flexed, with his head and eyes raised to maintain a wide peripheral view of his teammates. The height of the ball's bounce should vary as the purpose of the dribble varies. A speed dribble for fast-break situations should bounce belt high as opposed to a knee-high bounce for situations requiring control and deception when the player is closely guarded. The height of the bounce can be varied through the use of the "trap"—the meeting of the ball before it reaches the height of its bounce. Such a maneuver is used by all good dribblers to prevent timed contact by the defense that may result in a loss of the ball. Proper use of various feints

a.   b.   c.

FIGURE 6-4.   Reverse dribble.

will also aid control and prevent the stealing of the ball by the opponent.

Players must develop control in both hands as well as learn to transfer the ball safely from one hand to the other at varying speeds as in the front changeover or the behind-the-back dribble. The *front changeover* must be mastered by all players; however, it is a dangerous maneuver since the transfer occurs within the reach of the defensive player. A hard feint to the side of the ball as the ball is pulled back and across the body to the opposite hand will force the defensive player away from the danger point. The ball is then protected by the inside shoulder and body. The *reverse dribble* is a valuable technique when a player is completely blocked (Figure 6-4a). At this point, the inside foot (the foot nearest the center of the court) is planted hard on the floor and the body weight transferred to the outside foot as the ball is moved to the opposite hand while fully protected by a crouched body (Figure 6-4b). The reverse dribble is less dangerous than the changeover and is an effective offensive move. For good balance, the player's feet should be no wider apart than shoulder width; and the ball should be kept on the side away from the defender.

Shooting.   The techniques of shooting in basketball are extremely intricate, involving a multitude of details. The following instructions, however, apply to all types of shots and should be thoroughly mastered:

1. Distribute body weight evenly on the feet.
2. Face the basket with the shoulders and toes.

3. Position the ball between shoulder and eye level in the preshooting phase.
4. Decide upon a target area (center of the rim or backboard, if desired, on angle shots) and concentrate throughout all phases of the shot: the preparation, release and follow-through.
5. Utilize a grip in which the fingers and thumb are comfortably spread, providing a space between the palms and the ball.
6. Place the shooting elbow directly under the ball on one-handed shots.
7. Cock the wrist prior to releasing the ball.
8. Impart a slight backspin as the ball leaves the fingertips.
9. Follow through with a complete arm extension that also permits the wrist to collapse and the hand to drop down.
10. Choose an arc of approximately 45 degrees to provide an adequate target area.

The *jump shot* is the most effective, accurate, and difficult-to-defend maneuver in basketball. Within an area of 20 feet it remains a constant scoring threat should a defender not maintain tight enough pressure. Although the technique of execution varies somewhat among the great jump shooters, several principles are common to all. The jump shot can be taken from a stationary position, upon receiving a pass, or after terminating a dribble. Footwork will vary slightly in the three situations. After receiving a pass or terminating a dribble, the right-handed player plants the lead, or right, foot slightly ahead of the left and comes to a sudden stop, with his feet a shoulder width apart and his toes and shoulders facing the basket. The weight is evenly distributed as the knees flex to a prejumping position (Figure 6-5a). The ball remains in both hands between approximately shoulder and eye level as the shooter executes a vertical jump—he should avoid jumping to the side, forward, or backward. The supporting, or left, hand maintains contact with the ball until the maximum height of the jump is reached. The shooting hand then pushes the ball forward with fingertip control (Figure 6-5b). The follow-through consists of the complete extension of the shooting elbow, with the wrist collapsing and the hand falling forward and downward in a relaxed position (Figure 6-5c). The rim target should be sighted as the shot is initiated and the sighting should be held until the follow-through action has been terminated.

The *one-handed set shot* extends the potential scoring range to approximately 20 to 30 feet. The shooting and the supporting hands assume the same positions as described in the jump shot, with the shooting elbow placed close to the body in the pre-shooting or starting position. With a right-handed player, the right foot is slightly ahead of the left in a toe-instep relationship. As the wrist is cocked and the upward sweep begins, the elbow is actually in front of the ball and pointing toward the basket. The knees are slightly flexed and extend as the shot is taken, with a force commensurate to the distance and power needed.

The *two-handed set shot* appears to be a lost art in modern basketball. It is, however, an extremely effective shot from a long range and the use of it should be encouraged among young players of today. In the proper execution of this shot the knees are slightly flexed, with the left foot placed 2 to 4 inches ahead of the right. Both hands are placed on the sides of the ball, with the fingers and thumbs spread comfortably. The shot is initiated from the feet as the knees extend and the arm, elbow, and wrist actions begin. The ball is released from the fingertips with a gentle backspin, followed by a natural follow-through. The target is sighted in the starting phase, with the ball at shoulder and eye level, and eye contact is maintained throughout the execution of the shot.

a. Pre-jumping phase.   b. Vertical jump phase.   c. Follow-through phase.

FIGURE 6-5.   Jump shot.

The *hook shot* is a necessary shot for pivot players and can also be a powerful weapon for guards and forwards when they are closely guarded in the short range on fast-break and drive situations. It is one of the most difficult shots to master since the ball is held away from the medial plane of the body, preventing proper visual lineup. The inside foot, or foot nearest the center of the court, is planted, with a slightly flexed knee, to initiate the pivot action and to bring the left shoulder parallel to the basket. From a starting position at the waist, the ball is brought upward and overhead in a smooth, circular motion. The supporting hand serves to aid in the control and the protection of the ball. Proper release consists of a smooth wrist snap and fingertip control. On angle shots, the backboard should be used to improve accuracy.

The *lay-up* is a short-range shot, used after receiving a pass on a timed cut toward the basket or upon terminating the dribble. Such a shot is performed at high speed, adding to its difficulty. With a right-handed player, proper take-off is performed with the inside, or left, foot as a vertical jump is executed. The ball is held close to the body (away from the defender), brought overhead with a full extension of the shooting hand and wrist, and released with a slight backspin at the height of the jump. Follow-through and release parallel that of the one-handed push shot. At high speed, a release that places the back of the shooting hand toward the backboard improves the accuracy of the shot by eliminating the push action and providing backspin to the momentum already created by the body movement.

Free throw shooting has been performed successfully in many different manners; however, it is recommended that each player adopt a style similar to his shooting style from the floor. The one-handed foul shot is the most popular. In using this style, the feet should be placed a shoulder width apart, with the knees slightly flexed. Shooters should strive for complete relaxation, undivided concentration on the target area, a fixed head and neck, and for a smooth rhythm throughout the execution of the shot. The specific mechanics of the shot are discussed in the section on the one-handed shot. The two-handed set shot, the jump shot, and underhand shooting are additional shooting methods that have been successfully employed from the free throw line.

The *tip-in shot* is used in the congested area around the basket, when it is inadvisable to control the ball before shooting. Although the two-handed tip-in shot provides slightly better control, it is not possible to jump as high with it as with the more popular one-handed tip-in. In the tip-in shot, the ball should be met at the height of the jump with a cupped hand and relaxed wrist and fingers. A slight wrist snap provides both a cushion and the impetus to propel the ball against the backboard and into the basket.

Feinting. Mastery of the various feints is imperative if any phase of basketball is to be complete. Feints with the head, eye, shoulder, arm, and feet are employed prior to executing a pass, drive, shot, dribble, or cut. Without such maneuvers, the defensive player has a much easier task of preventing a score. Feinting is a part of every phase of the game and is just as useful for the defensive player in intercepting a pass or thwarting an offensive maneuver as it is for the player attempting to score.

Screening. Proper use of screening techniques is the heart of offensive basketball. Screening is performed by a player with or without the ball and can be executed toward or away from the ball, at various speeds, and from behind, in front, or either side of an opponent. Its purpose is to permit a teammate to gain an advantage through a dribble or cut that will result in a percentage shot, that is, a medium- to short-range shot with approximately a 50% probability of success. Should the defense execute a switching maneuver, in which a defensive player takes over his teammate's assigned opponent, the screener rolls toward the basket to receive a return pass. If a switch does not occur, the cutter should be free to move toward the basket or behind the screener to receive a pass. It is the responsibility of a cutter to force his opponent into the stationary screen set by a teammate. A screen may be set no closer than three feet from the defensive player.

Defensive Fundamentals

Man-to-Man Defense. Each player is assigned to an opponent of comparable size, speed, and quickness and given the task of preventing a score by closely guarding that man and assuming a position that will permit assistance to a teammate whenever necessary. The fundamentals of man-to-man defense must be thoroughly mastered as they represent basic skills employed in all types of zone, combination, and pressing defenses.

In the *basic stance* for man-to-man pressure defense, the knees are flexed, the feet a shoulder width apart, the body slightly crouched, the weight on the balls of the feet, the hands in a palms-up position

FIGURE 6-6. Basic stance for man-to-man pressure defense.

and moving fast, and the eyes looking at the opponent's belt area to provide a peripheral view of the entire body of the offensive player. The foot nearest the center of the court should be slightly forward in a heel-toe relationship with the other foot. This stance makes for a slight weakness toward the middle of the court where teammates are in a position to offer defensive assistance. It also provides for maximum defensive coverage of the vulnerable areas: over the head, by the feet, by the hips, and over the shoulders.

A basic slide consists of a two-step movement forward or backward, depending upon the action of the offensive player. Lateral movement is performed with a boxer's shuffle or slide, with the body slightly crouched while in the basic stance described above. Players should avoid crossing their feet.

When *guarding the dribbler,* the defensive player assumes the same basic stance between the dribbler and the basket, facing the dribbler and placing his shoulders parallel to the end line. Players should approach the dribbler with caution and should maintain a flashing, or fast-moving inside hand to discourage dribbling and changeover maneuvers. It is often possible to assume a position slightly closer to the strong dribbling hand. The defensive player should attack the dribbler with flashing hands and

quick foot movements, but he should be careful not to be caught moving forward as the drive is initiated. Proper defense of the dribbler includes coverage, or maintaining the guarding position described, and taking a stand to prevent further penetration before the dribbler reaches a good shooting range. The inside hand should remain active in an upward sweeping motion to bother the dribbler. If the dribbler goes by and the defender is not able to sprint to a legal guarding position, he should continue rapidly toward the basket and establish a position between the first free opponent and the basket in anticipation of the switch. If a dribbler passes to a teammate, the defender should execute a backward slide toward the basket to check give-and-go attempts. Dribblers should not be permitted to drive toward the baseline, but must be forced toward the middle of the court. In coverage, the importance of guarding with the feet as opposed to turning to the side of the offensive player and reaching in to grasp the ball cannot be overemphasized.

Guarding the cutter in the overplay position (see Figure 6-7) is the key to man-to-man pressure defense and is designed to cut off passing lanes and to force the opponent out of shooting range to receive the ball. When this occurs, the offensive player receives the ball at a great distance from the basket and can offer only the drive as a threat, thereby allowing the defender to slack off slightly in alertness. The inside hand and foot of the defender are extended in front of the offensive player between the ball and the man (ball-you-man), with bouncing overplay, or continuous thrusts forward and backward, in front of the passing lanes. If the offensive player cuts toward the basket, the proper action for the defensive player is to turn and face the ball by jerking his inside hand and leg back, pivoting on the outside foot, keeping his back to the offensive player, and gliding in between the ball and the cutter (see Figure 6-8). The defender must beat all cuts toward the basket by positioning himself in front of the cutter. The cutter should not be permitted to move in a straight line; proper coverage will force him to curve or "banana" his movement. A cutter moving away from the ball is executing this maneuver for one of three reasons: (1) to clear the area, (2) to screen for a teammate, or (3) to cut back hard toward the basket to receive a pass. In guarding a cutter moving away from the ball, the defender should drop off toward the center of the court, assuming a position to assist his teammates in this area and countering a timed cut by his opponent.

FIGURE 6-7.   Overplay position.

FIGURE 6-8.   Beating the cut and low post fronting.

When *guarding the pivot player* one of two basic positions can be assumed: at the side of the player where the ball is or in front of the player. In guarding the pivot player in the medium and high post areas (the high post area is around the free throw line, the medium post area is closer to the basket), the overplay position described previously is assumed (Figure 6-9a). Bouncing overplay, or continuous forward and backward thrusts, will aid in preventing a pass from entering the post area. As the ball moves from one side of the court to the other, the defender must slide "over the top" between the ball and the post player (Figure 6-9b) to assume an overplay position on the ball side (Figure 6-9c). If a pivot player does not impose a scoring threat from the high post area, the defensive player should assume a position behind the pivot player to prevent him from attempting a drive. In the low post area (three to eight feet from the basket), the defender places himself in front of the pivot player, reaching back continuously to reinforce his whereabouts.

a.

b.

c.

FIGURE 6-9.   Sliding over the top in medium post defense.

Defending against the jump shot is one of the most difficult tasks in basketball. The approach taken should vary depending upon the differences in size, reach, and speed of the defensive and offensive players as well as their proximity to the shooter. The defender should wait until the shooter's feet leave the floor before thrusting the hand nearest the ball upward in an attempt to block the shot. If the ball is not deflected, the defender should jump up and try to pressure the shot by "hanging" in the air in an attempt to force the shot, destroy the shooter's timing, or change the arc of the ball. If the shooter has used the dribble already, the defender should move in closely and jump up with the shooter. It may be wise to vary the defensive technique occasionally from the two methods mentioned to the utilization of a two-handed block or to the defender's ducking under and quickly out in an attempt to impair the shooter's concentration.

Switching is an essential maneuver to team defense and dictates that each player should always be prepared to pick up a teammate's assigned opponent should an advantage be acquired through a dribble, cut, or screen. As a switch occurs, proper position for the defense consists of immediate coverage of the area between the opponent and the basket. A *jump switch* is a power move in which the defensive player delays his action until the opponent with the ball approaches, then the defender springs quickly into his opponent's path to establish a legal guarding position. A well-executed jump switch should prevent further penetration. Switching may occur on lateral moves, on close exchanges, on breakthrough situations by a dribbler or cutter, and on screen plays. The verbal calling of a switch is performed by the *helper,* or the man in a position to assist his teammate, not by the player in difficulty.

The *double-up,* or the quick placement of two defensive men on the offensive player with the ball to prevent further dribbling and force a lob or a deflected pass, is an essential phase of team defense. Such action is a major part of man-to-man pressure defense, of all full- and half-court zone presses, and some regular zone defenses. It greatly increases the probability of interception and can be successfully employed anywhere on the playing court. The double-up can be used in several offensive situations: (1) a close lateral hand-off in a weave-type offense (Figure 6-10a), (2) a dribbler moving in such a way as to turn his back to a defensive player's weak side (Figure 6-10b), (3) a dribbler entering a second defender's territory (Figure 6-10c), and (4) a screen executed by an offensive player near the ball (Figure 6-10d). Players involved in the double-up have coverage, or the closing of all dribbling and passing lanes, as their primary responsibility. Their secondary purpose is to steal the ball through a lob or a deflected pass. Proper arm action consists of a complete sweep from the defender's knees to his maximum height overhead to block all passing lanes. Reaching in to grasp the ball should be minimized or eliminated.

Rebounding. The rebound is generally secured by the player who has been able to attain and hold the inside position (between the opponent and the basket). The following four phases of rebound techniques should be thoroughly mastered:

1. *Positioning.* The defender must screen or box out his opponent by floating toward the basket and turning to form a right angle with the basket as the shot is taken (maintaining eye contact with his opponent) before finally assuming a broad-based, spread position, with knees flexed and elbows out in preparation for the jump at the ball.

2. *Capturing the rebound.* The player should jump toward the basket rather than executing a perfectly vertical leap and increasing the probability of the rebound being taken from behind by a taller opponent.

3. *Protecting the rebound.* The ball should be brought down no lower than below the chin with elbows out, knees flexed, the body in a crouched position, and the head up and facing the sideline.

4. *Outlet pass.* The player should land with both feet simultaneously to permit a pivot in either direction. The foot toward the nearer sideline should be used to execute the pivot and the hook or baseball pass to the assigned pitchout area.

Man-to-Man Team Defense and Attack

Team defense consists of the application of the fundamentals of defense described previously. It also includes a helping defense in which each individual is responsible first for his assigned opponent and secondly for assisting a teammate in difficulty. Basic team position should include tight pressure on the ball, strong overplay on the next potential receiver, and the amount of pressure by the players increasing or decreasing depending on the proximity of the ball. As the ball approaches your area, pressure increases; as it moves away from your area, pressure decreases. The defensive triangle (ball-you-man) should be maintained at all times to provide a proper view of the total situation (see Figure 6-11). An attempt should be made to (1) decrease the number of shots taken, (2) prevent the ball from entering the pivot area, (3) minimize the number of second shots taken through proper boxing techniques, (4) decrease the number of shots within 15 to 18 feet of the basket through bouncing overplay, (5) prevent "cheap" baskets through proper defensive balance built into the offensive system, (6) pressure all shots, and (7) develop a helping defense through proper pick-up and recovery techniques.

Attacking the man-to-man defense may take the form of pattern or free-lance offense consisting of continuous movement, screening techniques, and adequate use of cutting and passing lanes. Numerous systems have been used to exploit individual offensive abilities as well as defensive weaknesses. Guard attacks consisting of spread-out 3–2 formations and

screening away from and toward the ball, screening by the forwards, and flash pivots will increase give-and-go maneuvers, driving, and outside scoring opportunities. Pivot attacks to exploit tall players may take the form of a single low or high post, a double low or high post, or a triple post offensive. A five-man, shuffle-type offensive, with four players overloading one side, is employed by a team without a superstar in order to distribute scoring and to provide an even, disciplined pattern of attack. Regardless of the system employed, constant movements of the

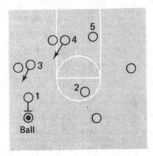

FIGURE 6-11.   Position of players in relation to the ball.

ball, cutting movements, screening, and floor balance are required. (See Figures 6-12 to 6-13 for examples of common, man-to-man patterns of attack.)

Zone Defense and Attack

As opposed to being assigned a specific player to guard as in man-to-man defense, in zone tactics certain areas are covered, with attention directed toward the ball. The five men are grouped in various formations in and around the free throw line in an attempt to eliminate the inside percentage shot. In covering cutters and dribblers, man-to-man defense principles must be followed if the zone defense is to be effective. The major advantages of zone defense are that: (1) inside or close-range shooting is kept to a minimum, (2) fewer fouls are committed, (3) rebounding is improved, (4) the execution of fast-break maneuvers is improved, (5) defensive mistakes by the weak player are kept to a minimum, (6) interception opportunities are encouraged, and (7) mastery of proper sliding is relatively simple. Among the major disadvantages are that: (1) susceptibility to outside shooting is increased, (2) ineffectiveness against stalling tactics late in the game is increased, (3) there is difficulty in placing blame for errors or

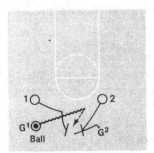

a.   Lateral exchange. As the left guard, G^1, dribbles to the hand-off, defensive player #1 jump switches on the right guard, G^2, to join his teammate for the double-up.

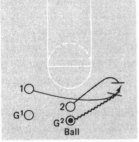

b.   The right guard, G^2, turns his back to defensive player #1 who trails. Player #1 leaves his assigned man, G^1, to clamp the right guard, G^2, as player #2 stops the movement of G^2 and forces G^2 to turn or reverse dribble.

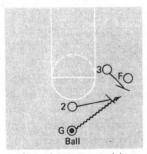

c.   A guard enters a second defender's area with the ball. Defensive player #3 executes a jump switch on the guard to complete the double-up with player #2.

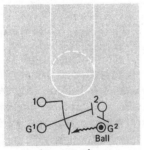

d.   The left guard, G^1, screens defensive player #2 for G^2, his teammate, who has the ball. Player #1 jump switches as the dribble is initiated to complete the double-up with player #2 who remains with his man, G^2.

FIGURE 6-10.   Offensive situations in which the double-up can be used.

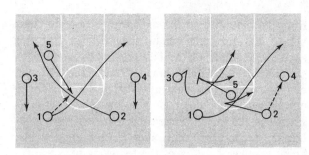

FIGURE 6-12. Single post offense. A variety of movements are permitted, such as the play shown on the left and the weak side screens and rollouts on the right. Clear situations are provided with a quick pass to #3, blind screens, double screens, free-lance moves, set plays, patterns, and other maneuvers from this versatile formation.

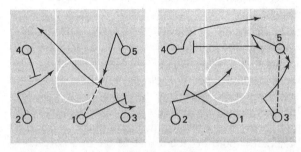

FIGURE 6-13. 3-2 guard attack. The open center area provides one-on-one situations, flash pivots, side exchange series, blind screens, 3-man weaves, free-lance moves, set plays, and other effective plays.

uncovering individuals responsible for scoring, (4) man-to-man defense fundamentals are somewhat less effective, and (5) overload tactics (more than one man in a defensive player's area), rapid movements, screening, and adequate use of cutting lanes are effective offensive maneuvers.

The more common types of zones and their basic weakness areas are shown in Figure 6–20a-d.

2-3 Zone (Figure 6-14a). Excellent rebound strength is coupled with strength in the corners and under the basket. This type of zone defense is very effective against poor shooting teams with weaknesses on the sides and in the middle and high post area.

1-3-1 Zone (Figure 6-14b). Since players tend to be more spread out than in most of the other zone formations, rebound strength is weakened. The corners and sides of the "chaser" are also weak. The strength of this type of zone defense lies in the pivot area since three men are stationed there.

1-2-2 Zone (Figure 6-14c). This zone formation is designed to stop a team with players who are excellent drivers. It is also stronger in the pivot area than is the 2-3 zone formation, but has major weaknesses on the sides and corners.

2-1-2 Zone (Figure 6-14d). In this formation, pivot or post defense is strengthened by the middle player who is capable of stopping attacks in this area. Good rebound strength is also combined with general strength around the basket. Major weaknesses are found at the sides and in the forward position.

Zone attack varies with the type of defense employed by the opponent and with the weakness areas specific to the zone formation and personnel. As a general rule, a 1–3–1 offensive alignment is used against even zone formations (2–3, 2–1–2) and a 2–1–2 offensive alignment against odd zone formations (1–3–1, 1–2–2). A sample zone pattern offensive—employing movement, maximum use of cutting and passing lanes, and a blind cutter—or player coming toward the ball from behind the zone—that can be altered to exploit zone weaknesses is shown in Figure 6-15a-c. As the ball enters the side area (2 passes to 4) opposite the pivot player, player #1 cuts down the center lane with the left hand raised above his head in preparation for the return pass. Player #4 has the option of feeding the ball to #1 in the middle, of shooting, or of passing to #1 in the corner before cutting to the opposite side, with the left hand high overhead in preparation for the return pass. Figure 6-15b shows the players' positions, with the ball in the corner of the court. Player #5 has timed his cut and receives the pass as he moves quickly toward the ball. Player #4 has assumed the position of a blind cutter behind the zone, which is now shifted to the far side. As #5 receives the pass, he turns to face the basket and shoots or feeds the ball to #4 or #3, who are stepping into the zone from behind. Figure 6-15c shows the proper ball revolvement should a pass not enter the pivot area.

The following basic principles are offered as a guide in attacking the zone defense:

1. Work for the percentage shot by forcing the zone to slide.

2. Utilize triangle formations to maintain rapid ball movement.

3. Do not hold the ball in the corners.

4. Use blind cutters that step toward the ball from behind the defense.

5. Shift the zone as far as possible to one side before revolving the ball to the weak side for the quick shot.

6. Use occasional screens on the weak side as the ball is revolved.

7. Look into the pivot area before passing elsewhere.

8. Drive into the zone to feed or to pick a hole for the quick jump shot.

9. Utilize movement and cutting lanes.

10. Sprint to proper offensive rebound positions.

11. Exploit individual weaknesses by driving the middle or baseline on defensive players unable to cover.

Offensive Against Pressing Defenses

There are different types of pressing defenses—full-court, three-quarter-court, half-court—that may be employed. Although a definite offensive plan is needed to counter man-to-man and zone pressing defenses, the following principles of attack are provided:

1. Turn and look upcourt immediately after receiving the ball.

2. Retrieve the ball quickly from the net after a free throw or field goal to execute a quick throw-in before the defense organizes.

3. Meet each pass.

4. Limit dribbling unless an opening is provided, in a man-to-man pressing defense, for an outstanding dribbler.

5. Attack the press, pushing for a field goal rather than just to move the ball over the 10-second or mid-court line.

6. Avoid passing back unless a definite plan is being used.

7. Stay out of corners by cutting away from these areas.

8. Keep all passes short and snappy, avoiding the lob pass.

9. Avoid telegraphing passes.

10. Execute "fishhooks" or drop-step maneuvers to receive the initial pass from out-of-bounds by sprinting away from the ball before coming to a stop and returning full speed toward the pass.

11. Pass the ball before the double-up forms.

12. Demonstrate poise and confidence.

13. Utilize the tall pivot player to cut to open areas in the middle to alleviate pressure from the guards.

14. Analyze the pressing defense in terms of what they would like you to do. Avoid such maneuvers.

15. Exploit defensive weaklings.

The Organized Fast Break

The fast break, or the rapid movement of the ball from the defensive to the offensive end of the court before the opponents set up their defense, requires superior handling of the ball and rebounding. Such an offense is carefully planned and practiced and demands the consistent application of disciplined movements. It should create a high number of 3-on-2 situations and should increase the probability of getting the second and third shots. The organized fast break involves mastery of the following phases:

1. *Quick accurate pitchout.* Players are instructed to execute the outlet pass (see the section on rebounding) to one of the assigned pitchout areas using the hook or baseball pass. No dribbling should be used prior to the pitchout, nor should a long full-court pass be thrown.

2. *Reception in the assigned areas.* The pitchout areas and the paths of the receivers are shown in Figure 6-16. The short sideline area is the best target for the outlet pass, followed by the long side areas and the middle. The receiver receives the ball with his back facing the sidelines to limit interceptions and to improve his view for the next phase of the fast break. It should be noted that as the ball is received in the pitchout area, all three lanes are filled.

3. *Centering the ball.* After the ball is received in the side area, it should be centered as shown in Figure 6-16. The ball is centered with a chest pass

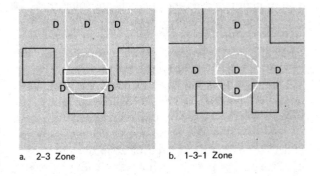

a. 2-3 Zone   b. 1-3-1 Zone

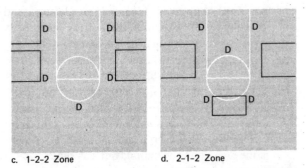

c. 1-2-2 Zone   d. 2-1-2 Zone

FIGURE 6-14.   Zone defenses and their weakness areas.

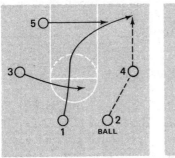

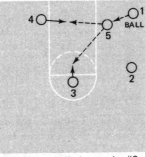

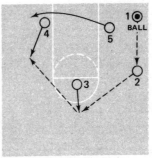

a. Basic cuts in the revolving zone pattern offense.

b. Use of blind cutter by #3 and #4.

c. Ball revolvement to the weak side.

FIGURE 6-15.   A sample zone pattern offensive.

or by a quick dribble toward midcourt should an opponent be in a position to intercept. If the dribble is used, the two players exchange lanes.

4. *Filling the lanes.* With the three lanes filled, the chest pass is used to advance the ball downcourt, dribbling only when players are under attack. No player should run away from the rebounder prior to a successful outlet pass.

5. *Spread.* Wingmen maintain a position 2 to 3 feet from the sideline until they reach the free throw line extended, at which point they both execute L cuts and try hard for possible lay-up shots. If they have not received the ball, both wingmen remain *if* they outnumber the defense. Otherwise, they cross and return to backcourt to set up the offensive attack (see Figure 6-17). The wingmen must see that the ball is in the hands of the middle man when he reaches the top of the circle.

6. *Trailer.* The use of only one trailer will provide proper defensive balance should a counterbreak occur. The fourth man downcourt should be slightly behind and to the right of the middle man, and he should time his cut for a hand-off from the foul line or a short pass for the jump shot.

7. *Full stop at the foul line.* The middle man stops at the foul line, unless he is able to split the defense or widen the lanes to set up the trailer who will crash between the lanes on the right side. Such a maneuver eliminates the charging possibility of the offense and permits the ball to be "triangled" when the defense is outnumbered.

8. *Defensive man.* The last man down the floor, the rebounder, stops at midcourt to maintain proper defensive balance.

The middle man has the alternatives of passing to either wingman, executing the jump shot from the foul line, driving down the middle to split the defense, or widening the lane to set up the trailer.

Defending against the fast break involves a combination of the following tactics: (1) controlling the pace or tempo of the game by employing slow-down tactics, (2) pressing the rebounder with one defensive player to slow the outlet pass, (3) covering pitchout areas, (4) running the collision course—that is, covering a player about to receive a pass by planting yourself three feet away from him—on the player receiving the outlet pass, on the player receiving the centering pass, or on the middle man in the scoring half of the court prior to his arrival at the foul line, (5) returning quickly to the defense without losing eye contact with the ball (side and back pedaling), and (6) covering to slow the dribbler when he moves the ball the length of the court outstandingly well.

Jump Ball Plays

Approximately seven to nine jump ball situations occur each game, making this an extremely important phase of basketball. Each team should develop a series of offensive and defensive plays for the center, the offensive, and the defensive circles. Either the diamond or box formation is used, with the basic man-to-man defense principles dictating the position of a player in relation to his opponent, that is, between his opponent and the basket. A signal calling system must also be developed which may take the form of: (1) the *clock method* in which the circle is assumed to be a clock face, with 12 o'clock directly ahead, 6 behind, and 9 and 3 to the left and right, and with the number called indicating the direction of the tap, should it be controlled, (2) *direction signals* in which the player touches the left hand to the front, back, or side of his clothing to indicate the direction of the tap, (3) *baiting* in which players purposely assume an alignment that invites an opponent to tap in a specific direction which will be filled as the ball is tossed into the air. Sample plays

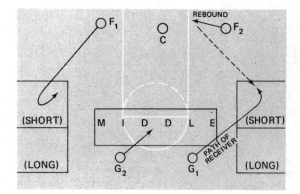

FIGURE 6-16. Pitchout areas and path of the receiver. Guard on side of rebound, G¹, moves to the pitchout area on that side. The off-side guard, G², moves to the middle area. The offside forward, F¹, has moved to the area on the other side and the three lanes are filled quickly and prior to the outlet pass. G¹ will center the ball to G². C becomes the trailer while the rebounder, F², stops at half-court. Should F¹ secure the rebound, the procedure is reversed with G² moving to the pitchout area on the rebound side, G¹ covering the middle, and F² moving to the offside area. C would become the tailer and F², the rebounder, would become the defensive man.

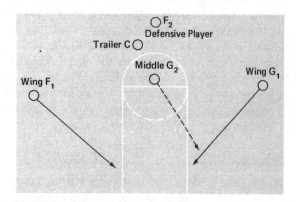

FIGURE 6-17. Execution in the scoring half of the court. Wingmen hold their positions near the sideline until they reach the free throw line. Note the full stop at the foul line and the positions of the trailer and defensive player.

from the diamond and box formation are shown in Figure 6-18a, b, and c.

SAFETY PRACTICES

1. Provide a minimum of six feet between any court line and the bleachers or other obstructions.

2. Keep the playing floor completely free from any film dust or dirt that may cause slipping. Make periodic inspection for splinters, nail heads, and other protruding objects.

3. To eliminate rough play, employ competent officials in all types of competition in the physical education, intramural, and recreational programs.

4. Tape weak ankles and lace shoes properly and snugly.

5. Attain proper levels of physical conditioning.

6. Maintain adequate lighting suitable for high-speed play.

WEIGHT TRAINING

A weight-training program for basketball players, other than the basic exercises for general body development, should be directed at the strengthening and the increasing of explosive power of the muscles used in jumping as well as the strengthening of the flexor muscles of the wrists. Vertical jumping ability has been shown to increase three to six inches following systematic, weight-training programs. The following exercises, designed to strengthen the legs and wrists, are recommended: the squat jump, heel raise, dead lift, wrist curl, and ¾-squat (see Chapter 17 for a description of these exercises).

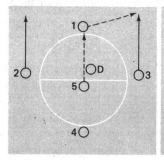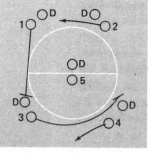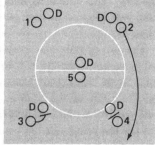

a. Offensive tap from the diamond formation. Position #1 should be filled by the tallest non-jumping player.

b. Defensive tap from the box formation. Players #1, #2, and #3 rotate one position to the right while player #4 drops back.

c. Back tap. Players #3 and #4 execute a screen as player #2 vacates his position to receive the tap in the backcourt area.

FIGURE 6-18. Sample jump ball plays from diamond and box formations.

EXERCISE   Definitions and List of Terms

1. A dribbler who throws or taps the ball into the air, touching it before it reaches the playing surface, has executed a legal _____.
2. An offensive player who receives a pass in the scoring half of the floor and then dribbles or passes to a teammate in the defensive half has committed a _____violation.
3. Team pressure defense, emphasizing the defensive triangle, the cutting off of passing lanes, and the use of overplay, is termed _____defense.
4. A maneuver designed to prevent an opponent from attaining the inside position near the basket following a field goal attempt is termed _____.
5. An offensive maneuver in which the dribbler makes a hard feint to one side as he pulls the ball back and across the body to the opposite hand is termed a _____.
6. The point man, or defensive player at the very front of a particular zone, is called the _____.
7. The most important defensive fundamental in basketball consisting of the attainment and the maintenance of a legal guarding position, with the head, shoulders, and feet completely facing the offensive player, is termed _____.
8. A defensive maneuver designed to force a lob pass by placing two individuals on one offensive opponent is referred to as a _____.
9. A pattern-type of offense in which there is constant movement and in which a team, for short periods of time, maintains control of the ball without scoring is referred to as a _____.
10. A defensive maneuver in which the defender assists a teammate in difficulty by picking up his assigned man and by sprinting to a legal guarding position just prior to the arrival of the opponent in order to prevent further penetration is called a _____.
11. A defensive strategy in which areas instead of men are assigned for defense and in which there is one single outside man is termed an _____.
12. Contact by an offensive player, with or without the ball, with a defensive player who has attained proper coverage is termed _____.
13. Following a rebound, the fast break must be initiated rapidly through an execution of what is termed the _____.
14. A tight guarding position in which the inside arm and foot are extended a half man in front of an offensive player who is in position to receive the next pass from a teammate is termed _____.
15. An offensive maneuver employed by a player with or without the ball to shut off the guarding path of a defender and permit an offensive advantage by a teammate is termed a _____.
16. A time infraction whereby an offensive player remains inside the lane (the area delineated by the lines leading from the endline to the free throw line) beyond the allotted time is termed a _____.
17. The offensive player who follows six to twelve feet behind and to the right of the middle man on the fast break, timing his cut to coincide with the middle man's full stop at the foul line, is termed the _____.
18. An offensive pattern in which three to five players perform close lateral exchanges in the backcourt area in an attempt to work the ball close to the basket for a drive or short jump shot is termed a _____.
19. A full-court, three-quarter court, or half-court press employing the use of assigned court areas and double-up action on the ball is called a _____.

1. Air dribble
2. Backcourt
3. Ball-you-man
4. Boxing
5. Changeover
6. Chaser
7. Coverage
8. Double-up
9. Freeze
10. Jump switch
11. Odd zone
12. Offensive charging
13. Outlet pass
14. Overplay
15. Screen
16. Three-second violation
17. Trailer
18. Weave offense
19. Zone press

QUESTIONS AND ANSWERS ON THE RULES

1. *Q.* What are the time allotments for the various actions?
   A.

Action	Time	Penalty
Throw-in	5 seconds	Loss of possession
Defensive player within six feet of a dribbling or stationary player who has the ball and who is not moving toward the basket	5 seconds	Jump ball
Replacing a disqualified player	1 minute	Charged time-out
Replacing an injured player	1½ minutes	Charged time-out
Crossing the backcourt line	10 seconds	Loss of possession
Shooting a free throw	10 seconds	Loss of possession
Remaining in free throw lane	3 seconds	Loss of possession
Time-out	1 minute	
Time between periods in high school basketball	1 minute	
Extra periods in high school	3 minutes	
Extra periods in college	5 minutes	
Length of periods in high school	8 minutes	
Time between halves in high school	10 minutes	
Time between halves in college	15 minutes	
Length of halves in college	20 minutes	

2. *Q.* What are the various types of fouls?
   A.

Infraction	Number of free throws awarded
Double foul	None—jump ball
Personal foul	One shot unless in the act of shooting when two free throws are awarded providing the shot was unsuccessful
Multiple foul	Two free throws
Player control foul	None—loss of possession
Technical foul	One free throw plus possession
Intentional foul	Two free throws
Flagrant foul	Two free throws plus disqualification

3. *Q.* Where is the legal position of a player who receives the ball while in the air?
   A. At the spot on the floor last touched by his feet. Should such a spot be in the backcourt or out-of-bounds, loss of possession would result regardless of the landing position.

4. *Q.* What are the proper positions of players when a shooter is shooting a free throw?
   A. The lanes adjacent to the endline are occupied by the opponents of the shooter, the next two positions are occupied by the teammates of the shooter, with the remaining two, at each side of the shooter, available one to each team.

5. *Q.* What are the most common rule violations resulting in loss of possession?
   A. Intentionally kicking the ball, double dribbling, carrying the ball, moving more than one step before releasing the ball, remaining in the backcourt area too long, remaining in the free throw lane for more than 3 seconds, and moving the pivot foot before the first dribble strikes the floor.

6. *Q.* How many fouls are allotted to each player? team?
   A. Five fouls result in individual disqualification. The sixth team foul in collegiate basketball results in the awarding of a second free throw if the first attempt is successful.

7. *Q.* If contact between a dribbler and a guard occurs, with whom does the responsibility for avoiding contact rest?

   A. With the dribbler. The guard is in a legal guarding position if he is facing the dribbler regardless of stance or length of time in that position.

8. *Q.* Is it a legal maneuver to jump into the air for the jump shot, and then to dribble instead of shooting or passing?

   A. No. This is a traveling violation distinguished by the fact that the ball did not strike the court surface before the pivot foot was moved.

9. *Q.* Does loss of possession result if the ball is accidentally kicked?

   A. No. The ball may accidentally strike a dribbler's leg, foot, or knee without being a violation; however, this terminates the dribble.

10. *Q.* A player is fouled in the act of an unsuccessful tap. How many free throws is he awarded?

    A. One. Tapping is not considered a try for a goal.

11. *Q.* What actions result in a technical foul?

    A. Coaching from the bench, unsportsmanlike contact, and sixth time-out result in technical fouls.

12. *Q.* Is grabbing the net or rim after a shot a technical foul?

    A. No. It is an automatic goal.

13. *Q.* May a team begin and end with less than five players?

    A. A team must start each game with five men; however, should no available substitutes be present after the game has begun, a team may continue with less than five players.

MAJOR DIFFERENCES IN GIRLS (DGWS) AND BOYS COLLEGE/UNIVERSITY RULES

Officials and their Duties

1. Officials notify players when game is in the last 2 minutes of the fourth quarter.
2. Timer shall notify official 3 minutes before each half and the scorers 2 minutes before game time.
3. A coach or any player on the court may request a team time-out from an official while her team has possession of the ball, regardless of any change of status about to occur. A coach may request a time-out from the scorer when the ball is dead, regardless of any change of status about to occur.
4. Successive team time-outs may be called after the expiration of the fourth quarter or each extra period.
5. If the ball is in flight on a try for field goal when time for the period expires, and the ball is subsequently touched, the field goal, if made, counts 2 points.
6. If the ball enters the basket from below and goes through and drops back into the basket, no goal is awarded and no violation is called.

Definitions

1. *Air dribble*—a play in which a player, after giving impetus to the ball once by throwing or tapping it may touch it again before it touches the floor or another player.
2. *Closely-guarded*—Within 3' of player with the ball.

Putting the ball in play

1. After each field goal or free throw, the player who initially positions herself behind the endline with possession of the ball must throw the ball into the court.
2. A player may lift the pivot foot while releasing the ball for a pass, goal try, or dribble. The ball must leave the hands before the pivot foot touches the floor again.

Out-of-bounds and throw in

1. A player without the ball may run out-of-bounds provided she does not return at a more advantageous position.
2. No player can cause the ball to go out-of-bounds by intentionally throwing or hitting the ball against an opponent.

Free Throw

1. Free throw(s) may be taken by any player who is in the game when the team foul was called (does not include substitues).
2. On the free throw line-up, at least one player from each team must line up on each of the lane lines.
3. If a player chooses not to take the 3rd lane space, the opposite team may not use that space.

Violations and Penalties

1. Disrupting the free thrower is a foul, not a violation.

Fouls and Penalties

1. Fouls are classified as individual and team. Any individual fouls may be a disqualifying foul if the situation is severe enough to warrant such action and one such disqualifying foul may remove a player from the game.
2. Free throws are awarded all fouls, except a double foul. No bonus "one and one" free throws are ever awarded.
3. During the final 2 minutes of the fourth quarter, all fouls are two shot fouls.

30-Second Clock

1. The assistant scorer normally acts as the 30-second clock operator.
2. On each possession, a shot must be taken within the 30-second time period. After each offensive rebound, an additional 30 seconds are allotted prior to the next shot attempt.

BIBLIOGRAPHY

Anderson, Forrest, and Albeck, Stan. *Coaching Better Basketball.* New York: The Ronald Press Company, 1964.

Bennington, John, and Newell, Pete. *Basketball Methods.* New York: The Ronald Press Company, 1962.

Bunn, John W. *Basketball Techniques and Team Play.* Englewood Cliffs, N. J.: Prentice-Hall, Inc., 1964.

Lindeburg, Franklin. *How to Play and Teach Basketball.* New York: Association Press, 1962.

McGuire, Frank. *Offensive Basketball.* Englewood Cliffs, N. J.: Prentice-Hall, Inc., 1958.

The Official National Collegiate Athletic Association Basketball Guide. New York: The National Collegiate Athletic Bureau, latest edition.

Ramsey, Jack. *Pressure Basketball.* Englewood Cliffs, N. J.: Prentice-Hall, Inc., 1965.

Sharman, Bill. *Sharman on Basketball Shooting.* Englewood Cliffs, N. J.: Prentice-Hall, Inc., 1965.

Wilkes, Glenn. *Basketball Coach's Complete Handbook.* Englewood Cliffs, N. J.: Prentice-Hall, Inc., 1965.

7

DANCE
(MODERN & SQUARE)

DESCRIPTION OF THE ACTIVITY
(MODERN DANCE)

Modern dance has been called by many names: natural dance, interpretive dance, free dance, and aesthetic dance. Since the time of Isadora Duncan, who is credited with being the first dancer to reject the set vocabulary of ballet movements and its traditional forms and themes, modern dance has continued to change. It is based on natural, expressive, and basic fundamental movements through which a dancer is able to express a wide range of emotions. Freedom of movement is always being stressed, but freedom within the framework of modern dance discipline. Most modern dance instructors use the standard five feet positions of ballet with the exception that the hip "turn-out" need not be as great as in ballet. Also, a parallel foot position, not recognized by ballet, is employed. In the parallel position the feet are not quite touching, the arms are in a long curve at the sides, and the middle fingers of each hand are in line with the side seam of the leotard or trousers. The torso is elongated but not stiff, the shoulders are down, and the hips are kept parallel and to the front. The knees must be directly over the center of the feet.

One of the purposes of modern dance is to permit the student to find his own means of creativity through the use of the modern dance vocabulary of movements. Therefore, it is essential that time and effort are devoted to movement exploration. Many of the techniques are performed on the floor in a sitting, lying, or kneeling position. The dancer rolls, crawls or uses the floor as a spring board for falls, recovery movements, and the like.

Contemporary modern dance has undergone several changes. Attention has shifted from using it as a form of propaganda to subject matter related to mythology, the Bible, and abstract movements. The avant-garde choreographer, in collaboration with an avant-garde pianist-composer, is experimenting with dancing to electronic music. Choreographers, like Alwin Nikolais, are experimenting with sound, color, light, bizarre props and shapes to create a remarkably theatrical set of illusion on the stage. Also, there now seems to be a trend in some companies to perform at least one dance in the nude.

EQUIPMENT

The woman modern dancer wears a leotard which covers the hips and trunk and is made of nylon or cotton. Men usually wear a T shirt. Black is usually the preferred color but leotards are made in many colors which is becoming more popular with the younger set.

Tights, which cover the legs, are worn by both men and women. Men also wear slacks or gymnastic pants. The tights are usually worn under the leotard, but some dancers prefer to wear them over the leotard. They come with or without feet and are made in many colors. Some dancers wear knitted legwarmers which cover the legs up to the middle of the thigh.

Shoes, except for a modern dance slipper that leaves the toes and heel exposed, are not worn. Ballet slippers may be used but they often cause slipping. Socks should never be worn as they are dangerous, causing accidents due to slipping.

In some instances, the teacher may require a long or short gored skirt to be worn over the leotard, or a Greek or wrap around tunic.

Drums and records are the most common means of accompaniment however, other percussive instruments like the piano, cymbals, and tambourines; and, the voice in song or prose may be used.

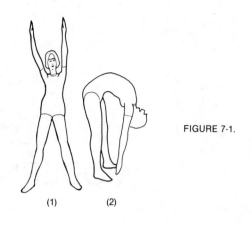

FIGURE 7-1.

(1)   (2)

SKILLS AND TECHNIQUES

Modern dance techniques are unlimited. They usually start with axial and progress to locomotion movements. As the student's vocabulary increases, time is alloted for exploration or creativity.

Axial Movements

Axial movements are those executed in one place and consist of three different types: percussion, sustain and pendulum. Percussion is a quick, sharp movement; sustain is a slow drawn-out movement; and pendulum is a swinging movement. Each of these movements is executed from three body positions; standing, on the knees, and sitting or lying.

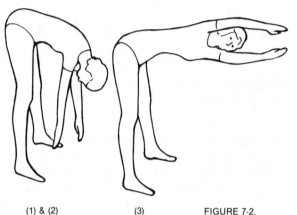

(1) & (2)   (3)   FIGURE 7-2.

Techniques in the Standing Position

Percussion and Sustain Standing Movements

Vertical Reach.   Stand in second position with both arms over the head. (1) Reach upward, as far as possible, with first the right hand and then the left. Keep the hips and heels down. Repeat 8 times. (2) Relax by flexing the trunk forward, and then repeat the reaching movement (see Figure 7-1).

Forward Bounce.   Stand in second position with the arms over the head and knees straight. (1) Drop the trunk forward, touch the hands, and even the elbows, to the floor. When skills permit the use of the elbows, flex them and turn the hands inward toward the body. (2) Bounce gently 4 times with the back rounded. (3) Staighten the spine, and return slowly in 4 counts to starting position, with the arms straight and held forward. Throughout the bounce, the knees remain straight (see Figure 7-2).

Side Bounce.   Stand in second position with the left arm raised over the head, the right arm across the body, and elbows and knees straight. (1) Bend directly to the right side, bounce 4 times and return to

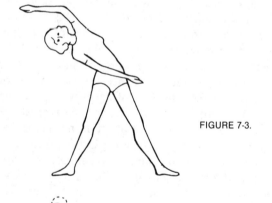

FIGURE 7-3.

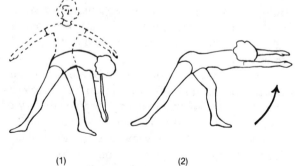

(1)   (2)

FIGURE 7-4.

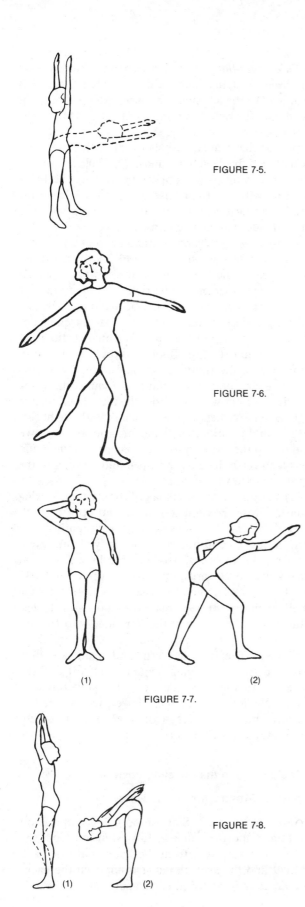

FIGURE 7-5.

FIGURE 7-6.

(1)   (2)

FIGURE 7-7.

(1)   (2)

FIGURE 7-8.

starting position. (2) Reverse the arms, bounce to the left, and return to starting position (see Figure 7-3).

Side Lunge. Stand in a side lunge position with the trunk rotated so that the chest is facing over the knee. Arms are in second position. (1) Collapse the trunk over the bent knee, with the arms relaxed and dangling from the shoulders. (2) Slowly raise the trunk in 4 counts until it is parallel to the floor, the trunk is still rotated over the knee, and the arms are forward and parallel to the floor, with the elbows straight. (3) Repeat steps 1 and 2 three more times, then reverse to the other side (see Figure 7-4).

Parallel Bounce. Stand in second position with both arms over the head, and elbows and knees straight. (1) Bend the trunk slowly forward from the hips, keeping the back straight until it and the arms are parallel to the floor. (2) Bounce the trunk 4 times and return to the starting position. The return may be a sustain movement or a percussive movement (see Figure 7-5).

Forward Lunge. Stand in first position, holding the arms in second position. (1) Relevé on both feet. (2) Lunge forward on the left foot, keeping the arms to the side and the trunk held high. The right knee is straight and rotated outward from the hip (2) Bounce from the left knee 3 times. (3) Pull the back right leg up to the left foot and at the same time, relevé on both feet. (4) Repeat the lunge with the right foot (see Figure 7-6).

Striking Lunge. Stand in first position, left arm in low second position and the right fist by the right shoulder. (1) Rise on toes (relevé). (2) Lunge forward on the left foot and at the same time, shoot the right fist forward (strike) and bend the left knee. (3) With a strong push off from the left foot, return the left foot back to the right foot into a relevé position for both feet. (4) Repeat the striking movement 3 more times, then reverse to the right foot with the left fist striking forward (see Figure 7-7).

Pendulum Standing Movements

Forward Pendulum. Stand in second position with the arms over the head and the body at full extension. (1) Swing the trunk and arms downward and bend the knees slightly, (count one). (2) As the arms follow through and up in back, the knees are straightened, (count two). The arms are swung on the outside of the legs and the head looks between the legs. (3) Recovery: the knees bend, then straighten as the arms, followed by the trunk, swings back to the full extension position, (count 3 and 4). The knees must plié and straighten with each part of the pendulum movement (see Figure 7-8).

FIGURE 7-9.

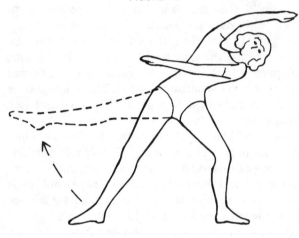

FIGURE 7-10.

Side Pendulum.   Stand in second position, weight on the left foot in a lunge position to the left side, left arm held to the left side, right arm extended over the head, and the right hip rotated outward. (1) Drop the trunk and arms over the left leg, (count one). (2) Continue the swing across the front of the body with both knees bent, (count and). (3) Follow through with the swing to the opposite side into the lunge position with the right knee bent, left arm over the head, right arm to the side, and left leg extended to the left side, (count two and). (See Figure 7-9.)

Cross Arm Pendulum.   Stand in second position, arms in low second position. (1) Plié both knees, and at the same time both arms swing down and across the trunk, (count one). The right arm continues it's arc over the head as the trunk bends to the left, and the weight shifts to the left foot. (2) At the climax of the arm swing, the knees are straightened, the right heel is raised off of the floor, and the toe remains in contact with the floor, (count and two). (3) Recovery: Plié with both knees and at the same time swing the right arm down and across the face, continue the right arm movement across the trunk to the right side into second position, while the left arm swings down and out to the left into second position, (count 3 and 4). (4) Reverse the cross arm pendulum swing to the right side (see Figure 7-10).

(5) Variation: At the climax of the cross arm swing (step 2), raise the right foot to second position.

Hip Thrust Fall.   Start with the feet slightly apart, arms at low second position, and body at full extension. (1) With the back straight, bend the knees and slowly sway backwards, (count 1, 2). (2) Reach backward with the left hand as the knees do a "grande plié", (count 3, 4). (3) Touch the floor with the left hand and slide out onto the left side, with the left hand preceding the trunk, (count 5,6). (4) Straighten the knees. The legs, left arm and trunk are fully extended along the floor, (count 7, 8). (5) Pull the knees up to the chest (count 9, 10), and roll over toward the left onto the bent knees, (count 11, 12). (6) Straighten the trunk, (count 13, 14) and stand, (count 15, 16). (See Figure 7-11.)

Techniques in the Kneeling Position

Sustain Movements on the Knees

Sway Backwards.   Start on both knees, hands on the thighs and the trunk at full extension from the knees. (1) Sway back from the knees with the back straight and the neck flexed. Do not arch the back. The knees may be together or apart, (4 counts). (2)

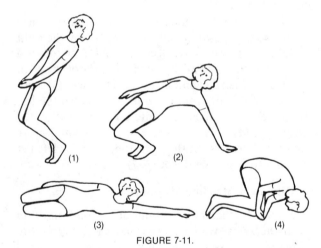

FIGURE 7-11.

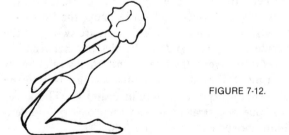

FIGURE 7-12.

Return to upright position in 4 counts (see Figure 7-12).

(3) Variation: With the knees apart and the back straight, sway backwards from the knees so that the trunk can lie on the floor between the legs. This movement involves a considerable amount of strength in the thigh muscles. Recovery: Contract the abdomen and thigh muscles, and with the back straight, return to full extension.

Sit on Heels. Start on both knees, arms in low second position and trunk at full extension. Knees may be together or apart. (1) Slowly lower the buttocks to the heels, (4 counts). (2) Slowly return to full extension, (4 counts). See Figure 7-13.

Curl Sit on Heels. Start on both knees, arms in low second position and trunk at full extension. (1) Slowly curl the trunk forward and lower the buttocks to the heels. The arms hang relaxed at the sides, (4 counts). (2) Slowly straighten the spine until the back is parallel to the floor and at the same time move the arms backward and parallel to the floor, (4 counts). (3) Raise the trunk from the knees to full extension, arms in low second position, (4 counts). (4) Repeat the "curl sit" three more times (see Figure 7-14).

Knee Fall. Start with both knees slightly apart, arms in low second position and trunk at full extension. (1) Slowly sway back from the knees with the back straight, and reach backward with the left hand until fingers touch the floor, (count 1, 2, 3). (2) Slide out onto the left side with the left arm preceeding the trunk, (count 4, 5, 6). (3) Straighten the knees so that the left arm, trunk, and legs are in a line, (count 7, 8). (4) Pull the knees up to the chest, (count 9, 10). (5) Roll over toward the left onto the bent knees, keeping the arms relaxed and to the sides, (count 11, 12). (6) Straighten the trunk, rising to full extension with the arms in low second position. The trunk is now facing the opposite direction, (count 13, 14, 15, 16). (7) Repeat the knee fall (see Figure 7-15).

Percussion Movements on the Knees

Fear. Kneel on knees, trunk at full extension, and arms in first position in front of the trunk. (1) Contract (tighten) the abdominal muscles, round the back, lift up the face, and sit quickly on the heels. At the same time shoot the arms upward with the palms facing and hiding the face, (count 1). (2) Return to starting position, (count 2). (See Figure 7-16.)

Stomach-ache. Kneel on knees, trunk at full extension, arms in low second position. (1) Contract the abdominal muscles, round the back, and flex the neck forward, (count 1). (2) Sit on the heels, and at

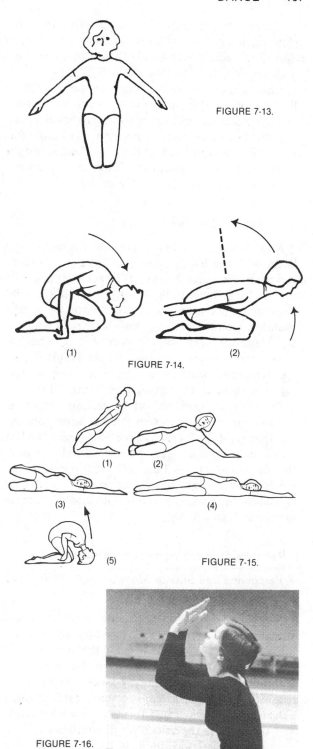

FIGURE 7-13.

FIGURE 7-14.

(1) (2)

(1) (2) (3) (4) (5)

FIGURE 7-15.

FIGURE 7-16.
Percussion
movement on
the knees (fear).

the same time, flex the elbows and cross the wrist close to, and in front of the trunk that is bent over as though in pain, (count 2). (3) Return to the starting position, (count 3, 4). (See Figure 7-17.)

Extension and Flexion. Kneel on the right knee, left foot on the floor and in front of the body, trunk at full extension, right fist at the right shoulder, and the left arm in low second position. (1) Lunge forward with the trunk and, at the same time, shoot the right first forward, (count 1). (2) Return to the starting position, (count 2). (See Figure 7-18.)

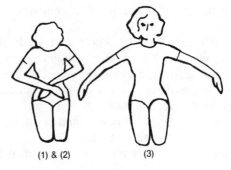

FIGURE 7-17.

Pendulum Movements on the Knees

Knee Swing. Assume a position on hands and knees with the hands directly under the shoulders, and the knees under the hips. The back is straight and the head is parallel to the floor. (1) Swing the right knee up to the chest as the neck flexes and the back is rounded, (count 1 and). (2) Swing the right leg back and high to full extension from the hip. The back is arched and the head is raised, (count 2). (3) Repeat the right knee swing three more times, then reverse the knee swing to the left leg (see Figure 7-19).

Knee Rock. Kneel on both knees, buttocks sitting on heels, trunk at full extension and arms forward and low. (1) Rock forward to the hands, with the feet raised in the back form the knees, and the neck flexed, (count 1). (2) Push off the floor with the hands and rock back to starting position, (count 2). (3) Repeat the rocking movement no more than three times (see Figure 7-20).

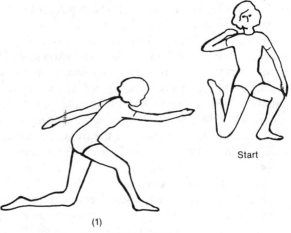

FIGURE 7-18.

Techniques in Sitting and Lying Positions

Percussion and Sustain Movements in Sitting and Lying Positions

Side Bounce. Sit in a straddle position, knees straight, trunk at full extension and the arms in second position. (1) Twist the trunk to the right, arms in first position, (count 1). (2) Grasp the right ankle with both hands and bounce 4 times over the right leg, with the back rounded, (4 counts). (3) Straighten or extend the back, reach forward with both arms, and slowly raise the trunk, which continues to face right to the starting position, (4 counts). (5) Reverse the bounce to the left (see Figure 7-21).

Parallel Bounce. Sit in a straddle position, trunk at full extension, and arms in second position. (1) Bend the trunk forward from the hips with the spine straight, arms sidewards toward the ankles, and bounce 4 times, (4 counts). Slowly return to starting

FIGURE 7-19.

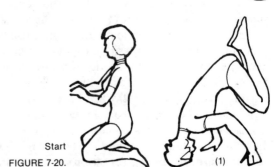

FIGURE 7-20.

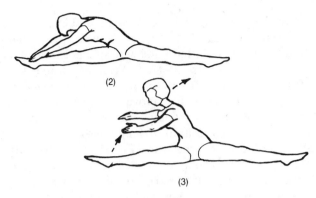

FIGURE 7-21.

FIGURE 7-22. Parallel bounce.

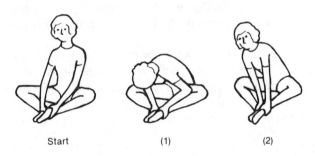

Start   (1)   (2)

FIGURE 7-23.

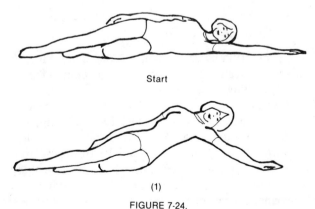

Start

(1)

FIGURE 7-24.

position, (4 counts). (2) Repeat the parallel bounce three more times (see Figure 7-22).

Soles Together Bounce. Sit with the soles of the feet touching, knees flexed, hands grasping the ankles, and trunk to full extension. (1) Flex the trunk forward, back rounded, elbows outward, neck flexed, and bounce 4 times, (4 counts). (2) Extend the spine, and slowly raise the trunk to full extension, (4 counts). (See Figure 7-23.)

Side Contraction. Lie on the left side, extend lower arm (left), resting head on the left shoulder, keep the upper arm (right) parallel to the extended right leg, and flex the left knee. (1) Contract the left rib cage so that the trunk is flexed to the left, and keep the head on the left shoulder, (1 count). (2) Relax by sliding the left arm and trunk back on the floor into the starting position, (1 count). Repeat 7 times (see Figure 7-24).

Chest Lift. Lie on the back with body at full extension, and arms in a diagonal position on the floor. (1) Contract the abdominal muscles and at the same time arch the back, and extend the neck, but keep the head and hands in contact with the floor, (1 count). (2) Relax by sliding the head, arms, and trunk on the floor to their starting positions, (1 count). Repeat three times (see Figure 7-25).

Chest Lift to Sitting Position. (1) Assume the starting position for the "chest lift". Contract the abdominal muscles, arch the back and slowly raise the trunk to a sitting (90 degrees) position. The arms remain behind the trunk, the hands in contact with the floor, and the neck extended, (2 counts). (2) Return to starting position by flexing the neck, looking at the feet, rounding the back, and sliding or rolling the trunk back to the floor. The arms precede the trunk, and the head is the last part of the body to touch the floor, (2 counts). (See Figure 7-26.)

Pendulum Movements in Sitting or Lying Positions

The Rocker. Lie on the abdomen, arch the trunk, extend the neck, flex the knees upward behind the trunk, and grasp the ankles with the hand. (1) Pull the feet toward the head, increasing the body arch, lift the legs higher in the air, and rock the body back and forth (see Figure 7-27).

Leg Swing. Lie on the back with the trunk and legs at full extensions, and arms at the sides. (1) Swing the fully extended right leg up and down with the right toe pointed. Repeat 8 times. (2) Repeat with the left leg 8 times (see Figure 7-28).

Side Sitting Pendulum Series. Sit on the right buttocks, right knee flexed in front, left leg extended

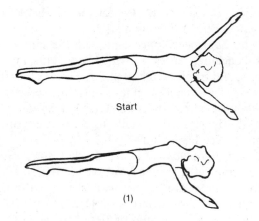

Start

(1)

FIGURE 7-25.

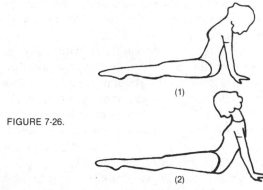

(1)

FIGURE 7-26.

(2)

FIGURE 7-27.   The rocker.

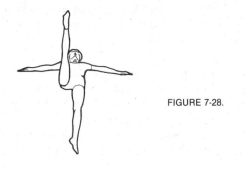

FIGURE 7-28.

to the left side with the knee straight, and leg rotated outward from the hip. Most of the weight is on the right hand, with the left hand in second position, and the trunk facing front. (A-1) Without turning the trunk, swing the left arm to the right side, down and across the chest ending above the head, (count 1 and). (2) Return by swinging the left arm down and back to starting position, (count 2 and).

(B-1) Start with the trunk facing front. The left arm is swung down across the chest and up over the head, as the trunk is raised onto the right knee. Right hand supports the body, and left toe is in contact with the floor, (count 1). (2) Return to starting position by swinging the left arm down across the body to the left side, and lowering the trunk to the side sitting position, (count 2). Repeat the kneeling swing 8 times.

(C-1) Start with the trunk facing front. Swing the left arm down across the chest and up over the head as the trunk is raised onto the right knee and the left leg, knee straight, is kicked sideward and upward, (count 1). (2) Return to the starting position by swinging the left arm down across the body, and to the left side, lowering the leg and trunk to the side sitting position, (count 2). (3) Repeat the kicking swing 8 times, then swing both feet to the right and sit on the left buttocks. (3) Repeat the side sitting pendulum series starting the swing with the right arm (see Figure 7-29).

Arm and Hip Swing.   Sit on the right hip, with the right leg extended, and the left knee flexed, and the left foot flat on the floor. The right hand is behind and in line with the right hip. (1) Swing the left arm upward as the hips are raised as far as possible off the floor. The weight is on both feet and the right hand. The neck is exended backward, (count 1). (2) Return to the sitting position, (count 2 and). (3) Repeat the swing three more times (see Figure 7-30).

Locomotion Movements

Locomotion is movement of the body through space by means of walking, running, hopping. sliding, galloping, and the like.

Walk.   It is a transfer of weight from one foot (right) to the other (left) in which one foot maintains contact with the floor. The movement is reversible.

Run.   It is a transfer of weight from one foot (right) to the other (left) in which both feet are momentarily off the floor at the same time. The movement is reversible.

Hop. It is a spring in which the take-off and landing is executed by the same foot. The movement is not reversible.

Jump. It is spring from one or both feet and a landing on both feet.

Leap. It is a spring from one (right) foot, to the opposite (left) foot in which distance is covered.

Slide. It is a step to the left side with the left foot, a leap left (together) with the right foot. The movement is not reversible unless an extra movement, such as a jump, leap or step, is taken by the left foot.

Gallop. It is a step forward with the left foot, leap forward (together) with the right foot. The left foot is always in front as the gallop is executed. The movement is not reversible unless an extra movement, such as a jump, leap or step, is taken by the left foot.

Skip. It is a step on the left foot, and a hop on the same (left) foot. It is reversible.

Prance. It is a modification of the run in which emphasis is placed upon the raising of a leg forward, with the knee flexed.

Triplet. It is a modification of the walk in which a step (left) is taken with the knee flexed (plié), followed by two walks (right, left) in relevé position. (Dip, toe, toe), (dip, toe, toe).

CREATIVITY

Creativity in dance is the initial performance of a movement which is new to the dancer. This personal innovation may be perfected or discarded.

There are several means by which creativity can be accomplished; two of these are: (1) combining two or more techniques (exercises) and, (2) improvising on a given technique.

Combining Two or More Techniques

An example is the uniting of the walk with the forward pendulum. Start with the right foot forward, arms above the head, and body in full extension. (1) Swing the trunk down as the knees bend, (count 1). (2) The arms follow through outside of the legs, and continue their arc up behind the back, (count 2). (3) The knees straighten, the head looks between the legs, (count 3). (4) Recovery: The knees plié, while the arms swing back toward the floor and the trunk returns to full extension, relevé, (count 1 and 2). (5) Step forward on the left foot, relevé, (count 3). (6)

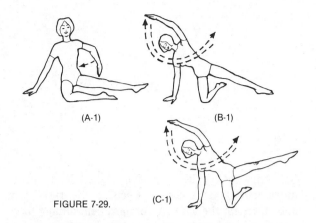

(A-1)   (B-1)

(C-1)

FIGURE 7-29.

(start)

(1)

FIGURE 7-30.   Arm and hip swing.

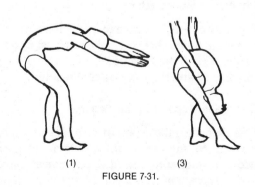

(1)   (3)

FIGURE 7-31.

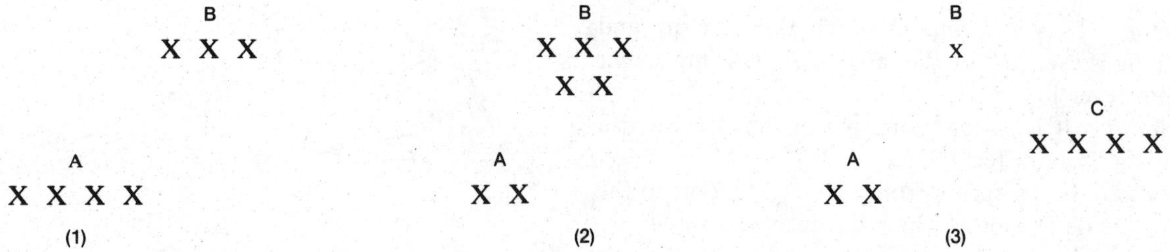

```
        B                          B                          B
     X  X  X                    X  X  X                        X
                                 X  X
                                                                            C
                                                                        X  X  X  X
        A                          A                          A
    X  X  X  X                    X  X                        X  X
       (1)                         (2)                         (3)
```

FIGURE 7-32.

Step forward on the right foot, right knee bends as movement 1 is repeated. Keeping the right foot ahead, repeat the walking forward pendulum 8 times (see Figure 7-31).

Improvising On A Given Technique

Using the "sitting side pendulum technique" as an example, the swinging leg may be swung forward with a straight knee, swung forward with a flexed knee, or swung backwards with either a straight or flexed knee. The swinging arm may follow the line, or be parallel with, the swinging leg. Another example can be demonstrated in the "forward pendulum" in which one or no arms may be swung, instead of two.

COMPOSITION

The ultimate purpose of technique and creativity is to provide the building parts from which dance composition is produced. It is at this level that dance makes its most important contribution to communication of ideas, ideals, feelings and emotions. Each composition is formed not only of techniques but also involves other elements like change in floor pattern, change in the number of dancers, change in focus, change in direction, and change in level. A brief description of the above elements follows.

Change in Floor Pattern

This movement is a change by dancers from one floor design to another. It can be achieved by changing from a circle to a diamond, to a square, or to a zigzag line in any sequence or combination.

Change in Number of the Dancers

This element is the action of dancers shifting from one group to another in order to produce a more varied and interesting composition. For example, a group of seven dancers is divided into two sections, A and B. In the first part of the dance, group A contains 4 dancers, and Group B has 3 dancers. As the groups progress into the second movement, two of the dancers join group B producing the relationship of 2 dancers to 5 dancers. And, during the third movement, 4 dancers leave group B and form a third group, C. The ratio then becomes 4-2-1 (see Figure 7-32).

A change in number may also be produced by having the groups move in opposition to each other, or in succession with each other.

Opposition. Opposition can create a very exciting and pleasing result. It is two or more groups moving contrary to each other. For example, group A starts the forward pendulum on the count of one. Group B begins the forward pendulum on count two. As each group continues the movement, group A will be swinging upward as group B will be swinging downward.

Another variation can be demonstrated by group A performing an axial movement, while group B executes a locomotive movement.

Succession. Succession is similar to a cannon or round in music. One group (a) starts a movement and on a designated count another group(s) B enters the composition with that same movement. In some instances this action is called "pick-up"—group B picks up the same movement that group A is doing.

Change in Focus

A dancer may look up, down, front, side, or diagonally. He may move to the right and look left, or move forward and look up. In many cases the focus will change the feeling of a movement from one of depression (looking downwards) to one of enlightment (looking upwards).

Change in Direction

A dancer changes bodily direction in relation to the room. He may face forward, backward, right or left sideways, right or left diagonally forward, or right or left diagonally backward.

Change in Level

Variety can be added by incorporating a change in level. There are 4 levels: standing, kneeling, sitting and lying.

These are just a few of the elements of composition which help to make a dance desirable and interesting.

EXERCISE   Definitions and List of Terms (Modern Dance)

1. A movement that is done in place is known as an _____ movement.
2. A _____ is a spring from one foot and a landing on that same foot.
3. A spring from one foot to both feet is known as a _____ .
4. A _____ is a spring from one foot to the other in which distance is covered.
5. A movement in which the body travels through space from one place to another by means of walking, running, and the like is known as _____ .
6. _____ is a swinging movement.
7. _____ is a quick, sharp movement.
8. The act of bending both knees is known as _____ .
9. A _____ is a modification of the run in which emphasis is placed upon the raising of a leg forward with the knee flexed.
10. The act of rising on the toes is known as _____ .
11. A _____ is a step on one foot and a hop on the same foot.
12. A _____ is a step with the left foot to the left side and a leap to the left with the right foot.
13. _____ is a slow, drawn out movement.
14. The transfer or weight from one foot to the other in which one foot maintains contact with the floor is known as a _____ .

1. Axial
2. Hop
3. Jump
4. Leap
5. Locomotion
6. Pendulum
7. Percussion
8. Plié
9. Prance
10. Relevé
11. Skip
12. Slide
13. Sustain
14. Walk

DESCRIPTION OF THE ACTIVITY (SQUARE DANCING)

American square dancing has its origin in England and France, but the system of calling is typically American and was created by Americans. The square, circle, line or reel (as in the Virginia Reel) are formations which are common to both the English and American dances. The French influence may be found in the use of such terms as promenade, balance, chasse, and allemande. It has been said that the American square dance forms illustrate a way of life in which the basic formation of a square is reminiscent of the village squares of New England. Those people who migrated south developed the Running Set, while those who traveled and settled in the west developed a faster and more complicated dance. Although the fundamental principles of these square dances are similar to those of the earlier years, the calls for the squares have changed considerably becoming more complicated in floor patterns and calls. Many of the new figures are now being called to popular tunes both new and old.

There are three types of calls: patter, prompt, and hash. A patter call is one in which the last word of a line rhymes with the last word of the preceding line and is sung. A prompt call is one in which there is no rhyme as a movement is called. A hash call is one in which the caller is not limited to a set pattern. He creates the pattern or formations as he goes along which challenges the listening power and skills of the dancers. He usually calls the patterns in the patter style.

EQUIPMENT

Costume

The costume has changed over the years. At first little thought was given to the costume by the participants but as square dancing became more and more popular there was developed a variety of costuming, ranging from every day dress to elaborate full skirted dresses for the women and silk shirts and dungarees for the men.

Instruments

The instruments most commonly used to accompany the dance and the singer were the "fiddle", banjo, and guitar. In many cases the musicians, as well as the "callers" or "prompters", were self taught. Today, orchestras and "callers" are trained just for square dancing. Classes for teaching square dancing are scheduled by community centers, public and private schools, colleges, and private square dance groups.

SKILLS AND TECHNIQUES

Fundamental Positions

Couple.   A couple is a gent and his lady partner. The lady is always on the gent's right.

Set.   A set consists of four couples who stand facing the center in the form of a square.

First Couple or Head Couple.   The first or head couple have their backs to the caller.

Second Couple.   The second couple is to the right of the first couple.

Third Couple.   The third couple is facing the caller and is opposite the first couple.

Fourth Couple.   The fourth couple is to the left of the first couple and faces the second couple.

Two Head Couples.   The two head couples are the first and third couples.

Two Side Couples.   The two side couples are the second and fourth couples.

Opposite Couples.   The couple directly across the set form the home position is the opposite couple.

Home Station or Home Position.   The station or place a gent and his lady stands at the start of the dance is home station.

Head Lady.   The lady with her back to the caller is head lady.

Head Gent.   The gent with his back to the caller is head gent.

Corner Lady.   The lady on the gent's left is the corner lady.

Opposite Gent or Lady.   The gent or lady standing directly across form the dancer's home station is the opposite gent or lady.

Visiting Couple.   The couple or couples who are progressing (active) around the set is the visiting couple

Type of Steps Used.   The beginner usually uses a walking step. The more advanced dancer uses the two-step or shuffle.

Fundamental Calls

Honor Your Partner (Salute).   The couples face each other; the gent bows, the lady curtseys.

Honor Your Corner.   Dancers face their corners; gent bows, the lady curtseys.

Eight Hands Around.   All dancers join hands. Each dancer clasps the hands of the dancers on each side of him (her).

Circle to the Left or Right.   Everyone holds hands and moves to the left or right.

Come on Back.   The direction of the circling motion is reversed.

Swing Your Partner or Corner.   The Buzz step is usually used to swing one's partner. Partners face each other in regular social dance position with the gent's right hand on lady's back, and his left hand holding her right hand extending sideways. The lady's left hand is on the gent's right shoulder. Place right hips together, and the right foot along the outside of partner's right foot. With the right foot ahead of the left, the left foot pushes as though on a scooter which rotates the body around in a clockwise manner. The left foot must be kept slightly behind the right at all times.

A more advance swing may be used. It is executed by partners taking a position facing each other with left hands joined. The lady's right hand is placed on gent's left shoulder; gent slips his right hand between the lady's left elbow and her hips and places his hand on her hip. The right hips are adjacent, with the right feet together. The dancer's rotate themselves in a clockwise direction by pushing the body around with the left foot.

Very young children may join right elbows and skip around each other in performing the swing.

Promenade. Partners, in a side by side position, walk counter clockwise around the set and back home. The hands may be used in two ways: (1) held in a skating position with both hands crossed in front of the dancers, or; (2) with the left hands joined in front, and the gent's right hand holding his lady's right hand behind her back.

Allemande Left with Your Corner. The gent runs and faces his corner lady. Taking her left hand with his left hand, they walk around each other counter clockwise and back home.

Allemande Right with Your Own. The gent takes his partner's right hand, and they walk around each other clockwise and back home.

Balance. There are two kinds. (1) Partners face each other and walk three steps forward, holding the fourth count, then three steps backwards, holding the fourth count. (2) Or, facing each other and holding right hands, take a step right with the right foot (count one), swinging left foot across as they hop on the right foot (count two). Repeat to the left stepping on the left foot and kicking the right foot across, hop on left foot.

Do-Si-Do (Do-Sa-Do). Partners start facing each other and walk forward passing right shoulders then passing back to back and without turning around, pass left shoulders to original position.

Grand Right and Left. Partners face each other, join right hands and walk forward passing right shoulders. Each gent joins left hand with the next lady and they advance passing left shoulders. The third lady is passed right shoulder to right shoulder with right hands joined and so on around the circle alternating hands and shoulders. Each dancer continues in this weaving manner, the lady clockwise and the gent counter clockwise.

Star by the Right. The gents (or ladies) walk to the center, join right hands and move clockwise around the circle.

Star by the Left. The gents (or ladies) walk to the center, join left hands and walk counter clockwise.

Head Ladies Chain. The head ladies walk toward each other, clasping right hands. As they continue across to the opposite gents, they drop hands and

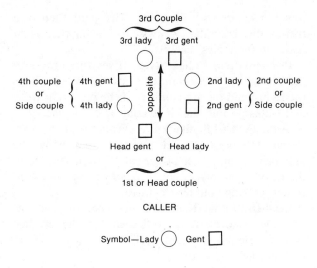

FIGURE 7-33.

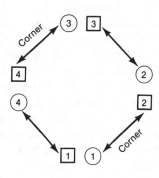

FIGURE 7-34.   Corners

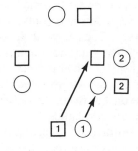

FIGURE 7-35.   Visiting Couple.

join left hands with the gents. The gents then turn them around counter clockwise by placing their right hand on the ladies' back.

Promenade in Indian Style. Everyone moves to the center and faces counter clockwise. Each places the right hand on the shoulder of the person in front and walks around the circle counter clockwise.

Swing the Girl Behind You. From the promenade Indian style position, each gent turns and swings the lady behind him. Then on the call "Promenade in Indian Style" he places her *in front* of him and continues walking counter clockwise.

Lead Out to the Right. A lady, gent, or couple as the caller denotes, moves to the center of the set, then faces the right hand couple. The next part of the call will tell them what to do.

Right and Left Back on the Same Old Track. Two couples face each other and give right hands to their opposites. They walk toward each other and pass by the right shoulders, turn and face their opposites again, join left hands, and pass left shoulders, and back home.

Right and Left Through. Two couples, as the caller designates, face each other and walk forward. Ladies pass each other by left shoulders, and at the same time the men pass right shoulders of their opposite lady. Upon arriving at the other couples' position, each of the men joins left hands with their partner and turns her half way around so that she is on his right and each couple faces its home position.

Side Ladies Chain Across. The side ladies advance toward each other and join right hands. They pass right shoulders, and continue across the set to the opposite gent. Each gent then clasps the left hand of the opposite lady in his left hand and turns her completely around counter clockwise.

Couple Separate. The head lady and head gent turn back to back and walk around the outside of the set; the lady moves to her right and the gent to his left. At the foot of the set (couple three's position) they pass right shoulders and continue on home.

Make a Basket. The ladies advance to the center and join hands. The gents join hands and move in behind and to the left of their partner. The gents raise their hands to form an arch while the ladies bow their heads and move backwards under the arch. The gents then lower their clasped hands.

Turn Basket Inside Out. Starting from the above formation, the gents raise their joined hands while the ladies bow their heads and walk forward under the arch.

Salute. The salute is the same as Honor.

Take a Peek. Couple one, holding inside hands,

FIGURE 7-36a.   Advance position for swing your partner.

FIGURE 7-36b.   Swing your partner (buzz step).

FIGURE 7-37.   Allemande left with your corner.

FIGURE 7-38. Grand right and left (partners have already passed right shoulders and are in the process of passing left shoulders).

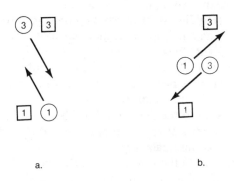

FIGURE 7-39. Head ladies chain across.

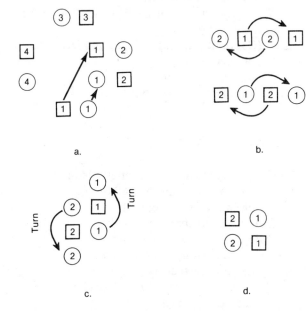

FIGURE 7-40. Right and left through.

advance to a couple. They lean forward and look around their opposites so they can see each other.

All Ladies Chain. All the ladies advance toward each other and join right hands. They walk clockwise half way around the center of the circle and join left hands with their opposite gent who turns each of them around with his right hand on her back.

Lady Go Gee, Gent Go Haw. Lady goes right, the gent goes left.

Dip and Dive. Couples one and two join hands. Couple two raise inside arms to make an arch, couple one ducks under the arch and takes a few steps through the arch, maintaining joined hands, and backs out. Couple two ducks under the arch formed by couple one and backs out.

Down the Center and Cut off Six. Head couple walks down the center of the set to couple three, and pass between them. Lady one walks to her right around the outside of the set and back home, while gent one walks to his left around the outside of the set and back home.

Down the Center and Cut off Four. Couple one walks down the center of the set. Lady one moves to her right between gent three and lady two; head gent moves to his left and walks between lady three and gent four. Each returns home.

Down the Center and Cut off Two. Head couple walks down the center of the set. Lady one walks between couple two and back home while head gent walks between couple four and back home.

INTRODUCTION CALLS

1. Honor your partner
   Honor your corner
   All join hands and circle to your left
   Come on back, you're on the wrong track
2. Honor your partner
   Honor your corner
   Now do-si-do with your corner
   And now with your partners all
      (Partners face and do-si-do)
3. Honor your partner
   Honor your corner
   Allemande left with your corners all
   Your right hand to your own
      (Partners face, join right hands and walk
      around each other)
   Swing your partner once around
   And square your set, come on
4. Honor your partner
   Honor your corner

FIGURE 7-41.   Take a peek.

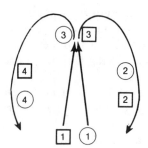

FIGURE 7-42.   Cut off six.

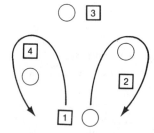

FIGURE 7-43.   Cut off four.

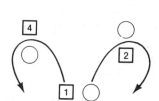

FIGURE 7-44.   Cut off two.

Swing your corner lady
Do-si-do your own
Now get ready for the call

BREAK CALLS
(Those calls that come at the end of a dance)

1. Allemande left with your corner
Allemande right with your own
Allemande left with your corner
Grand right and left the hall
2. Gents to the center back to back
(All gents into the center and stand back to back)
While the ladies go round on the outside track
(Ladies join right hands with their partner)
Balance with your partners all
(Holding right hands step right foot to right side and hop right, kick left foot across right. Reverse to left.)
It's on to the next with the curly hair
(Ladies progress to their right to the next gent and balance)
It's on to the next and don't be slow
(Ladies continue to progress right to next gent and balance)
It's on to the next and away we go
Swing your partner round and round, swing your gal up and down Promenade
3. Allemande left with corner
Grand right and left the hall
When you meet your partner, don't leave her there alone
(Continue with grand right and left until you meet your partner)
Swing her when you meet her
And promenade her home

SWINGING PATTER CALLS

1. Swing your Honey, that cute little miss
Give her a hug, and then a kiss
2. Swing that east, swing that west
Swing the girl that you love best
3. Swing her up, swing her down
Swing your Honey, around and around
4. Swing your partner by your side
Don't step on that old cow hide
5. Up that alley, down the lane
Swing your Honey just the same

6. Swing her out and watch her smile
   Bring her in and hug her awhile
7. Swing her high, swing her low
   Swing that gal in calico
8. Swing that little sugar plum
   Squeeze her boy, don't be dumb
9. Swing her low, swing her high
   Swing that gal until she cries
10. Right foot up, left foot down
    Swing your sweetheart round and round

PROMENADE CALLS

1. Promenade one and all
   Promenade around the hall
   With your right foot up
   And your left foot down
   Hurry up boys
   You'll never get around
2. Swing that darling little girl
   Swing her with a whirl
   Promenade your Honey
   The one with the little curl
3. Swing your little gal
   Swing her mightly hard
   Promenade your Honey
   Right in your own back yard
4. Swing your corner gal around
   Swing her up and down
   Promenade that same little corner
   Promenade the town
5. Promenade with your partner so sweet
   Lift that gal right off her feet
6. Promenade boys and away you go
   There's a chicken in the bread pan
   Picking up dough
7. Promenade when you get straight
   Chow's on the table, so don't be late

SQUARE DANCES

Texas Star

Tune: *Little Brown Jug*

1. Ladies to the center and back to the bar
   (Ladies walk into center, turn and walk
   back to place)
2. Gents go in with a right hand star
3. With a hey-diddle-diddle, the cat and the
   fiddle

(Gents continue the right hand star, moving
clockwise)
4. Back with your left, right in the middle
   (Gent turn, make a left hand star and walk
   counter clockwise)
5. Wink at your gal as you go by, pick up the
   next gal on the sly
   (Continue #4. *Do not drop left hands*. Gent
   passes his partner, extends his right arm
   sideways and, as he meets his right hand
   lady, places his right arm around her waist;
   she puts her left hand on the gent's right
   shoulder, and all continue walking counter
   clockwise)

Chorus:

6. Ladies swing in and the gents swing out
   (Gents drop hands, step backwards and
   swing ladies toward center where they join
   right hands to make a right hand star)
7. The other way and around about
   (Ladies continue walking clockwise with
   right hands joined)
8. The ladies swing out and the gents swing in
   (Ladies drop hands and step backwards,
   the gents walk to center, join left hands,
   making a left hand star)
9. The other way and you're off again
   (Gents continue walking counter clockwise,
   left hands joined)
10. Swing your partners, one and all
11. Promenade your Honey around the hall

The dance is repeated three more times. The
original partners will then be together. Variation calls
for the Texas Star are explained below. The movements remain the same.

1. Ladies to the center and back to the bar
2. Gents go in with a right hand star
3. With a diddle-da, diddle-da, diddle-da-do
4. Back with your left and away you go
5. Hurry now and don't be slow
6. Pick up the next gal and away you go

Chorus remains the same

1. Ladies to the center and back to the bar
2. Gents go in with a right hand star
3. Back with your left and how do you do
4. I'm just fine and how are you
5 and 6 may be the same as above

Chorus remains the same

Forward Up Six and Back

Tune: *Durang's Hornpipe*

1. First couple to the right, you circle four, you circle four
2. Leave that lady, go on to the next and circle three hands round
   (Head gent leaves his partner behind with gent two and continues to second couple. First lady is on gent two's left)
3. Take that lady along with you, circle four, circle four
   (Head gent takes a lady three with him to couple four and they circle to the left)
4. Leave that lady go home alone, oh the du-da-day
   (Head gent leaves lady three and returns home. Lady three stands to the left of gent four)

Chorus:

5. Forward up six and back
   (Ladies one and two and gent two walk forward four steps to meet ladies three and four and gent four, and all bow; then they walk backward to place)
6. Gents with a do-si-do
   (Gent one and three do-si-do)
7. Make that arch and make it high, pass the ladies below
   (Gent two and four raise their partners left arm into an arch, and, as ladies two and four walk toward their left in front of their partner, ladies one and three walk under the arch going to their right. Ladies three and two are now with gent one. Ladies one and four are now with gent three)
8. Forward up six and back
   Ladies one and three and gent one walk forward four steps to meet ladies one and four and gent three, and bow, then walk backward to place
9. Gent with a do-si-do
   (Gents two and four do-si-do)
10. With a hey and a hi and a little piece of pie, pass the ladies below
    (Gents one and three raise their right arms to make an arch; ladies three and one walk to their right under the arch, while ladies three and one walk to their right under the arch to gent two and four. Ladies two and four walk to their left to the side of gent two and four

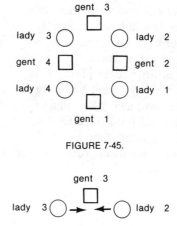

FIGURE 7-45.

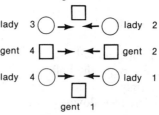

FIGURE 7-46.   Forward up six and back.

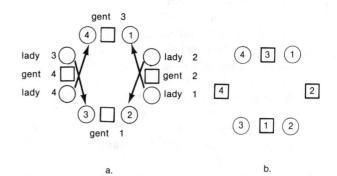

a.   b.

FIGURE 7-47.

FIGURE 7-48.   Forward up six and back.

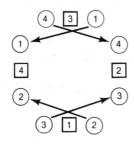

a.

12. Repeat calls 8, 9, 10

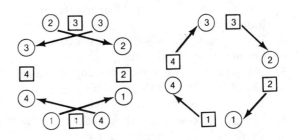

FIGURE 7-51.

c.

FIGURE 7-49.   Make that arch, make it high, pass the lady below.

13. Swing your partner
    (Gent's partner is now on his right)
14. Promenade

Couples two, three and four do the dance (1) through (14).

11. Repeat calls 5, 6, 7

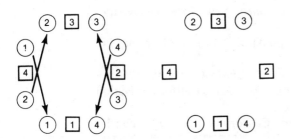

FIGURE 7-50.

Birdie in the Cage

Tune: *Mulberry Bush*

1. First couple to the right, you circle four,
     you circle four
2. Bird in the cage and close the door, circle
     three hands round
     (First lady steps into the center of the circle
     as the other three join hands)
3. The birdie jumps out, the crow jumps in, with
     a silly little grin
     (First lady steps out and joins hands with
     couple two, while the head gent steps into
     the center)
4. Then those two couples take a swing, you
     swing your birdie around
     (Each gent swings his partner)
5. It's on to the next and circle four, etc.
6. It's on to the last and circle four, etc.
7. Then everybody swing
8. Promenade

Couples two, three and four repeat the above pattern in turn.

EXERCISE   Definitions and List of Terms (Square Dancing)

1. In _____ , the gent takes his partner's right hand and they walk around each other.
2. It is called a _____ step when you step with your right foot sideways and kick your left foot across.
3. The swinging step which is most often used in square dancing is the _____ step.
4. Couple three is facing the _____ .
5. The prompters for square dancing are called the _____ .
6. The lady on the gent's left is his _____ .
7. The _____ is on the lady's right.
8. The _____ couple has their backs to the caller.
9. There are _____ couples to a set.
10. Couples one and three are the _____ couple.
11. On the call _____ the couple moves to the center of the set, then face the right hand couple.
12. When partners walk counter clockwise around the set in a skating position, it is called _____ .
13. The lady is always on the gent's _____ side.
14. In a do-si-do you always pass _____ shoulders.
15. Gents walk to the center, join right hands and move clockwise around the center is called _____ .
16. The couple facing the caller is the _____ couple.
17. _____ couples are the second and fourth couples.
18. The couple who is active is the _____ couple.

1. Allemade right with partner	7. Corner gent	13. Right
2. Balance	8. First	14. Right
3. Buzz	9. Four	15. Star by right
4. Caller	10. Head	16. Third
5. Callers	11. Lead to the right	17. Two side
6. Corner	12. Promenade	18. Visiting

BIBLIOGRAPHY (MODERN DANCE)

Books

Barrow, Billie, *A Method for Teaching Creative Dance*. New Haven Connecticut: Bartlett Hoffman, Inc., 1970.

Cheney, Gay and Strader, Janet, *Modern Dance*. Boston: Allyn and Bacon, Inc., 1975.

Ellfeldt, Lois, *A Primer for Choreographers*. Palo Alto, California: National Press Books, 1967.

H'Doubler, Margaret, *Dance, A Creative Art Experience*. Milwaukee: University of Wisconsin Press, 1966.

Hayes, Elizabeth, *An Introduction to the Teaching of Dance*. New York: University of Utah, Ronald Press Company, 1964.

Joyce, Mary, *First Steps in Teaching Creative Dance*. Palo Alto, California: National Press Books, 1973.

Lockhart, Aileene, *Modern Dance*. Dubuque, Iowa: Wm. C. Brown Company, 1966.

Penrod, James and Plastino, Janice, *The Dancer Prepares*. Palo Alto, California: National Press Books, 1970.

Sherbon, Elizabeth, *On the Count of One*. Palo Alto, California: Mayfield Publishing Company, 1975.

Winter, Shirley, *Creative Rhythmic Movement,* Dubuque, Iowa: Wm. C. Brown Company, 1975.

Records

Accompaniment for Dance Technique, Freda Miller. Northport, Long Island New York: Freda Miller Records.

Afro-American Jazz Dance, Johnny Frigo. Evanston, Ill.: Orlon.

Afro-American Jazz Dance, Gus Giordano. Deal, New Jersey: Kimbo Educational Records

Electronic Music, Otto Luening. New York: Columbia.

Improvisations for Modern Dance, Series I & II, Sarah Malament, New York: Sarah Malament.

Motivations for Modern Dance, Ruth White. Downey, California: Rhythms Productions

Music for Contemporary Dance, Vol. 2, Ruth White, Downey California: Rhythms Productions

Music for Modern Dance, Cameron McCosh. Waldwick, New Jersey: Dance Records, Inc.

Piano for Modern Dance, Quin Adamson. Ann Arbor, Michigan: Liberty Music Shop, Inc.

Rhythms for Modern Dance, Cameron McCosh, Great Neck, New York: Classroom Materials, Inc.

Strictly Percussion, Daniel Barrajanos. Waldwick, New Jersey: Hoctor Dance Records, Inc.

Films

Basic Movement, Perry-Mansfield Motion Pictures. Steamboat Springs, Colorado: Basic group exercises for flexibility.

Body Mechancis and Fundamental Movement, Mansfield Motion Pictures. Steamboat Springs, Colorado: Exercises for the individual and demonstrations.

Modern Dance Composition, Thorne Films. 1717 Hillside Rd. Boulder, Colorado: Elements of composition and technique.

Sound and Movement, Barbara Mettler Studio. 242 Newbury St., Boston: Movement improvisation accompanied by sound of voice, hands, feet and variety of instruments.

The Dancer's World, Rembrandt Films. 267 W. 25th St. N.Y.C. New York. Martha Graham explains the dancer's craft, while members of her company illustrate with dance.

Youth Dances, Contemporary Films. 267 W. 25th St. N.Y.C. New York. Depicts growth in benefits from training in modern dance; with students ages 4 through teenage.

BIBLIOGRAPHY (SQUARE DANCE)

Books

Kraus, Richard, *Square Dances of Today.* New York: McGraw-Hill Book Company, 1955.

Kraus, Richard, *Folk Dancing.* New York: McGraw-Hill Book Company, 1962.

Metheny, Eleanor, *Movement and Meaning.* New York: McGraw-Hill Book Company, 1968.

Phillips, Patricia, *Contemporary Square Dance.* Dubuque, Iowa: Wm. C. Brown Company, 1968.

Physical Education Activities for Girls and Women. Dubuque, Iowa: Wm. C. Brown Company, 1967.

Putney and Flood, H. H., *Square Dance.* Dubuque, Iowa: Wm. C. Brown Company, 1955.

Records

Honor Your Partner, Square Dance Associates, Ed Durlacher, caller.
Album No. 1
Susanna, Heads and Sides, Honolulu Baby, Do-si-do and Swing, Around the Outside and Swing, Two Head Ladies Cross Over
Album No. 2

Yankee Doodle, Sweet Alice Waltz Quadrille, Duck for the Oyster, Ladies Chain, Darling Nellie Gray, Push Her Away

Album No. 3

Loch Lomond, Ladies Grand Chain, Waltz Quadrille, Texas Star, Left Hand Lady Pass Under, My Little Girl, The Basket

Album No. 4

Forward Up Four, Six, and Eight, The Virginia Reel, Lady Walpole's Reel, The Grange Hall, Honor Your Partner

Album No. 8

Uptown and Downtown, Red River Valley, Portland Fancy, Bachelor Shack, Standard Waltz Quadrill, My Little Girl, Nellie Bly, Texas Star

Album No. 18

Ladies Chain the Mountain, Nine Pin, Hot Time in the Old Town, Progressive Three, Cross Trail, Around One, Back to Back, Old Kentucky Home, Back to Donegal

Let's Square Dance, R.C.A., Edited by Richard Kraus.

Album No. 1 (grades 3 and 4)

Honor, Circle, Swing, Promenade, Do-si-do, Grand Right and Left

Album No. 2 (grades 5 and 6)

Life on the Ocean Wave, Nellie Gray, Double Sashay, etc.

Album No. 3 (grades 7 and 8)

Right Hand Star, Captain Jinks, Coming 'Round the Mountain, Virginia Reel, etc.

Album No. 4 (grades 9 and 10)

Pattycake Polka, Swing Like Thunder, Texas Star, First Girl to the Right, etc.

Album No. 5 (grades 11 and 12)

When Johnny Comes Marching Home, Wearing of the Green, Hot Time in the Old Town, When the Work's All Done, etc.

Square Dances, Album A. 474 Decca, Al Macleod's Country Dance Band. Ed. Durlacher, caller.

She'll Be Comin' Round the Mountain When She Comes, Billy Boy, Grapevine Twist, Dip' N' Dive, Mademoiselle from Armentieres, Cowboys's Dream

Square Dances, R.C.A. Victor, Carson Robinson and his Pleasant Valley Boys, Lawrence V. Loy, caller.

Album P-155

Spanish Cavaliero, Irish Washerwoman, Solomon Levi, Comin' Round the Mountain, Jingle Bells, Paddy Bear, Golden Slippers, Turkey in the Straw

Square Dances, Set C-47 Columbia, Carson Robinson and his Old Timers, Lawrence V. Loy, caller.

The First Two Ladies Cross Over, Darling Nellie Gray, Buffalo Boy Go Round the Outside, Oh Susannah, Dive for the Oyster, Little Brown Jug, Possum in the Simmon Tree

Square Dances, Album 5 MGM, Carson Robinson and his Square Dance Music, Lawrence V. Loy, caller.

Bob's Favorite, Hook' in' a Whirl, Head Couples Seaparate, Lady Round the Lady, The Maverick, Pokeberry Promenade

Square Dances, Piute Pete and his Country Cousins.

Buffalo Gals, Red River Valley, Steam Boat, Looby Loo, Shoo Fly, Duck for the Oyster

Square Dance Films

American Square Dance, Coronet Instructional Films, 65 E. South Water St. Chicago. Positions and terms of square dance.

Let's Square Dance (6 reels), Audio-Visual Center, Indiana University, Bloomington, Indiana. Includes: "Forward Up Six", "Texas Star", "Take a Little Peek", "Split the Ring".

Promenade All, Western Square Dancing, Gateway Production. 1859 Powell St., San Francisco. Square dance figures.

Square Dancing, Bob Osgood. 462 N. Robertson Blvd., Los Angeles. Depicts fun of square dancing; some patterns and fundamentals shown.

8

FENCING

DESCRIPTION OF THE ACTIVITY

The original function of fencing, or dueling, was to inflict injury or kill the enemy. The objective today is to score points by a touch, or by making contact with the weapon within the legal target area to inflict a hypothetical wound as evidenced by a flexing of the weapon. The legal target areas for the three weapons are: (1) *épée*—any part of the body, (2) *sabre*—the upper body only, including the head and arms and the trunk to the groin, and (3) *foil* —the upper torso from the neck to the groin in front and from the neck to the waist in back, with the front and back connected by an imaginary horizontal line passing across the top of the hips to the groin. Points are scored each time a valid touch occurs or an opponent is forced off the end or side of the official area. The first competitor scoring five touches is declared the winner, with a bout limited to ten minutes. In the event of a tie, a "sudden death" tie breaker is employed in which the first fencer scoring a touch is declared the winner.

To initiate a match, fencers face one another in a position of attention at opposite ends of the strip, or fencing area, each holding the mask by the free, or left arm and the foil by the right hand. Competitors advance toward the center line, give the official salute to the president, the judges, and to each other, and then assume the on guard position. With the command, "Gentlemen, on guard," fencers cross blades and step back out of attack range. Once action begins, fencers observe the rule of *right of way,* that is, the first fencer to execute an offensive action by extending his weapon arm toward the target area may attempt to score a touch, with such action having to be parried by the opponent before

any counterscoring action is taken. Fencers also observe the rule of *phrase d'armes,* or the orderly exchange of blade action. The competitor scored upon acknowledges a touch by coming to a position of attention and pointing to the site of contact with his free hand. Touches are not indicated by the touched fencer until they are acknowledged by the president. Once the validity of the touch is determined by the president, competitors return to the on guard position at the center of the strip and resume action. If the touch is declared invalid, they return to the place where play ceased, and resume action. A halt is called and the sequence of play stopped after all touches. Attack maneuvers, parries, advances, lunges, retreats, and recoveries are used in an attempt to score five touches and thus win the bout. Competitors remove their masks and shake hands upon termination of the bout.

An official fencing area is shown in Figure 8–1. The surface is usually rubber—linoleum or cork mats are used in indoor championship matches— and must not provide an advantage to either competitor in relation to slope or lighting. The official strip varies in size ranging from 5 feet 10⅞ inches to 6 feet 6¾ inches in width and 40 feet in length. A 6 feet 6¾-inch extension is recommended at both ends to provide ample and equal retreating conditions for fencers who cross the rear limit. An official AFLA (Amateur Fencers League of America) fencing strip must possess five parallel one-inch lines across the width of the strip: (1) center line, (2) two on guard lines, and (3) two warning lines. The NCAA (National Collegiate Athletic Association) and ICFA (Intercollegiate Fencing Association) permit an alternate marking system with only three lines—a center line and two visual warning lines—

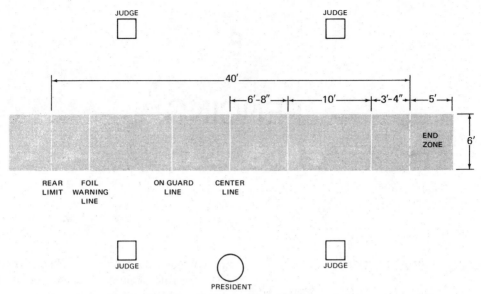

FIGURE 8–1. Fencing area and position of jury.

across the width, making the two on guard lines optional.

EQUIPMENT

Fencing attire is designed both for maximum protection and efficiency of movement. It varies slightly for the three weapons but consists basically of a mask, a jacket, a glove, and rubber-soled shoes. The uniform available for use with all three weapons consists of a fairly heavy, lined jacket, a three-weapon mask with heavy mesh in front and additional protection on the top and back of the head, a pigskin glove, and trousers that cover the knee. The uniform must be completely white. An improvised uniform for class purposes consists of a large-sized sweat shirt (arms quilted with cotton and muslin), old pigskin gloves, sweat pants with padding on the lead thigh, and tennis shoes. Equipment should be inspected periodically and kept in top condition if injuries are to be avoided.

Mask

The mask is made of wire mesh with a metal framework and a bib attachment of cloth at the lower edge, offering maximum protection for the face and neck. Additional leather padding on the sides and top provide protection from sabre cuts that often strike these areas. The mask should be light and cool and inspected thoroughly prior to each use.

Jacket

The jacket protects the arms and body and possesses a padded·front and a padded upper arm and armpit on the weapon side. The inner lining should reach from the shoulder to the elbow of the weapon arm. A half jacket, called a *plastron*, is used in practice sessions; however, it protects only the front and weapon side of the body. Jackets, made of gabardine, duck, or canvas material, should fit tightly and permit efficiency of movement.

Glove

The glove is optional protection for the weapon hand and arm and should always be used in practice to prevent minor cuts. A tight fit of pliable material, with padding on the back of the hand and double thickness at points of most wear—the end and the base of the thumb—is recommended. It should also have an attachment extending over the jacket sleeve to prevent blade entry up the arm.

Shoes

Light, rubber-soled, flat-heeled shoes, geared for traction and efficiency of movement are used with woolen socks. On a cork or linoleum piste, or fencing strip, special canvas or leather of soft composition should be used. With an electric foil, rubber-soled shoes must be worn.

Scoring Equipment

Red ink (for the épée), score sheets, and an electrical scoring machine have become a part of modern fencing competition. The ink is applied to a three-pointed button (*point d'arrêt*) which can be attached to the blade tip to aid in determining the validity of a touch in épée. At present, an electric sabre has not been perfected for competitive use. Electric épées and foils, with buttons at their points that depress on contact to register a touch on a central machine, remove much of the subjectivity and difficulty of judging. Foil fencers must wear a metallic jacket, over the regular fencing jacket, that covers only the legal target area. Since the legal touch area in épée covers the entire body, no special equipment is needed.

Weapons

The three basic weapons are shown in Figure 8–2. The French foil is somewhat more popular in modern fencing; however, equally strong arguments may be presented for the Italian foil. Advocates of the French foil feel that accuracy is increased through a lighter grip and improved balance. Proponents of the Italian foil argue that equal accuracy exists, with added strength provided by the strap and cross bar.

Foil.   The foil is considered the basic fencing weapon carried over from dueling practices in the past and is the concern of this chapter. Initial training with the foil will enhance skill with the sabre and épée. The foil blade is pointed and tapers from a thin, rigid section near the handle (*forte*) to a very thin resilient portion at the tip (*foible*). A 3-to 4-inch metal disc (*guard*) is attached to protect the hand. The overall length is approximately 34 to 35 inches. It has a wooden grip, or handle, terminating with a balance weight known as a *pommel*.

Épée.   The épée is also a pointed weapon although heavier and less flexible than the foil. The guard is approximately 4 to 5 inches wider to increase hand protection, while the blade is triangular to decrease blade flexibility without increasing the weight of the sword. Épée and foil fencing differ only in relation to scoring: in épée the right-of-way rule is eliminated and the target area is extended to the entire body. Épée fencing probably simulates a true fight more closely than does fencing with the

other two weapons; however, it has decreased in popularity in recent years mainly due to scoring imperfections that cause opponents to adopt the tactic of "beating the bell" by concentrating on quick touches rather than the daring attack and the more colorful, dangerous moves that could be employed in a life-death duel (a quick arm touch scores a point but is not very exciting fencing).

Sabre.   The sabre is a weapon similar to a cavalry sword. The blade is either triangular or T-shaped, with a point and simulated cutting edge that covers the entire front and one third of the back of the weapon. The guard extends to the very end of the

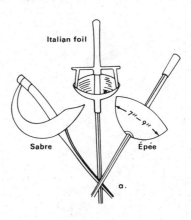

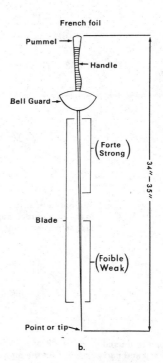

FIGURE 8–2.   Basic weapons.

handle to protect the hand and knuckles. The blade is light and flexible and must make clear contact within the legal target area for a valid score to occur.

SKILLS AND TECHNIQUES OF FOIL FENCING

Grip

A light, firm grip is recommended with the pommel at the center of the wrist and the arm becoming merely an extension of the foil. The handle of the French foil is curved and possesses a rectangular section that forms a natural site for the placement of the palm. The convex side of the curve is placed in

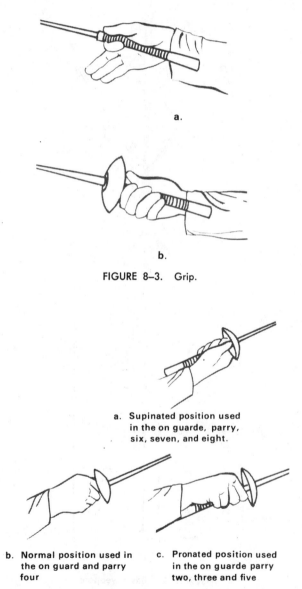

FIGURE 8–3. Grip.

a. Supinated position used in the on guarde, parry, six, seven, and eight.

b. Normal position used in the on guard and parry four

c. Pronated position used in the on guarde parry two, three and five

FIGURE 8–4. Basic hand positions.

the palm at the heel of the thumb; the index finger is hooked around the handle, with the area between the first and second joint resting on the shaft to oppose and touch the thumb; the thumb is placed on top of the shaft approximately one inch from the bell guard; and the remaining three fingers are wrapped around the handle, with the little finger resting on the shaft (see Figures 8–3 and 8–4 for grip technique and basic hand positions). The thumb and forefinger are the manipulators and provide the control in performing small movements of the blade tip, withdrawals, and high speed maneuvers. Fencers should avoid grasping the handle too tightly or curling the fingers too far around the handle, both of which hinder finger control and induce rapid fatigue.

Basic Positions

Salute. A position of attention is assumed prior to the initiation of the match to acknowledge the officials, the spectators, and one's opponent as well as to prepare for the on guard position. Feet are placed with the heels tightly together, forming a right angle, with the lead foot and the lead side of the body toward the opponent. The mask is held in the free hand at the hip, the foil, held in the weapon hand, points toward the opponent's feet, and the eyes face the opponent. To initiate the salute, the weapon is brought smoothly upward from the floor to a vertical position, with the palm toward the face, until the bell guard nears the level of the nose. The salute terminates with an extension of the foil horizontally toward the opponent (see Figure 8–5).

On Guard. The position of readiness is assumed to prepare fencers for maximum balance and efficiency of movement in all directions and also to decrease the target area for the opponent. The feet are placed a shoulder width apart (approximately fifteen inches) and at right angles to each other, with the knees slightly flexed and vertically in line with the instep or toes. The back is erect, the weight equally distributed over the feet, and the right side of the lead toe faces the opponent. The head remains erect and is turned slightly to the right. The free arm is raised behind the head to a position bringing the upper arm level or even with the shoulder, the elbow is flexed, forming a right angle with the upper arm, and the hand is flexed and relaxed behind the head. The weapon arm is partially extended, the elbow approximately six inches from the body, the palm upward, the blade tip aimed at the opponent's chin, and the hand at a point between the shoulder and the hip (on guard in sixth position).

Advance and Retreat. Gaining and breaking ground are basic movements in fencing used to approach an opponent for an attacking maneuver, to maintain the desired distance from an opponent when he moves back (the advance), or to force an opponent to advance by moving out of attacking range (the retreat). In both the advance and the retreat, fencers should avoid sliding the feet, raising the upper and lower torso, altering the on guard position in any way, or changing the distance between competitors. The advance is executed without a change in the spacing between the feet. The lead foot moves toward the attacker, the toe slightly raised and skimming the surface, and the back foot pushes off and moves forward, being lifted at the knee, to complete the action without a change in basic position. The retreat is performed in reverse order, with the heel of the lead leg providing the push-off as the back leg moves backward, followed by the front foot.

Balestra. The balestra is a variation of the advance in the form of a short jump forward, followed by a lunge. This involves a quick jump from the balls of both feet just above mat level. The fencer must adhere to the basic principles of the advance and take care not to alter the on guard position.

Flèche. The flèche consists of a short, rapid run to surprise attack an opponent who is out of lunge range. Since the attacker is off balance and open to a *stop hit,* or *riposte,* the touch must occur at the first possible opportunity. Body weight is shifted to the front foot as the weapon arm is extended and weight is thrown forward to the lead leg. The back leg leaves the piste, or fencing strip, and swings past the front foot, followed by quick running steps past the opponent. This maneuver should be used sparingly, be executed at the proper moment, involve rapid forward movement of the back leg, score a touch as the back leg leaves the mat, and should always include passing the opponent if a touch does not occur.

Backward Spring. The backward spring is a variation of the retreat and is used to move rapidly out of range of a touch after a lunge attack has failed. After performing the lunge, the fencer springs back quickly with his lead foot. He should land on his toes, with his lead foot beyond the spot originally occupied by his back foot. He then shifts or rocks his weight onto his back foot as his lead foot leaves the piste and assumes the proper on guard position.

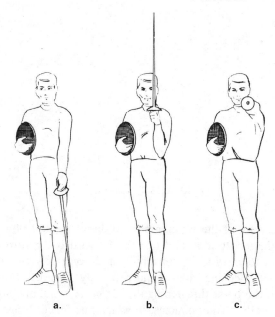

FIGURE 8–5. Salute.

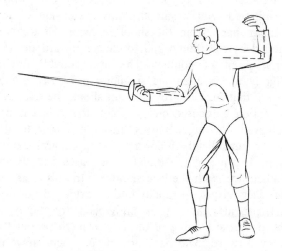

FIGURE 8–6. On guard position.

It is important to keep the weapon arm extended until proper position is reassumed and to strive for distance rather than vertical height in the spring.

Call. The call (*appel*) is used to indicate, to the opponent, a time out, or a stopping of the action. It consists of stamping the lead foot twice by raising the toes without shifting the weight completely to the back foot.

Lunge and Recovery

The lunge and the return to the on guard position stand as the most basic and important fundamentals of fencing. The two phases of the lunge are: (1) the

FIGURE 8–7. Lunge.

extension of the weapon arm to direct the foil point to the target area, and (2) the forward body movement to carry the point rapidly and accurately to the target. Fencing rules require a fully exended arm with the point threatening the target. A simultaneous hit by the two opponents, in which one fencer lunges with a flexed elbow and fails to establish the right of way, scores as a touch for his opponent. The lunge is initiated with a smooth, rapid extension of the weapon hand from the shoulder, with the weapon guided by the thumb and forefinger toward the desired point of contact. The arm should remain slightly higher than the shoulder and jerky movements that may destroy the aim should be avoided. Attention is focused on the point. If a touch is not achieved, the lunge moves the body closer to the target immediately following the rapid arm extension. The toe of the lead foot is raised slightly off the surface, with the heel skimming the piste, as the back leg pushes off rapidly into an extended position that provides the impetus and speed, together with the downward swing of the free arm, to propel the body forward. The back arm drops, palm upward, to a position parallel to and directly over the back leg. The action terminates with a flexed lead knee directly above the instep of the lead foot. Knee flexion beyond this point results in an overlunge and will hinder recovery while underflexion will result in a short reach and a failed touch attempt. In the lunge both feet are flat on the piste, the back leg and both arms are fully extended, the head is erect, and the weapon hand is at approximately eye level (see Figure 8–7).

The recovery phase begins immediately by transferring the weight of the body to the back leg and flexing the back knee. The toes of the lead foot are raised and a backward push is made with the heel as both arms return to the on guard position. These three movements—heel push, rear leg flexion, and upswing of the free arm—must be coordinated into one smooth action for maximum efficiency and protection against a counteraction. A *forward recovery* may be used should the opponent retreat. In this case the rear foot is brought forward to reestablish the proper base and reassume the on guard position.

Lines of Engagement

The legal target area in foil fencing, as delineated earlier, is the torso, from the neck to the groin in front (inside and outside high line) and from the neck to the waist in back, with the front and back connected by an imaginary horizontal line passing across the top of the hips to the groin (inside and outside low line). These four quadrants are classified into upper and lower lines with the bell guard serving as the divider. The inside lines lie toward the front of the body (to the left of the weapon from the fencer's viewpoint), and the outside lines lie toward the back (see Figure 8–8). These scoring areas obviously must be protected with the on guard position through either a palms up (supinated) or palms down (pronated) position of the weapon hand. The supinated position is more common in foil fencing. As the blade moves from high to low or from one side of the body to the other and as the weapon hand changes from a pronated to a half-supinated to a supinated position, the hand remains at the same, breast-high, guard position.

Each of the above mentioned quadrants have two guard positions, for a total of eight, which are named after the parry designed to protect this area. Of the

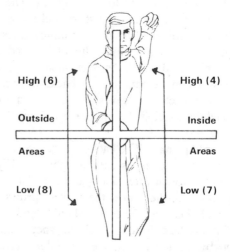

High (6)   High (4)

Outside   Inside

Areas   Areas

Low (8)   Low (7)

FIGURE 8–8. Target area and lines of engagement.

eight, four and six are most common (see Figure 8–9).

Blades are said to be engaged when the foibles of the two weapons are in contact as a protective action against a certain line. Thus, competitors may engage in fourth and sixth or other combinations depending upon the position of the weapons as contact is made. Engagement in sixte, for example, covers that line and deflects, without blade or body movement, any attempt to touch in that scoring area. The closing of one attack line allows a fencer to acquire a feel of the blade and predict somewhat more accurately his opponent's next move. Since a fencer decreases the target area with a parallel stance, the most vulnerable area is the pectoral muscle, which lies near the armpit and provides a flat surface for contact.

A change of engagement can be performed by merely passing the point under the opponent's blade to the opposite side through fingering and a small movement of the blade tip. Such a maneuver at the proper moment may upset an opponent's planned attack and force a change of tactics.

A double change of engagement—two in rapid succession—is even more effective in thwarting an attack. The final movement (point moves first) completely covers that line.

Fencing with the absence of the blade, or assuming the on guard position without crossing swords, is effective against opponents who are strong on blade techniques. Such tactics, although more common in

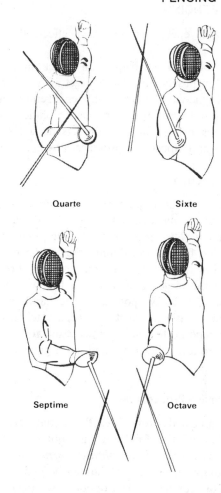

FIGURE 8–9. Basic on guard positions.

TABLE 8-1. Execution of guard positions.

Area	Guard Position	Execution
High inside line	Fourth guard position (garde en quarte)	The weapon hand moves to the left to a position where the blade tip points just over the opponent's near shoulder. The wrist moves, in a supinated position, slightly away from the pommel, with the handle remaining at the base below the thumb.
High outside line	Sixth guard position (garde en sixte)	The weapon hand moves to the right until the blade tip points just over the opponent's far shoulder. The hand rotates to the right until the knuckles of the thumb are directly to the side and the pommel is supported by the inside of the wrist.
Low inside line	Seventh guard position (garde en septieme)	The wrist breaks downward toward the piste as the weapon moves to a position just beyond the opponent's near knee.
Low inside line	Eighth guard position (garde en octave)	The blade moves to a position near the inside of the opponent's near knee as the wrist breaks downward toward the piste with the palm in a supinated position.

sabre and épée, can be used effectively in foil fencing.

An invitation, or baiting an attack in a desired line by purposely exposing a target area, can be used with absence of blades or by engagement and by exerting pressure on the opponent's blade to expose the opposite line. Such action sets up a score with a parry and riposte or provides attack openings.

Legal Touch

Fencing rules require the foil tip to strike the opponent clearly, distinctly, and with the quality of penetration. The fencer must "fix the point" through use of the fingers and thumb; the thumb forces the point downward and the index finger directs the point at the target. Such action is followed by a full extension of the weapon arm. The hand should be elevated slightly as the touch occurs to ensure the proper bend in the foil blade necessary for the judges to declare it a valid touch and not a graze or doubtful hit.

Offensive Procedures

As indicated previously, the initial attack—the extension of the foil arm and point toward the target area—begins the *phrase d'armes* and establishes the right of way, which can be ended only by an opponent's parry. The opponent's riposte, or return, then establishes his right of way, which also remains in effect until a succesful parry is executed. A phrase terminates with a touch (legal or illegal) or a separation of the two fencers.

Offensive attacks (described in Table 8–2) take the form of (1) *simple attacks*—single blade movements in the line of engagement or opposite line, (2) *compound attacks*—several blade movements, or feints, preceding the final blade action, (3) *blade attacks*—crossing blades to deflect the weapon from the target in order to open a particular line of attack, (4) *attacks taking the blade*—removing a menacing point from a line in preparation for an attack, (5) *renewed attacks*—designed to be parried by the opponent as a means of providing an opening for a successful counterattack, (6) *riposte*—a simple or compound return attack performed by a fencer who has parried an attack, and (7) *counterattacks*—offensive actions made on attacks by the opponent.

Simple Attacks. Simple attacks may be either direct and involve a single driving movement forward with one continuous action in the line of engagement, or indirect and be executed to a line opposite the original line of engagement in one continuous movement without a feint toward the target area. The most commonly used are the straight thrust, disengagement, counterdisengagement, and cut-over.

Compound Attacks. A compound attack is merely a combination of simple attacks such as a disengagement followed by a counterdisengagement or any number of other possible maneuvers combined into one action. The fencer must use the elements of surprise and timing successfully to perform two or more movements by feinting or controlling the opponent's blade thereby causing him to open a line. The initial action is designed to draw a premature parry by the opponent before the fencer thrusts in an open line. No blade contact should occur during the feints since such action would, under the rules, give the opponent the right to riposte and thus destroy the legality of the fencer's attack. By moving slightly ahead of the opponent as the compound attack is begun, blade contact can be avoided.

Compound attacks are executed either from a static position or progressively. From a *static* position, feints are performed without lunging until the final movement is completed, thereby enabling a fencer to observe the reaction of his opponent, diagnose the situation, and complete or alter the attack. A *progressive* compound attack is begun with feints as the blade point progresses and approaches the target in the initial attack stage. Once the attack is started, it is extremely difficult to alter plans since any hesitation provides the opponent with the opportunity to score with a stop thrust. The most common compound attacks are the one-two attack, one-two-three attack, and the double. The feint, or initial phase of any compound attack, is also described in Table 8–2.

Blade Attacks. Blade attacks serve one of two objectives: (1) to strike the opponent's blade out of line (the beat, the press, and the glide), or (2) to control the opponent's blade to touch (the bind and envelopment). Such attack procedures serve to open a line, control the blade, and invite an attack or feint prior to an attack and must be executed forte to the midblade of the opponent.

Attacks Taking the Blade. Attacks taking the blade, such as the bind and envelopment, differ from regular blade attacks and are designed to remove a menacing point by controlling the blade, removing

TABLE 8-2. Basic offensive procedures.

Action	Use	Execution
Simple Attacks		
Straight thrust (direct attack)	The straight thrust is used when an opponent is uncovered in a line, as the line opens and when an opponent changes a line of engagement, opens a line with absence of blade, or returns to the on guard position with an extension of the weapon arm.	From the on guard position, the weapon hand extends rapidly, slightly above shoulder level, toward the target area in the line a fencer is engaged to complete a straight lunge. A *coule*, or gliding of the blade along that of the opponent, may be used against a fencer who has only partially covered a line. The foil arm must be extended fully without hesitation to eliminate loss of touch due to insufficient reach or loss of right of way. A lunge may or may not follow depending upon the distance of the opponent.
Disengagement (indirect attack)	The disengagement is used when an opponent exerts pressure on the blade, changes engagements to cover a new line, returns to an engagement after fencing with absence of the blade, and to deceive lateral blade defensive movements.	The fencer passes his blade under that of the opponent, simultaneously extending his arm and utilizing finger control with a relaxed arm and shoulder, before thrusting to an open line with a lunge and covering the new line upon completion of the movement. Fine blade action keeps the two weapons close together at all times. Fencers must strive to decrease time and distance by combining the disengagement and lunge into one progressive attack rather than first executing one then the other in independent movements.
Counterdisengagement (individual attack)	The counterdisengagement is used when an opponent makes circular movements with the blade.	This maneuver is similar to the engagement; however, it terminates in the same line as the original engagement. It is initiated as an opponent changes his line by circling the blade around and extending the arm into the original line to encourage the opponent to take the blade. Finger play, arm extension, and the lunge must again be coordinated into one smooth progressive movement.
Cut-over (coupe)	The cut-over is used when an opponent pressures the blades, maintains a low point or guard, and to deceive lateral blade defensive movements.	This maneuver is less difficult to perform than the disengagement and involves opposite blade action. The entire weapon passes rapidly over the top of the opponent's weapon with minimum blade withdrawal through the use of the manipulators and a slightly flexed elbow and wrist. The blade moves to an open line immediately upon passing close to the opponent's blade through a full extension on the downward movement, followed by a lunge. Wide blade movements should be avoided in such a dangerous maneuver since it involves a flexed arm (right of way not established) and thus can be scored upon by a quick arm extension of the opponent.
Compound Attacks		
Feint	The feint is used to initiate a compound attack and to thwart an opponent who executes a stop thrust into the fencer's attack.	The feint is merely a fake attack, such as a straight thrust, cut-over, disengagement that must simulate the actual attack maneuver in every detail to draw a defensive response, or parry. The parry can be deceived, or thwarted, and followed by a thrust to an open line. Only aggressive, definite feints will draw defensive responses and set up compound attack maneuvers. A false attack is similar to a feint and is performed with either a partial or full lunge.

TABLE 8-2. (continued)

Action	Use	Execution
One-two attack	The one-two attack is used when an opponent makes a lateral parry in response to a feint of disengagement.	From the on guard position in sixth, the weapon arm is extended and disengaged from the open parry four. As the opponent attempts a parry four, the blade disengages under that of the attacker to assume the open sixth line and lunge toward the target area. The entire action consists of feinting a disengagement, deceiving a direct parry, and disengaging to score in an open line (two disengagements). Avoid permitting the parry to touch the blade, disengaging too deep, or lunging at the incorrect moment.
One-two-three attack	The one-two-three attack is used against very skilled fencers.	This maneuver is similar to the one-two attack with the addition of another disengagement to make two successive parries. From the on guard in sixth, the blade disengages, threatens an open line and acquires a parry four by the opponent. The parry is deceived by a disengagement into sixth and that parry also deceived by still another disengagement into the open four line to be followed by a lunge to the target area.
Double	The double is used when an opponent resorts to a circular or counterparry in response to a feint of disengagement.	A double is merely a disengagement followed by a counterdisengagement (two disengagements in the same direction). From the on guard position in sixth, the offensive fencer disengages into an open fourth line. A circle parry six occurs by the opponent to force the blade back to the closed sixth line. Prior to blade contact on the opponent's attempted parry six, a second disengagement is made into the open fourth line before lunging into that same open line.
Blade Attacks Beat	The beat is used to encourage an opponent to attack and thus secure an opening in an opposite line, to open a closed line. It is most commonly used from engagement in fourth and is weak and ineffective from sixth position.	All blade attacks are used to deflect the blade and secure an open line. Both the direct beat and the exchange beat (preceded by a change in engagement or circular movement to the opposite side) are executed with a sharp blow on the blade by an opening and closing of the last three fingers (opening reduces blade contact while closing permits a rapid beat on the blade). The weapon arm remains slightly flexed to permit blade contact forte to foible with the manipulators providing the control and force which varies from a *strong* beat (to provide an opening for a direct attack before the line is closed) to a *light* beat (to elicit a reaction that can be followed by an individual or compound attack). As the beat terminates, the foil arm must fully extend to acquire the right of way.
Press	The press is used to obtain a return press from the opponent to be followed by a cut-over or disengagement, to obtain an open line to touch with a release that moves the opponent's blade out of line, and during or immediately following a change of engagement.	The foil tip remains in line, fingers firmly in contact with the weapon, as only slight arm motion removes the blade from line by lateral pressure (not a striking action as described in the beat—merely pressure mid-blade to foible or midblade) before performing a full extension of the weapon arm for the hit. Mastery of the press also requires ability to diagnose the reaction of the opponent on the blade. The fencer must apply pressure accordingly and execute follow-up, offensive tactics in open lines.

TABLE 8-2. (continued)

Action	Use	Execution
Glide	The glide is used when an opponent maintains a light weapon hand or relaxes his guard and when he does not react to a beat or press.	Blades remain in contact as the foil arm is rapidly extended and moved to touch by sliding to the target area if the line is open and disengaging if the line is closed. The arm extends slightly, the last three fingers close, the wrist assumes a flexed, pronated position in preparation for a powerful graze along the blade, and a full arm extension occurs as the action terminates.
Attacks Taking the Blade		
Bind	The bind is used to remove an opponent's extended arm and threatening blade by forcing the tip out of line and establishing the right of way.	With blades engaged and continuous contact maintained, a half circular movement is used to carry the opponent's blade from a high to low line (sixth to seventh) on the opposite side of the target. Blade contact is made forte to foible as the point remains at hip level. The action is reversed from an engagement in a low line with the blade elevated (point slightly out of line) to force the opponent's blade upward and across to the opposite high line before the arm extension and lunge occurs for the touch. A fencer should avoid extending his arm prematurely and causing the opponent's weapon to contact the body or legs as it passes from a low to a high line.
Envelopment	The envelopment is used when an opponent uses a fully extended, rigid weapon arm and to deflect a threatening blade and obtain a blade position on top of the opponent's weapon.	The envelopment actually consists of two binds. It controls and moves the opponent's blade in a complete circle (in a high or low line), followed by a glide or similar offensive attack for the touch in the original engagement without loss of blade contact. Again, blade contact occurs forte to foible, with control maintained through use of the manipulators and a rotating wrist to ensure a small circle (away from the target—clockwise from on guard in sixth and counterclockwise from on guard in fourth). This attack is generally made from the on guard position in sixth and cannot be used against a flexed arm of an opponent.
Renewed Attacks		
Remise	The remise is used against an opponent who parries or avoids an attack in any manner and has opened a line without executing a riposte, when an attacker's first attempt to hit fails, and when an opponent uses a delayed or compound riposte.	A remise is a continuation of attack following the very same line of the original attack without withdrawing the weapon arm by performing additional blade movements or returning to the on guard position. This must precede the final action of a riposte in order to maintain the established right of way. Attempts should be made to execute the remise "covered" in order to deflect the riposte as it is executed.
Redoublement	The redoublement is used against an opponent who fails to riposte or delays his riposte after being parried, against an opponent who parries and also keeps the line closed, and after an opponent uses a compound riposte.	The redoublement is similar to the remise; however, it includes a new arm movement and is *not* a direct continuation of the original attack. The attacker remains in the lunge, bringing the opponent close, before executing a new attack from this position.

TABLE 8-2. (continued)

Action	Use	Execution
Reprise	The reprise is used when an attack has been parried, the on guard position assumed, and a riposte by the opponent is not used.	The reprise differs from the remise and redoublement since the fencer returns to the on guard position momentarily by withdrawing in a normal recovery or forward recovery to maintain proper distance in preparation for a return lunge. The reprise can be used with a simple or compound movement and should be performed quickly and smoothly.
Riposte Direct	The direct riposte is used against an opponent who flexes his weapon arm after returning to the on guard position.	The riposte, in general, is used as the attack is terminating. It is used in the low line against an opponent who maintains a high weapon hand or withdraws his hand to recover from a lunge. In the direct riposte, the blade moves in a direct thrust (shortest route) from the position of the parry to touch. A hit may occur through the use of a coule, or moving along the opponent's blade to a touch.
Indirect	The indirect riposte is used against a fencer who closes the direct line after a successful parry by the opponent.	An opponent who covers the line where he anticipates a direct riposte is susceptible in the opposite line to a cut-over or disengagement. Control is acquired through finger play and use of a partially flexed arm (due to closeness of competitors) until the defender's foil tip enters the new line.
Compound	The compound riposte is used when it is not possible to score with a direct or indirect riposte.	A compound riposte involves the use of one or more feints based on the direct thrust, cut-over, disengagement, and counterdisengagement. As indicated in the use of the direct and indirect riposte, fencers are extremely close making it necessary to execute feints with a slightly flexed elbow.
Counter	The counter is used as a planned technique to draw a parry and riposte in a desired line.	A counter riposte is an offensive action following a successful parry of the opponent's riposte or counter-riposte. All ripostes following the first are classified as counter-ripostes and are numbered consecutively in order of use. Counter-ripostes (compound or simple) are combined with a lunge, during recovery, or with a new lunge, depending upon the existing spacing between fencers. Refined arm movement and finger control as well as constant adjustment to distance are essential to success in the execution of a counter-riposte.
Counterattacks Stop thrust	The stop thrust is used against a slow opponent with poor timing, when an opponent attacks without extending his arm to establish the right of way, against an attack that is combined with an advance as the opponent's foot is lifted, when an opponent feints and moves his blade out of line, and when an opponent withdraws his weapon arm in advance.	The stop thrust is performed without an attempt to contact the opponent's blade. Major emphasis is placed on making contact ahead of the attacker whose blade tip may also move to touch. Proper form consists of a rapid, straight arm extension toward the target area, with or without the lunge, depending upon fencing distance. It is designed to take the *time* from a poorly executed attack and is valid if a touch occurs before the final movement of a compound attack.

TABLE 8-2. (continued)

Action	Use	Execution
Time thrust	The time thrust is used against a slow opponent with poor timing, against a simple or compound attack, against an attacker who does not wait for a reaction to a feint.	The time thrust is a less dangerous counterattack maneuver since the thrust is made with opposition (finding the opponent's blade) that closes the line of attack. Against a one-two or double attack, the thrust is executed as the opponent feints. An extension of the weapon arm or disengagement in the closed line to touch can also be used.

the tip from line, and initiating an attack. Blades must be engaged before these two attacks can be used to acquire the right of way by removing the threatening point.

Renewed Attacks. Renewed attacks are performed immediately after an original attack has failed and are merely a continuation of an original attack following a delayed parry or the absence of a riposte by the opponent. The type of return by the opponent must be anticipated and a decision must be made whether to return to the on guard position or to remain in the lunge and execute the offensive maneuver. The remise, redoublement, and the reprise are the most common renewed attacks.

Riposte. The riposte, actually a form of counterattack, is used by a fencer who has executed a successful parry. A fencer executes a riposte following a parry in an attempt to obtain a touch before his opponent can recover from his attack maneuver. Such action (successive parry) establishes the right of way over the continuation of an attack by the opponent and permits a valid touch. Either a static position or lunge can be used depending upon the proximity of the opponent. The four basic types of ripostes—direct, indirect, counter, and compound—may take the form of an *immediate* riposte—a rapid, direct thrust following the rebound from a parry—or a *delayed* riposte—one following a brief pause whereby a fencer breaks the cadence, changes tactics, and forces his opponent to use a premature response. A delayed riposte that follows a parry loses the right of way to an opponent who retakes the attack.

Counterattacks. A counterattack is an offensive action performed against an attack or one that follows a riposte that has been parried. The stop thrust and the time thrust are the most common and both involve the use of time. Ideally they are executed when an opponent attacks with a slow movement or fails to extend his weapon arm to establish the right

of way. Simple counterattack procedures are generally used to actually draw the attacker into the blade tip. The term "attacks on preparation" applies to such maneuvers when they are used just as the opponent initiates the forward movement of an attack.

Defensive Procedures

As with many other sports, the best defense is a good offense through aggressive, controlled attacks. However, mastery of defensive fundamentals is basic to sound fencing and may take the form of a simple parry (followed by a riposte and a touch), a deflection of the point from the target area, or a stopping of an attack as it is being prepared.

Blade defense of any type is called a parry and may involve a *block*—placement of the weapon merely to protect the body by contacting the opponent's foil—or a *beat*—striking the opponent's blade sharply. Aggressive parries take the right of way from the opponent. Parries must deflect the blade to the side, as opposed to up or down, and they serve the purpose of providing a barrier in the path of attack of the opponent.

The foil arm remains in the same relative position (in line) unless the opponent is extremely close and forces a withdrawal maneuver prior to the parry. Such procedure permits a quick return action through control of time and position. This is not possible on forceful attacks deflecting the blade.

In the best on guard position for the parry, the hand is at chest level with the elbow approximately a hand's breadth from the body. Blade contact is made forte to foible of the attacker's weapon (strong portion to weak) regardless of the type of parry employed. Before the parry is initiated, a slight retreat, which does not eliminate the effectiveness of a riposte, will decrease the probability of a hit should the parry be unsuccessful.

Two parries protect each of the four quadrants of the target area. Parries four, six, seven, and eight are performed with the hand in a supinated or half-supinated position while parries one, two, three, and five (rarely used in modern fencing) are performed with a pronated hand position (see Figure 8–4 for the basic hand positions).

Simple Parries. Parries falling into this classification (four and six) merely involve a rapid change of the on guard position and are designed to defend the high inside and outside lines. Simple parries are executed by *detachment*—the opponent's blade is released as soon as contact is made to permit the use of a riposte or the transfer of the blade to another line—or by *opposition*—maintaining contact with the blade to cover that line or to execute a riposte along the blade. The blade is contacted through the use of the fingers, wrist, and forearm with either a sharp beat, called the beat parry, or lateral pressure to move the point out of line. Opposition parries enable the defender to control the attack and feel the reactions of the opponent.

Semicircular Parries. A semicircular parry is an indirect parry taken from a high line engagement to present an attack into a low line or one from a low to a high line. The semicircular parry, in which the blade makes a half circle, is always executed when there is opposition from a low to a high line or high to low line on the same side of the target (on guard in sixth to seventh, fourth to seventh, seventh to fourth, seventh to sixth). The semicircular parries seven and eight are described in Table 8–3.

Circular Parries. A circular parry is merely a rapid change of the on guard position. A counter-parry exists for each of the target areas. The fencer's blade makes a circle around the opponent's blade and returns to the original line of engagement without a change in defensive position. The blade moves under the opponent's blade when there is an attack in a high line and over the opponent's blade in a low line attack. Fingering, or the execution of small movements of the blade, is the key to successful circular parries that provide defensive variety and often upset the offensive strategy of the opponent.

BASIC STRATEGY

The extent to which the many and varied strategic maneuvers are utilized depends upon mastery of the fundamentals outlined. In a sport such as fencing, strategy is based on split second decisions and therefore calls for the use of basic movements that have

been soundly mastered and can be executed correctly with rapidity and poise. In order to plan his strategy a fencer must test the physical reactions of his opponent—his speed, quickness of blade and foot, length of extremities, timing, and aggressiveness—and his skills—his strengths and weaknesses. He must uncover his opponent's attack and parry preferences in various situations: his responses to a feint, an attack on the blade, a change of engagement, a simple attack, a compound attack, a renewed attack, and a counterattack. He must maintain constant movement on the strip, control time and distance, concentrate on the target with proper peripheral vision, execute feints early in the bout in order to analyze his opponent's response, and avoid the establishment of fencing patterns.

Strategy deals with *what* action to apply, and *how* and *when* to apply it. The following additional suggestions are provided to supply beginning fencers with answers to these three aspects of competitive fencing:

Situation Strategy

1. Attack areas of weakness and avoid areas of strength, using the change of engagement to avoid contact against an opponent who prefers to fence with the blade, and fence with absence of the blade against an opponent who prefers constant use of blade attacks such as the beat.

2. Against a defensive fencer who fails to attack, attempt to force him to a position at the end of the strip. Vary actions with an occasional ballestra, redoublement, or retreat to attack as the opponent advances.

3. Risposte whenever possible to prevent an opponent from retaking the attack.

4. Make maximum use of the time thrust in counterattacking to close the opponent's line of attack.

5. Keep in mind that an opponent who does not react to a strong feint may be open to an explosive direct attack.

6. Use the advance attack against an opponent who constantly retreats with or without a parry.

7. Against a parry, with or without a riposte, use the one-two attack or the double to follow a direct parry or counterparry.

8. Test the speed of an opponent's blade by using a disengagement or a one-two attack and by moving quickly as the opponent responds to a beat or press in order to prevent him from finding your blade.

9. Remember that an opponent who does not re-

TABLE 8-3. Basic defensive procedures.

Action	Use	Execution
Simple Parries		
Parry four	The parry four is used to defend the high inside line.	From the on guard position in sixth and threatened by an attack in fourth, the foil moves laterally to the left (outside to inside) to close this line with a slight pivot of the elbow and wrist, thumb upward, hand in half-supination, with the elbow close to the body, and the blade tip at approximately eye level of the opponent. In the defensive guard position the strong portion of the blade makes contact with the opponent's blade. If a riposte is to follow, the point must first be deflected out of line.
Parry six	The parry six is used to defend the high outside line.	The hand, in half-supination, moves the blade laterally from left to right, inside to outside, to an on guard position in sixth.
Semicircular Parries		
Parry seven (low parry four)	The parry seven is used to defend the low inside line.	From the on guard position in fourth and threatened in the low line, the defender's blade makes a half-circle (clockwise) moving into the on guard in seventh. The action is performed with a relaxed last three fingers, firm manipulators, and a supinated hand and forearm and causes the point of the blade to be lowered to a position near the height of the opponent's knee and the attacker's blade to be deflected to the left. The level of the defensive guard remains constant throughout as the point of the blade is raised and extended to the target.
Parry eight (low parry six)	The parry eight is used to defend the low outside line.	From the on guard position in sixth and threatened in the low line, the blade makes a half circle (counter-clockwise) through the use of a relaxed last three fingers and the control of the manipulators to move the blade to an on guard position in eighth at approximately knee level of the opponent. The hand and forearm assume a supinated position as the blade is deflected to the right. The point can then be elevated under or over the opponent's arm and extend to the target to establish the right of way.
Circular Parries		
Circle parry six	The circle parry six is used against a disengagement, when the attack continuity of the opponent is in doubt, and to cause difficulty in the opponent's offensive strategy.	From the on guard position in sixth and threatened in the fourth line, the point is dropped under and around the blade of the attacker (a small circle clockwise) forcing it to a closed sixth line and returning to the original line of engagement.
Circle parry four	The circle parry four is used against the disengagement and when the attack continuity is unknown.	From the on guard in fourth and threatened in the sixth line, a small circle (counterclockwise) is made around the opponent's blade carrying it back to the original line of engagement through the use of the manipulators, finger play and proper wrist action.
Successive parries	Successive parries are used against a compound attack.	Successive parries are a series of maneuvers exhibiting variations in defensive actions. Adequate use of the manipulators and wrist action are essential if the opponent's blade is to be contacted at the correct position. Care must be exercised to keep blade movements small, to avoid following an opponent's wide blade movements in feints, and to avoid withdrawal of the weapon as the attacker's blade nears the target area.

spond to a beat or press is susceptible to a straight thrust.

10. Against an opponent who fails to respond to a change in engagement, feint a glide to elicit a response and then deceive the parry.

11. Use compound attacks from a static position against experienced fencers whose moves are difficult to anticipate.

12. An opponent who extends his weapon arm into a feint will probably favor the use of the stop thrust. Use a beat to gain the right of way or execute a false attack, parry the stop thrust, and lunge to touch.

13. Keep in mind that an opponent who attacks as you execute the beat or press can be encouraged to attack in a desired line that will prepare you a parry and riposte.

14. When the change of engagement is used, be prepared to parry and follow with a riposte when the opponent attempts to prevent you from taking or attacking the blade.

15. Against an opponent who prefers an advance or ballestra attack, vary your action by occasionally maintaining your position.

16. Learn to parry just prior to arrival of the point of the blade to touch, thus making compound attacks more difficult and delaying your intent.

17. Be alert to invitation, or the encouragement for you to attack in a certain line by blade pressure or by exposure of a target area.

18. As the opponent executes a cut-over, extend the arm rapidly to establish the right of way and attempt a touch as the opponent moves in to complete his movement.

19. Against an opponent who constantly prefers renewed attacks, use a simple riposte to gain the right of way.

20. Use the delayed or compound rispote against an opponent who generally returns to the on guard position following his parried attack.

21. Use a simple riposte against an opponent who is effective in the remise in order to obtain the right of way. A delayed or compound riposte does not establish the right of way over a remise.

22. The riposte by counterdisengagement in sixth is an effective maneuver against a left-handed opponent who returns to the fourth guard position following an unsuccessful attack.

23. Step back when executing a parry against a quick, superior opponent, taking the parry as the rear foot breaks ground and adjusting the retreat to the opponent's movement.

SAFETY PRACTICES

Fencing is a surprisingly safe sport, with an extremely low injury rate among participants in organized programs in physical education, recreation, and intramural and varsity athletics. The nature of the sport, however, does necessitate care and concern if injuries are to be avoided. The following suggestions are offered:

1. Avoid practicing any maneuvers, regardless of their simplicity, without a mask.

2. Always use a glove in practice sessions.

3. Avoid the use of damaged equipment such as badly worn masks that may puncture with hard contact. Repair or replace worn-out leather on the mask, worn-out neck cloth laces, and soiled neck pads. If a mask can be dented with the thumb, it should be discarded.

4. Utilize equipment recommended for that weapon (épée, sabre, or foil). Clothing specific to the weapon is designed for maximum protection against broken blades and weapon contact.

5. Jackets contain reinforced areas over the upper arm, armpit and breast on the weapon side. Avoid using jackets not designed for the dominant hand or the fencer will not be protected.

6. Use a rubber button or tape to offer additional padding over the foil tip.

7. Carry weapons with the point toward the floor.

8. Avoid stiff blades unless heavily padded jackets are worn.

EXERCISE   Definitions and List of Terms

1. An offensive maneuver executed as the opponent prepares for action prior to his initial movement is termed an _____.

2. A tie-breaking maneuver, fence-off, between two or more competitors is a _____.

3. The control of distance between fencers by retreating or advancing with both feet is termed _____.

4. A signal to the director to stop the bout by stamping the lead foot twice is termed the _____ .
5. An area of attack that is protected by the blade and arm is a _____ .
6. A series of actions involving the taking of the blade is termed _____ .
7. Body contact (clinch), or a closing of the guard that prevents normal fencing action, is called _____ .
8. A fencer who avoids an offensive or defensive action is said to have _____ that action.
9. An evasive action on an opponent's attempt to take the blade or attack the blade is called a _____ .
10. A series of actions involving the taking of the blade with loss of blade contact between each is termed a _____ .
11. A simultaneous hit by both fencers, declared invalid in foil competition, is termed a _____ .
12. An offensive action—generally a lunge—to elicit a response from the opponent without intent to score is called a _____ attack.
13. The distance maintained by the fencer as determined by reach, height, skill level, speed, and reaction time is termed the _____ .
14. The manipulation of the blade tip with the thumb and index finger is termed _____ .
15. Blade contact on the strong portion toward the blade with the opponent's weaker, flexible portion at the point half, is called _____ .
16. Contact on an opponent's blade to prevent a score by closing a line is termed _____ .
17. A hit that merely grazes the target, causing no bend in the weapon such as occurs in a square touch, is termed a _____ .
18. A number of offensive and defensive movements by one or both fencers that terminates with a break in the action is termed a _____ .
19. A blade that lands clearly ahead of the opponent's blade indicates that the attacker has controlled the _____ .
20. A term synonymous with "round" of tournament play, in which fencers are assigned to compete against each other in the preliminary, quarter-final or semi-final is a _____ .

1. Attack on preparation	8. Deceived	15. Forte to foible
2. Barrange	9. Derobement	16. Opposition
3. Breaking and gaining ground	10. Double prise de fer	17. Pass
4. Call	11. Double touch	18. Phrase d'armes
5. Closed line	12. False	19. Time
6. Compound prises de fer	13. Fencing measure	20. Pool
7. Corps-à-Corps	14. Fingering	

QUESTIONS AND ANSWERS ON THE RULES

1. *Q.* What are the common rule infractions and their corresponding penalties?

    A.

Infraction	Penalty
Corps-à-corps, or closing in body to body to avoid being hit	After a warning, one hit awarded per violation; disqualification for violent Corps-à-corps
Using the free hand to deflect the opponent's blade	After a warning, one hit awarded
Covering the target with another body part	One hit awarded if the protecting part is touched
Crossing the lateral limit on the piste	Loss of one meter of ground from the point crossed (two meters in épée or sabre)
Crossing with both feet over the rear limit	Warning, point if reoccurring

2. *Q.* When is a fencing bout completed?

   A. The first competitor to score five touches is declared the winner; however, a bout is limited to ten minutes, with time warning given when two minutes and one minute remain.

3. *Q.* What action is taken in the event of a tie?

   A. A sudden death period is declared. The score is changed to a 4-4, with the next touch deciding the winner.

4. *Q.* Are fencers restricted to a specific area?

   A. Yes, fencers are restricted to a strip approximately 6 feet 7 inches in width and 40 feet in length.

5. *Q.* How are bouts officiated?

   A. A jury of four is allotted one vote each in establishing the validity of a touch. A judge acknowledges all touches (valid or invalid) and signals the director to halt action. Jurors may vote "yes," "no," "abstain," or "foul." The president or superior official may vote one and a half times and takes the vote of the judges regarding validity of hits, giving priority to one of the fencers in accordance with the right of way rule. A touch is awarded only if a majority vote is obtained. Without such a majority, the rules favor the fencer who may have been touched and the hit is declared invalid. Two judges acknowledge all touches. If the two judges split their voting or both abstain, the president decides. The jury moves up and down the piste with the fencers.

6. *Q.* Who is awarded a point in a simultaneous touch situation?

   A. The fencer who had the right of way. A simultaneous touch by a fencer who maintained a flexed arm and another who used a stop thrust and an extended arm scores a point for the fencer who maintained the fully extended arm. Simultaneous hits involving no faulty action are nullified.

7. *Q.* Do fouls nullify all subsequent action?

   A. Only if they are a result of a right of way attack. Fouls resulting from a parry do not stop action that follows.

8. *Q.* What constitutes a legal touch after the right of way has been established?

   A. A legal touch consists of contact within the four quadrants, by the point of the blade with enough force to inflict a hypothetical wound as evidenced by a slight bending of the blade. Contact in the form of a graze with the point of blade is not a valid touch.

9. *Q.* May the target areas be shielded by the mask and arms to prevent a touch?

   A. A hit on the arm or mask when an opponent parries quarte, for example, would not be a valid touch since this represents a legitimate fencing movement and not a means of obstructing the target. On the other hand, if a fencer is hit on a body area not part of the valid target while trying to shield the valid area, a hit is scored. The same principle applies in a touch on a body part which is not a valid hit but would have been had it not been for displacement.

10. *Q.* Who is said to have the right of way?

    A. The fencer who first executes an offensive action by extending the weapon arm and point toward the target area has the right of way. A bent arm attack fails to establish the right of way. The first competitor to execute such action may score with this maneuver having to be parried by the opponent before any counteraction is taken. A blade tip that is not threatening the target area need not be parried.

11. *Q.* Does a parry terminate the attacker's right of way?

    A. Only if the riposte is immediate. A delayed riposte may lose the right of way.

12. *Q.* How do the rules differ for épée and sabre?

    A. Épée rules are similar to foil rules, with the following exceptions: (a) the piste size is 46 feet in length, (b) the weapon is the sole means of defense, (c) no priority is given to the first fencer to extend his weapon arm and threaten the target area, (d) both fencers are awarded points in a simultaneous hit, (e) if both competitors are hit with an elapse of time between hits ($\frac{1}{25}$ of a second), the first hit scores the point, (f) the entire body is the target area, and (g) there is no jury since the president detects and records all hits registered by an electric scoring apparatus.

Sabre rules are similar to foil rules, with the following exceptions: (a) the target area is extended to include the arms and head, (b) the piste is 46 feet in length, and (c) a jury of four judges and one president conduct the bout.

BIBLIOGRAPHY

Amateur Fencers' League of America, *Fencing Rules* (current ed.). New York: AFLA.
Castello, Hugo, and J. M. Castello, *Fencing*. New York: The Ronald Press Company, 1962.
Castello, J. M., *Theory and Practice of Fencing*. New York: Charles Scribner's Sons, 1961.
Crosnier, R., *Fencing With the Electric Foil*. New York: A. S. Barnes & Co., Inc., 1961.
De Beaumont, C. L., *Fencing: Ancient Art and Modern Sport* (rev. and enl. ed.). New York: A. S. Barnes & Co., Inc., 1971.
Palffy-Alpar, Julius, *Sword and Masque*. Philadelphia: F. A. Davis Company, 1968.
Vince, J., *Fencing* (2nd ed.). New York: The Ronald Press Company, 1962.

9

FIELD HOCKEY

DESCRIPTION OF THE ACTIVITY

Field hockey is a complicated field sport requiring highly developed skills and superior muscular and cardiovascular endurance. It is played on a field 100 yards long and 60 yards wide by two opposing teams of not more than eleven players (Figure 9-1). Each team attempts to score goals by propelling a hard ball into the goal cage using wooden sticks. In order to score a goal, the ball must be contacted by an offensive player in the striking circle. It may subsequently be deflected off a defensive stick before entering the goal.

The traditional hockey team of eleven players consists of five forwards: left wing, left inner, center forward, right inner, right wing; three halfbacks: right half, center half, left half; two fullbacks: right fullback, left fullback; and a goalkeeper. The five forwards act as the primary scorers. The two fullbacks are strong defensive players. The halfbacks, as intermediaries, play both offense and defense. Monumental changes are now occurring in the organizational make-up of the field hockey team. More and more coaches are abandoning the traditional system for the 'new system' which is diverse in its scope. It can vary from not labeling any players to dividing them into four fronters, two links, three thrusters, one sweep, and a goalkeeper. The 'new system' allows the flexibility needed to build a stronger attack and best utilize the talents of individual players.

Men's and women's field hockey has in the past differed because of four basic rules. The rule differences for men are: (a) use of a push-in instead of a roll-in; (b) two defending players as opposed to three between an attacker and the goal line to prevent offsides; (c) players on the defending team, not behind the goal line, must remain at the center line, as opposed to the 25 yard line, on corners; and (d) the use of the penalty stroke instead of the penalty bully. Women during this past season played with rules identical to the men on an experimental basis. These rule changes will now remain in effect until the Women's International Hockey Rules Board makes a decision on their permanent adoption. At the present time; therefore, there are no rule differences between men's and women's field hockey.

The game is started by a center bully between two center forwards or two opposing fronters. The two players stand with feet parallel straddling the center line. The ball is placed between the players with the blades of their sticks close behind the ball. The two opponents touch their sticks above the ball and then the ground. The bully is complete when the opponent's stick and the ground have been struck three times.

With the completion of the bully, the team gaining possession of the ball attempts to retain that possession and maneuver the ball to the goal and score. The ball is moved by either dribbling or passing. Four restrictions on advancing the ball make hockey a game of finesse and skill. One, only the flat side of the stick may be used in contacting the ball; two, no part of the stick may raise above the shoulder level; three, no player may position herself between an opponent and the ball and thereby obstruct the player from attempting to gain possession of the ball; and four, no player other than the goalkeeper may ad-

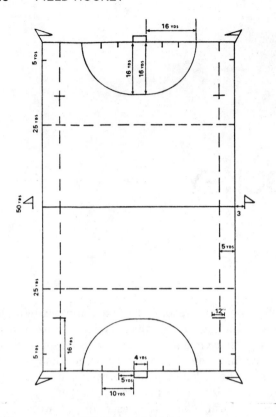

FIGURE 9-1. Field diagram.

vance the ball using any part of the body. The goal-keeper is allowed to kick the ball and utilizes this skill for clearing most shots on goal.

Play continucs with both teams attempting to keep possession and score a goal until the ball goes out of bounds, a goal is made, the half ends, or there is a rule infringement or injury to a player.

If the ball passes over the side line, the ball is put into play by the team not sending it out of bounds using a push-in*. If the ball is sent over the end line by an offensive player, a defensive hit is awarded to the opposing team. If the defense sends the ball over the line, the offensive team is awarded either a penalty corner or a corner.

For any rule infringement outside the circle, a free hit is awarded the opponents. Rule infringements by the defense inside the circle result in a penalty corner; infringements by the offense result in a free hit for the defense from anywhere within the circle. The penalty for preventing a sure goal by illegal means is a penalty stroke. A penalty stroke involves one offensive player seven yards in front of the goal and the goalkeeper. The offensive player may flick, scoop, or

*Experimental Rule

push the ball in an attempt to outwit the goalkeeper and score a goal.

Thirty five minute halves and the no substitution rule make hockey a grueling, but challenging and exciting sport. Possessing the skill and endurance to play a game of field hockey will certainly provide a sense of accomplishment to any hockey player.

EQUIPMENT

The basic equipment needed to engage in a field hockey game includes a stick, field shoes, shin guards, a hockey ball, and proper clothes.

The Uniform

The traditional and most popular uniform for field hockey includes a kilt or tunic worn with knee high socks; however, blouses and shorts are slowly becoming acceptable also. Leather shoes with rubber or synthetic cleats provide the grip necessary for quick changes of direction and starting and stopping on soft surfaces. A flat rubber soled shoe is usually better for frozen or "all weather" surfaces. Metal spikes, metal studs and nails are illegal. Padding is usually worn to protect the shins from careless stickwork by opponents. Shin guards can be purchased that either fit inside or outside the player's socks. Those worn outside the socks are somewhat clumsy, but offer greater protection for the ankles.

Sticks

Field hockey sticks are made of wood (ash or mulberry) and range in length from 31- to 37-inches. A rubber insert running the length of the handle prevents jarring when the ball is hit. Toweling is usually wrapped around the handle to assure a nonslip grip. The stick has a flat head on the left hand side and a rounded surface on the other. During play it is illegal to use the rounded side in contacting the ball. A stick may weigh no more than 23 ounces and must be thin enough so that a 2 inch ring can be slipped along its entire length. Players may choose between an Indian head or English head stick. The Indian head stick has become more popular because of its smaller head and greater mobility. When choosing a stick, there are several means for determining the proper length. The simplest seems to be grasping the stick at the top with two hands and while standing erect, swing the stick in an arc. If the stick barely touches the surface area, it is the correct length.

Balls

Several different quality balls may be purchased for use during practice and the game situation. The most economical is the plastic ball since it can be used for both practice and an official game. Other balls are either vinyl composition or leather. The ball must weigh between 5½ and 5¾ ounces, and have a circumference of not more than 9¼ inches and not less than 8¹³⁄₁₆ inches.

Goalkeeping Equipment

Sufficient protection and maximum mobility are the most important considerations in the selection of goalkeeping equipment. The goalkeeper most often prefers to wear pants rather than a kilt or tunic. A kilt or tunic often obstructs the goalkeeper's view of the ball and does not provide protection from the constant rubbing of the leg guard straps on the back of the legs.

Kickers. Kickers may be purchased with either a half sole or no sole. Those with a half sole are made from a hard leather and fit over a light shoe or boot. They provide a hard kick and protect the foot well, but are heavy and at times cumbersome. Those with no sole are canvas padded covers and should be worn

FIGURE 9-2. The dribble.

over boots with blocked toes. The no-soled kicker is more accurate than the half soled, but results in a less powerful kick.

Leg guards (pads). The goalkeeper's pads should be light, comfortable, and cover her thigh, leg and instep. The mobility required for bending at the knee is provided by two or three rolls at knee level.

Stick. A goalkeeper uses a short stick held in her right hand. If possible the stick weight should be concentrated in the head.

Glove. A padded left handed glove will prove to be an asset in stopping a scoop or flick shot at the goal. Now that the penalty stroke is occurring more frequently during a game, a left handed glove may prove invaluable.

The Goal

A field hockey goal is constructed from two perpendicular posts placed on the goal line four yards apart. These uprights are joined by a horizontal bar seven feet from the ground (inside measurements). A netting firmly attached to the goal posts prevents the ball from passing completely through the goal.

SKILLS AND TECHNIQUES

Grip

Without perfecting the proper grip on a field hockey stick, the beginning player will be unable to perform many necessary skills effectively. With the flat edge of the blade facing left, the stick is held with the palms facing each other. The left hand grasps or "shakes hands" about four inches below the left. The lower the right hand, the greater the control, but the more the player's vision is obstructed. From this position, the stick is merely turned to face forward. The player is now ready to maintain control whether dribbling, passing, or receiving the ball.

The left hand becomes the power hand when performing hockey skills. Since the left wrist is usually weak, the beginning player has a strong tendency to rotate the hand around the handle and attempt to let the right hand become the power hand. This limits the range of motion and makes skill movements difficult and awkward. Constant observation and correction of the grip is necessary to prevent the development of bad habits.

The Dribble

The dribble is a means to advance and control the ball while running. During a game, the dribble should be used sparingly for it is always faster to move the ball down field by controlling and passing. There are times, however, that one may be completely free and far ahead of her teammates and dribbling is the only option.

While dribbling (Figure 9-2), the left elbow is held high and almost level with the left shoulder. The left shoulder is kept slightly forward of the rest of the body. The right hand remains on the stick to stabilize and guide it. The ball is advanced using successive taps executed by the flexion and extension of the left wrist.

The most common errors during the dribble are tapping the ball too far ahead of the stick, and allowing the left elbow to drop close to the body. Unless the player is completely free, the ball should be within eight inches of her stick allowing an effective dodge or pass to be executed at any moment. If the left elbow is dropped while dribbling, it becomes impossible for the left wrist to provide the power necessary to propel the ball. Allowing the right hand to become the power hand decreases control and forces the player to hit and chase the ball.

Drive

The drive may be used for a square, angle or through pass, a free hit, a penalty corner or corner hit, or as a shot on goal. The drive has unfortunately come to be thought of as a hard stationary hit. The player, however, should develop this stroke so that it can be executed on the run either a short, medium, or long distance.

When driving, the right hand should slide next to the left during the backswing. The wrists should be cocked. The left shoulder, hip, and foot point in the direction of the intended drive. The head is kept over the ball until the actual completion of the hit. When contacting the ball, the arms and wrists should be stiff and straight, and the weight should be transferred to the forward foot. The arms and wrists remain straight on the follow through and the blade of the stick faces up. The intended direction of the drive varies the techniques used.

Left Drive. When making a flat pass to the left, the ball should be directly in front of the left foot. When driving left at an angle, the ball should be closer to the right side of the body.

Straight Drive. In order to drive straight ahead, the body must be rotated ¼ turn and the ball contacted nearer the forward foot. The straight drive is used for through passes, the free hit, and the penalty corner and corner.

FIGURE 9-3.   Drive to the right.

Right Drive. The right drive is the most difficult since the ball must be contacted when it is to the side of the right foot. Hip rotation is difficult, but increased flexibility and practice will make this stroke more comfortable.

The most common errors in performing the drive are: not looking at the ball long enough; failing to lock wrists on the follow through; and not transferring the weight while executing the stroke.

Push Pass

A short accurate pass with no backswing, the push pass has an element of deception and is much easier and faster to execute than the drive. The push pass can be made with either foot forward. With the ball in front of the player, the right hand lower on the stick, and the blade of the stick directly behind the ball, the left hand is pulled sharply toward the body and the right hand pushed directly forward.

The follow through is completed with the blade of the stick facing upward. The push pass is now being used for the push-in* following an out-of-bound infringement.

*Experimental Rule

Scoop

The scoop is short arched shot which may be effectively used as a dodge to the left or a short pass to the left when pressured by an opponent; a shot on goal; as a more reliable means of advancing the ball on wet playing areas; or as a surprise tactic on well blocked free hits. The scoop should always be practiced from a dribble. In order to scoop, the ball should be about three feet in front of the player's right foot. The hands remain in the dribble position with the right hand lowered for control and the right palm facing upward. The right knee is bent and forward. The tip of the blade is placed under the ball and the end of the handle is held to the left of the body. The right hand pulls up and forward in a shoveling action while the left hand exerts pressure downward. At the same instance that the ball is scooped, the knees should be extended for additional force. The completion of the follow through should be approximately at knee height.

Flick

The flick is an extremely difficult stroke to master, and is seldom learned by beginners. It is an effective

FIGURE 9-4. Push pass.

stroke in passing over an opponent's stick and as a shot on goal. From a dribble the flick is initiated similar to a push pass; however, the left arm is forcefully pulled back and down with the elbow being thrust between the knees. The wrists play an important part in this stroke as they are responsible for turning the blade of the stick down and over to impart spin to the ball.

Fielding

In order for a hockey player to effectively utilize the dribble, drive, and other skills, she must be able to receive and control the ball. Unfortunately, one of the most frequent sights during a hockey game is either the ball jumping over the player's stick, or the player attempting to field the ball and deflecting the ball directly to her opponent. The ball to be fielded may come from several directions; the front, the right, or from behind. The player must know how to handle each type of pass and begin her progress toward goal.

Receiving the ball in front. Receiving the ball from in front is relatively easy. The technique is very similar to catching a softball. The left foot is forward, the right hand is 6 to 8 inches down on the stick, the wrists are relaxed, and the stick is angled forward to prevent the ball from rolling over the blade or up the handle. If the received ball is traveling extremely fast, a few steps backward may be necessary to cushion the impact.

Receiving the ball from the right or left. If the ball comes from the left of a player, she must allow the ball to pass in front of her body and pick it up on the stick side of her body. When the ball comes from the right, the player must turn her stick to face the ball while keeping her left shoulder ahead of the body. Receiving the ball from the right is more difficult and beginners have a tendency to move their feet around instead of keeping them pointed in the direction of their goal.

Receiving the ball from behind. It is important to remember when receiving the ball from behind that the toes should point towards the goal being attacked. If one keeps this in mind, many obstruction calls will be avoided. When waiting for a pass, twist the body and look over the shoulder closest to the ball. The pass may come directly towards the player or into a space near. If the pass is ahead and to the right, the player merely follows the ball, picks it up on the stick, and controls it. If the pass is directly to the player, she should cut to meet the pass and pick it up on her stick side. If the ball is passed to a player's left, she must circle around the ball to pick it up on her stick side.

Tackles

When the opponents have possession of the ball, the means by which the ball is taken from them is referred to as a tackle. There are three basic tackles; the straight tackle, the left hand lunge, and the circular tackle.

Straight tackle. The straight tackle (Figure 9-5) is employed by the defense as the opponents' offense advances toward goal, or by the offense when a poor pass has been intercepted by the opponents' defense. The tackler should line herself up with the ball and approach the player using extreme caution so she does not become easy prey for a dodge. With her left foot forward, she should reach for the ball when it is not in contact with the opponent's stick. When reaching for the ball, all forward momentum should be stopped so that the body can pivot and procede in the opposite direction if the tackle is not successful.

FIGURE 9-6.   Left hand lunge.

ball, the tackler continues to a position behind the ball with her feet pointing toward her own goal.

Circular tackle. The circular tackle (Figure 9-7) might be considered the most difficult and frustrating tackle of the three. It is difficult since the tackler must wait until she is in full view of her opponent before executing the tackle, and frustrating because the attacker usually passes just as one is prepared to tackle. If one has forced the attacker to pass away from the goal or hurried her into making a poor pass,

FIGURE 9-5.   Straight tackle.

Left hand lunge. The left hand lunge (Figure 9-6) should be mastered by forwards, the center and right halfbacks, and the right fullback. By using the left hand lunge to tackle back, the right fullback and right halfback are able to stay between their opponent and the goal. The tackler must approach on her opponent's right side, or stick side. The lunge is executed using one or two hands; one hand is more frequently used since it affords a greater reach. Impetus is given to the stick with the right hand. Weight is on the left leg and the knee is bent. The stick travels forward, down and to the left. The left arm remains straight. Once the stick has come in contact with the

FIGURE 9-7.   Circular tackle.

her attempt at a circular tackle should be considered successful.

Used almost exclusively by the left half back, left fullback, left wing, and center halfback, the circular tackle is initiated on the non-stick side of the attacker. The tackler must overtake and actually pass the attacker. Once in this position, the tackler leads with the left shoulder and begins a semi-circular path in front of the attacker. Coming in front of the attacker, the tackler taps the ball from her stick and to the left in a corresponding semi-circle. Once clear of the attacker, a pass should be initiated immediately to prevent being retackled.

Dodges

If a pass cannot be initiated and an opponent is applying pressure, a dodge is the only possible evasive tactic. This situation may occur if a forward is ahead of the other players on her forward line or if a defensive player, after intercepting a pass, is being pressured by an attacking player. A dodge, successfully completed, allows the attacker to continue her progress toward the goal, or allows the defender to make a successful pass. Four dodges are frequently employed; the right dodge, the left dodge, the scoop, and the reverse.

Right dodge (push to the right). A right dodge is usually initiated by first dribbling slightly to the left, pulling the defense in that direction, then the ball is pushed to the right and non-stick side of the opponent. The ball tavels in a forward and slightly angled path no farther than 4 feet past the opponent. In order to prevent committing an obstruction foul, the dodger must go to the left or stick side of the opponent and retrieve the ball. Players on the right side of the field find this dodge most effective since the defense has a tendency to defend more on that attacker's left side to prevent the centering pass.

Left dodge (pull to the left). The left dodge, similar to the right dodge, should be initiated by dribbling in the opposite direction of the intended movement. Once the tackler is drawn to the right, it is an easy maneuver for the ball handler to pull the ball to the left while stepping left. She continues left until clear and then darts past the tackler. When pulling the ball left, the left elbow should drop close to the body and the blade of the stick should face left. The left elbow returns to its dribble position before continuing forward. Defenders on the right half of the field tend to play more on the players' right side, therefore, the players on the left half of the field find this dodge more successful.

Scoop. The scoop is an excellent surprise tactic. The procedure outlined under the dodge is utilized in executing the scoop. The ball is scooped a few inches above the blade of the tackler's stick. The scoop must be kept low to prevent the tackler from stopping the ball with her hand, and to insure against a dangerous hitting foul.

Reverse. The reverse dodge is a skill that should be learned by advance players only. If a player can not execute a satisfactory right and left dodge, she should not move on to a reverse dodge. To initiate the reverse dodge, the player dribbles left, drawing her opponent left. Reversing her stick and pulling the ball right frees her of her would-be tackler, and she continues forward. If done too late, it is easy to commit an obstruction foul.

Bully

At the beginning of each half and after each goal, a bully occurs at the 50 yard line. In the official rules established by the Women's International Hockey Rules Board, a penalty bully is provided for. The

FIGURE 9-8a, 9-8b.   Bully.

penalty bully, however, will be replaced by the penalty stroke and the defense hit if the present experimental rules are adopted.

The ball is placed on the center line. The center forwards or two fronters stand straddling the center line with their heads as much over the ball as possible (Figure 9-8). The stick is held with the right hand down a few inches and the blade behind the ball. All other players must be closer to their own goal than the ball. The two players participating in the bully must first strike the ground with their sticks, then raise their sticks above the ball and touch sticks. This procedure is repeated three times. After the third tap of the opponent's stick, both teams attempt to gain possession, keep control, and ultimately score a goal.

Some of the techniques for securing possession of the ball following the completion of the bully include:

1. Reverse the toe of the stick and pass back to a defensive player.

2. Lift the ball over the opponent's stick if the ball becomes wedged between the two sticks.

3. Pull the ball toward yourself, turn facing your goal, and make a pass to the left.

4. Pass the ball between the opponent's right foot and her stick.

A bully may also occur in two other infrequent situations; after a double foul, and following an injury not resulting from a foul.

POSITIONAL PLAY

The traditional positioning of team members, when the center bully is executed, is illustrated in Figure 9-9.

Wings

The two outside forwards are the left and right wings. These two players are usually the speediest players on the team and must possess an ability to dribble, dodge, field, and make centering passes. Since the wings play on the extremes of the field, they must be able to field balls well to keep them in play. The wing must have a high level of endurance and should be moving constantly posing herself as a threat to her opposing halfback.

In the defensive end of the field, the wings must be ready, if necessary, to spring back to field clear from the goalkeeper or the halfbacks. She then has the option of making a through pass up the alley for her inner to field or making a drive across field to her opposite wing who should be ready to begin her move up the field.

The sooner a wing can center the ball, the more effective the attack. An arbitrary centering pass; however, most often is intercepted by the defense. The wing must be aware of defensive positioning, and make her centering pass either into a space where it may be fielded by a teammate, or directly to her teammate.

If the wing reaches the 25 yard line and has not centered the ball, she has three options; take the ball into the circle and shoot if unchallenged, take the ball to the edge of the circle and pass flat across to the opposite side thereby forcing a confusing change for the defense, or if space allows, center the ball in front of her opposite inner.

If forced down to the endline, the wing can center a few yards in front of the goalkeeper or pass back to the top of the circle to a halfback.

A wing near the circle shoud never relax and watch her three inner forwards shoot for goal. She must be

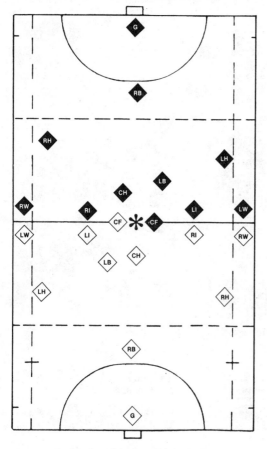

FIGURE 9-9.   Positioning of team members at the center bully.

constantly moving, picking up clears, covering spaces, and freeing herself for a possible shot on goal. The wing is also responsible for taking the corners on her side of the field, and push-ins beyond the 25 yard line in the offensive end.

Defensively, a wing should tackle back any defensive player who makes a successful tackle, and should mark the opposing wing on free hits and push-ins.

Inners

The inners should be considered the most free and devastating players on the forward line. Since the fullbacks are responsible for the inners, and one fullback is usually covering at the top of the circle, it leaves one player on the forward line, usually a wing, completely free. If the ball can be passed from inner to inner, this forces a defensive shift; the other fullback must come up to pick up her inner. If during this change, the fullbacks can be caught square, a through pass behind the center half for the center forward is very effective in initiating the attack.

Skills important for the inners to master are many and varied. They should be skilled dribblers, accurate passers, proficient at changing directions, be able to perform dodges effectively and possess a variety of shots on goal. Inners must be able to make effective triangular passes with their wings, and be aware of every opportunity to make an inner to inner pass, or inner to opposite wing pass.

In the defensive end of the field, the inners must be alert to open spaces through which they could receive a clear from their defense. If the ball is on the right side of the field, the right inner should drop behind the 25 yard line. A clear reaching the right inner should then be passed either to the left inner or to the center forward, if the center half has not yet had time to recover.

As the attack is initiated the inners should watch the defense carefully. She should watch to see if the defense is covering or marking. When in possession of the ball she has several options; she can pass to the wing, if the halfback comes off on her; she can pass to the opposite inner as the fullback drops back to cover; or wait for her own defensive fullback to challenge her and hopefully dodge her or catch the two fullbacks square. The left inner will find the left dodge more successful and the right inner the right dodge.

If the inner has possession of the ball at the edge of the circle, she should, if open, shoot immediately. If her fullback is marking her, she may either dodge and shoot, make a pass to an open forward, or back

pass to a halfback. After shooting, the inner should follow her shot hoping to pick up an ensuing clear and deflecting it into goal. Whenever any forward shoots, the inners are responsible for rushing the goal to pick up rebounds off the goalkeeper's pads.

The inners are also the principle receivers on corner hits. They should be able to control the ball and immediately shoot, or dodge the defender and shoot.

Center Forward

The center forward is responsible for starting the game with the center bully. A center forward should practice the bully and be proficient at all possible options that could lead to securing the ball. A center forward who most assuredly wins the bully is a great psychological advantage to the team.

When at the defensive circle, the center forward must be aware of the center half and the position of the fullbacks. If the center halfback shoots, either the inner or the center forward must drop back to help out the defense. By knowing which fullback is playing up, the center forward, if she receives a clear, can pass the ball to the wing on the opposite side of the field. In other words, if the opposing right fullback is playing past the center line, the center should pass forward to her right wing.

The center must constantly keep the center halfback occupied. By moving forward and back, and changing her pace, the center forward can free herself for the through pass, or pull the center halfback forward to allow the inner to inner pass.

If the center forward is playing down field toward the attacking circle and receives a pass from the clear, she may choose to dribble if she has left her center halfback by the defensive circle. She may dribble straight ahead hoping to draw the fullback and then pass to the free inner; she may dribble directly toward the fullback, while the inner interchanges with her, and receives a centering pass; or she may dribble toward the covering fullback forcing the fullbacks to changeup and back, and make a through pass down the center as the fullbacks become square.

Once reaching the attacking circle, the center forward should either dodge and shoot, or if not threatened with a tackle, drive for goal. Whenever any forward shoots, the center should rush to pick up the rebounds off the goalkeeper's pads.

Halfbacks

The halfback position is probably the most strenuous, but potentially the most satisfying also.

The halfback should not only be the strong defender backing up her offense, but a viable member of the attack. It should not be an unusual event when a halfback, especially the center halfback, drives toward goal.

The halfback on defense must be constantly adjusting to the position of the ball. The three halfbacks and the two fullbacks play what might be considered a zone defense as the ball is moved by the attack. The halfback on the ball side of the field plays the wing. The halfback on the non-ball side plays the opposing inner. The center halfback only covers the center forward. The center forward, being the most dangerous forward, is left no room to breathe. When in midfield, the halfbacks cover (Figure 9-10) to prevent as much forward movement as possible. When at the circle, the halfbacks mark closely to prevent the shot on goal. Each halfback should be aware of her forwards' positions so that clears will be well placed.

The halfbacks on offense follow their forward line anticipating clears made by the opposing defense. If a forward is tackled, the halfback must never rush in to tackle the tackler, for that leaves an opposing forward free for a pass. She must allow her forward to tackle back. If the forward is unsuccessful, the halfback is prepared to intercept the ensuing pass.

At the top of the attacking circle, halfbacks should anticipate the path of clears, be prepared for possible passes back to them from the wings or inners, and be aggressive enough, if the opportunity arises, to take the ball into the circle and shoot. Forward must be prepared to cover for halfbacks who shoot.

Fullbacks

The two fullbacks are purely defensive players. They are responsible for marking the two inners and preventing them from scoring a goal. The fullback on the ball side is marking her inner while the other fullback is covering near the top of the striking circle. The halfback picks up the inner for the covering fullback. When the ball has definitely changed sides of the field, the halfback drops off the inner and picks up the wing. The covering fullback moves to pick up her inner after she sees the other fullback is well on her way into the covering position. The two fullbacks must never be caught square across the field or they become easy prey for the through pass which leaves the goalkeeper facing three forwards and no help.

At the beginning of the game, the left fullback usually plays up to protect the non-stick side of the center halfback. When play is concentrated on the other end of the field, the up fullback plays as far toward the attacking circle as she feels allows her the margin to safely recover. She usually plays somewhere between the center line and the attacking 25 yard line.

Fullbacks have been notoriously known as the slowest members on a team. This poor conception of the fullback position should be dispelled. Fullbacks rushing the inners on corners must be as speedy and alert as any other team member. Remember, next to the goalkeeper, one of the fullbacks must be the last line of defense. No one wants to think of her fullback as slow at this moment.

Goalkeeper

Anticipating the strategy of the attack and squelching an attempt for goal is perhaps the ultimate reward for a goalkeeper. On the other hand, the most devastating and exasperating experience for a goalkeeper is when she sees the ball deflected off her own teammate's stick headed for a free forward.

Once a shot has been taken, that shot belongs to the goalkeeper. It is now her job to clear the ball. It is the defense's job to mark her opposing forward, staying between her and the goal and her and the ball, to prevent a follow-up shot.

A goalkeeper must have fast reaction times an aggressive determination to recover and be ready for the next shot, and an even temperament. The goalkeeper is the only player afforded the privilege of using her feet to control and direct the ball.

One will usually find the goalkeeper moving in a semicircular path in front of the goal line. A goalkeeper who stations herself on the goal line leaves a proportionately larger area open for the ball to pass over the goal line. There are certain instances when the goalkeeper is required to start behind the goal line; during a corner and penalty corner, and on

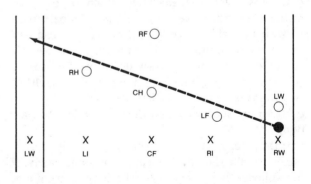

FIGURE 9-10. Defense covering in midfield.

the goal line; during a penalty stroke. When a corner is awarded, the goalkeeper should recover to her position in front of the goal as her teammates rush.

The skills necessary for the goalkeeper to master involve the use of her feet, stick and hand. She must learn to clear to the open space; to stop the bouncing ball, extremely hard drive, or hard shot to the corner of the goal cage; to use her hand on aerial balls; and understand the judicious use of her stick.

Basic positioning and movement. The goalkeeper should position herself three to four feet in front of the center of the goal. Her knees are bent and weight forward. As the ball shifts from side to side, the goalkeeper must side shuffle along her semicircular path to cover possible shots on goal. She holds her stick in her right hand with the blade at ground level.

There are two instances when the goalkeeper advances from her semi-circular path; one is when the free forward, having left the defense behind is advancing toward the circle; and the other is when a forward breaks free with the ball well within the circle. In both cases, the goalkeeper advances toward the forward cutting down the angle of a possible shot.

The Clear. The clear is executed by kicking the ball with the inside of the foot. A clear to the right is accomplished by using the right foot. In instances where the ball is near the end line, using the closest foot to the end line will prevent the ball from being sent out of bounds. A goalkeeper should first learn to clear the ball without stopping it. Emphasis at this time should be on keeping her body weight forward.

Stops. There are four basic stops which may prevent a goal from being scored. These four are: a stop using the pads, a lunge stop, a hand stop for aerial balls, and a stick stop.

When a goalkeeper wishes to stop a ball before clearing, she should advance directly in line with the ball and give when the ball comes in contact with the pads to prevent a long rebound. She should then immediately clear the ball.

If the ball is traveling toward the corner of the goal cage, a goalkeeper may have to execute a one foot lunge stop. The goalkeeper's pad is kept perpendicular to the ground, and the leg extended so that the thigh is parallel to the ground. The goalkeeper must be able to recover and clear the ball or attempt to clear as she stops it. The latter move is very difficult.

Aerial balls should be stopped by the left hand. The ball may be caught momentarily or allowed to strike the palm and drop. The goalkeeper should attempt to make aerial stops while the ball is still substantially in front of her so that the ensuing drop places the ball in a position where it may be cleared. Stopping the ball too close to the body means that the goalkeeper must back up before clearing the ball.

In some instances, a stick stop may be useful. If the goalkeeper has been pulled out of position or has fallen to the ground, a jab with the stick may produce favorable results.

Penalty stroke. The penalty stroke is now an experimental rule in effect until the Women's International Hockey Rules board makes a decision on its adoption. The penalty stroke replaces the previously used penalty bully.

At any time that an official feels that a goal would have been scored but for an illegal procedure by a defensive player in the striking circle, a penalty stroke is awarded. An attacking forward and the goalkeeper are the only participants. All other players must wait behind the 25 yard line. The goalkeeper must stand on the goal line. The ball is placed on a mark seven yards in front of and in the center of the goal. The forward is allowed one step and may push, flick or scoop the ball in an attempt to outwit the goalkeeper and score a goal. The forward may not touch the ball again. If the goalkeeper successfully stops the ball, play is continued with a free hit by the defense 16 yards in front of the center of the goal line.

BASIC STRATEGY

In field hockey, similar to all sport activity, knowledge of strategic principles plays an extremely important role in differentiating between the experienced and inexperienced team. All too many beginning players feel that once the skills have been mastered, the game has been mastered. Not true. Players must develop what is often termed "game sense"; the understanding of strategic principles and the ability to utilize or carry out these principles during a game situation.

At any one time during a contest, a player is either an attacker or defender; regardless if she is the center forward or the right fullback. If her team is in possession of the ball, she must assume an offensive posture. All her efforts are therefore channeled toward making the needed pass; angular, through, or square, fielding well, reaching the circle, making the best shot on goal and rushing that shot and ultimately to put the ball in the net. Making goals would be relatively simple if there wasn't a defense utilizing every possible means to foil the offense's plans. They are attempting to anticipate the offense's every move; forcing them to work for every yard they advance the ball, and waiting for the chance to tackle the player or intercept the pass and then initiate their own offense.

Many coaches are experimenting with new positional names and team formations. In the following discussion of offensive and defensive strategy, the traditional strategies will be described.

Defensive Team Strategy

Whenever the opposing team is in definite possession of the ball and driving toward goal, every player on the defensive team must know her role in preventing a goal. Many times, a goal could have been prevented by a forward who didn't tackle back the halfback initiating the attack.

Defensive players should concentrate on the following general guidelines:

1. When fielding the ball, the player should always have her feet pointing in the direction of her goal when actual contact with the ball is made. A player who fields a ball and finds herself facing the sideline or her opponents' goal is not in a position to initiate the offense and will usually commit obstruction before being able to pass the ball down field.

2. A defensive player should always be between her opponent and the goal and her opponent and the ball. This principle applies whether covering or marking.

3. Knowing where the opponent is likely to pass allows one to anticipate her actions. The ability to anticipate comes only through a thorough knowledge of game strategy.

4. Control the ball before clearing; either by deflecting it away from the approaching attack or by stopping it and dodging the attack.

5. A defensive player should always be aware of the offensive formation at the 25 yard line.

6. Without cardiovascular endurance, the most highly skilled defensive player will be left far behind.

7. The ability to sprint and change directions quickly should also be developed in the defensive player.

There are four basic defensive techniques of which all players must be aware. They are: marking, covering, tackling, and interchanging. Knowledge of these four techniques and the understanding of how to apply them makes the difference between a smoothly operating defense and one which is broken through

easily. The end result of which is a high score, for the other team.

"Marking" in field hockey means that the defensive player is on the ball side and goal side of her opponent and within a stick's length. When a defensive player marks an opponent she prevents the pass directly to the player and forces a pass forward into a space. The defense always marks her player near and in the circle. There are instances when forwards also mark. Forwards mark opposing forwards on free hits and push-ins so that the defense is free to cover the spaces.

Defensive players usually "cover" when the ball is in midfield. The defense is aware of their opponent's position; however, she plays deeper covering spaces through which a pass may be made. Covering delays the progress of the attack by only allowing square passes and inhibiting forward movement.

An offensive player will usually continue dribbling down field until she is forced to pass. The defensive player directly responsible for the offensive player with the ball must attempt to either take the ball away from the attacker or force a pass which hopefully can be interecepted by another defensive player. A defensive player accomplishes this by attempting a tackle; usually a straight tackle. If in spite of the defenses' clever deception, the opponent successfully dodges her, the defensive player should attempt to tackle back approaching her opponent on goal side.

There are occassions when a defensive player may get pulled out of position and it is necessary for another player to assume her position and duties. When this occurs, the player who found herself out of position must "interchange" with the other player. In other words, she must also assume the other players duties. Both players should remain in their new position until the crisis is over.

Offensive Team Strategy

Once a team has possession of the ball, all efforts are concentrated toward maneuvering that ball down field and into the net for a goal. Running from one end of the field to the other and consistently not scoring results in a frustrated, unsatisfied and extremely tired team. Keeping a few basic concepts in mind should start an offensive player on the way to success.

1. Advance the ball from the defensive end to the goal using as few passes as possible.

2. Bringing the ball down the center of the field is usually the quickest method; however, when defense is set, keep the ball out in the alleys in the defensive end, utilize cross field passing in mid-field, and center the ball before reaching the striking circle.

3. Through passes move the ball down field the fastest, however, the defense attempts to prevent them and force square passes.

4. Attempt to make passes or dodges when the defense has her weight forward.

5. Dribble in one direction, pass in another.

6. Be constantly award of spaces, either to pass into or to cut into to maneuver away from the ball.

7. Be aware of teammate's position; do not crowd her and therefore allow one defensive player to defend two offensive players.

8. Never follow your own pass; cut away from it.

9. Be aware of defensive positioning in the attacking end of the field to prevent offsides.

Depending on the area of the field in which the offensive player finds herself, there are many more tactics of which she must be aware. Moreover, in many cases, the offensive players have many options available to them. For example, while at the defensive twenty five yard line there are several forward line variations possible. The most common formations are the "V", the inverted "V", the "W", the diagonal, and the "M" formation (Figure 9-11). The "M" formation is usually considered the most defensive and the "W" formation the most offensive. While a team's goal is being beseiged by the opposing team, players in the forward line must learn to adjust formations depending on the strength of their defense. In addition, forward line players at the twenty five yard line must be prepared to cut back for clears as well as defend against the opposing halfbacks who shoot.

With a clear by the defense to a forward line player, the attack is initiated. At this point, a forward line player will either be moving downfield without the ball, moving to receive a pass, or moving downfield with the ball. Each of the three situations demand different offensive tactics.

The four forwards not in possession of the ball are responsible for opening spaces into which the ball can be passed or into which they may dart to free themselves for a pass. The forwards on either side of the player with the ball should pull away from the ball by moving ahead or behind the play. This maneuver should allow the offensive player with the ball the opportunity to either pass behind her own

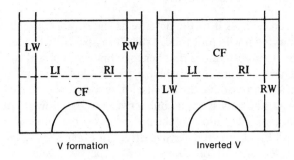

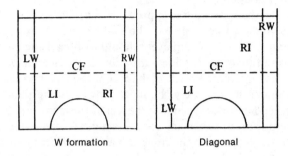

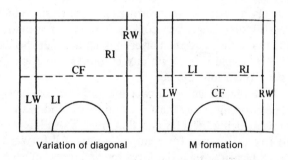

FIGURE 9-11.   Offensive formations at the 25 yard line.

teammate or behind her teammate's defender. In the offensive end of the field, an offensive player must be careful in moving ahead of the ball so that she does not commit offsides. As a general rule, in the defensive end of the field, the offensive players should play ahead of the ball when the defense is covering and on line with or behind the ball when the defense is marking.

Being aware of defensive positioning and the position of the player in possession of the ball should give one clues to where and when the ball may be passed. Be ready! Having anticipated the direction of the ball, rush to touch it and field it.

Once the ball is on the offensive player's stick, she should dribble only until she has a space or a teammate available to pass to. The hockey player who attempts to single handedly bring the ball downfield usually loses it to the defense as she is tackled or by making a wild hit (notice I didn't say pass), to the left or right with hopes that her teammate will pick it up. There are instances when a player should or must attempt to dodge the defense; however, a well placed pass not only is safer, but moves the ball downfield much faster, allowing the defense less time to recover and break up an offensive drive. In other words, the attack should be thought of as passes made into spaces or to a teammate with occassional dribbling and dodging.

As the forward line approaches the offensive twenty five yard line, the ball should be centered. At this point, all offensive players should rush as if the pass were for them. The ideal situation is to place the ball on a teammate's stick at the top of the circle so that she can immediately shoot. If, however, the player receiving the ball is not at the top of the circle and an opponent is advancing to tackle her, she can make a through pass into the circle and a teammate may rush to field the ball and make the shot on goal. Once the offense is near the offensive circle, the defense is usually marking so that through passes are more successful than square passes. As a shot on goal is made, the two inners and the player making the shot should rush the goal to pick up any rebounds and flick or scoop them into the net.

When in the circle, forwards should be constantly repositioning. They must move forward and back to prevent being offsides and they must move laterally to free themselves for a cut for a pass. All forwards should learn to feint one direction and move another.

Throughout the offensive drive, the halfbacks on the offensive team must back up the forward line. They must pick up passes before they reach opposing forwards and immediately direct them back to their own forward line. At the top of the circle they must cut off clears and if uncontested carry the ball to the top of the circle and shoot. If they draw a defender, they must pass to the free forward so that she may shoot. All to often, halfbacks simply pick up clears and direct the ball back into the "thick" of things. Halfbacks must learn to watch and if possible direct the play into an open area of the circle. In many cases, she may pass to another halfback or a forward on the other side of the circle. The halfback who will and is able to direct play, is the best asset a team can have. If a defense has to contend with three halfbacks that can and will shoot and can and do move the ball from one side of the circle to the other, they will be the first to admit that they will have to depend on their own forward line to help out on defense.

Pulling the defensive forward line down to help out on defense not only tires the opponents, but makes them less likely to be in an advantageous offensive position if and when a defender successfully clears the ball.

SPECIAL GAME SITUATIONS

Free Hit

A free hit is awarded to the opposing team for fouls committed outside the striking circle. No player other than the one taking the hit may be within five yards of the striker.

When defending against the free hit, tactics vary depending on the area of the field in which the hit occurs. If on the offensive end of the field, forwards should make a semicircle around the striker making a pass difficult.

If on the defensive end of the field, forwards should mark their opposing forward to prevent the direct pass, and defenders should cover the spaces through which a pass may be attempted.

On offensive free hits, the striker must make the hit as soon as possible to prevent the defense from being set. Other team members should be constantly moving to free themselves for a pass.

Corners

A penalty corner (Figure 9-12) occurs when any foul is committed in the striking circle by the defense

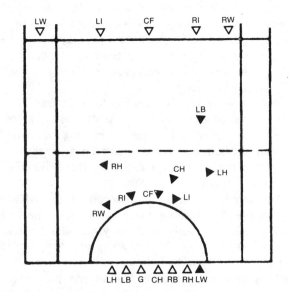

FIGURE 9-12.   Player position on penalty corner.

or if the ball is intentionally sent behind the goal line by a defensive player. A corner occurs if the ball is unintentionally sent behind the goal line by a defensive player. In both cases six defenders are allowed behind the goal line and the remainder of the defending team must wait beyond the center line until the ball is touched by another player other than the one taking the corner.* Members of the offensive team must have their feet and sticks outside the striking circle.

Defensive players lining up behind the goal line rush and mark their forward as soon as the ball is hit. A slow defensive line allows the forwards to get a shot off for goal.

Offensive players on the edge of the circle should control the ball and shoot for goal in one smooth motion. As the shot is taken the other two inside forwards should rush the goal.

Push-In*

A push-in is awarded to the opposing team when the ball is sent over the side line. No player may be within five yards of the player taking the push.

The most effective defense against the push-in is to ring the player who is taking the push making it difficult for her to find space in which to move the ball.

The most effective offense in the push-in situation is to take the push-in before the defense is set. In the defensive end of the field, one should attempt to move the ball down field toward the other goal as much as possible. In other areas of the field, one may take more liberties with the type of strategy utilized.

Rushing

Rushing refers to the fast movement toward the goal usually characteristic of the three inside forwards. Since it is more advantageous to shoot from the top of the circle, usually the center or one of the two inners will take the initial shot on goal. The remaining two players move (rush) toward the goal in an attempt to make a second shot if the ball is successfully deflected. The two inners rush toward the right and left goal posts and the center rushes toward the center of the goal. With the three inside forwards

*experimental rule

in this position they should be able to handle any deflections.

Triangular Pass

The triangular pass is one of the most effective means of passing a defensive player. It is usually employed as a wing to inner pass, but is effective on any part of the field. It is a combination of a flat pass and a diagonal pass forward, i.e. the wing, attempting to pass her defender, passes flat to her inner. The inner then passes the ball diagonally forward to be picked up by the wing who has now sprinted past her defending halfback.

SAFETY PRACTICES

When field hockey was first played it was intended that the game be played on a smooth surface similar to our present day golf green. However, few schools have fields where slopes are eliminated and the grasses well cut. This, as well as the unpredictable weather and the use of wooden sticks and a hard ball, make field hockey a potentially dangerous activity Adhering to a few basic safety rules, however, prevents injuries and allows the participant to enjoy the sport.

1. Always warm-up properly prior to a game. The warm-up should include stretching, jogging and stickwork practice.
2. Survey the field and determine possible hazards; i.e. sudden dips, gravel areas, or areas where grass is long.
3. Field shoes should be worn to prevent slipping when fields are wet.
4. Tennis shoes provide a better grip on artificial or frozen surfaces.
5. All extra balls should be removed from the field before starting stickwork drills or the game.
6. When scooping, keep the handle of the stick on the left side of the body to prevent the stick from jabbing into the stomach.
7. Avoid rough play, i.e. tripping, shoving, charging, or striking at an opponent.
8. If the ball is hit without controlling it, the ball often rises dangerously.
9. Do not drive the ball into the legs of an opponent who is close by.

EXERCISE   Definitions and List of Terms

1. When a player moves the ball in any direction using any part of the body, she is _____ .
2. A _____ is executed at the start of the game, the beginning of the second half and after each goal.
3. The player who plays between the two inners on the forward line is referred to as the _____ .
4. A _____ is usually made between the fifty and twenty-five yard line to increase attacking strength.
5. Kicking or driving the ball out of potential scoring area is referred to as _____ .
6. A _____ is awarded when the defense unintentionally sends the ball behind the goal line.
7. A _____ is awarded if the ball is sent over the end line, not between the goal posts, by an attacking player or unintentionally by a defender beyond the twenty-five yard line.
8. A _____ is a hockey skill which allows a player to maneuver the ball past an opponent and leave the player free to pass or dribble.
9. A _____ is executed by a series of short taps with the stick while moving at full speed.
10. A _____ is a two handed hit, hands together or apart, which is utilized for clears, shots on goal, and passes because of its potential speed and distance.
11. A shot on goal which rises slightly off the ground and has spin imparted to it is referred to as a _____ .
12. A _____ is an infringement of the rules, such as raising the stick above the shoulders, under cutting the ball, obstructions, or striking, hitting, holding, or interfering with an opponent's stick.
13. A _____ is awarded to a team when the opposing team has committed an infringement of the rules.
14. The _____ play between the halfbacks and the goalkeeper and are usually considered solely defensive players.
15. When the ball passes wholly over the goal line between the goal posts and under the cross bars a _____ is scored.
16. The _____ is the last line of defense.
17. Players which have heavy responsibilities both offensively and defensively are referred to as _____ .
18. When two players temporarily assume each others position and duties, it is referred to as _____ .
19. The forwards playing next to the outside forwards are referred to as _____ .
20. When a defensive player plays within a stick's length of her opponent and stays between her opponent and the ball and her opponent and the goal, the defender is said to be _____ .
21. When a player places her body between her opponent and the ball and thereby restrains her opponent from fielding the ball, she has committed an _____ .
22. When ahead of the ball, a player must have at least two defenders between her and the goal or she is considered _____ .
23. Directing the ball to a teammate or into a space where a teammate may move to field the ball, is referred to as _____ .
24. A _____ is awarded to the attacking team whenever the defense commits a foul in the striking circle or intentionally sends the ball over the end line past the twenty-five yard line.
25. A _____ is awarded when a goal would have most likely been scored if not for a breach of the rules by a defender.
26. When the ball passes over the side line, the team not responsible for its going out of bounds, is awarded a _____ .

27. When the stick is turned in the hands so that the toe of the stick points toward the ground, this position is referred to as _____ .
28. When a player runs toward the goal line following a shot on goal, she is said to be _____ .
29. A _____ is a stroke where the ball is lifted into the air during a dodge, a shot on goal, or to advance the ball on wet surfaces.
30. The area directly in front of the goal cage, where the ball must be hit by an attacker before a goal may be scored, is referred to as the _____ .
31. A _____ is an attempt by a player to take the ball from an opponent or force the opponent to pass.
32. When a teammate of the ball carrier positions herself between the ball carrier and her opponent, thereby not allowing her fair opportunity to secure the ball, it is referred to as a _____ .
33. A _____ travels through the defense down the field toward goal. Utilized when the defense is marking.
34. A _____ is a maneuver used by two players to bypass an opponent.
35. A _____ is the outside forward on the front line.

1. Advancing
2. Bully
3. Center Forward
4. Centering Pass
5. Clearing
6. Corner
7. Defense Hit
8. Dodge
9. Dribble
10. Drive
11. Flick
12. Foul
13. Free Hit
14. Fullback
15. Goal
16. Goalkeeper
17. Halfback
18. Interchanging
19. Inners
20. Marking
21. Obstruction
22. Offsides
23. Passing
24. Penalty Corner
25. Penalty Stroke
26. Push-In
27. Reverse Sticks
28. Rushing
29. Scoop
30. Striking Circle
31. Tackle
32. Third Person Obstruction
33. Through Pass
34. Triangular Pass
35. Wing

QUESTIONS AND ANSWERS ON THE RULES

1. Q. What is the duration of a field hockey game?
   A. A game consists of two thirty-five minute halves with time outs only allowed for injury.
2. Q. How much time is allowed between halves?
   A. Half time shall not exceed five minutes.
3. Q. How is a field hockey game started?
   A. A game is started by a center bully between two opposing fowards.
4. Q. What occurs if the center bully is not executed properly?
   A. The bully is repeated.
5. Q. What are the restrictions placed on the remainder of the players during a center bully?
   A. Every player must be nearer her own goal line that the ball and at least five yards from the players participating in the bully.
6. Q. How may the ball be played after the center bully?
   A. The ball may be propelled by dribbling or passing using only the flat side of the hockey stick (blade).
7. Q. How is a goal scored?
   A. The ball must be hit or glance off the stick of an offensive player in the striking circle

and pass completely over the goal line between the goal posts and below the cross bar. A goal is counted as one.

8. *Q.* How is play resumed after a goal is scored?

   A. Play is intiated again by a center bully.

9. *Q.* What is offsides?

   A. Offsides occurs whenever a player is ahead of the ball and there is not two defensive players between her and the goal. The opposing team is awarded a free hit.

10. *Q.* What is a foul during a field hockey game?

   A. There are several fouls, some of which include (a) raising the stick above shoulder level, (b) using the rounded side of the stick, (c) undercutting the ball, (d) interfering with an opponent's stick, (e) passing the ball between one's feet, (f) giving impetus to the ball other than with the stick, (g) handling an opponent by any means, and (h) obstructing an opponent.

11. *Q.* What are the penalties for a foul or an infringement of the rules?

   A. An infringement of the rules may result in several different calls by the officials depending on where the infringement occurred. It may result in a free hit, push-in, corner, penalty corner, defense hit, or a penalty stroke.

12. *Q.* What is a free hit?

   A. An uncontested hit by a member of the team not infringing the rules. No player may stand within five yards of the player taking the hit. A free hit is awarded when the infringment of the rules occurs outside the striking circle.

13. *Q.* What is a push-in?

   A. When the ball passes over the side line, the opposing team is awarded a push-in. No player may be within five yards of the player pushing the ball in.

14. *Q.* What is a corner?

   A. When the ball is unintentionally sent behind the end line by a defensive player, the offensive team drives the ball in from a point within five yards of the nearest corner flag.

15. *Q.* What is a penalty corner?

   A. For any breach of the rules by the defense within the circle or if the defense intentionally sends the ball behind the end line, the offense drives the ball from a point not less than ten yards from the goal posts. A goal may not be scored directly from a penalty corner.

16. *Q.* What restrictions are placed on players on a corner and penalty corner?

   A. The attacking team including their sticks and feet must be outside the circle. Six of the defending team including their sticks and feet shall be behind the end line. The remainder of the defending team must be behind the center line.

17. *Q.* What is a defense hit?

   A. When the ball is unintentionally sent behind the end line by an offensive player, the defense is awarded a hit opposite the spot where the ball crossed the goal line and sixteen yards from the inner edge of that line.

18. *Q.* What is a penalty stroke?

   A. A stroke awarded to the offensive team when a goal most likely would have been scored if not for a breach of rules by the defense.

19. *Q.* Who takes the penalty stroke?

   A. Any offensive player.

20. *Q.* How is the penalty stroke executed?

   A. The attacking player stands seven yards in front of the goal and may either push, flick or scoop the ball in an attempt to score. The goalkeeper must stand on the goal line. In making the stroke, the offensive player may take one step forward.

21. *Q.* What are the restrictions on the remainder of the players during a penalty stroke?

   A. All other players must stay behind the twenty-five yard line.

22. *Q.* How is play resumed after a penalty stoke?
    A. If a goal is scored, the game is restarted by a center bully. If a goal is not scored, the defense is given a hit sixteen yards from the center of the goal cage.
23. *Q.* What special privileges are the goalkeepers allowed?
    A. The goalkeeper is allowed to kick the ball or stop it with any part of her body but only in her own circle.
24. *Q.* When may a substitution be made?
    A. There are no substitutions allowed in field hockey except in the case of injury.

BIBLIOGRAPHY

All England Women's Hockey Association. *Coach Yourself Series Women's Hockey*. Marjorie Pollard Publications, LTD., The Deanery, Bampton, Oxford.

All England Women's Hockey Association. *Women's Hockey*. Educational Productions LTD., London, 3rd ed., 1969.

Cadel, Marjorie. *Coaching Hockey an ABC*. 2nd ed. Whilemilnes Kencot Lechlade Glos: Marjorie Pollard Publications Limited, 1974.

Clarke, Trevor. *Hockey Teaching and Coaching*. London: Lepus Books, 1976.

Hausserman, Caroline. *Field Hockey*. 4th printing, Boston: Allyn and Bacon, Inc., 1975.

Hickey, Melvyn. *Hockey For Women*. 2nd ed. London: Kaye and Ward Limited, 1970.

Meyer, Margaret H., Ph. E., Poindexter, Hally Beth, Ed. D. *Team Sports For Girls And Women*. 4th ed. Philadelphia: W. B. Saunders Co., 1965.

Poindexter, Hally B. W., Ed. D., Mushier, Carole L., Ph. B. *Coaching Competitive Team Sports For Girls and Women*. Philadelphia: W. B. Sunders Company, 1973.

Powell, Agneta. *Hockey Stick Work Games and Rotations.*, 1960.

Read, Brenda. *Better Hockey For Girls*. London: Kaye and Ward, 1971.

Taylor, Eileen. *Coaching Hockey in Schools*. 4th ed. The Deanery, Bampton Oxford: Marjorie Pollard Publications, LTD.

United States Field Hockey Association. *The Eagle*. Selected Team Positions, T.M. No. 5.

Vannier, Maryhelen, Ed. E., Poindexter, Hally Beth, Ed. D. *Physical Activities For College Women*. 2nd ed. Philadelphia: W. B. Saunders Company, 1969.

West, Barbara W. *Practices For Hockey Players*. The Deanery Bampton Oxford: Marjorie Pollard Publications, LTD.

10

GOLF

DESCRIPTION OF THE ACTIVITY

Golf is played on a course made up of units called holes. The basic pieces of equipment used are clubs and a ball. The ball is propelled along a designated route toward a hole by being struck with various clubs, each of which is designed for a specific purpose or distance. Each time the ball is hit with a club, one stroke is made. The object of the game is to get the ball into the hole with the least number of strokes. An official round is eighteen holes, however, there are many golf courses which have only nine holes.

Each hole on the course is made up of the teeing ground, or tee, the place from which the ball is first hit on each hole; the fairway, the maintained area between the teeing ground and the green; and the green, the special grass area that is designed for putting and that contains the hole. The area to each side of the fairway, where the grass is permitted to grow longer and where weeds, trees, and other obstacles are found, is called the rough. There may also be bunkers, sand traps, water, an other hazards within or to the side of the fairway. The purpose of the rough and the hazards is to form obstacles to handicap the players who make poor strokes.

Each hole is given a rating called par, which is, in general, based upon the length of the hole and is computed upon the number of strokes it would take an expert player to hole out, or get the ball into the cup, in errorless play, under normal conditions, with two putts allotted to each green. Par for any course is determined by adding the par for each of the eighteen holes.

The first stroke for each hole is made from the teeing ground. If it is a par four or five, a wood club would generally be used because it is designed to obtain distance. If it is a par three hole, an iron club may be used depending upon the distance. The first stroke on the par four and five holes is called the drive. The object of a drive is to hit the ball into the fairway as close to the green as possible. The second stroke, in which the player attempts to hit the ball on the green, is the approach shot. After the ball is on the green, the succeeding strokes are putts. The ball may be placed on a tee before it is hit from the teeing ground; however, after the first stroke with exceptions, it may not be touched, except by the club, until it is on the green where, under certain conditions, it may be picked up before it is holed out.

There are two general types of competition in golf: medal play and match play; but several adaptations of these two types are used. In medal play, competition is by strokes, with the winner being the player who takes the lowest total number of strokes for a given round or rounds. In match play, competition is by holes, with the winner in this case being the player who wins the most holes in a given round or rounds. A hole is won by the player who takes the least number of strokes to hole out. The match ends as soon as one player has won more holes than there are holes left to play. The total number of strokes per round in match play is not important. A player may lose a hole by one or many strokes. It is possible for the winner in match play to finish with a greater number of strokes for the round than the loser. Medal play is, therefore, more exacting than match play because each stroke is computed in the scoring.

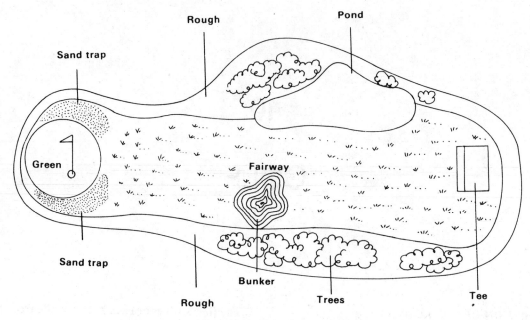

FIGURE 10-1. A typical golf hole.

A special kind of match play called the Nassau System is sometimes used. In this play a match is worth three points, with one point being given to the winner of the first nine holes, one point to the winner of the second nine holes, and one point awarded to the winner of the eighteen holes.

The Scotch Foursome is another type of competition in which a team of two play only one ball. Each of the team members strokes it alternately. However, practically all golf competitions and tournaments use medal play or match play to determine the winner.

Golf is one of the few sports which uses a system of handicapping to equalize competition among competitors of greatly varying abilities. This system operates by permitting the player with a higher average score to subtract a certain number of strokes from his total gross score which gives him a net score in medal play. In match play, this same player will subtract strokes from his total for certain holes designated as being the most difficult. In this case, if a player has a handicap of four, he would subtract one stroke from his total on each of the four most difficult holes on that particular course. The score card of most golf courses will give this rating.

TABLE 10-1. Par distance.

Par	Women Yards	Men Yards
3	up to 210	up to 250
4	211-400	251-470
5	401-575	471 and over

The golf course is the entire area in which play is permitted. The boundaries of the course and of each hole should be clearly marked. The par for a course is based upon eighteen holes and will generally be 70, 71, or 72, depending upon the total length of the course, its degree of difficulty, and the number of par 5 holes included.

EQUIPMENT

The basic equipment necessary to play golf is clubs, balls, a golf bag, tees, and proper clothing. Other gear, such as mobile carts, pull carts, folding seats, and putting tees, are used, but are not essential.

Clubs

The number, quality, and type of clubs recommended for use will vary with the degree of skill of the golfer. A beginner would do well to start out with a minimum number of moderately priced clubs, and use these until he has developed some skill. He can then sell these or trade them for a better and more complete set. A novice could learn to play the game well by starting out with four irons, numbers 3, 5, 7, and 9; a putter; and two woods, numbers 2 and 4.

Clubs need to be carefully used and maintained. They should never be hit into rocks or other solid surfaces, and after being used in the rain or in wet grass the should be dried. The face, head, and shank should be cleaned at regular intervals; the club should be cleaned, treated with a preservative, and stored in a clean, dry place at the end of the playing season. The heads of the wooden clubs should be waxed often to prevent absorption of moisture, and they should be kept covered with gloves designed for that purpose.

Balls

The vast array of golf balls on the market today is no doubt very confusing. Balls can be purchased for almost any price, ranging from 25¢ to $1.25 each. The official rules establish the following standards for balls: the weight cannot exceed 1.620 ounces, the diameter should be no more than 1.680 inches, and the maximum velocity must not surpass 250 feet per second as measured by the United States Golf Association apparatus. Good golf balls will cost more, but for the average player the most expensive balls may not give the service nor be any more functional than the less expensive balls because the more expensive balls have a very thin covering that is easily cut. They are made to develop great compression, necessary to get maximum distance which is needed by professional golfers. A ball with a some-what thicker cover may fall ten to fifteen yards shorter than a thinner-skinned ball, but the former will last longer and is more functional for the novice. In order for balls to retain true flight characteristics and to be easily visible, they should be kept clean.

Practice balls made of plastic and cotton are useful in the teaching and learning process because they are durable, economical, and provide the beginner with the opportunity to hit an object that is the same size as a real golf ball, but that will travel only a few yards. They are so light that they are not destructive to anything they may hit.

Golf Bag and Tees

A golf bag is necessary for carrying clubs, balls, and other items. They vary is size, material, cost, and shape. It is best to purchase the type that provides individual compartments for each club since this will decrease wear and tear on the clubs. If the player expects to carry his own bag, he should purchase one made from lightweight material.

Tees are made of many different kinds of material from wood to metal. Wooden tees are generally as functional as any other type.

Clothing

A player who expects to play or practice golf frequently should wear a glove on his left hand; otherwise the constant friction will cause blisters and calluses. The health and comfort of the feet are dependent upon the shoes and socks worn, therefore a good pair of shoes made with replaceable spikes is essential. Other necessary pieces of clothing should include a loose-fitting shirt, loose-fitting trousers, and a hat or cap to afford protection from the sun.

1. Putter
2. Pitching wedge
3. #9 iron ⎫
4. #8 iron ⎬ short irons
5. #7 iron ⎭
6. #6 iron ⎫
7. #5 iron ⎬ medium irons
8. #4 iron ⎭
9. #3 iron ⎫
10. #2 iron ⎭ long irons
11. Cleek (#4 wood)
12. Spoon (#3 wood)
13. Brassie (#2 wood)
14. Driver (#1 wood)

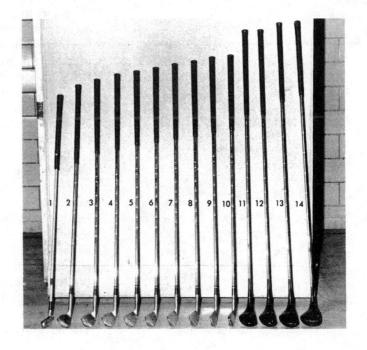

FIGURE 10-2.   The clubs.

SKILLS AND TECHNIQUES

Except for the putting motion, all golf clubs are swung with very similar, fundamental movements, which are neither natural nor inborn and must, therefore, be learned. Another essential concept to be grasped by the learner is that the golf swing must be learned and performed as a complete movement. Even though its parts—the stance, backswing, pause, downswing, and follow-through—can be discussed from an academic viewpoint, the swing itself must be a completely coordinated and continuous motion from the start of the backswing to the end of the follow-through.

In addition to the swing, golf skills include the knowledge of which club to use, the judgment of distance, the adjustment of stance, and the ability to read the contour of the green. However, none of these will be effective if the ability to stroke the club properly is absent. This does not mean that every individual should have an identical swing. There is no perfect swing. Actually, each person must develop his own swing as he interprets it, and as he modifies it to conform to his physical and psychological makeup. There are, however, certain generally accepted techniques of grip, stance, and body-arm movement and position that have proven effective in aiding the individual to stroke the ball with control, accuracy, and speed. The novice should not involve himself in the advanced and confusing refinements with which professional and highly skilled players often become preoccupied.

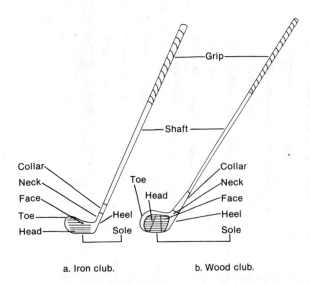

FIGURE 10-3.   Parts of the club.

FIGURE 10-4.   The grip. a. Correct left-hand placement on club handle. b. Right-hand position in relation to the left hand.

FIGURE 10-5.   The grip. a. The overlapping grip. b. the interlocking grip.

Grip

The purpose of the grip is to make it possible for the player to strike the ball with the greatest possible accuracy and power. With the correct grip, the hands work together to guide the club head under the force of powerful muscle contraction through the backswing, downswing, and follow-through into the proper position for achieving the desired flight of the ball. The correct grip is not natural, and it will feel awkward and uncomfortable to the novice when he first tries it.

The student should grip the club with the head of the club grounded and the shaft pointed up at the proper angle. (The correct grip from the left hand can be seen in Figure 10-4a.) The palm of the left hand should face directly back, away from the intended flight of the ball. Starting at the second joint of the index finger, the club handle is placed diagonally across the palm to the middle part of the heel of the hand, above the little finger. The fingers are closed around the shaft, with the index finger curled around it in a manner of gripping a pistol trigger. The last three fingers do most of the firm gripping.

This manner of gripping places the control in the fingers rather than in the palm. The thumb is extended down and slightly to the right of the top of the club shaft. When the grip is complete, the V formed by the thumb and index finger should point up toward the inside of the right shoulder, and the left hand should be located slightly on top of the club shaft with three of the third-knuckle joints visible to the student if he has the correct stance.

The right hand is placed below the left hand. The grip of the right hand is begun with the palm facing the intended line of the ball's flight. The club shaft is placed on the second joint of the index finger, and then diagonally across the palm at an angle similar to that across the left hand. The area at the base of the thumb and palm fits over the thumb of the left hand. The thumb of the right hand is pointed at a downward angle toward the left of the club shaft, and grips the shaft opposite the index and middle fingers. The V formed by the thumb and index finger points in the same direction as the V of the left hand. Most of the gripping is done with the thumb and first two fingers. The third and little fingers keep the right hand in position and help to coordinate the movement of the right hand with that of the left.

After the grip is completed, it can be checked for correctness by noting if the three following conditions exist: the V between the thumb and forefinger of each hand should point toward the inside of the right shoulder, three knuckles on each hand should be visible to the student, and both thumbs should point downward with the right one visible and gripping just to the left of the club shaft.

There are three different ways of joining the fingers of the right and left hands in the back of the grip: the overlapping, or vardon; the interlocking, and the nonjoining. Under ordinary conditions it is not advisable to use the latter grip; however, it is taught to persons who have small hands, short fingers, and weak wrists. Most experts seem to prefer the overlapping grip, although neither of the first two are sound. When one is chosen, it must be used consistently for some time before it becomes comfortable and efficient.

Overlapping Grip. The overlapping grip is made by placing the little finger of the right hand over the index finger of the left hand. At the same time the third finger of the right hand should be fitted snugly against the index finger of the left hand (see Figure 10-5a).

Interlocking Grip. In the interlocking grip, the little finger of the right hand and the index finger of the left hand are interlocked. This is accomplished by lifting both fingers away from the club shaft and placing each inside the other, and then closing them firmly (see Figure 10-5b).

Stance and Address

Three types of stances are used in golf: the square, the open, and the closed. The good golfer uses each for a specific purpose or in a particular situation.

In the square stance the feet are placed parallel to the intended line of flight of the ball. In the open stance the left foot is placed farther back than the right foot from the line of the flight of the ball. The closed stance is assumed by placing the left foot closer than the right foot to the line of the flight of the ball.

Stance consists of more than placement of the feet. It includes position of the club, distance of the feet from each other, position of the ball, and body and head alignment. For a full swing under tee or fairway conditions, the following stance should be taken. The

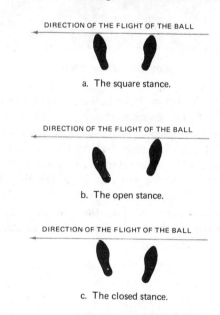

DIRECTION OF THE FLIGHT OF THE BALL

a. The square stance.

DIRECTION OF THE FLIGHT OF THE BALL

b. The open stance.

DIRECTION OF THE FLIGHT OF THE BALL

c. The closed stance.

FIGURE 10-6. Stances.

club is grounded so that the sole rests directly on the ground, the club faces in the direction of the desired flight of the ball, and the shaft is aligned with the left hand, arm, and shoulder. The feet are approximately a shoulder width apart, with the toes pointing out and the weight evenly distributed over the feet. The body leans to the ball, bending at the hips to adjust to the club length, and the knees are slightly flexed. The right shoulder is lower than the left. The head and eyes are pointed directly at the ball and remain in that position during most of the swing.

FIGURE 10-7.   The address.

The distance between the ball and the body will be determined by the length of the club and the height of the player, but the body should adjust itself so that the sole of the club rests flat on the ground. The placement of the ball in relation to an imaginary line drawn from toe to toe will vary from directly off the left heel to a point in front of the right heel. The novice should start out with the ball teed out at a point off the left heel and move it back as strength and skill are acquired.

Swing

The purpose of the grip and the stance is to establish a base for the swing which is made up of the backswing, the downswing, and the follow-through.

Backswing. The backswing is an unhurried, coordinated, weight-shifting movement in which the body and arms turn from left to right. It starts from the address position, with the head and eyes pointed down at the ball. Action is initiated by a unified movement of all parts of the body toward the right. This movement brings the club head back from four to six inches, keeping it low to the ground surface and directly in line with the intended direction of the flight of the ball. The body and arms continue to turn to the right, with little lateral movement, until the

hips form an approximately 45-degree angle and the shoulders a 90-degree angle with the desired line of flight of the ball. During this movement, the weight shifts toward the right leg, the right knee remains slightly flexed, and the left knee flexes and turns in toward the right leg. The flexion and the turning in of the left leg, caused by the pressure of the body twist, will force the heel to rise slightly from the ground. This latter action should never be exaggerated.

The arms become a part of the body rotation but with some turning and lifting action of their own. When the left arm is almost parallel with the ground, the wrists will start to cock and continue on smoothly until they are fully cocked at the height of the backswing. The wrist-cock direction is from the little finger side of the hand toward the thumb side, which places both hands below the club grip at the completion of the backswing. The left arm remains relatively straight throughout the backswing and the right upper arm is held in close to the right side. The right elbow is pointed downward at completion of the backswing.

When the backswing is completed, the hands are at about the height of the head, the club shaft is approximately parallel to the ground and pointed in the direction of the desired flight of the ball, the eyes are focused on the ball, the left shoulder is under the chin, and the weight is mostly on the right leg. There is always a slight pause at this point in order for the body to gather itself for the downswing.

Downswing. The downswing is a unified body movement in which there is a reversal of the pivot made in the backswing. The force is exerted in a downward direction. The purpose is to bring the club down in the same path by which it was taken up. The weight transfers from the right to the left leg and the hips and shoulders rotate to the left to aid the downward motion of the arms to the impact position where the wrists uncock and explode the club head through the ball, and on into the follow-through. It is essential for the hips to turn far enough to the left to clear out for the arms. The uncocking of the wrists should be delayed as long as possible.

The left side of the body takes the weight and becomes the pivotal point of the body's leftward rotation, and the stable line from which the stroke takes place. The right hip and shoulder turn to the left with the latter coming under the chin to replace the retreating left shoulder, the right elbow is tucked in close to the body, and the left arm stays relatively straight. These motions bring the club head into the hitting area from the inside. The club moves into the ball directly in line with the ball's intended flight and continues in that line as long as possible. The head remains steady throughout, and the eyes keep their focus on the ball and then on the spot where it lies until well after contact has been made. The head and eyes do not turn from this position until the follow-through has almost been completed.

Follow-Through. The follow-through is an essential phase of the swing in which the body completes its turn and the force of the downswing is dissipated. In the follow-through, the momentum generated by the downswing causes the hips and shoulders to continue to rotate to the left until the chest and abdomen face the intended flight of the ball, thus also causing most of the weight to shift to the left leg. The club head moves on through the hitting area, staying in the line of the flight of the ball as long as possible. The hands complete the circle by finishing at approximately the height of the head, with the club head pointing in the opposite direction of the flight of the ball.

Iron Clubs

The angle of the face of the iron clubs varies from the near straight angle of the long irons to the deep angle of the short irons and the pitching wedge. However, the swings for all iron strokes are essential-

TABLE 10-2.   Iron clubs and their distances.

Number of Club	Yards
1 Iron	190-210
2 Iron	170-190
3 Iron	160-180
4 Iron	150-170
5 Iron	140-160
6 Iron	120-140
7 Iron	110-130
8 Iron	90-110
9 Iron	80-100
Pitching wedge	60-90

ly alike. The difference is principally in the lengths of the backswing and of the follow-through. In the use of all the irons, the ball is hit as the club head is still traveling downward and before the club head moves into the turf. This action produces a backspin, which reduces the roll thereby giving better control. All irons are played to hit to the green.

Long Irons. The long irons are the numbers 1, 2, and 3 clubs. The number 1 iron should not be used by a novice because it is very difficult to control. The beginner and the average player should learn to use the number 3 first. The swing is identical with the one already described, and the ball is played from a point

a. The address.   b. The backswing.   c. Midway through the follow-through.   d. Completion of the follow-through.

FIGURE 10-8.   The full swing.

 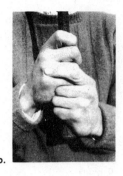

a.   b.

FIGURE 10-9. The putting grip. a. Front view. b. Back view: the reverse overlap that many good golfers use.

out from the left heel in a square stance. The maximum distance of a hit with a long iron will vary according to the individual, but one rule should be followed by all and that is to know what the distance is and never to press for a greater distance. If more distance is desired, a wood should be used.

Medium Irons. The medium irons are the numbers 4, 5, and 6 clubs. They are used mainly to make the approach shot to the green; however, they are also employed to get out of the rough or the hazards. The angle of the face of the medium irons is deeper than that for the long irons; therefore, they produce greater loft, more backspin, and less distance than the long irons. The club shaft is also shorter, which compels the player to take the stance closer to the ball and to bend more sharply at the waist. This type of stance will produce a swing which stays closer to the line of the intended flight of the ball. The ball should be hit from a point toward the middle of a nearly square stance.

Short Irons. The 7, 8, and 9 irons are generally classified as the short irons; the sand and pitching wedges can be included in this category even though they are designed for a special function. The general purpose of these clubs is to chip to the green from a distance of 60 to 145 yards; therefore, accuracy rather than distance is emphasized. The club shaft is shorter and the face is larger and has a steeper angle than that for the medium and long irons. These characteristics make the short irons more accurate and give them more loft than the other clubs. They also produce great backspin, which results in less run after the ball hits the playing surface. The stance taken by the player is generally opened and made slightly more narrow than that for the medium irons, and the ball is played from a point near the center of the stance. The backswing is reduced to a half or three quarters of the normal backswing, depending upon the distance desired. To get the best results

from these clubs, the club face should contact the ball on its downward arc and take turf after contact is made.

Putter. Half of the strokes for par golf is allotted to putts; therefore, the ability to putt well is probably the greatest stroke saver of all. Techniques for the grip, stance, and swing are different from those for all the other clubs, mainly because the aim is accuracy and finesse and not power and distance. The kinds of grip used vary a great deal, but there are some fundamental skills that are generally accepted by many teachers and good golfers.

The *grip* for putting is very similar to the one already described. The left hand is at the top of the club shaft, with the palm facing away from the intended line of the ball's roll. The club shaft angles across the hand from the second joint of the index finger to the heel of the hand, the fingers grip the shaft lightly, and the thumb is pointed straight down the club shaft. The right hand placement is below the left in very much the same position as for the irons and woods. The right palm is facing the intended line of the ball's roll and is opposite the left palm. The thumb is on the shaft, pointing directly down toward the club head (see Figure 10-10). The manner of joining the hands at the back of the grip is different from the one used for the woods and other irons. Several are used, but the one most often employed is the reverse overlapping. This is made by placing the index finger of the left hand over the little and ring fingers of the right hand.

The *stance and address* for the putt vary greatly; however, certain techniques are widely enough accepted to be worth copying. The body must necessarily be crouched low enough to use the short-shafted putter, the eyes and face are directly above the ball, the knees are slightly flexed, and most of the weight is on the left leg. The left elbow is bent and pointed out toward the desired line of the putt; the right arm is bent slightly, with the elbow pointed in the opposite direction of the desired line of the putt; and both arms are close to, but not touching the body. The stance is square and narrow, and the ball is teed on a point off the left heel or toe. Before starting the backswing, the putter should be placed behind the ball in the exact, desired hitting position.

The *stroke* is made by swinging the putter back low and directly in line with the desired path of the ball's roll. The forward motion and follow-through should remain in that exact line and low to the surface. At no time during the stroke should the putter blade deviate or rotate away from this line. The motion used for the putt is practically all arm movement as

FIGURE 10-10. The putting stroke.

the wrists are too unstable to be the controlling factor in making the putt. The ball can be struck with either a sharp tap or a kind of sweeping motion. The grip is loose but firm. The length of the backswing is determined by the distance the ball is to be putted, but it is always under control. The hands should never be behind the club head until after the start of the follow-through.

Wooden Clubs

The woods are designated by numbers from 1 through 5; the number 5, however is not used much. By name they are the driver (1), brassie (2), spoon (3), and cleek (4). The driver is used mainly for hitting a teed ball from the teeing ground; and the brassie, spoon, and cleek are employed for hitting long shots from the fairway, although professionals will occasionally use the driver for a fairway shot. The pitch of the face of the woods varies from 11 degrees for the driver to 19 degrees for the cleek. The novice should not attempt to use any wood until he has learned to hit with the irons, and he should learn to use the driver only after some experience with the other woods. He should use the brassie to hit the tee shot until he attains some consistency; and the spoon and the cleek for the long fairway strokes. Even for the woods, accuracy is more important than distance.

Grip and Swing. The grip and swing used for the woods are the same as the ones described above,

although there will be some variation because of the increased length of the club shaft and the larger and differently shaped club head. In general, the club face does not contact the ball on the downswing as is the case with the irons; instead the impact occurs at the bottom of the arc. A possible exception to this may occur with the number 4 wood. With this club the square stance is most generally used and the ball is teed at a point somewhere just off the left heel, back or slightly back toward the middle of the stance, according to the choice of the player.

Wedge Clubs

Two types of wedge are in general use: the pitching wedge and the sand wedge. The pitching wedge is used to hit short approach shots from the fairway to the green, and the sand wedge is imployed to stroke the ball out of sand traps that are located around the green. The two wedge clubs are similar in construction and are characterized by a broad, highly angled face, with a heavy, thick flange on the back and sole. The sand wedge is heavier and has more surface on its face. Both should be used from the beginning when learning the game.

Pitching Wedge. Certain basic techniques used with the pitching wedge are different from those used with the other irons. The ball is teed near the middle of the stance and closer to the golfer. There is less rotation of the hips and shoulders on the backswing,

a. Body and arm position at the top of the backswing.
b. Follow-through position, with the head down and the eyes focused on the ball.

FIGURE 10-11.   The pitching wedge stroke.

and the weight remains stable with slightly more weight on the left leg. The length of the backswing is determined by the distance required for the shot—the greater the distance, the more extreme the backswing. It is never sound, however, to swing the hands higher and farther back than about shoulder level. Regardless of the distance required, the wrists are cocked and the hitting is sharp and crisp but not powerful. The crispness results from the wrist snap. This shot will be ineffective if it is not hit in this manner.

Sand Wedge.   The sand wedge explosion shot requires a few special techniques. The feet must be well set in the sand in an open and somewhat broader stance than for the pitching wedge. There is little body rotation, the maximum backswing should not be greater than three-quarters, and the wrists are cocked more quickly than for most other strokes. The stance should be taken so that the position of the ball is at a point somewhere out from the middle of it. The club face will not hit the ball, but instead will contact the sand approximately two inches directly in back of the ball. It is important that the club head cuts through the sand and into the follow-through.

a. The backswing.

b. Start of down swing—weight is starting to shift to the left.

c. Just after contact—note that the head is well-down and eyes are still focused where ball lay.

FIGURE 10-12.   The sand wedge stroke.

BASIC STATEGY

The type of strategy used in team games does not apply to golf because the golfer plays his own ball in whatever way he thinks best, and his playing is not directly influenced by any act of his opponent. Although in some respects strategy and individual skill in golf are less distinguishable than in most other sports, certain actions performed by golfers can certainly be classified as strategy. It is generally wise when hitting with any of the clubs to aim for accuracy rather than for distance without control. It is much better to be in the fairway than in the rough even though the ball in the rough has been driven twenty yards father. Where both accuracy and distance are possible, the ideal has been attained.

Concentration in golf is difficult and requires much will power. In a round of eighteen holes, an average golfer will hit the ball from eighty to ninety times, and each of these shots requires a high degree of concentration. A golfer should make it a habit to go through all of the processes of judging distance, wind velocity, character of the target, the last bad shot, and of selecting the right club before taking his stance to hit the ball. When the stance is taken to hit the ball, all such matters should be forgotten, leaving the mind clear to concentrate on hitting the ball. Doubts about the club, the distance, the wind, or anything else must be wiped out. Many golfers will permit a bad shot or a poorly played hole to influence them mentally to the point where the next shot is made under mental duress, with resulting tension and anxiety. No player should permit a bad shot or the luck of a roll to determine his game. Each shot must be made as it comes up. Concentration on the immediate task is crucial. The act of making the club perform as it was constructed to perform is the highest kind of strategy and will make the difference of several strokes per round.

The choice of the correct club for each shot is important. This selection must be made not only upon the basis of the best information available from others, but also in terms of the player's own peculiarities and use of each club. It is impossible to copy anyone else exactly. After the club has been chosen, the ball must be hit with the confidence that it is the correct club for that particular shot.

If there is a water hazard on the hole, play away from it even though it means the sacrifice of a few yards. A ball in the water is a sure loss of a stroke.

In putting strategy, the lie of the ball, the distance to the hole, the break of the green, and the length and cut of the grass must be studied. After due consideration is given to these factors, and a decision reached, the putt must be made with the confidence that the decision is the correct one. It is generally best to putt long rather than shot since a short ball never falls. However, there may be situations which call for the lag-up within a foot of the hole.

The best golfers will frequently hit into a trap. The most important objective when trap-bound is to get out and on the green in one stroke and not to hole out.

SAFETY PRACTICES

Golf presents very few safety hazards; therefore, practices relating to safety are few and relatively simple. The greatest threats to health are found in the form of a flying club that has slipped from slippery hands, a ball that is hit too soon or wildly and that strikes another player, blisters, overexposure to the sun, or exposure to lightning from a thunderhead. Certain safety rules should be established to prevent or decrease injury occurring as a result of exposure to these hazards.

1. Be sure your hands are dry before making a stroke. This rule should be strictly enforced for group practice or practice indoors.
2. Do not hit the ball in a direction where people are close enough to be struck by it. Apply this rule to practice as well as play.
3. Sunstroke, or heat prostration can occur during very hot weather. Eat sufficient table salt to help the body retain liquids, and wear a head cover to protect against the direct rays of the sun. On hot days make short pauses between holes and drink water.
4. Thunderstorms often form suddenly during summer months. During one of these storms, do not take shelter under a single tree or use an umbrella out in the open since lightning seems to have an affinity for these. Seek protection and shelter at the club house. If this is not possible, a grove of many trees is much better than a single tree.
5. Even though golf is not an extremely vigorous sport, it does require endurance and toughness of the feet. Before playing a full round of eighteen holes after a layoff during the winter, there should be a gradual buildup. A conditioning process will help prevent blisters, pulled muscles, and undue fatigue.

WEIGHT TRAINING

Some top-notch golf players have employed selected weight-training exercises to help improve their game. An effective golf swing requires not only great finesse and coordination but also power and strength to obtain sufficient speed of the club head to propel the ball long distances. Furthermore, golf players must have great stamina and endurance which can only be acquired by hard work. Strong hands, fingers, wrists, arms, and upper trunk are essential for the swing; and strong legs are necessary for moving over the terrain of a golf course as well as establishing an effective hitting base.

Weight-training exercises appropriate for the development of skill in golf are: the clean and press, regular and reverse arm curls, wrist curls with palms up and with palms down, bent arm pull-over, toe raises, squats, rowing, and the bench press.

EXERCISE   Definitions and List of Terms

1. A hole-in-one is also called an _____ .
2. The position that a player takes before hitting the ball is the _____ .
3. The stroke that places the ball on the green is called the _____ .
4. That part of the golf course between the fairway and the green is the _____ .
5. The ball which is the greatest distance from the hole or the green is said to be _____ .
6. A hole played in one stroke less than par is a _____ .
7. One stroke more than par on a hole is _____ .
8. The number 2 wood is the _____ .
9. _____ is a term used to describe the roll of a putt which curves to the right or left because of a slope on the green.
10. A bare area on the fairway or near the green which contains sand is called a _____ or a _____ .
11. The distance a ball travels from the club until it hits the ground is the _____ .
12. Water which collects on a golf course from rain or a broken water main is called _____ .
13. The number 4 wood is called the _____ .
14. The entire area in which play is permitted is called _____ .
15. The strip of turf often cut up when making an iron stroke is a _____ .
16. _____ is used to describe a hole in which the green is hidden from view due to a bend of the fairway to the right or left.
17. In match play when one player is ahead of his opponent by the same number of holes as there are holes left to play he is said to be _____ .
18. Two strokes under par for a hole is an _____ .
19. A ball which curves slightly to the right near the end of its flight is said to _____ .
20. The part of the course between the teeing ground and the ground in which the grass is cut short is the _____ .
21. The pole which holds the flag and is placed in the hole as a marker is called the _____ .
22. _____ is the warning call or a golfer to persons who are in the way of play.
23. The caddie who goes in front of the players to watch the ball is the _____ .
24. The first nine holes of a course is the _____ nine. The last nine is the _____ nine.
25. That part of the course which contains the hole and is used for putting is the _____ .
26. _____ is a term used in match play to indicate that each competitor took the identical number of strokes to hole out on a particular hole.
27. Strokes given to higher-scoring players to equalize competition with lower-scoring players is called _____ .
28. Water, trees, bunkers, traps, and the like, included or built into a course in order to increase its difficulty are called _____ .
29. That division of the golf course which includes the teeing ground, fairway, and green is the _____ .
30. When the player puts the ball into the hole he has _____ .
31. The player who won the previous hole has the _____ and should be the first to hit his tee shot on the next hole.

32. The position in which the ball comes to rest after being stroked is its _____ .
33. Competition by holes is called _____ play.
34. Competition by strokes is called _____ play.
35. _____ is a type of golf competition in which one point is given to the winner of the first nine holes, one point to the winner of the second nine holes, and a third point is awarded to the winner of the eighteen holes.
36. The area in which play is not permitted is called _____ .
37. _____ is any stroke added to a player's total score because of a rule violation.
38. _____ is the number of strokes it takes an expert player to hole out on each hole under normal playing conditions.
39. A ball hit high to the green which develops much backspin and very little roll is a _____ shot.
40. In the winter, early spring, or when the fairways are in poor condition, local rules may permit a player to lift his ball and drop it in another spot. this is called _____ .
41. The part of the golf course that joins the fairways and that is not well maintained is the _____ .
42. It is called a _____ when the club head strikes the ground before impact with the ball.
43. _____ is a term describing a ball contacted with the heel and neck of the club.
44. A ball that travels to the right of the intended flight of the ball is a _____ . If it travels to the left of the intended line of flight it is a _____ .
45. The number 3 wood is called the _____ .
46. When a player places his feet in a certain relation to the intended line of the flight of the ball immediately preceeding the stroke, he has taken his _____ .
47. Each time the player hits the ball with the club a _____ is made.
48. The area from which the first stroke for each hole is made is the _____ .
49. The objects which mark the boundary of the teeing ground are called _____ .
50. A ball that is hit above its center and that rolls along the ground is said to have been _____ .
51. When a player is ahead of his opponent in either match or medal play he is said to be _____ . If he is behind, he is _____ .
52. _____ is a club with a steep pitch and heavy flanges on the head, used to hit the ball out of a sand trap.

1. Ace	19. Fade	36. Out-of-bounds
2. Address	20. Fairway	37. Penalty stroke
3. Approach	21. Flagstick	38. Par
4. Apron	22. Fore	39. Pitch shot
5. Away	23. Forecaddie	40. Preferred lie
6. Birdie	24. Front	41. Rough
7. Bogey	25. Green	42. Scuff
8. Brassie	26. Halved	43. Shanking
9. Break	27. Handicap	44. Slice
10. Bunker	28. Hazards	45. Spoon
11. Carry	29. Hole	46. Stance
12. Casual water	30. Holded out	47. Stroke
13. Cleek	31. Honor	48. Tee
14. Course	32. Lie	49. Tee markers
15. Divot	33. Match	50. Topped
16. Dog leg	34. Medal	51. Up, down
17. Down	35. Nassau	52. Wedge
18. Eagle		

QUESTIONS AND ANSWERS ON THE RULES

1. *Q.* Where is play permitted on the course?
   A. The ball may be played from any playable lie, except when outside the course boundaries.
2. *Q.* Are there restrictions related to club design?
   A. Yes. Some of these are very detailed, but in general all clubs must be constructed with a shaft and head, and no part may be moveable or adjustable.
3. *Q.* What restrictions are placed upon the ball?
   A. The weight of the ball shall not be less than 1.620 ounces, the diameter not less than 1.680 inches, and the velocity not more than 250 feet per second.
4. *Q.* How many clubs can a player have available for use during play?
   A. Only fourteen clubs may be carried during a round of golf.
5. *Q.* What kind of penalties result from rules violations?
   A. Penalties invoked vary according to the particular violation, and whether the violation is committed in match or medal play. Generally, penalties are one or two stroke, loss of hole, loss of distance, or disqualification. In situations where the penalty is loss of hole in match play, it will generally be two strokes in medal play.
6. *Q.* How is the golf game started?
   A. A game or round is begun by each player hitting a ball from the first teeing ground. The first player to hit the ball has the honor.
7. *Q.* What is the meaning of "the honor"?
   A. This is a term which designates the player who hits first from each tee. It is decided on the first tee by the order of the draw or by lot. After that the player with the lower score on the previous hole hits first.
8. *Q.* Do the rules permit a player to use his hands to touch or move a ball during play?
   A. Yes, under certain conditions; however, in general, the ball must be played as it lies after it comes to rest from a stroke. Some exceptions to this general rule, which permit the ball to be touched or moved without penalty, are: (1) if the ball needs to be checked for purposes of identification, except in a sand trap or hazard; (2) if it will interfere with the plan of another ball; (3) if it is in an unplayable lie or water hazard; (4) if it is unfit for play; (5) if it is moved when moving a movable obstruction; (6) if the ball is within two club lengths of an immovable obstruction; (7) if it comes to rest in casual water, in ground under repair, or in a hole made by a burrowing animal; (8) if it is one the green and needs cleaning, if there are ball marks in the turf that need repairing, if it has been struck and moved by another ball; and (9) if it lands on the wrong putting green.
9. *Q.* After a ball has been lifted how is it made ready for play?
   A. It may be dropped or placed, depending on the situation. Dropping is used through the green. It is performed by the player standing erect and dropping the ball behind him over his shoulder. He should drop it as near to the original spot as possible, but not nearer to the hole. Placing is used when the lifting occurs on the green. The ball is placed as near to the original spot as possible.
10. *Q.* Do the rules permit a player to move any object or objects which would interfere with making the stroke?
    A. Yes, under certain conditions. Any loose object may be removed without penalty; however, if the ball is moved in accomplishing this, a two stroke penalty is invoked.
11. *Q.* After the balls are hit from the teeing ground, which player hits first on the second and succeeding shots?
    A. The player whose ball is farthest from the hole hits first.
12. *Q.* In match play, what action is taken when an opponent's ball strikes a player's ball at rest and on the green?

A. There is no penalty. The ball may be replaced or played from where it was propelled by the other ball. If the ball is knocked into the hole, the opponent is scored as having holed out on the previous stroke.

13. Q. What action is taken when a fellow competitor's ball strikes a player's ball at rest on the green in stroke play?

A. When both balls lie within 20 yards of the hole a two stroke penalty is assessed against the player committing the violation. The other player's ball must be returned to its original position.

14. Q. Under what conditions is a ball declared unplayable?

A. The player himself will determine if it is unplayable. This can occur any place on the course.

15. Q. How does play proceed after a ball is hit out-of-bounds or is lost?

A. The player will play his next stroke at the spot from which the original stroke was made. If it was made on the teeing ground, the ball may be teed up; and if through the green or in a hazard, it will be dropped. To save time a provisional ball may be played in case the player knows beforehand that his ball is out-of-bounds or lost. If such is the case, he will continue to play the provisional ball until he holes out.

16. Q. What procedure is used when a ball is hit into a non-lateral water hazard?

A. Another ball may be dropped behind the hazard away from the green or it may be dropped at the spot from which the original ball was played. A one stroke penalty is assessed in either situation.

17. Q. What are the regulations when the ball strikes the flagstick?

A. The flagstick must be attended when the ball is being playing from the putting green. If it is not attended and the ball hits it, a violation has been committed. The penalty is two strokes in medal play and loss of hole in match play. The flagstick does not have to be attended or removed when the ball is played from off the green.

18. Q. When may a ball that is on the putting green be picked up?

A. It may be picked up to repair the ball marks on the turf, to be cleaned, when it interferes with another ball, when it is on the wrong green, or when it is struck by another ball.

19. Q. Is it legal to remove tall grass, leaves, branches, or other obstructions in order to provide better conditions to stroke the ball?

A. Loose obstructions may be removed; however, permanent and natural vegetation may not be broken, bent, or removed.

20. Q. How is it possible for some rules to be changed or modified for local golf clubs?

A. The United States Golf Association permits local golf clubs to modify certain rules to make play more enjoyable if there are specific abnormal conditions caused by weather and climatic conditions or by the nature of the course itself.

21. Q. What are the penalties for some of the more frequent rules violations?

A. The assessment of penalties for rules violations makes golf rules rather complicated because penalties for match and medal play vary. Some of the penalties are listed below.

Violation	Penalty	
	Medal Play	*Match Play*
Possessing more than fourteen clubs	2 strokes per hole, maximum of 4 per club	Loss of hole for each club at each hole violated
Moving or picking ball up in violation of rules	2 strokes	Loss of hole
Playing wrong ball (not in hazard)	2 strokes	Loss of hole
Dropping ball improperly	2 strokes	Loss of hole

Player, partner, or caddy stopping moving ball	None	1 stroke
Opponent stopping a moving ball	2 strokes	Loss of hole
Opponent touching or moving ball	None	1 stroke
Lost ball or ball out-of-bounds	1 stroke	1 stroke
Unplayable lie	1 stroke	1 stroke
Ball in water hazard	1 stroke	1 stroke
Ball striking flagstick or player's partner or caddy attending flagstick	2 strokes	Loss of hole
Ball striking unattended flagstick from the green	2 strokes	Loss of hole
Opponent's ball striking player's ball when both balls are on green	2 strokes	None

22. *Q.* What restrictions are placed on the putting stance?
    A. A player cannot putt using a stance astride the ball, or with either foot touching the line of the putt or its backward extension.
23. *Q.* What is the rule related to a lateral water hazard?
    A. The rule permit an option. It can be treated as a regular water hazard or a ball can be dropped within two club lengths from where the ball last crossed the edge of the hazard. The penalty is one stroke.
24. *Q.* Can a club be grounded previous to hitting a ball out of a hazard?
    A. No. In match play the penalty is loss of the hole; in stroke play it is two strokes.
25. *Q.* What is the penalty when a ball, played from the green, strikes the pin that has been removed from the hole?
    A. In match play the penalty is loss of the hole; in stroke play it is two strokes.
26. *Q.* What is the penalty when a ball that is played from a spot off the green hits an attended pin, a removed pin, or the person attending the pin?
    A. The penalty in match play is loss of the hole; in stroke play it is two strokes.
27. *Q.* What specific action can a player take when his ball is on the putting green?
    A. He can repair the ball mark left by his ball, lift his ball for cleaning, remove loose impediments between his ball and the hole, place his club head in front of the ball, and measure the distance to the hole to determine who is away. Otherwise, he cannot touch the surface between his ball and the hole.
28. *Q.* Is there a special rule concerning playing a ball that is buried so deep in a bunker or sand trap tha it is not visible?
    A. Yes. Enough sand or other debris can be removed to expose the top of the ball. The ball may be touched without penalty.
29. *Q.* What is the ruling on a ball in an unplayable lie?
    A. Two options are open. One, the player can go back to the spot from which the ball was hit and play another ball; two, he may drop a ball not more than two club lengths from the unplayable lie, and not closer to the hole. In either case it is a one stroke penalty.

BIBLIOGRAPHY

Bruce, B. and Davies, E. *Beginning Golf*. Belmont, Calif., Wadsworth Publishing Co., Inc., 1962.
Cheatum, Billye A. *Golf*. Philadelphia, W. B. Saunders Company, 1969.
Crogen, Corinne A. *Golf Fundamentals*. (rev. ed.), Palo Alto, California, National Press Books, 1964.

Finsterwald, D. and Robinson, L. *Fundamentals of Golf.* New York, The Ronald Press Company, 1961.

Gordin, Richard P. (editor) *Golf Coache's Guide,* Chicago, National Golf Foundation, 1975.

NAGWS, *Archer-Golf Guide.* Washington, D.C., AAHPER, 1975-77.

National Golf Foundation. *Twelve Comprehensive Professional Golf Lessons.* Chicago, The National Gold Foundation, 1972.

Abie Grossfeld,
Gymnastics Coach
Southern Connecticut State College

11

GYMNASTICS AND TUMBLING

DESCRIPTION OF ACTIVITY (MEN)

Gymnastics is a highly organized, competitive sport. It includes only certain, specific events, all of which are governed by well-defined and definite rules. These events have been accepted and adopted by the Fédération Internationale de Gymnastique (FIG), the governing organization for international competition including the Olympic Games, and by the Amateur Athletic Union of the United States. The standard events are floor exercise, side horse, rings, long horse vault, parallel bars, horizontal bar, and all-around. Tumbling and trampoline competition may be included as special events. Competition in the United States under the National Collegiate Athletic Association rules include all of the standard events.

Competitive gymnastics has great public appeal and acclaim and has its own dedicated following throughout the world. It offers a vast variety of activities that run the gamut of physical skills and fitness necessary to perform them. Throughout many years, skill and movement possibilities in the competitive events have been well explored and are thus highly developed today. The basis for measuring the improvement or skill level of an individual has, therefore, been standardized. Furthermore, in terms of the intensity of work required to develop great skill, the degree of danger involved in many of the more advanced tricks, the need for meticulous practice and work on details, and the dedication of its participants, gymnastics ranks very high among all sports. The more talented youth who becomes involved in gymnastics has the opportunity to set worthwhile goals and strive for a high level of performance.

Competition is conducted by requiring each contestant to perform in the event or events in which he is officially entered, and if he is entered in the all-around he must participate in all of the following events: floor exercise, side horse, rings, long horse vault, parallel bars, and horizontal bar. The Olympic rules require all contestants to compete in the all-around, and each contestant must execute both a compulsory and an optional exercise in all six of the above events. This procedure is continued in an orderly fashion until all contestants have completed their compulsory and optional exercises for all events. Each competitor is given credit for his personal score in each event. The team score for each event is computed by totalling the scores of its five highest scorers in each event. The winning team is the one whose members have amassed the highest combined points for all events. National Collegiate Athletic Association (NCAA) rules vary from Olympic rules in this area.

The order of events is established by the official rules for both dual and multiple team meets. The order of events for dual meets as established by the NCAA rules is: floor exercise, side horse, rings, trampoline, long horse vault, parallel bars, and horizonal bar. Events may be arranged somewhat differently for regional and championship meets in order to adjust to the needs of a situation involving a large number of contestants and teams.

The number of contestants from each team who may compete in each event and in the all-around competition and the number of events in which each contestant can participate are also established by rules. The NCAA rules allow a maximum of two all-around men and two specialists to participate in any specific event. Olympic rules permit six men from one team to compete in each event.

In dual-meet competition, the order in which members of opposing teams compete is fixed so that each team will have the last turn in every other event. A visiting team member will compete last in the floor exercise, rings, long horse vault, and horizontal bar. A member of the host team will compete last in the side horse, trampoline, and parallel bars. In Olympic competition, each country is given a set time of day to compete with five other countries. Six teams compete at once, rotating from event to event in the Olympic order.

Officiating is done for each event by four judges, one of whom is designated as the superior judge. In cases of emergency at collegiate dual meets, three judges may be used.

The scoring for all events is based upon a rating of 10 points for a perfect performance of an exercise. Each exercise is rated according to difficulty, combination, and execution. Execution of the exercise is weighted more heavily than either difficulty or combination. Points are deducted when a judge feels that any or all of these three criteria have not been perfectly met. For example, points are deducted for poor or incorrect execution, such as stops and weak positions; for technical faults, such as bent arms, bent legs, or touching the apparatus with wrong parts of the body; and for a weak start and end of a routine. A more complicated and dangerous trick is judged less severely than an easier one. The number of points that a judge may deduct can be either a whole number, a fractional part of it, or both. After a contestant has completed his routine, each of the judges rates him. These ratings are generally made without consultation. The scorer will then award a score to the contestant by eliminating the highest and lowest scores awarded by the judges, and averaging the two intermediate scores. For example, if the four judges have flashed individual scores of 8.1, 6.9, 7.8, and 7.6, the highest, 8.1, and the lowest, 6.9, are eliminated, and the average is taken for 7.8 and 7.6, which is 7.7. This last number is the score awarded to the contestant.

Every routine performed in each event is made up of many movements, each of which must be joined properly and smoothly with the subsequent movement, and each must start and end in a more or less specific manner. All of these movements must be in accord with the rules that prescribe the framework for the performance of an exercise for each event.

EQUIPMENT

A different piece of equipment is necessary for each gymnastic event, except for the long horse vaulting and the side horse competition, which use the same horse. Mats are essential for all events, including the trampoline. A gymnasium well-equipped for gymnastics will include the following items: chalk box, horizontal bar, mats of various types, mat racks, parallel bars, Reuther board, rings, side horse which is convertible to a long horse, trampoline, transporter, and spotting belts. An overhead harness for spotting purposes is also desirable.

Chalk Box

Containers to hold the chalk can be made or purchased. The size and shape of these boxes vary considerably; however, they should be large enough and deep enough to prevent the chalk from falling out on the floor when the hands are being chalked. The base should be covered with a material that will not mark the floor when the box is moved. A chalk box should be available for each piece of equipment that requires the use of chalk.

Horizontal Bar

There are many commercial brands of horizontal bars on the market. Most of the better horizontal bars are constructed to meet competitive specifications. Certain features should be present on all of them. The uprights should be adjustable from 42 inches to 98½ inches at 2-inch intervals. The bottoms of the uprights may be padded and flat or fit into a floor plate. The adjustment clamp which holds the upright at the proper height should be absolutely slip proof for obvious safety reasons. Four steel guy cables, anchored in floor plates and attached to the top of the uprights, should hold the bar steady and horizontal. The cables should be equipped with a turnbuckle so that they can be lengthened or shortened. Two of them should have a lock-and-release binder.

The crossbar should be 94½ inches long and 1⅛ inch in diameter. It should be constructed from high tensile steel with good resiliency so that it will always return to its straight form after use and give safe support to the competitors. Some of the more expensive bars feature a pivot type end which provides for greater resiliency.

Portable types of horizontal bars are now available, but they take up a great deal of space because of their large base. The bar should never be attached to the wall since that is hazardous.

Mats

Tumbling and gymnastics mats are available in various sizes, thicknesses, colors, and materials. The mats are filled with a mixture of animal hair, goat hair, polyethylene, vinyl, a felt and hair combination, or foam rubber. Goat hair, polyethylene, and vinyl seem to be the best. The mat covering is made of vinyl-coated nylon, vinyl-coated canvas, cotton canvas, or rayon plastic. Thickness of mats varies from less than an inch to four or more inches. The thicker and more resilient mats are needed in events in which the landing force of the participant is great and the danger of injury is high. Mat sizes vary. They can be made to order in almost any size, but more or less standard sizes can be purchased. These may come in 4-feet, 5-feet, and 6-feet widths and 4-feet, 6-feet, 8-feet, 10-feet, and 12-feet lengths. The mat for floor exercise should be a minimum of 42 feet by 42 feet and from ⅝ inch to 1 inch thick. The tumbling mat should be a minimum of 5 feet by 60 feet and from 2 inches to 4 inches thick.

Mats used immediately adjoining and under an apparatus can be cut out to fit snugly around the uprights and base, providing a safer landing area by eliminating the sharp drop-off at mat junctions where the mats are piled on top of one another.

Some mats are designed with special projections around the edges that can be attached to one another to prevent separation. This feature makes it possible to join several mats without the danger of their slipping apart during activity. Except for the very light or short ones, mats should have two, three, or more strong handles securely attached to each of the long sides. These handles are essential for moving the mats from one place to another.

Mat Racks

Mat racks are essential equipment and are available in a horizontal or vertical design. The horizontal type requires less effort when placing the mat, but the vertical design requires less space and is generally more convenient. The rack should be mounted on swivel, ball bearing type casters that are large enough to roll easily. The rolling surface of the casters should be equipped with a material that prevents the rack from marking up the floor surface.

Parallel Bars

Parallel bars should meet official specifications if they are to be used for competition. The competitive rules require that each bar must be $66^{15}/_{16}$ inches high and have a width adjustment span from 16 inches to 22 inches. However, because this apparatus is generally used for teaching students of different ages and skill levels, the height should be adjustable down to approximately 48 inches and the width should be adjustable from 12 inches to 24 inches. Most parallel bars on the market will meet these specifications.

The metal parts of the bars are made of steel. The finish varies according to the manufacturer; some have a chrome or paint cover, while others are stainless steel or have other special coloring.

Bars are constructed from laminated wood, compressed wood with or without a steel rod center, or fiber glass. The fiber glass bars have more resiliency than the wooden ones, but they do not seem to have the same feel to the hands as the wooden ones. The laminated or compressed wooden bars seem to be preferred.

Each of the four upper, cylindrical uprights should be so constructed that the bars can be moved up or down in degrees of 50mm and secured safely at each of these levels. Each manufacturer has its own patented device for locking the uprights in place. The upper cylinder should also be easily adjustable to the limits of the widths given above.

The base should be wide enough and heavy enough to provide for sufficient stability. The floor contact points of the base should be covered with rubber pads to prevent the marking up of the floor and slipping or sliding during activity on the bar. Most manufacturers will also have an adjustment on the bottom of one of these pads to level the base if the floor is uneven.

Personal Equipment

Participants should be equipped with a loose-fitting uniform that will permit freedom of movement of all parts of the body. For protection against blisters and bruises, hand or palm guards made of leather are essential for most apparatus work. Special lightweight shoes or slippers, made of canvas with leather soles or leather with soft, rubber soles, are helpful.

Reuther Board

The Reuther board, used as a base in takeoffs for vaults, is generally made of laminated hardwood, and provides enough resiliency to soften the shocking jar of a takeoff. It is approximately 2 feet by 4 feet, with a top surface that is covered with a nonskid material or that has a tread. All floor contact points should be covered with a material that prevents skidding and the marking up of the floor. Some types are adjustable.

A beat board may be used as a takeoff base; however, it does not have the resiliency of the Reuther board.

Rings

The rings may be suspended directly from a pipe or girder attached to the ceiling or from a portable frame supported by steel guy wires that are anchored in floor plates. There is also a completely portable frame available, which has a movable base and is not attached to the floor by guy wires, but which takes up a great deal of floor space.

Rules for competition require the rings to be 8 feet 2½ inches above the floor. However, because the rings will generally be used for instruction at different age levels, they should be adjustable to a much lower level. This is sometimes done by installing a pulley system. For competition, the pulley system has not proved to be satisfactory; a strap extension is preferable.

The rings should be attached to an adjustable canvas or nylon web strap which is connected to the ends of steel cables. The other ends of the cables should be attached to a pipe, girder, or frame by a clamp and a ball bearing, swivel device.

The rings themselves should be constructed according to rule specification of the rings and other measurements. The best type is made from laminated hardwood, although they can also be made of an iron core covered with hard rubber. The rings are attached to the loops at the ends of the web strap.

Side Horse

The body of the side horse should measure 13¾ inches in diameter and 63 to 64⅛ inches in length. It is constructed of wood or metal, padded with hair

or other material, and covered with leather, vinyl, or naugahyde. Its height is usually adjustable from approximately 40 inches to 60 inches above the floor. A safe device for locking the uprights at the desired height is essential. Competitive rules require the top of the pommels to measure 48 inches from the floor. Pommels are usually made of laminated hardwood, are removable, and should be adjustable in their width from 15¾ inches to 17¾ inches.

The base of the horse should be large enough and of sufficient weight to provide stability. It may be necessary to anchor the base to the floor during competition. The floor contact points of the base should be covered with a material that prevents skidding and the marking up of the floor. Some manufacturers also equip one of these floor pads with an adjustable leveler.

The side horse can be converted to a long horse for vaulting by removing the pommels and placing the appropriate markings on the body.

Trampoline

Trampolines are manufactured in several sizes, ranging from the mini-tramp to the Olympic size. Three standard sizes are available: a 7- by 12-foot frame with a 5- by 10-foot bed; a 9- by 15-foot frame with a 6- by 12-foot bed; and a 10- by 17-foot frame with a 7 by 14 foot bed. Each of these trampolines should fold up into a compact unit and should be equipped with a portable truck that is easily assembled and removed. The bottom surface of the truck and the points at which the trampoline rests on the floor should be covered with a material that prevents skidding and the marking up of the floor.

The bed may be made of a 1-inch nylon web, a 1¾-inch nylon web, or a solid piece of canvas. The 1-inch size is more resilient than the 1¾-inch size, and is required for competition. Both are much more resilient, as well as more costly, than the solid canvas.

Either steel springs or elastic rubber cables can be used to attach the bed to the frame and to increase resiliency of the bed. Steel springs are required by competitive rule. The smaller trampolines will have from 80 to 100 of these, and the larger ones will have 110 to 115. Pads should be used to cover the top of the frame and the springs.

Auxiliary Equipment

Twisting belts and spotting belts should be available for use to provide greater safety for the more advanced stunts during the learning stages. The twisting belt permits the gymnast to rotate around two axes during a sequence of movements. Both of these belts can be attached to an overhead harness that may either be stationary or movable.

Because of the weight and size of the heavy apparatus, it is necessary to have some means of moving it from place to place. Each manufacturer has developed a transporter that is especially designed to fit his own equipment. The transporters are equipped with ball bearing, swivel casters that rotate 360 degrees. The casters should be large enough to roll easily, and their outer surface should be covered with a material that will prevent the marking up of the floor.

SKILLS AND TECHNIQUES

The skills for each event are listed and described in a progressive order from the simple to the more difficult. They should, therefore, be taught and learned in the order in which they are presented. Basic mechanics and essential safety features are considered. A basic routine for each event can be made up of a combination of the individual skills presented for any particular event. Each student is thereby provided with an opportunity to learn and perform a routine, and to be evaluated through actual gymnastic judging. The student should not be satisfied with a crude performance, but should strive for good form while learning each stunt.

Floor Exercise

Flexibility Skills

Piked Seat–Chin to Knees. While seated, grasp the soles of the feet or the ankles and attempt to touch the chin to the shins. Attempt to keep the back flat rather than hunched.

Straddle Seat–Chin to Floor. While seated with the legs spread apart, grasp the soles of the feet or the ankles and exert an effort to touch the chin and even the shoulders to the floor.

Wide-Straddle Stand. While standing, keep the legs straight and bend the body forward from the hips so that the back is flat and horizontal.

Back Bend. 1. Assume a supine position, with the palms on the floor over the shoulders, the fingers pointing outward, and the knees deeply flexed.

2. While keeping the palms and the soles flat on the floor, push and arch the body up as high as possible off the floor, and straighten the arms.

3. Rock back and forth, moving the feet as close as possible to the hands. Then rock forward and up to a stand.

4. Note: The spotter helps by lifting the performer at the small of his back.

Agility Skills

Jump Full Twist (Tour). Make a jump upward, accompanied by a twist of the shoulders and hips in the direction of the arm thrust. The landing should be balanced.

Jump Straddle–Toe Touch. While jumping, hold the chest erect, keep the legs straight, lifted as high as possible, and spread apart, and touch the toes. Recovery should be made in an erect stand.

Front-Support Squat Through to Back Support. Perform an arch in front support and lift the hips causing the chest to hollow. Then push down on the mat and squat the legs between the arms and extend into a back support.

Single-Leg Circles. Squat down on the right leg with the hands on the mat on both sides of the right foot and the left leg extended backward. Circle the left leg clockwise, lift the hands over the circling leg and return the hands to the floor, lean on the arms and jump over the left leg with the right foot, and continue circling the left leg.

Neckspring (Kip)

1. Start from an inverted pike, lying position on the neck, with the hands tucked over the shoulders so that the palms are on the mat.

2. Thrust the feet far upward, extending the hips at about a 45 degree angle.

3. Arch the back and land in a back-bend position.

4. Then, eliminate step 3 by following through with a hand-push and shooting the legs down under the body which should result in an arched-foot stand.

Mule Kick (Snapdown)

1. Start from a three-quarter handstand with the arms vertical, the back arched and the knees bent.

2. Snap feet down to the mat by straightening the knees and flexing the hips, and simultaneously push off the mat with the hands.

3. Land on the balls of the feet in an erect position.

Balance Skills. Keep the following hints for learning the balance skills in mind: (1) Holding the positions for five seconds rather than two seconds will enhance the learning of these skills. (2) When

FIGURE 11-1.   Single leg circles.

FIGURE 11-2.   Neckspring.

the hands are used as a base of support, they should be placed about a shoulder width apart on the floor, with the fingers spread. (3) When the head is a base of support, the front part of the top of it is placed well in front of the hands so that the hands and head form a triangle.

V-Balance from Sitting-Tuck Position. Grasp the soles or the ankles with the hands. Lift the legs then straighten and hold them.

Knee-Elbow Headstand

1. Place the hands about a shoulder width apart with the fingers spread.
2. Place the inside of the knees on top of the elbows.
3. Lean forward and place the head on the floor about a foot in front of the hands so that the hands and head form a triangle.
4. Lift the feet off the floor and hold.

Knee-Elbow Handstand

1. Steps 1 and 2 are the same as for the knee-elbow headstand.

FIGURE 11-3. Headstand.

2. Lean forward slowly until the forearms are approximately vertical.
3. Lift the feet off the floor and balance on the hands and hold.

Headstand

1. From a kneeling position, place the hands on the floor slightly ahead of the knees.
2. Place the head on the floor well in front of the hands.
3. Straighten the legs so that the hips are raised, and walk the feet toward the head until the hips are above the head.
4. Slowly raise the bent legs up toward an inverted, straight-body position.
5. If the student has trouble lifting the legs together, he can lift one leg up as high as possible and slowly lift the other leg to join the first.
6. Note: The headstand may be performed from other starting positions such as a straddle stand and front support.

Handstand

1. Place the hands about one foot from a wall.
2. Keep one leg straight and the other one bent under the body.
3. While keeping the arms straight, with the eyes focused constantly on the section of the mat between the hands, swing the straight leg vigorously upward toward the wall and at the same time push vigorously off the mat with the bent leg.
4. Bring both legs to the wall and keep them straight. Keep the arms vertical and the eyes looking at the section of the mat between the hands.
5. After a good handstand position is attained, move one leg away from the wall and slowly edge the other leg away from the wall. Shift the weight and *fight* to maintain balance by bending the arms and leaning the shoulders back and forth or pressing down with the fingers.
6. Note: After the wall handstand is mastered, the student can practice away from the wall with a spotter standing at his side ready to catch him and regulate his positioning. If the kick is too hard and causes overbalance, recovery can be made by ducking the head, tucking, and rolling forward, or by walking one hand forward, turning on the stationary arm, and landing on one foot.

Front-Leg Scale

1. Stand with the arms out to the side, then lift one leg backward off the floor by arching the body.

2. As the heel of the lifted leg rises, the trunk is forced forward to a horizontal position.

3. The final position is a stand on a straight leg, with the body arched horizontally, the heel of the raised leg at least as high as the head, the eyes looking forward, and the arms straight out sideways.

Double-Elbow Planche. From a front support on the hands with the fingers pointing outward, place the elbows under the abdomen by slightly bending the arms, lean forward until the legs rise off the floor. Keep the body straight and horizontal.

Floor Exercise Routine

1. Front handspring.
2. Jump straddle–toe touch.
3. Back roll shoot through handstand.
4. Come down on one leg, make a quarter-turn, a cartwheel, a quarter-turn.
5. Kick to handstand, hold momentarily.

FIGURE 11-4. Handstand.

6. Forward roll out to wide straddle stand.
7. Press to headstand and hold.
8. Lower to two single leg circles to front support.
9. Squat through between arms to rear support.
10. Pull back and sit, touch head to straight knees.
11. Sit up, push to L, and hold.
12. Roll back to neckstand and kip to stand.
13. Make two steps, roundoff jump, and stand erect.

Tumbling

Forward Roll

1. Take a deep-tuck stand with the hands on the floor in front of the feet.

2. Support the body weight by leaning on the arms, push with the feet, duck the head, roll and land on the back of the head. Keep the knees drawn against the chest.

3. Roll forward to a stand by grasping the shins just prior to standing on the feet.

Straddle Roll Up. Speed throughout the roll makes up for lack of flexibility. Similar mechanics should be employed if the roll is to be performed in a piked position except that the hand-push would be beside the knee area. Perform steps 1 and 2 as in the forward roll above.

1. As soon as the head makes contact with the mat, straighten and straddle the legs.

2. Place the hands between the legs as the body continues forward.

3. Push on the mat as long as possible, driving the head down and forward in coming to a straddle stand.

4. Note: To simulate a rolling-body position and action, assume a tuck position with the hands on the shins, and rock backward and forward on the spinal area.

Dive Roll

1. Start from a standing, two-feet takeoff.

2. The catching or supporting of the body weight on the arms is of vital importance in this skill, therefore, this technique should be developed through small dives. The dives can be slowly lengthened as control is gained. The jump from the feet should start low.

3. The height of the jump can be increased and eventually the body can be arched before rolling. Do not perform this roll over objects or persons.

Backward Roll. Start from a deep-tuck stand, with the chin on the chest and the palms up over the shoulder; roll backwards forcibly, keeping the knees to the chest. Roll over head to foot stand with the palms on the mat.

Piked Sit Down–Back-Roll Extension

1. From a standing position, sit down with straight legs by bending the trunk forward and reaching back to the mat so that the thighs are between the arms.
2. Roll onto the back and place the palms up over the shoulders.
3. As the feet roll over the head, shoot them up and extend the hips.
4. As the roll over the head occurs, the arms push down on the mat so that the body passes through a straight-arm handstand.

Headspring

1. Start like a tuck, forward roll but place the head on the mat at the hairline between the hands.
2. As the hips pass the top of the roll, straighten the legs and shoot the feet upward at about a 45-degree angle.
3. There is a follow-through with a hand-push and an attempt to land on the balls of the feet in an arched position.
4. Note: It is simpler to learn this skill by placing the hands and head on a rolled mat. As the action is performed, a spotter places one hand under the performer's shoulder and the other hand under his back.

Cartwheel. The performer should perform a cartwheel to the same side as the leg with which he pushes off the floor when kicking up to a handstand.

1. Start from a side stand with the legs straddled and the arms spread overhead, then look at the mat

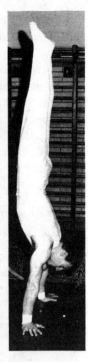

FIGURE 11-5.   Back roll extension.

to the right and bend over placing the right hand near the right foot.
2. Kick up through a spread-arm, straddled-leg handstand.
3. Come down on the far side with the left leg followed by the right leg.
4. Note: The rhythm of the contact of the hands and feet with the mat should be even. The performer should strive to perfect cartwheels by doing three or four in sequence rapidly. The spotter should stand behind the performer and hold his waist with crossed arms.

FIGURE 11-6.   Headspring.

Skip Step. From a slow, striding run, hop on one foot, step onto the other foot, bend over, and perform a hand spring or a one-legged aerial skill. This preparatory movement is necessary in order to obtain maximum control and power.

Tinsica. This movement is initiated from a forward run and a skip step. First perform a slow cartwheel and execute a quarter-turn out or away from the cartwheel. Then perform it rapidly by placing the hands on the mat in a staggered or cartwheel fashion and immediately execute the quarter-turn out.

Roundoff. The roundoff is also initiated from a forward run and skip step.

1. First place the hands on the mat in a manner similar to a cartwheel and execute a quarter-turn in toward the cartwheel.

2. Then place one hand on the mat, pirouetting forcibly on that arm, and place the other hand on the mat past the 180-degree turn.

3. Join the legs and snap them down vigorously while pushing the trunk high off the mat with the hands.

4. Make the foot rebound high, straight, and symmetrical.

5. Note: A slow approach facilitates learning the proper techniques. Also, a one (near) arm roundoff enhances learning the pirouetting action of the arm.

Forward Handspring. This stunt is initiated from a forward run and a skip step.

1. Bend over with straight arms and place the hands on the mat well in front of the shoulders. Do not dive onto the hands.

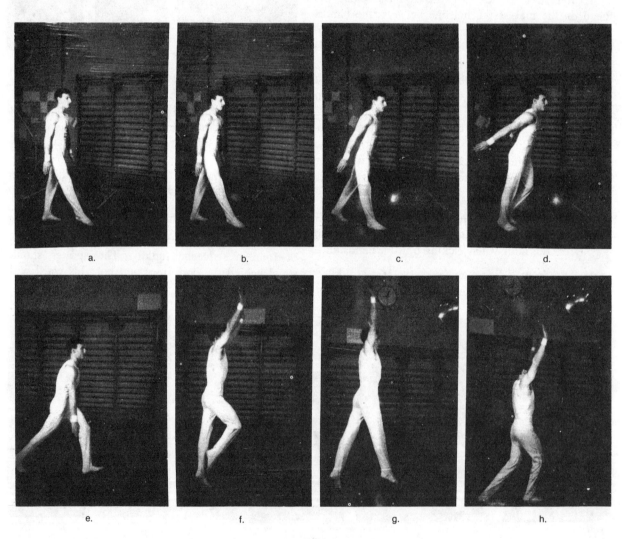

a.   b.   c.   d.

e.   f.   g.   h.

FIGURE 11-7. Skip step.

2. Kick up forcibly through a stretched-handstand position. Keeping the head up and looking between the hands helps to prevent the shoulders from drifting forward too soon or before the body reaches the handstand position.

3. Follow through with a hand-push and endeavor to land on the balls of the feet in an arched stand.

Side (Pommeled) Horse

When performing on the side horse the legs are always straight, and the support position is always on the hands with arms kept straight. The shoulders are depressed rather than hunched. The use of snug, stretchable pants reduces friction between the horse and the legs.

Basic Leg Cuts

1. Start from a front support.
2. Cut the left leg forward to a stride support, then cut the left leg backward to a front support.
3. Repeat this with the right leg.
4. Cut the left leg forward, then cut the right leg forward to a rear support.
5. Cut the left and right leg alternately backward to a front support.

FIGURE 11-8.   Roundoff.

FIGURE 11-9.   Forward handspring.

Single-Leg Travel

1. Start from a stride support with the left leg forward, the left hand on the end, and the right leg backward. Place the right hand slightly forward on the pommel.

2. Lift the right leg forward around the right arm.

3. Cut the left leg backward and simultaneously place the left hand in back of the right hand on the pommel.

4. Lift the right leg backward, switching the right hand to the other pommel.

5. Finish in a front support in the middle zone of the horse.

6. Note: This skill may be performed from the middle to the end of the horse also.

Lateral Leg-Swinging in Stride Support. Swing both feet evenly together. As the legs swing to the left side, lean well on the right arm and lift the legs and hips as high as possible to both sides.

Forward Undercut. The first attempt should be made from a stand on the mat, with the hands grasping the pommels.

1. Jump the legs up to the right side, lean on the left arm, and cut the left leg forward under the right hand and over the right pommel. Regrasp the pommel.

2. After this is accomplished, perform the movement from a front support. Swing the legs and hips up to the right side, lean on the left arm, and cut the left leg forward under the right hand and over the right pommel.

Modified Back Scissor

1. Start from a stride support outside the right arm, with the right leg in front and the left leg in back.

2. Swing the legs up and to the right, push off the right arm with the right leg, and simultaneously

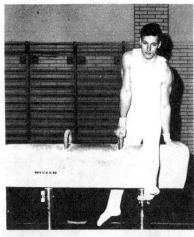
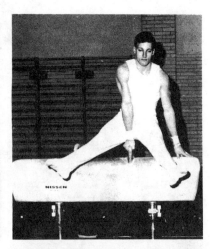

FIGURE 11-10.   Single leg travel.

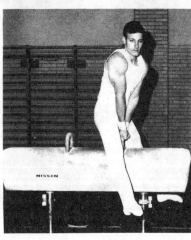
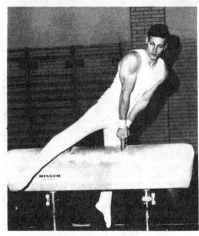
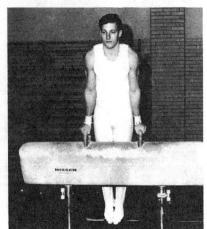

FIGURE 11-11.   Back scissor.

lean on the left arm and switch or scissor the legs. Cut the right leg backward and the left leg forward.

3. As the legs swing downward, regrasp the pommel with the right hand as the stride position between the pommels is attained.

Back Scissor

1. From a stride support between the arms with the right leg in front and the left leg in back, swing the legs and hips to the right and push off with the right hand, leaning on and bearing down on the left arm.

2. As the legs approach the peak of the swing, switch, or scissor, them and extend the hips.

3. Regrasp the pommel with the right hand as the stride position between the pommels is attained.

Front Scissor

1. From a stride support between the arms with the right leg in front and the left leg in back, swing the legs and hips to the left, push off with the left hand, and lean on and bear down on the right arm.

2. As the legs approach the peak of the swing, switch, or scissor, them and extend the hips.

3. Regrasp the pommel with the left hand as the stride position between the pommels is attained.

4. Note: Single-leg cuts, undercuts, and scissors should be learned in both directions.

Single Rear Dismount from One-Arm, Straddle Support

1. From a straddle support around the right hand, with the left hand on the left pommel, swing the right leg back, make a half-turn to the right, and place the left hand on the right end of the horse.

2. Continue swinging the right leg in a clockwise direction until it joins the left leg which pushes off the horse.

3. Both legs are swung over the end of the horse by pushing off the horse with the left hand and leaning on the right hand.

4. Execute a quarter-turn to the left so that the legs pass over the horse to a cross stand.

Loop Mount. From a cross stand in line with the end of the horse, with both hands on the end, jump over the end with a quarter-turn to a rear support leaning on the end arm. Place the other hand on the pommel.

Backward Undercut. From a rear support, swing the legs up to the left, push the left hand off the

FIGURE 11-12.   Front scissor.

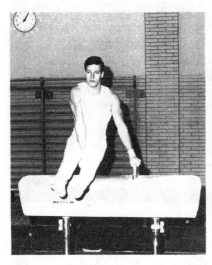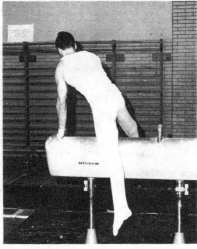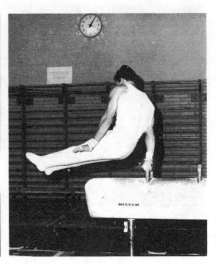

FIGURE 11-13. Single rear dismount.

pommel, or end, and cut the right leg backward under the left leg and over the pommel, or end, by leaning on the right arm. The left leg is in front and the right leg is in back.

Forward-Leg Cut with Half-Turn Mount

1. From a stand with the right hand on the left pommel and the left hand on the horse, jump, pushing with the left hand and supporting the weight on the right arm.

2. Lift the right leg forward over the horse with a half-turn left.

3. Finish with the left leg forward and the right leg backward in a stride position.

4. Note on spotting: Where applicable, a spotter may hold a performer's waist from behind and give assistance in the performance of the stunt by lifting.

Side Horse Routine

1. Travel from left end to center.

2. Cut left leg forward, cut right leg forward around right hand, cut left leg back and perform a back scissor (modified) to right side.

3. Cut left leg back, undercut left leg forward, cut left leg back.

4. Cut right leg forward, make a front scissor to left side, swing right leg forward around right hand.

5. Swing right leg back, make a half-turn with the body, place left hand on end, make a half circle for-

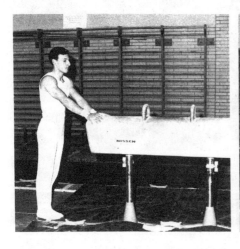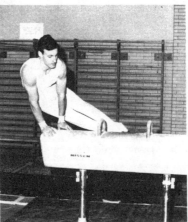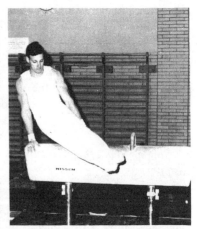

FIGURE 11-14. Loop mount.

ward (clockwise), and make a quarter-turn left (rear vault) dismount.

Horizontal Bar

When spotting on the horizontal bar, move in the direction of the swing and watch the performer's grasp.

Swing and Dismount

1. From a stand slightly behind the bar, jump to a hang with a slight pendulum swing. Keep the body straight and make it as long as possible.

2. As the body passes the bottom of each forward swing, lift the legs upward and forward.

3. Release the bar just after the end of the backward swing and immediately before the body swings forward.

Single Knee Rock Up

1. From a one-knee hang between a double overgrip, with the unhooked leg extending under the bar, kick the unhooked leg downward, pull the trunk up with the arms, lunge the shoulders above the bar.

2. Assume a straight-arm, stride support.

3. Note: It may take two or three rocking actions to gain ample swing to complete the rock up.

Stride Support, Leg Cut, Quarter-Turn, Dismount. Lift the rear leg over the bar, make a quarter-turn in the direction of the forward leg, and drop to a stand.

Stride Support, Leg Cut, Half-Turn to Front Support. With the left leg to the rear and the right hand turned to an undergrip, lift the left leg over the bar and make a half-turn to the right. Finish in a front support.

Pull-Over to Front Support. This stunt should be first attempted from a stand next to a bar that is about shoulder height.

1. Stand on one foot under the bar, with an overgrip or undergrip and the arms well bent.

2. Kick the free leg up over the bar and at the same time pull the bar into the waist and finish in a front support.

3. After accomplishing the above movement, perform the stunt from a hang on a higher bar, pull up, lift the legs up and over the bar, pull the bar into the waist, and finish in a front support.

4. The head should be kept forward and facing the legs to best facilitate a constant arm pull and a circling of the legs over the bar.

Backward Hip Circle

1. From a piked, front support, using an overgrip and touching the lower abdomen against the bar, hyperextend the hips and push about sixteen inches off the bar with the abdomen and the arms.

2. Then, just as the lower abdomen is about to make contact on its return to the bar, lean the shoulders slightly backwards, thus offsetting the front support balance.

3. With the feet leading, pike slightly, allowing backward rotation of the body around the grasp and the lower abdomen.

4. Finish with a straight body in a front support.

Forward Hip Circle

1. From a high, straight-body, front support, using an overgrip and resting the upper thighs on

FIGURE 11-15.
Pull-over to front support.

a.

b.

c.

FIGURE 11-16. Backward hip circle.

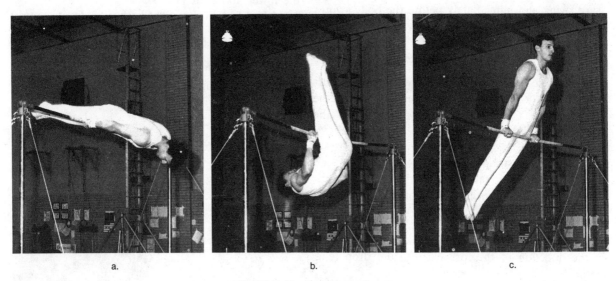

FIGURE 11-17. Forward hip circle.

the bar, fall forward, keeping the body straight until it is horizontal.

2. Then pike by bringing the head toward the feet and rotate the hands around the bar. While circling, keep the lower abdomen in contact with the bar.

3. During the final phase of the circle, pull down on the bar with the hands, thus facilitating the circling of the shoulders over the bar.

4. As the shoulders circle over the bar, stop them in the support position while the trailing leg moves down to a straight-body, front support.

Underswing from Front Support

1. Keep the arms straight, drop the hips, invert the trunk, and pike, allowing the knees to come next to the bar.

2. As the shoulders swing forward under the bar, shoot the feet far upward.

3. To dismount from this position: reinforce the shooting upward of the feet by pulling down on the bar with the arms; as the body shoots upward and away from the bar, release the grip and arch the body during its flight, and land in an erect position.

Underswing from Front Support with a Half-Turn Dismount

1. Perform the movements in steps 1, 2, and 3 above.

2. As the body shoots upward, twist the hips, executing a half-turn.

3. Land erect facing the bar.

4. Note: Spotters should stand at the sides of the performer ready to facilitate a firm foot landing.

FIGURE 11-18. Half-turn dismount.

FIGURE 11-19. Under bar cast mount.

Under Bar Cast Mount

1. From a stand slightly behind the bar, jump to a hang with a pendulum swing.

2. As the body swings backward, pull up.

3. Just as the body is about to swing forward from the pulled up position in back, invert the body and lift the legs to the bar, forming a pike.

4. As the shoulders swing forward under the bar, shoot the legs forward and upward.

5. Note: It is best to teach this skill on a bar that is about shoulder height. From a stand facing the bar, with an overgrip, jump off the floor and proceed as in steps 3 and 4.

Kip

1. Just before the end of a straight-body, forward swing, pike and lift the feet upward next to the bar.

2. As the shoulders begin to swing backward, shoot the feet forward and upward at about a 45-degree angle, simultaneously pulling the bar, with straight arms, along the legs to the waist.

3. Make the rise to the front support with a slight pike, thereby facilitating the casting up of the body from the bar.

Horizontal Bar Routine

1. Pull over.
2. Underswing.
3. Swing backward.
4. Swing forward and kip.
5. Perform a front hip circle.
6. Perform a back hip circle.
7. Underswing with a half-turn dismount to a stand.

Rings

Safety precautions are important when teaching stunts on the rings. Magnesium carbonate should always be used on the hands, and two spotters, one on each side of the performer, should be required. Because of the strength necessary, this is usually the most difficult event for beginners.

Pendulum Swing. From a hang, keeping the arms straight, swing the body forward and backward from the shoulders. As the hips pass the bottom of the forward swing, lift the legs forward, causing a slight pike. At the moment the hips pass the bottom of the backward swing, drive the legs backward from the pike, causing a body arch.

Skin-the-Cat

1. From a hang, keeping the arms straight, lift the legs up over the head through a piked, inverted hang.

2. Keeping the knees near the face, continue turning over backwards, lowering the hips and legs straight down as far as possible to an extended, reverse (inlocate), hang.

3. Pull the hips and legs up through a piked, inverted hang and lower to a straight-body hang.

Piked, Inverted Hang. Pike the body well, with the legs horizontal over the trunk and the eyes looking at the knees.

Straight, Inverted Hang

1. Lift the legs up to a piked, inverted hang.

2. Keeping the eyes on the feet, extend the legs upward, place the feet on the straps, and straighten the body.

3. Then look at the mat below and slowly bring the legs together, removing one foot at a time from the straps.

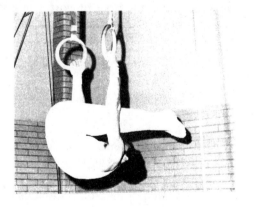

FIGURE 11-20. Piked inverted hang.

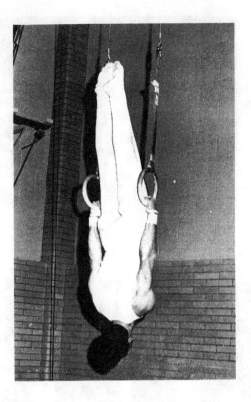

FIGURE 11-21. Straight inverted hang.

Back Lever

1. From an inverted hang, with straight arms held close to the sides, lift the head and lower the front of the straight body toward the mat.

2. When the horizontal position is reached, keep the upper arms under and against the latissimus dorsi muscle, stop and hold for three seconds.

3. After the position is held, pike the body and lower it to a reverse hang.

Single-Leg Kip

1. From a piked, inverted hang, place the right leg over the right arm.

2. Then shoot the left foot forward and upward at approximately a 45-degree angle, and pull up to a support with the right leg over the right handhold.

3. Return to the starting position.

Front, Single-Leg Cut, Quarter-Turn Dismount

1. From a piked, inverted hang, shoot the legs forward and upward, with the right leg over the right arm.

2. Pull down on the rings and release the right ring after the right leg contacts the right arm and rocks the trunk erect.

FIGURE 11-22.   Back lever.

3. As the right leg cuts past the right arm, execute a quarter-turn.

4. Release the left ring and come to a stand.

5. Note: This trick should be spotted under the upper back.

Muscle (Pull) Up to Support

1. From a straight-body hang, pull up slightly and obtain a false grip by placing the heels (of the little-finger sides) of the hands over the rings. This places the hands in a support grasp position while the body is in a hang.

2. With the palms facing each other, pull up as high as possible.

3. Turn the rings outward and lean the chest forward, simultaneously pushing the rings beneath the shoulders to a bent-arm support.

4. Continue pushing up to a straight-arm support.

L-Support. From a straight-arm support, keep the trunk vertical, lift the legs until they are horizontal, and hold. Make sure the palms are facing each other.

Front Uprise. As the legs approach the end of a hang, swing forward with a fairly straight body, pull the trunk upward and lean the chest forward, causing the body to pike. Push the rings under the shoulders, passing by a bent-arm support to a straight-arm support.

Piked, Forward Roll

1. From an L-support, lean forward, bending the arms and lifting the hips.

2. Roll forward to a piked, inverted hang with a false grip.

3. Continue rolling and pulling the trunk upward through a bent-arm support.

Kip Dismount

1. From a piked, inverted hang, shoot the legs forward and upward, extending the hips completely.

2. Bring the body to an erect position with a follow-through and a hand-pull.

3. Release the rings and come to a stand.

4. The dismount may be performed with a half-turn.

Kip

1. From an open-piked, inverted hang, bring the legs down to the trunk, closing the pike.

2. Shoot the feet forward and upward at about a 45-degree angle, simultaneously pulling down on

FIGURE 11-23.   Front uprise.

FIGURE 11-24.   Back uprise.

the rings so that, with the arms slightly bent, the shoulders rise above the rings to a straight-arm support.

3. A false grip aids in the learning of this skill.

Back Uprise

1. As the hips, with a slight pike, pass the bottom of a large, hanging, swing backward, unpike and pull down vigorously on the rings so that the body rises to a straight-arm support.

2. Note: Spotters should lift the performer by the thighs during the learning stages.

Inlocate. While standing on the floor, go through the inlocate on low rings. Then have spotters lift the performer through the action on the regulation rings.

1. As the hips pass the bottom of a large, hanging, swing backward, spread the arms, duck the head, and pike.

2. Finish in a piked, inverted hang.

3. Note: Spotters should lift the performer by the abdominal area.

Shoulder Stand

1. From an L-support, lean forward, bending the arms and lifting the hips slowly above the head.

2. Keep the eyes looking straight down, the elbows close to the sides, and the hands in front of the chest.

3. Raise the straddled legs and place them on the cables.

FIGURE 11-25. Shoulder stand.

4. Slowly move the legs together one at a time, and hold with a straight body. If the performer falls forward or backward, bring the knees to the chest and roll to a hang.

Back, Flyaway Dismount

1. From a large, hanging swing forward, lift the legs over the head through an open-piked, inverted hang.

2. Continue to turn backward and drop off to a stand.

3. Eventually the feet may be shot backward and upward before releasing.

4. Note: Spotting should be done under the shoulder, and the hands kept in front of and behind the performer in order to help prevent overrotation or underrotation.

FIGURE 11-26. Back straddle dismount.

Back, Straddle Dismount

1. From a large, hanging, swing forward, lift the legs overhead through a straddled open-piked, inverted hang.

2. Continue turning backward, and as the rings reach the crotch, release and drop off to a stand.

Rings Routine

1. Execute a pendulum swing and front uprise to an L-position.

2. Press to shoulder stand.

3. Lower to a piked, inverted hang, swing legs down to inlocate.

4. Raise the legs to a straight, inverted hang and hold.

5. Lower to back lever and hold.

6. Lower to reverse hang (skin-the-cat), pull up and around to a piked, inverted hang.

7. Swing down and back to a flyaway dismount.

Parallel Bars

The right or left directions given in the learning steps are to clarify explanations.

Hand-Support Hopping. From a cross, hand support, bend the arms slightly and straighten vigorously, hopping off the bars and traveling slightly forward. When learning this skill, take short hops as large hops will tend to cause one to go off balance.

Straddle Travels

1. From a cross, straight-arm support, swing the legs forward and straddle them over the bars.

2. Rock the trunk forward and swing the arms forward and regrasp the bars in front of the legs.

3. Repeat steps 1 and 2 down the length of the bars.

Straight-Arm Support Swing. Keep the arms straight and swing the body from the shoulders. The tendency to pike on the forward swing and arch on the backward swing is permissible but should be only slight. Keeping the head up on the backward swing and down on the forward swing enhances control during the learning stages.

FIGURE 11-27.   Upper arm stand.

Rear Vault (Forward Swing) Dismount

1. From a straight-arm support, swing forward to a high V-position so that the rear of the body passes over the right bar.

2. Switch the left hand behind the body to the right bar and lift the right hand outward away from the bars.

3. Land erect with slightly bent knees.

Rear Vault with Quarter-Turn Inward

1. As the rear of the body passes over the right bar, execute a quarter-turn (90-degree turn) left or into the bar.

2. Land erect, facing the bar, and with both hands grasping it.

Rear Vault with Half-Turn Inward

1. As the rear of the body passes over the right bar, execute a half-turn (180-degree turn) left or into the bar.

2. Bring the right hand over the body to the right bar as the half-turn is made.

3. Land erect with slightly bent knees.

Front Vault (Backward Swing) Dismount

1. From a straight-arm support, swing backward above the horizontal line so that the body passes over the right bar.

2. Switch the left hand to the right bar and lift the right hand outward away from the bar.

3. Keep the body arched until the landing, which should be made with the chest erect and the knees slightly bent.

Upper-Arm Stand. The first attempt should be made on very low parallel bars, with a mat draped over the distant half of the bars.

1. From a cross, kneeling position, lean forward and place the top of the upper arms on the bar about ten inches in front of the hand grasp. The draped mat should be next to the back.

2. Keep the upper arms horizontal so that the elbows are straight out sideways, and keep the eyes looking directly down.

3. Straighten the knees, thereby raising the hips, and walk the feet up to the trunk, thus raising the hips above the shoulders.

4. Draw the knees to the chest and lift the legs slowly until the knees and hips are straight.

5. Hold the balance with a straight or slightly arched body.

6. After learning this stunt on the low parallel bars, make the next attempt on the higher parallel bars from a straddle-seat position, with the hand grasp next to the thighs. Lean forward, placing the upper arms about ten inches in front of the grasp. Keeping the legs straddled, raise the hips above the shoulders and then raise the legs slowly to the straight-body position and hold. Note: If the performer cannot raise the hips from a straddle-seat position, he should place the feet on the bars and then raise the hips.

Roll Forward from Upper-Arm Stand. From the upper-arm stand, duck the head and look at the knees and pike. (Tuck is permitted at the start.) Release the hand grasp, keeping the upper arms horizontal, and roll forward to an upright, upper-arm support, with hands grasping the bars, and straddle legs, rolling to straddle seat.

Swing to Shoulder Stand

1. Swing straight body backward in a straight-arm support above the horizontal line.

2. As the straight body approaches the peak of the backswing, lean forward, thus dipping the shoulders down to the bars and inverting the body, and simultaneously spread the upper arms horizontally.

3. Note: The body should remain straight throughout this stunt; however, the performer usually must execute a pike during the early, learning stages of this skill.

Cartwheel Dismount from Upper-Arm Stand. Lean the body directly to the right side, rotating on the right upper arm. Keep the head tilted to the right to avoid hitting the left bar with it. Land erect with the right hand grasping the bar.

Uprise

1. From an upper-arm support, rise to a straight-arm support by bearing down on the bars with the upper arms and hands, shifting the body weight and shoulders forward above the hand grasp.

2. Once the upper arms lift from the bars, straighten the elbows.

3. Finish in a straight-arm support.

Front Uprise. Be prepared to rise from an upper-arm support to a hand support before the legs pass the bottom of the forward swing. Then, bear down on the bars with the upper arms, raising the shoulders above the hands and simultaneously driving the hips forward rather than upward.

Back Uprise

1. From an upper-arm support, swing the body backward with a slight pike.

2. Just as the legs pass the bottom of the swing, unpike vigorously into an arch, simultaneously bearing down vigorously with the upper arms and hands.

3. Continue to raise the body as the arms attain a straight-arm support.

4. Note: The higher the body rises above the bars when the arms attain a straight-arm support, the better.

Forward, Swinging Dips. As the forward swing of the straight-arm support begins, bend the arms as

FIGURE 11-28. Forward roll from upper arm stand.

FIGURE 11-29. Front uprise.

FIGURE 11-30.   Back uprise.

the body swings downward and straighten them as the body swings upward. Note: Swinging dips may also be performed on the backward swing.

Upper-Arm Kip

1. From an upper-arm support, lift the legs to a horizontal position over the trunk (inverted pike).
2. Rocking slightly forward, thrust the feet, extending the hips at about a 30-degree angle forward and upward and simultaneously bear down on the bars with the upper arms, rising to a straight-arm support.
3. Note: For safety purposes, first perform this skill in a straddle-seat position.

Single-Elbow Planche

1. From a side seat on the right bar, place the right hand in front of the left leg.
2. Turn the body to the left so that the abdomen is placed on the right elbow while the left hand maintains a grasp on the left bar.
3. Lean the right elbow forward, keeping the chest and head up, and lift the legs so that the body is horizontal and straight.
4. Note: First attempt this stunt from a straddled-squat stand on the one-foot high, parallel bars.

Drop Kip

1. From a cross, standing position, with an inner grasp at the end of the bars, jump upward lifting the legs and dropping to an inverted, pike position with the ankles between the hand grasp.
2. As the shoulders begin to rock back from the

drop, shoot the feet out, extending the hips at about a 45-degree angle forward and upward.
3. Simultaneously bear down with the hands on the bars, keeping the arms straight.
4. Raise the shoulders above the hands to a straight-arm support.
5. Note: An auditory cadence of "one, two" helps to attain the proper timing for thrusting out the legs. The first cadence "one" would be the drop as the feet move between the hands, and "two" would be the start of the rock back when the legs should be thrust out. This stunt may be performed to a straddle seat.

Backward, Upper-Arm Roll. At first this stunt should be performed from a straddle seat without hip extension.

1. From an upper-arm support, swing the legs up over the head through an inverted pike.
2. Extend the legs backward and upward, and continue swinging downward and grasp the bars as in a regular, upper-arm support.

FIGURE 11-31.   Single elbow planche.

3. The bars may be grasped so that the downward swing is performed in a hand support.

4. Note: For safety, spot from under rather than over the bars when parallel bars are high. Use a sweatshirt to offset the friction between the upper arms and the bars.

Parallel Bars Routine

1. Start with front uprise swing to shoulder stand.

2. Roll over, back uprise, swing legs forward over the bar, turn onto elbow.

3. Do an elbow planche.

4. Press to shoulder stand and hold.

5. Roll down backward and up to piked, inverted, upper-arm support and upper-arm kip.

6. Swing back over the bar to front, vault dismount.

Trampoline

The first time the student is introduced to activity on the trampoline, he should mount it, taking care not to fall through the springs, and walk around the bed, but not too near the edge, until he becomes somewhat accustomed to its resiliency. After he has done this, he should assume the following positions.

1. *Stand:* Stand erect with the legs a shoulder width apart.

2. *Seat:* Sit with the trunk erect, the legs horizontal and straight, and the palms flat on the bed by the hips.

3. *Hand and knee:* Kneel with the knees slightly apart, toes pointed, and thighs and straight arms vertical. The body weight should be distributed between the shins and hands.

4. *Knee:* Kneel with the knees slightly apart, toes pointed, and hips straight.

5. *Front:* Take a prone position with the toes pointed and the chest and face held up from the bed. Keep the arms well bent, with the forearms and palms flat on the bed below the head.

6. *Back:* Assume a supine position with the head held off the bed and the legs piked well over the trunk.

After the student has become somewhat familiar with the above positions, he is ready to start the rebounding movements.

Foot Bouncing

1. Standing erect at the center of the bed, with the feet a shoulder width apart, jump upward by bending and straightening the knees causing the bed to depress and rebound.

2. Keep the eyes down at the forward end of the bed.

3. As the body ascends, lift the arms forward and upward, and as the body descends, lower the arms.

4. Circle the arms backward once for each bounce.

5. Keep the bounce low in order to maintain control.

Stop (Break-Fall). The springing action of the bed is absorbed and stopped by bending the knees at the moment of the foot landing.

Straddle Toe Touch. From a foot bounce, keep the trunk erect and lift the legs straight and straddled to a horizontal level. Touch the toes with the hands and lower the legs to a foot landing.

Foot Bounce, Full Turn. From a foot bounce, execute a 360-degree turn to the right by swinging the left arm and shoulder to the right. Finish in a balanced foot landing.

Seat Drop

1. From a stand, raise bent legs forward to the horizontal level and then straighten them.

2. Keep the trunk vertical and drop it straight down. Land with the seat where the feet were.

3. Then, perform from a low bounce.

4. Eventually keep the legs straight while raising them to the horizontal level.

5. Make the seat landing flat on the legs, with the palms beside the hips.

6. Rebound by pushing off the bed with the hands.

Seat Drop, Half-Turn to Seat Drop (Swivel Hips)

1. From a seat drop, push off the bed with the hands, bringing the legs back down under the trunk.

2. Make a half-turn to the right by raising the arms overhead and twisting the head and left shoulder to the right. Land in a straight, foot-bounce position.

3. From a foot bounce, make a half-turn to the right by raising the arms overhead and turning the head and left shoulder to the right. Land in a seat drop.

4. Combine steps 1, 2, and 3 by raising the legs after the half-turn in step 1. Land in a seat drop. (See Figure 11-32.)

Seat Drop, Full Turn to Seat Drop. Learn step 1 of the front drop before attempting step 1 for this trick.

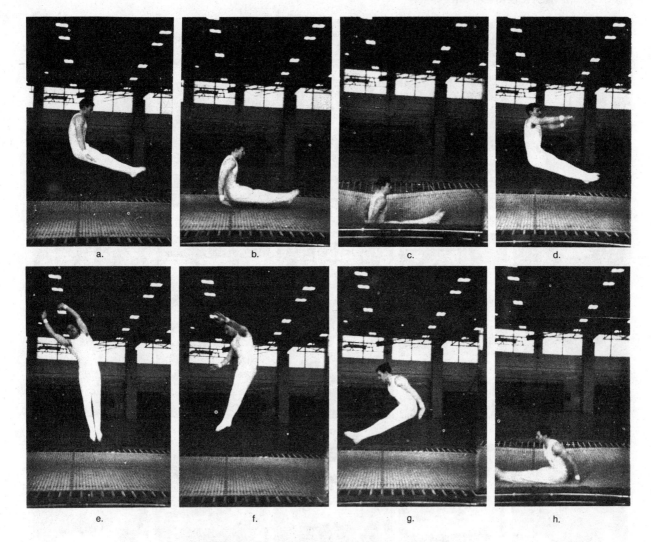

FIGURE 11-32.   Seat drop half-turn to seat drop (swivel hips).

1. From a seat drop, thrust the hips forward so that the body straightens horizontally, half-turn to the right by looking over the right shoulder. Land in a front drop. A slight, backward, trunk lean facilitates the forward thrust of the hips (see Figure 11-33 a. through j).

2. From a front drop, half-turn to the right by turning the head and right shoulder to the right, and pushing off the bed with the hands so that the landing is made in a seat drop (see Figure 11-33 a. through o.).

3. Eliminate the front drop and continue turn to right to a seat drop landing.

Hand and Knee Bounce. Bounce by pushing on the bed with the hands and knees. Keep the bounce very low until both hands and knees rebound with control and simultaneously from the bed. Then increase the height of the bounce.

Hand and Knee Drop. From a stand, bounce up, lean the trunk forward, bend the hips and knees, and drop onto the hands and knees. Land with the knees where the feet were rather than forward of this spot.

Front Drop

1. From a hand and knee bounce, extend the knees and hips so that the hips drop straight down rather than forward, and land on the front.

2. Then perform a hand and knee bounce to a front drop, and return to hand and knee bounce alternately.

3. From a stand, drop to hands and knees, drop to front, return to hands and knees, return to a stand.

4. After step 3 has been perfected, start from a stand. Lift the hips by bending them and drop onto

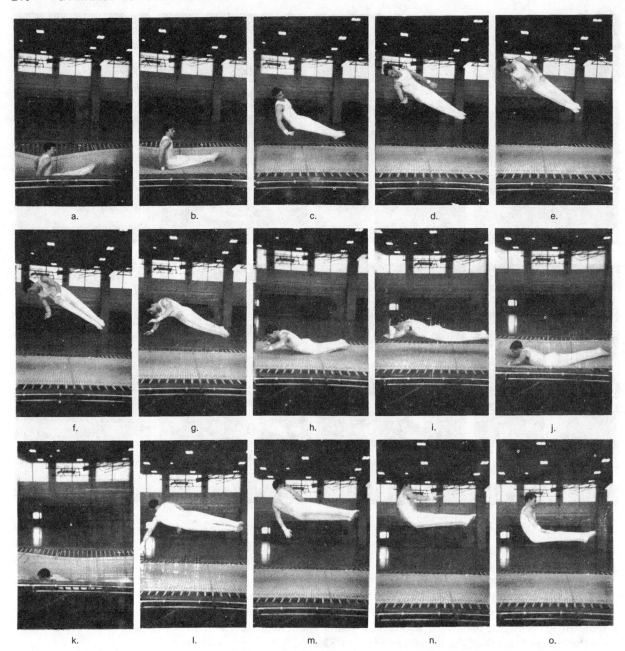

a.   b.   c.   d.   e.

f.   g.   h.   i.   j.

k.   l.   m.   n.   o.

FIGURE 11-33.   Seat drop half turn to front drop followed by a half turn to a seat drop.

the front. After control is gained, perform with straight legs.

Front Drop, Half Turntable

1. From the rebound of a front drop, tuck the legs under the body, keeping the trunk horizontal.

2. Initiate the turn in the horizontal plane by a hand-push and the turning of the head and shoulders laterally.

3. After the 180-degree turn, land on the front again. (Figure 11-34.)

4. Note: At first only a partial turn may be completed. This turn may be worked up to a 360-degree and even a 720-degree turn. A 180-degree turn in one direction followed by a 180-degree turn in the opposite direction is well within the capabilities of novice performers.

Half-Turn to Front Drop. From a stand, look over the right shoulder and turn the left shoulder 180 degrees to the right and drop onto the front.

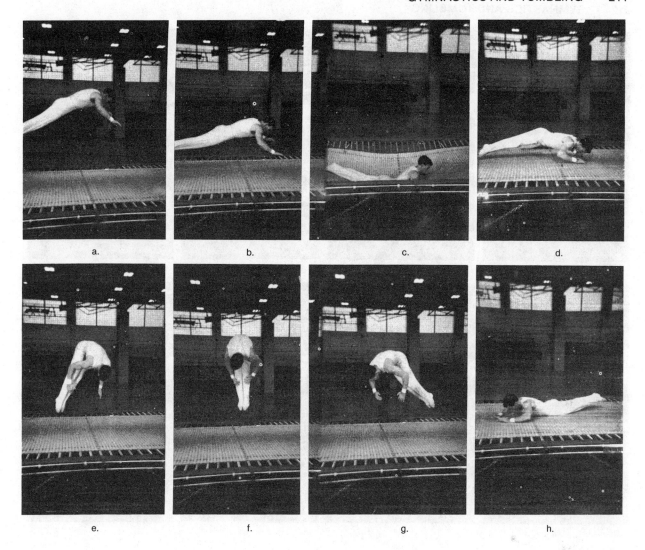

a.   b.   c.   d.

e.   f.   g.   h.

FIGURE 11-34.   Front drop half turntable.

Back Drop

1. From a hand and knee bounce, push the trunk backward and land on the middle of the back, with the head forward and the legs piked over the trunk. Upon rebounding from the back, shoot the legs forward and upward and land in a stand.

2. From a stand, lift one leg up as high as possible, which causes the loss of balance of the supporting leg and the dropping of the trunk straight down to the back-drop position.

3. Then attempt this move from a stand with the legs together, being careful not to dive backward, but rather to drop easily onto the back.

Cradle. As the rebound is made from the back drop, extend the hips, thrust the feet down under the body, and land in a front drop. Perform this stunt with a half body twist just before the front drop and land in a back drop.

Mule Kick. From a knee drop, bounce to a hand support and return to a knee drop. Perform this sequence at least three times. Make the hand support approach a handstand.

Forward Somersault

1. From a knee drop, bounce to a handstand and roll forward.

2. From a knee drop, bounce over past a piked handstand and land on the back.

3. From a knee drop, rebound, lifting the hips well over the head and land on the seat.

4. Then perform a knee drop forward by lifting the hips and ducking the head. Land on the feet.

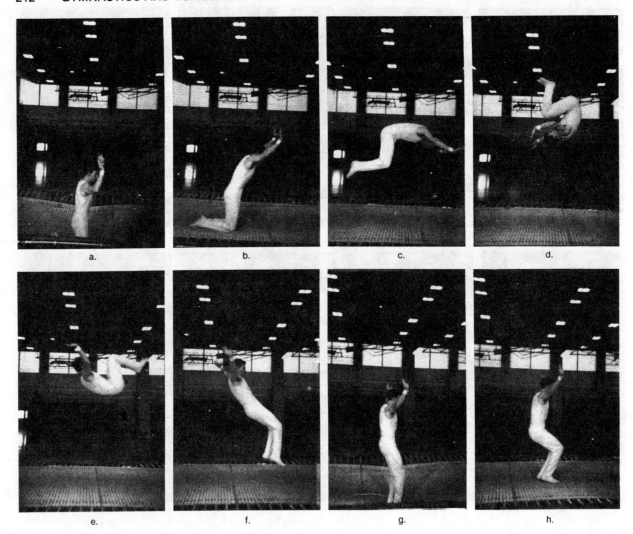

FIGURE 11-35.   Forward somersault.

5. Perform steps 3 and 4 from a stand.

6. Note: During all of the above steps keep the arms overhead.

Back Pull-Over

1. Perform a backward roll, with the hands over the shoulders.

2. From a squat stand, drop onto the top of the seat and pull the legs over the head and roll backward to a stand.

3. As control is attained, perform from a straight stand before performing from a low bounce.

4. Note: During all of the above steps keep the arms overhead.

Trampoline Routine

1. Straight bouncing, swivel hips, one bounce.

2. Half-turn to front drop.

3. Turntable.

4. Hands and knees bounce.

5. Back drop, two bounces.

6. Seat drop, full turn to seat drop.

7. Knee drop.

8. Two mule kicks.

9. Knee, front somersault (with hands in overhead position) to foot stand.

Safety on the Trampoline

The following safety rules are essential for learning and performing on the trampoline.

1. During the learning stages, keep the bounce low.

2. Never jump off the trampoline.

3. Make sure the frame is padded.

4. Make sure activity on the trampoline is supervised.

5. When not in use, keep the trampoline folded and locked.

6. Position spotters around each end and side of the trampoline during the learning stages.

Long Horse Vaulting

Long horse vaulting consists of the approach, the hurdle, the takeoff, the preflight, and the postflight.

The Approach. The distance of a run may vary from nine to thirteen steps. It is begun from a specific point, which should be marked for reference, and is executed by taking normal, running strides rather than shortened ones. During the first part of the run, focus the eyes alternately on the board and the horse; approximately two strides before the hurdle is made, focus them on the horse.

The Hurdle. This is a movement in which the performer jumps from the one-foot stride to the two-foot landing on the Reuther board. Make it low, flat, and more an extension of the run rather than an upward jump onto the board.

The Takeoff. The takeoff is initiated from the middle of the Reuther board, which should be depressed with the balls of the feet. Keep the chest erect and start sweeping the arms forward toward the horse before the feet leave the board. Since there is a tendency to jump directly forward, the beginner should try to jump upward, allowing the momentum of the run to carry him forward. Note: In order to develop adeptness, the gymnast should practice the run, hurdle, and takeoff from the Reuther board, and use a three-foot thick mat or trampoline with a mat over the edge as a landing surface.

The Preflight. Immediately following the takeoff, swing the arms forward and reach for the top of the horse so that when contact is made by the hands on the surface of the horse, the shoulders are well behind the hands. From this position, push vigorously downward with the hands thus helping to elevate the body and keep it erect as the hands leave the horse.

The Postflight. Following the hand-push, the body is raised well above the horse and travels out away from it. Just after the hand-push—regardless of whether the vault is from the neck or croup, or in a squatted, stooped (piked), or straddled position—extend the knees and hips fully before the erect foot landing. The first attempt to vault should be on a buck or a side horse without pommels.

Learning Stages of Vaulting from the Neck. During the primary stages of learning to vault, place the

a. The approach.

b. The takeoff.

c. The post flight.

FIGURE 11-36.   Long horse vault.

Reuther board only about one or two feet from the croup end of the horse. Learning to perform the vault can be enhanced by the following progressive steps.

1. Practice with a short, slow run, jumping upward, landing on the horse on a hand support, and lowering the body to a straddle seat.
2. On each succeeding vault, attempt to place the hands farther along the horse until the neck is reached.
3. Then lengthen the run and attempt to clear the horse by pushing vigorously down with the hands on the neck of the horse and straddling the legs.
4. As control and flight are acquired, the preflight should be executed in a layout position, with the legs higher than the shoulders and body, approaching a 30-degree angle as the hands make contact with the horse.
5. Reference should be made to suggestions listed above under the preflight and postflight phases.

Learning Stages of Vaulting from the Croup. In the initial course of learning, place the Reuther board approximately one and one-half to three feet from the croup end of the horse. The learning sequence should include the following.

1. From a short run and also at the time of the takeoff, extend the arms forward and incline the trunk slightly forward.
2. Push the croup down vigorously with the hands and lift the tucked legs between the arms. This action brings the feet on the horse in a standing position.
3. On each succeeding vault, make the attempt to land on the feet farther along the horse until the neck is reached.
4. After the above has been accomplished, lengthen the run and try to clear the horse in a squat position.

5. As better control and flight are acquired, try to straighten the knees before the body passes over the horse.
6. After step 5 is learned, attempt a straddle vault from the croup.
7. Reference should be made to the suggestions under the preflight and postflight stages.

Drills for Concentrating on Specific Phases of Vaulting. The ability to perform a good hand-push can be developed by practicing the following exercise. From a half-squat stand on a mat, execute a dive forward onto the hands with the body arched up at a 45-degree angle, then snap the legs down, push off the mat with the hands, and land standing on the spot where the hands were.

To improve the squat, straddle, and stoop, start from a front support on the floor and perform a squat, straddle, or stoop action by making sure that the legs shoot between the arms and the hands push off the floor so that the participant lands in a sitting position.

Safety Suggestions. Use rock rosin on nonslip, firm, gymnastic shoes. Never make vaults in socks. If the surface of the horse is slippery, treat it with a good spray adherent.

WEIGHT TRAINING

Weight training can help to develop the strength and stamina necessary to perform well in gymnastics and tumbling. However, any weight-training program used should be scientifically planned to move the participant through a series of exercises that gradually increase in severity. Participation in weight training should be restricted to three days a week and principally to off-season or light-work periods. Appropriate exercises can be found by consulting Chapter 17.

EXERCISE   Definitions and List of Terms (Men)

Unlike the procedure in the other chapters, in this chapter each term is included with its definition. This procedure has been adopted because numerous gymnastic terms are likely to be unfamiliar to many people.

1. *AAU* are the initials for the Amateur Athletic Union of the United States.
2. *"A" parts* is the rating given to simple, basic, and definite skills.
3. *Alignment* refers to the line made by the arrangement of the legs and feet, the arms and hands, and the trunk and head.

4. *Arch* is the hyperextension of the hips and spinal column in which the back side of the body forms a concave curve.

5. *Around:* is a movement on the side horse in which the leg is moved laterally and around one arm.

6. *"B" parts* is the rating given to skills of medium difficulty.

7. *Back* is a term used to refer to the back side of the body.

8. *Back support* is a hand-support position in which the posterior surface of the body faces and may be leaning on the apparatus.

9. *Backward* is a word used to refer to the direction in which the backside of the body leads.

10. *Break* is an error or mishap in execution which breaks the continuity of the routine.

11. *"C" parts* is the rating given to skills of extreme or maximum difficulty.

12. *Cast* is a means of obtaining a bodily swing on the parallel bars, horizontal bar, and rings by shooting the legs up and outward, away from the point of support.

13. *Compulsory* exercise is a routine and/or a vault that is prescribed and required for a specific competition.

14. *Croup* is the near-end zone of the long horse and the right-end zone of the side horse.

15. *Cross position* is a term used to describe the position of a gymnast in relation to the parallel bars, horizontal bars, and horse, in which the gymnast's body is perpendicular to the longitudinal axis of the apparatus.

16. *Cut* is the action of passing one or both legs between the hand grasp and the apparatus.

17. *Execution* is the form (posture), technique (mechanics), and style (expression) of a performance.

18. *Exercise* is a drill for increasing fitness or skill level. It is also a series of stunts or a routine.

19. *False grip* is a front-hang position on the rings in which the grasp is high with the outer heel of the hand above and diagonally across the ring so that the hand is essentially in the same position after the body rises to the support position.

20. *FIG* are the initials for Federation Internationale de Gymnastique (International Gymnastic Federation), which is the governing body for international gymnastic competition.

21. *FIT* are the initials for the International Trampoline Federation, which was founded in 1965.

22. *Feint* is a preparatory position or movement.

23. *Flank* refers to a lateral vault whereby the side of the body passes over the apparatus.

24. *Flip* is a somersault.

25. *Floor exercise* is an all-around event performed on a matted floor. It is sometimes called free exercise or free calisthenics.

26. *Form* is the term used to describe trunk posture and limb and head positioning and alignment. It is usually exhibited by pointed feet, straight legs, and specific head and limb positions.

27. *Forward* refers to the direction in which the front of the body leads.

28. *Front* refers to the anterior surface of the body.

29. *Front support* is a hand-support position in which the anterior surface of the body faces and may be leaning on the apparatus.

30. *Giants* are large bodily revolutions around the horizontal bar or rings using the hands as the fulcrum.

31. *Hand support* is a position in which the shoulders are above the hands and the body weight is borne by the hands as they rest on the apparatus. Hand stands and planches are included in this group.

32. *Hang* is a position in which the shoulders are below the point of support. Levers are included in this group.

33. *Hecht* (swan) is a straight or arched body position throughout a vault or a dismount over the parallel or horizontal bars.

34. *Hold parts* are phases of an exercise in which the body should be held perfectly stationary for a duration of two seconds on the parallel bars and during floor exercise, and three seconds on the rings.

35. *Hurdle* is a movement made by leaping onto two feet for a double foot takeoff, or the hop or skip step before a roundoff or forward handspring.
36. *Jump* is a two-foot spring from the floor or board.
37. *Kip* is a vigorous hip extension from an inverted, pike position which culminates in a hand support or handstand.
38. *"L"* is a position in a support or a hang whereby the trunk is vertical and the legs are horizontal.
39. *Layout* is a straight- or arched-body position in somersaulting and vaulting.
40. *Lever* is a hand-hanging, horizontal, straight-body, held position.
41. *Magnesium carbonate* (carbonate of magnesia) is the chalk used on the hands to absorb perspiration and prevent slippage of the grip.
42. *NCAA* are the initials for the National Collegiate Athletic Association.
43. *Neck* is the name for the far-end zone of the long horse and the left-end zone of the side horse.
44. *Optional exercise* is a particular routine of the performer's own choice. It is usually composed of the performer's best stunts.
45. *Overgrip* is a hand grasp in which, when taken from a hang on the horizontal bar, the thumbs face each other and the palms face away from the performer.
46. *Part* indicates a definite skill, stunt, trick, position, or movement.
47. *Pike* is a body position in which the hips are flexed and the legs are straight.
48. *Pirouette* is a turning movement of the body about its longitudinal axis from a leg or arm support.
49. *Planche* is a hand-supported, horizontal, straight-body, held position.
50. *Pommels* are the two curved handles, usually made of wood, on top of the side horse.
51. *Postflight* is that part of the flight in long horse vaulting from the hand-push until the foot landing on the mat.
52. *Preflight* is that part of the flight in long horse vaulting from the foot takeoff to the hand contact on the horse.
53. *Press* is a movement in which the body is slowly lifted by the strength of the arms to a shoulder stand, handstand, or planche.
54. *Rear* refers to the back or posterior side of the body.
55. *Reuther board* is the official, slightly resilient, wooden, takeoff board used for vaulting.
56. *Roll* is a revolution in which the body continuously contacts and moves along the surface of the floor or parallel bars, or one in which the midsection of the body moves smoothly around the horizontal bar or hand grasp on the rings.
57. *Roundoff* is a forward, half-twisting, hand-springing skill, which efficiently converts forward movement to backward movement yet maintains momentum.
58. *Saddle* is the middle zone of both the long horse and the side horse.
59. *Somersault* is a 360-degree, bodily revolution in flight through the anteroposterior or lateral plane around a transverse, horizontal axis.
60. *Spotting* is the procedure used to guard one against injury and a teaching aid to manipulate or to assist a performer through a stunt.
61. *Stoop* is the act of passing straight legs between the arms by flexing the hips.
62. *Straddle* is a position in which straight legs are spread apart laterally (abduction).
63. *Stretch* is a phase of the technique of execution. It refers primarily to the extending or lengthening of the trunk or arm reach.
64. *Stride* is a straddled-leg position in which one leg is forward (hip is flexed) and the other leg is backward (hip is hyperextended).
65. *Style* is the individualistic expression and character of performance aside from the technique of execution.
66. *Support* is a position where a good portion of the body, usually the shoulders, is above the point of contact with the apparatus.

67. *Swing time* is the action of performing a sequence of stunts on the trampoline without taking intermediate or extra bounces.

68. *Technique* is a term which describes the mechanics of execution exhibited by efficiency, amplitude, and control.

69. *Tinsica* is a hand-springing skill. It is a cross between a cartwheel and a front handspring.

70. *Travel* is a movement in which the body is transferred along the longitudinal axis of the apparatus from one zone to another.

71. *Tuck* is a body position in which the thighs are drawn to the chest and the lower legs are drawn to the thighs by flexing the hips and knees respectively.

72. *USGF* are the initials for The United States Gymnastic Federation.

73. *Undergrip* (reverse grip) is a hand grasp taken from a hang in which the little fingers face each other and the palms face the performer.

74. *Upper arm support* is a position in which the bodily weight is borne by the upper arms resting on the parallel bars.

75. *Uprise* is a movement in which the body rises to a hand-support position from the end of a forward or backward swing while the body is in an upright hang or upper-arm support.

76. *V* is a support in an upright, hand support or seat position in which the trunk and legs form a V.

77. *Vault* is a leg-springing or hand-swinging skill in which the impetus over the apparatus is received from a hand-pull and/or hand-push.

QUESTIONS AND ANSWERS ON THE RULES (Men)

1. *Q.* What are the Olympic, gymnastic events?
   A. The Olympic events are floor exercise, horizontal bar, long horse vault, parallel bars, rings, side horse, and all-around.

2. *Q.* Are the NCAA events identical with the Olympic events?
   A. Yes.

3. *Q.* Are the Olympic rules for competition identical with the NCAA rules?
   A. No. These differences will be explained in the following pages.

The questions and answers which follow below will be in accordance with the Olympic or FIG rules.

Floor Exercise.

1. *Q.* What are the basic rules for floor exercise?
   A. The floor exercise area is a square 39.44 by 39.44 feet, covered by a firm mat from $\frac{5}{8}$ to 1 inch thick. Each participant has a time limit of fifty to seventy seconds in which he must complete the routine. The routine is made up basically of tumbling, balancing, flexibility, strength, and agility skills, which are performed with rhythm and harmony. No spotters are permitted.

Side Horse

1. *Q.* What are the official, competitive measurements for the side horse?
   A. The body of the side horse must be 63 inches long and $13\frac{3}{4}$ inches in diameter. The top surface must be $43\frac{3}{8}$ inches from the floor and the top of the pommels must be 48 inches above the floor.

2. *Q.* What are the rules for competitive, side horse exercises?
   A. Exercises must be a continuously moving routine, consisting of split-leg, pendular swings and joined-leg, circular swings. The routine should be composed predominately of double leg, circular movements with forward and backward scissors, one of which must be per-

formed at least twice in succession. The center, right, and left side of the horse must be used in a routine. Spotters are not permitted.

Rings
1. *Q.* What are the required dimensions and measurements of the rings?
   A. The cable from which the rings hang must be attached to a swivel $216\frac{1}{2}$ inches above the floor. The rings must be $98\frac{1}{2}$ inches above the floor surface, and $19\frac{5}{8}$ inches apart. The diameter of the inside circle of the ring is 7 inches and the diameter of the wooden ring is $1\frac{1}{2}$ inches.
2. *Q.* What movements and positions are required by the rules for the rings?
   A. The ring routine is composed of moving and static skills above and below the rings, without causing a pendular swing of the cables. A minimum of two handstands are required, one of which must be done from a press and the other from a swing. In addition to the handstands, at least one other difficult, strength position must be held.

The Long Horse Vault.
1. *Q.* What dimensions and measurements do the rules require for long horse vault?
   A. The length of the body of the horse must be from 63 to $64\frac{1}{2}$ inches, and the height of its top surface must be not less than $53\frac{1}{8}$ inches and not more than $53\frac{3}{8}$ inches. The minimum length of the run, including the take off board, is 65.6 feet.
2. *Q.* How is the body of the horse marked?
   A. It is marked by $\frac{3}{8}$-inch wide lines placed $15\frac{3}{4}$ inches and $23\frac{5}{8}$ inches from each end. The area between these lines are the zones.
3. *Q.* What kind of takeoff device is used for the long horse vault?
   A. The Reuther board, which is $23\frac{5}{8}$ inches wide, $47\frac{1}{4}$ inches long, and $4\frac{23}{32}$ inches high at the front end, is used.
4. *Q.* Explain the movement requirement for a competitive vault?
   A. The vaulter must place his hands in either the near- or far-end zone without touching the dividing lines. In the cartwheel vault only the forward hand is considered in evaluating the grip. One point per zone will be deducted for improper hand placement. Vaulters must show height, distance, and specific body positions (pike, arch) and body angle of not less than 30 degrees on neck vaults. The body angle is a line through the ankle, shoulder and top of horse.

The Parallel Bars.
1. *Q.* What measurements are required for the parallel bars?
   A. The top of each bar must be $66\frac{15}{16}$ inches above the floor, and the width between the bars must be set between 16 and 22 inches.
2. *Q.* What are the movements required by the rules for parallel bar competition?
   A. The movements consist of a swinging routine accompanied by vaults, with a maximum of three held positions, a strength part, and a simultaneous hand release either above or below the bar of at least "B" difficulty.

Horizontal Bar.
1. *Q.* What are the required measurements for the horizontal bar?
   A. The top of the cross bar must be $98\frac{1}{2}$ inches above the floor. The bar must be $1\frac{1}{8}$ inch in diameter and $94\frac{1}{2}$ inches in length.
2. *Q.* What are the movements required by the rules for the horizontal bar?
   A. The movements must be put together in a continuously moving routine, usually embracing circular movements that are small or near the bar and large or away from the bar, turns, vaults, other hand releases, and a dismount away or over the bar.

The trampoline and tumbling are called special events and are not included in the standard Olympic competition. Competitive rules related to them are discussed below.

Trampoline
1. *Q.* What kind of bed is necessary?
   A. The bed must be constructed from 1-inch wide, interwoven, nylon web. It is suspended from the frame by 110 to 115 steel springs.
2. *Q.* What safety procedures are required by the rules?
   A. Protective pads covering the frame and mats covering the surrounding area to a minimum distance of 5 feet are required. Furthermore, spotters must be stationed at the ends and sides of the trampoline.
3. *Q.* In general, what kind of movements are required in trampoline competition?
   A. The routine must be one sequence and consists of forward and backward somersaults, combined with twists, one of which is done so that some part of the body other than the feet makes contact with the bed.

Tumbling
1. *Q.* What equipment is required for competitive tumbling?
   A. Mats at least 5 feet wide, 60 feet long, and from 2 to 4 inches thick are required.
2. *Q.* What kind of activity is required?
   A. A routine is limited to four tricks of not more than two-minutes duration. Tumbling is not a NCAA event.

This portion of rules discussion will consider the primary differences between the Olympic and NCAA gymnastic rules.

1. *Q.* What is the difference in the number of events required?
   A. (1) Under Olympic rules all contestants must compete in the all-around. They must perform six compulsory and six optional exercises.
   (2) According to the NCAA rules a contestant may compete in any number of events.
2. *Q.* In what manner is the champion of the individual event determined?
   A. (1) Under the Olympic rules a contestant must attain at least an 8.0 average for the all-around in order to be eligible for a place in the finals or a medal.
   (2) According to the NCAA rules no all-around qualification score is necessary. Specialist compete in the individual events.
3. *Q.* What is the maximum number of men that may compete on one team?
   A. (1) Olympic rules permit six men to compete.
   (2) NCAA rules permit a maximum of fourteen men to compete.
4. *Q.* What is the maximum number of men from a team that may enter each event?
   A. (1) Olympic rules allow six men to compete in each event.
   (2) NCAA rules allow four, two all-around men and two specialists.
5. *Q.* How is the team champion determined?
   A. (1) According to the Olympic rules, the highest five of the six compulsory and optional exercise scores in the six events are totaled. The lowest score in each compulsory and optional exercise is deleted. The highest total determines the winner. The maximum total is 600 points.
   (2) Under the NCAA rules, the highest three of the four competitors' scores in each of the six events are totaled. The lowest score in each event is deleted. The highest total determines the winner. The maximum total is 180 points.
6. *Q.* What time limit is set on the duration of floor exercise?
   A. (1) Olympic rules require a minimum of fifty seconds and a maximum of seventy seconds.
   (2) NCAA rules set no time limit.

7. *Q.* How are Olympic and NCAA rules different in the long horse vault?

   A. Under the Olympic rules in the preliminaries the second performed vault may be the same or different from the first vault. The best score of the two vaults will count. In the finals, competitors must perform two vaults from different categories in order not to receive a deduction in points. The scores of both vaults are averaged. The NCAA is now using the same rules as are used in the Olympic finals.

The following section distinguishes the difference between AAU and NCAA rules for the trampoline.

1. *Q.* How many bounces may a contestant take during his routine on the trampoline?

   A. (1) Under AAU rules, ten to twelve bounces are counted aloud after the first skill of the routine has been executed.

   (2) According to the NCAA rules, bounces are not counted aloud, but a minimum of eleven skills are required.

2. *Q.* What is the ruling if a contestant falls off the trampoline, touches the springs or frame, or is supported by the spotters?

   A. (1) Under the AAU rules, his routine is terminated at that point and he shall be scored on the basis of the number of bounces completed.

   (2) The NCAA rules require him to rest up to thirty seconds and continue with a one-point, penalty deduction. He is permitted preliminary bounces, without further penalty, to regain his height before resuming his routine.

3. *Q.* What is the final position at the conclusion of a routine on the trampoline?

   A. (1) Under the AAU rules, the performer may jump once in a stretched position after his final stunt.

   (2) According to the NCAA rules, the performer's last landing must be a stationary foot landing on the bed.

The section of rules discussed below are those established for judging gymnastic events.

1. *Q.* What is the general procedure for scoring an exercise?

   A. A contestant starts an exercise with 10.0 points, the number given for a perfect performance. Points are deducted in units of tenths for variations from good form as defined in the rules. Four judges are used, each awarding a score to each contestant of each performance. The final score for each performance is obtained by eliminating the highest and lowest scores of the judges, and averaging the two intermediate scores. However, the difference between the two intermediate scores must not exceed 0.1 if the average is 9.6 or higher; 0.2 if the average is between 9.0 and 9.55; 0.3 if the average is between 8.0 and and 8.95; 0.5 if the average is between 6.5 and 7.95; 0.8 if the average is between 4.0 and 6.45; 1.0 in all other cases.

2. *Q.* Are deductions classified in any manner?

   A. Yes. There are three general categories: difficulty, combination, and execution.

3. *Q.* What procedure is followed for judging difficulty?

   A. Difficulty, in all events except vaulting, includes a minimum number of eleven parts to obtain the maximum score for a routine. There are six "A" parts, valued at 0.2 each; four "B" parts, worth 0.4 each, and; one "C" part, valued at 0.6. If a "C" part is replaced by a "B" part, the difficulty is reduced by 0.2 point, thus the maximum score would be 9.8 points. Total deductions for difficulty cannot exceed 3.4 points.

4. *Q.* How are combinations judged?

   A. Combinations include the type of exercises that are adapted to the apparatus with basic harmonious composition and parts which present marked originality and great risk. Deductions, not to exceed 1.6 points, are made for extra (intermediate) swings and counterswings, ineffective mounts and dismounts, worthless or too simple parts or connections in relation to the difficulty and character of the exercise as a whole, optional sequences that are noticeably similar to the compulsory exercises, improper duration of floor exercise routine, and performing within the boundaries of the floor exercise area.

5. *Q.* What is the procedure used for judging execution?

   A. Execution deductions, not to exceed 5.0 points, are made for: (1) improper technique that includes interruptions, instability, or lack of balance (falling); scraping; too short duration of the held parts; swinging of the rings during held parts; lack of harmony, rhythm, amplitude, and extension; (2) poor form such as unwarranted bending of the leg and arm, malaligned body, and failure to point the toes.

6. *Q.* In what way is judging long horse vaulting different from judging other events?

   A. The judging of long horse vault is divided into four components: (1) the degree of difficulty of the vault; (2) the grip or position of the hands; (3) the flight before (preflight), the flight after (postflight), and the hand support; and (4) execution (holding) of the body.

DESCRIPTION OF THE ACTIVITY (WOMEN)

Women's gymnastics can be traced to the early part of the nineteenth century when women wore long skirts and high collars and were equipped with hand apparatus. In the latter part of the nineteenth century, women gymnasts evolved into members of rigid marching troupes. It wasn't until the early 1950's that the arrival of the present-day sport of gymnastics for women occured.

The evolution of gymnastics can be thought of as paralleling the evolution of women into free, equal and separate beings who are a great deal less delicate and feeble than formerly believed. The sport, today, epitomizes the uniqueness of women and their special characteristics of beauty, grace, poise, flexibility, strength, power, coordination, agility and balance, all in harmony with the feminity of the woman performer.

Competitive women's gymnastics includes four specific events governed by well-defined rules established by the following organizations: Fédération Internationale de Gymnastique (FIG), the United States Gymnastics Federation (USGF), the Amateur Athletic Union (AAU), and the Association for Intercollegiate Athletics for Women (AIAW). Although there are some discrepancies in the regulations of the above four organizations, they are basically similar and all follow prescribed standards. The standard events are floor exercise, uneven parallel bars, balance beam and side horse vaulting. Depending upon the level of competition, a girl may either compete in one or more events, or train for all-around as is mandated of Olympic and International competitors.

Most gymanstic competitions involve performance of compulsory or prescribed routines, which change every four years, and optional or original routines which also must meet certain standards to achieve maximum score.

Collegiate competition now limits the number of performers per team, per event to six in dual meets. Four rated (USGF) officials must preside over the competition. International order of events should be followed and include the vault, bars, beam, and floor exercises. Optionals, only, are performed at this level. Optional scoring of all events is based upon a rating of ten points broken down as follows.

A. **Five points for composition**
1. Value of the elements of difficulty—
   3 superior elements at .6 each 1.8
   4 medium elements at .3 each 1.2
                                                    ___
                                                    3.0

2. Originality and vaue of the links 1.5
3. Value of the general composition 5

B. **Five points for execution**
1. Execution and amplitude 4.0
2. General impression 1.0
                                                    ___
         Total 10.0

The above applies to all optional bar, beam and floor exercise routines. Vaults are scored on the basis of their listed value with faults deducted from that value.

Penalties for falls at all apparatus result in the following deductions:

1. Fall on the apparatus or on the ground 5
2. Touching the floor with the hand 5
3. Fall on the buttocks 5
4. Touching the floor (hand) on landing 3
5. Touching the apparatus after landing 3
6. Fall on the knees 3

Floor and beam routines should include locomotor movements such as leaps, hops, skips, runs as well as turns, variety of levels and moods, balance or poses, flexibility, suppleness as well as tumbling elements. Floor routines should cover the entire floor area and beam routines should move along the entire length of the beam with varied placement of the elements of difficulty from one end to the other. Exercises performed on uneven parallel bars are primarily swinging, circling and kipping movements with releases and regrasps used as the performer changes from bar to bar. A maximum of three stops on balance beam and no stops on uneven bars are permitted in a routine. Stops should only be used briefly as passing positions.

All exercises should show amplitude, originality, good connections, variety, lightness, continuity, difficulty and impeccable form. Attainment of the 10.0 routine or vault should be the ultimate goal in performance of all gymnasts. The striving for perfection at all levels can only result in the growth and development of the sport as well as the individual.

Equipment

A well-supplied gym area should include a floor exercise mat, a large selection of apparatus mats, crash pads of varying thicknesses, a trampoline for lead-up purposes, at least two sets of uneven parallel bars, two high balance beams and several low carpeted beams, at least one good vaulting horse and several reuther boards. Supplementary materials should include chalk and chalk stand(s), rock rosin, sand paper, stop watches, record players and tape recorders, towels (wet for gymnast's feet and dry for the equipment), and a rubber vaulting runway. Transporters for all apparatus should be on hand as well as spotting belts and an overhead harness.

Many gymnastic suppliers manufacture uneven parallel bars which come with either cable supports or base extensions with a strong triangular bracing system. All systems are designed to meet competitive specifications. The height of the upper bar is 2.30 meters (7'6.5"), the height of the low bar is 1.50 meters (4'11"). New regulations permit the raising of the high bar one or two notches. The width of the bars may be adjusted by the competitor to achieve regulation width (21.26"-30.74"). Rails of uneven bars are generally made of laminated wood for optimum resiliency and strength. Fiberglas rails are rapidly gaining acceptance world wide.

Balance beams are constructed of fine laminated wood with a steel base. New designs include diagonal legs and braces for increased stability. Beam's are 16'5" long and approximately 47 inches high. The beams are adjustable so that skills can be learned and practiced at lower heights. A non-skid lacquer is applied to provide sure footing. Padded and vinyl beams are now being used at all levels of competition. Wooden beams must also be made available at competitions in which padded or vinyl beams are employed.

The vaulting horse will be 47" high from the mat to the top of the horse. The horse is 13¾" in diameter and 63 to 64⅛" inches in length. The men's pommel horse quickly converts to a long horse or women's vaulting horse by simply removing the laminated wood pommels and inserting special flush rubber plugs into the pommel holes.

Women's boards should be covered with a foam rubber pad and either a vinyl or carpeted surface to reduce the shock of take-off.

Gymnastic Personal Equipment

The leotard should not be to flashy as it may detract from the actual performance.

Women gymnasts generally wear some type of footwear which varies with the event and individual preference. Types of footwear include a cotton blend footie with criss-cross elastic from heel to instep; a leather shoe with rubber pads on the ball and heel of the shoe; heavy canvas shoe with a rubber sole (generally for vaulting); and an all nylon shoe with a rubberized bottom.

For descriptions of specifications on types of trampolines see the Men's Gymanstics section.

Dance in Gymnastics

Dance plays a very important role in both the composition and the quality of gymnastic movement. Proper body carriage, grace and skill are developed through practice of dance technique.

Gymnastic "walks" as well as other locomotor movements should consist of a body in perfect alignment with sufficient turnout of the pelvic girdle, legs and toes. The walk is performed with a toe-heel action. The arms should swing freely in opposition from the shoulder with the index finger an extension of the arm. The torso should be erect and controlled; the steps should be small.

A gymnastic "run" should generate energy efficiently. The run should be on the balls of the feet with the arms swinging in opposition to the legs. The angle of the arms should be decreased as they go forward and the fist should not come any higher than the shoulder. The arms should never cross in front or in back of the body. Knees should come forward first. Strides should be even and the movements smooth and free.

A "hop" is a transference of weight from one foot to the same foot and usually follows another movement such as a step or a jump. The knee should be lifted in front of the body and well turned out with the heel turned in and forward of the knee. The arms are optional but often are posed in opposition to the lifted leg. The head and chest are lifted for maximum height.

A "skip" is simply a combination of a step and a hop.

"Jumps" involve taking off from two feet and landing on both feet. Variations of jumps are: the cheerleading or "c" jump; the tuck jump; the squat jump; the straddle or "Russian" jump; the arch jump; the entrechat. Jumps should always start low and increase in height. All jumps should appear explosive. Arms should be used to assist in gaining maximum amplitude.

"Leaps" involve take-off from one foot or both feet and a landing on the opposite foot. Leaps cover distance and are slower than runs because they also involve elevation and suspension. Some varieties of leaps are: the sissone, (two foot take-off with a one foot landing); stag or deer leap; stride and split leaps; scissors leap, (switch legs in the air); "Pas de Chat" or cat leap.

FLOOR EXERCISE

Nature of the Activity

A floor exercise routine must thoroughly cover the entire 12 meter square area with curvilinear as well as straight paths arranged in an interesting pattern. The floor exercise routine must be lively and exciting. Change in the quality and pace of movement and variety in the types of movement selected must be evident. Each sequence should add to the total impression of poetry in motion with the careful coordination of diverse rhythms. The attributes of the gymnast should be dramatized in each sequence. The performance should possess originality as well as individual character. Difficult elements should be well spaced throughout the routine with the most spectacular stunt coming at the climax of the exercise. Additional skills to be utilized include: tumbling, acrobatics, pivots on the feet or hands, leaps, jumps, hops, balance on the feet or hands, running steps, trunk movements, and selected movements from ballet, modern dance, folk dance or jazz dancing.

Selected floor exercise movements

Body Wave

A body wave can be performed from a squat, half squat, or slight flexion of the body. The sequential action of the parts of the body from a contracted squat to a stand is as follows:

1. Knees and ankles move forward as the arms start downward and backward.
2. The hips move forward.
3. The rest of the trunk moves forward as the arms continue backward and upward.
4. Shoulders move backward and the head is in neutral position.
5. The finish is on the toes in releve with the arms held in a high oblique position.

The movement must be fluid and supple.

Japanese Split

In a Japanese split, both legs must be stretched directly to the side. The split should be flat unless it is

FIGURE 11-37a. Back walkover.

FIGURE 11-37b. Back walkover, inverted position.

to be called a Straddle Stand. The hips should be backward with the seat well turned under. Movements into and out of this must be carefully designed so as not to appear awkward.

Press Handstand

A woman's press handstand must be performed with straight arms and must not be confused with the man's muscular push-up press. Counterbalance is achieved at the shoulders. The hips should be directly above the support with shoulder forward lean occurring as the leg lift begins (either tucked or piked). The movement must be fluid and appear easy.

Back Walk Over

The gymnast starts in a stretched stand with one leg elevated forward to a 90° angle at the hip. This extended leg moves backward concurrent with the upper body movement backward. Extension in the inverted position must be very hard in the shoulders. Both legs should be split 180° (see Figure 11-37a, b).

Valdez

A valdez is executed from a long sit position with one leg extended and the other leg bent with the foot placed close to the hips. Either arm is placed on the floor behind the hips, palm flat and fingers pointing backward. The other arm is extended forward to be used for the lift upward and backward. The bent leg pushes forcefully against the floor and extends. The straight arm and leg lift up and reach backward. The body passes through a momentary arch position into a handstand.

FIGURE 11-38. Dive roll-pike.

Tumbling Movements

Forward Roll (see Men's section)

Dive Forward Roll-Pike Position

From a semi-squat position with the arms backward obliquely, the arms are thrust forward as the feet push to extend the legs and lift the hips. The body will leave the mat and be momentarily suspended in the air. The hands will then contact the mat and support the body weight; the elbows will immediately bend enabling the shoulders to contact the mat. The rest of the roll proceeds as in the forward roll-pike (see Figure 11-38).

Balanced Handstand (see Men's section)

Backward Roll From Straddle to Straddle

From a straddle stand, sit backwards gently by piking sharply at the hips. Place hands on the mat between the legs and behind the feet to soften the landing of the hips. Upon hip contact, bring the legs overhead and place the hands on the mat next to the ears (elbows are bent, palms down and fingers are pointing toward the hips). As soon as the palms contact the mat, push with the hands to extend the arms and return to the straddle stand position with the head lifted.

Backward Roll Extension (see Men's section)

Cartwheel (left side) (see Men's section)

Dive Cartwheel

This skill is usually preceeded by a hurdle. The movement differs from a cartwheel in that it involves a stronger pushing action; a lifting of the head and chest; a reaching forward and upward before hand placement on the mat and an almost simultaneous contact of the hands with the mat.

Front Handspring (see Men's section)

Tinsica

A tinsica is executed just like a handspring step-out except that hand placement on the mat is different.

In a right foot take-off, the right hand is placed on the mat about 18″ in front of the right foot. The left hand is then placed about a foot in front of the right.

The eyes spot the hands as they are placed. The legs are kept in a wide stride position. The hips

FIGURE 11-39. Cartwheel.
a. Starting position.

b. Lunge.

c. Inverted position.

d. Completion.

a. Starting position—lunge.

b. Hand placement.

c. Inverted position.

d. Completion.

FIGURE 11-40.   Tinsica.

remain elevated and the head well back throughout the skill.

Round-Off (see Men's section)

Back Handspring

The starting position is with the feet together and in a straight stand.

The knees and hips are flexed and start moving backward as if sitting in a chair. The arms are moving down and backward at the same time.

When balance is lost, the legs push vigorously and the arms are thrust up overhead.

The head is tilted back and the shoulders are extended. The reach is for the mat with the hands. The body is momentarily airborne before hand contact.

The body passes through the handstand position and then the legs are snapped sharply to the mat as the head and upper body are lifted (see FIGURE 11-41 a, b).

a. Starting position.

b. Hand contact.

FIGURE 11-41.   Back handspring.

Cartwheel—Aerial (left side)

Horizontal momentum must be blocked and transferred into vertical momentum in order to affect an aerial.

The block is achieved after the run and hurdle by a step forward on the left foot with the left knee flexed over the left foot; the head and chest are held high and not ahead of the foot position. At this time the right leg swings backward and upward forcefully.

There is then an immediate strong push from the left leg.

The arms pull up on the hurdle and swing down toward the sides of the body as the leg action begins.

As the right foot lands, it is quickly followed by the left foot. The head and chest are lifted.

Backward Somersault

From a straight stand, the legs are flexed slightly and the ensuing action is a vertical spring.

The arms are thrust vigorously upward to assist in gaining height.

At the peak of the jump, the knees are driven to the chest and the head is arched backward to cause rearward rotation. As the eyes contact a spotting point, the legs are extended and the upper body raised. The knees flex slightly to absorb the landing.

Composing a Floor Exercise Routine

The floor exercise event allows for the greatest exploration and originality of movement of the four competitive events. Even the beginning student may compose a floor routine which can later be upgraded to include more difficult elements.

There are several techniques for composing a floor routine; the following is just one:

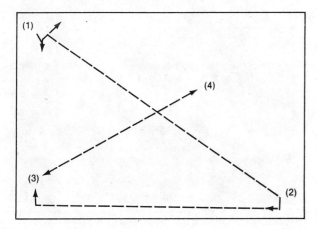

FIGURE 11-42.   Floor pattern—beginning floor exercise routine.

1. Find a selection of music that the student can relate to and likes.
2. Draw up a sample floor pattern which is simple and short at first. Make sure the pattern covers the entire floor area and has curvilinear as well as straight paths.

List tumbling skills, dance skills, balance skills and transitional skills the student can perform.

Listen to the music and create combinations from the list that suit particular passages of music. Keep the following ideas in mind when creating the routine:

1. The opening sequence should be lively and exciting.
2. A variety of types of movement and levels of movement must be employed to avoid monotony.
3. The style of movement must suit the personality of the performer and not be copied from someone else.
4. Change pace and direction where it is least expected. Vary the quality of movement (e.g. sharp vs. flowing movements).
5. The ending should be the high point of the routine with the most spectacular or unusual skill contained within the final pass.

Sample Beginning Floor Exercise Routine

1. Step left; kick right; go into a deep lunge. Bring left foot to right in a deep squat; body wave up onto ½ toe. Balance right, balance left. Run, run, run *Cartwheel* jump 210° turn.
2. Chassé, chassé; *dive forward roll-pike position;* step, scale; Swedish fall; ½ turn on mat; "V" seat, long sit; *backward roll-pike;* to long lying (prone); 1½ log rolls to the left. stag sit to knee spin up (360°). 135° pivot turn on ½ toe.
3. Two châiné turns; step *handstand; forward roll-out* to stand. Hitchkick; step stag leap; land in an abstract scale as a final pose (4).

UNEVEN PARALLEL BARS

Nature of the Event

The uneven parallel bars offer women the opportunity to use more flowing and swinging movements than strength movements. Uneven bar exercises can be characterized by swinging, circling, kipping movements with releases and regrasps employed during the changes from bar to bar. Elements should be linked without unjustified pauses or stops. Most routines consist of 12 to 18 movements without any time limit.

Specific Techniques

Mounts

Straight Arm Support Mount

Facing the low bar, hands are placed on bar in an overgrip shoulder width apart. A jump is then executed while simultaneously pressing down on the arms to straighten the elbows. Weight should be resting at the base of the hips with the back slightly arched and the hips, legs and toes totally extended (see Figure 11-43).

Back Hip-Pullover-Mount

Stand facing the low bar with the hands shoulder width apart in an overgrip. Kick one leg forward and upward over the bar as the arms flex, pulling the hips to the bar. The support leg immediately joins the first leg and the body finishes in the front support position described above.

Squat on Mount

Place the reuther board directly in front of the low bar. A short run and low, long hurdle are executed with a two foot take-off. The hands reach for the low bar in an overgrip as the hips are elevated. The knees are then quickly drawn to the chest in a tight tuck position as the body is elevated above the bar. Both feet are then placed on the bar in between the hands. The hands may then regrasp the high bar to begin the routine (see Figure 11-44).

Straddle Over Low Bar-Catch High Bar Mount

The reuther board is placed just in front of the low bar. A short run and low, long hurdle are executed. The hands reach for the low bar as the hips are elevated and the legs begin to straddle. As the body moves over the bar in a straddle position, the arms push down on the low bar and the hands release the bar and catch the high bar. The grip on the high bar can be an overgrip or mixed (one overgrip; one undergrip) depending upon the nature of the subsequent movement (see Figure 11-45)

Glide Kip Mount

Facing the low bar on either side about double arms length away, the performer jumps into the air

FIGURE 11-43.   Straight arm support mount.

FIGURE 11-44.   Squat on mount.

FIGURE 11-45.   Straddle over low bar—catch high bar mount (board take-off).

a. starting position.

b. Full extension glide.

c. Completion (straight arm support)

FIGURE 11-46.   Glide kip mount.

reaching for the bar in an overgrip while driving the hips upwards and backwards. The body then glides forward, completely extending, with the feet just a few inches above the mat. Upon reaching the fully extended position, the legs are piked sharply with the ankles brought to the bar. The legs are then forcibly kicked outward and downward as the arms pull strongly. The body finishes in a straight arm support (see Figure 11-46a, b, c).

Balance or Held Positions

Squat Stand

From a straight arm support on the low bar, the legs are swung forward and then forcibly backward to a free front support position (see cast-swinging movements). At the height of the backswing, the knees are brought to the chest and the toes are placed on the bar between the hands.

Swan Balance

This movement may be performed facing inward or outward on either bar. From a straight arm support position, the balance point or fulcrum of the body is located. The body is kept well arched and the arms are lifted off the bar sideways or upwards. The fulcrum of the body is on the hips or upper thighs. A front hip circle is a good movement to follow this position (see Figure 11-47).

Side Handstand

From a swan on the high bar, facing inward, reach forward and grasp the low bar in an overgrip. Push the body off the high bar by swinging the legs under it and then upward and rearward until the handstand position is achieved. A suggested following movement might be a straddle down into a back hip circle on the low bar.

Circling Movements

Back Hip Circle

From a free front support position (cast) the hips are then brought to the bar as the head drops backward. When in the inverted position, the body is slightly piked to shorten the radius of rotation, and return the body to the straight arm support position.

Front Hip Circle

From a straight arm support position, the body leans forward with the chest in the lead. The arch of

FIGURE 11-47. Swan balance.

the body is held as long as possible. The body sharply pikes at the bottom of the circle. This will provide sufficient momentum for the return to the straight arm support position.

Seat Circle Backward

Sitting on either bar with the hands in an overgrip on either side of the body (rear support position), the body is lifted from the bar taking the weight on the hands. The body is in a tight pike position and drops backward, completely circling the bar. To slow rotation, the body opens as it returns to the rear support.

Mill Circle Forward

The performer is in a stride support position with the hands in undergrip on either side of the body. The weight is lifted off the bar. The legs are kept rigid. The chest leads as the front leg steps forward and then downward circling the bar with the bar resting on the rear leg. The bar is kept close to the crotch.

Straddle Sole Circle Backward

From a free front support position (cast), at the height of the backswing, pike sharply at the hips and straddle the legs placing the soles of the feet (insteps) on the bar. From this position, drop backward and circle completely around the bar ending in the original position.

Swinging Movements

Cast (free front support position)

From a straight arm support position on either bar in either direction, the hips are flexed slightly. This causes the legs to swing forward under the bar. The legs are then extended to the rear and upward with the shoulders shifted well forward and the body lifted into the free front support position. The elbows slightly flex and then extend to assist in pushing the hips from the bar. The body then returns to the starting position with the hips fully extended (see Figure 11-48).

Cast Off High Bar, Wrap Low Bar

From a straight arm support position on the high bar facing inward, a cast into a long hand is executed. The body swings downward and forward. When the hips meet the low bar the legs whip into a pike position around the low bar and the hands instantly let go of the high bar and grasp the low bar. The back hip circle is completed when the body is in a straight arm support on the low bar.

Eagle Catch

From a cast wrap, the arms are swung upward and backward to catch on the high bar in an eagle grip.

FIGURE 11-48. Cast.

Kipping Movements

Double Leg Stem Rise

From a long hang on the high bar facing inward, hands in overgrip, the legs are tucked placing the soles of the feet on the low bar. The feet push off as the hands are rotated forward and the arms press downward causing the body to finish in a straight arm support position on the high bar.

Stationary Kip to High Bar

From a rear lying rest position on the low bar with the hands in overgrip on the high bar, the legs are sharply piked drawing the ankles to the high bar. At this point, the legs are snapped sharply downward and outwards as the arms pull. The body finishes in a straight arm support position on the high bar.

Back Uprise

From a cast to a long hang from the high bar, the body swings into the low bar and then sharply pikes. As the hips swing backward, the body straightens. When the body is under the high bar, a slight pike is executed at the hips as the arms pull hard. This should snap the body into a front support on the high bar (see Figure 11-49a, b, c).

Connecting and Miscellaneous Movements

Back Hip Pullover, Low to High Bar

From a rear lying position on the low bar, bend one knee, placing the sole of the foot on the low bar. Kick the other leg straight rearward and upward over the high bar as the foot on the low bar pushes. The bent leg immediately joins the straight leg as the arms pull the hips close to the high bar. The circling is continued about the high bar until the body arrives in a straight arm support position.

Double Leg Shoot Through

From a free front support position, the knees are tucked at the height of the backswing and then extended sharply through both arms to arrive in a sitting position on the bar.

Leg Scissors on Low Bar

From a rear lying position on the low bar, grasping the high bar in a mixed grip (e.g. right hand overgrip, and left hand undergrip). The left leg is kicked up into the air and passes over the right leg as the body

a. Bar beat.

b. Start of uprise.

c. Completion.

FIGURE 11-49. Back uprise.

twists to the right. The right hand is removed at this point and regrasps as the body arrives in a crotch seat facing the high bar. The scissors action is then continued as the right hand is again removed and the left leg continues its circle back to the starting position continuing to twist to the right. The right hand finishes in overgrip on the high bar.

Stomach Whip

From a straight arm support on the high bar, facing outward, a cast-push away is executed. The body maintains a rigid extended position as it descends toward the low bar. Upon arrival on the low bar, the hips immediately pike to absorb the landing force. The legs swing under the bar and then upward again permitting a wide variety of subsequent movements.

Dismounts

Cast Off to Rear

At the height of a cast on the low bar the arms push and the body jumps backward. This and all landings must be performed with bent knees to absorb the force of the landing.

Pike Position-Shoot Off Dismount

From a rear support on the low bar, sharply pike the body and cast the body away from the bar by pushing off the hands.

Underswing From High Bar Over the Low Bar

From a straight arm support position on the high bar, facing inward, the legs are sharply piked under the bar as the body drops downward. The legs then swing upward as the body straightens and then extends fully. The swing is continued until the hips are arched and the hands release the high bar. The performer lands facing outward from the front of the low bar.

Stomach Whip to Back Tuck Somersault-Dismount

A stomach whip is executed. As the legs swing upward off the low bar the hips are piked and the legs straddle so they may pass over the low bar. As the body swings under the high bar, the legs are brought together. At the height of the forward swing, the knees are sharply tucked as the head drops backward and the hands push off the high bar causing back-

ward rotation. The body opens as the eyes focus on the mat resulting in a fully extended landing.

BALANCE BEAM

Nature of the Event

Balance beam, today, has evolved into floor exercise in an elevated and confined area. A well performed beam exercise makes the spectator forget that it is being performed on an area only 5 meters long and 4 inches wide. The exercise consists of a mount, locomotor skills, poses or held positions, turns, tumbling and acrobatic movements and a dismount. Routines must be one minute 20 seconds to one minute 45 seconds in length. Deductions occur if routines are too short or long.

Specific Techniques

Mounts

Crotch Seat Mount

Facing the side of the beam, run and jump to a front support while swinging one straight leg over the beam. The body will then execute a one-quarter turn to arrive in a sitting position with one leg on either side of the beam (see Figure 11-50).

FIGURE 11-50. Crotch seat mount.

Forward Roll Mount

The reuther board is placed just under the end of the balance beam. The hips lift high before the head is tucked. A forward roll is executed with the elbows squeezing tightly against the sides of the head to maintain control (see Figure 11-51a, b, c).

a. Board take-off

b. Landing on back of neck.

c. Completion.

FIGURE 11-51.   Forward roll mount.

Squat Mount

Jump and push off to straight arm support with the hips elevated. The knees are tucked at the height of the jump. The feet are then placed on the beam landing between the hands.

Step on Mount

The board is placed perpendicular to the side of the beam. A short run and one-foot take-off is executed. The landing occurs on the beam with the opposite foot in either a squat or upright position (see Figure 11-52).

Handstand Mount

The board is placed perpendicular to the side of the beam. After a short run, the hands are placed on the beam and the arms are straight. The hips are elevated to right over the beam. The legs then press up to a fully stretched handstand.

Locomotor Skills

Cat Leap

This is used as a forward movement rather than a sideward movement as in dance. Take off is executed from the right foot; the bent left leg is kicked high in the air; as it descends, the bent right leg kicks upward. Landing is on the left foot.

Stag Leap

Take off is executed from the left leg. The right leg kicks upward and bends so that the right foot touches the left knee giving the illusion of pushing the extended left leg higher. Landing is on the right leg.

Hitchkick

The right leg is kicked straight forward and upward in the air. As it descends, the left foot ascends in the same manner. Landing is on the right foot.

Chassé (forward)

A chassé is a step-together-step with the together phase occuring in the air, above the beam. The legs

FIGURE 11-52.   Step-on mount.

FIGURE 11-53.   Croisé.

FIGURE 11-54.   Abstract scale.

are drawn together in the air fully extended. Landing is on the back foot. The same foot an remain in the lead for succeeding chassés or they can switch.

Step-Hop

Step on the left foot and hop on it while the right foot is held in a croi sé position.

Poses

"V" Sit

A tight pike is performed by bending only at the hips. The legs can be lifted in a tuck and then extended or there can be a straight leg lift into the "V" sit position.

Croisé

Stand on one foot. Lift the other leg with the knee high and the leg turned outward from the hip. The toe of the elevated leg crosses slighty in front on the supporting leg (see Figure 11-53).

Abstract Scale

Stand on one leg and lift the other leg rearward as high as possible. Simultaneously, the trunk bends forward. The support leg bends slightly and the extended leg bends slightly with the knee turned outward. Arm position may vary (see Figure 11-54).

Forward Split

The forward leg is turned outward so that the foot will slide forward and down to a split on the beam. Both hips should be in line with each other and perpendicular to the length of the beam.

Turns

Jump Turn

For a jump turn as well as all turns and pivots on the balance beam, execution must be with good alignment of body segments and weight over the base of support.

In the jump turn, spotting is especially important. Good amplitude is necessary to achieve full value of the difficulty rating. The turn begins with slightly flexed legs which straighten upon take off, with good body stretch in the air. Landing is executed after the turn is completed.

One and One Half Turn In the Lunge

The left leg is stretched and the right leg is in a deep squat. The arms are held over the left leg and swing towards the right foot to initiate the turn. The left leg lifts off the beam and touches down on the beam as each 180° turn is executed. The extended left leg never drops below the level of the beam in executing the turn.

Piqué Turn

A step is performed onto the ½ toe of the straight right leg and the turn is initiated by the arms swinging from left to right. The body is held in good alignment over the right toe and the head spots a convenient point throughout the turn.

Pivot Turns

Pivot turns can be performed in either an upright or squat position with the feet placed one in front of the other and close together. When the right foot is in front, the turn will be executed to the left. Arms assist in the execution of the turn as described in the piqué turn above. All pivot turns should be performed on ½ toe.

Tumbling and Acrobatic Skills

Forward Roll

From any starting position (squat, kneeling, lunge, scale), reach forward with the hands; elevate the hips; bend the elbows and tuck the head between the arms as the base of the neck and shoulders are placed on the beam. The elbows control the movement by squeezing against the sides of the head.

Backward Roll

From a single leg squat with the other leg extended forward to the horizontal, sit on the beam and reach over head to grasp the top of the beam. The elbows squeeze against the sides of the head as the support leg joins the extended leg in a pike position. Both legs move backward and upward until the hips are over head. The thumbs then push and the hands press to the side of the beam assisting in clearing the head. The movement can be finished in several positions (squat, knee scale, kneeling, etc.)

Cartwheel (sidewards)

The cartwheel is executed similarly to the floor cartwheel (see section on floor exercise) except that a slightly oblique preparation is recommended. The rhythm of the cartwheel must be a definite 1-2-3-4 (hand-hand-foot-foot) with the first foot landing closer to the hand than on the floor.

Back Walkover

This movement is also similar to the back walkover executed in floor exercise except that the hands are only placed 4 inches apart and not shoulder width. The first foot lands close to the hands and the second leg is stretched as high as possible before coming to the upright position.

a. Starting position.

b. Handstand.

c. Roll-out.

FIGURE 11-55.   English handstand.

English Handstand-Forward Roll

Facing the length of the beam, the performer bends forward placing the hands on the beam, thumbs on top and fingers on the sides. Simultaneously she kicks up to a handstand. The roll-out is accomplished by bending the elbows and piking the body. The chin is well tucked to permit primary contact with the beam by the back of the neck and shoulders. The elbows remain close to the sides of the head throughout the roll (see Figure 11-55a, b, c).

Handstand-Straddle Down

Cartwheel into a side handstand with good body stretch and alignment. The legs are then straddled as the hips pike. The feet are placed on the beam outside the hands. During the downward motion of the straddled legs, the shoulders shift slightly forward of the hands to counterbalance the weight going backward.

Free Forward Roll

From various starting positions, the hips are elevated and the back of the neck is placed on the beam. The arms are extended sidewards as the body rolls over in a pike position. To achieve full difficulty, the roll must finish in a stand or a continuous whip up to a squat.

Dismounts

Round-Off

Stand facing about 2-3 feet from the end of the beam. Step onto the right foot and swing the left leg upward and backward. Both hands are placed on the beam, one at a time, with the fingers directed down the right side of the beam. Push with the right foot and bring both legs together in the inverted handstand position. Execute a one-quarter turn with the body; pike at the hips and push off with the hands after the feet have passed the inverted vertical.

Cartwheel-¼ Turn Off

This skill is executed with the same preparations as the round-off. As the body passes the side handstand position, the left hand is released and the head is turned to the left. The right hand is then released and both arms are joined overhead. A one-quarter turn is executed in the air to land with the back to the beam.

Backward Somersault

From a stand at the end of the beam on the balls of the feet, the arms reach up lifting the chest and hips up in front of the body. A good tuck position is achieved as the knees are brought up to the chest. The head comes into play during the second half of the dismount; it is tilted backward to cause backward rotation. The body then stretches for a good landing.

Handspring

Step into an English handstand position on the end of the beam and push from the shoulders. Keep the head well back for a good arch. Stretch the body for a smooth landing.

Barani

A barani is an aerial round-off. A one-quarter turn is made on the initial take-off and then a one-quarter turn is executed after passing vertical. A good solid block is needed with fast leg action. The eyes should spot the dismount area on the mat. The chest should be lifted as the legs pass the head position.

SIDE HORSE VAULTING

Nature of the Event

To vault is to go over. Women's vaulting has become very exciting in recent years due to the downward grading of the values of the common vaults. To perform a vault worth 10.0, there must be at least a 180° twist (the hecht vault is the exception to this rule). All vaults must be performed with the placement of the hands on the horse. For compulsory vaults as well as optional vaults, the gymnast is allowed two tries, the best one counting. For optional vaults, the two vaults must be different. The difficulty of the vaults is fixed according to the annexed scale.

All vaults consist of a run or approach; a take-off or hurdle and board contact; preflight; on horse contact; after flight and landing. Generalizations about vaulting follow.

The Approach

Run on the balls of the feet. Spring training is very beneficial as the run should generate energy efficiently. To get rid of the hesitation before contacting the board, keep the distance of the run consistent and count the number of steps. Bear in mind that as speed increases, the steps will be longer.

Take-off

The hurdle should be long and low so as not to decrease forward momentum. The feet should be ahead of the body's center of gravity as board contact is made. There is a slight knee bend at this point. The arms reach forward and upward to give height. The knees and ankles are extended fully and the toes leave the board last.

Pre-flight

Positions for pre-flight vary with the vault. It is necessary, however, that there is a visible time in flight between board take-off and horse contact. During the pre-flight, the center of gravity must rise and the body must rotate around it.

Horse Contact

The arms should always be straight with the shoulders in line with the hands. The hands should be flat (not on finger tips) and shoulder width apart. The weight is on the hands and the push-off is very quick. The push-off should cause the center of gravity to rise higher than in pre-flight. The push-off is from the shoulders.

After-flight and Landing

The head should be up with eye focus ahead and upward slightly. The height of the after-flight is greater than the pre-flight for the new vaults. Repulsion from the horse must be very strong for good after-flight. A good body stretch in the air must be achieved before landing. The landing must be solid with no additional steps taken. Shock is sequential absorbed by the toes, heels and knees which bend.

Examples of Vaults

Bent Hip Ascent (New Ratings)
Squat 4.5
Straddle 5.0
Stoop 5.0

Straight Body Ascent (New Ratings)
Squat (Layout) 8.0
Stoop (Layout) 8.5
Straddle (Layout) 8.5
Handspring 9.2
Yamishita................................ 9.4
Cartwheel-¼ Turn 9.4
Tsukahara 10.0
Hecht 10.0

EXERCISE   Definitions and List of Terms

Dance and Modern Rhythmic Gymanstics

1. *Arch jump*—(body stretched with legs together or body arched with rear foot to head height)—hollow jump or sheep jump.
2. *Cabriole*—leap with beat of the legs.
3. *Cat leap*—leap with flexing of legs in front.
4. *Corkscrew 1½ turn*—1½ turn on one leg descending from stand to squat.
5. *Scale*—(an arabesque performed with the upper body lowered forward and balletically termed an arabesque penchee)—arabesque or low arabesque (balletically; an arabesque is performed with an erect torso and free leg raised at least to right angle to support leg).
6. *Scissors leap*—ciseaux or hitchkick.
7. *Series*—2 or 3 movements in succession and refers to medium and superior elements.
8. *Stag leap*—deer leap.
9. *Stag-split*—bending, then stretching of forward leg.
10. *Split leap (180°)*—grand jete.
11. *Stride leap*—denotes less than 180° split during leap.
12. *Tuck jump*—squat jump with legs bent forward in front of body.
13. *Waltz*—three moving steps in rhythm.

Gymnastic and Acrobatic Movements, Supports and Mounts

1. *Arabian*—jump with ½ turn into somersault forward piked, tucked, stretched, with step-out.
2. *Aerial walkover*—free walkover.

3. *Bridge stand*—crab stand.
4. *Cartwheel forward*—Cartwheel forward or ¼ turn into cartwheel, ¼ turn out of cartwheel facing start (inward).
5. *Flic-flac*—back handspring or back flip.
6. *Flic-flac step-out*—flic-flac on one leg.
7. *Flic-flac or handspring*—denotes landing on two legs.
8. *Flyspring*—denotes handspring from 2 legs (tuck or pike) to step-out.
9. *Step-out*—a separation of legs during the flight phase and landing on one leg (in particular the flic-flac and handspring).
10. *Illusion*—turn on one leg passing through a scale forward into a scale backward.
11. *Knee scale*—knee stand.
12. *Kneeling lunge*—kneeling sit on one leg with the other leg stretched backward.
13. *Limber*—turnover backward or forward with the legs together.
14. *Needle scale*—vertical standing split with forward grasp.
15. *Pike-stretch somersault*—pike somersault.
16. *Pike support (clear)*—"L" support or leg lever support.
17. *Press*—raise legs to handstand without spring.
18. *Roll backward or handstand*—back extension roll.
19. *Round-off*—arabspring.
20. *Snap-down*—courbette or ½ flic-flac.
21. *Split sit*—split.
22. *Split forward*—cross or transversal split.
23. *Split lateral*—split sideward.
24. *Stands*:
    (1) Cross—when the breadth axis of the gymnast is at right angles to the length axis of the apparatus.
    (2) Side—when the breadth axis of the gymnast is parallel to the length axis of the apparatus.
25. *Stag handstand*—lunge handstand.
26. *Straddle support (clear)*—straddle "L" support.
27. *Stretched somersault*—layout somersault or hollow back somersault.
28. *Thief mount*—jump passing one leg stretched, the other bent to a rear support.
29. *Tinsica*—arabwheel.
30. *"V" support (clear)*—kid support.
31. *Valdez*—bacward tinsica to or through handstand position from sit or tuck stand.
32. *Walkover*—turnover forward or backward from 1 leg stand to 1 leg stand.
33. *Whip back*—flic-flac without hand support.
34. *Wolf mount*—squat stand with support leg bent and free leg stretched sidewards.

Terms and Definitions

1. *Aerial*—denotes a tumbling or acrobatic movement performed in the air.
2. *Clear*—designates a position with a hands support with body and legs not touching apparatus or floor.
3. *Free*—designates a position or movement accomplished without hand support.
4. *Turn*—used when a minimum of ½ turn is described and specifically used to describe a revolution around the long axis in vaulting.
5. *Twist*—used to describe a full revolution around the long axis in tumbling and in uneven bar movements where a full turn is demanded.
6. *Pirouette*—used to describe a full turn on one foot or tour en l'air in dance or occasionally to describe a full turn to catch high bar on the uneven bars (around long axis).
7. *To squat (verb)*—to tuck.
8. *To stoop (verb)*—to pike.

9. *Kip-up*—(uneven bars) designates a kip onto the bar to a front or rear support.
10. *Kip*—(uneven bars) designates a kip movement only, not onto the bar to a support.

The above definitions were taken from: ENGLISH TERMINOLOGY COMMITTEE, Representing 13 Nations, Mrs. Jackie Fie, Chairman USA, printed in *USGF News,* March 1976, pp. 28-30. This terminology is a key to the terminology which precedes each event in the 1976 English Edition of the *FIG Code of Points.*

QUESTIONS AND ANSWERS ON THE RULES

1. *Q.* What is Olympic Order in a women's gymnastic competition?
   A. Vault, uneven bars, balance beam, floor exercise.
2. *Q.* How many officials should preside at any gymnastic meet?
   A. All compulsory and optional exercises should be evaluated by four judges and one head judge.
3. *Q.* How is the final score calculated?
   A. The four judges shall write their scores independently from another and hand their score to the head judge for examination and computation. The highest and lowest of the four scores are eliminated. The two middle scores are averaged.
   The difference between the middle scores may not exceed:

   0.30 for scores between 9.50-10.00
   0.50 for scores between 8.50-9.45
   1.00 for scores . . . . in all other cases

   During finals on each apparatus, the separation between the scores will be:

   0.20 for scores between 9.50-10.00
   0.30 for scores between 8.50-9.45
   0.50 for scores . . . . in all other cases

   The head judge will score all exercises, but her score will only then be considered when the difference between the scores of the four judges is too great. In such a case, she will call the four judges together and determine the base score using her score as foundation.
   (*Base score*—average score plus the score of the head judge divided by two.)
4. *Q.* What are some of the functions of reserve judges?
   A. They are permitted to work:
   (1) As line judges for floor—the deduction is made by the head judge from the average score.
   (2) As time keeper for beam and floor—deduction is made by the head judge from the average score.
   (3) To count number of optional same vaults performed by each team.
   (4) To count the number of same mounts and dismounts by each team on bars and beam.
   These judges do not judge. It is their duty to record all faults and to signal the penalty to the head judge after the work of either a team or individual gymnast. The deduction concerning time limits on beam and floor as well as penalties for same optional vaults, will be made by the head judge and communicated to the secretary of the jury. The deductions will be taken from the final score of the gymnast or team.
5. *Q.* What is the division of the 10.00 points for optional exercises on the uneven bars, balance beam and floor?

A. Composition of the exercise — **5.00 points**

Value of difficulty	3.00
3 superior difficulties at 0.60 points each	1.80
4 medium difficulties at 0.30 points each	1.20
Originality and value of connection	1.50
Value of general composition of exercise	0.50

Execution — **5.00 points**

Execution and amplitude	4.00
General impression	1.00

6. *Q.* What are the new (1975) standardized deductions for falls from the apparatus and dismounts on all apparatus during optional and compuslory exerices?

   A.

Fall from apparatus	0.50
Fall during the dismount	0.50
Steps and hops	0.10 to 0.20
Fall on the knees	0.50
Fall on the seat	0.50
Support with one or two hands	0.50
Slight touch with one or two hands	0.30
Fall against the apparatus	0.50
If the gymanst falls at the end of the exercise and the dismount is missing	0.50
If the missing dismount counts as a difficulty, there is a further deduction in case of superior difficulty	0.60
For a medium difficulty	0.30

7. *Q.* How can deductions for general faults pertaining to incorrect body position be summarized for all 4 apparatus?

   A.

Small errors	deduction 0.10 to 0.20 points
Medium errors	deduction 0.30 to 0.40 points
Serious errors	deduction from 0.50 points

8. *Q.* What is the deduction for incorrect attire of the gymnast?

   A. 0.30 points.

9. *Q.* What are the deductions that a coach can incur from her gymnasts score?

   A.

Coach blocks the view of the judge	0.30
Coach signals gymnast	0.30
Coach touches apparatus during exercise	0.30
Assistance from coach during exercise	1.00
Assistance during landing	0.50
Assistance during vault	vault void
Coach stands between rails or runs underneath apparatus	0.50
Coach gives verbal assistance during exercise	0.50

   Coach may talk to gymnast after fall from apparatus to inquire if the gymnast is injured.

10. *Q.* What are the vault deductions for all types of vaults.

    A. **First Flight**

Insufficient pre-flight	up to 1.00
Body bent	up to 0.50
Legs bent, straddled or open	up to 0.50

    Support

Too long in support	0.20
Support with arched body	up to 0.30
Arms slightly bent	0.20
Arms fully bent	1.00

Second Flight Phase

Insufficient height	up to 0.50
Insufficient stretch of the body	up to 0.50
Poor direction	up to 0.50
Poor body position (legs bent, straddled or open)	up to 0.50
Turn to early or too late	0.30
Turn not completed	0.50

11. *Q.* What are the different structure groups from which elements must be taken in composition of an uneven bar routine?
   A. (1) Arriving in support or suspended hanging position through circling movements.
   (2) Kipping movements.
   (3) Elements with swing to handstand.
   (4) Elements with turns around longitudinal axis (pirouettes).
   (5) Elements with turns around horizontal axis (somersaults).
   (6) Counter swings with grip changes (passing from one bar to another).

12. *Q.* How many stops are permitted on uneven bars and what is the penalty for additional stops?
   A. No stops are permitted and each stop is penalized 0.20 points.

13 *Q.* How long does the gymnast have to remount the bars after a fall?
   A. 30 seconds, after that time period the exercise is considered terminated.

14. *Q.* What is the penalty for extra swings?
   A. 0.50 points.

15. *Q.* How many stops are permitted in a balance beam exercise and what is the nature of these stops?
   A. Three stops are allowed. Stops are:
   (1) Planned technically good and conscious held positions.
   (2) Acrobatic stands (handstand, shoulder stand, headstand).
   (3) Gymnastic stands with accented holds in the end phase.
   Pauses are to be avoided before and after acrobatic elements or otherwise be penalized each time 0.20 points.

16. *Q.* What is the duration of the balance beam exercise and what is the penalty for an exercise too long, too short?
   A. 1:15 to 1:35. The stop watch will be started when the gymnast's feet leave the floor or springboard. They will be stopped when the gymnast's feet touch the floor again after completion of the exercise. A signal warns the gymnast at 1:30 and again at 1:35. All elements executed after 1:35 will not be evaluated.

The penalty for an exercise too long	0.30 points
(for each missing second) too short	0.05 points

17. *Q.* How long does the gymnast have to remount the beam after a fall?
   A. 10 seconds. After 10 seconds have elapsed, the exercise is considered finished.

18. *Q.* What is the penalty for music being against regulations in floor exercise? (Only one instrument—usually piano—is allowed.)
   A. 1.00

19. *Q.* What is the penalty for the absence of an acrobatic series (need at least two) during a floor exercise routine?
   A. 0.20 each time.

20 *Q.* What is the duration of the floor exercise event?
   A. 1:00 to 1:30. The deductions for a routine too short or too long are the same as balance beam.

The above rules were taken from the International Gymnastics Federation, Women's Technical Committee, *Code of Points,* Copyright FIG, 1975 Edition.

BIBLIOGRAPHY (MEN)

AAU Official Guide and Handbook. New York: Amateur Athletic Union of the United States, 1965.

Claus, Marshall. *A Teacher's Guide to Gymnastics.* Palo Alto, Calif.: The National Press, 1967.

Code of Points (Men's Section). Technical Committee of the F.I.G., 1964. (distributed by the American Athletic Union of the United States)

DeCarlo, Tom. *Handbook of Progressive Gymnastics.* Englewood Cliffs, N.J.: Prentice-Hall, Inc., 1963.

Farkas, James. *Age-Group Gymnastic Workbook.* Tucson: U.S. Gymnastic Federation, 1964.

Griswold, Larry. *Trampoline Tumbling.* New York: A. S. Barnes and Co., Inc., 1962.

Hughes, Eric. *Gymnastics for Men.* New York: The Ronald Press Company, 1966.

Johnson, Barry L. *A Beginner's Book of Gymnastics.* New York: Appleton-Century-Crofts, 1966.

LaDue, F., and Norman, J. *This Is Trampolining—Two Seconds of Freedom.* Cedar Rapids, Ia.: Nissen Trampoline Company, 1956.

NCAA Official Gymnastic Rules. Phoenix: College Athletic Publishing service, 1968.

O'Quinn, Garland. *Gymnastic for Elementary School Children.* Dubuque, Ia.: William C. Brown Company, 1967.

Yeager, Patrick. *Science of Coaching and Teaching Gymanstics.* Statesboro, Ga.: Wide World Publications, 1964.

BIBLIOGRAPHY (WOMEN)

Bowers, C., Fie, J., Kjeldsen, K., and Schmid, A. *Judging And Coaching Women's Gymanstics.* Palo Alto, Calif.: The National Press, 1972.

Carter, Ernestine Russell. *Gymnastics For Girls And Women.* Englewood Cliffs, New Jersey: Prentice-Hall, Inc., 1969.

Cooper, Phyllis. *Feminine Gymnastics.* Minneapolis, Minn.: Burgess Publishing Company, 1973.

Drury, B. and Schmid, A. *Gymnastics For Women.* Palo Alto, Calif.: The National Press, 1970.

International Gymnastics Federation, Women's Technical Committee, *Code of Points,* FIG, 1975.

Hughes, Eric. *Gymanstics For Girls.* New York: The Ronald Press Company, 1971.

Kjeldsen, Kitty. *Women's Gymnastics.* Boston, Mass.: Allyn and Bacon, Inc., 1975.

National Association for Girls and Women in Sport. *June 1975-June 1977 NAGWS Guide—Gymnastics.* Wash. D.C.: American Alliance for Health, Physical Education, and Recreation, 1975.

Official Publication of the United States Gymnastics Federation. *USGF News.* Tucson, Arizona: The USGF, March 1979.

12

HANDBALL/ RACQUETBALL

DESCRIPTION OF THE ACTIVITY (HANDBALL)

There are two types of handball that have gained popularity: four-wall handball and one-wall handball. In this discussion emphasis will be given to the four-wall version; however, the one-wall game will be explained briefly under a separate heading. The four-wall game is played indoors in a completely enclosed area. The one-wall courts may be constructed outdoors against the walls of buildings or inside gymnasiums. In many situtations, they are laid out on both sides of a specially designed wall.

Four-Wall Game

The four-wall game is played in an enclosed area that has four solid walls and a ceiling. It should measure not less than 20 feet in width, 40 feet in length, and 20 feet in height, with a back wall at least 10 feet high. The floor is divided into a front and back court of equal size by a line in the middle known as the short line. Another line, drawn 5 feet in front of and parallel to the short line, is the service line. These two lines are joined by two lines, each of which is 18 inches from and parallel to the right and left walls respectively. The areas between the lines and the side walls are known as the right and left service boxes. In doubles play, these lines mark the area where the partner of the server must position himself while the service is being delivered.

The ball can be struck only on each return or serve, and it must be played with one hand only, but may be struck with either the right or left hand on any one specific play. It is a fault to catch the ball or to permit it to rebound from any part of the body except the hands.

The game is begun by the player of one team making a service. After the serve has been delivered, the ball must be played by either of the opposing players (or player if it is a singles game). Play is continued by each member of a team or player striking the ball alternately until one side commits a foul or fails to make a good return. When this occurs, the opposing player or team either scores a point or a hand is out, whichever is applicable.

To deliver the service, the server must be within the area between the short line and the service line. He drops the ball and strikes it on the rebound from the floor. The ball must strike the front wall before making contact with any other surface, and it must touch the floor in back of the short line either before or after hitting one of the side walls. The opposing team may play the ball on the volley or after it has made one contact with the floor. They cannot play the ball after it has touched the floor a second time. In doubles, the partner of the server must be in the service box while the serve is being made, and the opposing players must take a position at least 5 feet in back of the short line. The server does not have to hit the ball into any specific area, nor do the receivers have to alternate in receiving the service. For the team that serves first, only one member gets to serve before the side is out. After the first serve, both team members serve before giving up the ball to the opponents.

After the serve, any returned ball may first strike either or both of the side walls, the ceiling, the back wall, or the back wall and side wall before it hits the front wall. After it makes contact with the front wall,

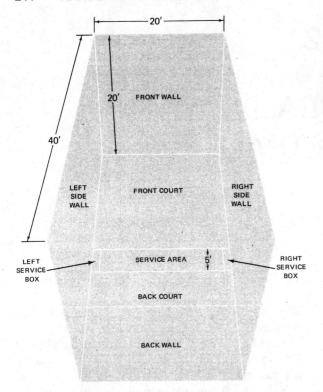

FIGURE 12-1.   Four-wall handball court.

Besides the singles and doubles games, there is a third type of unofficial competition called "cut-throat," in which the fundamentals and rules are identical with the singles and doubles except that three players compete. The server plays against the other two players, with the service alternating, each player keeping his own score, and the winner being the one who first makes 21 points. This can be a very strenuous and exciting game.

The One-Wall Game

The size of the official court for one-wall handball is 20 feet wide and 34 feet long, with a wall at the front 16 feet high. The short line is marked 16 feet away from and parallel to the base of the front wall. The serving court is a rectangular area 9 by 20 feet, which is bounded at the front by the short line and at the back by markers 9 feet in back of the short line.

The fundamental skills for the one-wall game are the same as those for the four-wall version. The served ball must hit the front wall before hitting the floor, and must rebound far enough from the front wall to touch the floor in back of the short line on the fly. It must also strike the playing surface on or within the side and end boundary lines, and it must be returned before it hits the playing surface twice. The cross-court and hop services are effective in this game.

In the regulations for the one-wall game, screening is permitted and is not considered a hinder. The

it may strike any of the above-mentioned surfaces, or a combination of them, but it must do this before it touches the floor for the second time. Either team member may play the ball—they do not have to alternate in hitting it. The short line and service line have no function after the service.

A game is won by the side that first scores 21 points. Points can only be scored by the serving team; therefore, there is no score when a hand out or side out occurs. A point is scored by the serving team each time the receiving team fails to return the ball against the front wall, violates a rule, or makes other errors.

During play, each player must have a clear path to play and to see the ball. Therefore, if a player *unintentionally* obstructs the movement of an opponent when the opponent is attempting to play the ball or shuts off his opponent's view of the ball, a hinder is declared and the point is replayed. If the blocking is *deliberate,* a point is won or a hand out is called. The side which last struck the ball must provide the opponents with a fair chance to make a play.

The play in singles and doubles is the same except for the regulations governing team play during the service and other specific game conditions such as hinders.

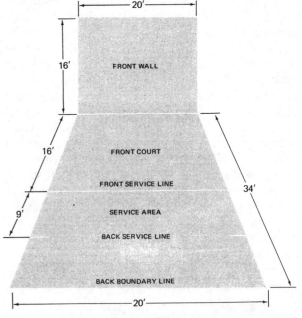

FIGURE 12-2.   One-wall handball court.

player may, therefore, play the ball in such a way that the opponent's view is obstructed or that his direct route to the ball is blocked.

EQUIPMENT

The equipment necessary to play handball consists of loose-fitting cotton shorts and shirt, woolen socks, a good pair of sneakers, a ball, and a pair of handball gloves. Some players even dispense with the gloves; however, this is not recommended.

Gloves

Gloves of many types and varieties are used, but leather gloves made especially for handball are the most functional. They can be purchased with or without padding in the palm. The type without padding is better because it gives the player greater feeling and more control over the ball. After the play is finished, gloves should be laid out in an open and airy place to dry. Frequent treatment of the gloves with saddle soap and an appropriate oil will add to their life and usefulness.

Ball

The official ball is made of black rubber and is 1⅞ inches in diameter. In ordinary play, however, many other types of balls may be used, especially during the learning stages and on courts smaller than regulation. The ball should be kept clean and dry at all times, and stored in a warm, dry place.

Court

The playing court should have regulation measurements, and all playing surfaces should be smooth and free from splinters, projections, cracks, and other handicapping or hazardous features. Light fixtures should be in the ceiling, recessed flush with the surface. The door should have a small window in it placed at eye level and made of unbreakable glass flush with the inside surface. If there is a gallery, it should be located above the back wall and screened from the court with fine mesh wire. The playing surface of the back wall should be at least 10 feet high.

SKILLS AND TECHNIQUES

Body Position and Footwork

Correct footwork and body position for all strokes are decisive factors in developing good playing skill because handball requires quick body reactions, sudden movements, and rapid changes of direction. The ready position is taken with the knees flexed, the weight equally divided on the balls of the feet, the feet approximately a shoulder width apart with one slightly in advance of the other, the arms hanging relaxed at the sides, the body bent slightly at the waist, and the eyes focused on the ball. This position will enable the player to move quickly in any direction. Depending on which movement can best be performed, the first foot movement to meet the ball should be a pivot, a push-away step, or cross-over step.

Except in rare situations, when the ball is played with the left hand the right foot should be in front of the left and in the direction of the desired flight of the ball. When the ball is played with the right hand the left foot should be forward. The hitting position should be reached with the last step short and most of the weight on the back leg so that the forward motion of the arm can be accompanied by the shifting of the weight from the back to the front foot. After the stroke is completed, the player must move quickly to the most strategic floor position. For singles play this position is generally in the center of the court just behind the short line. For doubles play it is in the center of the half of the court for which the player is responsible.

Strokes

The shaping of the hand determines to some extent the character of the ball's flight. The hand may be held relatively straight, with the thumb tucked in against the outside of the forefinger and the four fingers quite close together. It may also be partially cupped, with the fingers slightly flexed and held lightly together and the thumb a little away from the index finger. In either of these positions the ball makes contact with the hand in the well-cushioned area at the base of the fingers. The third manner of holding the hand is in the shape of a fist. In this case the fingers are flexed against the palm and the thumb is extended over the top of the flexed index finger. The ball contacts either the heel of the hand or the knuckle surface of the flexed fingers.

Players should develop power, placement and change of pace for all strokes. The essence of a good power stroke is made up of several elements. In general, its execution is very similar to throwing a baseball. The arm, wrist, shoulders, trunk and hips are synchronized into one sequential and unified movement. The body starts the motion behind the

a. Contacting the ball.

b. Follow through.

FIGURE 12-3. Basic stroke.

ball and a step is taken into it as the movements of the other body parts are coordinated with the overall forward motion. After all strokes, the player should return immediately to the ready stance in the best court position.

Underhand Stroke. There are several variations of the underhand stroke, but the one generally used is an underhand motion similar to the underarm delivery of a baseball pitcher. To execute it the player faces the side wall and shifts his weight from the back to the front leg on the forward motion and the follow-through. He brings the arm back in the backswing to approximately shoulder height, with the elbow and wrist slightly flexed. With the downward and forward motion he brings the arm in front of the body where the hand makes contact with the ball at knee height or lower. Holding the hand either cupped or flat, he snaps the wrist into motion just before contact and slightly increases the elbow flexion. The motion is made through the ball and carries the hand and arm into the follow-through in the direction of the flight of the ball.

In the proper execution of this stroke the body bends forward steeply from the hips and the knees

are well flexed so that the ball can be contacted at the low point. It is essential that the hips, trunk and shoulders rotate as the arm swings through the hitting area into the follow through.

There are two variations of this stroke. One is a forearm-circling, wrist-snapping motion in which the elbow is flexed approximately 90 degrees. In this stroke most of the power is a result of the circular motion of the forearm and the snapping of the wrist. The other variation of the underhand stroke is executed with the body partially facing the front wall rather than the side wall, the arm relatively straight, and the hand flat. The motion is similar to that of a submarine baseball throw. This stroke is not very powerful and is used for shots requiring more exact placement.

Side Arm Stroke. It is used to hit a ball that is traveling at a level between the hips and shoulders, too high to use the underhand stroke and too low for the overhand stroke. The body is held more erect than for the underhand shot. The arm is kept relatively straight and is swung through approximately parallel with the floor. However, the elbow is flexed slightly and the wrist is relaxed until it is snapped into the ball just before contact is made. The rotation of the hips, trunk and shoulders is more pronounced than for the underhand stroke.

Overhand Stroke. The bent-elbow, overhand stroke is made with an arm motion quite similar to the service stroke in tennis. The feet are in a staggered stance, the body faces the front wall, the arm is brought up and back until the hand is behind and at the same level as the head, the hand is cupped, and the wrist is cocked. From this position, the forward motion is initiated which carries the hand into and through the ball. Just as the hand moves into the hitting area, the wrist and elbow joints are flexed into the motion. In the follow-through the hand moves out and downward finishing near hip level on the left side of the body if the right arm is being used and vice versa. This stroke is used when the ball must be played at or above shoulder height. To reach for a high ball, it is sometimes varied by extending the elbow joint almost fully.

Hook Shot. The right and left hook shots are used for serving as well as for return strokes. To execute the left hook a slight variation is made in the regular underhand motion. The elbow is flexed to about a 90-degree angle, and kept into the body, the arm is brought through on the forward swing, with the elbow leading and the palm turned outward and upward, and the hand makes contact with the ball in the area where the fingers and palm join. After contact is made, the hand slices around the inside of the ball, causing it to slide out either between the index finger and thumb or direclty over the thumb, which imparts the spin that gives the ball a hopping motion. There is a pronounced forearm and wrist snap in the proper execution of this stroke.

The right hook is executed in a manner similar to the left hook except that the palm of the hand faces into the body and moves across the outside surface of the ball, causing the ball to slide off the little-finger side of the hand, near the base, and thus imparting the spin to the ball. The elbow is flexed less than in the left hook, but the forearm and wrist snap are as essential in the proper delivery of this stroke.

Serve Stroke. The same basic body and arm positions and movements that are used for the overhand and underhand strokes and hook shots are used in the delivery of the service. The most effective serve for the beginner is the bent-arm, underhand stroke. The position of the feet and the body is almost identical to that used in the return stroke. However, in making the service the forward bend of the body at the hips should be more pronounced so that the ball can be hit at a low level. The hand is usually cupped, but the fist may be employed. The server can drop the ball from either hand, although it is usually better to drop it with the nonserving hand. He should, however, drop and not throw the ball and he should stroke it as it rebounds from the floor.

The *placement of the ball* when serving is more important than the speed with which it is driven. The player should strive to obtain sufficient control and accuracy to place the serve into the area of the court

a. Waiting position.

b. Preparation.

c. Follow through.

FIGURE 12-4. Overhead stroke.

a. Starting position.   b. Foot action.   c. Ball contact.

FIGURE 12-5. Service.

he desires. In relation to ball placement and speed, there are three types of serves which should be mastered: (1) the parallel to side wall serve, (2) the front wall-side wall combination, and (3) the hop serve. Each of these serves may be utilized on both the right and left side of the court, and each may be delivered with either the right or left hand. Using a variety of serves increases deception.

The *parallel to side wall service* has two variations, namely, the low service and the lob service. The low service is one driven hard and low into the front wall near its junction with the side wall in such manner that the ball touches the floor just behind the short line and near the side wall. The ball should die before it reaches the back wall. In the low service the position of the server should be approximately three feet from the side wall.

In the *lob service,* the ball is stroked more softly and placed high on the front wall very near its junction with the side wall. The ball also touches the floor just behind the short line, rebounds high at a high steep angle, but falls to the floor before reaching the back wall. The lob service is very effective on the left side when playing against a right-handed player because it will usually force him to hit an overhand, left-handed stroke, which is usually a defensive return.

The *front wall-side wall combination* has at least two distinguishable variations. The first is a sharp-angled stroke in which the ball contacts the front wall

near the side wall, angles sharply into the side wall, and rebounds close to the server to touch down near the center of the court and behind the short line. The ball then strikes the side wall, rebounds against the back wall, and drops to the floor. It can also be placed so that it dies near the crotch, or junction, of the side wall and floor or the back wall and floor. The server's position should be to the left or right

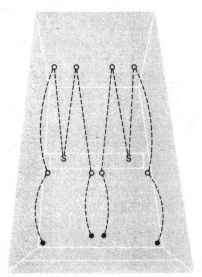

S — SERVER
--- PATH OF THE BALL'S FLIGHT
O — SPOT WHERE THE BALL TOUCHES THE SURFACE

FIGURE 12-6. Low drive service.

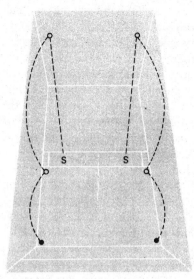

S — SERVER
--- PATH OF THE BALL'S FLIGHT
O — SPOT WHERE THE BALL TOUCHES THE SURFACE

FIGURE 12-7.
Lob service.

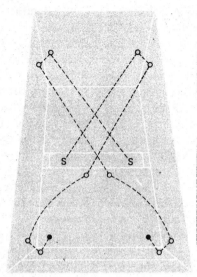

S — SERVER
--- PATH OF THE BALL'S FLIGHT
O — SPOT WHERE THE BALL TOUCHES THE SURFACE

FIGURE 12-7.
Sharp angle service.

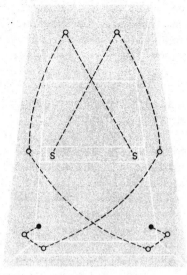

S — SERVER
--- PATH OF THE BALL'S FLIGHT
O — SPOT WHERE THE BALL TOUCHES THE SURFACE

FIGURE 12-8.
Double wall to back wall service.

side of the service area, depending upon whether he serves to the left or right side.

In the second variation of the double wall service, the ball is driven to the front wall, four or five feet from the side wall, causing it to rebound and make contact with the side wall at the height of approximately four feet and near the short line. From there it caroms to the floor, bounces into the back wall, and then to the side wall where it drops to the floor. This stroke is also very effective if the ball can be hit so that it dies at the crotch of the floor and back wall. The position of the server is the same as that for the sharp-angled shot.

The *hop service* is made with the same body position and arm motion as the hop shot. The ball can be made to hop either to the left or to the right, and the service is effective when hit short to the center of the court as well as down the side walls. The ball should be delivered so that it hits the floor just behind the short line since the service loses some of its effectiveness if it is hit too long. The right and left hop are made with a similar arm motion.

A — LEFT HOP SERVICE
B — RIGHT HOP SERVICE
S — SERVER
--- PATH OF THE BALL'S FLIGHT
O — SPOT WHERE THE BALL TOUCHES THE SURFACE

FIGURE 12-9.
Right and left hop service.

BASIC STRATEGY

Returning the Ball (Volleying)

After the service is delivered, the remainder of shots made before a point is scored or a hand out or side out is declared are returns. The player must be able to ex-

ecute all the various shots from more or less difficult positions and must, therefore, concentrate on using the most effective stroke for each particular situation as well as achieving accurate placement and deception.

Making good returns also involves maintaining good floor position, knowing the location of the opponent, playing the ball at a desirable height, using kill strokes only when in a good position, and employing the fly and half-fly strokes when necessary. The back corner return, kill return, ceiling stroke, and passing stroke need to be described in greater detail because they require somewhat different techniques and movements than those already set forth in the description of strokes.

Back-Corner Return.   Because of the nature of four-wall handball, the back-corner return must be mastered early since it will be employed many times in each game.

When the ball is played so that it is on a back-corner course and the receiver cannot play it before it passes him, he must turn and face the corner, a few feet away from the crotch, and must assume a square stance, ready to pivot to the right or to the left. He should bend the body forward deeply at the waist, focus the eyes on the ball, and hold the hands comfortably away from the body to give added balance. If the ball rebounds from the back wall to the right, the player should pivot about a quarter-turn on the left foot and make the play with the left hand. If the ball caroms to this left, he should perform a quarter-turn to the left an use his right hand to hit the ball.

FIGURE 12-10.   Preparation for back wall shot.
See Figure 12-18 for sequence in racquetball.

Kill Return.   Kill, as used in handball, means a ball that contacts the front wall so low or at such an angle that a return is impossible. The best arm motion to use in executing this stroke is the underhand one with the hand in the flat position, which permits the ball to roll off the ends of the extended fingers. The body is deeply crouched so that the ball can be met at a level below the knees. In the kill, speed is desirable, but a change of pace may be employed by occasionally making a soft return. The punch shot is used by some players to acquire speed for the kill.

The kill is best employed from the offensive position when a player is in the center of the floor and has a clear opening to stroke the ball or when the player plays the ball as it rebounds from the back wall. The most common kill returns are the straight-away shot, which hits the front wall very low; the low, side wall-front wall angle; and the front wall-side wall angle. The latter two are generally most effective.

Ceiling Stroke.   It is used to score and to move an opponent away from the center of the court. A high ball is generally hit with an overhand stroke so it will strike the ceiling approximately one and one half feet from its junction with the front wall. It should be placed so that it carries close to the side wall without touching it. The speed of the ball should be sufficient to cause it to hit the floor in the service area, rebound high, fall sharply into the back wall or back corner, and drop quickly to the floor. If the ball strikes the back wall so hard that it rebounds far out, it makes for an easy return, therefore, the speed and angle must be such that it dies as it strikes the back or side wall. In order to play a ceiling shot, the attacker should go back and hit the ball on its downward flight as it rebounds from the floor.

Passing Stroke.   The object is to hit the ball so it will be out of range of the opponent and low enough so he cannot play the rebound from the side or back wall after it has passed him. Any kind of stroke can be used, however, the ball should be hit hard enough to get by him, but no so hard that it rebounds well out into the court from the back or side wall. The good shot is one which falls to the floor after it passes him, or just before it touches either wall. It is most effective when the opponent is caught out of position.

The Fly Stroke.   It is used to play a ball when a player gets caught out of position, especially up in the front court, and to play lobs, sharp angle and ceiling returns under certain conditions. The fly results in a quick return and may catch the opponent off guard or out of position.

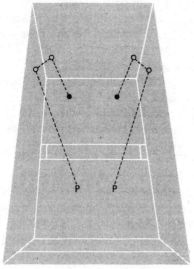

a.   Side wall-front wall

P — POINT FROM WHICH THE BALL WAS HIT
--- PATH OF THE BALL'S FLIGHT
O — SPOT WHERE THE BALL TOUCHES THE SURFACE

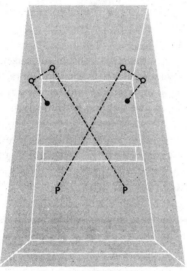

b.   Front wall-side wall

FIGURE 12-12.   Kill returns.

Planned tactics are an essential element in a well-played handball contest. Any planned action that is used to obtain an advantage over an opponent can be termed strategy. Such planning may vary from a quick judgment related to the placement of a particular shot to a continued study of the playing patterns and potential of an opponent.

It is essential strategy for the player to learn as much as possible about the opponent's techniques and preferences so that he can direct play toward the opponent's weaknesses and away from his strengths.

If the opponent likes to play up close to the front wall, the player should use side wall and other passing shots; if the opponent likes to play back, the player should use low shots; if the opponent is a rusher, the player should put some twist on the ball; if the opponent favors fast balls, the player should use many lobs. However, the player should not overdo the play to the opponent's weak point but should use it when a point is needed or the opponent may compensate for his weakness.

Every player should learn to change the pace by varying the speed of shots and by mixing a variety of placements to keep the opponent off balance. He should calculate the placement and control the speed of each shot.

Floor position will help to determine the outcome of any match. The most desirable spot is the offensive position in the middle of the court. It is from here that the player has the greatest advantage over his opponent and that he can use the kill shot most effectively. The player should maneuver the opponent out of this area by the use of passing shots that will require him to move in order to make a good return. The player should make most defensive shots with the purpose of forcing the opponent out of this area. One of the advantages of being the server is that the server can place his service to accomplish this purpose.

The player should learn to play both offense and defense. He should use defensive placements in order to move to the offensive position from where kill shots must be made. He should rarely attempt a kill from a defensive position as it will usually result in a weak return and leave an opening for the opponent to make a kill.

Singles Strategy

One of the keys to both offensive and defensive effectiveness is to hold the center position on the court, and to maintain a good ready stance that permits movement in any direction. After a shot has been made, instead of watching the results, the player should move to the center position, and if possible, stay in front of his opponent. The ball should be kept in the range of vision, but if this cannot be done, the eyes should be focused on the front wall where the ball must eventually hit. Experience will help the player determine what kind of shot his opponent is making without the need for looking back. However, if a player must look back, he should do so by looking underneath one or the other arm so that he has some protection against being hit in the face.

If the opponent hits many kill shots, a position should be taken farther up toward the front court than normal; if he hits numerous passing shots, a position should be taken toward the back court. The opponent should be kept moving and off balance by using a variety of shots, change of pace, different styles and good placement.

Doubles Strategy

All of the strategic moves discussed above under singles play apply to doubles. Teammates generally take a side-by-side position on the court where each is responsible for balls that rebound into his half of the area. If both teammates are right handed, the one on the left will play most shots that are returned down the middle, and each will take the balls that rebound toward them from the opposite wall. Partners will cover for each other when one is forced out of position, and both will play defensively until they regain the good court position to go on offense. A right and left handed partner will generally be weak against balls that rebound down the center of the court, therefore, the one with the strongest off hand should take most of these shots. Every effort should be made to maintain a position in the center of the court and in front of the opponents as well as to prevent a passing shot. Tactics for doubles call for a variety of strokes with emphasis on the sharp angled shots and hop drives down the center. Good serving is important because after the first inning, both team members get a term of service before the side is out.

SAFETY PRACTICES

1. Precede competition by a thorough warm-up.
2. Use gloves to protect the hands. If glasses are worn, protect them with a guard.
3. Never look back while the opponent is playing the ball behind you unless the shoulder is raised and the arm is covering the face. A player seldom needs to take such a backward look.
4. Pick up a dead ball and give it to the proper person. Never hit it.
5. When a ball must be played while it is close to the wall, place the hand against the wall so the hitting motion is away from or parallel to the wall and not into it.
6. Never enter a handball court without first determining whether it is in use.
7. The entrance door into the court should have an observation window in it.
8. The light switch for each court should be on the outside.
9. Move out of the path of an opponent who is charging the ball.

WEIGHT TRAINING

Good general muscular and cardiovascular conditioning are essential for high-level participation in handball. It is an activity which requires stamina, quick reactions, and strength of the legs, forearms, wrists, hands, and fingers. General weight-training activities, such as military and bench presses, trunk raises, half-knee bends, leg lifts, and dead lifts, are effective. Because of the importance of the arm, wrist, hand, and finger action, bent and upright rowing, arm curls, finger and wrist curls, and bench presses could be of special value in developing and improving the ability to play handball.

EXERCISE   Definitions and List of Terms (Handball)

1. When a service is so fast or deceptive that it eludes the receiver completely it is an _____ .

2. The section of the playing area to the rear of the short line is the _____ ; the part in front of it is the _____ .

3. A ball which hits the junction of any two playing surfaces simultaneously is called a _____ .

4. _____ is a three-man, handball game in which each plays against the other two when he is serving.

5. After a point is won or a hinder or violation occurs, the ball is declared _____ .

6. A service which violates the rules and involves a penalty is a _____ . When two of these are served consecutively, it is a _____ which results in a hand out.

7. Any move made by one player to draw his opponent out of position is a _____ .

8. A ball stroked before it rebounds from the floor is a _____ .
9. When a player receives the ball for his first serve in any inning, it is a _____ .
10. When a player loses his service it is a _____ .
11. When a player unintentionally interferes with his opponent as the latter is attempting to play the ball, or when the ball strikes his opponent, it is a _____ .
12. _____ and _____ are terms used to describe the action of a ball that has been stroked so that is spins, causing it to jump suddenly to the left or right when it strikes the floor.
13. When both players in singles and all players in doubles have served an _____ has been played.
14. _____ is a return hit so low or at such an angle on the front wall that it is impossible to return it.
15. A _____ is a kind of return or service in which the flight of the ball is very high.
16. A service in which the ball rebounds from the front wall to the back wall before hitting the floor is a _____ .
17. _____ is a shot that gets by the player and does not hit the rear wall.
18. When a handball is stroked with the fist, it is said to be a _____ .
19. A ball struck so that it rebounds from one side wall to the back wall to the other side wall is a _____ shot.
20. _____ is a legal tactic used in one-wall handball in which a player may place himself between the ball and his opponent.
21. The court area in which the partner of the server in doubles stands during the service is the _____ .
22. The line that marks the forward boundary of the service area is the _____ . The line that marks the rear boundary is the _____ .
23. The area between the short line and the service line is the _____ .
24. _____ is a violation of the service rule in which the ball fails to carry from the front wall to the area behind the short line on the fly, hits two wall surfaces, or hits the ceiling before striking the floor in the back area.
25. When both members of the doubles team have lost their serves, it is called _____ .
26. _____ is the term used to describe play from the time of the service until a hand out, side out, point, or dead ball is declared.

1. Ace
2. Back court
3. Crotch ball
4. Cutthroat
5. Dead
6. Fault, double fault
7. Feint
8. Volley
9. Hand in
10. Hand out
11. Hinder
12. Hop or hook
13. Inning
14. Kill
15. Lob
16. Long ball
17. Pass shot
18. Punch ball
19. Run-around shot
20. Screening
21. Service area
22. Service line, short line
23. Service box
24. Short
25. Side out
26. Rally

QUESTIONS AND ANSWERS ON THE RULES (Handball)

1. *Q.* How is the game begun?
   A. The game is begun by a player serving the ball to his opponent(s).
2. *Q.* How must the service be delivered?
   A. The server must stand within the service court, and as the ball rebounds from the floor, he must strike it with one hand. The ball must first hit the front wall, after which it may hit one side wall, but must touch the the floor behind the short line.

The server may drop the ball to the floor not more than three times before hitting it. In doubles, the server's partner must stand in the service box facing out, and the opponents must be at least five feet in back of the short line.

3. *Q.* How many walls may the ball strike after the service?
   A. After the service, the ball may make contact with any number of walls before or after its first contact with the floor and after it strikes the front wall as long as the ball contacts the wall or walls before it strikes the floor for the second time. It may also hit these walls before striking the front wall, but it may not hit the floor until contact is made with the front wall.

4. *Q.* When is a game won?
   A. The first player or team to score 21 points wins the game.

5. *Q.* How is a point made?
   A. A point is scored by the serving player or team each time the opposition is unable to return the ball or violates a rule. No point is scored on the exchange of service.

6. *Q.* In what manner is the ball played?
   A. The ball can be played with one hand only, but it can be hit alternately with either hand. The fist and back of the hand are legal. The wrist and arm may not be used. It must be hit and not caught and thrown.

7. *Q.* How many players can play in a game?
   A. There are three types of competition in handball: singles, doubles, and cutthroat. In singles play, one player plays against one; in doubles, two play against two. In cutthroat, three players compete, with the service alternating and the server playing against the other two.

8. *Q.* What is the ruling in doubles when the served ball strikes the server's partner?
   A. If he is in the service box, the ball is dead and there is no penalty. The ball is served again. If he is outside the service box, if is a fault.

9. *Q.* How many times can a player serve?
   A. A player continues to serve until he fails to return the ball or violates a rule. When either of these situations occurs, his hand is out. In some violation cases he has two attempts to serve on each point, but on others he has only one. In the following situations two successive faults result in a hand out: (1) the ball fails to hit the floor in back of the short line, (2) the ball hits two or more walls after hitting the front wall and before bouncing from the floor, (3) the server steps out of the service court when serving, and (4) the partner is not in the service box in doubles, (5) the ball hits the ceiling after hitting the front wall, (6) the ball rebounds from the front to the back wall before touching the floor, (7) the ball goes out of the court, (8) the ball is screened by the server's body. In the following situations only one illegal move is required to retire the server: (1) the server serves with both hands, (2) the ball touches the server, (3) the ball strikes the partner when he is not in the service box, (4) the ball hits the ceiling, floor, or side wall before contacting the front wall, and (5) a crotch ball, (6) server bounces the ball more than three times, (7) server misses the ball, (8) in doubles partners serve out of order.

10. *Q.* What is the system of serving in doubles?
    A. The first team to serve in each game has only one hand in. After the first hand is out, the serve goes to the opponents who gets two hands. Thereafter, both team members serve before the service is relinquished.

11. *Q.* Must the server alternate his serves to that one goes into the right and the other into the left service court?
    A. No. There is no right or left service court. In both doubles and singles, the server may hit the ball into any area of the court he chooses as long as it strikes the floor in back of the short line. The players do not have to receive the service alternately.

12. *Q.* What is the ruling if a player swings at the ball and misses it during a volley?

   A. The ball is still in play until it hits the floor for the second time or until another violation occurs.

13. *Q.* What is the ruling when, during a volley, the ball strikes an opponent or a partner?
   A. If it strikes an opponent it is a hinder and there is no penalty. The point is replayed. If it hits a partner, it is a fault and becomes a point or had out, whichever is appropriate.

14. *Q.* What is a hinder?
   A. A hinder occurs when an opponent is struck by a returned ball and when there is an unintentional obstruction or interference with an opponent that prevents him from playing the ball properly. In both cases, the point is replayed. It is the responsibility of the side that last played the ball to move out of the way of the opposition. Players must have an unobstructed opportunity to see and to play the ball.

15. *Q.* May the player receiving the service move across the short line to play the ball?
   A. No. He is warned on the first violation. If another infraction of this rule occurs, the opponent is awarded a point.

16. *Q.* Is any item of clothing required by the rules?
   A. Yes. Gloves must be worn. These may not be webbed.

17. *Q.* How many officials are used?
   A. Officials are not used except in tournament play. When used, a referee and a scorer are required. Linesman may be used.

18. *Q.* Is it legal for a server to hit a quick serve to surprise his opponent?
   A. No. The receiver must be ready.

19. *Q.* What is a fly return?
   A. When a player strokes the ball before it rebounds from the floor.

20. *Q.* What is a volley?
   A. It is any legal return made after the serve.

21. *Q.* Is a serve good when the ball rebounds from the front wall and hits the short line?
   A. No. It must touch the surface in back of the back edge of the short line.

22. *Q.* When the serve is being delivered, what is the penalty for the receiver taking a position closer than five feet from the short line?
   A. A point is awarded to the server.

23. *Q.* How many time outs are allowed each side during a game?
   A. Each team is allowed three time outs. A time out cannot exceed thirty seconds in length.

DESCRIPTION OF THE ACTIVITY (RACQUETBALL)

The four-wall handball court has often been the practice ground of tennis players. In the 1930's, such an observation by Earl Riskey of the University of Michigan led to the development of paddleball (solid wood paddle) and raquetball (short handled stringed racket). In recent years, the short-handled stringed racket has increased in popularity and is used by the majority of participants. The two games or racquetball and paddleball are nearly identical with both being played on a handball court with similar skills, techniques, strategies, and rules. Although some minor differences do exist, the term racquetball will be used to designate both games.

Racquetball provides competitors with a vigorous workout in a relatively brief time. With the shorter handle, beginners experience much earlier success at keeping the ball in play than in tennis. In fact, the shorter racket is often used with young children as a tennis lead-up activity.

Racquetball can be played by two (singles), three (cutthroat), or four (doubles) players on a one, three, or four-walled court. This chapter deals with four-walled racquetball (official handball court).

An official four-walled and single-walled racquetball court is shown in Figures 12-1 and 12-2. Three-wall dimensions are the same as the one-wall court with two side walls sloping downward from the front wall before reaching a height of only six feet where they terminate at the short line.

To begin a game, the server stands anywhere within the service zone, bounces the ball once, and strokes it onto the front wall. The ball must rebound from the front wall and land behind the short line to be in play. It may also rebound from one or both side walls (not the ceiling or back wall) providing it contacts the front wall first. If the first serve is not legal, a second attempt is granted. Another illegal serve results in loss of service. The opponent (receiver) may return the ball off any combination of walls (sides, back, ceiling) providing the ball contacts the front wall prior to hitting the floor. Play continues until one player fails to return the ball legally to the front wall. If the server fails to make a legal return, the receiver then becomes the server. Only the server can score. A game ends when one player receives 21 points.

In doubles competition, each player serves before a loss of team service occurs. The only exception to this rule is the initial service of each game when only one partner serves before a loss of team service takes place. Either player on a doubles team may return the ball with returns alternating from one team to another A match generally consists of two out of three games.

EQUIPMENT

Racquetball equipment is designed for maximum efficiency of movement. For tournament play, all parts of the uniform (shirt, shoes, shorts, and socks) must be white to make the ball more easily seen by both competitors.

Paddle Racket

A short-handle racket is used. In national competition, a solid wooden racket must be used. In actual practice (socially, YMCA competition) the stringed racket is more popular. The wooden racket is less expensive; however, control and speed are sacrificed. The racket may not exceed 16 ounces in weight, must be approximately 8 inches wide and 16 inches in length. A leather strap is attached to the handle and

slipped over the wrist to avoid "throwing" the racket when hands become damp.

Ball

The official ball, developed by General Tire-Pennsylvania Athletic Products Company is dark gray, 7.2 inches in circumference, weighs 1.5 ounces, and bounces approximately 3.5 feet when dropped from a height of six feet.

SKILLS AND TECHNIQUES

Body Position and Footwork

Correct footwork and body position for all strokes parallel that explained in the handball section of this chapter. The ready position is shown in Figure 12-13. With the player facing the front wall, racket extended in front, a simple tennis pivot manuever moves one to the proper forward or backhand stroking position.

FIGURE 12-13.   Ready position.

a. Preparation.

b. Ball contact.

c. Follow through.

FIGURE 12-14.   Forehand sequence.

Strokes

The Eastern or "handshake" grip is used to execute the forehand drive and the serve. For the backhand drive, the racket is rotated one-quarter turn counterclockwise toward the thumb. The knuckle of the index finger should be aligned down the center of the racket handle. Some players place the thumb directly up the handle to reinforce the wrist. Since the game of racquetball is fast and furious, often allowing little or not time to change grips, some players choose the continental grip which permits either a backhand or forehand shot without altering the grip. This grip in racquetball has the same limitations as a tennis continental grip, requiring a strong wrist and creating a more suitable racket angle for the backhand than the forehand drive. For a complete review and discussion of grips, see Chapter 15, Tennis.

Forehand Stroke.   The forehand stroke is similar to the forehand drive in tennis with a few exceptions: (1) the backswing and follow-through are shortened due to the speed of the ball, need for quick reaction, racket preparation, and to lessen the danger of injuring an opponent, and (2) knees and upper body are much more flexed to "get down to the ball" and use a low return. After ball contact, follow-through carries the body back to the "ready position."

Backhand Stroke.   From the "ready position," the right-handed player steps back with the left foot as the ball approaches, before drawing the racket back and stepping torwad the front wall with the right foot. Ball-racket contact occurs just ahead of the first foot. With little time to react, the backswing

must be shortened and the wrist used to generate the power. Weight transfer, arm action, and ball contact are similar to the tennis stroke.

Overhead Stroke.   High bounding balls must be returned with both the backhand and forehand stroke. The overhead smash resembles the flat serve in tennis. It is used when a ball rebounds off the front wall or ceiling high and above the receiver's head. The overhead smash is not the devastating power shot of tennis. In some cases, it may be a better choice to either allow the ball to rebound off the back wall or to drop to knee level before executing a forehand or backhand drive.

Underhand Stroke.   While in the front court, a player may await the ball with the racket held directly under the hitting hand. This position is effective for quick reaction and use of a half volley return (forehand or backhand) on a low, fast ball. With considerable wrist action, the racket passes close to the lower leg in a motion similar to an underhand throw from the shortstop to the second baseman.

Serving

Both the "power" serve and "lob" serve have numerous variations in terms of combinations of wall contact and strategy. See Figures 12-6 through 12-10, in the handball serving section for details. Few serves produce outright point winners. A more realistic approach is to develop serving combinations that produce an advantage on your next shot.

Power Serve.   A forehand racket grip is assumed as the server takes a position 1-2″ behind the short line. The body is turned to the right (left shoulder

a. Preparation.

b. Ball contact.

c. Ball contact.

FIGURE 12-15.   Backhand sequence.

a. Preparation.

b. Ball contact.

c. Follow through.

FIGURE 12-16.   Overhead sequence.

toward front wall) with feet at the shoulder width parallel to the line and knees slightly bent.

The ball is dropped just in front of the left foot by extending the arm at waist height and merely releasing the ball with the palm toward the floor. Racket preparation and backswing are similar to the forehand stroke in tennis. The racket is drawn back even with the body as weight shifts onto the rear foot. As the forward swing begins, weight is transferred onto the front foot. Ball contact is made at the height of the bounce in front of the lead foot just below waist level. After impact, the racket continues forward then to the left of the body without resisting this natural flow. The follow-through is completed with a pivot on the lead foot and a step forward with the rear foot until the player is now facing the front wall.

Power serve variations and wall placement are shown in Figures 12-6, 12-8, 12-9 and 12-10. The ball is generally hit to the front wall slightly off center to allow a low trajectory to the rear corner (backhand or forehand side). The ball should not reach the back wall.

Lob Serve. The lob serve is shown in Figure 12-7. The ball is hit as high and close to the wall and back corner as possible to prevent the opponent from executing a full swing.

The Eastern forehand grip (one-quarter turn to the right) is used with the thumb resting on top of the handle. The server faces the front wall from a position one to two inches behind the service line and between the service and short line. Feet are spread at shoulder width, left foot slightly forward in a heel-

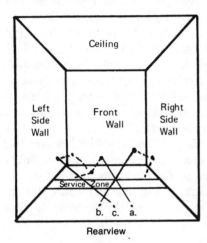

FIGURE 12-17.   Placement of Kill Shots. a. Front Wall Kill; b. Front Wall-Side Wall Kill; c. Side Wall-Front Wall Kill.

toe alignment, and knees slightly flexed. Little weight transfer occurs as the arm directs the ball with little wrist involvement.

As the ball is dropped on the floor, the racket is drawn down behind the rear leg. Ball contact is made just ahead of the front foot. The racket follows through forward and upward until the racket is overhead and slightly to the left.

Kill Shots.   The kill shot is the most effective shot in paddleball. It is executed with either a forehand or backhand stroke. Ball contact must be made below the knees. A ball hit at waist height will be nearly impossible to kill off the front wall since the downward trajectory will result in a rather sharp angled upward bounce back to the opponent. The player must assume a crouched position with knees and hips flexed. Contact is made when the ball bounces or drops to a position six to twelve inches from the floor. The ball is aimed approximately six inches from the floor.

The three basic placements for the kill shot are shown in Figure 12-17. The front wall kill is the most commonly used, however, the side wall/first wall and front wall/side wall kills are effective, depending upon the position of the opponent.

Back-Court Kills.   Advanced players effectively use the kill shot from the back court. With the opponent in a waiting position in the front court, a near perfect shot is needed or the shot will be returned easily before recovery from the back court is possible. If the opponent is also in the back court, a low near kill will be just as effective.

a. Waiting position.   b. Racket preparation.   c. Ball contact.

FIGURE 12-18.   Backwall sequence.

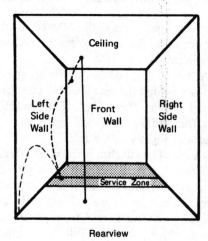

Rearview

FIGURE 12-19. Ceiling Shot.

Back-Wall Kill.   Most advanced players are very adept at hitting a kill shot off the back wall. Providing a back wall shot of almost any type to some players is an almost certain loss of point or side. To execute the back wall kill, move quickly to a position-facing the side wall and begin racket preparation early, as the ball drops to knee height or lower.

Soft Kill.   A softly hit ball to the low front wall dies quickly and is a valuable shot. It is also difficult to master. It is used when the opponent is in the back court or is moving backward. The shot is usually aimed toward the corner.

Fly Ball.   Hitting the ball before it bounces from the floor can catch the opponent out of position. The secret is to allow the ball to descend before executing the stroke. Such a manuever also allows one to hold the front court position and control play.

Passing Shots.   Passing shots are hard hit strokes that attempt to force the opponent to swing without being fully prepared or to have the ball rebound and pass the opponent completely. The ball must be hit low enough on the front wall to avoid reaching the back wall and at such an angle that it does not contact either side wall. The shot is used when a player is out of position and is effective with the opponent stationed in the front court.

Ceiling Shot.   The ceiling shot is used to force an opponent to retreat to a back court corner where a strong return is difficult to make. The ball is hit upward to contact the ceiling three to six inches from the front wall at an angle causing the ball to then contact the front wall before rebounding high off the floor. A properly hit shot will drop into the back corner with a high arch and make only slight contact with the back side wall.

Lob Shot.   The lob and ceiling shots differ only in the order of contact with the ceiling and front wall. The front wall is contaced high to cause a rebound to the ceiling and placed in the corner spot as described for the ceiling shot.

Drop Shot.   The drop shot is aimed to the front corners in a manner that will result in little rebound. It is used to force an opponent caught in the deep back court to run the full court distance. Little follow-through is used in executing the drop shot.

BASIC STRATEGY

Racquetball singles and doubles strategy parallel handball strategy described in this chapter.

QUESTIONS AND ANSWERS ON THE RULES OF RACQUETBALL

1. *Q.* How is the first server of the match determined?
    A. In official play, by a toss of a coin. In informal competition, players "lag" for serve by throwing the ball against the front wall and determining which ball rebounds closest to the short line. The receiver of the first game becomes the server at the start of the second game. The server calls the score (server's score first) prior to each serve.
2. *Q.* When may the server leave the service zone?
    A. He must remain somewhere in the zone with no part of his feet over the line (may touch the line) until the ball passes the short line.
3. *Q.* What constitutes an illegal serve?
    A. Stepping over a service zone line during the serve, failure to rebound the ball behind the short line (short serve), striking anything but the front wall first, contacting the ceiling with the ball, contacting three or more walls before the ball contacts the floor, contacting the back wall before the ball contacts the floor (long serve), and a

foot fault (stepping out of the service zone). A serve-out occurs after two illegal serves are delivered.

4. *Q.* What constitutes a serve-out serve?
   A. Bouncing the ball more than twice before striking, hitting the side wall before contacting the front wall, dropping the ball and hitting it into the air, swinging and missing a dropped serve, touching the ball to the server's body, causing the ball to simultaneously strike the front wall and the floor, ceiling or side wall.

5. *Q.* What restrictions govern serving in doubles?
   A. The side starting each game receives only one serve-out, thereafter, both players on each side serve until a serve-out occurs. Once a service order is established, it must be followed throughout the game. Serving out-of-order results in a serve-out. The ball may be served to either receiver and alternating receivers is not required. The server's partner must stand in the service box (back against the wall) until the ball passes the short line. Failure to maintain this position results in a serve-out. If the partner is hit with the ball while in the service box, a dead ball is declared. If the ball passes behind the player, it is a hinder and must be served over.

6. *Q.* What constitutes a legal waiting position for the receivers?
   A. Receivers must remain at least five feet from the short line until the ball is touched by the server. The ball must be returned on the fly or after the first bounce to the front wall with no part of the body crossing the short line. An illegal return results in a point for the server.

7. *Q.* What constitutes an illegal volley?
   A. Once the ball is in play it must be hit with the paddle in one or both hands with the safety throng around the wrist. The ball may not be touched with the arm, hand, or other body part. The ball may be touched only once on each volley.

8. *Q.* What is an unintentional hinder?
   A. Unintentional hinders are replayed. Such is the case when a player unavoidably interferes with an opponent's opportunity to hit the ball. After striking the ball, a player must get out of his opponent's way and view immediately. In addition, any unnecessary crowding of an opponent is a hinder. Other unintentional hinders include:
   1. Striking the opponent on the fly with a returned ball.
   2. Striking a part of the court that is considered a dead ball area under local rules.
   3. A ball going between the legs of an opponent (straddle ball).
   4. A served ball that nearly brushes the server as it passes by and interferes with the opponent's vision.

   Remember that it is not a hinder when a player hinders his partner. Also, no hinder can be called unless the interference took place before or simultaneously with the contact of the ball with the paddle.

9. *Q.* What is an intentional hinder?
   A. An intentional hinder occurs when a player fails to move sufficiently to permit a fair shot, pushes an opponent, or blocks the movement of an opponent by stepping into his path.

10. *Q.* What is the ruling if a ball breaks during play?
    A. The point is replayed.

11. *Q.* Are rest periods permitted?
    A. A two-minute break is allowed between the first and second game. Players must remain on the court. During the 10-minute break between the second and third game, players may leave the court area.

12. *Q.* Can a time-out be called?
    A. Yes. Two time-outs per game are permitted. Play must be continuous. Deliberate stalling results in either a point or side-out. Play may also be disrupted for any injury. Failure to return within 15 minutes results in a forfeit.

BIBLIOGRAPHY (HANDBALL)

O'Connell, C. J. *How to Play Handball.* New York: American Sports Publishing Company, 1935.

Phillips, B. E. *Fundamental Handball.* New York: A. S. Barnes and Co., Inc., 1940.

Seaton, D. C., and others. *Physical Education Handbook,* 4th ed. Englewood Cliffs, N.J.: Prentice-Hall, Inc., 1965.

Shaw, J. H., and others. *Individual Sports for Men,* rev. ed. Philadelphia: W. B. Saunders Company, 1955.

Sports for Recreation. Mitchell, E.D., ed. New York: A.S. Barnes and Co., Inc., 1952.

U.S. Handball Association. *Official Handball Rules.* Skokie, Ill.: The United States Handball Association, 1976.

BIBLIOGRAPHY (RACQUETBALL)

Allsen, Phillip E. and Alan Witbeck. *Paddleball.* Dubuque, Iowa: Wm. C. Brown, Co. Publishers.

Kozare, A. J., Trambeau, R. J., and Riskey, E. N. *Beginning Paddleball.* Belmont, CA: Wadsworth Publishing Co., Inc., 1967.

O'Connell, C. J. *Handball Illustrated.* New York: The Ronald Press Co., 1964.

Official Handball Rules. New York: The Amateur Athletic Union (current edition).

Official Paddleball Rules. Ann Arbor, Mich.: Sports Building, 1970.

Stafford, Randy. *Raquetball.* 4327 Walnut Grove, Memphis, Tenn., 1975.

Varner, Margaret and Bramall, Norman. *Squash Racquets.* Dubuque, Iowa: Wm. C. Brown Co. Publishers, 1967.

Yessis, Michael. *Handball.* Dubuque, Iowa: Wm. C. Brown Co. Publishers, 1966.

Jack Schiltz, ED.d.
Associate Professor of Physical Education
Virginia Commonwealth University

13

SKIN AND
SCUBA DIVING

DESCRIPTION OF THE ACTIVITY

Three quarters of the world is covered by water and most of it is unexplored. In recent years man has challenged this exciting and adventurous frontier. Skin diving and scuba diving are experiences which can never be adequately described. They can only be truly appreciated by those who become part of the underwater world of exploring, collecting, photographing and just playing.

Paralleling diving's phenomenal growth in the last twenty years has been the establishment of certifying organizations offering instruction in safe diving. In the late 1950's and early 1960's three organizations came into national prominence—YMCA, National Association of Underwater Instructors (NAUI), and the Professional Association of Diving Instructors (PADI). All three offer courses whose successful completion is represented by a ''C'' card. Swimmers can now receive certification in skin diving (representing competency in the use of mask, fins, snorkel and buoyancy compensator) and/or scuba (additional competency with Self-Contained Underwater Breathing Apparatus).

With the unusual physical and psychological demands which are made on the underwater swimmer, a high level of fitness and skill must be maintained at all times. The YMCA has established the following proficiency test which swimmers must pass before participating in its (Scuba) course:

1. Tread water, feet only, for three minutes.
2. Swim 300 yards without fins.

3. Tow an inert swimmer 25 yards without fins.
4. Stay afloat for 15 minutes without accessories.
5. Swim 15 yards underwater without fins and without pushing off from the wall.

One interested in diving should be able to perform the preceding test with ease and, in addition, pass a thorough medical examination.

EQUIPMENT

The selection of properly fitting equipment is imperative to the diver. Ill-fitting equipment can result in discomfort, loss of efficiency or injury. The novice should consult an experienced diver or professional dive shop before purchasing gear. It should be noted that diving is not as expensive as many adult leisure sports. A mask, fins, snorkel and buoyance compensator can launch the beginner on his way.

Mask

A wide variety of quality masks are currently available to the diver. Final selection should be based on comfort, size, shape and seal. Essential features should be:

1. A tempered lens secured with a non-corrosive metal band.
2. An adjustable head strap split in the back for better fit.

FIGURE 13-1.   Equipment.

3. Finger or nose pockets to aid in clearing the ears. .

4. Black rubber composition, for its added strength and durability.

Many instructors prefer a beginning diver to refrain from purchasing a mask with a purge valve, which is essentially a drain valve in the base of the skirt. It is feared that the diver may never acquire sound mask-clearing skills. The valves also tend to leak. To check for proper fit place the mask on the face without the headband and inhale slightly through the nose. The mask should stay on the face by itself if it fits properly. (See Figure 13-2.)

Snorkel

Basically, all snorkels are J-shaped, 12-to 14-inch tubes made of plastic or rubber. new-fangled gimmicks such as mask-snorkle combinations, ping pong balls and purge valves can only create problems. The diver should select a large-bore snorkle with simple lines and a mouthpiece that fits comfortably when attached to the mask with a keeper.

Fins

Selecting fins requires the same careful attention to detail as other pieces of equipment do. The primary decision confronting the diver is whether to choose the slipper fin or the adjustable strap fin. Each style has its strong points; however, the trend is toward the

latter. A second trend is toward the "vented" fin which supposedly redirects water flow to the end of the blade, resulting in more power and greater efficiency.

When selecting fins, try them on while wearing diving boots. If the novice diver does not wish to purchase the boots at first, two pairs of socks will suffice.

Buoyancy Compensator

The buoyancy compensator burst upon the sport diving scene rapidly. Today many skin diving instructors and virtually all Scuba instructors consider them required equipment. In addition to acting as a safety or life vest to the scuba and skin diver, the buoyancy compensator allows the scuba diver to manipulate his own buoyancy. Minimum features to look for when selecting a vest are: (1) a drain plug, (2) an oral inflator and (3) a 16-gram or larger CO_2 cartridge and (4) an over-inflation valve commonly referred to as a dump valve. Until the diver is sure of his love for the sport, the less expensive vest should be purchased.

Scuba Tank

Because of stringent regulation by the United States Department of Transportation, it would be very difficult to obtain a new tank of inferior quality. Tank selection is based more on the size, pressure, and type of metal, lining and color desired. Tank volume varies from 20 to 100 cubic feet, with the 71.2 cubic foot tank the most popular among adult sport divers. Until 1970 virtually all tanks were made of steel. Today the diver can choose not only between aluminum and steel tanks but also from among various protective and decorative coatings.

The diver has a choice of two types of on-off air valves for his tank, the "J" valve or the "K" valve. The "J" valve allows for an extra margin of approximately 500 psi of reserve air. Traditionally it has been felt that the "J" valve makes tremendous safety sense. Yet, recently its safety value has been questioned. Some diving experts feel the J-valve gives a false sense of security because it can be knocked into the down position without the diver's knowledge.

It is also wise to purchase a rubber or plastic boot for the bottom of the tank to protect it. A backpack for the tank is a necessity. It should have a wide band to secure the tank, a handle for carrying and quick-release shoulder and waist straps.

All tanks should be visually inspected every year and must be hydrostatically inspected once every five years.

Scuba Regulator

There are basically two types of regulators being used in sport diving—the single hose and the double hose. The trend in the last few years has been toward the single hose regulator. Its compact design, durability, lower purchase price and maintenance costs make it more popular with the average diver. A relatively new device that many experienced divers would not dive without is the underwater pressure gauge. It attaches to the regulator so that the diver can instantly and continuously check his air supply.

Weight Belt

A weight belt of about 10 to 20 pounds will meet the needs of the average diver. The best should be two to three inches wide with weights that lay flat against the surface of the body. A critical feature is the quick-release buckle, so the belt may be released immediately in an emergency.

Wet Suit

The purpose of protective clothing is to decrease body heat loss. Although there are generally three types of underwater clothing (wet suits, absorbent clothing and dry suits), the wet suit is normally used by the sport diver.

A wet suit is designed to allow for a thin layer of water between the skin and suit. Once this water has been warmed by body heat it no longer draws as much heat as would cold water continuously passing by the skin's surface.

If the diver plans to swim in water below 75° he must wear a wet suit. It extends underwater time and protects the skin from sharp objects.

Wet suits are sold in a variety of thicknesses and designs. One can be completely covered with hood, gloves and boots or select just a short sleeve top.

After determining the type of suit that meets his needs, the diver should examine the neoprene material carefully. It should be covered inside and out with stretchable nylon, which makes it stronger and easier to get into. Zippers at the ankles and wrists also make dressing easier. A well-fitted suit should feel snug all over the body without binding or pinching.

MISCELLANEOUS TOOLS AND EQUIPMENT

Watch

A watch is a necessity for those divers planning to descend below 30 feet. At depths below 30 feet time becomes a critical factor. Select only a watch which specifically indicates it has been *pressure* tested not just water proof. Such watches usually have a "bezel" around the watch face so the diver can keep track of his bottom time.

Depth Gauge

Although there are three types of depth gauges (capillary, bourdon tube, and oil or gas filled), the capillary type is undoubtedly the best all-around gauge for the sport diver at relatively shallow depth. It literally has no moving parts and is extremely accurate to 33 feet and reasonably accurate to 99 feet. It is also the least expensive. Some watches include a capillary gauge on the outside of the face next to the bezel. At greater depths, however, the capillary gauge becomes difficult to read.

Knife

The knife is one of the most versatile tools a diver has. It is virtually everything *but* a weapon. Divers have been known to use their knives as levers, crow bars, screwdrivers, hammers, cutting tools, eating utensils, saws and rulers. The knife should be made of stainless steel, and the sheath should have durable stretchable straps with a strong retainer.

SKILLS AND TECHNIQUES

Donning Gear on Land

Mask. To keep the mask from fogging, rub saliva, a cut raw potato, tobacco, an apple slice or a commercial defogging substance on the inside surface of the lens. Rinse, and the lens should remain clear. Place the mask on the face over the eyes and nose, and stretch the headband over the back of the head.

Fins. Wet the fins before putting them on. Make sure not to wear the fins while trying to walk. Walking short distances can be accomplished by walking backwards.

Buoyancy Compensator. Put the vest on over the head. Although each vest clips on differently, the waist strap is adjusted and attached first. The crotch strap is then secured. The CO_2 cartridge and all valves should be checked prior to each use.

Tanks. The diver should put his tank on while his partner holds it. Once the harness is secured the mouthpiece can be brought over the right shoulder to a ready position. Some divers prefer to position the tank in front of them, with the valve toward them.

Placing both arms through the straps, the diver lifts the tank over his head onto his back. The weight of the tank makes this procedure both cumbersome and possibly dangerous. This procedure is often used in donning the tank in the water.

Other Equipment. Once all other equipment is donned the weight belt is put on. Remember, it *must* be the last piece of equipment on, so it can easily be discharged, in an emergency.

Clearing the Mask

One of the most important skills the novice diver must acquire is draining the water from his mask while underwater. To clear the mask of water, press it tightly against the face with slightly more pressure at the top. Tilt the head backward and exhale through nose slowly. The exhaled air will force all water out of the lower portion of the mask. (See Figure 13-2.)

FIGURE 13-2.   Clearing mask.

Clearing the Ears

Clearing the ears is a procedure used to equalize the pressure between the inner ear and water. As soon as the diver descends, he may experience pressure on his ears. As he goes deeper it may turn to pain unless he pressures inside and outside the ear are

equalized. Some divers find that simply slowing the descent alleviates the problem. Others pinch the nostrils tightly shut using the finger or nose pockets in the mask and *gently* try to "blow their nose." Other methods which seem to work are yawning with the mouth closed, swallowing, wiggling the lower jaw, and "clicking the ears." Because the ear drum is sensitive to pressure changes the skill of clearing the ears is imperative.

Clearing the Snorkel

The snorkel should be attached to the left side of the mask strap using the rubber loop called a keeper. It should be adjusted in such a manner that when the diver is swimming on the surface the snorkel points upward or slightly backward.

Once the diver submerges the snorkel will fill with water. When surfacing he should exhale sharply through the snorkel to blow the water out. Caution should be exercised when taking the first breath, in case some water is not expelled. A second method of clearing the snorkel is to tilt the head upward and blow out gently just before surfacing. Just as the diver surfaces he should tilt his head down, raising the cleared snorkel into the air.

Swimming Skills

Kicking. Only two kicks are presently being used by skilled divers. The first is the traditional flutter kick. Important points to remember are (1) kick from the hip, (2) keep the knees straight with slight flexion on the down part of the kick, and (3) kick slowly and steadily. (See Figure 13-3.) The second kick is the dolphin kick, in which both legs move in a simultaneous kick, similar to the undulating motion of a fish tail.

Arm pull. Although an arm pull is not necessary while swimming underwater, several can be used. The breaststroke pull is advocated by many divers, for it requires a minimum expenditure of energy. A second arm pull is the underwater dog paddle. Most instructors, however, emphasize minimum use of the arms due to the increased energy expenditure and the use of the arms for other purposes.

Descending

To descend, three surface dives are used at various times and for various reasons. These are the feet-first, tuck and pike surface dives.

Feet-first surface dive. The feet-first surface dive is used when a diver wishes to descend only 6 to 12

FIGURE 13-3.   Proper swing style.

feet or when visibility is limited. It is performed by bringing the body into a vertical position similar to treading water. Once in a vertical position the diver executes one large scissors kick, bringing the legs together while pushing the hands to the side. These movements bring the diver up out of the water. He then turns his palms out and slowly brings his arms from the side upward over his head, keeping his legs straight with fins pointed downward to eliminate resistance as he descends.

Pike surface dive. The pike surface dive is used when greater depths must be attained. The dive automatically places the diver in a swimming position. While swimming in a horizontal position the diver brings his hands down to his side with the palms facing down. Forward momentum can be retained by kicking. He then bends at the waist until a 90° angle is formed. The straightened legs are flipped into the air while the diver presses the arms slowly from his side to an extended position over the head. The weight of the legs forces the diver downward.

Tuck surface dive. The tuck surface dive entails the same preliminary positions as the pike surface dive, with the arms to the side, palms down and the legs kicking slowly. Once the head is brought to the vertical position, the diver tucks the knees and extends them into the air. Again, the weight of the legs forces the diver downward.

Ascending

Several important points must be remembered when surfacing. For obvious reasons the diver must inform his partner of his desire to ascend. He should

look upward and swim slowly to the surface while rotating 360° to see if any obstructions exist. One hand should be extended over the head. Ascent must be slow (approximately the speed of the diver's bubbles) when using scuba to prevent pressure problems. The scuba diver must also remember to breathe regularly. As he comes closer to the surface, the diver should bleed his buoyancy compensator if he inflated it at depth. Another procedure is to flare out, which is simply placing the body in a position parallel to the surface of the water. Once on the surface the snorkel can be used so air in the tank can be conserved.

Donning Gear in Water

Once the diver has mastered the basic swimming skills he should practice putting his gear on underwater, starting with the mask, fins, and snorkel. Holding the fins in one hand with the mask strapped over the same arm, the diver enters the water. While sitting on the bottom he puts the fins on first, followed by the mask. Once the mask and snorkel are in place, the diver clears the mask, surfaces and clears his snorkel.

The tank can then be added to the equipment. The diver holds the mask, fins and snorkel in one hand and the tank in the other. Once submerged, the tank's valve is turned on and the regulator mouthpiece put into the mouth. To clear the mouthpiece the diver can simply exhale through the mouth or place his tongue over the orifice and press the purge button on the regulator mouthpiece. The diver can then don the tank and other equipment at his own pace. The process of donning equipment underwater is commonly referred to as the NAUI bail-out.

Entering the Water

The diver can safely enter the water several different ways. Regardless of the method selected, the diver should *never* enter the water without a partner.

One of the safest entries is wading into the water backward with the fins on or forward with fins in hand. This method is primarily used in beach areas. Entries from a platform or boat require different skills. The stride entry, allows the diver to remain at the surface while a second entry, the feet-first jump, lets the diver submerge immediately. In both entries the diver holds his mask with one hand and his tank with the other. (See Figure 13-4.)

Two more different entries for the novice are the forward and backward rolls. When performing the forward roll the diver stands at the edge of the water and bends forward with the knees slightly flexed. He

FIGURE 13-4.   Platform entries.

then rolls forward holding his mask with one hand, the tank with the other, and lands on his shoulders. The backward roll is performed similarly to the forward roll. From the crouched (some prefer to sit) the diver merely falls backward, landing on the tank.

EMERGENCY SKILLS

Buddy Breathing

If for some reason a diver's scuba fails, the skill of buddy breathing may save his life. Recently the use of buddy breathing has been challenged. Some leaders in the field feel that the dangers of buddy breathing (if performed incorrectly) make it inappropriate for the novice diver. Others, however, maintain the skill may be the only alternative open to a diver in distress and therefore should be taught.

Once the recipient diver (diver in distress) informs the donor diver of his plight, the donor diver must move quickly, making no errors. The two divers face each other. The donor holds his mouth piece in his right hand and grasps the recipient's buoyancy compensator with his left hand. The recipient diver places his left hand over the donor's right hand (which is on the regulator mouth piece) to assist in guiding the mouthpiece to his mouth. The recipient's right hand grasps the donor's buoyancy compensator for added stability. The donor then takes two deep breaths and places the regulator in the recipient's mouth. It is imperative that the donor retain control of the regulator. The recipient takes two deep breaths and releases the regulator to the donor. This procedure is continued until the divers reach the surface. (See Figure 13-5.) Because buddy breathing should normally be used only while the diver in distress is returning to the surface, strict adherence to ascending rules is necessary. (See SKILLS AND TECHNIQUES section.)

Emergency Ascent

If a diver expends his air supply he should not take his mouthpiece out. He should drop his weight belt

FIGURE 13-5.   Buddy breathing.

and, using normal ascent procedures, surface, exhaling to prevent over-expansion of the lungs. Pulling the CO_2 cartridge in the buoyancy compensator is another alternative for emergency ascent. The primary thing to remember is to flare out or slow your ascent when nearing the surface. Over expansion of the lungs is most likely at this point. A third alternative is to buddy breathe with both divers exhaling into the oral inflating valve of their buoyancy compensators. The expanding buoyancy compensator will aid the ascending diver, thus conserving his energy.

Rescuing Another Diver

If the buddy system is strictly adhered to, a diver in trouble should be noted almost immediately. Yet accidents do happen. If they do—determine where the diver was last seen and scan the surface for bubbles. A team should search the bottom right away using a (a) circular, (b) grid, (c) progressive overlap or (d) rank pattern. (See Figure 13-6.)

If the diver in distress has managed to surface but is still struggling, several assist procedures can be used. The safest method is to extend a floatable object to the victim. A second approach is to inflate his vest Removing his weight belt may also help. The diver can then be towed in by the rescuer, who grasps the victim's wrist or tank valve.

The victim may also surface in an unconscious state. Chances are he will not be breathing. Inflate his vest and yours, drop his weight belt and start mouth-to-mouth resuscitation. The rescruer can slowly swim to shore while continuing resuscitation.

A diver in distress may also be found under water. When bringing the unconscious diver to the surface, keep the victim's head back so exhalation can occur. If bubbles are not coming from the victim's mouth or nose it is often helpful to press on the victim's lower chest with the head to force air out. This is not necessary under normal circumstances, however.

Hand Signals

Many emergency situations can be avoided by the use of hand signals. Some of the most common are noted in Figure 13-7.

LAWS AND PRINCIPLES OF PRESSURE AND THEIR EFFECTS ON DIVERS

Because a diver is composed of matter, laws relating to pressure and its effect on matter become

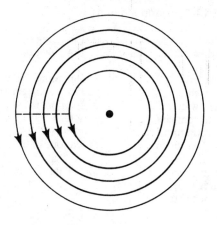

a. Circular search pattern

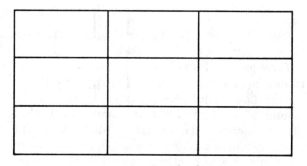

b. Grid search pattern

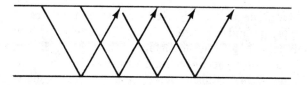

c. Progressive overlap search pattern

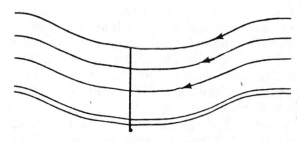

d. Irregular shore search pattern

FIGURE 13-6. Search patterns.

FIGURE 13-7.   Hand signals.

Thumbs up	I'm going up
Thumbs down	I'm going down
Pointing in a given direction	I'm going this way
Pointing to ears	I'm having ear trouble
Pointing to watch	It's time to go up
Pointing to compass	Which way
Pointing to mouthpiece and then removing	I'm out of air
Holding both hands, palms up, to side	"What do you mean?"
Both hands held in clinched fists	Hold still
Banging on tank	Attention
Bring hand across throat	I'm fouled, help
One or two hands on throat	I'm hurt—get me up!

crucial. The pressure of gases and liquids affect virtually all parts of the diver's body.

Three physical laws cover the majority of pressure-related circumstances divers encounter. The first is Boyle's Law: If temperature remains constant, the volume of gas decreases at the same rate that the pressure increases. The second is Dalton's Law: The total pressure of a gas mixture is equal to the sum of the partial pressures of components making up the gas. The third is Henry's Law: Gases will enter into a liquid in proportion to the partial pressure of the gas.

The effects of pressure while descending

Both air and water have force, which is expressed in psi (pounds per square inch). One square inch of air extending from the surface of the earth to the top of the atmosphere exerts a pressure of 14.7 psi. The value of 14.7 is also referred to as one atmosphere. The diver must only descend 33 feet below the surface of the water to experience two times as much pressure, 66 feet to experience three times the pressure, and so on. Accordingly, the diver's air volume at the surface is cut in half when he descends only 33 feet underwater and is reduced to one quarter at 66 feet, and so on (Boyle's Law). Consequently, the diver must always take into account not only the amount of air he has in his tank but also the depth at which he plans to dive.

In addition to the air in the diver's tank, air pockets such as sinus, intestines, ears, and mask are affected by pressure when descending. The volume of air in these pockets is also reduced, creating a suction effect with the water environment. Such a condition

is termed "squeeze". Sinus squeeze occurs when the suction becomes so great that the soft tissues in the sinuses break open and blood is sucked from the broken blood vessels into the sinuses. Pain can be considerable under such circumstances. Sinus squeeze can be prevented by *not* diving with a cold. Ear squeeze is created when a similar difference in air pressure occurs between the inner ear and the water. Normally, this can be eliminated by clearing the ears, a skill discussed previously. If the diver is unable to clear his ears, the delicate timpanic membrane or the blood vessels of the ear may rupture. The diver must not descend if he can't clear his ears. Gas formed in the stomach or intestines just prior to descending

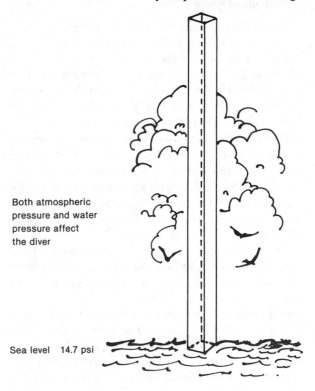

Both atmospheric
pressure and water
pressure affect
the diver

Sea level   14.7 psi

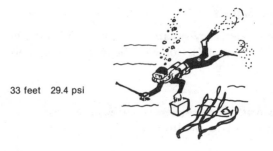

33 feet   29.4 psi

FIGURE 13-8.   The effects of pressure.

can, on occasion, cause intestinal squeeze. It can also result in considerable discomfort for the diver. The possibility of intestinal squeeze can be reduced by avoiding gaseous foods and drinks. Squeeze can even occur in air spaces outside the body. One such example is face mask squeeze, which can happen to the novice diver without his knowing it until later, when he looks in a mirror to see two "shiners" staring back at him. Face mask squeeze can be eliminated by blowing through the nose into the mask until a few bubbles leak out the edge of the mask. Because the diver has no way of equalizing goggles, they should not be included as scuba equipment.

The effects of pressure at depth

As the diver remains underwater, and, consequently, under pressure, greater amounts of air are absorbed by the blood and tissue. Air, which has a total pressure of 14.7, is composed of nitrogen, with a partial pressure of 11.5 psi; oxygen, 3.1 psi; and carbon dioxide, .003 psi (Dalton's Law). As air is absorbed, its components are also absorbed proportionally (Henry's Law). As the diver descends further or remains under longer, more and more nitrogen is absorbed into the tissues until its narcotic effect is felt. This is termed nitrogen narcosis. It should be noted that normally oxygen and carbon dioxide do not have a toxic effect because oxygen is burned by the body and carbon dioxide is given off through the lungs. Scuba divers have a rule of thumb for nitrogen narcosis: Every fifty feet the diver descends is equivalent to drinking one martini.

Oxygen and carbon dioxide poisoning can occur under unusual circumstances and are usually associated with closed circuit scuba. At a depth of 25 to 30 feet or more, the breathing of pure oxygen can cause unconsciousness and death. Carbon dioxide poisoning normally occurs when the regulator malfunctions. It is recommended that the sport diver not use closed circuit scuba.

The effects of pressure while ascending

As the diver ascends, air in his lungs expands (Boyle's Law). Delicate lung tissues can be damaged if the lungs over-inflate. The small air sacs in the lungs called alveoli rupture and several things occur. Air enters the blood stream and causes a cerebral air embolism, mediastinal and subcutanneous emphysema (in which air bubbles collect in the tissues of the neck) or pneumothorax (when air enters the pleural cavity and the lung collapses).

FIGURE 13-9.   Martini's law.

A second effect may be noted in the intestinal tract. The opposite of intestinal squeeze can occur on ascent. If gas is formed in the intestine while the diver is submerged, it will increase in volume as the diver ascends and the pressure decreases (Boyle's Law). Again, the easiest way to prevent intestinal problems is to avoid consumption of gaseous foods and drinks.

When the diver breathes air at particurly great depths, large amounts of nitrogen are absorbed into the blood. If he ascends slowly enough, the nitrogen returns to the blood stream and is given off by the lungs. If he ascends too quickly, the nitrogen expands and small bubbles start forming in the blood and tissue. These bubbles can cause pain (particularly in the joints), obstruction of circulation, dizziness, unconsciousness and, unless treated in time, paralysis and death. This phenomenon is commonly called the "bends". Whenever a diver goes deeper than 33 feet below the surface of the water, he should consult the Navy Air decompression charts to determine how long he can safely remain at that depth. The sport diver should be discouraged from making dives deep enough for the bends to occur. Divers going deeper than 33 feet often use a decompression meter in conjunction with the decompression tables. The meter indicates the amount of nitrogen absorbed in the tissues.

Hyperventilation and Anoxia

Anoxia, lack of oxygen, can occur while skin diving. The prolong dive time, many divers breathe deeply several times before submerging. This deep-breathing technique is called hyperventilation. In essence, it reduces the amount of carbon dioxide in the blood, which results in a diminished urge to breathe. Contrary to common belief, breathing deeply does not allow the body to store more oxygen.

Because the diver has no urge to breathe, he loses consciousness due to a lack of oxygen, before normal mechanisms are alerted. If the diver takes fewer than five deep breaths, hyperventilation can be an effective and safe means to increase dive time.

EXERCISE   Definitions and List of Terms

1. *Absolute pressure.* The total air and water pressure exerted on the diver. The addition of 14.7 p.s.i. to the indicated gauge pressure gives absolute pressure.
2. *Air.* A highly compressable mixture of gases. Approximately 78 percent nitrogen, 21 percent oxygen, and trace amounts of carbon dioxide and rare gases.
3. *Air embolism.* An obstruction in the circulation of the blood.
4. *Anoxia.* A lack of oxygen.
5. *Artificial respiration.* Mechanical method of forced expiration to an individual who has stopped breathing. Also called resuscitation.
6. *Atmospheric pressure.* The pressure exerted by the pressure of air. This is expressed in pounds per square inch. One atmosphere is 14.7 p.s.i.
7. *Barotrauma.* Injury due to effects of pressure.
8. *Back pack.* A back pack-like apparatus designed to hold a scuba tank in a stable-comfortable position on the diver's back.
9. *Bends.* A condition resulting from dissolved nitrogen-forming bubbles in the blood stream. Also called Caisson disease or decompression sickness.
10. *Bezel.* A ring around the watch face which allows the diver to keep tract of the total time he is under water.
11. *Boyle's law.* The volume of gas varies inversely with its absolute pressure when temperature remains constant.
12. *Buddy.* Diving partner.
13. *Buddy breathing.* An emergency rescue technique in which two divers share a single scuba tank and regulator.
14. *Buddy line.* A line connecting diving partners.
15. *Buoyancy.* The upward force exerted on a floating or immersed body by a fluid.
16. *Buoyancy compensator.* An inflatable vest that allows the diver to float safely in a face-up position. It is also used to control buoyancy at various depths.
17. *Caisson disease.* (See Bends).
18. *Closed circuit.* Diving equipment that is primarily used by commercial and military divers in which pure oxygen is breathed into a bag with a carbon dioxide absorbant. Not recommended for sport diving.
19. *Compressor.* A machine pump used to compress gas for filling scuba tanks.
20. *Cylinder.* A steel receptacle used to hold the compressed air in sport diving. A scuba tank.
21. *Dalton's law.* Gas in a mixture exerts the same pressure that it would exert if it occupied the same volume alone.
22. *Decompression.* The release of nitrogen by body tissues when the surrounding pressure is decreased.
23. *Decompression meter.* An instrument which indicates the level of residual nitrogen in the tissues of a diver and the stops required for decompression.
24. *Decompression sickness.* (See Bends).
25. *Decompression tables.* Tables used to determine the number and length of stops, following underwater a swim of considerable depth and duration.

26. *Doffing equipment*. Taking off equipment underwater.
27. *Donning equipment*. Putting on underwater equipment while on the bottom.
28. *Dry suit*. A rubberized suit which covers the body and keeps it completely dry.
29. *Equalizing pressure*. The process of balancing pressure in the internal air spaces or mask with the pressure of the water.
30. *Hemorrhage*. Discharge from blood vessels due to injury.
31. *Hyperventilation*. Increased deep breathing resulting in a decreased urge to breathe when preparing to dive underwater.
32. *Keeper*. A small rubber strap used to attach the snorkel to mask.
33. *Mediastinal Emphysema*. A collection of air bubbles in the mediastinum due to ruptured alveoli.
34. *Narcosis*. A state of decreased efficiency, accompanied by dizziness, disorientation, and an inability to think clearly.
35. *Nitrogen narcosis*. Dizziness, disorientation and inability to think clearly resulting from the body's absorption of excessive amounts of nitrogen.
36. *Open circuit*. A diving apparatus that exhausts exhaled air into the water. Recommended for sport diving.
37. *Partial pressure*. The pressure exerted by a gas in a mixture of gases, such as the pressure of oxygen in the air.
38. *Safety line*. A line attached to the diver and a surface station.
38. *Scuba*. Self-contained underwater breathing apparatus. Two types—open and closed.
39. *Shock*. A depressed condition of many of the body functions due to failure of sufficient blood to circulate through the body following serious injury.
40. *Sinus*. Air spaces in the front part of the bones of the skull.
41. *Skin diver*. A diver diving without self-contained breathing apparatus.
42. *Spear gun*. Rubber-, spring-, or gas-operated gun used to launch spears.
43. *Spontaneous pneumothorax*. A collapsed lung that results when air from ruptured alveoi enters the space between the lung and chest wall.
44. *Sport diver*. One who skin or scuba dives for recreational purposes.
45. *Squeeze*. A decrease in pressure in air spaces resulting in pain and often hemorrhage.
46. *Subcutaneus emphysema*. A collection of air bubbles under the skin in the neck region, from ruptured alveoli.
47. *Vertigo*. Dizziness frequently accompanied by nausea.
48. *Wet suit*. A rubberized suit that allows water to form an insulating layer between the suit and the diver's skin.
49. *Weight belt*. A belt with adjustable weight used to obtain a desired buoyancy in the water.

BIBLIOGRAPHY

American National Red Cross. *Lifesaving and Water*. Garden City, M.J.: Doubleday and Co., 1974.

Bennett, P. B. and Elliot, D. H. *The Physiology and Medicine of Diving and Compressed Air Work*. Baltimore: Williams and Wilkins, 1969.

Carrier, R. and B. Carrier. *Dive: The Complete Book of Skin Diving*. New York: Funk, 1963.

Council for National Cooperation in Aquatics. *The New Science of Skin and Scuba Diving*. New York: Association Press, 1974.

Darby, J. and G. Beardsley. *Scuba Rescue and Recovery*. Hanover Park, Ill: Illinois Scuba Rescue and Recovery Unit, 1972.

Dueker, C. W. *Medical Aspects of Sport Diving*. New York: Barnes, 1970.

Hogan, W. F. *Safe Scuba*. Minneapolis, MN: Printing, Inc., 1971.

Strauss, R. H. *Diving Medicine*. New York: Grunet & Stratton, 1976.

Tillman, A. A. *Skin and Scuba Diving*. Dubuque, Iowa: Brown, 1962.

Tzimoulis, Frey, Hank and Paul. *The Complete Guide to the Art and Science of Underwater Photography*. New York: Association Press, 1968.

United States Government. *U.S. Navy Diving Manual:* NAVSHIPS 0994-001-9010, Superintendent of Documents. Washington, D.C.: U.S. Government Printing Office, March 1970.

Cousteau, J-Y and Diole, Philippe. *Life and Death in a Coral Sea*. New York: Doubleday, 1974.

Hannau, H. W. *In the Coral Reefs of the Caribbean, Bahamas, Florida, Bermuda*. New York: Doubleday, 1974.

Parker, Gene. *Gene Parker's Complete Handbook of Skin Diving*. Fort Lee, N.J.: Little Book Co., 1971.

Allen, Barry. *Skin Diving and Snorkeling*. Philadelphia: Lippincott, 1973.

Cramer, J. L. *Skin and Scuba Diving, Scientific Principles and Techniques—Manual*. New York: Bertwall Prod., 1975.

14

SOCCER

DESCRIPTION OF THE ACTIVITY

Soccer is a goal game played on a rectangular field by two opposing teams composed of not more than eleven players each. The object of the game is to propel a soccer ball through the opponent's goal in a legal manner. When this is done the team scores one point.

A regulation soccer field has the following areas and equipment. All areas should be clearly marked with white lines.

The *center line* divides the field into two equal halves. From a point directly at the center of this line, a *circle* 10 yards in radius should be drawn and clearly marked.

A *goal area,* located at each end of the field, is marked by two lines drawn perpendicular to the goal line and 6 yards from each goal post. These lines extend 6 yards into the playing field, and at that point are connected by a 20-yard line drawn parallel with the goal line. All goal kicks are taken from this area.

The *penalty area* is also located at each end of the field. It is marked by two lines perpendicular to, and 18 yards away from each goal post. These lines are extended into the playing field for 18 yards and connected at the end of this extension by a line 44 yards long and parallel with the goal line. During a penalty kick, no player except the goalkeeper and the kicker may be in this area until the ball is kicked. Certain fouls committed by the defense in this area are penalized by a penalty kick.

A *penalty kick mark,* two feet in length, is located 12 yards out and at right angles to the midpoint of the goal line. This line should extend one foot on each side of the midpoint. The ball may be placed at any point on this mark for the penalty kick.

A *restraining line* for penalty kicks is marked by drawing a 10-yard arc from the center of the penalty kick mark so that it intersects the front line of the penalty area at a right and left point. During a penalty kick no player except the kicker and the goalkeeper may be inside this line until the ball is kicked.

The *corner area* is marked by a one-yard arc drawn from the point of junction of the goal and touch lines. It extends into the field of play and intersects both the touch and goal lines one yard out from their junction. All corner kicks are taken in this area.

The outside dimensions of the field have been established by the rules committee. Measurements have been set with a maximum length of 120 yards and width of 75 yards, and a minimum length of 110 yards and width of 65 yards. The goals are 8 feet high and 24 feet wide, and are set directly in the center of the goal line. All markings and dimensions of the playing field are given in Figure 14-1.

A maximum of eleven players may participate on one team during a game. By position, these players are five forwards: (strikers) inside left, inside right, outside left, outside right, and center; three halfbacks: (midfielders) right, center, and left; two fullbacks: right and left; and one goalkeeper. The outside forwards are commonly known as wing forwards or wings, and the right and left halfbacks are generally called wing halfbacks.

A game is begun with a kickoff, which is executed by a player of the kicking team from a point at the center of the field on the line dividing the field into two equal halves. The official places the ball on the kickoff mark and the player chosen to take the kick starts play by place-kicking the ball from that point. At the time of the kickoff, each player must be in his own half of the field, and no opposing player may take a position closer than ten yards to the ball. The ball must be kicked forward into the oppoennt's half of the field, a distance of at least the length of the ball's own circumference. The kickoff is considered

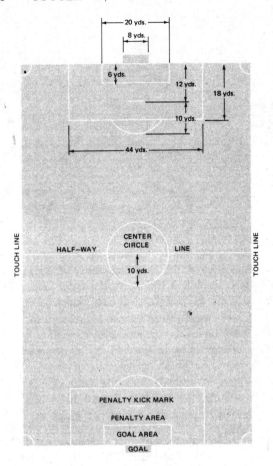

FIGURE 14-1. Soccer playing field.

The National Collegiate Athletic Association rules set the duration of the game at two-45-minute halves. However, rules for scholastic competition are written especially for this level of play, and the length of a game may be set by the mutual agreement of the coaches involved.

A goal is made when the ball is sent through the goal in a legal manner, and may occur during play or from a penalty kick. Both have a one-point value. The team that scores the most goals wins.

The rules governing play provide for some bodily contact; however, a contestant may not trip, kick, strike, hold, push, or jump at an opponent at any time. Charging is permitted, but an opponent may not execute this move in a violent or dangerous manner or when a player has both feet off the ground. When a player commits any one of these illegal actions, his team is penalized by the awarding of a free kick to the opposing team. If an illegal action is committed by a defensive player in his penalty area, a penalty kick is given to the opposing team.

When the ball passes completely over a touch line, it is put in play by a throw-in executed by a player of the team that did not last touch the ball before it went out-of-bounds. When an offensive player causes the ball to go out-of-bounds over the goal line, the defense puts the ball in play with a goal kick. If a defensive player last touches the ball before it goes out-of-bounds across the goal line, but not betwen the goal posts, it is put in play by a corner kick.

to have been completed as soon as the ball has been kicked, and at that time players can move any place on the field and the ball can be propelled in any direction. A goal, however, cannot be scored directly from the kickoff. This method of putting the ball into play is used after each score, and to start each period and overtime period.

After the kickoff, the ball may be played by any player, using any part of his body except the hand and the arms from the shoulders down. However, the restrictions on the use of the hands and arms do not apply to the goalkeeper when he is within the penalty area. Each team attempts to advance the ball to a favorable position close enough to the opponent's goal so that a score can be made. In accomplishing this objective, the ball may be propelled with the head, shoulders, chest, back, thighs, knees, legs, or feet. Play continues in this manner until the ball goes out-of-bounds, a goal is made, the ball touches the referee, a period ends, or the referee stops play for any reason because of a rule infringement or an injury to a player.

EQUIPMENT

Elaborate and expensive equipment is not essential for playing soccer. The uniform may be a light shirt and trunks. Shoes, probably the most important item of personal equipment, should be safety cleated with rubber or a synthetic material and should provide ample protection for the feet, especially the toes and arches. They should be oiled periodically and especially when used in the rain or on a wet playing surface. It is best to dry them at room temperature and then oil them.

The soccer ball may be constructed from leather sections or it may be a solid rubber formation. The leather type is preferred by good players; however, the rubber ball is durable and serviceable for class play. When in use it should be inflated according to the manufacturer's recommendations. When the leather ball becomes wet from the rain or from surface water, it should be partially deflated, oiled, and stored in a dry, cool room that has good air circulation. However, there is now a waterproof, plastic-coated, leather ball available.

A good grade of shin guards made of a synthetic material or of leather should be worn during competitive play. They are generally placed inside knee-length socks.

The goal is constructed so that it has two uprights with inner edges 24 feet apart and set an equal distance from the junction of the touch and goal lines. These uprights should be high enough to support a crossbar whose lower surface is 8 feet from the ground. The width and depth of the crossbar and uprights should not exceed 5 inches.

A net should be attached to the goal posts, the crossbar, and the ground behind the goal. It should be arranged in such a way that it provides sufficient space for the goalkeeper to move freely. The top of this net should extend two feet in back of and on the same level with the crossbar. The sides of the net should join the goal posts, and the net should then angle to the ground and be securely fastened so that the ball cannot go under it.

Each of the four corners of the soccer field should be marked by a flag mounted on a blunt-topped post that is not less than 5 feet in height and that is constructed of rigid material.

SKILLS AND TECHNIQUES

Kicking

Kicking, in all of its forms, is the most essential and frequently used of all soccer skills. It is employed to pass, clear, shoot, center, put the ball in play at the start of each quarter of the game, and on all free kicks, penalty kicks, corner kicks, and goal kicks.

In spite of the fact that there are many different types of kicks, certain basic fundamentals apply to most of them. If the flight of the ball is to be straight, the ball must be struck with the foot at a point on a vertical plane running from the ball to the target. If the flight of the ball is to be curved, the foot must contact it at a point away from this central area or move at an angle across the central area. Only the highly skilled player should attempt the curved flight. In order for a player to make accurate contact with the correct spot on the ball, he must focus the eyes on that point and see all else as background. The elevation of the ball can range from a ground shot to an extremely high flight. The elevation is determined by the point of contact, the degree of ankle flexion or extension, the follow-through, the distance the

nonkicking foot is placed from the ball, and the flight of the ball before the kick is delivered. Placement of the ball in the desired spot is more important than speed or distance; therefore, accuracy is a first objective. Players must also remember that the arms and body are used in coordination with the feet and legs to maintain good balance.

Description of techniques will be given for kicking a stationary ball. The same or similar skills are employed when the ball is moving on the ground or in the air; however, under such conditions the timing is more difficult and some of the preliminary moves, made when kicking a stationary ball, may have to be eliminated.

Instep Kick. There are three variations of the instep kick depending on the area of the foot that contacts the ball. These are: the full instep kick, the inside of the instep kick, and the outside of the instep kick.

The *full instep kick* is used for shooting, clearing, free kicks, goal kicks, and passing. When executing this kick, all movements of the body during the preliminary run, or motion into the ball, should be in line with the intended flight, and the ball should be struck by the foot directly on top of the longitudinal arch, extending from a point at the base of the toes to the junction of the ankle and lower leg. The following techniques are important when kicking a stationary ball.

1. One or several steps should be made directly in line with the desired flight of the ball. The last stride is longer than the others, but it is a regular running stride. The nonkicking foot is placed alongside the ball, and 6 to 8 inches away from it.

2. The head is down and the eyes are focused on the ball at the point where the foot is to make contact.

3. As the nonkicking foot is being moved into position, the backswing of the kicking leg is executed by sharply drawing the leg back at the hip and flexing the knee to an angle of approximately 75 degrees. These movements carry the foot high in back of the thigh.

4. The weight is balanced over the nonkicking leg, the body leans slightly forward at contact, and the arms are coordinated with the legs.

5. The forward swing of the kicking leg is initiated from the hip. As the knee is pointing at the ball, the lower leg is snapped quickly forward bringing the foot into the ball. The knee is not fully extended into a locked position.

6. The ankle joint is extended before contact is

made with the ball. This action causes the toe to point toward the ground so that the ball can be contacted squarely on the top of the instep. The ankle joint must be kept firm at the time of contact and follow-through.

7. If a high flight is desired, the nonkicking foot can be placed in back of the ball so that the knee of the kicking foot is behind the ball at the time of contact. If a low flight is desired, the nonkicking foot is placed parallel with the ball.

8. The follow-through of the foot and leg is in line with the desired point of placement and should carry the body beyond the original position of the ball.

The *inside of the instep kick* is a kind of chip kick used to elevate the ball for a placement just over the head of a player or for a short pass. When perform-

a. The start.

b. The follow-through.

FIGURE 14-2.   Instep kick.

ing this variation of the instep kick, the foot makes contact with the ball on the inside of the instep from a point near the base of the great toe to the area just in front of the ankle bone. It is executed in much the same way as the full instep kick except for the following variations:

1. The preliminary movement into a stationary ball is at a slight angle rather than linear. If the left foot is the kicking foot, the direction of approach to the ball is from the right at an angle to the desired flight of the ball, and vice versa if the right foot is to be the kicking foot.

2. The nonkicking foot is placed farther away from the ball laterally than it is for making the full instep kick.

3. The kicking leg is turned slightly outward on the backswing, and the forward swing is slightly circular rather than exactly linear.

The *outside of the instep kick* is another variation of the full instep kick. It is accomplished very much as the two kicks described above except that the ball is contacted by the outside area of the instep on the linear surface from the little toe to the outside projection of the ankle joint. The kicking foot is turned inward slightly in a pigeon-toed manner, but the approach and forward swing are linear.

Inside of the Foot Kick.   The inside of the foot kick is used especially for accurate passing, but can be effectively employed for other purposes. The ball makes contact with the inside of the foot on a broad triangular area extending from a point near the heel, along the edge of the sole, to a point in back of the side base of the big toe, to the front of the junction of the lower leg and ankle. The ball, however, should not touch the toe or the heel, but should contact the foot in the middle of the instep. In order to develop a sound technique for the inside of the foot kick, the following movements must be learned.

1. The nonkicking foot is placed comfortably close to the lateral side of the ball.

2. During the backswing of the kicking leg, the leg is rotated outward at the hip so that the foot turns out and can be driven into contact with the ball on the inside surface of the foot. If the foot position is correct, the longitudinal axis of the foot is perpendicular to the intended line of the ball's flight.

3. The knee is flexed slightly, the body is bent forward a bit at the hips, the head is tilted downward, and the eyes are focused on the ball.

4. The forward swing of the kicking leg is initiated

FIGURE 14-3.   Inside-of-foot kick.

FIGURE 14-4.   Outside-of-foot kick.

in the hip joint, the leg is turned out, the knee is flexed and relaxed until just before contact at which time it is set.

5. The toe of the kicking foot is turned out and slightly upward, the sole is parallel with the ground surface, and the ankle is locked.

6. The extent of the follow-through varies with the distance and speed desired.

Outside of the Foot Kick.   The outside of the foot kick is employed mostly for short flick-like passing because very little power can be initiated from such a position. For this reason it is not used as frequently as other types of kicks. The techniques are similar to those employed for the inside of the foot kick except that the ball is contacted by the foot along the thin lateral edge at the junction of the sole from near the little toe area back to the middle of the long arch. The backswing is taken across and in front of the nonkicking leg, and is, therefore, restricted in length. The forward motion is a kind of flicking jab into the ball.

Heel Kick.   Kicking with the heel is a difficult skill to perform and is not employed except in special situations. It is sometimes used when a ground ball has rolled past a player in the direction of is own goal and he wants to reverse its direction. In this situation,

the player will run in the same direction as the ball and, after overtaking it, he will step ahead of it with the nonkicking foot and swing the free leg back driving the heel into the ball. This kick may also be utilized when a high ball drops over the head of a player and he cannot reach it except by kicking upward and backward. The use of the heel kick is not recommended.

Volley Kick.   There are situations during a game when the ball should be kicked with a volley kick while it is still in flight. When the ball is coming directly at a player, the instep is generally used; however, the heel kick or the side of the foot kick may be employed. The following are the techniques for executing the volley kick with the instep:

1. The distance of the backswing of the kicking leg is less than when one is kicking a stationary ball.

2. The ankle joint is extended before contact with the ball.

3. The eyes are focused on the ball and follow it until the kick is made.

4. The height of the trajectory is determined by the type of kick and where the foot makes contact with the ball.

5. The weight is placed over the nonkicking leg, and the arms are used for balance.

Side Volley Kick. This kick can be used defensively for clearing and offensively for shooting. When it is used defensively to clear the ball and a change in direction of the ball's flight from straight-away is desired, the player should execute a pivot in the desired direction by placing the toe of the non-kicking foot so it is pointed in that direction, lift the kicking foot to the desired height and contact the ball on its side-bottom. When it is used to shoot, the foot should make contact directly at the back center of the ball, or if a downward flight is desired, contact should be made at the top center.

Half Volley. The half volley is executed just as the ball rises after having made contact with the playing surface. The instep or the side of the foot kick are most generally used. Proper timing is essential. The placement of the nonkicking foot is determined by the intended destination and elevation of the ball. The eyes must be focused on the ball until the kick is completed.

Pivot Kick. The purpose of the pivot kick is to propel the ball at an angle to the right or left of the direction in which the player is traveling when approaching the ball.

1. The nonkicking foot is placed farther away from the ball than for the straight instep kick, and the weight is carried well over the nonkicking foot.

2. The kicking leg travels in a circular motion and contacts the ball on the instep at a point in the arc which will give the desired direction.

3. The body pivots on the nonkicking leg, and turns in the direction of the kick.

Trapping

Trapping, or receiving and bringing the ball under control, is essential to good soccer play. By using some part of his body, the player should be able to gain control of the ball when it comes to him on the ground or in the air. This skill should be developed to such a degree that the player can stop the ball within reach of his feet so that he has time to make a play before an opponent rushes in and interferes, or that the player can pass to a teammate who is in a favorable position. The different types of traps are identified according to the part of the body used to make the stop.

Inside of the Foot Trap. The surface of the foot employed to make contact with the ball in the inside of the foot trap is the same as for the inside of the foot kick. The weight of the body is balanced over the nontrapping leg, the knee is flexed lightly, and

the trunk is bent slightly toward the approaching ball. The movements and the coordiantion of the trapping leg are accomplished in the following manner:

1. As the ball nears the player, the trapping leg is rotated outward and is moved forward with all joints relaxed.

2. As the ball makes contact with the foot, the entire leg is relaxed and moves with the ball but at a somewhat slower speed, thereby absorbing the shock of the ball's momentum and causing the ball to stop without any great rebound. The foot must not be in contact with the ground. It is difficult to stop a fast-moving ball dead but it can be kept under control.

3. When the player receives a ball that bounces up from the ground, the trapping leg is moved backward so that the inside of the leg forms a 40- to 60-degree angle with the ground. The foot or the inside of the leg may then be used to make contact with the ball which should be wedged between the leg or foot and the ground.

Outside of the Foot Trap. When the ball moves toward the player from either side, the foot on that side will become the trapping surface. Techniques are similar to those of the inside of the foot trap except that the ball makes contact with the lateral surface of the longitudinal arch of the foot. As the ball ap-

FIGURE 14-5.   Inside-of-foot trap.

FIGURE 14-6.   Outside-of-foot trap.
The starting position.

FIGURE 14-7.   Sole-of-the-foot trap.

FIGURE 14-8.   Thigh trap.

FIGURE 14-9.   Chest trap.

proaches from the player's left, the relaxed left leg is moved slightly toward it, but when the ball makes contact with the outside of the foot, the leg gives with the momentum of the ball. As it moves across and in front of the right leg, the left leg forms an angle with the ground and slows the ball gradually until it come to a stop.

Sole of the Foot Trap. This type of trap is most generally used to receive a ball coming directly at a player in a roll or a low bounce. When performing preliminary movements for receiving the ball, the trapping leg is raised from the hip, the knee is bent to approximately 90 degrees, and the ankle is flexed so that the sole of the foot will receive the ball, slow it down, and deflect it downward between the bottom of the foot and the ground. Care must be taken to keep the heel low enough to the ground so the ball will not slide under it and out behind.

Thigh Trap The thigh trap is utilized mostly to receive balls coming directly at a player at any height. As a high arcing ball approaches, the trapping leg is lifted until the thigh is approximately parallel with the ground with the knee flexed accordingly. When the ball makes contact with the front surface of the thigh, the thigh is lowered to absorb the speed of the ball. The knee remains flexed enough to permit the foot to pass behind the vertical plane of the body. In this way it is possible to decelerate the ball so that it will fall dead at the feet. However, the thigh can be stiffened so that the ball rebounds upward or forward, according to the purpose of the trapper.

When the ball is approaching at a horizontal plane and at a lower level, the knee is dropped quickly upon contact and the thigh is moved quickly backward. These movements deaccelerate the ball causing it to lose speed to the extent that it drops slowly to the surface.

Chest Trap. When the ball is propelled toward the player at chest height, the player can receive it with the surface of the chest so that is bounces slightly upward or downward. The downward trap is accomplished by taking a stride stance, with the trunk leaning backward. As the ball comes into the trapping area and makes contact with the chest, the hips are jerked back, the front leg is drawn back, and the chest and shoulders are quickly bent forward, pushing the ball toward the ground. The ball can be blocked upward by holding the original position and allowing the ball to strike the chest while the trunk is leaning backwards. The ball may also be trapped with the surface of the stomach if the same movements are used as in the chest trap.

Heading

The purpose of heading the ball is to pass or shoot for the goal; therefore, it is employed both as an offensive and defensive move. In heading, the safest way to use the head and still be able to follow the ball with the eyes practically until the ball contacts the head is to use only the surface of the forehead to contact the ball.

Heading, like kicking and trapping, can occur under many different situations. The player may be moving or stationary; and if moving, he may be running at full speed, at half speed, backward, or to the side; or he may be jumping from one or both feet. The ball may be coming at any speed, from any angle, and from any altitude. For each of these conditions, the player will have to adapt the basic technique of the skill to fit the needs of the particular situation. However, certain movements are common to all of these. When heading the ball directly forward from a stationary position, the following technique should be employed.

1. The feet are placed in a stride position, with the knees flexed slightly and the legs angled forward to the hips.
2. The trunk is bent backwards at the hips.
3. When the ball moves into the heading area, the trunk springs foward quickly and the front of the forehead is driven into the ball. The neck is used as an extension of the back and must remain firm. The forward and upward movement originates in the back.
4. If a high trajectory is desired, the forehead is angled up. If a low flight is desired, the forehead is straight ahead or downward—the latter position sometimes being used to shoot for the goal. It is also possible to extend the head far enough to the rear to propel the ball in backward direction. If the player desires to direct the ball to the side, he will turn his head in that direction and twist the body accordingly.

Heading when running is similar to heading when in a stationary position, but the movements and the timing are more difficult to execute correctly. The speed of the run will provide the force to obtain the necessary acceleration of the ball. When running, the player can execute the heading motion by jumping with both feet or with only one foot. However, he must also use the upper trunk and the neck to give added impetus to the ball. When landing from a jump, the player should keep the feet spread apart so

Body position when the ball is moving directly into the player. The ball has already made contact with the front of the forehead.

FIGURE 14-10.   Heading the ball.

that he will maintain good balance for the next move.

The *side of the forehead* can be employed to head the ball. In performing this skill from a stationary position, the leg lean forward is the same as for the front head, but the trunk is bent sideways and the side is turned in the direction of the intended flight of the ball. This position turns the body so that the head can be held in its natural front position, and the ball can be struck with the side of the forehead. The movement of the head should be in the direction of the desired flight of the ball.

Dribbling

Dribbling is a method of propelling the ball with the feet and is employed to move the ball on offense or defense, to make an opponent shift so a pass can be completed to an open teammate, and to establish a more strategic position for a shot at the goal.

However, it is the slowest way to move the ball and should never be used if a pass is possible. If the dribble is employed, complete control must be maintained so that loss of possession to a tackle does not occur. In the dribble, the sole, the outside, the inside, and the full instep of the feet are used.

The *inside of the foot dribble* is the most common and is accomplished in the following manner:

1. The surface of the foot that makes contact with the ball is the same as that for the inside of the instep kick.
2. The dribbling leg is rotated out from the hip so that the toe is pointed outward.
3. As the player moves downfield, the ball is played alternately from the inside of one foot to the inside of the other foot. The ball is usually kept close to the feet and under the complete control of the dribbler.
4. The upper trunk leans forward slightly. A highly skilled player will dribble without looking directly at the ball, thereby making it possible for him to see both his teammates and his opponents and to detect more easily an opening for a pass to a teammate or a shot at the goal than if his eyes were focused on the ball.

The ball may also be dribbled with the outside of the feet. In this case the toes are rotated inward and the ankle is kept loose. Which type of dribble is used will depend upon the position of the opponent, the desired speed of the dribble, the deceptive elements involved, and the adeptness of the dribbler in the use of this skill.

Tackling

Tackling is primarily a move by a player not in possession of the ball to gain possession of it from an opponent who is using the dribble. Even if possession is not gained, tackling may cause the dribbler to make a bad pass or to slow down his progress. Tackling may be executed from the front, side, or rear.

Front Tackle.   Because of the nature of the game the front tackle is probably the one most frequently employed. It is executed in the following manner:

1. As the player moves into position, the tackler shifts his weight to the nontackling foot, which should be placed parallel to the ball.
2. He keeps the arms near the sides to avoid fouling, and leans the body slightly forward.

3. He turns the tackling foot out and toe slightly up to present broader surface to block the ball.

4. The tackler attempts to block the ball with the foot nearest to the dribbler. He must avoid being faked out of position and must make feints of his own in order to gain a favorable position to one side of the dribbler.

5. He moves the tackling leg swiftly forward into the ball to block it in such a way that the dribbler loses control and the tackler gains possession. If possible the tackler pushes the ball in back of the dribbler and then moves on downfield with it.

Side Tackle.   Body contact of some kind is almost unavoidable when tackling from the side. The tackler reaches the dribbler from the side and, using the leg closest to the intended line of the dribble, he moves the side of the foot in quickly to intercept the ball and propels it to the opposite side or to the rear of the dribbler. The tackler must take care not to trip or to foul the dribbler in some other way. A split tackle is often made from the side position. In this move, the tackler attempts to contact he ball with the sole of the foot and shake it loose from the dribbler. When executing the split tackle, the tackler usually falls down and is out of any succeeding play. A slide tackle from the side may also be used, but should be attempted only as a last resort.

Rear Tackle.   When the tackler is behind the dribbler he must overtake him, and as the tackler draws slightly ahead of him, he must move his inside foot, or the foot nearest to the dribbler, into the ball just as the dribbler pushes the ball ahead. The tackler should place his inside foot between the dribbler and the ball, and then, using the charge, move in front of the dribbler and take possession of the ball. Side-to-side body contact is generally necessary when making this tackle.

Charging

Charging is a legal move and an important skill of soccer. It can only be employed to help gain possession of the ball when tackling and should be executed in the following manner:

a. The player on the right has executed a front tackle without making body contact.

b. The player on the right has made a front tackle using shoulder-to-shoulder body contact.

FIGURE 14-11.   Front tackles.

FIGURE 14-12. Side tackle.

FIGURE 14-13. Rear tackle. The player on the left has come up from behind. As he pulls slightly ahead of his opponent his inside foot is thrust in to intercept the ball.

1. The arms and hands must be kept close to the body and away from the opponent.

2. The rules require that contact must be made shoulder height to shoulder height.

3. Contact is most effective when the opponent's weight is on his outside leg.

4. Concentration should be centered on securing possession of the ball.

Feinting

The purpose of feinting is to elude, fake out, or outmaneuver an opponent. It may be executed with or without possession of the ball, and as an offensive or defensive weapon. When used defensively, a feint attempts to prevent or discourage the opponent from making his intended move. If attempted offensively, it is employed to outmaneuver an opponent who is defending against the dribble, the pass or the shot at the goal. The player doing the feinting has a distinct advantage because he alone knows what his ultimate move will be; his opponent can only guess.

In general, a feint consists of making a false move with the body, a part of the body, or the ball in one direction then making the real move in the desired direction. It can also be used by varying the speed with which a move is made. Some examples of feints are: inclining the body in one direction and then moving in the opposite one; rushing at an opponent who is in possession of the ball then quickly stopping or retreating; kicking at the ball, but intentionally missing it so it will roll by for a teammate to play; and faking a kick with one foot, then kicking with the other. For most feints, the center of the weight of the body must be balanced well over the legs, and the body must be kept as low as possible.

Feinting while in possession of the ball includes both moving the body and maintaining control of the ball. Many variations of the feint may be performed.

1. The trunk can be moved in one direction while the ball is dragged or cut with the feet in the opposite direction.

2. The foot can be dragged over the ball as if a dribble is to be started in a particular direction. The same foot is repositioned and the dribble is begun with the opposite foot in another direction.

3. When the potential tackler is in front of the dribbler, the dribbler can place his foot on the ball, draw the ball back to him, turn his body to protect the ball, and move off in a different direction.

4. When the dribbler is being hard pressed by an opponent who is rapidly drawing up to his side, he

can place his foot on the ball, stop his forward movement completely, and let the opponent speed by him.

5. The dribbler can push the ball around an opponent on one side and then run by him on the opposite side.

Passing

The moving of the ball by a player to a teammate is an essential feature of soccer. Each time this is done, a pass has been made; therefore, every kick except a penalty kick and a shot at the goal, is a pass. Accuracy, speed, and timing are the most important features of a good pass. The ball must be directed to the man in the open so that he can play it effectively, or into an open area so a teammate can move in for the play. Passes may vary in distance from a short flick pass, executed with the outside of the foot, to a long pass across the width or down the length of the field.

Throw-In

The throw-in may be executed from a standing position or from a run, but in either case the ball must be thrown with an overhead motion. The ball is held with the hands gripping it from the side to the back and with the thumbs and index fingers behind the ball. A cup-like pocket in which the ball rests is thereby formed. The throw-in must be one continuous motion and is exectued as follows:

1. The feet are usually placed in a stride stance; however, a square stance may be used.

2. The backswing of the arms is made by moving them back over and behind the head. The elbows are flexed, the trunk is bent backward over the rear leg, and the knees are slightly bent.

3. The forward motion is a coordinated and powerful movement of the arms and trunk, accompanied by the extension of the knees and the shifting of the weight in the direction of the throw.

4. The ball is propelled from the hands with a final flip of the wrist.

5. Both feet must maintain contact with the ground until the ball has been thrown.

BASIC STRATEGY

Strategy consists of the best use of soccer skills in developing coordinated defensive and offensive patterns. Each player must have a specific function to perform, a certain area to cover, and at the same time

FIGURE 14-14.   The throw-in.

he must know what each of his ten teammates is doing and where each is located on the field. The ability to use strategy depends upon the technical skill of the players, their knowledge of the game, the weather conditions, and the size and condition of the field. Strategy must always be limited by the level of skill and knowledge possessed by individual players.

Position Play

Center Forward.   The center forward is an important attack player on the team, and, unless he is used for some other specific purpose, he will spearhead most of the offensive drives. He rarely moves beyond the offensive half of the field. He must be adept at shooting, passing, eluding, feinting, controlling, and heading into the goal, and he must know when and where to use these skills. He must be able to move crossfield to his left or right as well as forward and backward. Under certain conditions, he will switch positions with another forward and pull out of the center area in the scoring territory in order to make an opening for a teammate to shoot for the goal.

When the ball is in the scoring area, he must continually attempt to free himself for a pass and a possible shot at the goal.

Inside Forwards. Since the inside forwards have both offensive and defensive responsibilities in most play patterns, they need to be well conditioned. They must attempt to feed the ball to the center and outside forwards, and will play somewhat behind them on offense. They will usually take the wing halfbacks in a man-to-man defensive situation. Like the center forward, they must be able to perform all the necessary skills well, especially passing, kicking, dribbling, trapping, and controlling the ball.

Outside Forwards. The outside forwards work with the center forward to spearhead the attack, and will have limited defensive responsibilities. In general their position is to the outside of the field on or very near the touch lines. If the ball is on the opposite side of the field, however, the outside forward on that side plays farther away from the touch line and on the same line as the center forward. They will often switch with the inside forwards or with the wing halfbacks. They must bear much of the responsibility for bringing the ball downfield into the scoring area and centering it to the center forward for a scoring kick, or passing it crossfield to a teammate. In order to perform these functions effectively, they must be fast, have good control of the ball, be adept at the dribble and the long pass, and be able to beat a fullback.

Halfbacks. The two wing halfbacks have both offensive and defensive responsibilities, but in most plays, the center half is mostly defensive unless he interchanges with another halfback or forward. The halfbacks must be well conditioned, and highly skilled in the ability to control the ball. When man-to-man type of defense is used, the wing halfbacks take the inside forwards, and the center half is responsible for the center forward. The positions of these three men depend upon the location of the ball as well as the location of the men for whom they are responsible. When the offensive opponent has possession of the ball on the right side of the field near the center line, the left halfback plays up toward his man and the ball, the center marks his forward, and the right halfback is toward the center and near the front of the penalty area. They should always be alert to intercept crossfield passes and tackle offensive men in order to get control of the ball so that it can be passed out to their wings to start a counterattack. The wing halfbacks must be able to interchange and switch positions on both offense and defense. The center half should protect the center of the field in

the scoring area, and should not be drawn out of this position unless he is sure that a teammate is moving in to switch with him. The wing halfbacks should take most of the throw-ins.

Fullbacks. The two fullbacks are primarily defensive men. They must be able to maintain a position between the opponent in possession of the ball and the goal, without backing into their goalkeeper and obstructing his vision. Therefore, they must mark their man, and as soon as he moves into the danger area with the ball, he must be tackled or driven out to the sideline. The intent of the tackle is to get possession of the ball and to pass it out to a halfback or wing forward in order to start an offensive play. However, under no circumstance should the pass out of the defensive zone be made across and in front of the goal.

The two fullbacks must work in coordination with each other as well as with their other teammates and especially with the center halfback. When one is moving out for the tackle, the other should give support by falling back toward the goal and to the center of the field in order to be in a better position to intercept a shot or to intercept the player if the latter has eluded the other fullback. They should also be ready to interchange with the center halfback if the attacking team switches offensive positions, One of them will take most the goal kicks.

Goalkeeper. The basic responsibility of the goalkeeper is to keep the ball from going through the goal. He also directs the defense. He is permitted to use his hands and arms as long as he is in the penalty area to help prevent goals. In performing this function, he may hurry the offensive player so that his shot goes wild or is blocked, he may deflect the ball to the side or over the crossbar, or he may gain possession of the ball and clear it out to his forwards. After preventing the score, his next most important job is to get possession of the ball and clear it out of the scoring area to the best advantage of his team. He can accomplish this by either a throw or a kick, both of which should be executed accurately and quickly. In general, the goalkeeper should clear the ball out toward the touch lines as far downfield as possible so that it can be played by a teammate, usually a wing forward.

The goalkeeper must be a master of many skills. He must be able to catch, throw, kick, jump, dive, and punch; maintain the proper field position in and out of the goal; and field all types of balls from the rolling to the high flying, and from the slow lob to the powerful line drive.

The goalkeeper must keep his body between the

ball and the goal on all shots from all positions on the field. If this is not possible, he must then extend himself as far as possible with both arms outstretched. If he still fails to each the ball, he must stretch out with the stronger arm. As a final desperate move, if he still cannot reach the ball, he must dive for the ball with his arms fully extended. Even then he may be forced to punch the ball in order to prevent a score. He should angle the dive away from the goal so that if he contacts the ball, it will be propelled outward and not driven in for a possible score.

The goalkeeper must maintain a balnced stance when the ball is within the danger zone. The feet should be spread about a shoulder width apart, the knees flexed, and the weight well forward on the balls of the feet. The arms should be out at the sides, with the foreharms held out and up. The trunk should lean slightly forward, the head should be up, and the eyes should be focused on the ball. The goalkeeper should take this position approximately a foot in front of the goal line.

The goalkeeper must be able to field the ball well. When he can catch the ball with his hands, he should bring it quickly in to the abdomen and chest area and hold it in a cradle-like grip with his arms until he can start the clearing move. The goalkeeper must always keep his legs or body between the ball and the goal. If the ball comes in low, he must kneel down on one or both knees; if its flight is higher, he must jump up to get the upper part of his body behind it. If he has dived and gained possession of the ball, he must quickly regain his feet to clear it as fast as possible.

After gaining possession, the goalkeeper must clear the ball by throwing or kicking it. He can execute the throw with an overhand baseball motion or with an underhand movement. If the ball is to travel some distance in the air, he should use the baseball throw. If a rolling ball is desired, he can use the underhand movement. The punt is generally used if a kick is thought to be best. Regardless of the tactic chosen, accuracy is more important than distance, and the speed with which the ball is cleared is very essential if the opponent's defense is to be caught off balance.

The goalkeeper may be forced to go out of the immediate goal area to make a play. If one of opponent's offensive players breaks through the defense and dribbles unchallenged toward the goal, the goalkeeper has no choice but to move out to play him. In doing this, he must cover the short side of the triangle if the opponent is coming in from the side. If the oppponent is moving in toward the middle of the goal, the goalkeeper must move out quickly to meet him when the dribbler is at the penalty kick arc, or 18 to 20 yards away. When he is within 6 to 8 yards from the dribbler, the goalkeeper should attempt a tackle and try to gain possession of the ball or divert the dribble or shot. As the goalkeeper moves out toward the attacker, he narrows the distance, on each side of him, that he must cover to intercept a shot at the goal. In some cass, this advantage may be counterbalanced by the speed of the shot at the goal.

The goalkeeper must also know the angles at which the ball has the most space to enter the goal. The widest angle is in front of the center of the goal. If the ball comes from either side, the angle within which the ball must travel to enter the goal decreases. From a percentage point of view, the shots from the widest angles are more likely to be good and are more difficult to defend against. In most cases, the goalkeeper should overplay a bit to the short side of the triangle, about a yard out in front of the goal line. Therefore, he should stand where the angle formed by the ball and the two goal posts bisects.

Offensive Team Strategy

Long Passing Game.   The basis for an attack is usually the long pass, the short pass, or a combination of the two. Some teams like to use the *long pass-*

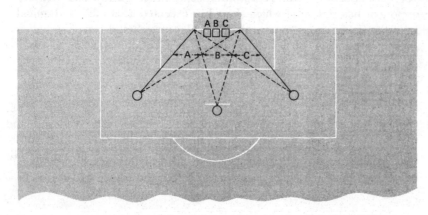

FIGURE 14-15.   Degree of angle shots. Angle B provides the widest and most favorable angle from which to make the shot at the goal. The goalkeeper's position for each angle is indicated by the letters A, B, and C which correspond to the angles that they mark.

ing game because it gets the ball downfield more quickly than the short passing game. When this offensive strategy is employed, the ball is moved out to one of the wings and then quickly on a long pass to the center forward who is cutting toward the touch line. The center forward can then make a crossfield pass from which a shot at the goal may be executed. This quick-striking system keeps pressure on the defense and compels several players to play defense at all times.

Short Passing Game. The short passing game depends more upon individual skill to move the ball into scoring territory and, to set up a shot at the goal. This offensive strategy depends a great deal upon players working together as a unit within the team structure. The supporting pattern and the crossfield pass are employed to work the ball downfield. The supporting players may be made up of the right outer, the right inner and wing halfback, or other combination.

Switching Positions. To confuse the opposing team's man-to-man defense, switching positions can be used as an offensive strategy when players are in the attack area. The wings may switch positions with the center forward as well as with the halfbacks, and the inside forwards may exchange positions with the center forward. Other switches can be made. If the opposing team is playing man-to-man defense, when the offensive men make an exchange of field positions the defensive men covering them will have to switch also or check their assigned men to each other. During the exchange by the defense, the opposing team may have an opportunity to move the ball in for shot.

Pulling Out and Filling. It is sound offensive strategy for an offensive player to pull out of a position when he is in the danger area in order to move his defensive man out with him, and, at the same time, for a teammate to run into the vacant position to receive a pass and to set up a possible scoring shot at the goal. This action can be coordinated between the center and inside forwards by the center moving quickly out to the side, and, as the ball is passed into the area he vacates, the inside forward moving in for the shot.

Team Formations. There are several basic formations into which the players may be arranged for both offensive and defensive purposes. Three of these are the 5-2-3, the 4-2-4 and the 4-3-3. None of these are rigid but are fluid and flexible.

In the *5-2-3 formation*, used by many teams, the inside forward must play both offense and defense, the wing halfbacks must give support to the forwards

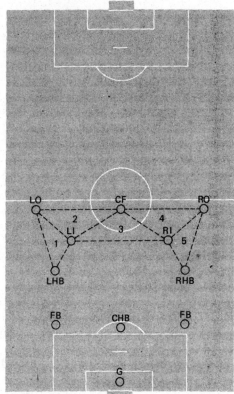

KEY FOR ALL DIAGRAMS

○	–	OFFENSIVE PLAYERS
□	–	DEFENSIVE PLAYERS
●	–	POSITION OF BALL
---	–	PATH OF BALL
——	–	DIRECTION OF PLAYER'S MOVEMENT

CF	–	CENTER FORWARD
LI	–	LEFT INSIDE FORWARD (OR LW LEFT WING)
RI	–	RIGHT INSIDE FORWARD (OR RW RIGHT WING)
LD	–	LEFT OUTSIDE FORWARD
RO	–	RIGHT OUTSIDE FORWARD
LHB	–	LEFT HALFBACK
RHB	–	RIGHT HALFBACK
CHB	–	CENTER HALFBACK
LFB	–	LEFT FULLBACK
RFB	–	RIGHT FULLBACK
G	–	GOALKEEPER

FIGURE 14-16. Triangle pattern. Five triangle patterns are shown in the above W formation.

and control the play in the middle of the field, and the fullbacks and center halfback are primarily defensive. The center halfback must protect the center area in front of the goal and should not be drawn out of this position. When the ball is on one side of the field, the fullback and halfback playing on the the opposite side of the field should drop back and move in toward the center so that they may be in a position to help out on defense. This is one of the simplest patterns, and is based on the use of triangular patterns. Regardless of the position of the

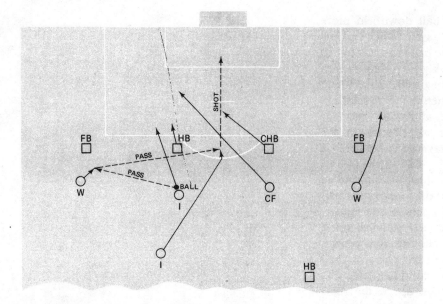

FIGURE 14-17. Offensive pulling and filling. The center forward cuts through the middle. The lead inner forward passes to the wing. The back inner moves up to receive the pass from the wing for the shot.

ball, there is always the support of three players who can pass the ball to each other, for example the wing, inner, and center forward or the halfback, wing, and inner.

In the *4-2-4 formation,* the normal or traditional positions of some of the players are changed. The center forward, wing forwards, and one inner form an offensive line of four men who become the spearhead for the attack and have, by and large, only offensive responsibilities. The purpose of this fourman front line is to put an extra offensive man up front so that it is possible to obtain a two-on-one situation against a basic three-man back-line defense. As a defensive pattern, it places an extra man in back to pick off passes, to recover loose balls, and to cover any opponent who eludes his defensive man. The two middle men are the connecting link between the defense and offense and initiate the attack by getting the ball up to the front line. When on defense they should mark and delay the offense until a forward comes back to help. When man-to-man defense is played, the fullbacks take the outside forwards, and the two middle men in the four-man back line take whichever men lead the attack.

The *4-3-3 formation* arrangement of players places the outside forwards, one inside forward, and the center forward in the forward line; the wing halfbacks and an inner forward in the middle area; and the center halfback and two fullbacks in the back defensive line. In this formation, the wing halfbacks and inner forward must perform offensive and defensive duties. When their team moves to the attack, they give support to the front-line attack men. The inner forward moves up into the front line either

to the center or to the sides on offense, and drops back to his central position on defense. The wing halfbacks cover the center as well as the sides and move to play any ball that is nearer them than to any other teammate. The wing forward will remain near the side lines. The center halfback is responsible for

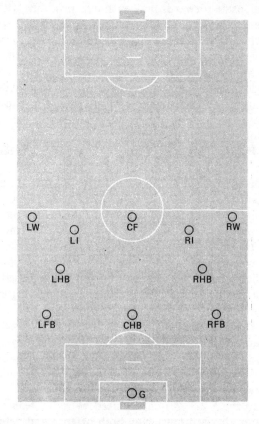

FIGURE 14-18. 5-2-3 or W formation.

defending the area directly in front of the goal.

Strategy for the *kickoff* is varied. It is designed to take advantage of the defensive alignment of the opposing team or the strength of the kicking team. The ball may be kicked short to an inside forward, who will kick it back to a wing halfback, who will then make a long pass to one of the attack men. This move provides time for the forwards to get downfield into good scoring positions. However, the ball may be passed in a shallow kickoff to a wing forward, who is moving into the opening between the halfbacks and forwards, or it may be passed in a deep kickoff to a wing forward if the defensive halfbacks are playing up near their forwards.

Defensive Team Strategy

Modern soccer defensive strategy includes man-to-man defense, zone defense, and combintaion patterns. Zone defense seems to provide the best general coverage of all spaces in the scoring area. Man-to-man defense gives coverage anywhere on the field and is particularly suitable for close coverage at all times and places. Combination zone and man-to-man, especially where a team can move from one to the other at any time, can cause a great deal of confu-

sion to the opposition's offense, and can be upsetting to individual players.

The effectiveness of defensive team strategy depends upon the knowledge and skill of the individuals who make up the team; therefore, basic defensive skills should be learned by each player. Most of these skills have been presented under the discussion of player positions; however, attention should be given to several necessary and basic defensive moves.

Defensive Position.   In most situations in which an offensive player has the ball within his scoring area, the defensive man must maintain a position between the man he is guarding and the center of the goal. His purpose is to block the path of the ball and/or the man who is in control of the ball, to intercept and gain possession of the ball, and to clear it out to his wing forward. However, when the ball is located on the opposite side of the field, the defensive player must drop back toward his goal and toward the ball so he will be in a position to help his teammates if the offensive man gets by them or passes the ball past them. In this situation the defensive man must at all times know the position of the man assigned to him.

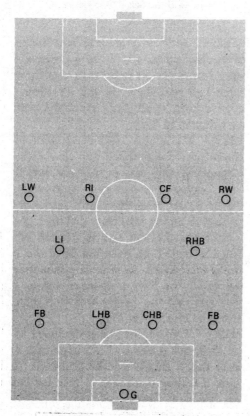

FIGURE 14-19.   4-2-4 formation.

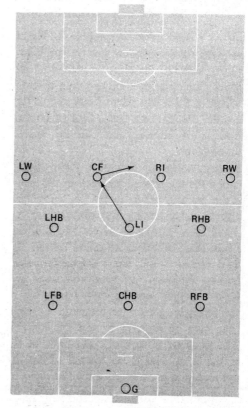

FIGURE 14-20.   4-3-3 formation.

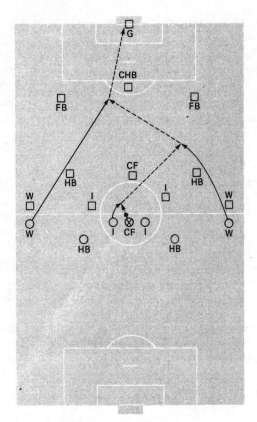

FIGURE 14-21.   Shallow kick-off.

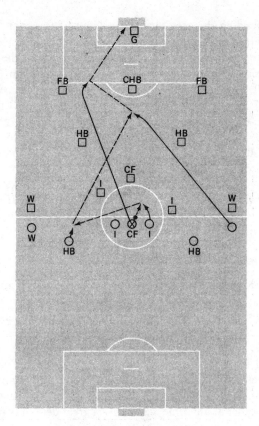

FIGURE 14-22.   Deep kick-off.

Marking.   Marking is a defensive tactic in which a defensive player will watch and stay with his assigned opponent, who may or may not have the ball, while the opponent is not in a dangerous scoring position. It is the defensive man's responsibility to attempt to prevent his man from making a good pass if the latter has the ball and to prevent him from receiving the ball if he does not have the ball. In performing these tasks, the defensive man may guard his man closely or from a distance, but as the opponent moves into the danger area with the ball the defensive man must cover him.

Tackling.   Tackling has been discussed as an individual skill, but it has such an important function in defense that it should also be explained from this viewpoint. Tackling is a move to take the ball away from an opponent who is dribbling or passing. The easiest way to get the ball is by intercepting a pass. The player can do this by timing the move into the intended path of the ball just as the ball leaves the opponent's foot or another part of his body. The next most opportune moment to make the tackle is just as the opponent receives the ball on a pass, since at that time the opponent is usually concentrating on gaining control of the ball. After the tackle is made, the

defensive man must attempt to gain control of the ball and pass it out of the danger area to an open teammate so that a counterattack can be initiated. All balls should be cleared toward the touch lines and away from the area in front of the goal.

Man-to-Man Defense.   Each defensive man is assigned an opponent for whom he is responsible. The fullbacks are usually assigned the wing forwards, the wing halfbacks take the inside forwards, and the center halfback covers the center forward or his counterpart if the offensive formation presents a four-man attack line. The inside forwards cover the wing halfbacks in most situations. The center halfback should keep his position in the middle area of the field directly in front of the goal and should seldom let himself be drawn out of this position even though the man to whom he is assigned pulls out. If his assigned man moves out, the center halfback should change positions with a teammate whose assigned man moves in to fill.

The center halfback may be used in defense in other ways than that described above. He may play the center forward in a close man-to-man position at all times or he may cover the middle zone and mark the center forward. In this case he is called a sweeper.

In general, when the ball is in the center area of the field, the members of the team in possession should be covered and tackled if possible, but as the offense moves the ball into the danger area, the man with the ball must be charged and tackled. All other defensive men should move a bit toward the ball and then back toward the goal in order to congest the shooting lanes and attempt to intercept the ball when it is passed. There should always be a defensive player ready to back up his teammate in case the attack man eludes him. In this case there must be a defensive switch. The defensive player whose man has eluded him must cover his teammate's assigned man as quickly as possible. The two defensive players will not exchange men again until it is safe to do so. The center halfback should not be forced into making this switch as it could leave the middle open.

Zone Defense.   In zone defense each defensive player is assigned a certain area which he must protect when an opponent moves into it. The opponent becomes important only when he has the ball or when a pass to him is imminent. This type of defense

and should not leave his position until he can judge the flight and placement of the ball. If the kick is short, he must move forward. If the ball is kicked in front of the goal and within the penalty area where he can reach it before an opponent does, the goalkeeper must rush out and intercept it or punch it to the side. Each of the fullbacks should take his position against the goal upright on his side. The center halfback should cover the center forward, and the wing halfback should cover the inside forward. The defensive inside forwards should guard the offensive halfbacks, and one of the wing forwards should fall back to guard the offensive outside forward who is not taking the kick.

Corner Kick Offense.   Offense for the corner kick can be varied in many ways. The most common strategy is to loop the ball over the reach of all players to a point near the penalty kick mark where an offensive player attempts to head it into the goal. The ball may also be kicked fast and low to the right inside who lets it pass him so the cutting left inside can take the shot (see Figure 14-25). Another option

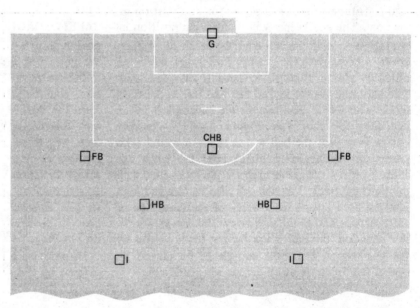

FIGURE 14-23.   Zone defense; alignment.

makes switching or interchanging unnecessary and is very effective if employed in combination with man-to-man defense.

Offensive and Defensive Formations for Special Situations

Corner Kick Defense.   To defend against the corner kick, the goalkeeper should take a position just in front of the goal line and a few feet inside the goal post farthest from the kicker. He should be facing the kicker, should have an unobstructed view of him,

is to pass the ball to the inside forward, who passes out to the left halfback after the latter has shaken off his defensive man by interchanging with the right halfback. The ball can also be directed high into the area just to the outside of the front line of the goal area and to the side away from the kicker. In this situation, the ball is too far out to be caught by the goalkeeper, but close enough to be played by one of the forwards or by the far wing halfback.

Penalty Kick Offensive and Defensive Formation.   The goalkeeper must take a position in the center of the goal with his feet on the goal line. He must be in a balanced position, ready to move in any direction. He should hold his arms out from his sides to narrow the area of the kicker's vision. It is not possible for the goalkeeper to actually cover the goal area from the uprights to an imaginary line parallel to them and four to five feet in toward the center; therefore, he must make every effort to cause the kicker to be inaccurate. (See Figure 14-27 for the player arragement for both the offense and defense during a penalty kick.)

Free Kick. When either the direct or indirect kick is taken within the danger area, the offensive strategy selected will depend upon the defensive tactics and the distance of the kick from the goal. The defensive team attempts to block out as much of the goal as possible and the offensive team tries to open up a wide angle for the shot.

If the kick is taken within the area between the outer boundary of the penalty zone and four to six yards beyond it, the defense will usually place three or more men between the kicker and one side of the goal to form a wall of protection for that portion of the goal. The goalkeeper will then take a position in the center or at the point of the best angle of that portion of the goal not covered by his teammates who form the wall. This arrangement decreases the goal area that the goalkeeper must cover. The defensive men, who form the protecting wall, should take their position as close to the ball as possible so that only a kick that produces a lob ball flight could possibly propel the ball over their heads and into the goal. In this situation the defensive wing forwards are brought back to cover the offensive wings (see Figure 14-28.)

In order to eliminate the advantage given to the defense by the wall, the offense can make the kick by involving two men in the play. The first kicker should pass the ball to his teammate who moves quickly over to a point that will given him a wider angle of possibility for a shot at the goal. (The lineup of players for this strategy is shown in Figure 14-29.)

When the offense makes the move described above, the three-man wall should move as a unit in front of the second kicker to block his shot at the goal.

When an *indirect kick* is given to the offense within the penalty area, the defense should move enough defense men into the goal to make a solid wall across its entire length (see Figure 14-30).

Free kicks taken farther away than 22 yards from the goal necessitate the use of offensive and defensive strategies different from that used for closer kicks. The same two-man pass and kick may be executed as for the near kick, but it is often expedient to make a second pass to the center or inside forwards who have cut quickly around behind the wall. If a team has tall forwards, it may be advantageous to lob the ball to them. During the long free kick, the ball may also be passed to an inside forward who is cutting into an open space.

SAFETY PRACTICES

If soccer is played correctly on a well-graded and well-maintained surface, it is a relatively safe sport. Ignorance of the rules, lack of skill, and the desire to win often lead to action that may cause accidents and consequent injuries.

WEIGHT TRAINING

A combination of the weight-training exercises performed by track men and those perfomed by basketball players should be of value to soccer players. A soccer player needs the agility, the strength, and the ability to change direction of the basketball player, and the endurance for running of

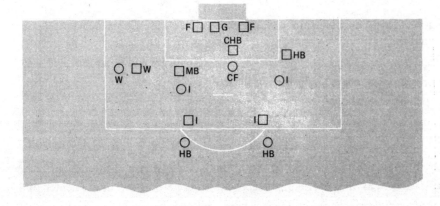

FIGURE 14-24.   Corner kick defense.

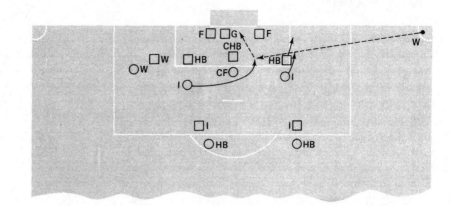

FIGURE 14-25. Corner kick to inside forward. The kick is made low and hard to inside forward who permits ball to pass him so it can be played by the moving left inside.

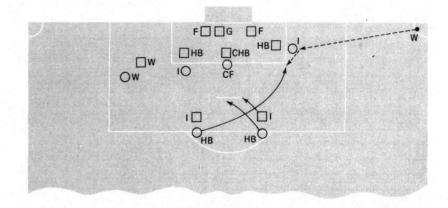

FIGURE 14-26. Corner kick to half-back.

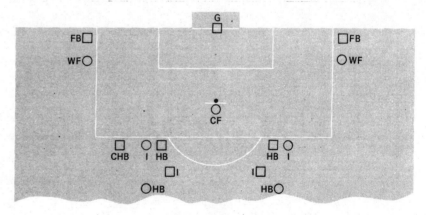

FIGURE 14-27. Penalty kick formation.

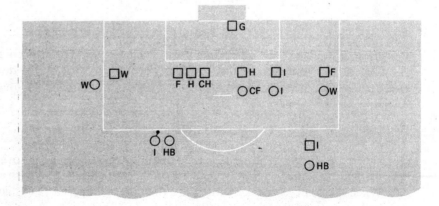

FIGURE 14-28. Defense against a short free kick. Three-man wall made up of the fullback, halfback, and center halfback protect a half of the goal. This placement leaves the goalkeeper only one half of the goal to defend against the free kick.

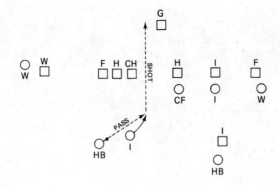

FIGURE 14-29. Offensive strategy on the short free kick. The offensive halfback taking the free kick pushes the ball far enough into the center of the field to bypass the three-man wall and to provide an open shot at the goal. the inner forward takes the shot.

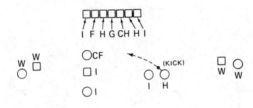

FIGURE 14-30. Defense against the indirect free kick in penalty area. Seven defensive men make a wall across the goal. The wing forwards come back to cover the opposing wings and one inside forward covers the middle area and waits for rebounds.

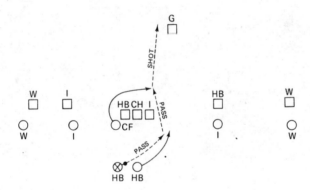

FIGURE 14-31. Center forward around wall offensive strategy. The center forward cuts around the wall to take a pass from the halfback.

the distance runner. The clean and press, squat, pullover, reverse arm curl, regular arm curl, bench press, trunk raise, heel lift, leg lift, and angle rotation could be incorporated into a weight-training program to develop the qualities mentioned above. This program is best employed during the off-season period.

EXERCISE   Definitions and List of Terms

1. When one defensive player moves behind his teammate, who is covering the man with the ball, he is said to be _____ .
2. When the goalkeeper takes more steps than the rules permit, he is guilty of _____ the ball.

3. A player is _____ his opponent when he makes contact shoulder-to-shoulder with him.
4. _____ is the action of throwing, kicking, or heading the ball outward and away from the goal.
5. A _____ is awarded to the offensive team when the defense causes the ball to go out of bounds over the goal line and a score does not occur.
6. The _____ is the part of the goal that is attached to the top of each of the goal posts and extends between them.
7. When a member of a team kicks the ball from one side of the field across to the other side it is called a _____ .
8. A _____ is a defensive technique used by a team during a free kick in which three or more men are placed side by side between the kicker and a part of the goal.
9. A _____ is a free kick from which a goal may be scored directly.
10. A _____ is a soccer skill in which a player kicks the ball back and forth between his feet as he moves down or across the field.
11. A _____ is used to start the game after a temporary suspension of play.
12. When a score results from regular play it is called a _____ .
13. _____ is a term used to describe the strategy in which one offensive player pulls out of a position and a teammate moves in after him.
14. A _____ is an infringement of the rules that results in a penalty of some kind.
15. _____ is a place-kick awarded to a team after a foul, or violation committed by an offensive player or by any player outside his team's penalty area.
16. The area from which the goal kick is taken is he _____ .
17. When a member of the offensive team causes the ball to go out of bounds over the goal line and no score results, the defense is awarded a _____ .
18. The lines at each end of the field which form the end boundary lines are the _____ .
19. When a player kicks the ball just as it raises from the ground it is a _____ .
20. An _____ is a kick in which a goal cannot be scored unless the ball is touched by another player in addition to the kicker.
21. The forwards that play next to the outside forwards are sometimes called the _____ .
22. _____ is a kind of strategy in which two or more offensive or defensive players will exchange positions or assigned men.
23. The _____ is an indirect free kick used to put the ball in play to start the game and in certain other situations.
24. The official who assists the referee when the ball is out of play is the _____ .
25. _____ is defensive strategy in which a defensive player watches his assigned man who is not at that moment in a position to shoot for a goal. The defensive player may play close to or some distance away from his assigned man.
26. The halfbacks are also known as _____ .
27. When a player who is not playing the ball runs between an opponent and the ball or positions his body so that it blocks his opponent's path he is _____ .
28. When a player is nearer the opponents' goal line than the ball is at the time the ball is being played by a teammate and there is only one opponent between him and the goal line he is _____ .
29. The penalty for a personal foul made by a defensive man in his own penalty area is a _____ .
30. The area from which the penalty kick is taken is the _____ .
31. Any infringement of the rules that is penalized by a direct free kick is a _____ .
32. Strategy in which a player of the offensive team moves out of his regular field position to permit a teammate to fill in is called _____ .
33. A player whose action on the field is dangerous and likely to cause injury to others is said to be guilty of _____ .
34. When the goalkeeper makes a stop of a shot at the goal he has made a _____ .
35. The forwards are also called _____ .

36. A center halfback who covers the central zone and marks the center forward on defense is called _____ .
37. Another term for interchanging is _____ .
38. _____ is a playing skill in which a player moves in and attempts to get the ball away from an oponent.
39. The side boundary lines of a soccer field are called the _____ .
40. When the ball accidentally makes contact with the hands or arms of a player other than the goalkeeper it is called _____ .
41. The outside forwards are often called the _____ .

1. Backing up
2. Carrying
3. Charging
4. Clearing
5. Corner kick
6. Crossbar
7. Cross kick
8. Defensive wall
9. Direct free kick
10. Dribble
11. Drop ball
12. Field goal
13. Filling
14. Foul
15. Free kick
16. Goal area
17. Goal kick
18. Goal lines
19. Half-volley kick
20. Indirect free kick
21. Inners
22. Interchanging
23. Kick-off
24. Linesman
25. Marking
26. Midfielders
27. Obstructing
28. Off side
29. Penalty kick
30. Penalty mark
31. Personal foul
32. Pulling out
33. Rough play
34. Save
35. Strikers
36. Sweeper
37. Switching
38. Tackling
39. Touch lines
40. Unintentional handling
41. Wings

QUESTIONS AND ANSWERS ON THE RULES

When a rule is identical for both men and women no sex designation will be noted. When a rule is different for the two sexes each will be identified by name and explained.

1. *Q.* How is a soccer game started?
   A. It is begun by a kickoff. The ball is placed in the center of the field by the referee. When he gives a signal, one of the players of the kicking team place-kicks the ball into the opponent's half of the field. The ball must travel at least the distance of its circumference.
2. *Q.* In case of an illegal or improper kickoff, what action is taken?
   A. *Men:* The ball is again placed at the center of the field and the kickoff is retaken by the same team that took the original kickoff. In case of willful encroachment over the 10-yard line or repeated improper kickoffs, the player involved is warned and if he again fails to perform a proper kickoff, he is ordered off the field.
   Women: An indirect free kick is awarded to the opponents at the center of the field.
3. *Q.* Are restrictions placed upon players at the time of the kickoff?
   A. *Men:* Yes. All players of both teams must be in their own half of the field, and no player of the opposing team may be within ten yards of the ball until it is kicked.
   Women: Yes. Players of either team may be anywhere in their own half of the field, except that all defenders must be behind their restraining line and all attackers behind the centner line until the ball is kicked.
4. *Q.* How is the ball played after the kickoff?
   A. The player who kicked off may not play the ball again until it has been touched by another player. However, after another player has made contact with the ball, it

may be legally kicked or propelled in any direction and players may move freely to any part of the field.

5. *Q.* What parts of the body may be used to play the ball?

A. For all players except the goalkeeper, the ball may be played with any part of the body except the hands and the arms up to the shoulder joints. The goalkeeper may use his arms and hands to play the ball as long as he is in the penalty area. When he moves out of the penalty area, he may not play the ball with his hands or arms. Players may dribble, volley, trap, block, head, and pass the ball.

Women: For purposes of blocking, the arms may be folded across the chest but may not be raised from this position when playing the ball.

6. *Q.* How is play started after a goal has been scored and at the beginning of the second, third, fourth, and extra periods?

A. In each of the above situations play is initiated by a kickoff taken under the same conditions as at the start of the game. When a goal is scored, the team against which the score was made takes the kickoff. In the second, third, fourth, and extra periods, the opponent of the team that took the kickoff the previous period will take it.

7. *Q.* Is provision made for teams to change ends of the playing field?

A. Yes, teams will change ends of the field at the start of each period, including any overtime period.

8. *Q.* At the start of a game, what is the manner of determining which team will kick off and which goal they will defend?

A. This will be determined by a toss of a coin. The team that wins the toss will have its choice.

9. *Q.* How is a score made and what is its value?

A. A score may be made by either a field goal or a penalty kick. A field goal results when the ball is legally propelled through the goal between the uprights and beneath the crossbar. The ball must be completely across the goal line to become a score. The goalkeeper may be behind the goal line and catch the ball in front of it without a score resulting. If the goalkeeper moves the ball so that it has completely crossed the goal line, a score results. It is the ball's position that determines if a goal is scored. A penalty kick is good when the ball goes into the goal directly from the kick or as a result of deflection by another player. Each score counts one point.

10. *Q.* What is the length of a game?

A. *Men:* The National Collegiate Athletic Association rules stipulate two, 45 minute periods. These rules also provide for two extra periods of five minutes each in case of a tie. Provisions are made for the shortening of the time for a high school game.
Women: The rules stipulate four, ten minute quarters, but time may be decreased as much as four minutes per quarter by mutual consent. In case of a tie score at the end of a game, two extra periods of three minutes each are played. Three minutes are allowed between the end of the game and the first overtime, and two minutes between the first and second overtime. If no score is made during the overtime periods the tie stands.

11. *Q.* How much time is permitted between periods

A. *Men:* The halftime interval must not exceed ten minutes.
Women: The are two minute intervals between the first and second, and third and fourth quarters, and a ten minute period a half time.

12. *Q.* How is time determined?

A. An official timer operates a clock that registers playing time. During the last three minues of the third and fourth quarters and throughout the duration of all overtime periods, the clock is stopped on all dead balls and started when the ball is put into play. The clock is always stopped when a goal is scored and is not restarted until the kickoff.

13. *Q.* What is the penalty for infringements of the rules?
    A. There are a variety of penalties that are enforced as a result of a player infringing the rules. Depending upon the nature, the severity, and the location of the violation of the rule, the following penalties may be enforced: (1) direct free kick, (2) indirect free kick, (3) penalty kick, (4) warning only, (5) expulsion from the game, and (6) drop ball.
14. *Q.* What is a direct free kick?
    A. It is a place-kick executed by a player of the team against which the infringement was made. A goal may be scored directly from this kick.
15. *Q.* What offenses are penalized by a direct free kick?
    A. Practically all fouls of a serious nature are penalized by a direct free kick, for example, intentionally handling the ball, holding, pushing, striking, jumping at an opponent, kicking, tripping, kneeing, charging dangerously, and charging the goalkeeper.
16. *Q.* What are the conditions under which a direct free kick is executed?
    A. It is taken from the spot where the foul was made by a player of the team against which the foul was made. The ball may be kicked in any direction. No opposing player may be closer than ten yards (five yards for women) to the ball at the time of the kick, unless he is standing on his own goal line between the goal posts. Any member of the team fouled against may execute the kick. The kick cannot be made until the referee gives a signal. The ball is not in play until it has traveled the distance of its circumference, and it may not be played by the kicker a second time until it has been touched by another player.
17. *Q.* What is an indirect free kick?
    A. It is a place-kick, but, unlike the direct free kick, no goal can be scored directly from it. In order for a goal to be scored, the ball must be touched by a player other than the kicker before it passes through the goal.
18. *Q.* What offenses are penalized by an indirect free kick?
    A. The most common offenses penalized by an indirect free kick are being off side; interfering with the goalkeeper while he is clearing the ball; obstructing illegally; leaving the field of play during the game without consent of the official; a player playing the ball a second time before it is played by another player after a kickoff, throw-in, free kick, corner kick, and goal kick; the goalkeeper's carrying the ball; the goalkeeper delaying in getting rid of the ball; substituting illegally; and coaching from the side lines. Women's rule includes all those listed plus infringement of the rules governing goalkeeper privileges and defense kick.
19. *Q.* How is the indirect free kick executed?
    A. Under the same conditions as the direct free kick.
20. *Q.* What procedure is required when a free kick is awarded to the defense in the penalty area?
    A. All opposing players must be outside the penalty area and ten yards award from the ball. The player of the defensive team taking the kick must propel the ball beyond the penalty area.
21. *Q.* What is a penalty kick?
    A. It is a direct kick taken from the penalty kick mark, which is twelve yards directly in front of the goal. Only the goalkeeper may defend against this kick, and a goal may be scored directly from it.
22. *Q.* What offenses are penalized by a penalty kick?
    A. *Men:* If a defensive player is in his own penalty area when he commits any of the offenses for which normally a direct free kick is given, the penalty is a penalty kick taken by one of the opposing players. These include holding, jumping into, striking, kicking, pushing, tripping, high kicking, unnecessary roughness and intentional handling the ball.

Women: They include: more than two time outs, illegal substitution, and failure to notify the official when substituting the goalkeeper, as well as those listed above for men.

23. *Q.* How is a penalty kick taken?

    A. The ball may be placed at any point on the penalty kick mark. All players except the goalkeeper and the kicker must be outside the penalty area but in the field of play and at least ten yards (five yards for women) away from the ball. Other conditions required by this situation are as follows:

    (1) The goalkeeper must stand, without moving his fect, on his own goal line between the goal posts until the ball has been kicked.

    (2) The player taking the kick must kick the ball forward at least the distance of its circumference and may not play it a second time until it has been touched by another player.

    (3) If the ball rebounds from the goal posts, crossbar, or the goalkeeper, it is in play.

24. *Q.* What are the penalties for an infringement of the penalty kick rule?

    A. If a member of the defending team infringes the rules and a goal has not resulted, the kick will be retaken. If a goal is made, no penalty is enforced. If a member of the attacking team, other than the kicker, infringes the rules, the kick will be retaken if a goal has resulted. If the player taking the kick commits a rule violation, the opposing team is awarded an indirect free kick from the spot of the foul.

25. *Q.* When is a player expelled from the game?

    A. *Men:* When, in the judgment of the referee, a player is engaging in dangerous play, he may be expelled from the game. The referee may or may not warn the player. A player may also be ordered off the field if he is guilty of using foul and abusive language, or other unsportsmanship-like conduct.

    Women: Women's rules include those listed for men, and in addition, a player may be expelled from the game for intentionally charging the goalkeeper.

26. *Q.* In what manner may the goalkeeper play the ball?

    A. The goalkeeper may use his hands and arms as well as all other parts of the body to play the ball, as long as he is within the penalty area. However, he may not carry the ball more than four steps without bouncing it, and he may bounce if four times. He must not delay in getting rid of the ball, and he may not be interfered with while he has possession of it.

27. *Q.* How is the ball put back into play after going out-of-bounds over the touch line (sideline for women)?

    A. *Men:* If a ball passes completely over a touch line either on the gound or in the air, it is thrown in at the point of exit by a player of the team opposite the one which caused it to go out. The player executing the throw-in must face the field of play with both his feet on the ground, on or outside the touch line, hold the ball with both hands, and make the throwing motion directly over the head. A goal may not be scored directly from a throw-in.

    Women: Sideline is used instead of touch line. The player taking the throw-in may use any type of one or two hand throwing motion, and may take two or more running steps preceeding the throw as long as both feet are on the ground and outside the sideline at the time the ball is released. All players must be five yards distance from the thrower.

28. *Q.* How is play begun after the ball goes out-of-bounds over the goal line without a score resulting?

    A. If a member of the defending team last touches the ball, it is put into play by a member of the attacking team with a corner kick. If a member of the attacking team last touches the ball, play is begun with a goal kick (defense kick for women) taken by a player of the defending team from the goal area.

29. *Q.* What procedure is used for a corner kick?

A. *Men:* The ball is placed within the quarter circle at the corner, and a place-kick is taken by an attacking player. No opposing player may be within ten yards of the kicker. The ball must be kicked the distance of its circumference, and it cannot be played a second time by the kicker until it has been touched by another player. A goal can be scored directly from a corner kick.

Women: The ball is kicked from the corner kick mark located on the goal line, five yards in from the near corner. The defending halfbacks, fullbacks and goalkeeper must stand on or behind the goal line until the ball is kicked. Attackers can be anywhere in the field of play but not closer to the kicker than five yards. A goal can be scored direct from this kick.

30. *Q.* What procedure is used for the goal kick?

A. *Men:* The ball is placed in the half of the goal area nearest to the point where it went out-of-bounds. From this point, it is kicked by a defensive player so that it is propelled beyond the penalty area. All opposing players must be outside the penalty area until the ball has crossed the boundary marking that area. The ball must be kicked from place and a goal cannot be scored directly from it.

Women: Defense kick is used instead of goal kick. The ball is placed on the nearest point of the quarter circle marking the penalty area. It must be kicked forward from place at least the distance of its circumference. No player may be within five yards of the kicker.

31. *Q.* When is a drop ball used?

A. When the officials stop the game for any reason except for a free kick, throw-in, goal kick, and the like, play is restarted by dropping the ball between two opposing players. It must touch the ground before it can be played. It is also used when two opposing players touch the ball simultaneously as it goes out-of-bounds over the touch line. In this case the ball is dropped five yards in from the touchline. A goal can be scored direct from a drop ball.

Women: In addition to the stipulations above, according to women's rules, if a drop ball is called within five yards of the goal it must be taken just outside the penalty area.

32. *Q.* What is the off-side rule?

A. *Men:* The off-side rule has several facets. In general, a player is off side if he is in the opponent's half of the field, has less than two opponents between him and their goal, and is ahead of the ball when it was last played by one of his teammates. A player cannot be off side when he is in his own half of the field; there are two opponents between him and their goal; he is behind the ball when it was last played by a teammate; he receives the ball from an opponent; and on a corner kick, goal kick, drop ball, and throw-in.

Women: The offside conditions are the same as stated above, but no penalty is enforced unless the offside player is playing the ball, interferring with another player, or gains an advantage from being offside.

33. *Q.* When may a substitution be made?

A. Substitution may be made on goal kicks, corner kicks, after a goal, between periods, before a penalty kick, when the ball is out of bound, during time-out, and when an injury occurs.

34. *Q.* What officials are necessary to officiate a soccer game?

A. Two referees, two linesmen, and a timekeeper.

35. *Q.* How many time-outs are permitted during a game?

A. Each team is permitted to take two time-outs. Each time-out is two minutes in length.

36. *Q.* How many players are on an official team?
    A. Eleven players make up an official team. There are five forwards (strikers); left and right wings, left and right inners, and center; three halfbacks (midfielders); left, center and right; two fullbacks, left and right, and; a goalkeeper.

BIBLIOGRAPHY

Bailey, Charles I., and Teller, Francis L. *Soccer.* Philadelphia: W. B. Saunders Company, 1970.

Batty, Eric. *Soccer Coaching the Modern Way.* London: Faber and Faber, 1969.

Csanadi, Arpad. *Soccer.* Budapest: Corvina Press, 1965.

Graves, J. *Soccer Techniques and Tactics.* New Rochelle, N.Y.: Wide World Book Center, 1964.

NAGWS. *Soccer, Speedball, Flag Football Guide.* Washington, D.C.: AAHPER, 1974-76.

National Collegiate Athletic Association. *Soccer Guide.* New York: National Collegiate Athletic Bureau, 1976.

United States Soccer Football Association. *Soccer Football Rules.* New York: Soccer Sports Supply Company.

Robert G. Davis, Ph.D.
Assistant Professor of Physical Education
Virginia Commonwealth University

15

TENNIS

DESCRIPTION OF THE ACTIVITY

Tennis is an extremely popular lifetime sport that can be played by children as young as eight or nine years of age and adults in their eighties. Since it is a game of skill, more so than strength and endurance, players are capable of continuing throughout life long after more vigorous sports must be dropped. Although tennis was once a game of the rich, it has now come out of the country clubs to be enjoyed by all. Much of tennis' recent popularity is owed to television and increased professionalism and big prize money. Its popularity, however, has resulted in a shortage of public courts and an increase in the cost of lessons.

Two players can play opposite each other in a game of singles or two individuals can team up to play opposite another team in doubles. The doubles court is nine feet wider than the singles court since the 4½-foot alleys are used. The server begins the game by standing behind the base line and to the right of the center service line; he puts the ball in play by tossing it into the air and striking it with the racket in such a way that it falls within the right service court of the opponent. The server has two chances to place the ball in this area. A ball that fails to land in the proper service court is classified as a *fault* and is not played. Two such failures would result in a *double fault* and a loss of point for the server. A served ball that strikes the net and falls into the proper service court is called a *let serve* and is played again; it is not a fault. The object of the game is for the players to continue returning the ball across the net after each serve until either the server or the receiver fails to make a legal return. After the first point has been won, the server moves to the left of the center service line, behind the base line, and makes a service to the left service court of the opponent. He alternates service courts accordingly after each point throughout the game. Upon completion of the first game, the receiver becomes the server as the players change sides of the court. Players continue to change sides after every odd game throughout the match, changing at the close of the first and every two subsequent games.

EQUIPMENT

Selection of equipment should be made carefully keeping in mind that "you get what you pay for."

Footwear

Selecting a tennis shoe should not be too difficult since it is almost identical to buying regular shoes. Improper fitting can cause blisters or twisted ankles, particularly, in the early stages of learning. Shoes come with a variety of soles, some of which are better for play on certain surfaces than others. The basketball shoe, however, is unacceptable for tennis and could cause harm to the player and the playing surface.

Racket

The variety of sizes, shapes, colors, weights, grips, and material can overwhelm even the experienced player. Cost is usually the best criteria for quality,

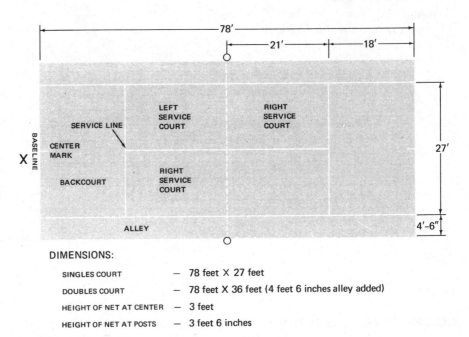

FIGURE 15-1. Diagram of tennis court. 4½-foot alleys not used in singles. X indicates position of the server at the start of the game. Server will attempt to place the ball into the opponent's right service court.

DIMENSIONS:

SINGLES COURT	— 78 feet X 27 feet
DOUBLES COURT	— 78 feet X 36 feet (4 feet 6 inches alley added)
HEIGHT OF NET AT CENTER	— 3 feet
HEIGHT OF NET AT POSTS	— 3 feet 6 inches

but quality is only one aspect of the selection process. For the beginning player, the wood racket is recommended since it tends to give more success on off center hits. The steel and fiberglass rackets, however, are growing in popularity. For very small children (earliest recommended starting age is seven years old) a paddle racket (see Chapter 12) should provide more immediate success. As better hand-eye coordination develops, the junior racket is recommended.

Rackets normally come in three weight categories: light, medium, and heavy with the distribution or balance of the weight differing in each racket. Although personal preference is the key, it is suggested that heavy rackets be avoided in favor of light or medium since the lighter rackets tend to cause less arm trouble. The trend is toward lightweight rackets for both men and women. Balance of the racket is another factor which is usually determined by feel, although it is recommended that the racket head feel slightly heavy when holding the racket at the extreme end of the handle.

Selection of the proper size racket handle is important in terms of playing quality and hand fatigue. Sizes usually vary from 4⅜ inches to around 4¾ inches. The best way to determine your grip size is to shake hands with the racket being sure the first and second fingers are spread apart and the thumb is wrapped around the handle. To check grip size, you should just be able to fit the index finger of your free hand between the third finger and meat part of the thumb on the hand holding the racket. If you are slightly between the standard grip sizes, it is suggested you select the smaller grip. The pro shop can, however, build up or shave down the grip size to suit your needs.

Strings for rackets also come in a variety of types and sizes, and can be strung to different tensions. The two most popular types are nylon and gut. Rackets which are pre-strung for sale in department stores are equipped with nylon which is at a tension or poundage of 45-50. Nylon is favored by the majority of players for its durability and cost. Gut, on the other hand, is used almost exclusively by tournament players since it has a better playing quality than nylon. Gut, however, is more expensive, does not last as long, and is ruined if exposed to wet conditions. No matter what type of string is selected, it must be placed in the racket head under tension. This tension is referred to as poundage and usually varies from 50-65 pounds of pressure. For the nonprofessional player, 50-55 pounds is recommended in order to avoid elbow and/or shoulder problems.

To protect your racket, a press for wood rackets and a cover for all rackets is suggested. The press which comes in both metal and wood is a must to keep wood rackets from losing their shape. Metal rackets do not require a press, but should, like the wood racket, be protected by some sort of water resistant cover.

Balls

A number of companies produce tennis balls which, although approved by the United States Tennis Association (USTA), have very different playing qualities. To determine the best ball for you, experimentation with a number of different brands is suggested. How long they last will depend upon how hard you hit them and the type of surface on which you play. New balls come packed under pressure in cans, and the distinct sound of escaping air pressure should be heard upon opening. If it is not heard, immediately test the new balls by squeezing them. Even with a very hard squeeze, you should not be able to indent a good ball more than a fraction of an inch. A ball incorrectly packaged or one that has sat around too long will flatten out considerably when squeezed. Balls begin to lose their playing quality as the pressure is released from inside the ball and the surface area of the ball is worn away by friction.

SKILLS AND TECHNIQUES

Grips

There are three basic grips in tennis: the eastern, the western, and the continental. Although the eastern forehand and backhand are the most popular, each one of the three basic styles will be dealt with briefly. All grips will be described for right-handed players.

Eastern grip. The eastern grip is recommended for all players, especially beginners. The grip is assumed by shaking hands with the racket while the racket head is perpendicular to the ground. The "V" made by the first finger and thumb should be on top of the racket handle. The first and second fingers of the hand should be spread apart so the racket is an extension of the arm. An incorrect grip with all the fingers together will cause a 90 degree angle between the arm and the racket, resulting in very poor shot production. See Figure 15-2a for the correct eastern forehand grip. The eastern backhand is assumed by turning the racket one-fourth of a turn so the knuckle of the first finger is on the top of the handle. As in the forehand grip, the fingers are spread so the racket is an extension of your arm. See Figure 15-2b for the correct eastern backhand grip.

Western grip. A forehand grip which is used by some players and may be effective for high bouncing balls is the western grip. To assume a western grip, first take the eastern forehand described above, and then turn the racket approximately one-fourth to the left which would be opposite the turn for the eastern backhand. See Figure 15-2c for the western grip.

Continental grip. A number of players have adopted the continental grip which can be used for

FIGURE 15-2a.
Eastern forehand.

FIGURE 15-2b.
Eastern backhand.

FIGURE 15-2c.
Western grip.

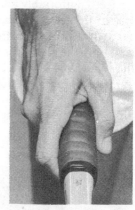

FIGURE 15-2d.
Continental grip.

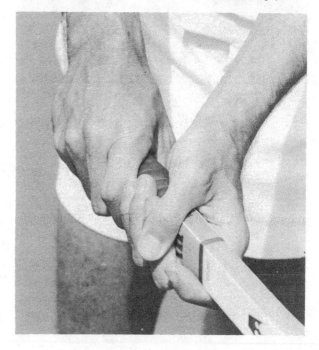

FIGURE 15-3. Common two-hand backhand grip.

both forehand and backhand, thus eliminating the necessity to change grips for these two strokes. It is also the grip used for the serve. To take a continental grip, assume the eastern forehand and turn the racket one-half the distance betwen the eastern forehand and the eastern backhand. The knuckle of the first finger will be on the small ridge between the top of the racket and the right side of the racket. See Figure 15-2d for the continental grip.

The Ready Position

After every shot, the ready position is assumed and thus is the starting point for all strokes except the serve. To assume the ready position, face the net with the feet comfortably spread and the weight on the balls of the feet. The racket is held with both hands and is straight out in front of the body. The right hand is on the grip while the left hand is on the shaft. The right hand should be loose in order to rest the arm muscles between shots while the left hand is used to turn the racket to either the forehand on backhand grip depending upon the return. See Figure 15-3 for the ready position.

FIGURE 15-3.   Ready position.

Basic Strokes

When learning basic strokes such as the forehand, the backhand, and serve it is desirable to practice at the speed one wants to eventually achieve when playing the game. Slow motion practice, although necessary initially for development of the proper techniques, will have limited transfer value with regard to speed. Players should increase speed to the desired playing level as soon as possible in the early learning stages. Beginning players tend to hit the ball softly in order to get it in the court which they perceive as success. This practice can lead to incorrect skill development and will be difficult to correct later when the player wants to stroke the ball harder. If a skill is done properly, the ball will go in the court even when stroked hard. By swinging at the correct speed, one will usually find out immediately if the technique is right or wrong.

Forehand

Since most people who play tennis right-handed also bat right-handed, the forehand is easier to master because of the similarity between these two skills. As soon as you realize the ball is on the forehand side, turn sideways placing the shoulders perpendicular to the net with the left shoulder closer to the net than the right. While turning, the left hand adjusts the racket to the eastern forehand grip. The right arm with the wrist bent back draws the racket behind the body preparing for the forward swing. The racket head should be kept slightly higher than the hand, with the eyes on the ball throughout the entire stroke.

The stroke is executed by swinging the racket as level as possible with a slightly bent elbow while shifting the weight from the right to the left foot. A slight step with the left foot will facilitate this weight shift process. The swing is accompanied by a distinct rotation of the shoulders until, upon the completion of the stroke, the chest is almost facing the net. Contact with the ball is made in front of the left foot. This contact should be made at the height of the ball bounce with the racket face flat and the wrist locked (see Figure 15-4). The racket swing should be kept level on both high and low bouncing balls. The knees are bent for low balls and the arm and racket raised for high bouncers. The player should drive through the ball trying to keep the ball on the racket as long as possible.

The follow-through will determine to a great extent the height, direction, and spin of the ball. To hit the ball deep into the opposite court, the ball should be

FIGURE 15-4a. Preparation.

FIGURE 15-4b. Ball contact.

FIGURE 15-4c. Follow through.

FIGURE 15-4. Forehand sequence.

aimed three to five feet over the net. To achieve this height, the racket head should end up higher than the left shoulder. The racket face is gradually turned from the flat ball contact position to a closed position which will cause a slight amount of top spin. During follow-through, the racket head should continue toward the path of the ball. A properly stroked ball should land within three feet of the baseline. When passing as opponent standing at the net, however, the ball should be aimed just over the top of the net causing it to land near the service line.

Beginning players usually make many of the same errors on the forehand. One of the most common is slowness in getting into the preparatory, racket back position. Timing can be adversely affected by lack of preparation, and it is helpful to turn as soon as you know on which side the ball will approach. Another common error is dropping the racket head and swinging up through the ball rather than level. Poor weight shift and lack of shoulder rotation are two more errors. And lastly, stroke through the ball; do not punch.

Backhand

As in the forehand, the backhand is begun from the ready position. The preparation phase of the one-handed backhand using the eastern backhand grip is begun with a turning of the body until the right shoulder is facing the net. To accomplish this posi-

tion, place the right foot in front of the left as shown in Figure 15-5. This is known as a closed stance. The racket should be drawn back with the right hand gripping the handle and the left on the shaft as a guide. The racket face should be open and higher than the hands, the eyes should be on the ball, and the weight on the left foot.

The execution or swing of the racket is similar to a left-handed batters swing only using one hand on the bat. One the forward swing, the weight is shifted from the back foot to the front and a small step can be taken. The racket is swung in a level position and the racket face is turned from the open position to a flat position for ball contact. The turn of the racket face should be done at the shoulder joint keeping the arm slightly bent and the wrist locked. The ball should be contacted at the height of its bounce eight to ten inches to the right of the lead foot.

In the follow-through, the racket head should follow the direction of the ball and end up higher than the right shoulder. The racket head should be perpendicular to the court upon completion of the stroke. Strategy for handling high and low bouncing balls and aiming points for the backhand are the same as those for the forehand.

Most players experience more difficulty with the backhand than the forehand by committing similar errors. One of the most common errors is not turning sideways enough causing the ball to go out of court to the right. Another fault is hitting the ball with an

FIGURE 15-5a.   Preparation.

FIGURE 15-5b.   Ball contact.

FIGURE 15-5c.   Follow through.

FIGURE 15-5.   Backhand sequence.

open face racket or swinging up through the ball rather than level and the resulting tendency for the ball to go high.

Two-Handed Backhand

The two-handed backhand is essentially the same as the one-hand, except more power is possible and top spin is usually essential. The top spin required is achieved by turning the racket face from a square position to a closed position during the follow-through phase of the stroke. The disadvantage of the two-handed shot is the lack of reach possible with both hands on the racket. Younger children, however, will be able to achieve more success with the two-hand due to increased strength, power, and racket movement.

Service

The serve is the only stroke which you have complete control over. Unlike other strokes, you get to control the flight of the ball. It is unique also in its importance, for if you are unsuccessful serving, there is no way you can play the game as it was intended. Since you must both toss the ball and swing the racket simultaneously, the coordination of the stroke would seem to be more difficult. When one con-

siders, however, the possible combination of factors such as ball spin, court surface, weather, and speed, which occur on other shots, the coordination of the serve is mild by comparison.

The attention and importance placed on the serve often leads to anxiety among both students and teachers which frequently leads to modified teaching methods to bring about early success. These methods usually include a shortening of the racket motion by beginning with the racket behind the back and the hand above the head. Although this will bring about early success for the beginning player, the transfer value in learning the full stroke will be limited and may even bring about negative learning. It is suggested, therefore, that the total racket swing be practiced and not shortened in the early stages of learning.

The grip for the top spin serve is between the eastern forehand and eastern backhand, and is assumed by placing the knuckle of the first finger on the small ridge between the top and side planes of the racket hand (see Figure 15-2d—continental grip). As in the other grips, the fingers should be spread to allow the racket to become an extension of the arm.

The serve has a preparation, an execution, and a follow-through. The preparation phase begins with the placement of the feet. The toe of the left foot, placed about 12 inches to the right of the center line several inches behind the baseline is pointed toward the right net post. The right foot is approximately 18 inches behind the left, and is nearly parallel to the baseline. This foot placement creates a sideways position with the left shoulder pointing toward the opponent's right service court.

The starting point for the racket is in front of the body with the ball held against the racket face with the left hand. The racket can be used as an aiming device by sighting over the top of the racket head just before beginning the down swing. To begin the swing, both arms are dropped down with the racket moving beside and finally behind the body in a natural pendulum motion. Little muscular action is required in this phase of the swing. The ball hand goes down with the racket and then up again in front of the body in coordination with the racket. The hands work in unison, both going down, then up before fully extending overhead. As the left hand reaches its highest point, the ball is pushed up to a point just above the highest reaching point of the racket. The racket now fully extended above the head is dropped behind the head and across the back in a

rotary movement. The racket drop is accomplished by bending both the elbow and wrist. This loop behind the head is critical to racket velocity and power. The loop is completed by extending the racket fully above the head and making contact with the ball in front and to the right of the body. The entire swing is nearly identical to throwing a ball. As in throwing a ball, the weight is shifted initially to the back foot and then to the front foot. The swing should be a continual motion with no stopping or hesitation.

The most important part of the serve is the ball toss. If the ball toss is off, there is little chance for real success or consistency. A properly tossed ball, if allowed to hit the ground, should land 8-10" in front of the lead foot. The height of the ball toss is also important. A toss that is too low or too high can be a problem. The idea is to toss the ball high enough that you have to stretch to hit it, but not high enough to cause you to wait for it to come down. A ball coming down is a moving target and difficult to hit with control. A ball at the right height will be momentarily suspended in air to provide a good target.

FIGURE 15-6. Service sequence.

The ball should also be free of spin on the toss. This is accomplished by holding the ball with the fingers and thumb rather than the palm of the hand. Pushing the ball rather than swinging the arm up in an arch and releasing it will also cut down on spin and produce a more consistant ball toss. If the left arm is held straight to produce an arching motion of the hand, the ball will also arch above and behind the head when released. The left arm should therefore be bent, bringing the hand up close to the body followed by an upward extension of the arm and a push of the ball upward.

The final part of the serve is to actually contact the ball and follow-through. The ball should be hit just to the right and in front of the left foot. The racket face should hit on the top, right of the ball at the one o'clock position. This will produce a necessary spin causing the ball to curve down into the service court. The follow-through of the racket is across the body, ending beside the left leg. The forward momentum caused by the weight shift and racket follow-through will cause you to move forward into the court. To catch your balance, bring the right foot forward. This step should be taken only after the ball has been hit. Remember, it is a rule violation to touch the baseline or the playing surface prior to contacting the ball.

The Lob

There are two types of lobs, the offensive lob and the defensive lob. The offensive lob, when well disguised, can be very effective against an opponent standing at the net. The offensive lob should simulate a normal forehand passing shot, until, at the last instance, the racket head continues traveling on an upward path, causing the ball to go just over the reach of the opponent. The swing is almost identical (except for the lifting of the ball) to the forehand described earlier. The force placed on the ball must be reduced (as compared with the forehand) when lobbing or the ball will go beyond the baseline. To help bring the ball down onto the court, an offensive lob should be hit with top spin by closing down the racket face at the end of the swing. A frequent error is to let up too much causing either a miss hit or a very short lob and an easy winner for the opponent.

The defensive lob is used when you are in trouble. You may be out of position, off-balance, or have any number of other problems which occur during a game forcing you to hit a lob. When in difficulty, the defensive lob is a good shot. It will probably not win any points for you outright, but it will give you a

chance to recover from an awkward position. Unlike the offensive lob, the defensive lob does not have to be disguised. It is hit by drawing the racket back low and swinging from a low to high position putting top spin on the ball by closing down the racket face on the follow-through. Like the offensive lob, force is of major concern, and hitting the ball too easy is a common fault. There is no rule governing how high you can hit the ball, so aim high and hit through the ball.

The Overhead

The stroke used to counter the lob is the overhead. The execution of the overhead is similar to the serve, however, the flight of the ball does need to be controlled. There are basically two types of overhead hits: one is made after the ball bounces and is usually associated with the defensive lob; the other is hit prior to the bounce of the ball and is usually associated with the offensive lob. As was pointed out earlier, the defensive lob is much higher than the offensive lob and is usually coming nearly straight down at the court. It is, therefore, safer to let the defensive lob bounce before trying to hit it. It is very difficult to coordinate the racket head with the rapidly descending ball. By allowing it to bounce, the speed is greatly reduced. The ball should then bounce to just about the right height to hit the overhead as you would a serve. A low bouncing ball can sometimes be handled effectively by bending the knees to get under the ball to allow for a service type swing with the racket.

The good offensive lob will be more difficult to hit since you will most likely be traveling backward while swinging. Timing is crucial—swing too late and it goes into the net; to early the ball goes long. Although the stroke is similar to the final phase of a service, the preparation is quite different. The ready position finds the racket behind the head ready for a overhead swing forward. The ball should be traveling almost right at your head when the swing is executed. The sideways position is essential and a jump kick which is shown in Figure 15-7 is required on the execution of the stroke in order to coordinate the shot.

The Volley

A volley is any shot taken prior to the ball bouncing on your side of the court. It is normally executed anywhere from the service line to the net since volleys from further back often result in errors. The volley is most closely associated with net play. The advantage of being able to volley at the net is related to the angle which can be placed on the ball. The angle at which the ball can be hit increases as you approach the net. Since angle, not speed, is the key, very little swing is necessary. The ball approaches quickly necessitating the use of only one grip for forehand and backhand volleys. Attempting a backswing or changing grips while playing net will usually result in a racket error. The best choice of grips is the service grip between the eastern forehand and backhand. The swing should be a pressing motion moving the racket and the body toward the net. The action is similar to catching the ball with the end of the racket. The angle on the face of the racket will determine the direction of the ball and a fast approaching ball requires little forward swing of the racket while slower moving balls can be stroked by a pushing type motion in the direction you want the ball to travel. As in other strokes, the sideways position of the body is essential. Often, there is only time to rotate the shoulders because of the speed of the approaching ball. Some sort of a sideways position, however, must be achieved in order to successfully and consistently volley the ball.

Drop Shot

The drop shot is one in which the ball just clears and drops very close to the net on the opponents side. The shot can be executed from anywhere on the court although it is most effective when it is hit close to the net, giving the opponent less time to react to the shot. It is executed by undercutting the ball and producing a great deal of backspin. The shot is very delicate since sufficient force must be put on the ball along with the backspin to get the shot over the net without hitting it too long. A long drop shot will usually result in a winner for the opponent, whereas, one which is hit just a little too easy will not clear the net. The drop shot is used sparingly since it is most effective when it is unexpected.

Playing the Game

Before beginning play, a few things must be decided: (1) who will serve, and (2) on which side should a player choose to receive. Who serves is usually determined by a spin of the racket with one side of the racket being heads and the other tails. Since most rackets have different markings on each side, heads and tails is easily defined. The winner of the spin can choose to serve or select the side on which he wishes to receive. Since the server usually has an advantage in tennis, the winner of the spin will usually elect to serve, thus giving the choice of side to the other player. Selection of side can be crucial particularly under certain sun, wind, or lighting conditions. Since the players switch after the first game, it

FIGURE 15-7a. Preparation.

FIGURE 15-7b. Ball contact.

FIGURE 15-7c. Follow through.

FIGURE 15-7. Overhead sequence.

FIGURE 15-8a.   Forehand volley.

FIGURE 15-8b.   Backhand volley.

FIGURE 15-8.   Volley.

is usually desirable to select the poorer side to receive on for the first game of the set, thereafter providing two games in a row on the good side. The poor side is usually the side in which you must look into the sun. Wind is another factor, and knowledge of your game and your opponent's will determine which side to select under certain conditions.

Scoring

Scoring in tennis has always been a problem for the beginning player since there seems to be little logic to it. In fact, when the game was originated by and for royalty, the scoring system was deliberately made complicated to exclude the peasants. Attempts to change the scoring system have met with moderate success due primarily to television.

Some changes have been made in set scoring. A player must still win a minimum of six games, and must be ahead by at least two games to win a set. Thus, scores of 6-4, 6-3 would indicate completed sets while a score of 6-5, would not. In most competition with the game score is 6-6, a tie breaker of nine or twelve points is played, and the final score of the set is recorded as 7-6 or 6-7. The easiest tie breaker to learn is the nine point. The person scheduled to serve the thirteenth game begins the tie breaker by serving two points; the opponent then serves two, after which the players switch sides of the court. The first server again serves two, and the opponent gets to serve the next three. Should the tie breaker go to the ninth point, the receiver has the option to select the side on which he wishes to receive. The first player to win five points wins the set. The next set is begun with the player who served the last complete game before the tie breaker as the receiver of the service.

Matches are usually best of three sets with some of the major tournaments still retaining the best of five sets for men's competition. Match scores are recorded with the winning players score in each set appearing first, i.e., 6-4, 2-6, 6-3. In this example, the winner won the first and third set while losing the second. The score of the tie breaker is often recorded along with the set score—6-2, 6-7, (5-2), 6-4. The eventual winner in this example lost the second set in a nine point tie breaker 5-2.

Playing Surfaces

At one time, grass was the exclusive playing surface, however, with the cost of upkeep and better all-weather surfaces, grass is being phased out of even the biggest tournaments. Surfaces now in use include hard surfaces such as concrete, asphalt, and specially prepared surfaces, and soft surfaces such as clay and composition. The hard courts are easier to care for, and are generally considered to be "all weather." The soft courts in contrast are unplayable under wet conditions, require more upkeep, and generally a longer waiting period is necessary after rain before play can begin. Generally one can play for longer periods on clay or composition, and equipment such as balls, shoes, and wooden rackets last considerably longer.

Court surface alters playing strategy. Hard court play is characterized by a fast paced, hard hitting attack type game. The serve and volley game in which the serving player attacks behind his serve by rushing the net is typical of high caliber play on hard courts. The ball tends to skid on this surface and stay low necessitating speed and quickness in order to keep the ball in play.

On the slower soft courts, the pace of the game is dramatically different. Since the ball tends to come up off the court more, time is available to get to it for a return. Attacking behind the serve will usually result in the server losing the point. A player, therefore, must work his way to the net slowly by taking advantage of short returns by his opponent. Games on clay and composition characteristically include long rallies.

Singles Strategy

Each court surface requires a different type of strategy; but since the hard surface court is most prevalent, this discussion will deal with play on hard courts. Play begins with the service, and success can only come if one can get the ball into play. A player should strive to get a minimum of 60 percent of his first serves in and at least 90 percent or more of the second serves. The first serve should be hit harder than the second, but neither should be too hard or soft—remember the percentages. A very soft second serve, although successful, will often lead to a winning return from the opponent. Development of a second serve should not be neglected by beginning players. Once the first serve is developed, a player should try to follow it to the net. The strategy in both singles and doubles is to get the advantage at the net and angle off a winning shot. To secure the advantage, the serve should be hit toward the outside corner of the service court which will tend to force the opponent off the court freeing the remainder of the court for a volley from the net for a winner. When following the serve, the server should end up midway

between the sideline and the center of the net. This position protects against a shot down the line. When receiving against a person who is attacking behind the serve, hit the ball very low over the net, aiming at the opponent's feet. Try to make the opponent volley the ball upward which should allow an easy passing shot or lob.

The second slower serve is not usually followed to the net. It should be aimed, therefore, at the opponent's weakness, usually the backhand. A good deal of top spin should be put on the ball to cause it to drop into the service court. A rally usually results from a second serve necessitating strategy to keep the opponent off the net while trying to get to the net yourself.

Successful points off of a rally are a result of playing an opponent's weakness and using percentage tennis. Try to make best use of your strengths by forcing the opponent into playing your game. If you rally well, keep him off the net by hitting shots deep. When you do get into trouble, use a percentage shot. Since the middle of the net is six inches lower than the sides, cross court shots represent percentage tennis. Deep cross court shots should be returned cross court which will take the ball over the center of the net and increase the chances for success.

There are a number of other general rules to follow in percentage tennis including keeping the ball deep. As mentioned earlier, the advantage is achieved by getting to the net and short shots can easily be hit and followed to the net. Also, short shots lead to greater angle on returns, which results in considerably more running. In addition to keeping the opponent off the net, a deep ball cannot usually be returned for a winning shot. Winning a point, therefore, is usually determined by who makes the mistake of hitting a short ball.

Direction of the ball is another important consideration in percentage tennis. As mentioned earlier, cross court to cross court is a general rule when rallying from the baseline. Shots down the line should only be hit when returning a short ball when the opponent is out of position. An obvious opponent weakness, however, should be fully exploited.

Doubles Strategy

Doubles is an extremely complicated game, and only basic information can be provided in this section.

The obvious difference between singles and doubles is the number of players on the court. The difference between singles and doubles is comparable to the difference between checkers and chess. Getting the first serve in is extremely important in doubles and double faulting is a cardinal sin. The first serve, therefore, is usually similar to the top spin second serve used in singles. With the reduced force on the ball and added spin, this represents a much higher percentage serve than the hard flat first serve in singles. The serve is usually directed at the backhand of the receiver since there is no advantage to drawing an opponent off the court. Both the first and second serve should be followed to the net. With the addition of the alleys in doubles, the server may move to the sidelines to serve if desired.

Basic strategy in doubles includes getting to the net, holding the net position, and keeping the opponents in the backcourt area. Whether at the net or back, teammates should play side by side. The serving team attempts to achieve the side-by-side position by having the server attack behind his serve. The receiving team attempts to execute a good return with the hitter moving up beside the partner already stationed halfway to the net at the service line. If the serving team acquires the net advantage, the non-receiving opponent who has been standing at the service line should retreat immediately to the baseline side-by-side position with his partner. The "one up, one back" formation generally results in a loss of point against a good doubles team.

When in the position of defense or back position in doubles, a team must work its way to the net. Ground strokes should be kept low, forcing the net players to volley the ball upwards, and shots should be aimed at the middle of the court where the net is six inches lower. The ball should also be directed at the weaker player whenever possible. The lob is also a very effective weapon to get the opponents off the net. No matter what method is used, however, the team that is off the net must work its way up if it hopes to win.

A real threat in doubles is the "poacher," the net player particularly on the serving team that moves along the net and hits a service return right at the feet of non-receiving opponent. A good poacher who is skillful enough to disguise his moves can completely destroy the opposition. A poacher can be thwarted by: (1) lobbing the service return over his head, (2) hitting a weak serve right at him or trying to hit behind him (where he was) as he goes across the net, or (3) having both players on the receiving team stand at the baseline to return a poached ball. A poacher plays a cat and mouse game with the opposition. When an incorrect guess is made, the point is generally lost. Poaching is usually only necessary when the non-poaching member of the team is weak. It can be very successful against a person with a weak return or against a team that does not know how to defend against the poaching player.

SAFETY PRACTICES

Tennis is not considered a dangerous sport although accidents will occur occasionally. Most injuries are brought about by falls. Such injuries can be kept to a minimum through mastery of proper footwork coupled with proper body balance at all times. However, fatigue, off-balance attempts, and last resort tries will occur in the course of a tournament and injuries will result.

Blisters can be eliminated through the selection of proper tennis sneakers and the use of two pairs of woolen socks. A special inner sole, recently developed and available at most sporting goods stores, has proven nearly 100 percent effective in preventing blisters. It also permits an athlete to continue playing while recovering from a blister. Proper warm-up through both calisthenics and rallying is an individual matter and may or may not aid in the prevention of muscle strain.

WEIGHT TRAINING

The use of weight training in tennis is becoming increasingly more popular. A large percentage of Australian players have been training regularly with weights for years, indicating the importance of strength as well as agility, explosive power, speed, endurance, and coordination.

Exercises with the wall pulley and dumbbells that require movements similar to tennis strokes are recommended. The following exercises, designed to strengthen the entire body with special emphasis on the wrists, arms, and shoulders, are recommended: the wrist curl, reverse wrist curl, wrist adduction and abduction, straight-arm pull-over, upright rowing, lateral raise, bent-arm pull-over, dips, and chinning.

EXERCISE   Definitions and List of Terms

1. A successful serve that completely eludes the receiver is an _____ .
2. The score of a game after either side has won a point from deuce is _____ .
3. The strip of the court located between the sidelines for singles and doubles is referred to as the _____ .
4. The basic stroke made from the left side by a right-handed competitor is called the _____ .
5. "English" applied to a ball that results in a backward spin toward the stroker is called _____ .
6. The style of play in which the player uses hard drives from behind the endline is termed the _____ game.
7. The theory calling for a return to the deep center of the court to eliminate angle returns is called the _____ .
8. Holding the racket closer to the striking service or shortening the grip is termed a _____ .
9. The stroke used to apply backspin by drawing the racket down sharply when striking the ball is the _____ stroke.
10. The forehand grip, in which the V formed by the thumb joining the hand is 45 degrees to the left of the position in the eastern grip, is termed the _____ grip.
11. A return in which the ball is stroked diagonally across the court is called a _____ shot.
12. The area of the court just inside the base line or in the middle of the court is termed the _____ .
13. A tie score of 40-40 and any subsequent tie score is referred to as _____ .
14. A server who drives both balls into the net or over the service line has committed a _____ .
15. A volley that is made at a level between the shoulders and the head with a longer backswing than the conventional volley is a _____ .
16. A backspinning shot that requires delicate wrist action and that results in the ball dropping just over the net with a limited bounce is a _____ .
17. A forehand in which the V formed by the thumb joining the hand is over the plane of the handle is called the _____ .
18. A server who steps on or over the service line before stroking the ball has committed a _____ .
19. A stroke made by hitting the ball immediately after it bounces is called a _____ .
20. A serve that touches the net and falls into the proper service court, a serve that is made when the receiver was unprepared, or a volley that is interrupted by outside interference result in a _____ .
21. A successful shot placed over the opponent's head is termed a _____ .
22. A shot that is stroked immediately as it contacts the court and that is placed over the head of the opponent is a _____ .
23. The term used to indicate a score of zero is _____ .
24. A series of legal returns by both players is called a _____ .
25. The overhead stroke used to put the ball into play is called the _____ .
26. A player who has won six games, providing he is at least two games ahead of his opponent, has completed one _____ .
27. An overhead stroke performed by hitting forward and downward from the highest point above the head during a volley is termed a _____ .
28. A shot made before the ball contacts the court is a _____ .

1. Ace
2. Advantage
3. Alley
4. Backhand stroke
5. Backspin
6. Base line
7. Center theory
8. Choke
9. Chop
10. Continental
11. Cross-court
12. Danger zone
13. Deuce
14. Double fault
15. Drive volley
16. Drop shot
17. Eastern grip
18. Fault
19. Half volley
20. Let
21. Lob
22. Lob-volley
23. Love
24. Rally
25. Service
26. Set
27. Smash
28. Volley

QUESTIONS AND ANSWERS ON THE RULES

Singles

1. *Q.* What is the correct sequence of scoring?
   A. Four consecutive points by any player will complete a game. The server's score is always listed and called first.

Server	Receiver	Score	Serving From
1 point	0 points	15—love	left side
2 points	0 points	30—love	right side
3 points	0 points	40—love	left side
4 points	0 points	Game—Server	
3 points	1 point	40—15	right side
3 points	2 points	40—30	left side
3 points	3 points	Deuce	right side
4 points	3 points	Adv.—Server	left side
5 points	3 points	Game—Server	

2. *Q.* How many games constitute a complete set?
   A. Any player who wins six games is declared the winner of the set, providing he has won by a margin of at least two games over his opponent. Play is continued until a two-game margin is secured by either player.
3. *Q.* How many sets constitute a complete match?
   A. The maximum number of sets in men's play is five.
4. *Q.* How are the choices of court sides and server or receiver determined?
   A. The player winning a coin toss or the racket spin (place the racket head down on the court and spin it with the opponent calling "rough" or "smooth," determined by the trim at the top and bottom of the racket) may choose or require his opponent to choose (1) the right to serve or receive, with the other player choosing the court side; or (2) the side, with the other player choosing to serve or receive.
5. *Q.* Do players continue throughout the match without a change of sides?
   A. No. Players change sides at the end of the first, third, and every subsequent odd game of each set until the match is completed.
6. *Q.* What constitutes a legal serve?
   A. The server must stand behind the base line within the imaginary marks of the center mark and the sidelines and toss the ball by hand into the air, striking it with the racket before it hits the ground without first having touched the base line or the playing area with either foot, without changing position by walking or running, and without losing contact with the ground behind the base line.
7. *Q.* Is a fault recorded if a server catches a tossed ball and retosses it?
   A. No, providing the server did not attempt to strike the ball with the racket.
8. *Q.* Is a fault recorded if a server misses a tossed ball completely in attempting to strike it?
   A. Yes.

9. *Q.* Is it a fault if the served ball touches a permanent fixture (other than the net, strap, or band) before it hits the court?

A. Yes.

10. *Q.* Is a fault recorded if the server stands to the left of the center mark behind the base line when serving to the opponent's right service court?

A. Yes. however, a fault may not be claimed if the second serve has been delivered.

11. *Q.* What is a double fault?

A. A double fault is declared if the server fails to place the ball into the proper service court in two attempts or violates the procedures for serving as described in rule six.

12. *Q.* When is a receiver classified as being ready?

A. If the receiver attempts to return the service, he is deemed prepared. If he states that he is not ready, he cannot claim a fault should the serve not fall within the service court since it then becomes an automatic let.

13. *Q.* Does a player who serves out of turn forfeit all points scored during this period?

A. No. At the end of the first game the receiver becomes the server and the server becomes the receiver, continuing alternately in all subsequent games. However, if a player serves out of turn, play is stopped as soon as the error is discovered, the correction is made and the game continues with all points scored prior to the discovery of the error reckoned. If a full game is completed, the service order remains as altered.

14. *Q.* What constitutes a let?

A. A let does not pertain to a serve alone in which the ball touches the net, strap, or band, and falls into the proper service court. A let is also claimed if a service or fault is delivered when the receiver is not prepared as described in rule twelve, or outside interference occurs. The point or serve is replayed without penalty. Any number of let serves may occur without penalty.

15. *Q.* Is a ball falling on the line classified as inside the playing area?

A. Yes.

16. *Q.* Is it legal to throw the racket at and hit the ball?

A. No.

17. *Q.* Is it legal to strike the ball with the racket more than once?

A. No.

18. *Q.* Does a loss of point result if a player touches the net, posts, cord or metal cable, strap or band, or ground within the opponent's court during play with the racket or any part of the body?

A. Yes.

19. *Q.* May a ball be touched with any part of the body?

A. No.

20. *Q.* May a ball be played before it passes over the net?

A. No. A loss of point results.

21. *Q.* Who is awarded the point if a ball in play, stroked by player *A* to player *B*, touches the net, posts, cord or metal cable, or strap or band after it has hit the court within the playing area?

A. Player *A*.

22. *Q.* Is it a legal return if a ball touches the net posts, cord or metal cable, or strap or band and passes over and into the playing area?

A. Yes.

23. *Q.* Is it a legal return if the ball, served or returned, hits the ground within the proper court and rebounds back over the net, and the player whose turn it is to strike the ball reaches over the net to play the ball without touching any part of the net or posts?

A. Yes.

24. *Q.* Is it a legal return if the player's racket passes over the net after he returns a ball from his side of the court?

   A. Yes.

25. *Q.* Who is awarded the point if player *A* returns a volley into the proper area of player *B* and it strikes another ball lying in the court?

   A. Player *A*.

26. *Q.* In a tournament match, with whom does the final authority rest?

   A. The umpire. If a referee is appointed, an appeal shall be made to him.

Doubles

27. *Q.* How is the order of service determined?

   A. The pair who is to serve in the first game of each set must decide which partner will do so and the opposing pair must decide for the second game. The partner of the player who served in the first game will serve in the third and the partner of the player who served in the second game will serve in the fourth, with this pattern continuing until the termination of the set.

28. *Q.* How is the order of receiving determined?

   A. The pair who is to receive in the first game must decide who is to receive the first service, and that player must receive on very odd game throughout the set. The same procedure is followed for the opposing players.

29. *Q.* Does a partner who serves out of turn forfeit all points scored prior to the discovery of the error?

   A. No. See rule thirteen.

30. *Q.* Do partners who alter the order of receiving forfeit all points prior to the discovery of the infraction?

   A. No. See rule thirteen.

31. *Q.* Are players entitled to a rest period at any time during the match?

   A. Yes. Play is continuous unless, after the third set, either player desires a rest. The rest period should not exceed ten minutes.

BIBLIOGRAPHY

American Association for Health, Physical Education, and Recreation, *Group Instruction Manual for Tennis.* Washington, D.C.: Government Printing Office, 1963.

Broer, Marion R., *et al.,* eds., *Individual Sports for Women* (5th ed.). Philadelphia: W. B. Saunders Company, 1971.

Plagenhoef, Stanley, *Fundamentals of Tennis.* Englewood Cliffs, N. J.: Prentice-Hall, Inc., 1970.

Talbert, William F., and Bruce S. Old., *The Game of Singles in Tennis.* Philadelphia: J. B. Lippincott Company, 1962.

Tilden, Bill, *How To Play Better Tennis.* New York: Simon & Schuster, Inc., 1957.

United States Lawn Tennis Association, USLTA, *Official Tennis Guide and Yearbook.* New York: USLTA.

16

VOLLEYBALL

DESCRIPTION OF THE ACTIVITY

Volleyball is played on a rectangular court 30 feet wide and 60 feet long. The height of the top of the net is 7 feet 4½ inches for women and 8 feet for men. A team is composed of six players; three forwards and three backs. The forwards take floor positions in front of their respective backs, in proper rotation order, until the server hits the ball. After the serve is executed players may switch positions. Players on a team rotate one position clockwise each time their team receives the ball to start a serve.

The game is begun when the right back serves the ball over the net into the opponents' court. After the serve, each team attempts to propel the ball back over the net into their opponents' court before it strikes the floor. The ball is generally played with the hands or forearms, however, USVBA rules permit play with other parts of the body. It may be hit, tapped or batted not more than three times by each team on its side of the net. A team must be serving to score. A point is scored by the serving team each time the opponents fail to return the ball across the net in a maximum of three hits, commit a foul or make an error. The game is won by the team that has a minimum lead of 2 points and is the first to score 15 points, or that is at least 2 points ahead after eight minutes of play. However, if the score reaches a 14-14 tie and there is still time to play, or the teams have decided to omit the time rule, the winning team must score a minimum of 2 consecutive points.

The serve initiates action and is performed by the player striking the ball with the hand, fist, or forearm with sufficient force to send it over the net into the opponents' court. The ball is then hit back and forth over the net until one team faults. If the serving team faults, the serve goes over to the receiving team and no point is scored.

The development of power volleyball introduced techniques like the dive, roll, bump pass and multiple offense that changed the game from one in which the ball was hit back and forth over the net in most any manner to one with difficult individual skills, and complicated defensive and offensive strategy.

The rules, skills and strategy for volleyball are similar for women and men. For this reason no separate treatment of these areas for the two sexes will be included. However, full explanations of variations will be noted where significant differences exist. The USVBA rules govern all open play, men and women, and college play for men. The NAGWS rules govern women collegiate competition.

EQUIPMENT

The Ball

The ball is a sphere, with or without a bladder, covered with leather or other suitable material made up of 12 or more pieces. It measures not less than 25 and not more than 27 inches in circumference, and weighs between 250 and 280 grams. It must be inflated so that it will have a vertical rebound of not less than 60 and not more than 65 inches when dropped to a concrete floor from a height of 100 inches.

The leaher ball is preferred, however, the rubberized cover is used and is durable and serviceable.

The Net

The net is 3′ wide and 32′ long with a 2″ wide, white or orange canvas strip of double thickness attached to the top, bottom and ends. A quarter inch steel cable, with a tensile strength of 3000 pounds, runs through the top strip, and; a similar cable, one-eighth inch in diameter with a tensile strength of 1000 pounds runs through the bottom strip. The two end strips have openings through which a wood or metal dowling may be inserted. The net is fabricated in four inch square mesh. When installed for play, the net is stretched tightly across the middle of the court at the proper height. The bottom should be drawn tightly so that the ball will rebound properly when it is hit into it.

Net Antenna

Each antenna is identical. It is made of break resistant, flexible material not more than ⅜ inch in diameter and long enough to extend not less than 2½ nor more than 3½ feet vertically above the top of the net. It can be constructed to extend from the bottom of the net. One antenna is located at each end of the net, 8½″ from the outside edge of the vertical extension of the side line. The upper part should be marked in alternate white and red or orange bands that measure between 4″ and 6″ long.

The Standards

The standards which hold the net should be located at least 3 feet outside the sidelines, and made of material that gives sufficient strength to sustain the tightly drawn cable supporting the net. This cable must be drawn taut enough across the court above the center line so that there will be no more than a quarter inch sag, and the height of the top of the net at the center of the court will be fixed to be in accord with the rules.

The Court

The playing court should be free from obstructions and should have an overhead clearance of at least 26 feet. Its outside boundaries are marked by white lines 2 inches wide. Measurement is taken from the outside edge of these lines. A line 4 inches wide is drawn across the center of the court. An a 2-inch-wide line is drawn from sideline to sideline, parallel to the center line and 10 feet from the center line, on each side of

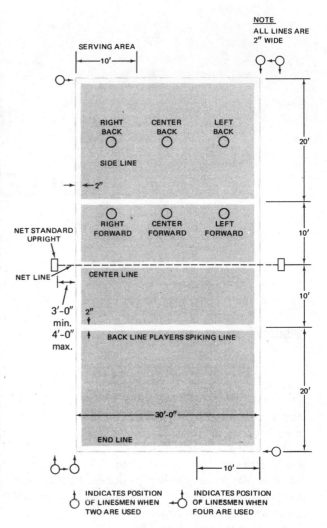

FIGURE 16-1.   The volleyball court.

SOURCE: From the *Official Volleyball Rules and Reference Guide*, United States Volleyball Association, 1967.

the net. These last two lines are restraining lines for the spikers who spike from the back position. There should be a 6-foot deep space, 10-foot wide on the right side of the court in back of the endline for the service area.

SKILLS AND TECHNIQUES

The Underhand Pass

This two-arm, underhand pass in which the ball is bounced off of the forearms is used to play the ball when it is at a height below the waist. It is employed generally to field a spiked ball, to receive the service, to recover a net ball, or when the ball falls beyond a player's normal reach.

The pass may be executed by making a fist, thumb up, with one hand; and, joining the other hand to it by curling the fingers around the fist, and placing the thumbs in a parallel position. The second method is to place one open hand, palm up, into the palm of the other hand, and curl the fingers of the bottom hand around those of the other hand, with the thumbs up and parallel. In both hand positions, the thumbs and fingers should be pointed toward the floor and the elbows rotated inward so that the soft surface of the forearms will make contact with the ball.

The body position should be behind the ball. This is generally accomplished by using a slide step, and if necessary, a stretch. The back is straight with the upper body leaning slightly forward. The knees are flexed, placing the body in a squatting position so the ball can be hit at about waist level. When it is impossible to get the body behind the ball in the normal manner, the player must move sideward by pushing off with one leg and flexing the other leg sharply under the body weight. The leg used to push off is to the side. In situations where the player cannot move the body behind the ball in any manner, he may have to play it from a lateral position. In this case, as the ball is contacted, the upper body is turned in the

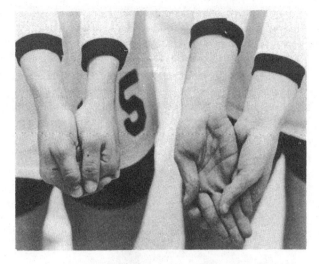

a. Closed fist thumbs parallel.   b. Open hand, palms up.

FIGURE 16-2.   Hand and arm positions for the underhand pass.

direction of the target, and the inside shoulder is lowered.

One Arm Underhand Dig Pass

This is usually an emergency technique and is employed when the ball cannot be reached with the

a. Body directly behind the ball.

b. The stretch to move body behind the ball.

c. Lateral position without getting body behind the ball.

FIGURE 16-3.   The underhand pass.

FIGURE 16-4.   The underhand dig pass.

FIGURE 16-5.   Backward two arm bump pass.

two-arm pass. If possible, the ball should be played off the wrist or forearm of either arm, however, the fist or hand may be used. If it occurs on the first or second play it should be hit high to a teammate so it can be played effectively.

Backward Two-Arm Bump Pass

This pass is used in two situations: when a player cannot play the ball facing the net, and secondly, to make a set to a spiker behind the passer. It is executed in a similar manner to the normal underhand bump pass except tht the ball is contacted at a higher level, the upper body leans slightly backward, and the shoulders are elevated as the ball is hit.

Dig and Roll Pass

It is usually employed when the ball cannot be reached in any other manner or when it has been driven so hard there is no other way to react. It is executed by taking a long stride with one leg toward the ball. The weight is moved over the opposite leg which is flexed under the body. From this position the ball is played either with the normal two-arm technique, or if necessary with one arm. When balance is lost after contact with the ball, a rolling motion to the flexed leg side is begun. The roll is continued until the player contacts the floor surface with the appropriate shoulder, back and buttocks in that

a. Just after the ball has been passed.

b. The roll after the ball has been passed.

FIGURE 16-6.   The dig and roll pass

order. The knees are kept flexed as the roll is continued, turning the body over to a front position, and subsequently to a ready stance.

Dive and Pass

This movement should first be practiced on mats to the point where sufficient skill and strength have been developed to perform it without danger of body injury. It is performed by jumping in a horizontal manner and playing the ball during the suspended flight. The ball may be played with the normal forearm pass or the forearm or wrist of one arm. The back of the hand is used by some players. The objective is to hit the ball high so a teammate can play it.

After the ball has been played, the hands are lowered to make contact with the floor, the back is arched, the legs are flexed back and upward, and the head is lifted with the chin pulled inward. The shock of the fall is taken by the hands, chest and abdomen in a rocking, or roll-down tumbling motion. The roll-down should end with the body weight on the hands and extended feet. From this position the player pushes up to a ready position.

The Set

The set may be executed with either an overhand or an underhand forearm pass, however, the overhead set is used by most players when possible. The purpose of the set is to place the ball where an effective spike can be made. There are two types of overhand sets; the front and back. Most sets are made to either the left or right side of the court near the net.

The Front Set. The hands are held in front of the face, the fingers are spread and slightly flexed, and the thumbs located about three or four inches apart and pointing toward each other at a slight angle. The wrists are extended backward, and the elbows are held just about shoulder level. Contact with the ball is made with the second joints of the fingers and padding of the hand.

The body is moved under the pass so that the player is directly behind the ball with the feet in a stride stance, knees flexed, back straight, and the front foot pointed toward the placement of the set. As the ball hits the hands, the fingers and wrist give a bit to absorb the shock. This is followed immediately by a coordinated upward movement of the body, arms and hands which propel the ball upward and into the spiking area. The arms are thrust upward and the fingers and wrist extended with a follow through in the direction of the flight of the ball.

FIGURE 16-7.   The dive and pass. First contact with the floor after the ball has been passed.

FIGURE 16-8.   The overhand front set.   FIGURE 16-9.   The overhand back set.

The Back Set. The back set is employed to deceive the opposing blockers, and in play situations where the ball has been poorly passed, forcing the setter to turn his back to the spikers.

The position of the body is similar to the stance for the front set, except it should be moved somewhat farther under the ball. The wrist and hand extension is somewhat greater than in the front set. The ball is contacted above the forehead. The back is arched, the shoulders raised and the face should be turned in an upward direction. The hands move up and backward above the head in a follow-through.

The Jump Set. It is an advanced technique used while feinting an attack at the net or in an emergency when there has been a bad pass and the ball may cross over the net. When the first pass propels the ball into a favorable spiking position, the player makes the jump set move by jumping up in a spiking action. If the blockers do not respond for the block, he may spike. If the blockers go up for the block, he sets the ball to a teammate who makes the spike.

Advanced (Specific) Sets. The height and angle of the ball can be varied with each of the sets discussed. The ball can be set low and very near the net so that it can be spiked on its upward flight. The threat of this kind of spike keeps the blocker in place and helps prevent the double block. This is sometimes called an *one-set* or *Japanese set*. The ball can be set 2-3 feet above the net, approximately the same distance in front of the blocker where it can be driven down into the opponents court. This also holds the blocker in place. This is called a *two-set*. The flight of the ball can be directed at a crosswise angle to the net, and 3-4 feet above it, so that it will drop approximately 5-6 feet from the sideline. It can be spiked in between the blockers. This move can set up a spike without blocker opposition if delivered quickly. This is a *three-set*. The fourth type is executed by directing the flight of the ball 3-5 feet above the net and at a sharp angle crosswise to the net so that it will drop on or near the sideline. This isolates one defense player on the spiker because the center forward is held in place by the threat of a center spike. These specific sets require setter and spiker in order to develop the timing necessary for success. The setter will generally call the signal for these plays as the team is preparing to receive the serve.

The Spike

It is an offensive technique in which a front line player executes a high vertical jump, hits the ball with the hand, and drives it down into the opponents'

a. Player at maximum height just before contact.

b. Body position just after contact.

FIGURE 16-10.   The spike.

court. It is generally the third hit and follows the set. It's effectiveness is dependent upon a good set. The speed of the ball and the angle of its flight will vary according to the situation and the type of spike. A spiker must learn to jump as high as possible, be able to make several different type of spikes, and know the weak areas in the defense. The spike can be executed more effectively when the ball is set up from the on-hand side of the spiker. For a right hand player, the right side is the on-hand side, and the left side is his off-hand side.

The spiker should start his preliminary approach 8-12 feet back from the net, and facing it. Generally three or more steps are taken before the jump is initiated. The jump is started with a two-foot take off at the end of the last stride, the trailing foot is brought up the lead foot with the heels hitting first, followed by a rocking motion up to the toes. At the same time the arms are moved vigorously in an outward and upward motion from a position behind and below the shoulders to a position above the head. The right knee is lifted strongly upward. As the body reaches near maximum height, the right arm and wrist are cocked, placing the hand behind and below the head level, with the elbow pointing outward and slightly upward. The left arm is lowered in front of the body with the forearm near the belt level.

The striking motion is made by moving the right hand down into the ball in a baseball catcher's throwing motion, with the elbow leading. The ball is struck with the open hand above its horizontal axis. Contact is first made with the heel and palm and then with the fingers as the wrist is snapped through. The elbow is straight at the time of contact. The hand and arm may follow through over the net, but no part of the body may touch it. If the player makes the spike near the net, the ball will be contacted above head level and out in front of it. If the spike is made farther back away from the net, contact with the ball will be made farther back over the head.

The Dink. It is a soft hit made to confuse the blockers and ruin their timing when a hard spike is expected. The initial body and arm movements are identical with the hard spike except the speed of the arm movement is reduced, the wrist is held rigid, and contact with the ball is made with the fingers. The ball is directed into a weak defensive area.

The Off-speed Spike. The speed of the ball can be varied from the very fast high-speed spike to a slow dink or high lob. The purpose of this change of pace is to confuse the defense, especially the timing of blockers. This kind of spike should be used infrequently and placed into a weak area in the defense.

Advanced Spiking Techniques. Direction of any ball can be varied by rotating the hands to the right or left as contact is being made. In this way the ball may be directed to any part of the opponent's court. The spiker may also deliberately drive the ball into the blocker's hands at such an angle to cause it to rebound out of bounds. This is called a wipe-off. He may also hit the ball at different heights above the net, and cooperate with the setter, who can place the ball at a specific height and in a designated place. These kinds of spikes are difficult to control and should be learned only after the basic hard and soft ones are under control.

The Block

The block is used either as a defensive or an attack maneuver, depending on how the spike is delivered and the manner in which the block is performed. Some good teams score as many as 50 percent of their points with the block. Rules permit the blockers to reach across the net as long as no part of the body makes contact with it, or the ball is not touched on the opponent's side of the net before it is played by an opposing player.

Stance. The best spot for the block is near the net for all but the very short player who must take three or four steps in order to obtain sufficient vertical height to block well well. The forearms should be parallel to, and approximately six inches from the net with the hands pointing upward. The vertical jump should be made with a two-foot take off by squatting, dipping the arms slightly, springing upward, and thrusting the arms up, forearms parallel with the net, into the blocking position. At the height of the jump the arms will be fully extended. The angle of the arms and hands will depend upon the type of rebound desired.

The Block. When the blocking position has been reached at the apex of the vertical jump, the hands and forearms are held close enough together to prevent the ball from sliding through them. The fingers are slightly flexed, and the thumbs are pointed toward each other and nearly touching. The arms are fully extended upward and outward so that the hands are about a foot in front of the head. The eyes should follow the ball into contact with the hands. For the offensive type of block, the hands are extended above the head and across the net into the opponent's court, the wrist set, and the hands are flexed and rigid. Execution of the defensive block requires the wrist to be slightly extended backward so that the ball will rebound into the blockers court. In either case, the ball should rebound from the hand without any aggressive movement of the hands into the ball.

Timing. The blocking position must be reached in time to intercept the spiked ball just before or just after it crosses over the net. The jump phase should be initiated by watching the spiker's take-off. Generally, the blocker will start his jump immediately after the spiker starts his jump. However, in the case of a very high jumping spiker, or one who delays the spike, the blocker must time his jump accordingly, and delay the jump. Also, in case of a low set, or the delivery of the spike some distance from the net, timing adjustment must be made by the blocker. The blocker's eyes are first focused on the spiker, and then after the jump, on the ball.

The Serve

The serve is important because it starts play for each point or change of service, and no score can be made by the non-serving team. It is delivered from behind the back line within an area extending 10 feet in from the right side line and at least 6 feet beyond the backline. A good serve must clear the net and fall within the opponents' court, or be played by an opponent. Four types of serves will be described. These are: (1) Underhand, (2) Overhand floater, (3) Overhand spin, and (4) Roundhouse.

Underhand Serve. At the start of the serving motion, the body is in a stride stance with the knees flexed slightly and the left leg forward and facing about 45 degrees toward the net. The ball is held in the palm of the left hand, and the left arm is relatively straight and pointed toward the net in front of the hitting hand. The right hitting hand is hanging loosely downward from the shoulder.

The delivery is a coordinated movement of the trunk, legs, arms and hands. The right arm is swung directly backward beyond the hip with the elbow relatively straight. The weight is shifted back over the right leg. The weight then begins to shift forward, accompanied by a forward, underarm motion of the right arm. As the right arm moves into the hitting area, the ball is dropped into its path by the left hand. Contact with the ball is made just below the center, midline with either the heel, fist, or half fist of the right hand. The arm follows through in the direction of the serve.

The ball can be directed to the right or left side of the opponents court by contacting it to either side of center. The eyes must be focused on the ball throughout the delivery.

a. Starting motion.

b. Just after contact.

FIGURE 16-11. The overhand floater serve.

Overhand Floater (Punch). The ready body position is a stride stance, left leg forward, with the left shoulder pointed toward the net. The right forearm and hand are back of and above the shoulder, in a position similar to the baseball catcher arm when throwing to second base. The left hand, palm up and holding the ball, is held in front of, and at face level.

The hitting motion is a synchronized movement in which the weight is shifted back over the right leg, then forward over to the left. At the same time the right arm is cocked and the ball is tossed from 3 to 5 feet above, and in front of the head and striking hand. The right arm is brought vigorously forward over the shoulder with the elbow leading. The hand, with the wrist stiff, is forced into the ball as it reaches the proper height. There is little or no follow through of the hand after contacting the ball. This is essential if the ball is to have a knuckle-ball, floating action. Contact with the ball is generally made by the hand with the fingers together and slightly flexed, however, the heel of the hand and fist can be used.

The position of the inflating valve in the ball affects its flight. The ball will break toward the side of the valve location, when hit so it floats in this manner. When sufficient accuracy is attained in performing this serve, the placement of the valve can be used effectively. The floater serve is probably the one most frequently used in modern volleyball. It is difficult to pass because of its flight fluctuations.

Overhand Spin. The stance and other fundamental skills are almost identical to the overhand floater, however, in order to produce the overspin, the action of the hitting hand is different. In executing this serve, the first contact with the ball is made below the mid-center with the heel of the hand, followed by a wrist snap which brings the fingers up and over the ball to impart the overspin. The overspin causes the ball to develop a dropping direction as it crosses the net into the opponents' court. It is also possible to produce a right or left curve in the flight of the ball by striking it on its respective right or left side.

Roundhouse. This is the most difficult of the serves to learn and should not be attempted until the others are mastered. The preliminary body stance and initial arm position for delivery is similar to the overhand floater, except for the left shoulder, which is pointed more squarely toward the net.

As the delivery begins, the weight is shifted back over the right leg, the right hand drops back and down to about knee level with the palm pointed outward. As the ball is tossed upward, the weight begins to shift forward, and when the ball reaches the pro-

per altitude, the right arm is brought forceably forward in an elbow-locked, overhand, windmill-like motion. The hand contacts the ball almost directly above the right shoulder as the body weight moves over the left leg.

Two types of ball action can be produced, depending upon how the hand is used. To induce a dead ball flight, contact with the ball must be made at its back, center with the heel of the hand. To produce overspin, the ball is struck slightly below its midline, with a slightly flexed hand and a follow through that brings the fingers over the ball.

Net Recovery

The ball is sometimes hit into the net on the spike, pass, or recovery play. In such cases, unless it has already been played three times, it may be recovered and put into play. The ball reacts differently depending upon which section of the net it strikes: if it strikes the net near the top, it will slide down in a nearly perpendicular manner; if it strikes the middle portion of the net, it will rebound out one or two feet; if it strikes the bottom portion of the net, it will hang for a brief moment and then rebound out several feet.

When a net ball occurs, the player takes a position with one side to the net at a distance determined by where the ball hits and its speed. If the recovery is made on the second hit, the attempt for the set should be made; but if it is made on the third hit, the ball must be played over the net. Usually the situation requires the use of either the one-handed dig or the forearm bump pass. In either case, the player must take a low squatting position and get set before the ball rebounds from the net.

TEAM DEFENSE

The team that is not playing the ball is on defense. Strategy must be developed for this phase of the game. The block and court position of non-blocking players are essential elements in any type of defense, however, other factors to consider are: covering a free ball, changing from offense to defense and vice versa, type of spike, and changing types of defense during play.

The Block

The purpose of a block is to play a hard driven ball back into the opponents court, or cause it to rebound so a non-blocking teammate can play it. The rules place limitations on blocking strategy. Only the three front players can block, no player may touch the net with any part of his body, and no player may touch the playing surface on the opponents' side of the net.

Individual blocking techniques have been discussed previously. However, it should be emphasized that blockers should start the jump from a position close to the net with the forearms up parallel to the net, and approximately 6 inches away from it. The jump is made from a deep knee flexion, and the legs drive upward, the arms are pushed up to a fully extended position, with the fingers spread, and thumbs nearly touching. If time permits, lateral movement should be executed with a slide step, otherwise the cross over step must be used.

When team blocking is executed to the right or left side of the court, the outside player sets the block and is joined by the center front player. The hands of the blockers are positioned with respect to the direction they wish the ball to rebound after contact. The outside player will turn the palms slightly inward toward the center of the court to prevent the spiked ball from rebounding out-of-bounds when the spiker attempts a wipe-off. The palms and fingers will be extended slightly upward and backward if they want the ball to rebound into their own court. If the object is to cause the ball to rebound into the opponents' court in a downward direction, the blockers will reach over the net and flex the wrists. The block is also set to prevent the spiker from directing the ball into certain areas on the court, and to encouage him to hit it into other areas that are well protected by a non-blocking teammate.

The type of offense may influence the number of players who can block. Generally, it is relatively easy for two players to block against a 4-2 offense because the spike is usually delivered from the extreme right or left side of the court. However, the two-man block is more difficult to execute against the 6-0 offense because the spike can be hit by any one of the three front line players. This possibility holds the blockers in their respective positions until it is sometimes too late to move over to participate in the block. This is especially true against a low or quick set, and other deceptive moves by the setter and spikers.

Defensive Patterns

Two team defense alignments are in general use. These are distinguished by the court position of one of the backs, usually the CB When the CB plays the back court area it is called a man-back or 2-4 defense.

When the back positions himself up behind the block, it is called the man-up or 2-1-3 defense.

The Man Back Defense (2-4). It is strong against balls hit hard directly over the block, but weak against soft shots and dinks. The diagrams below show player position for the two-man block because it is the one most frequently used.

When the two-man block is set to the right, the non-blocking players are aligned as described below. The RB aligns himself outside of the outside blocker's hands, and moves to a position three quarters distance from the net, close to the right sideline. He must play all balls hit down his sideline alley, and all dinks and soft shots that fall to his side of the block. The CB is responsible for playing all balls hit into the back court area. This includes spikes hit over the block, rebounds, lobs hit into his area, and spiked balls hit through the block. He has no responsibility for playing dinks or short shots. The court area a few feet in front of him and up toward the block is the weakest area of this defense. The LB is assigned to the area called the power alley, where most of the hard angled spikes are directed. His initial position is 6-10 feet in from the left sideline, up near mid-court, so that he is aligned just off the left shoulder of the inside blocker. He will be required to use the dig or bump to pass hard driven spikes. The LF (off-side blocker) positions himself approximately 10 feet back from the net and three feet into the court toward the blockers. If the spike is made from a position in toward the center of the opponents' court, he will move to about 5 feet from the left sideline to play the ball; if the spike is delivered from near the left sideline of the opponents' court, he will move farther in toward the center upon contact. He is responsible for playing all sharp-angled spikes down along the net; and dinks, rebounds and off-speed shots to the left of the block.

When the two-man block is set to the left, the player assignments are reversed except for the CF and CB The backs can switch positions after the serve, and, good teams may have their backs switch so the player with special skill in fielding the hard spike can play the power alley position. Other switches can be made to take advantage of player ability. The blockers can switch also in order to get the best blocker in the most favorable position.

Changing from Man-Back Defense to Offense. The manner of this change will be dictated to some degree by the type of offense the team is using. When switching to the 4-2 offense, the first pass is to the CF position. If the setter has been blocking in a LF, RF or off-side blocker position, he will switch with the

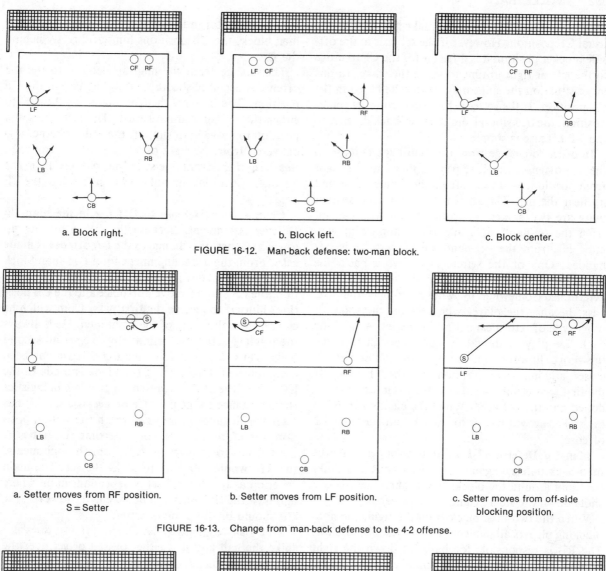

a. Block right.

b. Block left.

c. Block center.

FIGURE 16-12.   Man-back defense: two-man block.

a. Setter moves from RF position.
S = Setter

b. Setter moves from LF position.

c. Setter moves from off-side
blocking position.

FIGURE 16-13.   Change from man-back defense to the 4-2 offense.

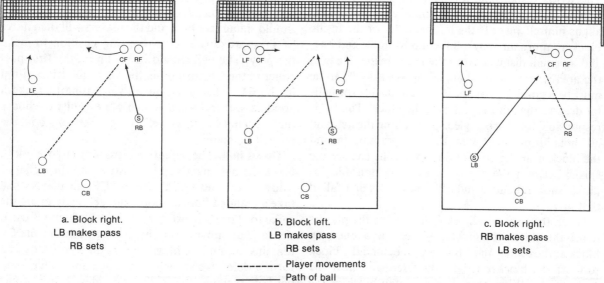

a. Block right.
LB makes pass
RB sets

b. Block left.
LB makes pass
RB sets

c. Block right.
RB makes pass
LB sets

- - - - - - -   Player movements
——————   Path of ball

FIGURE 16-14.   Change from the man-back defense to the 6-0 offense.

player in his position so he can make the set from the usual CF position. However if the setter is in the off-side blocker position it is difficult for the CF to move to the left or right in time to make the spike. In this latter situation the spike may have to be hit from the CF position. If the setter is blocking from the center position, the transition from the man-back defense to the 4-2 offense is simple.

In order to change from the man-back defense to the 6-0 offense, the first pass is made to the right front position, 8-10 feet in from the right sideline and up near the net. The set is made by a back so that there are two spikers in front of him who can hit from the on-hand side, and one behind him who must hit from the off-hand side unless he is left handed. One of the setters is always a back line player, however, the back player who makes the set is determined somewhat by who must play the first pass, because the player who receives the spike or other type of return cannot make the set. Any of the back line players should be quick enough to make this move, however, the player in the RB position is closer, and in a better position than the other two. If the first pass is not a good one, the 6-0 must be abandoned and the 4-2 used. When the back setter plays the spike, he will pass it to the CF and start the 4-2 offense.

Man-Up Defense (2-1-3). It is stronger than the man-back defense against off-speed balls and dinks over and around the block, but weaker against long shots down the sideline and into the center.

When the two-man block is on the right, the non-blocking players align themselves as described below. The RB is responsible for balls hit down the right sideline, and to the right of the middle court. The LB aligns himself just off the left shoulder of the inside blocker, approximately 6-8 feet up from the end line, and an equal distance from the left sideline. He is in the area where the hard angled spikes are hit, so he must be a good dig passer. He is responsible for balls hit deep to the left of, and over the block. The LF is responsible for sharp angled spikes along the net, and all shots hit into that area. the CB comes up behind the block near the 10-foot line so that he can see the spiker between the blockers. He is responsible for dinks, short rebounds and off-speed shots that fall in that area.

When the two-man block is to the left the players make the shift accordingly. If there is a one-man block at the center, the CB moves in behind the block just off the blocker's right shoulder, and near the 10-foot line. When there is a two-man block at the center, the CB must cover for the front line player who participates in the block. If all three front line men block, the CB positions himself directly behind the CF.

The change from the man-up defense to the 4-2 offense is accomplished by setting the ball to the CF position. The set can then be made by the CF to either the left or right forward. The CB is now in position to move in to support the spike whether it is delivered from the right or left side of the court. In this case, if the front line setter has blocked from the RF or LF positions, he will have to switch into the CF area.

Change from Defense to Offense in the Man-Up Defense Alignment. Because the CB is playing up toward the net, the change to the 6-0 offense is made easy. From the usual alignment for a two-man block right, the CF slides from the block to the CF position, the LF and RF move into place and the CB positions himself to receive the first pass, from which he can set the ball to any of the front men. He is always the primary setter and will attempt to set all second balls. Thus, the change to the 6-0 offense has been accomplished. However, if the block is made to the left side of the court, it presents a problem in logistics for the change to the 6-0 offense because the CB has a greater distance to move to reach the setting position, therefore, the RB would become the setter. If the CB has to receive the ball from the opponents, the RB. would move up to make the set. The main criterion as to who will set is dependant upon where and how the first pass will be executed, however, the CB should be the primary setter.

Free Ball Alignment. When the offense does not spike the ball and it is either passed or set over the net, one of the defense players, usually the CF, should signal free ball, and the players will then move to an approximate serve-receiving position to make the play. The ball should be set up on the first pass either to the CF position in the 4-2 or the RF position in the 6-0. This situation provides time to make a good pass, therefore, a greater opportunity to choose the best kind of set, as well as the spiker to whom the set will be made.

Down Ball. The defensive team may choose not to block the opponent's spike. Instead, on the signal of "down" or "no block" by the CF, all players will take a planned floor position and get ready to dig the spike to start their offense. If the 4-2 offense is used, the set man moves up to his setting position, the CF remains up, and all other players take positions that form a defensive semicircle on the court. This manner of playing the spike provides better court coverage than the one, two or three-man block.

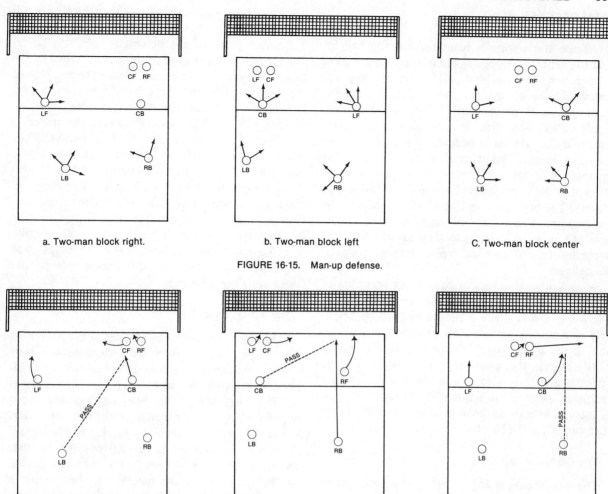

a. Two-man block right.

b. Two-man block left

c. Two-man block center

FIGURE 16-15.   Man-up defense.

a. From block right.

b. From block left when CB receives ball.

c. From block center.

FIGURE 16-16.   Change from the man-up defense to the 6-0 offense.

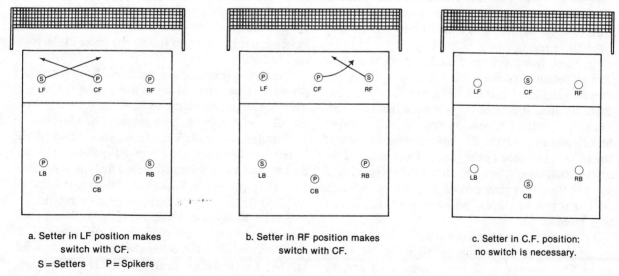

a. Setter in LF position makes switch with CF.

S = Setters   P = Spikers

b. Setter in RF position makes switch with CF.

c. Setter in C.F. position: no switch is necessary.

FIGURE 16-17.   The 4-2 offensive alignment.

TEAM OFFENSE

Offense starts when a team receives the ball hit over the net by the opposing team either from a serve or a return of any kind. Offensive strategy for volleyball, like other team sports, can be designed from the simple to the complex, for beginners to the highly skilled. Any attack is dependent upon delivering the ball to the setter accurately and at the most favorable height. The offense selected should fit the capabilities of the participants. It is a mistake to attempt to use a complicated offense with low skilled players. The higher the skill level of the players, the more complicated the attack can be made. The purpose of any good attack is to take advantage of the strengths of the offense and exploit the weaknesses of the defense.

Several different types of offensive alignments or systems are in use. The three included here are the 6-6, 4-2 and 6-0. The 6-6 should be used by beginners, and as skill increases, change should be made to one of the other two. However, it should be emphasized that the most important aspect of any volleyball offense is to master the skills of service reception, passing and setting. The proper execution of these skills provide the only means whereby the set man can place the ball for effective spiking.

The 6-6 Offense

The 6-6 offense is the lowest level attack system and does not provide for specialization. Each player must perform all the skills of passing, setting and spiking. Therefore, the CF is always the setter regardless of which player is in that position. This compels each player to learn each skill. This system is more suitable for physical education classes than either the 4-2 or 6-0. It is not used by varsity and competitive teams.

The three front and three back players take their normal rotation position on the court. The serve reception is passed into the CF position, several feet above the net, and from 1-4 feet back from the net. The player in the CF position sets the ball to either the LF (on-hand side) or RF (off-hand side) forward. The spike is executed by the forward who receives the set. The ball should be set so that it falls into an area either to the left or right side of the court bounded by the last 6 feet of the net and approximately 5 feet back from it.

If the first pass comes to the setter from his left, he should set to the LF; if from his right, he should set to the RF However, as skill increases, the setter, by

using the back pass, can set to either the RF, or LF and thereby add some deception to the offense.

Another phase of any offense is providing coverage for the spiker in case of a blocked return of the spike. When the spike is made from the left side of the court, the LB and CF move in close to, and slightly behind the spiker. The RF moves over to his left and the CB and RB move up toward the spiker to play the balls blocked high over the LB and CF The player who receives the ball, if it is blocked back over the net after the spike, should pass it to the CF position so it can be set up for the spike. Therefore, all players on a team must move quickly from one formation to another. The adjustment from the spike coverage to offense must be accomplished speedily, as well as the movement from the service reception to the attack formation. For this reason, players are continually on the move.

The 4-2 Offense

This offense depends upon specialization for its effectiveness. Two players are designated as setters and four men as spikers. The set is made by the designated set man who is a front line player in the normal rotation alignment. The two setters are placed diagonally opposite each other in the rotation order. A match is generally begun by placing one in the LF position and the other in the RB position because USVBA rules require a team to rotate before serving for the first time in the match. The best setter is generally started in the LF spot. The two best spikers are placed in a similar manner, but start the match in the LB and RF positions. Therefore, when the offense team serves for the first time the players rotate so that the LB moves into the LF position. This is done so that each one of them gets to spike from the LF (on-side) position during two rotations if the switch is used. They also follow the setter in the rotation order.

The switch (exchange of positions by two or more players) is an essential technique in the 4-2 attack. This is necessary in order to have the set made from the CF position by the two players who specialize in performing this skill. Therefore, when either of the setters are in either the LF or RF position, he will switch with the CF immediately after the server hits the ball for the serve. When the setter is in the normal rotation CF position there is no need to switch.

Service Reception. Players must be in their proper rotation position until after the serve is executed. They may not overlap either horizontally or vertically. The LF (spiker) is near the middle of the court,

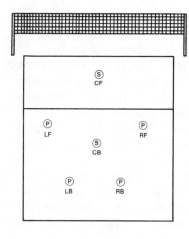

FIGURE 16-18.
Serve reception for 4-2 offense.

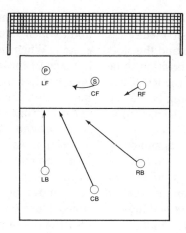

a. Spike made from the left.

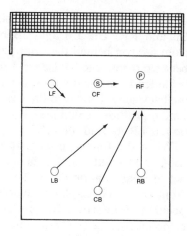

b. Spike made from the right.

FIGURE 16-19. Supporting the spiker in the 4-2 offense.

and 3-5 feet from left sideline. The CF (setter) is in the center, near the net. The RF (spiker) is near the middle of the court, and about 6-7 feet in from the right sideline. The CB (setter) plays near the center of the court, slightly behind the LF and RF The RB and LB (spikers) split the gap between the front men and the CB and position themselves 6-8 feet in from the back line.

The front setter moves up to the net so he can receive the pass and set the ball facing the best spiker. The spikers do not start moving to their attack positions until they are certain the pass is played effectively. One of the back men always backs up the player who receives the serve.

Supporting the Spiker. As the spike is being executed, the spiker's teammates move into position to protect against a blocked return of the spike. When the spike is delivered from the left, the setter, LB and CB move into semicircle around the spiker. The RF moves back and in toward the spiker and the RB moves up toward the middle of the court. It is the duty of the RF and RB to cover the bulk of the court area. All players stay low with knees flexed and hands down in a ready position. When the spike is made to the left, the responsibilities of the players are reversed.

The 6-0 Offense

It is distinguished by several characteristics. Each player becomes a spiker when he rotates into the front line, one of the back men executes the set, and the set is made from the RF position, approximately 8-10 feet in from the right side line. This provides

much more opportunity for deception than in the 4-2 attack. It gives the opposing blockers little time to determine the area from which the spike will be delivered, therefore, it makes the multiple block more difficult to perform, and provides more opportunity for the spiker to have only a single blocker opposing him. The set is made from the right side of the court, thereby enabling two spikers to hit the spike from the on-hand side. Further deception is possible by the setter using the back set to the RF who may have no blocker opposing him.

Although this system generally requires that all players must be able to perform the spike, two players are designated as setters and are placed diagonally opposite each other in the rotation order so that one of them is in a back position at all times. The CB is generally in the best position to make the set, but it can be made from either of the other back positions. However, it is difficult for the LB to move cross court to the RF position, therefore, either the RB or CB will generally make the set. If the best set man is not in the CB or RB position, he can switch to that area after the serve, therefore, it is possible to have the set made by the CB or RB at all times. The strength of the 6-0 depends upon deception, accurate passing, and setting the ball to the best spikers. See Figure 16-20 for basic 6-0 alignment.

Serve Reception in 6-0 Offense. Either four or five players may be designated as receivers. In the five-player alignment, when the setter is in the RB position, the front players take positions at mid-court. The LF is near the left sideline; the RF moves toward the center of the court and several feet from the right sideline; and, the CF splits the distance between the LF and RF. The LB and CB position themselves from 6-8 feet behind the front players, and the slots between them. The RB (setter) takes a position so he is hidden from the opposing server by the RF When the back setter rotates to the CB position, he takes a similar position behind the CF, and on the next rotation as LB, behind the LF

When the four-man serve reception alignment is used, a back setter and front spiker play up near the net in legal rotation order. The position of the two front and two back players depend upon the rotation position of the setter. The primary setter and his corresponding spiker will take the front position.

Supporting the Spiker in the 6-0. Strategy depends upon which side of the court the spike has been executed. When the spike is made by the LF from the left side of the court, the other players should move into position to play the ball in case a successful block sends the ball back into their court. The setter and two front players move quickly to form a semicircle around the spiker. The two remaining backs move up toward this semicircle to play a blocked ball that rebounds over the front players, or that passes them. After the block has been played all players must move quickly into their normal attack positions. However, if the ball has been blocked back into the opponent's court, they must move into the

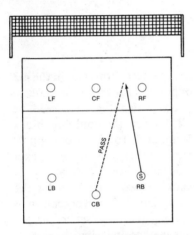

Setter is generally the CB or RB

FIGURE 16-20.
Basic 6-0 offensive alignment.

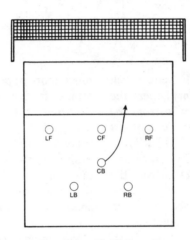

a. 5 receivers with CB the setter.

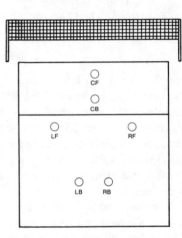

b. 4 receivers with CB the setter and CF the best spiker.

FIGURE 16-21.   Service reception alignment for the 6-0 offense.

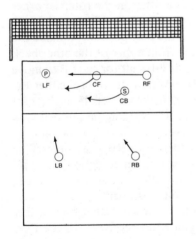

a. Spike delivered from LF position.

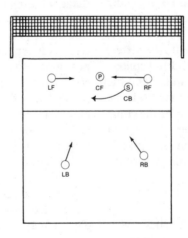

b. Spike delivered from CF position.

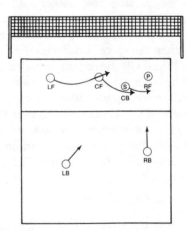

c. Spike delivered from RF position.

FIGURE 16-23.   Supporting the spiker in the 6-0 offense.

defense alignment to receive a possible spike. When the spike is made at the center or to the left, players take comparable positions.

Play Systems or Patterns

When players reach a sufficiently high level of individual skill in performing the basic fundamentals or receiving, passing, setting and spiking, team play patterns and systems should be developed so that all players know where the set will be placed, the type of set, as well as the type of spike and player positions. In order to accomplish this goal, a team may have a system whereby the placement of the serve, spike and other situations will dictate the play sequence and player movement, or have special signals called by the primary setter to designate the placement of the set as well as the type of set to be executed. This situation provides the setter and spiker an opportuni-ty to use the high, low and shoot types of sets and the appropriate spike which they dictate.

WEIGHT TRAINING

Weight training can be used to develop strength, endurance, flexibility, explosive power and other qualities necessary to play volleyball well, just as it is used for many other sports. For volleyball, particular attention should be directed to exercises that will increase endurance, flexibility, quickness, balance, vertical jump, and strength and toughness of the hands, wrists, shoulders and arms. Exercises recommended to develop these and other desirable qualities are: heel and toe raise, half and full squats, dead lift, pull-over, bench press, overhead press, wrist curls, rowing, arm curls and other similar exercises. See Chapter 17 for the proper execution of these exercises.

EXERCISE   Definitions and List of Terms

1. A serve that a receiver cannot play is called an _____ .
2. An _____ is any situation in which a team is playing the ball.
3. The players occupying the three positions in the back court in normal rotation order are called _____ .
4. When one team member takes a position behind a teammate to give him support when he is playing the ball, he is said to be a _____ man.
5. That portion of the court generally occupied by the three back court players that extends from mid-court to the back line is called the _____ .
6. A set that is passed to a spiker located behind the setter is called a _____ .
7. The _____ is a means of playing the ball just before or as it crosses the net after a spike.
8. A pass in which the ball makes contact with the forearms, wrists or fist is called a _____ .
9. A spiked ball that travels at a sharp angle across the court toward the side line is called a _____ .
10. _____ is the action taken by one team to keep the opponents from scoring or getting the serve.
11. A one-handed pass used to field a low ball that is impossible to reach by usual methods is called a _____ pass
12. A soft hit by a spiker that propels the ball just over the top of the block, or to either side of it, is called a _____ .
13. A _____ is a tumbling movement made by a player attempting to play a ball beyond normal reach. It is generally followed by a slide.
14. When players on opposing teams commit simultaneous fouls a _____ is called.
15. When the ball makes two or more contacts with the same player it is called a _____ .
16. The action of a player who moves in to make a spike, but does not make it is called a _____ .
17. A serve hit so that the ball travels without any spinning motion is called a _____ .
18. A pass made by striking the ball with the forearms is called a _____ .
19. Any violation of the rules is called a _____ .

20. A low set, one that is not more than four feet above the net, that travels at a sharp angle crosswise to the net and drops near the side line is called a _____ .

21. A weak return of the ball over the net by the opposing team that provides a team with a favorable attack opportunity is called a _____ .

22. That part of the court from the midline to the net, and generally occupied by the forwards, is called the _____ .

23. A play in which the overhand pass is used to make a set, and the ball is hit upward in front of the setter is called a _____ .

24. When a ball comes to rest on, or in the hand, or hands which is judged to be in violation of the rules, it is called _____ .

25. A set executed by a player from a jumping movement is called a _____ . It is often made to deceive the defense.

26. A _____ is a ball driven down into the opponents' court with such great speed that the defense is not able to return it.

27. The _____ is a pass in which the ball travels slowly and with a high arc.

28. A defensive alignment in which one of the backs, usually the CB is responsible for playing all balls hit into the deep back court is called _____ defense.

29. A defensive alignment in which one of the backs, usually the CB plays up close behind the block is called the _____ defense.

30. A _____ is two out of three or three out of five games.

31. The action taken by team in possession of the ball to attempt to score or get possession of the serve is called _____ .

32. When a ball is set to a right hand spiker from his left, it is said to be set to his _____ side.

33. When a ball is set to a right hand spiker from his right, it is said to be set to his _____ side.

34. The front line player who does not participate in the block is called the _____ blocker.

35. A ball hit by the spiker at less than full speed is called an _____ ball.

36. A ball set very low and close to net so it can be spiked by the spiker on its upward flight is called a _____ .

37. An illegal alignment of players before the serve is delivered is called an _____ .

38. A _____ is the action of a player hitting the ball to a teammate.

39. A _____ is a unit of scoring which can be made by the serving team only.

40. The area to the inside of the right or left block that extends cross court to the respective back line and side line, into which most hard spikes are made, is called the _____ .

41. Continuous play from the serve to the time when a point is scored, a side out is declared, play is stopped, or the ball is declared dead is called a _____ .

42. A tumbling rolling movement made by a player after making a lunge or dive to play the ball is called a _____ .

43. _____ is the clockwise movement of players one position, when the ball is received for delivering the first serve, and by the team getting possession of the ball after a side out is called.

44. _____ is a type of serve delivered by using a straight arm swing in an overhand manner. It is sometimes used to make the spike.

45. _____ is a violation made during an underhand pass in which the ball comes to rest on the hands.

46. A _____ is used to put the ball into play to start a game, after each foul, and following each point.

47. The area extending a minimum of 6 feet behind the back line and 10 feet in from the extension of the right side line, from which the serve is delivered is called the _____ .

48. A _____ is the act of passing the ball into a specific area, and at a suitable height to be spiked.

49. The _____ is another name for the four-set.

50. A _____ is called when the serving team loses its serve.
51. A _____ is the name of the technique in which a player jumps right into the air, and forceably hits the ball down into the opponents' court.
52. The player who makes the spike is called the _____ .
53. Any action or maneuver made by one team to help it win a contest is called _____ .
54. A _____ is a legal move in which to or more players change position as the serve is delivered.
55. The _____ is a set in which the ball travels at a crosswise sharp angle to the net, and from 3-4 feet above it, and drops from 5-6 feet from the side line.
56. A _____ is a set in which the ball is passed from 2-3 feet above the net, and about the same distance in front of the spiker so that he can spike it on the rise.
57. A _____ is the name applied to a play in which the spiker his the ball directly into the hands of the blockers so that it rebounds out-of-bounds.

1. Ace	20. Four-set	39. Point
2. Attack	21. Free ball	40. Power alley
3. Backs	22. Front court	41. Rally
4. Back-up	23. Front set	42. Roll
5. Back court	24. Holding	43. Rotation
6. Back set	25. Jump set	44. Roundhouse
7. Block	26. Kill	45. Scooping (lifting)
8. Bump pass	27. Lob	46. Serve
9. Cut shot	28. Man-back defense	47. Service area
10. Defense	29. Man-up defense	48. Set-up
11. Dig pass	30. Match	49. Shoot-set
12. Dink	31. Offense	50. Side out
13. Dive	32. Off-hand side	51. Spike
14. Double foul	33. On-hand side	52. Spiker
15. Double hit	34. Off-side blocker	53. Strategy
16. Fake	35. Off-speed ball	54. Switch
17. Floater	36. One-set (Japanese)	55. Three set
18. Forearm pass	37. Overlap	56. Two set
19. Foul	38. Pass	57. Wipe-off

QUESTIONS AND ANSWERS ON THE RULES

1. *Q.* How is the game begun?
   A. The game is begun by a player of one team serving the ball to the opposing team. The first team to serve in a game shall be determined with the toss of the coin by the referee. The team not serving first in the first game of a match will serve first in the second game.
2. *Q.* What are the regulations governing the delivery of the serve?
   A. The serve is made from the service area by the player occupying the right back position. The server cannot touch the lines bounding the service area or the floor outside these lines at the time the ball is hit on the delivery of the service. The ball may be struck with fist(s), hand(s), or arm(s). It must clear the net on its flight into the opponents' court. Each player will become the server when he rotates into the right back position. The server continues to serve until he or his teammates make a foul or the game is completed.
3. *Q.* What position must all players other than the server take when the ball is being served?

    A. All players except the server must be in their rotation serving order, with each of the forwards nearer to the net than his respective back when the ball is hit for the serve. No player shall place his feet so that one or both are completely in front of or behind (whichever is applicable) the foremost point of the foot or feet of his respective teammate.

4. *Q.* When does the receiving team serve?

    A. When the serving team commits a foul, completes a game, or otherwise fails to make a good return, the ball is given to the opposing team. According to USVBA rules, the team receiving the ball for the serve will rotate one position clockwise, and the player rotating from the right forward position to the right back becomes the server. According to NAGWS rules, there is no rotation until after the first RB player serves her turn.

5. *Q.* How many attempts does the server get to make each serve?

    A. Only one try is permitted.

6. *Q.* What is a service foul?

    A. The server commits a foul when he steps on or outside the lines marking the boundary of the service area, throws or scoops the ball, fails to make the ball clear the top of the net, hits the ball out-of-bounds, fails to hit it clearly, or propels it under the net.

7. *Q.* How is the ball played after the serve is completed?

    A. The ball must be played by the receiving team before it touches the playing surface. According to USVBA rules it may be played with any part of the body above, and including, the waist. AIAW rules do not permit the ball to hit the body. It must be hit, struck, or rebound sharply from the body part. It is a foul to permit it to come to rest momentarily on any part of the body. It may not be thrown, lifted, or carried. It must be cleanly hit.

8. *Q.* Explain the scoring system in volleyball?

    A. Only the team serving can score. It scores one point each time the opponents commit a foul or fail to return the ball across the net. No point is scored when a side out occurs.

9. *Q.* When does a team win?

    A. A game may be won in two different ways: by points only, and by points and time. If two teams are using the points-only choice, the team that first scores 15 points and has a 2-point lead wins. When the points-and-time choice is made, the team that scores 15 points with a 2-point lead before eight minutes are up wins. However, if the teams are compelled to play the full eight minutes, the team that has a 2-point lead wins regardless of the total score.

10. *Q.* When does a net foul occur?

    A. A foul occurs when a player touches the net while the ball is in play, except when the force of the ball drives the net into a player. The hand(s) of blockers or attack players may pass over the net; however, the hand(s) of the blockers or attack players may not touch the ball until after the attacking player(s) has made contact with the ball.

11. *Q.* Is one player limited in the number of times he can hit the ball on his side of the net?

    A. Yes. He may not play the ball twice in succession, except that if he plays a hard-driven spike that has not been played by a teammate, he may make successive contacts. He may also play the ball again after he has contacted it simultaneously with a teammate or with an opponent. He may also play the ball after it has been played by one of his teammates.

13. *Q.* What is a match?

    A. A match is two out of three or three out of five games.

14. *Q.* What players are eligible to spike?

A. Any player on the team may spike; however, players occupying the three back positions must take off for a spike from behind the 10-foot line but may land on, or in front of, this line after making the spike. A back line player can play the ball in the front court but must contact it below the level of the top of the net.

15. *Q.* What is the manner of rotation?

A. According to NAGWS rules, after the first RB player serves for each team in each game, all players will rotate one position clockwise when the ball is received the second time for the serve. USVBA rules require rotation to start before the first serve in each game.

16. *Q.* What is the substitution rule?

A. A player may re-enter the same game not more than three times, including the starting line-up, and must re-enter in his original position. If this rule is violated and the violation is discovered before the opponents serve, points scored by his team while the player was playing in the wrong position will be deducted and side out called if his team is still serving. He may not remain in the game unless he assumes his original position. A team is limited to 12 substitutions in one game. The substitute must take the position of the player for whom he is substituted.

17. *Q.* Is it legal to play a net ball?

A. Yes. Any ball driven into the net may be played except on the serve, or after it has been played three times.

18. *Q.* What is screening?

A. Screening is any move made by a player to conceal the start of his teammate's serve by obstructing the view of an opponent. It is illegal.

19. *Q.* Explain the blocking rule?

A. Not more than three players may execute a block, and none of these may come from the back line players.

20. *Q.* May a player cross the center line while the ball is in play?

A. Any part of the body may touch the center line, and the foot or feet may extend into the opponents' court as long as some part of the foot or feet remains on or above this line. Any part of the body may be in the air below the net and beyond the center line if there is no interference with the play of the opponents.

21. *Q.* What is a double foul?

A. When two opposing players commit simultaneous fouls, a double foul has been committed. In this case, no points are scored and the play is taken over.

22. *Q.* How many time-outs are permitted during a game?

A. Each team has two time-outs of thirty seconds in each game. A foul is charged for any time out in excess of two per game. Time allowed for injury or adjustment of apparel is not considered a charged time-out.

23. *Q.* Can a team compete with less than six men?

A. No. A team will less than six players must forfeit.

24. *Q.* When is a serve good?

A. It is good when it crosses above the top of the net between the antenna or their extension, and does not touch the net, antenna, any surface, object or person before touching an opponent or the playing surface.

25. *Q.* What is the size and location of the service area?

A. It extends from the right sideline 10 feet along the endline, and a minimum of 6 feet in back of the endline. If the playing area does not provide enough space for the 6-foot depth, the service area should be extended into the court far enough to give this depth.

26. *Q.* Where is the location of the spiking line for the back players?

A. It is drawn across each half of the court 10 feet from, and parallel to, the middle of the center line.

27. *Q.* When is the ball in play?
    A. The ball is in play from the time it is hit for the serve until a point is scored, side out is called, or play is suspended for any reason.
28. *Q.* What is a foul?
    A. A foul is any encroachment of the rules or any failure to play the ball as prescribed by the rules.
29. *Q.* Describe how the ball must be hit?
    A. The ball must be cleanly hit. If it comes to rest when it contacts the player, a foul has been committed.
30. *Q.* When is the ball out-of-bounds?
    A. The ball is out-of-bounds when it touches any surface or object outside the boundary lines of the court, or touches the net outside the antenna. If any part of the ball touches a boundary line or the antenna, it is in bounds. If it is caught, hit, or otherwise played by a player before landing out-of-bounds, it is not out-of-bounds.
31. *Q.* When is the ball dead?
    A. When it touches the playing surface, goes out-of-bounds, or the referee blows the whistle for any reason other than starting play.

BIBLIOGRAPHY

Cherebetiu, Gabriel, *Volleyball Techniques.* Hollywood, Calif.: Creative Sports Books, 1969.

Coleman, James E. and Liskevcn, Taras N., *Pictorial Analysis of Power Volleyball.* Hollywood, Calif.: Creative Sports Books, 1972.

Cohen, Harlan, *Power Volleyball Drills.* Hollywood, Calif.: Creative Sports Books, 1971.

DGWS, *Volleyball Guide.* Washington, D.C.: AAHPER, 1975-77.

Egstrom, Glen H. and Schaafsma, Frances, *Volleyball.* Dubuque: Wm. C. Brown Company, 1966.

Keller, V., *Point Game Match.* Hollywood, Calif.: Creative Sports Books, 1968.

Scates, Allen E., *Winning Volleyball.* Boston; Allyn and Bacon, 1972.

Shondell, Donald and McManama, Jerre, *Volleyball.* Englewood Cliffs, N.J.: Prentice-Hall, Inc., 1971.

Slaymaker, Thomas and Brown, Virginia H., *Power Volleyball.* Philadelphia: W. B. Saunders Company, 1970.

Thigpen, J., *Power Volleyball for Girls and Women.* Dubuque: Wm. C. Brown Company, 1970.

United States Volleyball Association, *Volleyball Official Guide And Rule Book.* Berne, Ind.: USVBA Printer, 1975.

17

WEIGHT LIFTING AND
WEIGHT TRAINING

DESCRIPTION OF THE ACTIVITY

Weight training has become an important part of both physical education and athletic programs for total bodily development, increased physical capacity, and muscular efficiency specific to the activity. Research on its value in developing strength, endurance, explosive power, flexibility, and speed of muscular contraction as well as in the rehabilitation of injured parts of the body has been overwhelmingly favorable. The once-prevalent concept that weight training tends to develop muscles that are thick, heavy, and slow to contract is rapidly diminishing. Weight training possesses the versatility of permitting specific muscular development in preparation for a movement in a particular sport, general bodily development, increased physical capacity, the increasing or losing of weight, and the improvement of the efficiency of practically any muscle group within a short period of time. It is a systematic training program whereby muscles are gradually provided with increased resistance in weight and intensity, or work per unit of time to tax and improve the functioning of the systems of the body.

Weight lifting also applies the principle of progressive resistance exercise; however, the program is directed, through the use of much heavier weights, mainly toward the development of strength and explosive power in preparation for the three basic competitive lifts: the two-hand press, the two-hand snatch, and the two-hand clean and jerk. Competition is equalized for men of all sizes and weights through their division into the classes shown in Table 17-1.

Strength, not overall bodily development, is of primary importance in weight lifting. Workouts require heavy lifts and limited repetitions.

Weight-training and weight-lifting exercises can be performed in a small area with minimum equipment. A typical workout may last from forty-five minutes to two hours, with actual lifting time approximately two to six minutes.

EQUIPMENT

Platform

A square platform, 4 by 4 meters in length, with sides of heavy wood capable of supporting heavy weights that are dropped meets international specifications for weight lifting. For weight training, practically any area, such as a room, a hallway, or a locker room, can be converted into an efficient station.

Barbell

The official, international weight-lifting barbell is a maximum of 7 feet in length and 1 inch in diameter;

TABLE 17.1   Division of classes in weight lifting.

Class	Maximum Weight
Bantamweight	123¼ lbs.
Featherweight	132¼ lbs.
Lightweight	148¾ lbs.
Middleweight	165 lbs.
Light-heavyweight	181¼ lbs.
Middle-heavyweight	198 lbs.
Heavyweight	Unlimited

TABLE 17.2   Equipment used in weight-training program.

Equipment	Purpose
Abdominal board	Execution of a variety of abdominal exercises with and without weights.
Bench	A bench 10 to 12 inches wide, 18 inches high, and 4 to 6 feet in length is basic to the performance of numerous exercises requiring a supine position.
Calf machine	Muscle development in the back of lower leg.
Chest expanders	Provides isotonic resistance to practically any body area.
Head strap	Strengthening of neck muscles.
Incline bench	Development of chest and arm muscles.
Iron boots	Development of leg and abdominal muscles.
Knee bench	Development of knee extensor muscles.
Latissimus dorsi machine	Development of shoulder and upper back.
Lifting belt/wrist band	Assists in supporting heavy weight; provides back and wrist rigidity.
Lower leg flexor/extensor table	Strengthening of supporting muscles of the knee.
Multi-purpose bench	Aids performance of squats and exercises requiring the supine position.
Portable power rack	Permits isometric and isotonic exercises and chinning, with exceptional safety features.
Shoulder rest support (padded)	Cushions extremely heavy weight in the shoulder rest position and permits the squat and semi-squat walk without undue discomfort.
Weight Machine	Permits 10 individuals to perform simultaneously in a variety of exercises. One-piece apparatus with all weights permanently attached.
Wall Pulleys	Development of arms, shoulders, and upper back; capable of simulating exact movements of a specific activity.
Wrist Roller	Development of grip and forearms.

weighs 45 pounds, including the weight of two fixed inside collars; and has rotating sleeves at each end to secure the discs and permit rotation during competition. The 5-pound outside collars prevent the weights from sliding from the bar. The bar, together with the two inside and the two outside collars, weighs 55 pounds. For weight training, a bar 4 to 7 feet in length and 1 inch in diameter is sufficient. Dumbbells, 14 to 18 inches in length and also 1 inch in diameter, are essential to a good training program.

Weights

Weights are graduated in pounds ranging from 2½, 5, 10, 25, 35, 45, to 75 and 100. European sets are graduated in kilograms and deviate slightly in poundage at each of the above weights.

Uniform

An official uniform, consisting of trunks and a T-shirt or V-neck shirt, permits complete freedom of movement for competitors as well as adequate vision of all parts of the body involved for the judges. A low-heeled lifting shoe for competitors using the split movement or a high-heeled lifting shoe for competitors using the squat style is recommended.

Numerous accessory equipment is available for use in weight-training programs, with each item contributing to bodily development. (See Table 17-2.)

SKILLS AND TECHNIQUES

Basic Grips

The choice of grip varies with the exercise being performed and the various difficulties encountered in supporting the barbell. Although official weight-lifting rules dictate grips for the basic lifts, *weight trainers* make use of several styles.

Pronated. In the pronated, or overhand, grip, which is the most common grip, the bar is grasped until the thumb wraps around and meets the index finger. The thumb may be placed next to the index finger without wrapping around the bar if so desired for a particular lift.

Supinated. In the supinated, or underhand, grip the bar is grasped with the palms turned upward away from the body. The fingers and thumb are wrapped around as indicated above.

Alternate. The alternate grip is a combination of the above two styles, with one hand assuming a pronated and the other a supinated position in order to reduce finger strain in heavy lifts such as the dead lift.

Competitive Lifting

In three basic international lifts discussed below, each competitor is granted three trials for each event with the highest total weight determining the winner.

Two-Handed Military Press. In the starting phase, both hands are placed slightly more than a shoulder width apart on the bar, which lies on the platform just in front of the feet. The head remains up, the neck erect, the back nearly straight, both arms extended, and the knees flexed. The toes must

FIGURE 17-1.   Semisquat.   FIGURE 17-2.   Split.

remain parallel and no more than 16 inches apart. In one continuous motion the bar is raised to chest level as the body drops under through the use of a spring and drop to a semisquat position (see Figure 17-1) or of a lunge by thrusting the legs into a split position (see Figure 17-2). With the feet no more than 16 inches apart, the bar at chest level for at least two seconds, and the body completely motionless, the second phase is initiated immediately after the referee claps his hands. At this point the bar must be pressed overhead in one continuous motion until both arms are fully extended, simultaneously and evenly. The body and head may not alter or deviate from the vertical position, the heels may not be raised from the floor, and the legs must remain completely extended. After a two-second pause in this position, the final phase, or return to the starting position, is rapidly performed. Although any type of grip is permitted, the pronated style is most efficient.

Two-Handed Snatch. With the bar and the body in the same positions as for the two-handed military press, the hands assume a pronated position without a restriction on width. However, the grip may not be altered during the entire movement. The bar must now be raised in one continuous motion to an ex-

FIGURE 17-3.   Two-handed military press.

FIGURE 17-4.   Two-handed snatch.

tended position overhead, with the feet aligned and no more than 16 inches apart and the bar must be held for two full seconds with the legs and arms extended. No part of the body other than the feet may contact the platform nor may a jerky or slowing action occur until the wrists turn over, which takes place after the bar passes the height of the head. A split movement or sprint and drop to a squat position explosively lowers the weight of the body under the bar. It is helpful to place the hands slightly wider apart than for the two-handed military press, pull the bar upward and close to the body, and keep the body directly under the weight after utilizing either the split or squat to drop the weight of the body under the bar.

Two-Handed Clean and Jerk. The bar must be brought in one continuous motion up to, but not contacting, the chest through the use of the split or squat before aligning the feet to the limiting width and completely extending the legs. In the final phase, the bar must be raised overhead, with the arms and knees locked, and held for two seconds. The raising force is attained by an explosive flexion and extension of the legs, with the arms simultaneously joining

FIGURE 17-5.   Two-handed clean and jerk.

in the effort. The lift is invalid if any part of the body other than the feet contact the platform, the bar touches the body as it moves to the chest position, the elbows contact the thighs as the bar is moved overhead, or the extension overhead is not held for a full two seconds.

Training Variables

Prior to the initiation of any type of weight-training program, the basic objectives of training should be established in terms of what the desired outcomes are, which will assist in determining the alteration of variables discussed below. The exercises chosen must utilize the movements that will develop the major muscle groups desired.

Repetitions. The number of times an exercise is performed without any intervening rest period should be gradually increased from the lower to the upper limit, that is, from no less than two to no more than ten repetitions within each period of three to five training days. A greater number of repetitions tends to produce greater changes in endurance whereas a fewer number of repetitions with heavier weights tends to favor the development of strength. For the development of both strength and endurance the lower and upper limits of six to ten repetitions are recommended.

Sets. The frequency or the number of times the above group of repetitions are performed each training day is referred to as a set, or bout. Sets may be completed one to five times for each exercise, with each interrupted by a brief rest period, or interval. Although training varies from one to twenty repetitions and one to ten sets, all programs have produced significant increases in strength. In order to save time, all exercises should be performed once before repeated sets are performed. One to three sets are recommended under ordinary conditions.

Interval. The interval variable applies the principle of "work per unit of time." It is essential in the development of all the systems of the body, and gives weight training tremendous versatility and potential for cardiovascular development as well as providing adequate gains in physical capacity through short workouts. The principles of circuit training (see Chapter 3) can be adapted to weight training in order to form a vigorous program. This variable should be slowly decreased in order to provide minimum amount of rest between sets and exercises, thereby increasing the intensity of the program. This gradual decrease is an important factor in achieving peak conditioning in weight training as well as in interval training for distance runners. The interval (I) and weight (RM) should not be decreased simultaneously. After the subject is able to perform three sets of ten repetitions, the interval is reduced to thirty seconds between sets in three workouts before weight is added and the subject returns to six repetitions (lower limit).

Weight (RM–Repetitions Maximum). The weight with which an individual is capable of performing a specific number of repetitions of an exercise is termed the RM. The 10RM, then, is the amount of weight with which a subject can perform an exercise a maximum of ten times. The use of lighter weights will permit more rapid contractions and a greater number of repetitions for the improvement of endurance. Heavy weights, slower contractions, and fewer repetitions will tend to develop strength more so than endurance; although both are developed concurrently, they are not developed in the same proportion. When the goal for a particular exercise, in terms of the maximum number of repetitions chosen, is attained, additional weight is added and the subject again returns to the lower limit of repetitions. A starting weight should be chosen that permits an individual to perform three sets of eight repetitions, when he is utilizing six to ten repetitions as the lower and upper limits. The starting weight obviously varies with the choice of lower and upper limits of repetitions.

Speed of Contraction. The time required to complete one repetition or movement is also an important variable affecting muscular development. Slower contractions produce greater fatigue than do rapid movements that fully utilize the starting momentum to flex and return to the normal position. The choice of slow, moderate, or rapid contractions depends upon the training objectives of strength, local muscular endurance, cardiovascular/respiratory endurance, and increased muscle contractual speed. If speed is the desired outcome, rapid contractions should be used.

Exercises. Weight-training movements are chosen on the basis of their contribution to the development of various muscle groups. When applicable, exercises should simulate movements of the activity for which training is designed. For total bodily development, a variety of exercises are needed to tax most of the systems of the body and activate different areas of the body. Heavy explosive movements, such as repeated squat and clean and jerk exercises, are needed to improve cardiovascular development.

Breathing. Proper breathing and its importance in bodily development and lifting performance is a point of controversy. Basically, it is recommended that inhalation occur while the muscles are contracting and exhalation occur while the muscles are relaxing. The only apparent value of loud and timed breathing may be its possible assistance in fixating the chest walls, which in turn aids shoulder girdle and arm movement. Forced breathing undoubtedly contributes nothing to cardio-respiratory development and may actually impair a highly refined and efficient mechanism. Breathholding should be avoided. Beginners are recommended to leave breathing adaptation during the stress of exercise to nature.

Basic Weight-training Programs

The variables described above can be altered in numerous ways and adapted to individual needs and objectives, providing the following principles are employed: progressive resistance; frequency—two to four times weekly on alternate days to permit adequate recovery; intensity—a minimum and reducing rest interval between sets and exercises; and duration —forty-five minutes to two hours depending upon the intensity variable.

A variety of programs are in use today and have proven effective.

Program I. For each exercise a starting weight is chosen that allows the subject to perform one set of eight repetitions. The progressive resistance method is then applied and when each subject can perform three sets of ten repetitions, an additional five to ten pounds for arm exercises and ten to twenty pounds for leg exercises are added and the subject returns to three sets of six repetitions. This program increases strength, endurance, cardiovascular-respiratory efficiency, and explosive power; and is applicable where performance in a sport can be improved through increased strength without increased muscle mass.

Program II. Maximum power is performed once weekly. The first set of ten repetitions is completed using half of the 10RM, the second set with three-quarters of the 10RM, and the final set with the 10RM.

Program III. The first set of ten repetitions is performed using the 10RM, the second set with an increase of five to ten pounds for a maximum number of repetitions, and the third and subsequent sets also with weight increases of five to ten pounds each set, with subjects completing as many repetitions as possible until the 1RM, that is, the amount of weight with which an individual can perform one repetition, is reached. It is obvious that this program will pro-

TABLE 17-3. Basic weight-training programs.

Desired Physical Outcomes	Variable Control
Cardiovascular endurance	Moderate to heavy weight, rapid contractions, the use of repeated power exercises such as the clean and jerk and squats, 6–10 repetitions for 3 sets.
Local muscular endurance	Light weight (10RM), 10–15 repetitions, 3 sets, moderate contractions, and minimum rest inverval.
Explosive power/speed	Moderate weight, 1-3 repetitions, rapid contractions, decreasing rest interval, 1–3 sets, and use of power exercises.
Flexibility	Moderate weight, slow contractions, 6–10 repetitions, 1–3 sets, carrying each exercise to the extreme range of motion and applying static pressure for several seconds before returning to the starting position. Avoid ballistic movements that force the joints quickly beyond the normal range of movement.
Muscle mass or bulk	Heavy weight, maximum number of repetitions, 2 sets, slow contractions, repeated heavy or maximum lifts, use of "flushing," or activation of the same muscle groups repeatedly to provide a prolonged flow of blood to a specific area.
Rehabilitation of injured muscles and joints	Light weights, slow contractions, 6–10 repetitions after initial training sessions involving no weight and 3–5 contractions, 3 sets, utilizing exercises that activate the supporting muscles of a joint such as those of the ankle, knee, and shoulder. Also helpful for prevention of injury to these areas.
Strength	Heavy weights (2-5RM), low repetitions, slow contractions, minimum rest beween sets and exercises, maximum lifts, Groves' Super-Overload Method.
Strength and endurance (general body development)	Moderate weight (8RM), 6–10 repetitions, moderate contractions, decreasing rest interval, 3 sets, varied exercises to activate all major muscle groups.

duce a great increase in strength as well as in muscle mass.

Groves' Super-Overload Method. A technique developed by Dr. Barney Groves of Virginia Commonwealth University provides a major breakthrough in strength/power training. The Groves method requires you to add 25% to the true maximum weight you can lift one time. This now becomes so heavy that you are incapable of performing even one repetition using the traditional method. The Groves' method differs considerably, however, since you: (1) begin each exercise in the up position (bench press begins with weight lifted by you and a partner to a starting position overhead), (2) start leg press exercises at a 90° angle (angle from which jumping and explosive sprint action begins) rather than a full squat position, and, (3) perform each repetition by flexing the arms or legs only slightly, never bringing the weight the entire way back. The method has the advantage of permitting you to work with very heavy weights in the ideal position or angle for leg exercises that will provide maximum benefit to the sprinter. Most sprinters will be capable of

beginning this method with 50-100 pounds more weight than had been previously used. Progression occurs by completing 3-9 repetitions, returning to 3 and increasing the weight when two sets of nine repetitions can be performed

Basic Exercises

The exercises discussed in this chapter represent a cross section of the variety of movements possible with the barbell, dumbbells, and iron boots. In relation to the position of the body and lifting hints, the following principles apply to practically all exercises and will not be mentioned for each specific exercise:

1. In the basic stance, the feet are slightly more than a shoulder width apart, with the toes parallel in a straight line. Primary considerations are balance (maintaining the weight directly above the medial plane of the body) and agility. The strongest leg is sometimes placed back in a heel-toe alignment depending upon individual preference.

2. In the starting phase of exercises where the barbell is resting on the floor, the toes should be

placed under the bar, with the bar against the ankles.

3. Unless the back is the muscle group being exercised, maintain an erect back, with the head up and the eyes looking straight ahead.

4. Grasp the bar with the hands approximately a shoulder width apart and the weight equally distributed on each hand. Utilize the alternate grip when heavy weights must be supported by the arms as in the dead and straddle lifts.

5. Avoid leaning backward to assist the completion of a repetition designed to strengthen the arm muscles.

6. Do not alter the stabilizing parts of the body after the exercise is initiated.

7. Stress the mechanical disadvantage of levers in arm exercises.

8. Carry each repetition to the full range of movement.

The arm exercises (1 to 12 in Table 17-5) can also be performed with dumbbells. From the exercises described, a wide variety of programs can be developed to meet the specific goals of the individual. Programs should be varied to avoid boredom and failure to activate and develop the majority of muscle groups. A basic weight-training program and two alternate programs designed for general bodily development and increased physical capacity is provided in Table 17-4. The three exercise groups may be used concurrently, with the basic program performed the first training day, Alternate I the second, and Alternate II the third; or, several weeks to months may be devoted to the basic program before changing to the alternate groups.

Weight Machines

Weight machines are important parts of weight lifting and weight training programs. Such apparatus is in use by professional, college and high school teams throughout the country. A weight machine eliminates the time consuming task of changing

TABLE 17-4. Basic and alternate exercise programs for general bodily development and increased physical capacity.

Exercises	Repetitions	Sets	Starting Weight	Speed of Contraction	Interval
Basic Program					
Two-arm curl	6–10	1–3	8RM	Moderate	3 min.–30 sec.
Military press	6–10	1–3	8RM	Moderate	3 min.–30 sec.
Sit-ups (flexed)	25–50	1–3	30RM	Rapid	3 min.–30 sec.
Rowing (upright)	6–10	1–3	8RM	Moderate	3 min.–30 sec.
Bench press	6–10	1–3	8RM	Moderate	3 min.–30 sec.
Squat	6–10	1–3	8RM	Rapid	3 min.–30 sec.
Heel raise	15–25	1–3	20RM	Rapid	3 min.–30 sec.
Dead lift	6–10	1–3	8RM	Rapid	3 min.–30 sec.
Pull-over (straight arm)	6–10	1–3	8RM	Moderate	3 min.–30 sec.
Alternate I					
Reverse curl	6–10	1–3	8RM	Moderate	3 min.–30 sec.
Triceps press	6–10	1–3	8RM	Moderate	3 min.–30 sec.
Sit-ups (flexed)	25–50	1–3	30RM	Rapid	3 min.–30 sec.
Shoulder shrug	6–10	1–3	8RM	Moderate	3 min.–30 sec.
Squat jump	15–25	1–3	20RM	Rapid	3 min.–30 sec.
Knee flexor	6–10	1–3	8RM	Rapid	3 min.–30 sec.
Knee extensor	6–10	1–3	8RM	Rapid	3 min.–30 sec.
Pull-over (flexed)	6–10	1–3	8RM	Moderate	3 min.–30 sec.
Alternate II					
Wrist curl	6–10	1–3	8RM	Moderate	3 min.–30 sec.
Dead lift (overhead)	6–10	1–3	8RM	Moderate	3 min.–30 sec.
Side bender	6–10	1–3	8RM	Moderate	3 min.–30 sec.
Lateral raise	6–10	1–3	8RM	Moderate	3 min.–30 sec.
Straddle lift	6–10	1–3	8RM	Rapid	3 min.–30 sec.
Supine leg lift	6–10	1–3	8RM	Rapid	3 min.–30 sec.
Hip flexor	6–10	1–3	8RM	Rapid	3 min.–30 sec.
Leg abductor	6–10	1–3	8RM	Rapid	3 min.–30 sec.
Forward raise	6–10	1–3	8RM	Moderate	3 min.–30 sec.

TABLE 17-5.   Description of basic exercises.

Exercise	Equipment	Basic Movement	Helpful Hints	Muscle Groups Activated
Arm				
1. Bench Press	Barbell, bench rack	Pronated grip, lying on the back on a bench or floor, with both knees raised, the bar is slowly lowered to the chest and pressed back to the starting position.	Keep both feet flat on the floor; avoid lifting the buttocks; extend the arms fully.	Arm and shoulder extensors
2. Bent-arm pullover	Barbell, bench rack	Pronated grip; from the same position as above the bar is placed at the chest and lowered behind the end of a bench (arms flexed) as far as possible before a return arch brings the bar back to the starting position.	Flex the arms during the entire movement; pass the bar close to the face on the return phase.	Shoulder flexors Shoulder extensors
3. Two-arm curl	Barbell	Supinated grip; with the bar resting at the thighs and the arms fully extended, the bar is raised to chest level and returned.	Keep all parts of the body erect and motionless throughout.	Upper arm flexors, wrist flexors, long finger flexors
4. Reverse curl	Barbell	Pronated grip; the same movement as above with only the grip altered.	Use less weight than in the two-arm curl.	Upper arm flexors, hand extensors, finger extensors
5. Forward raise	Barbell	Pronated grip; from a standing position, with the bar resting at the thighs, the arms remain straight and move upward to the height of the shoulders and return in the same arch.	Keep the entire body erect at all times, vary the exercise by continuing the movement to the overhead position.	Shoulder flexors, anterior and middle deltoid.
6. Military press	Barbell	Pronated grip; the bar is slowly pushed overhead from chest level until both arms are fully extended.	Maintain an erect neck and back, and extended, locked knees; avoid jerky movements or lean.	Shoulder abductors, flexors, and arm extensors.
7. Upright rowing	Barbell	Pronated grip; with the bar resting at the thighs and the arms and legs extended, the bar is raised to the chin and returned to the thigh rest position.	Use a narrow grip with the hands 6 to 8 in. apart; keep the elbows higher than the hands; maintain an erect stationary position.	Shoulder abductors, arm flexors

FIGURE 17-6.   Bench press.

FIGURE 17-7.   Bent-arm pull-over.

FIGURE 17-8.   Upright rowing.

FIGURE 17-9.   Shoulder shrug.

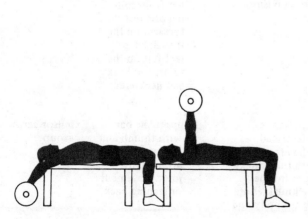

FIGURE 17-10.   Straight-arm pull-over.

FIGURE 17-11.   Tricep press.

TABLE 17-5.   (continued)

Exercise	Equipment	Basic Movement	Helpful Hints	Muscle Groups Activated
8. Shoulder shrug	Barbell	Pronated grip; with the bar resting at the thigh and the body erect, both shoulders are elevated until they nearly contact the face before relaxing and permitting the bar to return to the starting position.	Keep the extremities fully extended; heavy weight will insure more rapid strength gains.	Shoulder girdle elevators
9. Straight-arm pull-over	Barbell	Pronated grip; lying on a bench, with the head at the very edge, the barbell resting on the floor, and both arms extended, the bar is raised overhead and returned to the floor.	Maintain fully extended arms; do not elevate the lower back or remove the feet from the floor.	Pectoralis muscles, triceps, latissimus dorsi, serratus anterior
10. Tricep press	Barbell	Pronated grip; the bar is placed in the shoulder rest position and then pressed slowly overhead until both arms are fully extended.	Place the hands 9 to 12 inches apart; follow hints for the military press; tilt the head forward to prevent bar contact as the movement is initiated.	Arm extensors
11. Wrist curl	Barbell, bench or chair	Supinated grip; with the bar held by the final joint of the fingers and the wrists in a position of maximum extension, both palms are brought toward the body as far as possible and returned to the starting position.	Grasp the bar as far toward the end of the fingertips as possible; curl the fingertips to prevent the bar from rolling off; rest forearm on the thighs; keep feet flat on the floor, and back and neck erect.	Flexor carpi group
12. Reverse wrist curl	Barbell, bench or chair	Pronated grip; from the position described in #11, the hands are reversed with the knuckles pointed toward the floor. The knuckles are raised toward body and returned.	Support the bar with thumb and end of fingers; avoid elbow joint movement or leaning back.	Extensor carpi group

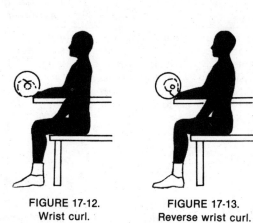

FIGURE 17-12.
Wrist curl.

FIGURE 17-13.
Reverse wrist curl.

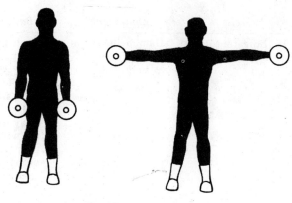

FIGURE 17-14.   Lateral raise.

FIGURE 17-15.   Side bender.

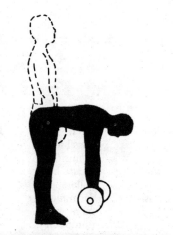

FIGURE 17-16.   Straight-leg dead lift.

FIGURE 17-17.   Trunk flexor.

TABLE 17-5. (continued)

Exercise	Equipment	Basic Movement	Helpful Hints	Muscle Groups Activated
13. Forearm rotator	Dumbbells, weight on one end only.	Supinated grip; from a sitting position with forearm resting on a table, wrist and hand extended over, and the weighted end of the dumbbell away from the body, the wrist is rotated from a supinated to a pronated position and returned.	Do not raise the forearm from bench or table; and maintain an erect upper torso.	Pronator-supinator group
14. Lateral raise	Dumbbells	Pronated grip; both arms are extended from the thighs outward to head level and lowered to the starting position.	Maintain an erect upper-lower torso; avoid flexing arms; vary with the leaning raise (same movement with trunk flexed at right angles) or supine position (lying on back on floor or bench).	Abductors, shoulder horizontal flexors
15. Wrist abductor	Dumbbells, weight on one end only.	Pronated grip; the bar is held parallel to the floor, with the weighted end pointing away from the body; the arm is extended and to the side. The weighted end is slowly lowered until it points toward the floor before it is returned to the starting position.	Place a dumbbell in each hand and alternate movements; keep the body erect at all times.	Wrist abductor
16. Wrist abductor	Dumbbells, weight on one end only.	With the weighted end now behind the body, the weight is lowered until it points directly at the floor.	Same as for #15.	Abductors
Abdominal 17. Side bender	Barbell	Pronated grip; with the bar in the shoulder rest position, the upper torso is alternately tilted to the right and left and brought back to the starting position.	Tilt as far as possible to each side; secure bar collars; perform movement with dumbbell in each hand.	Lateral flexors

TABLE 17-5.   (continued)

Exercise	Equipment	Basic Movement	Helpful Hints	Muscle Groups Activated
18. Sit-ups (bent leg)	Barbell or disc	Pronated grip; from a supine position on the back, with the bar or weight held firmly behind the neck with both hands, the upper torso is raised until both elbows contact the knees.	Bring heels up tight with the buttocks; flex the neck forward to initiate the movement; hook feet under a bar.	Rectus abdominis
19. Sit-ups (straight leg)	Barbell or disc	Pronated grip; from the position described in #18 the upper torso is raised until both elbows contact the knees.	Same as for #18; vary by alternately touching opposite elbow to opposite knee.	Hip flexors, psoas major
Back				
20. Dead lift (straight leg)	Barbell	Alternate grip; with the bar at the thigh rest position, the hips are flexed to lower the bar without flexing the legs.	Maintain arms and legs fully extended; use light weights.	Back and hip extensors
21. Dead lift (overhead straight leg)	Barbell	Pronated grip; from a standing position, the upper torso lowers to grasp the bar, with the arms fully extended, before raising the weight in a semicircle to a position overhead.	Extend legs and arms; avoid jerky movements; use light weight.	Back and leg extensors, shoulders flexors anterior and middle deltoid.
22. Dead lift (flexed knees)	Barbell	Alternate grip; with the bar resting on the floor, a crouch position is assumed, the knees are flexed, the arms and back extended; the bar is raised to the thigh rest position and lowered.	Maintain extended arms and erect back; lift weight by extending the knees and hips and moving to a standing position; keep the shoulders back to protect the back muscles.	Thigh, lower leg, and back extensors; quadriceps; hamstrings, gluteus maximus
23. Trunk flexor	Barbell	Pronated grip; from a standing position, with the bar in the shoulder rest position, the upper body is bent forward to a right angle, parallel to the floor, and then returned to the upright position.	Keep the head up; avoid bending the knees; alter the movement with hyper-extension of the trunk and/or twisting to the right or left as the body is returned to the starting position.	Back extensors

TABLE 17-5.   (continued)

Exercise	Equipment	Basic Movement	Helpful Hints	Muscle Groups Activated
24. Heel raise	Barbell, 2 to 3 inch board	Pronated grip; with the bar in the shoulder rest position, the toes together elevated on a 2 to 3 inch board, the body is raised upward to the maximum height of the toes.	Alter toe position from straight ahead, to pointed in and out; keep the body erect.	Foot plantar flexors
25. Squat	Barbell, squat rack, bench, 2 to 3 inch board	Pronated grip; with the bar in the shoulder rest position, the body is lowered to a sitting position by flexing the legs until the buttocks contacts the chair or bench placed underneath the body.	Avoid bending the back; keep the head up; point the toes outward slightly with heels elevated on a 2 to 3 inch board.	Thigh and lower leg extensors
26. Squat jump	Dumbbells	Pronated grip; with the feet in a heel-toe alignment and the body in a squat position, (dumbbell in each hand) a forceful jump, or extension, is performed that completely extends and raises both legs from the floor. Foot position is reversed in midair before the body is returned to the starting position.	Maintain an erect position throughout; strive for maximum height on each jump; work from the balls of the feet.	Lower leg, thigh, and back extensors
27. Squat walk	Barbell, padded shoulder rest support	Pronated grip; with the bar in the shoulder rest position, short steps (1 to 2 feet) are taken while squatting down toward the rear heel after each step until the thigh of the front leg is parallel to the floor.	After each step and squat, raise the body to a normal walking position; number of steps fulfill the repetition variable.	Thigh and lower leg extensors
28. Straddle lift	Barbell	Alternate grip; from a standing position, the upper torso is lowered to grasp the bar, with the arms fully extended before the legs are extended and the body is returned to the starting position. One leg is placed on each side of the bar at shoulder width apart.	Grasp the bar with one arm toward both ends; keep head, back, and shoulders erect.	Thigh, lower leg, and back extensors

TABLE 17-5.   (continued)

Exercise	Equipment	Basic Movement	Helpful Hints	Muscle Groups Activated
29. Hip flexor	Iron boots	From a standing position, the knees are alternately pulled toward the abdominal area and returned.	Perform this movement with explosiveness; combine with alternate knee extensor.	Hip flexors
30. Knee extensor	Iron boots, bench or table	From a sitting position, with the lower legs extended over a table, the foot is raised by extending the knees alternately.	Maintain an erect back; stabilize the body by grasping the sides of the table.	Quadriceps group
31. Knee flexor	Iron boots	From a standing position, the knees are alternately flexed to move the boot as close to the buttocks as possible.	Can also be performed lying flat on the stomach; keep the body erect.	Hamstrings
32. Leg abductor	Iron boots	Lying on one side with the boot secured to the top, the weight is raised upward as far as possible and returned to the starting position.	Stabilize the body by resting the head on a bent arm, maintaining floor contact with the other hand.	Abductors
33. Supine leg lift	Iron boots	Lying on the back, the legs are alternately raised, with the knees straight, to a vertical position.	Keep the lower back in constant contact with the floor; grasp a weighted barbell overhead to stabilize the upper torso.	Quadriceps, hip flexors.

weights, greatly decreases the risk of injury, eliminates the need for spotters, reduces the size of the workout area, provides six to twelve stations and is less expensive in the long run.

The choice of exercises is almost as plentiful as with barbells. The weight machine does, however, have a major drawback; it does not make allowances for the extreme differences in limb length. With the seat as far back as possible on the leg press station, the long legged basketball player's knee are almost fully flexed. In this position, only mimimal weight can be pushed. With the legs straightened weight can be handled. This angle is also much closer to the angle involved in the specific tasks of jumping, sprinting from starting blocks, sprinting and other common sports skills. In the fully flexed position, the legs are at a serious anatomical disadvantage. One solution to this problem is to have an assistant help with the weight until the 90° angle is reached. At this angle, the desired number of repetitions can be performed alone. With such a procedure, you are working with much more weight, and, even more importantly, you are working at the same angle involved in your sport's skill.

FIGURE 17-18.   Heel raise.

FIGURE 17-19.   Squat.

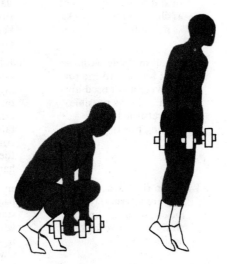

FIGURE 17-20.   Squat jump.

FIGURE 17-21.   Straddle lift.

FIGURE 17-22.   Hip flexor.

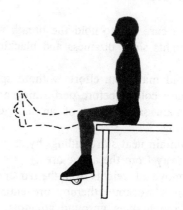

FIGURE 17-23.   Knee extensor.

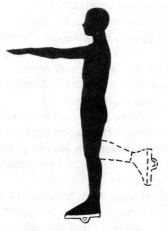

FIGURE 17-24.   Knee flexor.

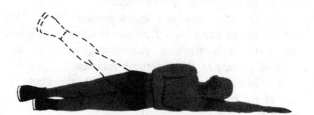

FIGURE 17-25.   Leg abductor.

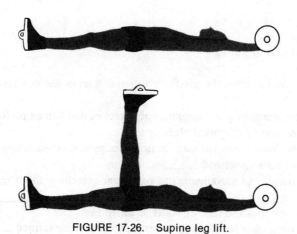

FIGURE 17-26.   Supine leg lift.

SAFETY PRACTICES

1. Take care not to hold the breath while lifting heavy weights since dizziness and blacking out may occur.

2. Avoid maximum efforts without spotters.

3. Secure collars before performing any exercise.

4. Remain safely clear of an individual in the act of lifting.

5. Maintain neat surroundings by stacking unused weights away from the active area.

6. Remove all weights from the bar upon the completion of a workout, thereby preventing incoming groups from making unsound attempts.

7. Utilize mats around the lifting areas.

8. Form the habit of returning the bar to the floor or rack gently.

9. Avoid distracting an individual in the act of lifting through noise or movement. Avoid resting in the area of activity. Keep occupied as a spotter or loader in preparing for the exercises to follow.

10. Group individuals using similar weights together in the same squad on the basis of maximum lift tests, with students progressing to more advanced groups as their strength increases.

11. Maintain an active squad, with simultaneous use of the barbell, boots, and dumbbells where space permits.

12. Stress the principle of intensity and rapid movement from one individual to another.

13. Utilize periodic lifting competition as a self-testing device.

14. Design programs for optimum increase in physical capacity and improvement of areas of physical weakness.

15. Include power exercises to increase cardiovascular efficiency.

16. Have the individual in each group who uses the least weight for a particular exercise initiate activity. Have spotters, who also serve as loaders, adjust the barbell for the next performer immediately after he calls out his desired weight.

17. Arrange matted areas in such a position that individuals can benefit from demonstrations and the correction of form.

WEIGHT TRAINING IN ATHLETICS

The value of weight training in athletics during the three major coaching phases—off-season, preseason, and in-season—is well established. Weight training has a definite place as an adjunct to training in the off-season and preseason and as a supplement to in-season training and competition.

After a careful analysis of the sport for which training is designed, exercises are chosen on the basis of their contribution to the muscle groups used. Sample objectives or desired outcomes, such as those listed previously, are outlined and the training variables altered accordingly.

A weight training program for basketball players, for example, would emphasize strength development in the muscles involved in jumping, in wrist flexor strength, in local muscular endurance, and in the general development of the body.

A similar procedure is followed in developing a weight-training program for any sport. It must be remembered, however, that the principle of "specificity of training" indicates that physical conditioning is specific to the sport. Weight training, therefore, must always be considered as only a supplement to, and not a replacement for, actual athletic training.

EXERCISE Definitions and List of Terms

1. The rapid movement of the bar from the platform to chest level in one continuous action is termed a _____.

2. A weight-training program consisting of a sequence of exercises that can be performed in succession with little or no change of weights is utilizing a _____.

3. The grouping of exercises that activate the same muscle groups in succession to provide a prolonged flow of blood to one area is termed _____.

4. Performing a maximum number of movements in a particular exercise without regard to form is termed _____.

5. The rest period between exercises and sets, or bouts, is called the _____.

6. Exercises that include both muscle tension and external movement are termed _____.

7. An explosive movement of both the upper and lower torso to press the bar to the overhead position is termed a _____.

8. The total number of consecutive times an exercise is performed before an exercise pause, or rest, is referred to as _____.

9. The amount of weight with which an individual is capable of performing a maximum of eight repetitions is referred to as the _____.

10. The movement of the barbell in one continuous motion from the floor to an overhead position, through the use of the upper and lower torso and the split or squat, is termed a _____.

11. The rapidity with which a bar is moved through the complete range of movement and returned to the starting position is referred to as the _____.

12. A movement of the lower torso, used in competitive lifting, in which the weight of the body is lowered under the barbell by dropping one foot to the rear and the other forward is termed a _____.

13. A similar movement used in competitive lifting to lower the body under the bar by an explosive drop to a low sitting position is termed a _____.

14. The capacity of a muscle to exert force either statically or through a range of movement for a short period of time is called _____.

15. Holding the breath while pressing heavy weights tends to compress the chest, produce great intrathoracic pressure, increase blood pressure, and deter the return flow of the venous blood to the heart. Such a condition produces a dizzy or faint feeling and is known as the _____.

1. Clean	6. Isotonic exercises	11. Speed of contraction
2. Combination exercise routine	7. Jerk	12. Split
3. Flushing	8. Repetitions	13. Squat
4. Forced repetitions	9. 8RM	14. Strength
5. Interval	10. Snatch	15. Valsalva phenomenon

QUESTIONS AND ANSWERS ON THE RULES

1. *Q.* What are the three official competitive lifts?
   A. The two-hand military press, the two-hand snatch, and the two-hand clean and jerk. The International Amateur Weight Lifting Federation recognizes these three and four additional lifts: the one hand snatch with the right arm, the one-hand snatch with the left arm, the clean and jerk with the left arm, and clean and jerk with the right arm. The USAAU recognizes five odd lifts: the upright row motion, the two-hand bench press, the squat, the two-hand curl, and the two-hand clean and press behind the neck.

2. *Q.* What restrictions are placed on competitive uniforms?
   A. The uniforms must fit tightly, with the legs and arms uncovered, to permit the judges a clear view of total movements and positions.

3. *Q.* How many attempts are permitted for each lift?
   A. Three, regardless of the weight attempted, but no preliminary trials on or near the platform are permitted. Once a lift is successfully completed, a contestant may not repeat the lift at the same weight. If the attempt is unsuccessful, a maximum rest period of three minutes is provided between attempts.

4. *Q.* What restrictions govern the barbell grip?
   A. A contestant may hook the fingers over the thumb or grasp the bar in a normal manner.

5. *Q.* What actions, other than successful completion of the movement, constitute a trial?
   A. Stepping off the 4 by 4 meter platform during the lift, any attempt where muscular strain is evident, or a violation of restrictions common to each lift.

6. *Q.* What tie-breaking methods are employed within each weight class?
   A. The lightest competitor is declared the winner.
7. *Q.* What restrictions are placed on the equipment in competitive lifting?
   A. (a) A 4 by 4 meter platform must be used. (b) Only one barbell set that meets official specifications may be used throughout the competition. (c) The bar must be weighed on standard platform scales prior to the start of competition.
8. *Q.* What regulations govern the choice of starting and adding weights?
   A. (a) The starting weight for the first trial is determined by each competitor and may not be altered for the next trial if the attempt is unsuccessful. (b) A minimum weight increase of ten pounds between the first and second trials and five pounds between the second and third trials is required. The third trial is eliminated if there is an increase of less than ten pounds between the first and second trials. Every subsequent lift must be performed with additional weight.
9. *Q.* May a competitor, who fails to make his weight class, enter a heavier competitive group?
   A. No competitor may enter a weight class lighter or heavier than the one in which his weight officially places him. Competitors are weighed no more than one hour prior to competition. If a competitor does not make his weight class, he may enter the new class commensurate with his weight only if a vacancy exists.
10. *Q.* What procedures are a prerequisite to the establishment of a national or district AAU record?
    A. (a) A minimum of two contestants must have participated in the weight class in which the record lift was performed. (b) Both the barbell and the lifter must again be weighed, with the weights officially approved by the referee and two judges. (c) A minimum of one pound must exist between the new and the existing record. (d) The barbell is weighed in half-pound increments. If the total weight does not reach an even power of halfs, the lower half-pound increment is counted.
11. *Q.* Is an explosive leg movement permitted?
    A. Yes. Unless forbidden in the specific restrictions of the lift, an explosive lunge of the legs is a legal action.
12. *Q.* What constitutes a completed movement for the three basic lifts?
    A. The bar is held overhead, with both arms fully extended and the feet spread a maximum of sixteen inches apart and parallel, for a minimum of two seconds and is lowered on the referee's signal.
13. *Q.* How is the individual scoring determined by the officials?
    A. After each lift is completed, the referee requests the decision of the two judges. The judges give their verdict independently without consultation by nodding the head or making a thumbs-up motion for "good" and making a thumbs-down motion for "not good." The referee votes in the event of a split decision by the judges. The contestant's score is the total weight lifted in each of the three lifts.

BIBLIOGRAPHY

Amateur Athletic Union. *Weightlifting–Official Rules.* New York: latest edition.

De Lorne, Thomas. *Progressive Resistance Exercise.* New York: Appleton-Century-Crofts, 1951.

Fallon, M. *Weight Training for Sports and Fitness.* New York: Soccer Associates, 1957.

Gresham, William L. *The Book of Strength.* New York: The John Day Company, Inc., 1961.

Hoffman, Bob. *Weight Training for Athletics.* New York: The Ronald Press Company, 1961.

Hooks, Gene. *Application of Weight Training to Athletics.* Englewood Cliffs, N. J.: Prentice-Hall, Inc., 1962.

Leighton, Jack R. *Progressive Weight Training in Athletics.* Englewood Cliffs, N. J.: Prentice-Hall, Inc., 1956

Massey, Banjamin H., and others. *The Kinesiology of Weight Lifting*. Dubuque, Ia.: William C. Brown Company, Publishers, 1959.

Murray, J., and Karpovich P. *Weight Training in Athletics*. Englewood Cliffs, N. J.: Prentice-Hall, Inc., 1956.

Pullum, W. A. *Weight Lifting Made Easy and Interesting*. New York: Soccer Associates, 1951.

Sills, Frank D., and others. *Weight Training in Sports and Physical Education*. Washington, D. C.: American Association for Health, Physical Education and Recreation, 1962.

PERSONAL RECORD SHEET

Name _____ Institution _____ Date _____

Local Address _____

Height _____ Weight _____

Class and Activity	Physical Fitness		Skills Test		Written Tests		Performance Rating	Final Grade
	Pre	Post	Pre	Post				
Total								
Total								
Total								
Total								

Swimming Requirement _____

Physical Fitness Requirement _____

Grading System _____

_____

_____

_____